Great Britain A·Z Road Atlas

EDITION 29 2015

Copyright © Geographers' A-Z Map Company Ltd.

Telephone: 01732 781000 (Enquiries & Trade Sales)
01732 783422 (Retail Sales)

A-Z A·Z AtoZ
registered trade marks of Geographers' A-Z Map Company Ltd

www./az.co.uk

C000008624

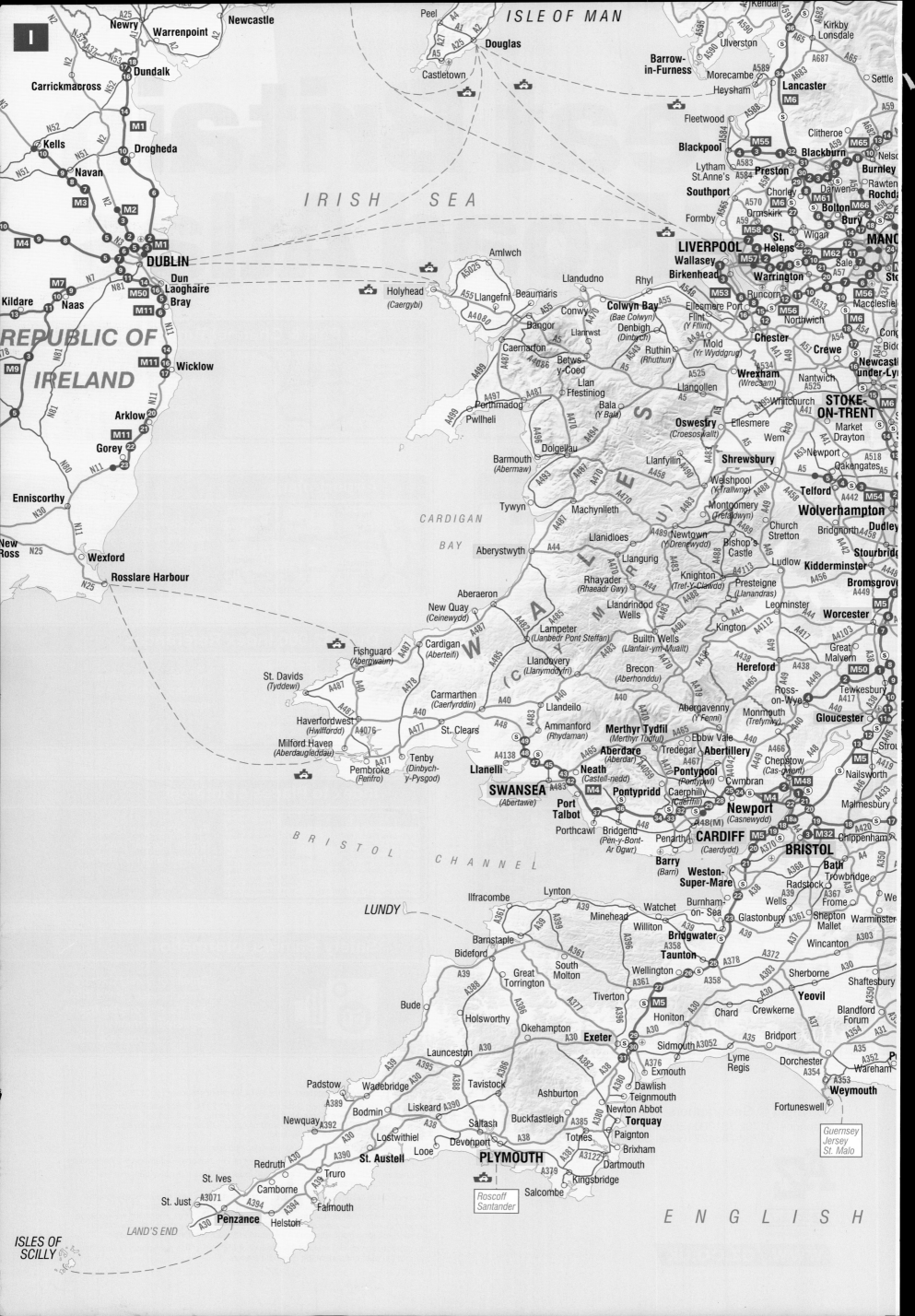

REFERENCE

MOTORWAY WITH NUMBER	M4 — s — Service Area
MOTORWAY (Under Construction/Proposed)	—————
MOTORWAY JUNCTIONS	5 — 23a
PRIMARY ROUTE	A5
A ROAD	A272
NATIONAL BOUNDARY	————
TOWNS SHOWN IN THE MILEAGE CHART	NORWICH

SCALE

0 10 20 30 40 Miles
0 10 20 30 40 50 60 Kilometres

Jersey and Guernsey lie 85 miles south of Weymouth

GUERNSEY — St. Peter Port

JERSEY — St. Helier

UNST

YELL

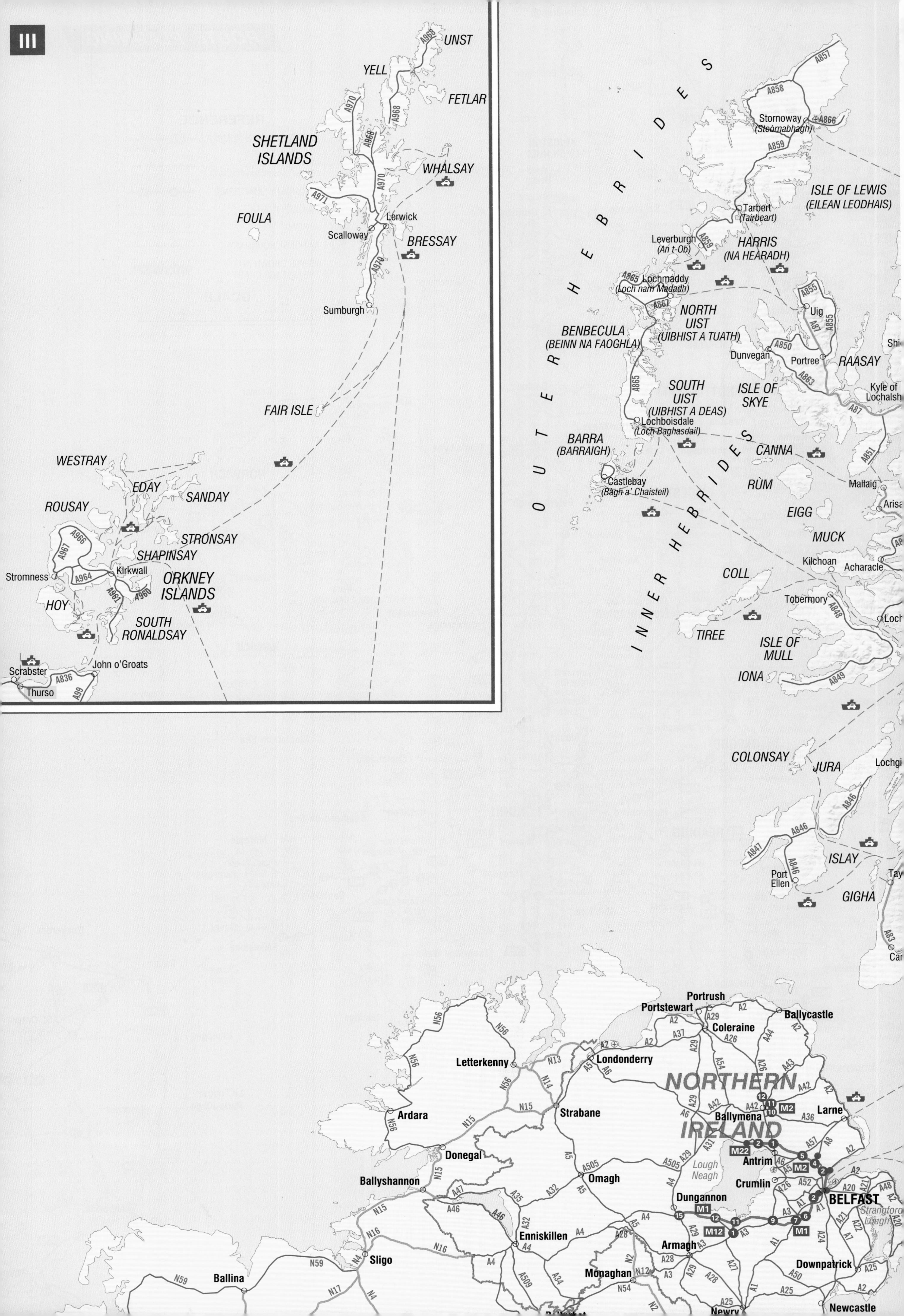

FETLAR

A968

A970

A968

SHETLAND
ISLANDS

WHALSAY

A970

A971

Lerwick

Scalloway

BRESSAY

FOULA

A970

Sumburgh

FAIR ISLE

WESTRAY

EDAY

SANDAY

ROUSAY

STRONSAY

SHAPINSAY

A966

A967

Kirkwall

ORKNEY
ISLANDS

A964

Stromness

A961

A960

HOY

SOUTH
RONALDSAY

Scrabster

Thurso

A836

A99

John o'Groats

A857

A858

Stornoway
(Steòrnabhagh)

A866

A859

ISLE OF LEWIS
(EILEAN LEODHAIS)

Tarbert
(Tairbeart)

Leverburgh
(An t-Ob)

A859

HARRIS
(NA HEARADH)

A865 Lochmaddy
(Loch nam Madadh)

A861

NORTH
UIST
(UIBHIST A TUATH)

A855

Uig

A865

BENBECULA
(BEINN NA FAOGHLA)

Dunvegan

Portree

A850

A81

A855

RAASAY

SOUTH
UIST
(UIBHIST A DEAS)

ISLE OF
SKYE

A863

Kyle of
Lochalsh

A87

Lochboisdale
(Loch Baghasdail)

BARRA
(BARRAIGH)

CANNA

RÙM

Mallaig

Arisa

Castlebay
(Bàgh a' Chaisteil)

EIGG

MUCK

Kilchoan

Acharacle

COLL

Tobermory

A848

Loch

TIREE

ISLE OF
MULL

IONA

A849

COLONSAY

JURA

Lochgi

A846

A847

A846

A846

ISLAY

Tay

Port
Ellen

GIGHA

A83

Car

O U T E R   H E B R I D E S

I N N E R   H E B R I D E S

Portrush

Portstewart

A29

A2

Ballycastle

A2

A37

A29

Coleraine

A26

A44

N56

A7

A2

NORTHERN

Letterkenny

N13

Londonderry

A6

A2

A26

A42

A2

N56

N14

A29

A54

A2

M2

A42

Larne

N15

Strabane

A6

A505

12

11

10

M2

A36

Ardara

N56

N15

Ballymena

2

1

IRELAND

A57

A8

M22

Antrim

5

M2

2

Donegal

A5

A32

Omagh

A505

A29

4

A6

A26

A52

Crumlin

A2

Ballyshannon

N15

A505

A4

Lough
Neagh

A20

Dungannon

15

M1

12

1

9

7

6

BELFAST

N15

A47

A46

A35

A4

A29

1

3

7

A1

Strangfor
Lough

Enniskillen

A46

A32

A28

M12

1

A3

M1

A21

A22

N16

A4

Armagh

A29

A27

Downpatrick

A48

N59

N16

Sligo

N4

A5

N2

Monaghan

N12

A3

A28

A29

A25

A25

A50

N59

Ballina

N17

N54

A34

A509

A4

Newry

Newcastle

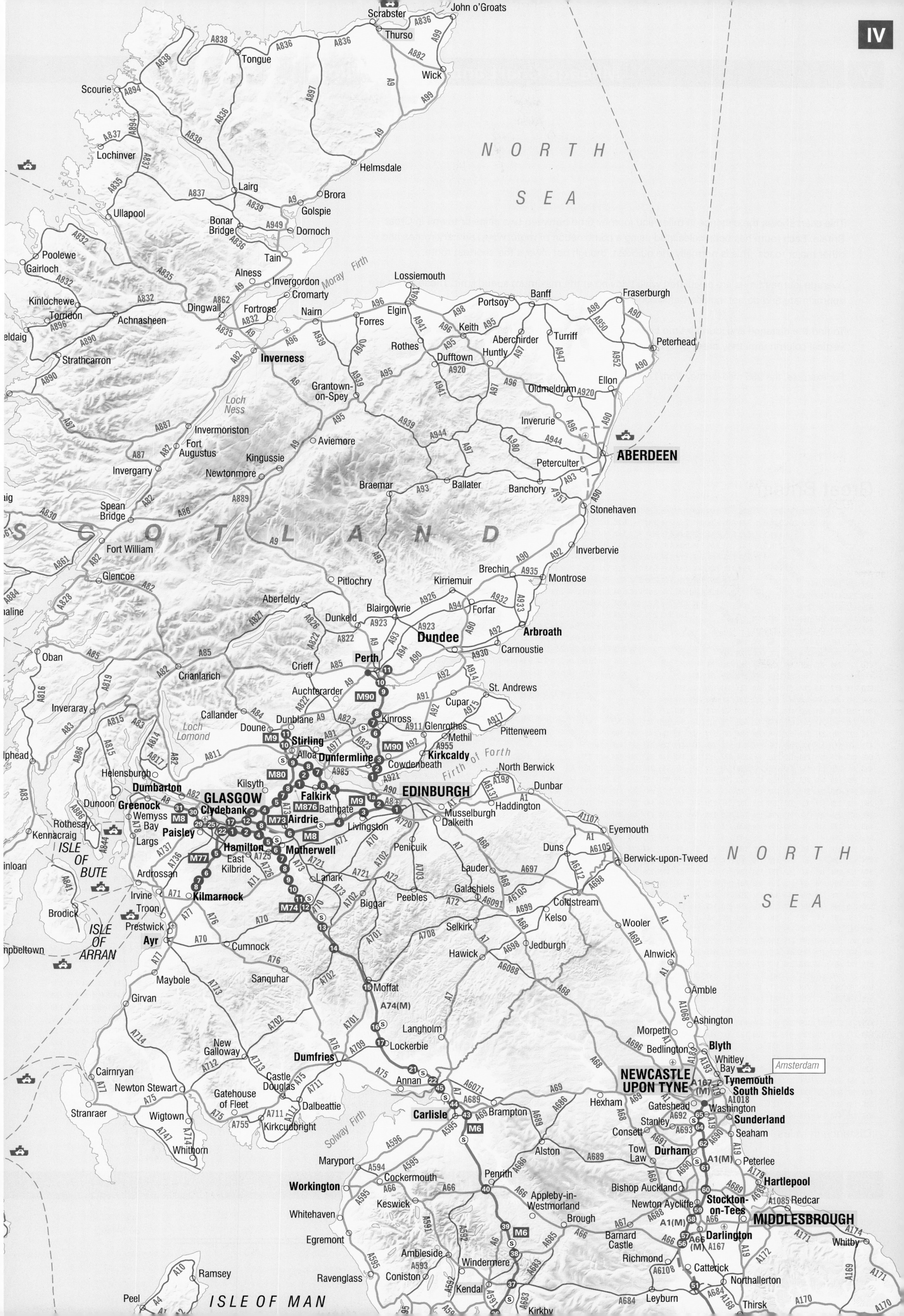
NORTH SEA
SCOTLAND
John o'Groats
Scrabster
Thurso
Wick
Tongue
Scourie
Lochinver
Helmsdale
Lairg
Brora
Golspie
Ullapool
Bonar Bridge
Dornoch
Tain
Poolewe
Gairloch
Alness
Invergordon
Moray Firth
Cromarty
Kinlochewe
Torridon
Achnasheen
Dingwall
Fortrose
Nairn
Lossiemouth
Elgin
Forres
Portsoy
Banff
Fraserburgh
Keith
Turriff
Aberchirder
Peterhead
Rothes
Huntly
Dufftown
Strathcarron
Inverness
Grantown-on-Spey
Oldmeldrum
Ellon
Loch Ness
Invermoriston
Inverurie
Fort Augustus
Aviemore
ABERDEEN
Invergarry
Kingussie
Peterculter
Newtonmore
Braemar
Ballater
Banchory
Spean Bridge
Stonehaven
Fort William
Inverbervie
Glencoe
Pitlochry
Brechin
Montrose
Kirriemuir
Aberfeldy
Blairgowrie
Forfar
Dunkeld
Arbroath
Dundee
Carnoustie
Oban
Perth
Crianlarich
Crieff
St. Andrews
Auchterarder
Inveraray
Cupar
Callander
Kinross
Glenrothes
Loch Lomond
Doune
Dunblane
Pittenweem
Methil
Stirling
Kirkcaldy
Alloa
Dunfermline
Firth of Forth
Cowdenbeath
North Berwick
Helensburgh
Kilsyth
Dunbar
Dumbarton
GLASGOW
Falkirk
EDINBURGH
Dunoon
Greenock
Clydebank
Bathgate
Haddington
Wemyss Bay
Musselburgh
Rothesay
Airdrie
Dalkeith
Paisley
Livingston
Eyemouth
Kennacraig
Largs
ISLE OF BUTE
Hamilton
Motherwell
Penicuik
Duns
Berwick-upon-Tweed
East Kilbride
Lauder
Ardrossan
Lanark
Galashiels
Coldstream
Irvine
Kilmarnock
Peebles
Kelso
Troon
Biggar
Brodick
Prestwick
Selkirk
Wooler
ISLE OF ARRAN
Ayr
Cumnock
Jedburgh
Campbeltown
Hawick
Alnwick
Sanquhar
Maybole
Moffat
Amble
Girvan
Ashington
Langholm
Morpeth
Bedlington
Blyth
Lockerbie
New Galloway
Whitley Bay
Amsterdam
Dumfries
Cairnryan
Castle Douglas
Annan
NEWCASTLE UPON TYNE
Tynemouth
South Shields
Newton Stewart
Gatehouse of Fleet
Dalbeattie
Hexham
Gateshead
Washington
Carlisle
Brampton
Stanley
Sunderland
Stranraer
Wigtown
Kirkcudbright
Consett
Seaham
Solway Firth
Whithorn
Alston
Tow Law
Durham
Maryport
Peterlee
Penrith
Cockermouth
Hartlepool
Workington
Bishop Auckland
Keswick
Appleby-in-Westmorland
Newton Aycliffe
Stockton-on-Tees
Redcar
Whitehaven
Brough
MIDDLESBROUGH
Barnard Castle
Darlington
Egremont
Whitby
Ambleside
Windermere
Richmond
Catterick
Ramsey
Ravenglass
Coniston
Northallerton
Peel
Kendal
Leyburn
ISLE OF MAN
Kirkby
Thirsk

This chart shows the distance in miles and journey time between two cities or towns in Great Britain. Each route has been calculated using a combination of motorways, primary routes and other major roads. This is normally the quickest, though not always the shortest route.

Average journey times are calculated whilst driving at the maximum speed limit. These times are approximate and do not include traffic congestion or convenience breaks.

To find the distance and journey time between two cities or towns, follow a horizontal line and vertical column until they meet each other.

For example, the 285 mile journey from London to Penzance is approximately 4 hours and 59 minutes.

Great Britain

Journey times

Distance in miles

| | | 0 | 1 | 2 | 3 | 4 | 5 | | 10 | | 15 | | 20 | | 25 | | 30 Miles |
| 0 | 1 | 2 | 3 | 4 | 5 | | 10 | | 15 | | 20 | | 25 | | 30 | | 35 | | 40 | | 45 Kilometres |

Limited Interchange Motorway Junctions

Limited Interchange Motorway Junctions are shown on the mapping pages by red junction indicators 2

M1

Junction	Direction	Restriction
2	Northbound	No exit, access from A1 only
	Southbound	No access, exit to A1 only
4	Northbound	No exit, access from A41 only
	Southbound	No access, exit to A41 only
6a	Northbound	No exit, access from M25 only
	Southbound	No access, exit to M25 only
17	Northbound	No access, exit to M45 only
	Southbound	No exit, access from M45 only
19	Northbound	Exit to M6 only, access from A14 only
	Southbound	Access from M6 only, exit to A14 only
21a	Northbound	No access, exit to A46 only
	Southbound	No exit, access from A46 only
24a	Northbound	Access from A50 only
	Southbound	Exit to A50 only
35a	Northbound	No access, exit to A616 only
	Southbound	No exit, access from A616 only
43	Northbound	Exit to M621 only
	Southbound	Access from M621 only
48	Eastbound	Exit to A1(M) northbound only
	Westbound	Access from A1(M) southbound only

M2

Junction	Direction	Restriction
1	Eastbound	Access from A2 eastbound only
	Westbound	Exit to A2 westbound only

M3

Junction	Direction	Restriction
8	Eastbound	No exit, access from A303 only
	Westbound	No access, exit to A303 only
10	Northbound	No access from A31
	Southbound	No exit to A31
13	Southbound	No access from A335 to M3 leading to M27 Eastbound

M4

Junction	Direction	Restriction
1	Eastbound	Exit to A4 eastbound only
	Westbound	Access from A4 westbound only
21	Eastbound	No exit to M48
	Westbound	No access from M48
23	Eastbound	No access from M48
	Westbound	No exit to M48
25	Eastbound	No exit
	Westbound	No access
25a	Eastbound	No exit
	Westbound	No access
29	Eastbound	No exit, access from A48(M) only
	Westbound	No access, exit to A48(M) only
38	Westbound	No access, exit to A48 only
39	Eastbound	No access or exit
	Westbound	No exit, access from A48 only
42	Eastbound	No access from A48
	Westbound	No exit to A48

M5

Junction	Direction	Restriction
10	Northbound	No exit, access from A4019 only
	Southbound	No access, exit to A4019 only
11a	Southbound	No exit to A417 westbound
18a	Northbound	No access from M49
	Southbound	No exit to M49

M6

Junction	Direction	Restriction
3a	Eastbound	No exit to M6 Toll
	Westbound	No access from M6 Toll
4	Northbound	No exit to M42 northbound No access from M42 southbound
	Southbound	No exit to M42 No access from M42 southbound
4a	Northbound	No exit, access from M42 southbound only
	Southbound	No access, exit to M42 only
5	Northbound	No access, exit to A452 only
	Southbound	No exit, access from A452 only
10a	Northbound	No access, exit to M54 only
	Southbound	No exit, access from M54 only
11a	Northbound	No exit to M6 Toll
	Southbound	No access from M6 Toll
20	Northbound	No exit to M56 eastbound
	Southbound	No access from M56 westbound
24	Northbound	No exit, access from A58 only
	Southbound	No access, exit to A58 only
25	Northbound	No access, exit to A49 only
	Southbound	No exit, access from A49 only
30	Northbound	No exit, access from M61 northbound only
	Southbound	No access, exit to M61 southbound only
31a	Northbound	No access, exit to B6242 only
	Southbound	No exit, access from B6242 only
45	Northbound	No access onto A74(M)
	Southbound	No exit from A74(M)

M6 Toll

Junction	Direction	Restriction
T1	Northbound	No exit
	Southbound	No access
T2	Northbound	No access or exit
	Southbound	No access
T5	Northbound	No exit
	Southbound	No access
T7	Northbound	No access from A5
	Southbound	No exit
T8	Northbound	No exit to A460 northbound
	Southbound	No exit

M8

Junction	Direction	Restriction
8	Eastbound	No exit to M73 northbound
	Westbound	No access from M73 southbound
9	Eastbound	No access, exit only
	Westbound	No exit, access only
13	Eastbound	No access from M80 southbound
	Westbound	No exit to M80 northbound
14	Eastbound	No access, exit only
	Westbound	No exit, access only
16	Eastbound	No exit, access only
	Westbound	No access, exit only
17	Eastbound	No exit, access from A82 only
	Westbound	No access, exit to A82 only
18	Westbound	No exit, access only
19	Eastbound	No exit to A814 eastbound
	Westbound	No access from A814 westbound
20	Eastbound	No exit, access only
	Westbound	No access, exit only
21	Eastbound	No access, exit only
	Westbound	No exit, access only
22	Eastbound	No exit, access from M77 only
	Westbound	No access, exit to M77 only
23	Eastbound	No exit, access from B768 only
	Westbound	No access, exit to B768 only
25	Eastbound & Westbound	Access from A739 southbound only Exit to A739 northbound only
25a	Eastbound	Access only
	Westbound	Exit only
28	Eastbound	No exit, access from airport only
	Westbound	No access, exit to airport only

M9

Junction	Direction	Restriction
2	Northbound	No exit, access from B8046 only
	Southbound	No access, exit to B8046 only
3	Northbound	No access, exit to A803 only
	Southbound	No exit, access from A803 only
6	Northbound	No exit, access only
	Southbound	No access, exit to A905 only
8	Northbound	No access, exit to M876 only
	Southbound	No exit, access from M876 only
Junction with A90	Northbound	Exit onto A90 westbound only
	Southbound	Access from A90 eastbound only

M11

Junction	Direction	Restriction
4	Northbound	No exit, access from A406 eastbound only
	Southbound	No access, exit to A406 westbound only
5	Northbound	No access, exit to A1168 only
	Southbound	No exit, access from A1168 only
8a	Northbound	No access, exit only
	Southbound	No exit, access only
9	Northbound	No access, exit only
	Southbound	No exit, access only
13	Northbound	No access, exit only
	Southbound	No exit, access only
14	Northbound	No access from A428 eastbound No exit to A428 westbound
	Southbound	No exit, access from A428 eastbound only

M20

Junction	Direction	Restriction
2	Eastbound	No access, exit to A20 only (access via M26 Junction 2a)
	Westbound	No exit, access only (exit via M26 Jun.2a)
3	Eastbound	No exit, access from M26 eastbound only
	Westbound	No access, exit to M26 westbound only
11a	Eastbound	No access from Channel Tunnel
	Westbound	No exit to Channel Tunnel

M23

Junction	Direction	Restriction
7	Northbound	No exit to A23 southbound
	Southbound	No access from A23 northbound

M25

Junction	Direction	Restriction
5	Clockwise	No exit to M26 eastbound
	Anti-clockwise	No access from M26 westbound
Spur to A21	Northbound	No exit to M26 eastbound
	Southbound	No access from M26 westbound
19	Clockwise	No access, exit only
	Anti-clockwise	No exit, access only
21	Clockwise & Anti-clockwise	No exit to M1 southbound No access from M1 northbound
31	Northbound	No access, exit only (access via Jun.30)
	Southbound	No exit, access only (exit via Jun.30)

M26

Junction	Direction	Restriction
Junction with M25 (M25 Jun.5)	Eastbound	No access from M25 clockwise or spur from A21 northbound
	Westbound	No exit to M25 anti-clockwise or spur to A21 southbound
Junction with M20 (M20 Jun.3)	Eastbound	No exit to M20 westbound
	Westbound	No access from M20 eastbound

M27

Junction	Direction	Restriction
4	Eastbound & Westbound	No exit to A33 southbound (Southampton) No access from A33 northbound
10	Eastbound	No exit, access from A32 only
	Westbound	No access, exit to A32 only

M40

Junction	Direction	Restriction
3	N.W bound	No access, exit to A40 only
	S.E bound	No exit, access from A40 only
7	N.W bound	No access, exit only
	S.E bound	No exit, access only
13	N.W bound	No access, exit only
	S.E bound	No exit, access only
14	N.W bound	No exit, access only
	S.E bound	No access, exit only
16	N.W bound	No exit, access only
	S.E bound	No access, exit only

M42

Junction	Direction	Restriction
1	Eastbound	No exit
	Westbound	No access
7	Northbound	No access, exit to M6 only
	Southbound	No exit, access from M6 northbound only
8	Northbound	No exit, access from M6 southbound only
	Southbound	Exit to M6 nothbound only Access from M6 southbound only

M45

Junction	Direction	Restriction
Junction with M1 (M1 Jun.17)	Eastbound	No exit to M1 northbound
	Westbound	No access from M1 southbound
Junction with A45 east of Dunchurch	Eastbound	No access, exit to A45 only
	Westbound	No exit, access from A45 northbound only

M48

Junction	Direction	Restriction
Junction with M4 (M4 Jun.21)	Eastbound	No exit to M4 westbound
	Westbound	No access from M4 eastbound
Junction with M4 (M4 Jun.23)	Eastbound	No access from M4 westbound
	Westbound	No exit to M4 eastbound

M53

Junction	Direction	Restriction
11	Northbound & Southbound	No access from M56 eastbound, no exit to M56 westbound

M56

Junction	Direction	Restriction
1	Eastbound	No exit to M60 N.W bound No exit to A34 southbound
	S.E bound	No access from A34 northbound
	Westbound	No access from M60
2	Eastbound	No exit, access from A560 only
	Westbound	No access, exit to A560 only
3	Eastbound	No access, exit only
	Westbound	No exit, access only
4	Eastbound	No exit, access only
	Westbound	No access, exit only
7	Westbound	No access, exit only
8	Eastbound	No access or exit
	Westbound	No exit, access from A556 only
9	Eastbound	No access from M6 northbound
	Westbound	No exit to M60 southbound
10a	Northbound	No exit, access only
	Southbound	No access, exit only
15	Eastbound	No exit to M53
	Westbound	No access from M53

M57

Junction	Direction	Restriction
3	Northbound	No exit, access only
	Southbound	No access, exit only
5	Northbound	No exit, access from A580 westbound only
	Southbound	No access, exit to A580 eastbound only

M58

Junction	Direction	Restriction
1	Eastbound	No exit, access from A506 only
	Westbound	No access, exit to A506 only

M60

Junction	Direction	Restriction
2	N.E bound	No access, exit to A560 only
	S.W bound	No exit, access from A560 only
3	Eastbound	No access from A34 southbound
	Westbound	No exit to A34 northbound
4	Eastbound	No exit to M56 S.W bound No exit to A34 northbound
	Westbound	No access from A34 southbound No access from M56 eastbound
5	N.W bound	No access from or exit to A5103 southbound
	S.E bound	No access from or exit to A5103 northbound
14	Eastbound	No exit to A580 No access from A580 westbound
	Westbound	No exit to A580 eastbound No access from A580
16	Eastbound	No exit, access from A666 only
	Westbound	No access, exit to A666 only
20	Eastbound	No access from A664
	Westbound	No exit to A664
22	Westbound	No access from A62
25	S.W bound	No access from A560 / A6017
26	N.E bound	No access or exit
27	N.E bound	No access, exit only
	S.W bound	No exit, access only

M61

Junction	Direction	Restriction
2&3	N.W bound	No access from A580 eastbound
	S.E bound	No exit to A580 westbound
Junction with M6 (M6 Jun.30)	N.W bound	No exit to M6 southbound
	S.E bound	No access from M6 northbound

M62

Junction	Direction	Restriction
23	Eastbound	No access, exit to A640 only
	Westbound	No exit, access from A640 only

M65

Junction	Direction	Restriction
9	N.E bound	No access, exit to A679 only
	S.W bound	No exit, access from A679 only
11	N.E bound	No exit, access only
	S.W bound	No access, exit only

M66

Junction	Direction	Restriction
1	Northbound	No access, exit to A56 only
	Southbound	No exit, access from A56 only

M67

Junction	Direction	Restriction
1	Eastbound	Access from A57 eastbound only
	Westbound	Exit to A57 westbound only
1a	Eastbound	No access, exit to A6017 only
	Westbound	No exit, access from A6017 only
2	Eastbound	No exit, access from A57 only
	Westbound	No access, exit to A57 only

M69

Junction	Direction	Restriction
2	N.E bound	No exit, access from B4669 only
	S.W bound	No access, exit to B4669 only

M73

Junction	Direction	Restriction
1	Southbound	No exit to A721 eastbound
2	Northbound	No access from M8 eastbound No exit to A89 eastbound
	Southbound	No exit to M8 westbound No access from A89 westbound
3	Northbound	No exit to A80 S.W bound
	Southbound	No access from A80 N.E bound

M74

Junction	Direction	Restriction
1	Eastbound	No access from M8 Westbound
	Westbound	No exit to M8 Westbound
3	Eastbound	No exit
	Westbound	No access
3a	Eastbound	No access
	Westbound	No exit
7	Northbound	No exit, access from A72 only
	Southbound	No access, exit to A72 only
9	Northbound	No access or exit
	Southbound	No access, exit to B7078 only
10	Southbound	No exit, access from B7078 only
11	Northbound	No exit, access from B7078 only
	Southbound	No access, exit to B7078 only
12	Northbound	No access, exit to A70 only
	Southbound	No exit, access from A70 only

M77

Junction	Direction	Restriction
Junction with M8 (M8 Jun.22)	Northbound	No exit to M8 westbound
	Southbound	No access from M8 eastbound
4	Northbound	No exit
	Southbound	No access
6	Northbound	No exit to A77
	Southbound	No access from A77
7	Northbound	No access from A77 No exit to A77

M80

Junction	Direction	Restriction
1	Northbound	No access from M8 westbound
	Southbound	No exit to M8 eastbound
4a	Northbound	No access
	Southbound	No exit
6a	Northbound	No exit
	Southbound	No access
8	Northbound	No access from M876
	Southbound	No exit to M876

M90

Junction	Direction	Restriction
2a	Northbound	No access, exit to A92 only
	Southbound	No exit, access from A92 only
7	Northbound	No exit, access from A91 only
	Southbound	No access, exit to A91 only
8	Northbound	No access, exit to A91 only
	Southbound	No exit, access from A91 only
10	Northbound	No access from A912 Exit to A912 northbound only
	Southbound	No exit to A912 Access from A912 southbound only

M180

Junction	Direction	Restriction
1	Eastbound	No access, exit only
	Westbound	No exit, access from A18 only

M606

Junction	Direction	Restriction
2	Northbound	No access, exit only

M621

Junction	Direction	Restriction
2a	Eastbound	No exit, access only
	Westbound	No access, exit only
4	Southbound	No exit
5	Northbound	No access, exit to A61 only
	Southbound	No exit, access from A61 only
6	Northbound	No exit, access only
	Southbound	No access, exit only
7	Eastbound	No access, exit only
	Westbound	No exit, access only
8	Northbound	No access, exit only
	Southbound	No exit, access only

M876

Junction	Direction	Restriction
Junction with M80 (M80 Jun.5)	N.E bound	No access from M80 southbound
	S.W bound	No exit to M80 northbound
Junction with M9 (M9 Jun.8)	N.E bound	No exit to M9 northbound
	S.W bound	No access from M9 southbound

A1(M)

Junction	Direction	Restriction
Hertfordshire Section		
2	Northbound	No access, exit only
	Southbound	No exit, access from A1001 only
3	Southbound	No access, exit only
5	Northbound	No exit, access only
	Southbound	No access or exit
Cambridgeshire Section		
14	Northbound	No exit, access only
	Southbound	No access, exit only
Leeds Section		
40	Southbound	Exit to A1 southbound only
43	Northbound	Access from M1 eastbound only
	Southbound	Exit to M1 westbound only
Durham Section		
57	Northbound	No access, exit to A66(M) only
	Southbound	No exit, access from A66(M)
65	Northbound	Exit to A1 N.W bound and to A194(M) only
	Southbound	Access from A1 S.E bound and from A194(M) only

A3(M)

Junction	Direction	Restriction
4	Northbound	No access, exit only
	Southbound	No exit, access only

Aston Expressway A38(M)

Junction	Direction	Restriction
Junction with Victoria Road, Aston	Northbound	No exit, access only
	Southbound	No access, exit only

A48(M)

Junction	Direction	Restriction
Junction with M4 (M4 Jun.29)	N.E bound	Exit to M4 eastbound only
	S.W bound	Access from M4 westbound only
29a	N.E bound	Access from A48 eastbound only
	S.W bound	Exit to A48 westbound only

Mancunian Way A57(M)

Junction	Direction	Restriction
Junction with A34 Brook Street, Manchester	Eastbound	No access, exit to A34 Brook Street, southbound only
	Westbound	No exit, access only

Leeds Inner Ring Road A58(M)

Junction	Direction	Restriction
Junction with Park Lane / Westgate	Southbound	No access, exit only

Leeds Inner Ring Road A64(M) (continuation of A58(M))

Junction	Direction	Restriction
Junction with A58 Clay Pit Lane	Eastbound	No access
	Westbound	No exit

A66(M)

Junction	Direction	Restriction
Junction with A1(M) (A1(M) Jun.57)	N.E bound	Access from A1(M) northbound only
	S.W bound	Exit to A1(M) southbound only

A74(M)

Junction	Direction	Restriction
18	Northbound	No access
	Southbound	No exit

Newcastle Central Motorway A167(M)

Junction	Direction	Restriction
Junction with Camden Street	Northbound	No exit, access only
	Southbound	No access or exit

A194(M)

Junction	Direction	Restriction
Junction with A1(M) (A1(M) Jun.65) and A1 Gateshead Western By-Pass	Northbound	Access from A1(M) only
	Southbound	Exit to A1(M) only

Reference

Motorway
Autoroute
Autobahn

Motorway Under Construction
Autoroute en construction
Autobahn im Bau

Motorway Proposed
Autoroute prévue
Geplante Autobahn

Motorway Junctions with Numbers
Unlimited Interchange **4**
Limited Interchange **5**

Autoroute échangeur numéroté
Echangeur complet
Echangeur partiel

Autobahnanschlußstelle mit Nummer
Unbeschränkter Fahrtrichtungswechsel
Beschränkter Fahrtrichtungswechsel

Motorway Service Area (with fuel station) **S**
with access from one carriageway only **S**

Aire de services d'autoroute (avec station service)
accessible d'un seul côté

Rastplatz oder Raststätte (mit tankstelle)
Einbahn

Major Road Service Areas (with fuel station) with 24 hour facilities
Primary Route **S**   Class A Road **S**

Aire de services sur route prioritaire (avec station service) Ouverte 24h sur 24
Route à grande circulation   Route de type A

Raststätte (mit tankstelle) Durchgehend geöffnet
Hauptverkehrsstraße   A- Straße

Truckstop (selection of) **T**
Sélection d'aire pour poids lourds
Auswahl von Fernfahrerrastplatz

Primary Route **A41**
Route à grande circulation
Hauptverkehrsstraße

Primary Route Junction with Number **5**
Echangeur numéroté
Hauptverkehrsstraßenkreuzung mit Nummer

Primary Route Destination **DOVER**
Route prioritaire, direction
Hauptverkehrsstraße Richtung

Dual Carriageways (A & B roads)
Route à double chaussées séparées (route A & B)
Zweispurige Schnellstraße (A- und B- Straßen)

Class A Road **A129**
Route de type A
A-Straße

Class B Road **B177**
Route de type B
B-Straße

Narrow Major Road (passing places)
Route prioritaire étroite (possibilité de dépassement)
Schmale Hauptverkehrsstraße (mit Überholmöglichkeit)

Major Roads Under Construction
Route prioritaire en construction
Hauptverkehrsstaße im Bau

Major Roads Proposed
Route prioritaire prévue
Geplante Hauptverkehrsstraße

Safety Cameras with Speed Limits
Single Camera **30**
Multiple Cameras located along road **50**
Single & Multiple Variable Speed Cameras **V** **V**

Radars de contrôle de vitesse
Radar simple
Radars multiples situés le long de la route
Radars simples et multiples de contrôle de vitesse variable

Sicherheitskameras mit Tempolimit
Einzelne Kamera
Mehrere Kameras entlang der Straße
Einzelne und mehrere Kameras für variables Tempolimit

Fuel Station
Station service
Tankstelle

Gradient 1:5 (20%) **& steeper**
(ascent in direction of arrow)
Pente égale ou supérieure à 20% (dans le sens de la montée)
20% Steigung und steiler (in Pfeilrichtung)

Toll *TOLL*
Barrière de péage
Gebührenpflichtig

Mileage between markers **8**
Distence en miles entre les flèches
Strecke zwischen Markierungen in Meilen

Railway and Station
Voie ferrée et gare
Eisenbahnlinie und Bahnhof

Level Crossing and Tunnel
Passage à niveau et tunnel
Bahnübergang und Tunnel

River or Canal
Rivière ou canal
Fluß oder Kanal

County or Unitary Authority Boundary
Limite de comté ou de division administrative
Grafschafts- oder Verwaltungsbezirksgrenze

National Boundary
Frontière nationale
Landesgrenze

Built-up Area
Agglomération
Geschloßene Ortschaft

Village or Hamlet
Village ou hameau
Dorf oder Weiler

Wooded Area
Zone boisée
Waldgebiet

Spot Height in Feet • *813*
Altitude (en pieds)
Höhe in Fuß

Relief above 400' (122m)
Relief par estompage au-dessus de 400' (122m)
Reliefschattierung über 400' (122m)

National Grid Reference (kilometres) 100
Coordonnées géographiques nationales (Kilomètres)
Nationale geographische Koordinaten (Kilometer)

Page Continuation
Suite à la page indiquée **48**
Seitenfortsetzung

Area covered by Main Route map **MAIN ROUTE 87**
Répartition des cartes des principaux axes routiers
Von Karten mit Hauptverkehrsstrecken

Area covered by Town Plan **SEE PAGE 94**
Ville ayant un plan à la page indiquée
Von Karten mit Stadtplänen erfaßter Bereich

Tourist Information

Airport ✈
Aéroport
Flughafen

Airfield ✈
Terrain d'aviation
Flugplatz

Heliport 🚁
Héliport
Hubschrauberlandeplatz

Battle Site and Date ⚔ 1066
Champ de bataille et date
Schlachtfeld und Datum

Castle (open to public) 🏰
Château (ouvert au public)
Schloß / Burg (für die Öffentlichkeit zugänglich)

Castle with Garden (open to public) 🏰
Château avec parc (ouvert au public)
Schloß mit Garten (für die Öffentlichkeit zugänglich)

Cathedral, Abbey, Church, Friary, Priory ✝
Cathédrale, abbaye, église, monastère, prieuré
Kathedrale, Abtei, Kirche, Mönchskloster, Kloster

Country Park 🌳
Parc régional
Landschaftspark

Ferry (vehicular, sea) ⛴
(vehicular, river) ⛴
(foot only) 🚶

Bac (véhicules, mer)
(véhicules, rivière)
(piétons)

Fähre (auto, meer)
(auto, fluß)
(nur für Personen)

Garden (open to public) ✿
Jardin (ouvert au public)
Garten (für die Öffentlichkeit zugänglich)

Golf Course (9 hole) 🏌9   (18 hole) 🏌18
Terrain de golf (9 trous)   (18 trous)
Golfplatz (9 Löcher)   (18 Löcher)

Historic Building (open to public) 🏛
Monument historique (ouvert au public)
Historisches Gebäude (für die Öffentlichkeit zugänglich)

Historic Building with Garden (open to public) 🏛
Monument historique avec jardin (ouvert au public)
Historisches Gebäude mit Garten (für die Öffentlichkeit zugänglich)

Horse Racecourse 🏇
Hippodrome
Pferderennbahn

Lighthouse 🗼
Phare
Leuchtturm

Motor Racing Circuit 🏎
Circuit Automobile
Automobilrennbahn

Museum, Art Gallery 🖼
Musée
Museum, Galerie

National Park
Parc national
Nationalpark

National Trust Property
(open) *NT*
(restricted opening) *NT*
(National Trust for Scotland) *NTS* *NTS*

National Trust Property
(ouvert)
(heures d'ouverture)
(National Trust for Scotland)

National Trust- Eigentum
(geöffnet)
(beschränkte Öffnungszeit)
(National Trust for Scotland)

Nature Reserve or Bird Sanctuary 🦆
Réserve naturelle botanique ou ornithologique
Natur- oder Vogelschutzgebiet

Nature Trail or Forest Walk 🍃
Chemin forestier, piste verte
Naturpfad oder Waldweg

Place of Interest *Monument* •
Site, curiosité
Sehenswürdigkeit

Picnic Site ⛱
Lieu pour pique-nique
Picknickplatz

Railway, Steam or Narrow Gauge 🚂
Chemin de fer, à vapeur ou à voie étroite
Eisenbahn, Dampf- oder Schmalspurbahn

Theme Park 🎡
Centre de loisirs
Vergnügungspark

Tourist Information Centre 🛈
Syndicat d'initiative
Information

Viewpoint (360 degrees) 🔆   (180 degrees) 🔅
Vue panoramique (360 degrés)   (180 degrés)
Aussichtspunkt (360 Grade)   (180 Grade)

Visitor Information Centre **V**
Centre d'information touristique
Besucherzentrum

Wildlife Park 🦌
Réserve de faune
Wildpark

Windmill 🪟
Moulin à vent
Windmühle

Zoo or Safari Park 🐘
Parc ou réserve zoologique
Zoo oder Safari-Park

Please note: symbols have been enlarged for clarity

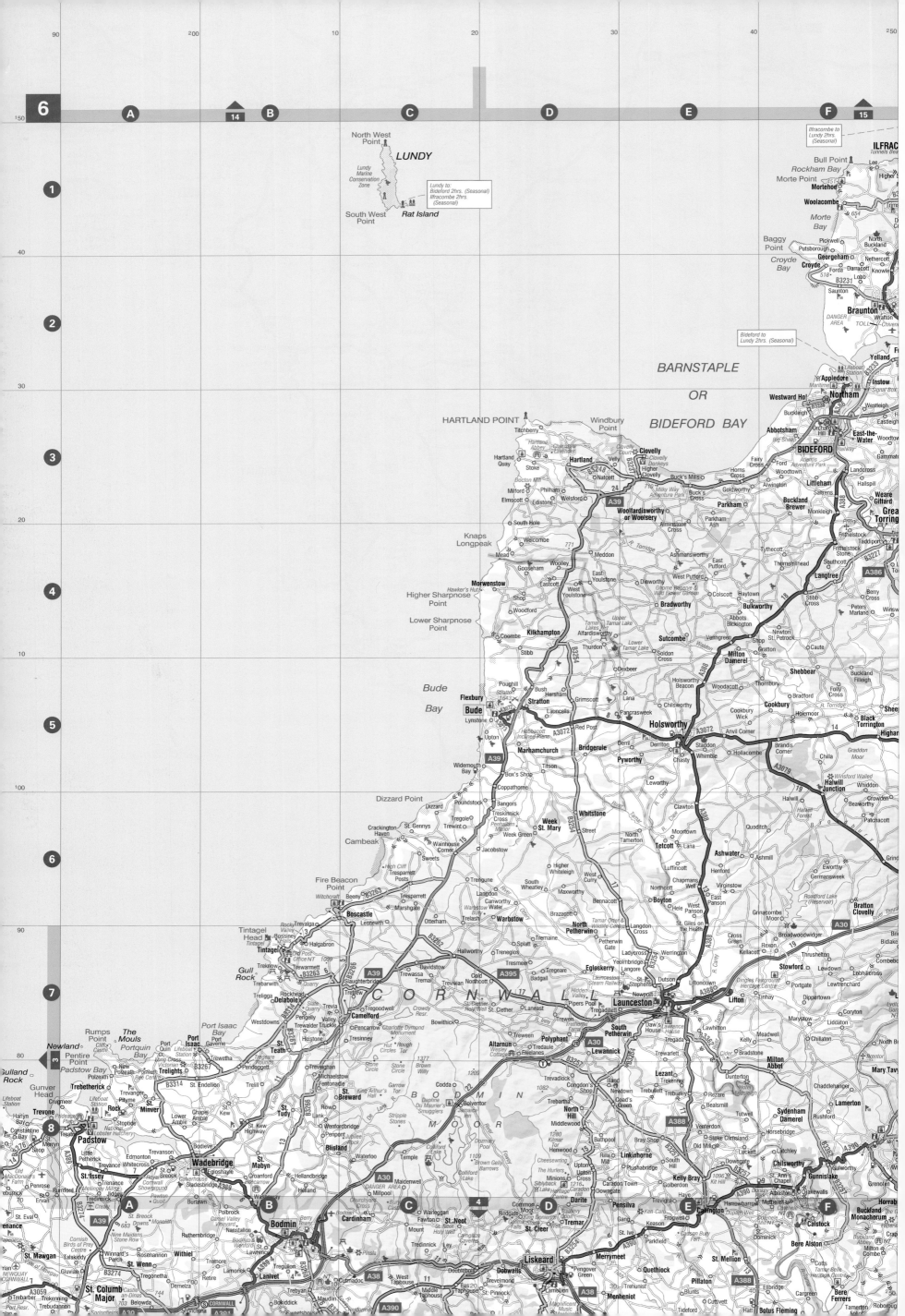

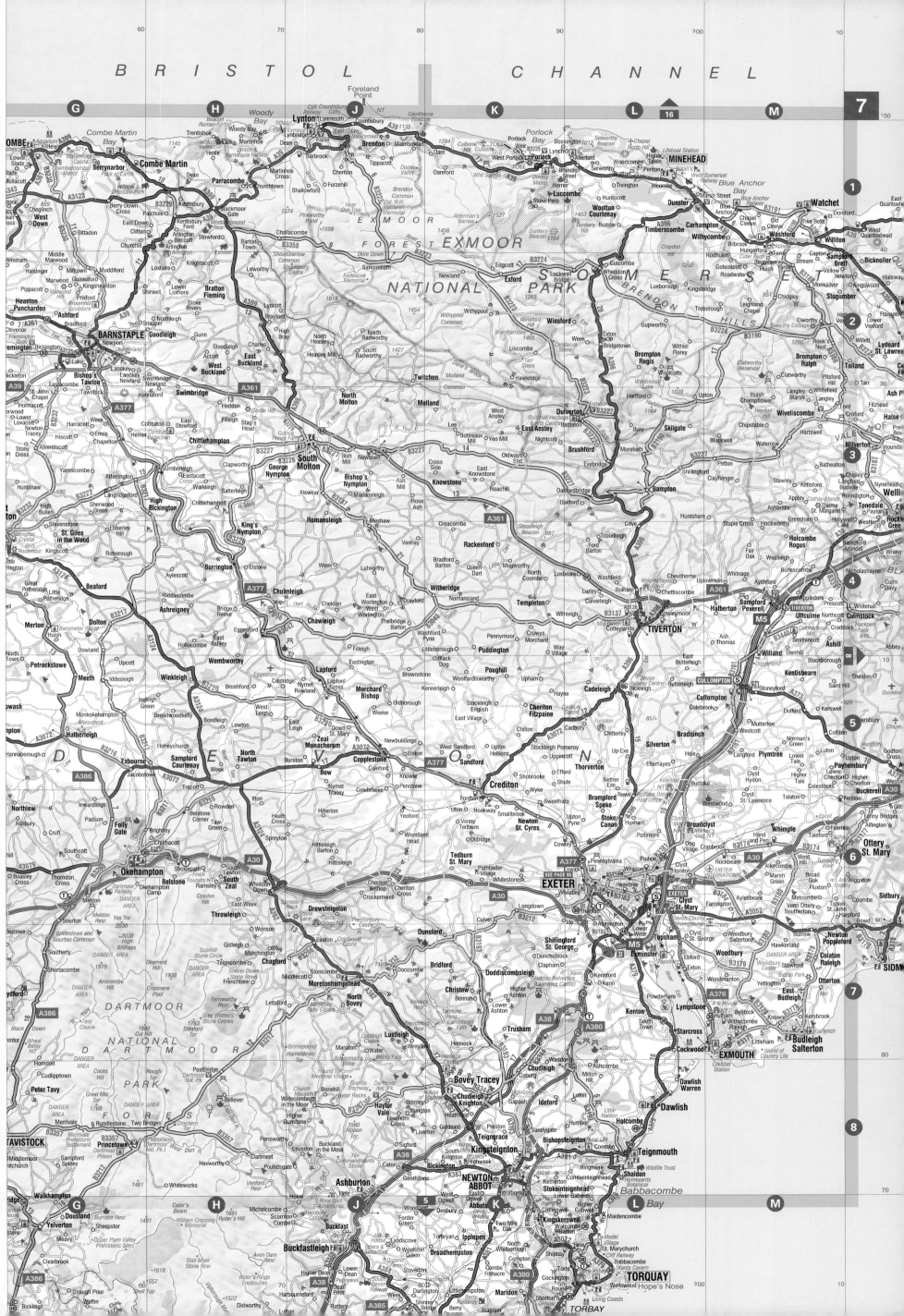

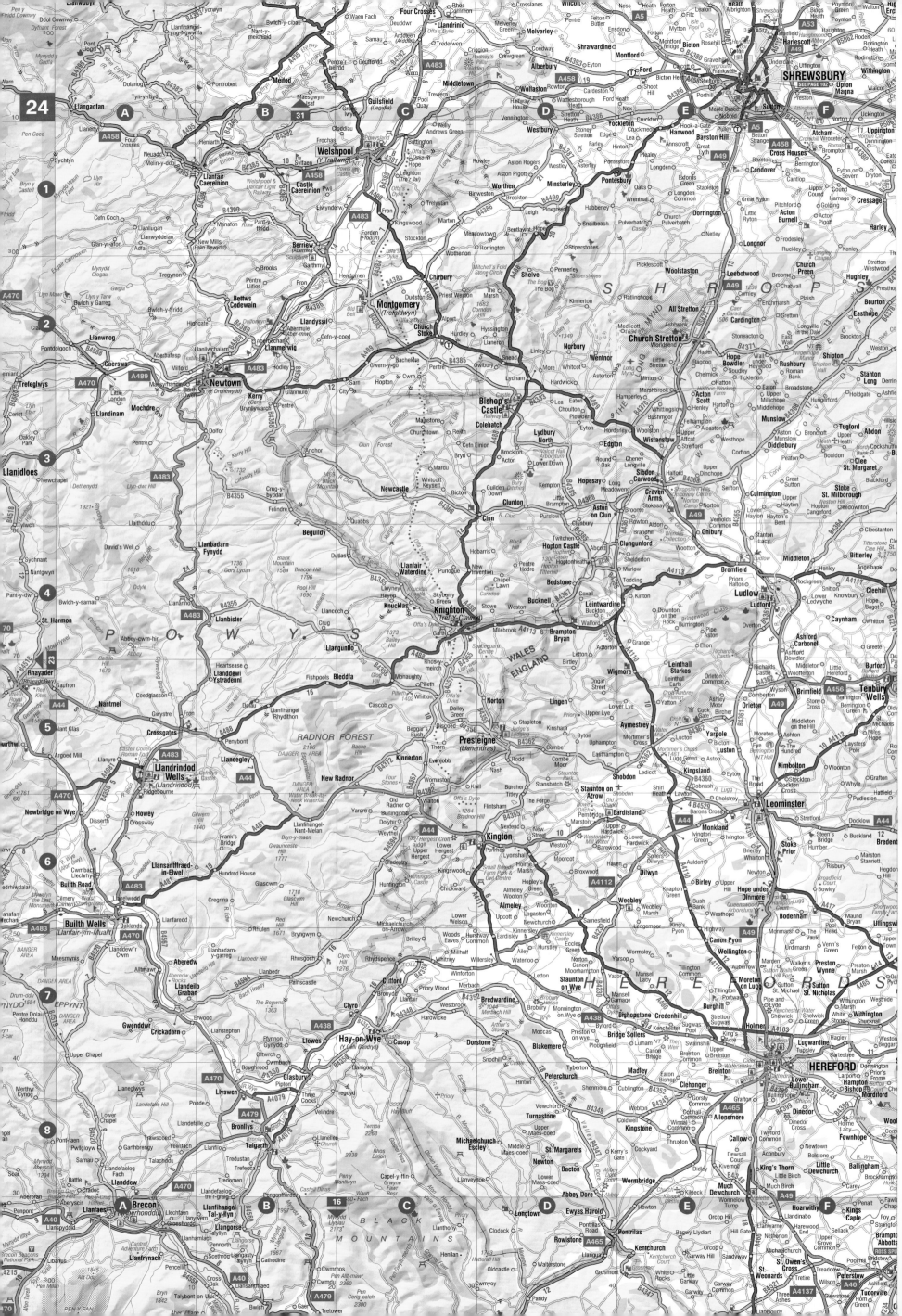

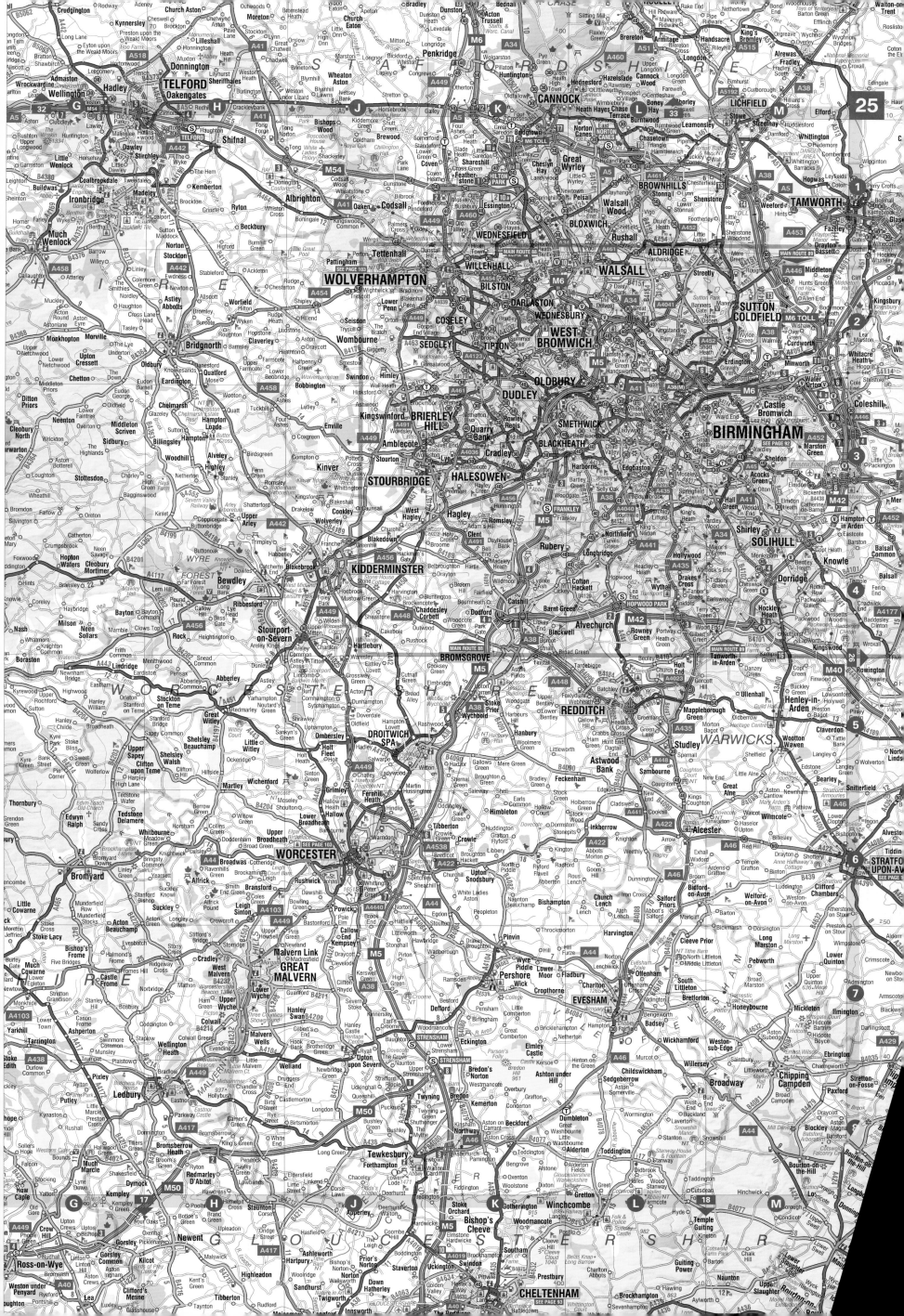

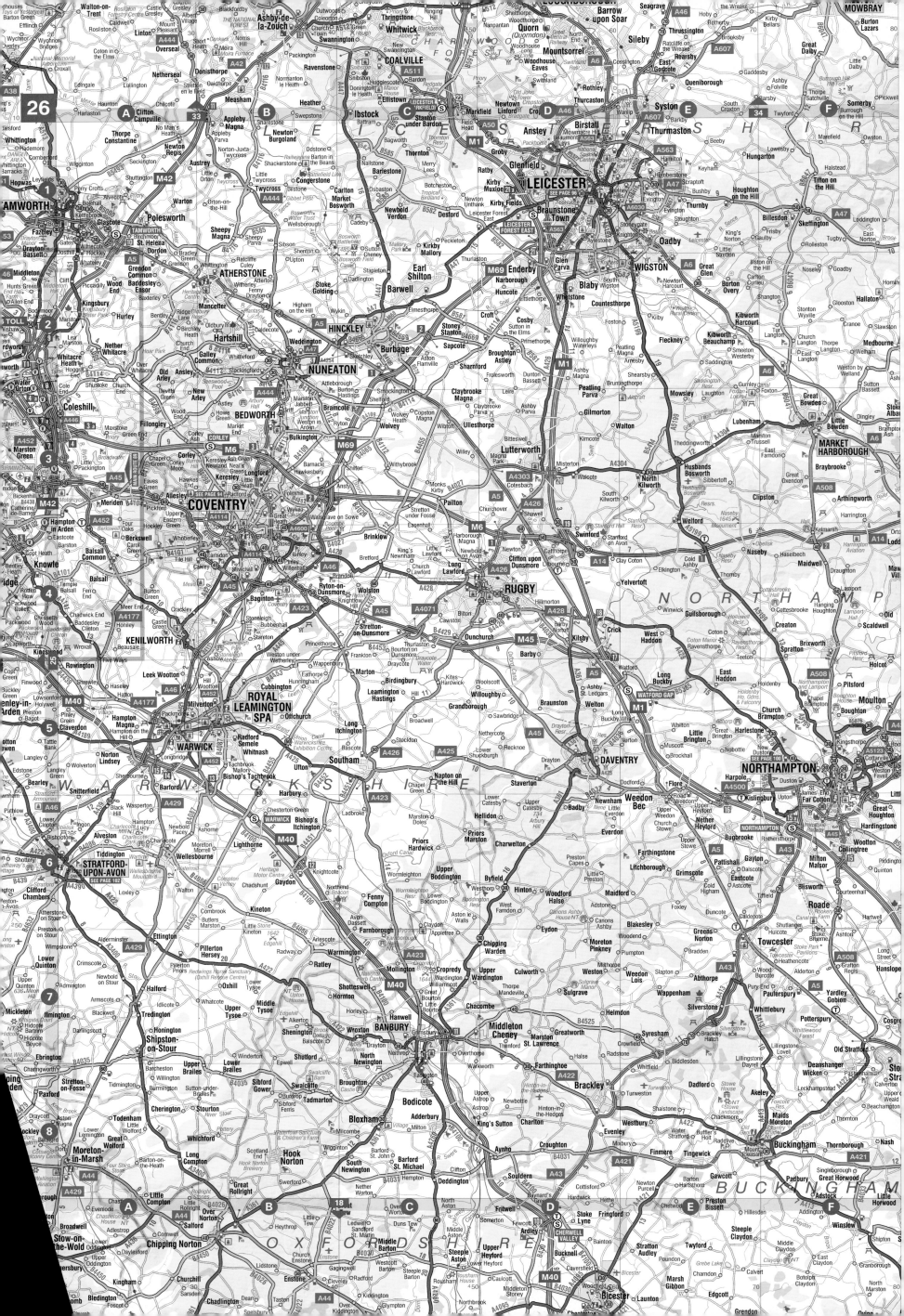

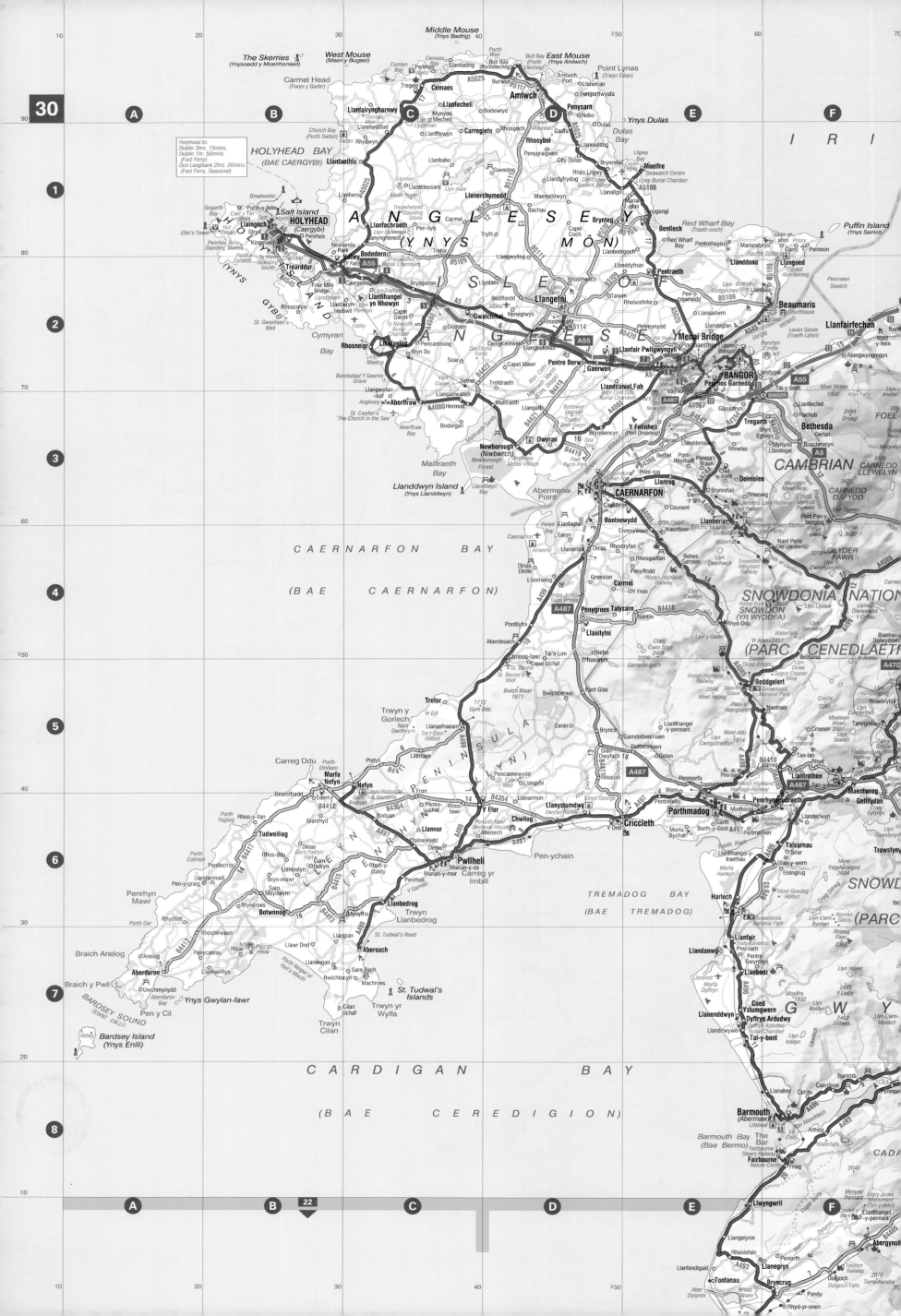

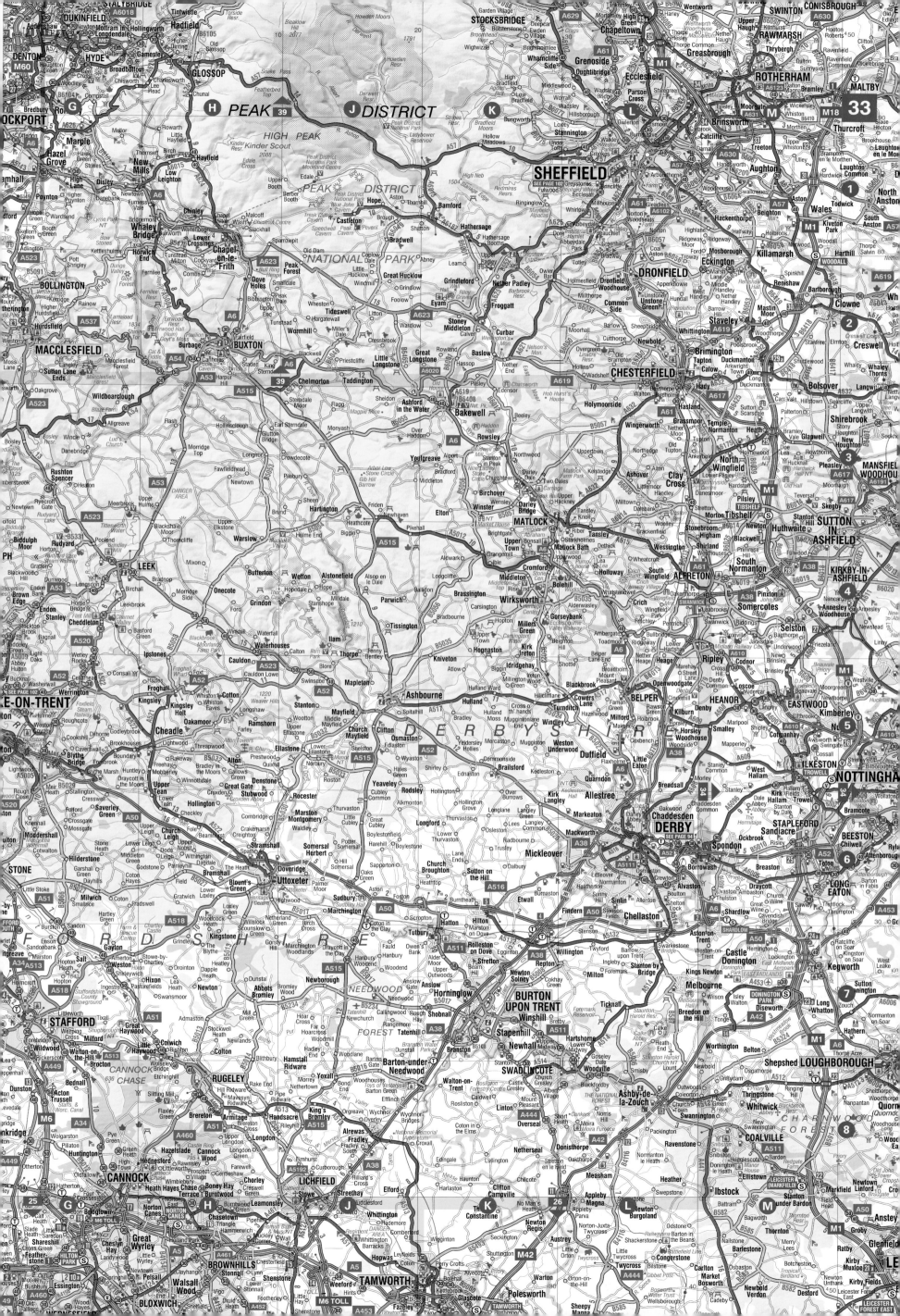

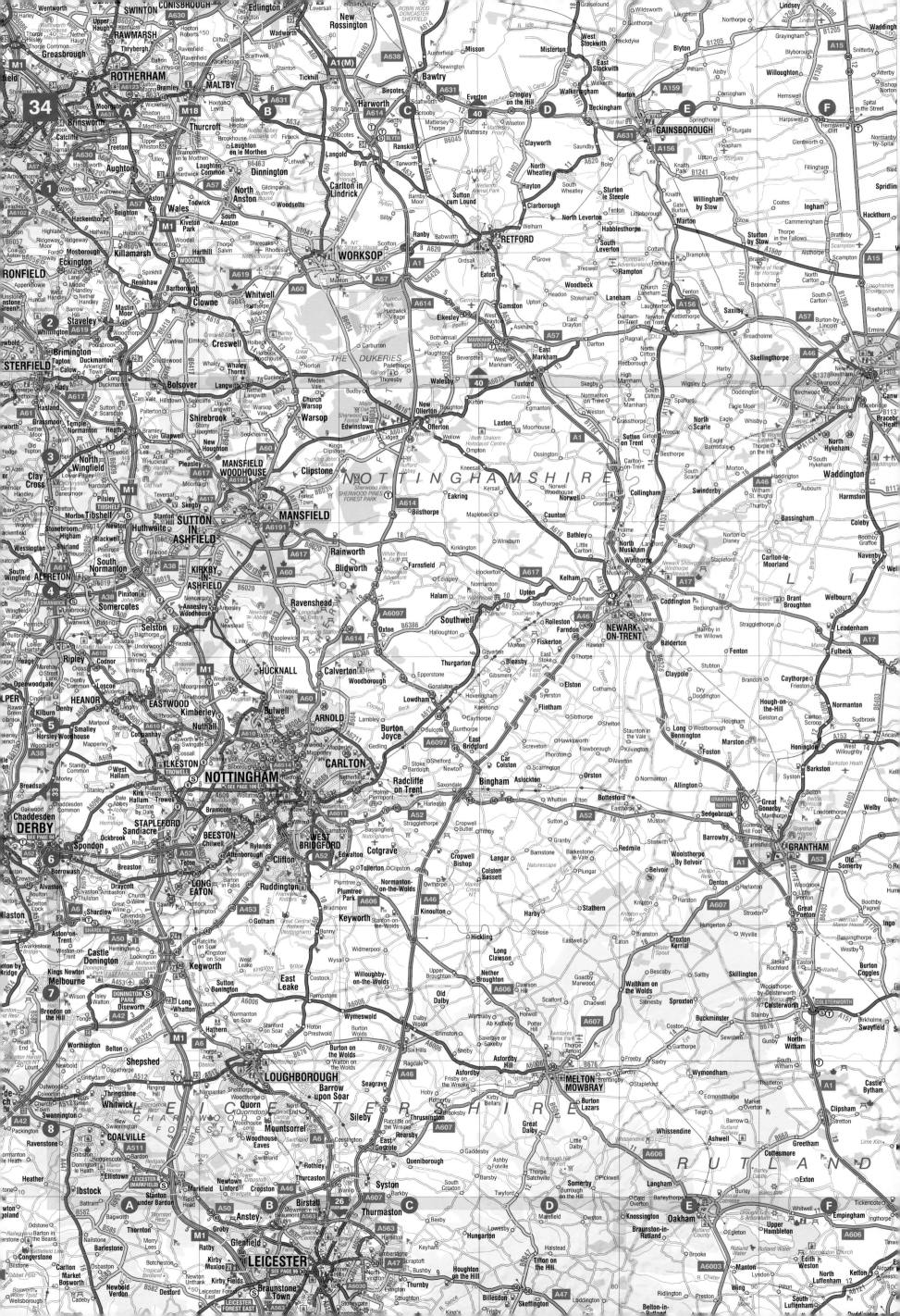

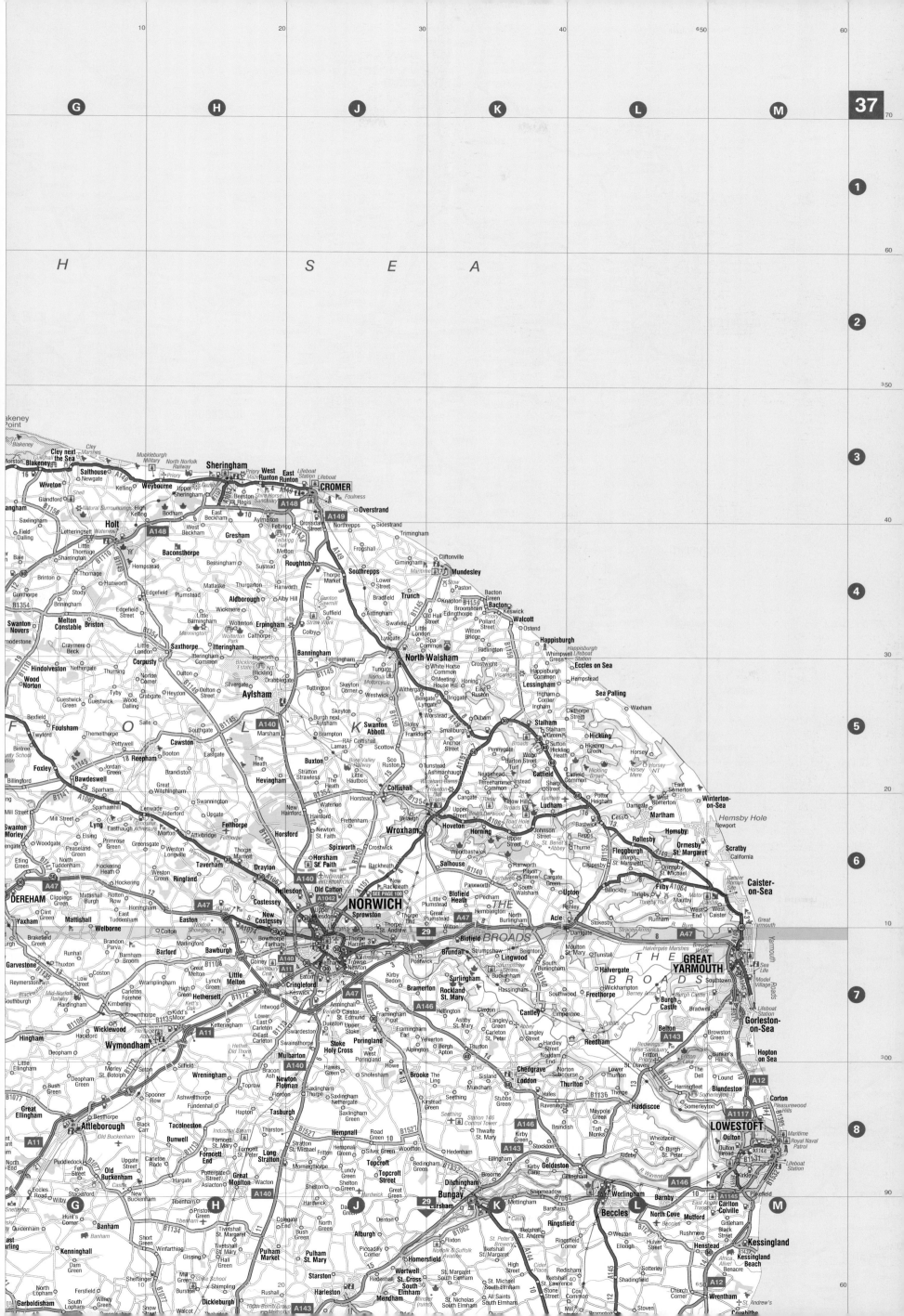

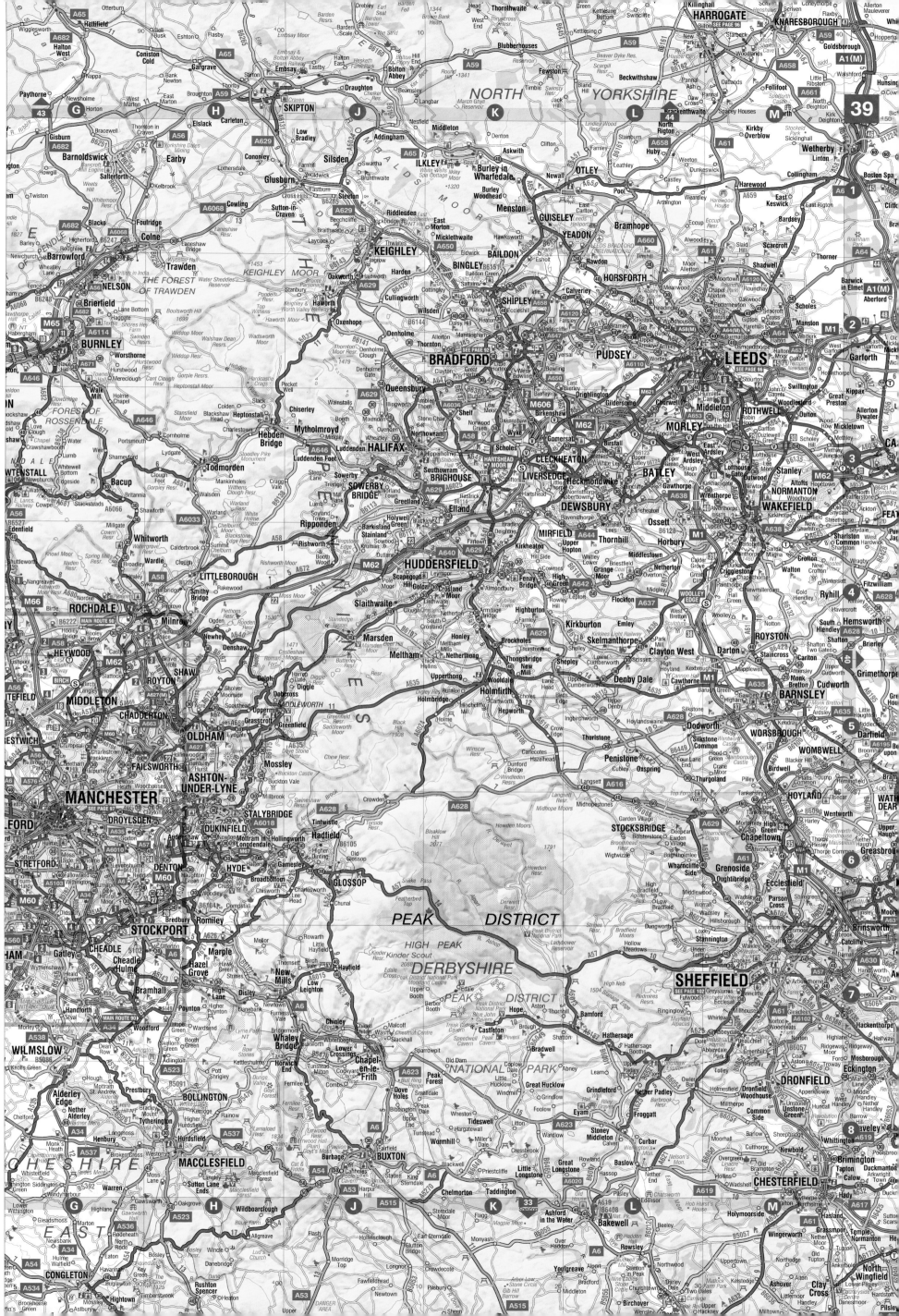

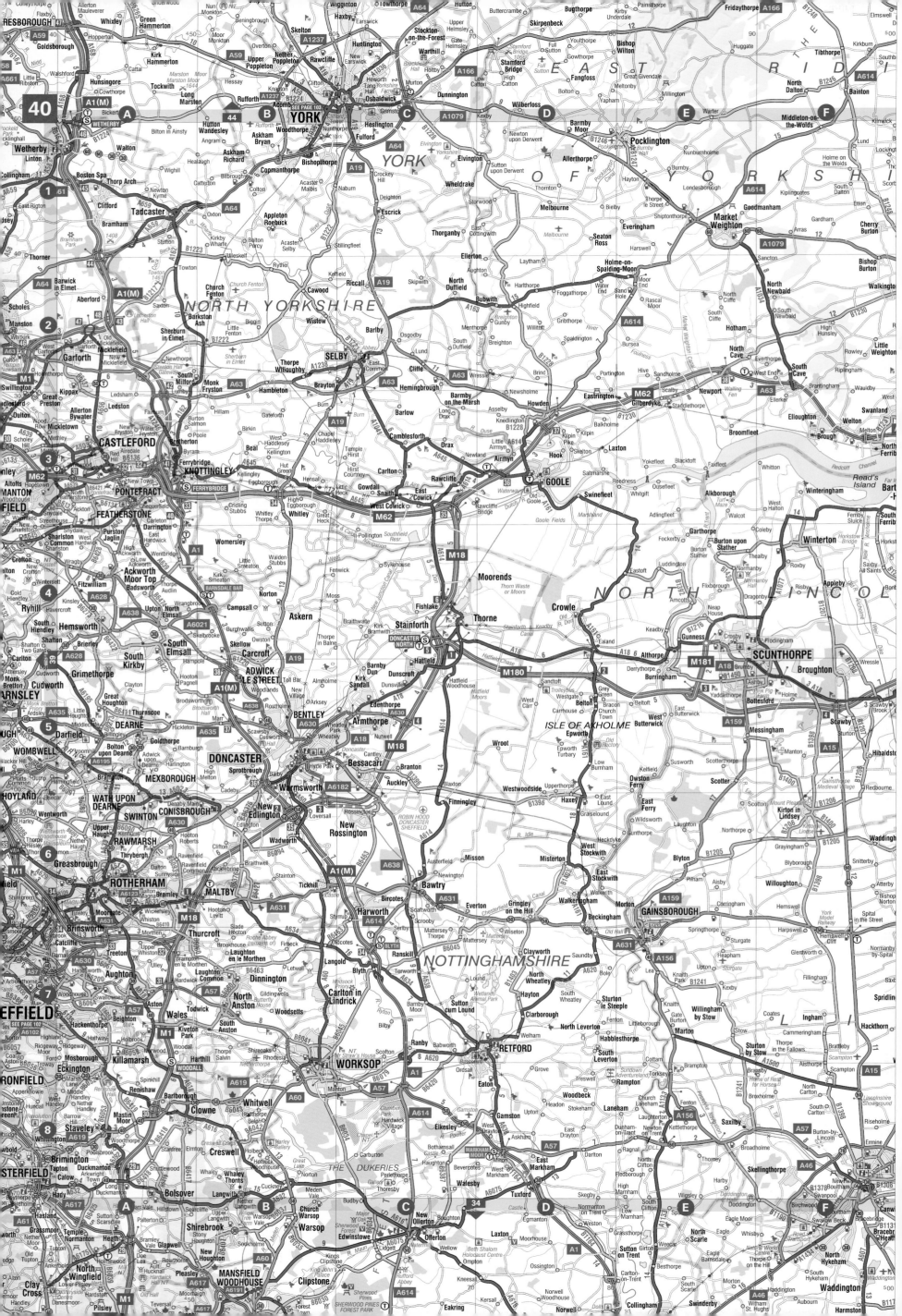

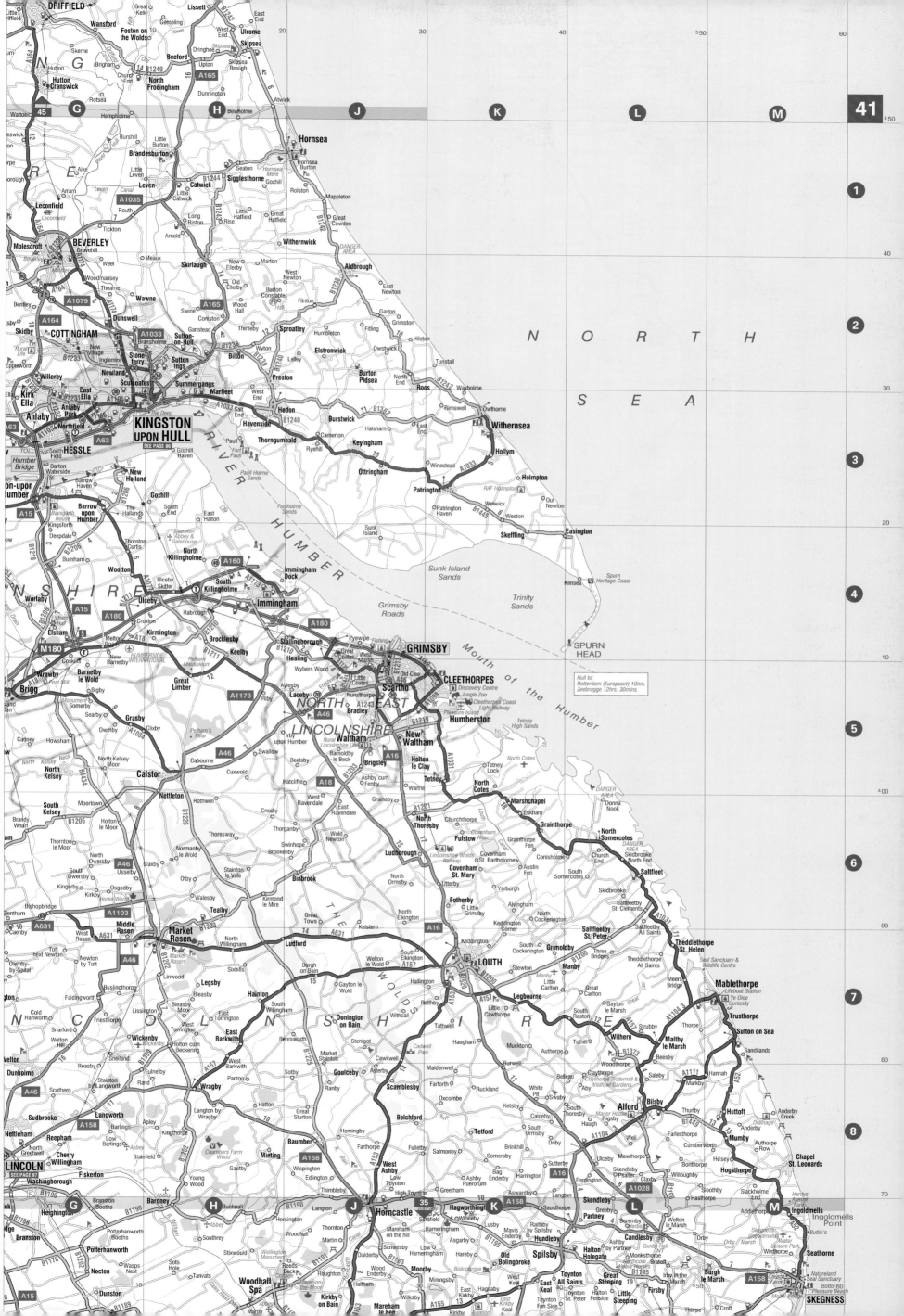

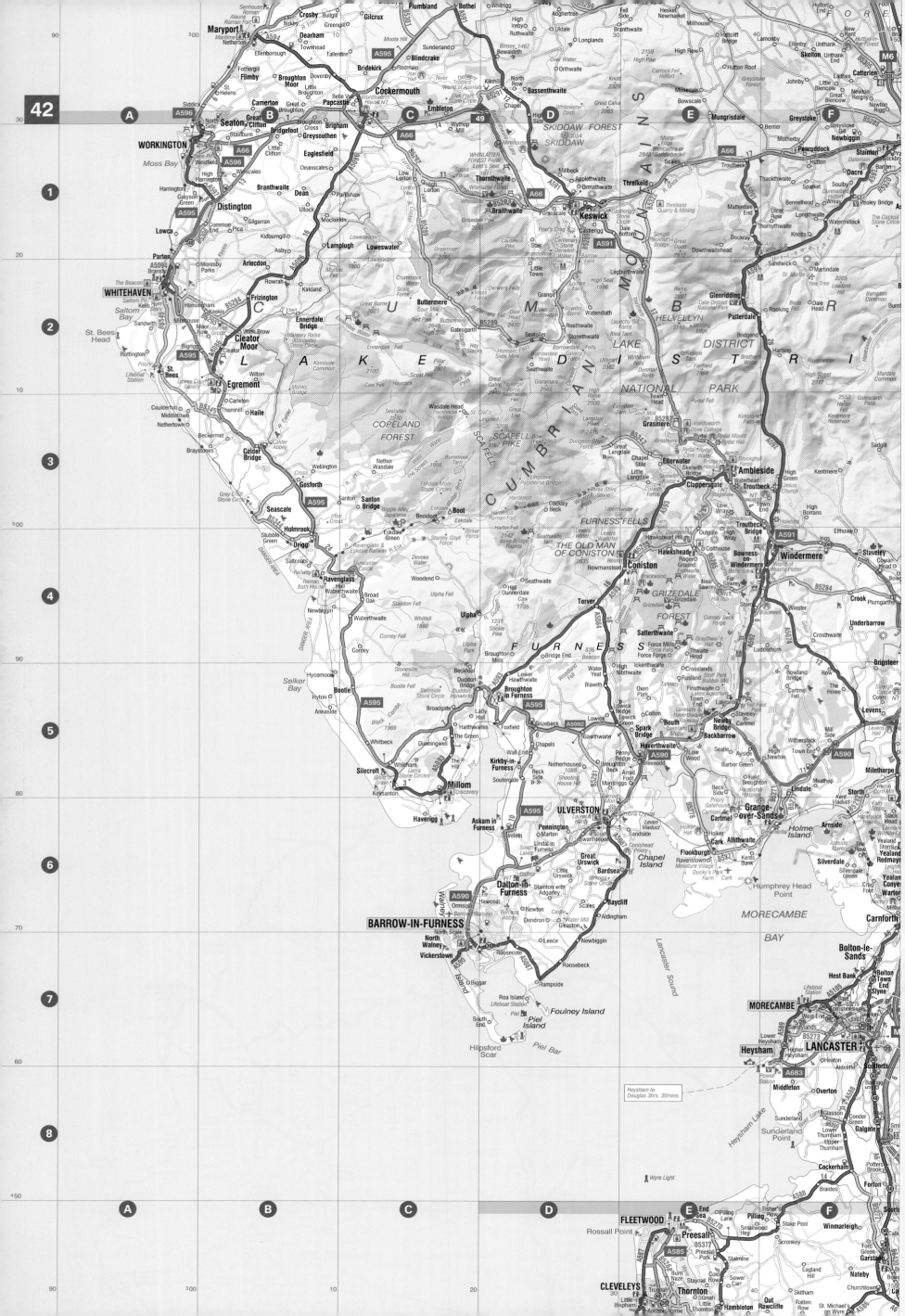

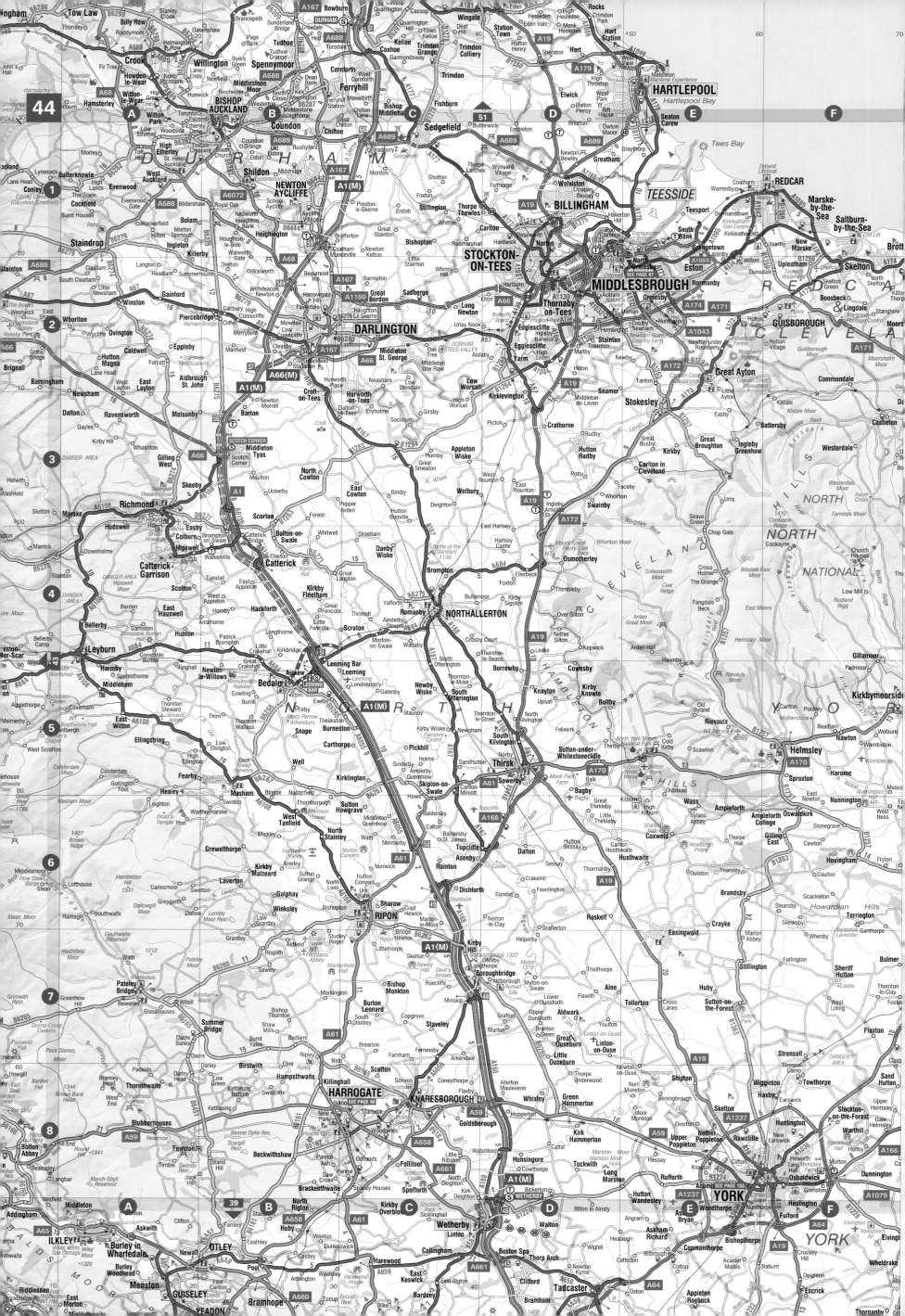

IRISH SEA

NORTHERN IRELAND

DUMFRIES & GALLOWAY

SOUTH AYRSHIRE

CARRICK

CHANGUE FOREST

LUCE BAY

Campbeltown to
Ballycastle 1hr. 30mins.
(Seasonal)

Cairnryan (Loch Ryan Port) to
Belfast 2hrs. 15mins.
(Fast Ferry, Seasonal)

Cairnryan to
Larne 2hrs.

PAGE NOT CONTINUED

Maybole

Stranraer

Girvan

Ballantrae

Portpatrick

Port William

Drummore

MULL OF GALLOWAY

Mull of Galloway

Ailsa Craig

Achinhoan Head

Johnston's Point

Sheep Island

Sanda Island

Cove Point

Polliwilline Bay

Macharioch

Corsewall Point

Dunure

Maidens

Turnberry

Kirkoswald

Crossraguel Abbey

Dailly

Barr

Lendalfoot

Colmonell

Pinwherry

Barrhill

Cairnryan

Kirkcolm

Leswalt

Lochans

Stoneykirk

Sandhead

Ardwell

Port Logan

Kirkmaiden

Glenluce

Dunragit

New Luce

Donaghadee

Copeland Island

Loch Ryan

Ballantrae Bay

Downan Point

Currarie Port

Finnarts Bay

Glen App

Broadsea Bay

Black Head

Cairngarroch Bay

Money Head

Float Bay

Ardwell Point

Mull of Logan

Port Logan Bay

Cairnywellan Head

Clanyard Bay

Laggantalloch Head

Crammag Head

Maryport Bay

Port Kemin

Cailliness Point

Kilstay Bay

Balgowan Point

Terally Point

Chapel Rossan Bay

Low Ardwell

Logan Botanic Garden

Logan Fish Pond

Logan House

Kildonan

Kirklauchline

Port of Spittal Bay

Dunskey Castle

Lifeboat Station

Knockdolian

Garleffin

Heronsford

Glenwhilly

Chirmorie

Polbae

Glenwhan Challoch

Castle Kennedy

Innermessan

Aird

Mark

Stairhaven

Auchenmalg

Milton

Kilfillan

Auchenmalg Bay

Garheugh Port

Milton Point

Barsalloch Point

Big Scare

Little Scares

Scares

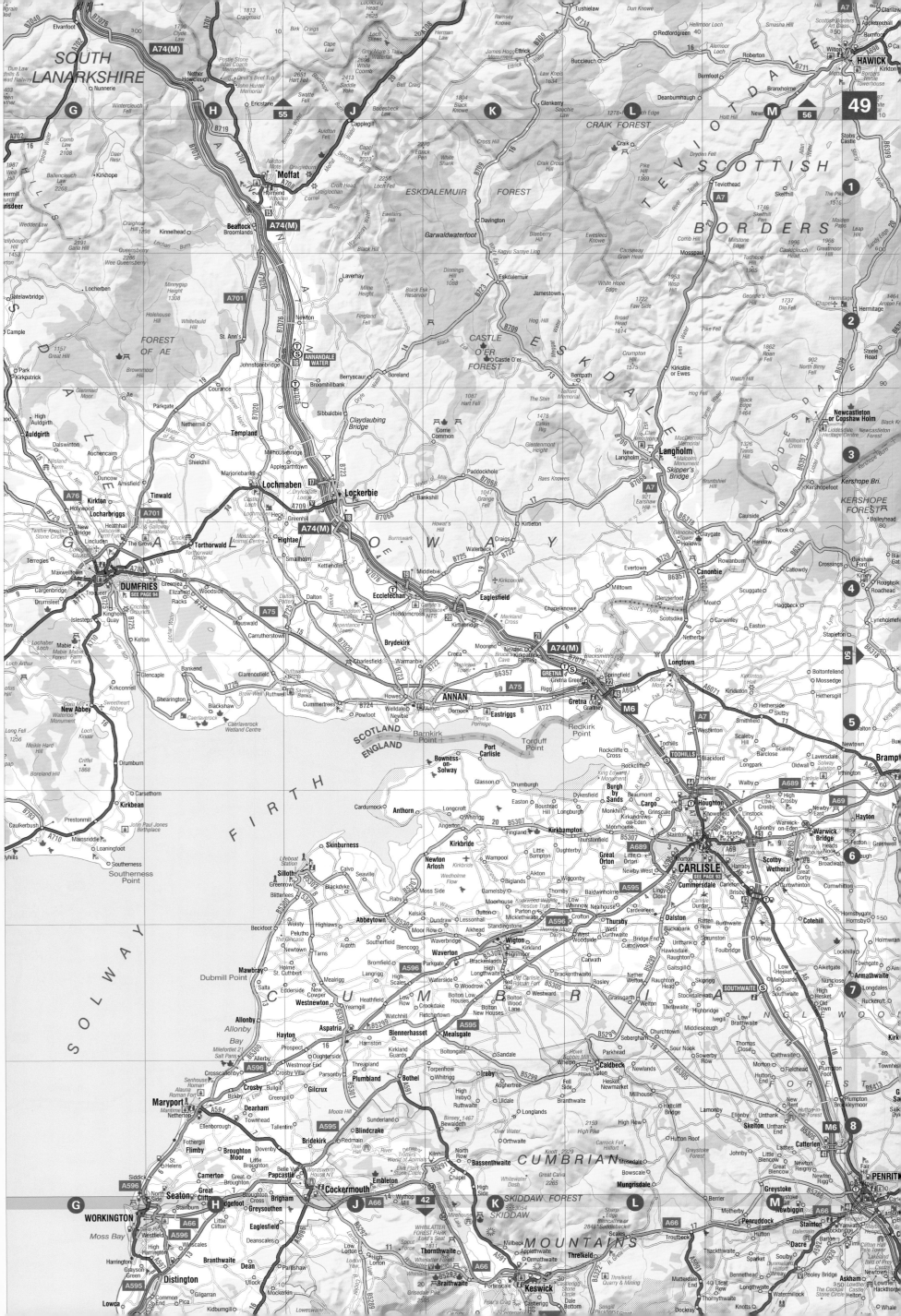

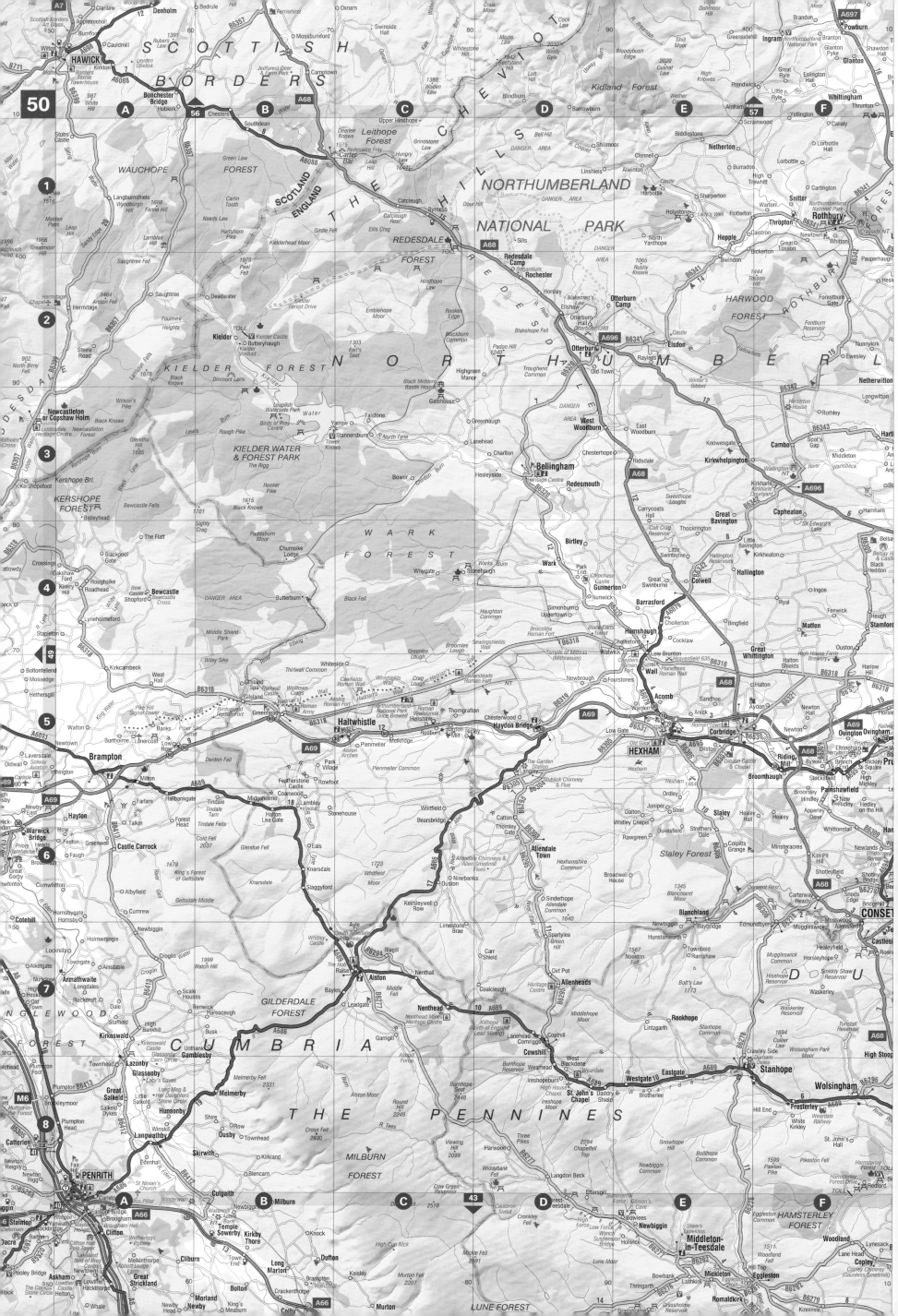

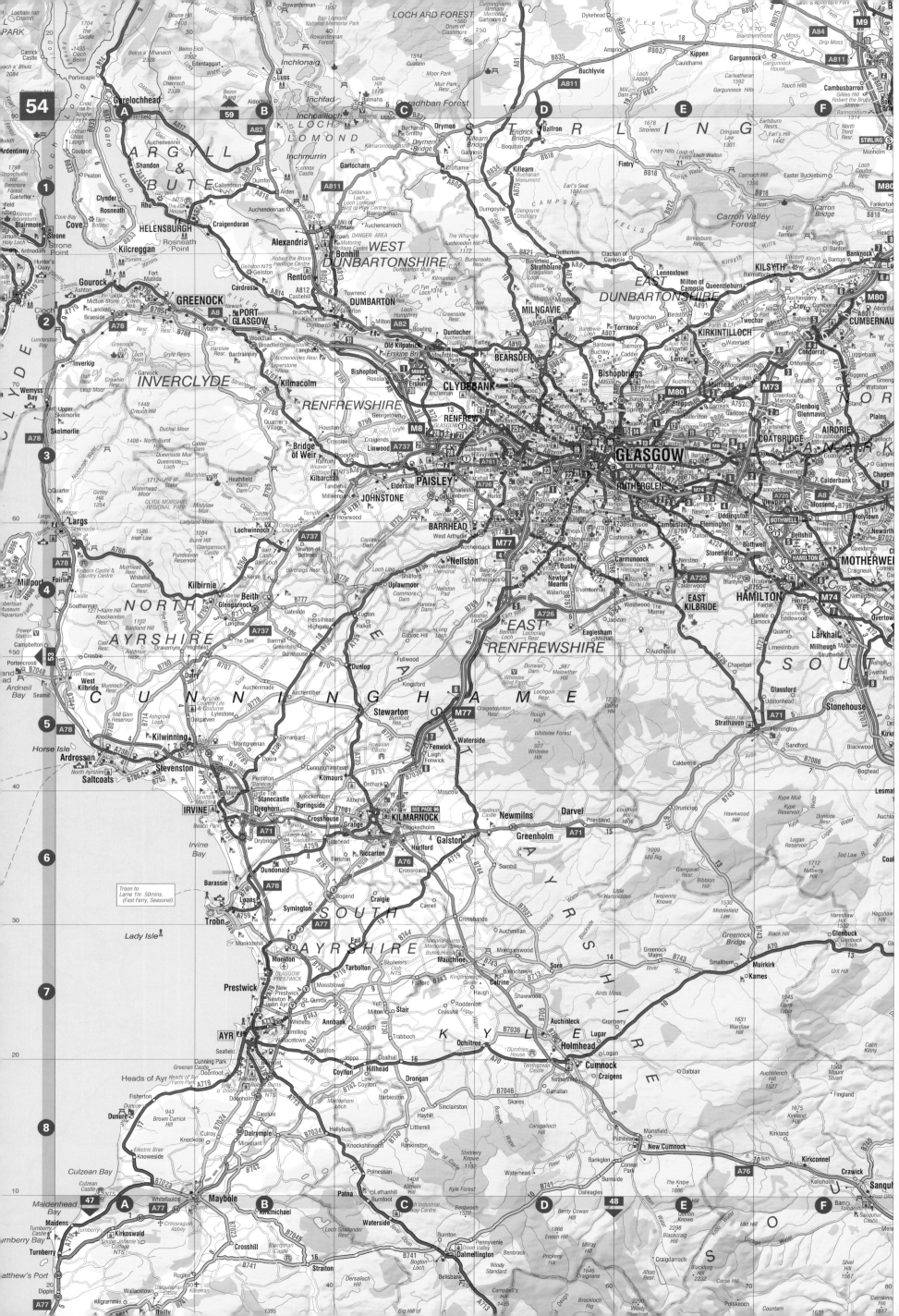

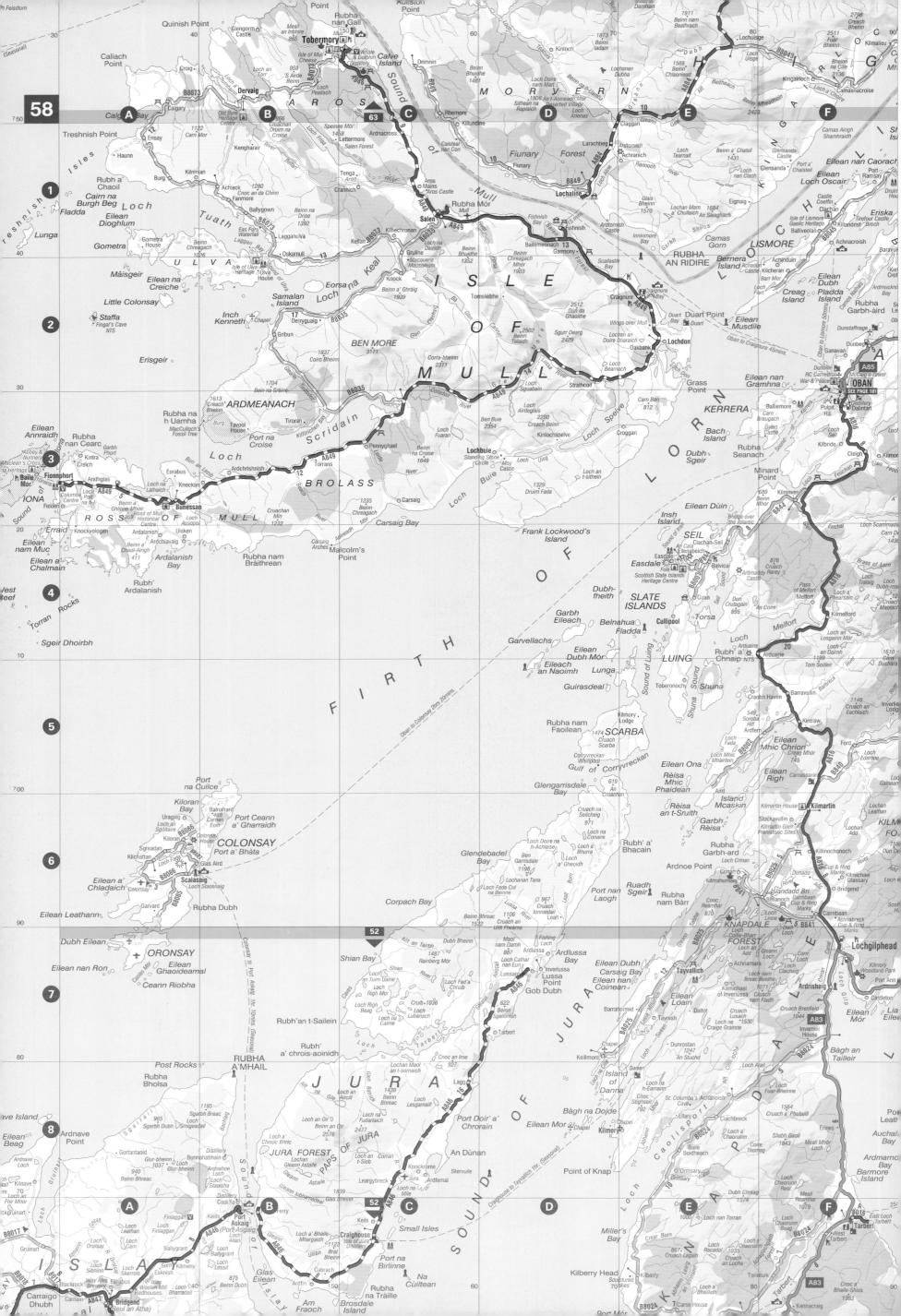

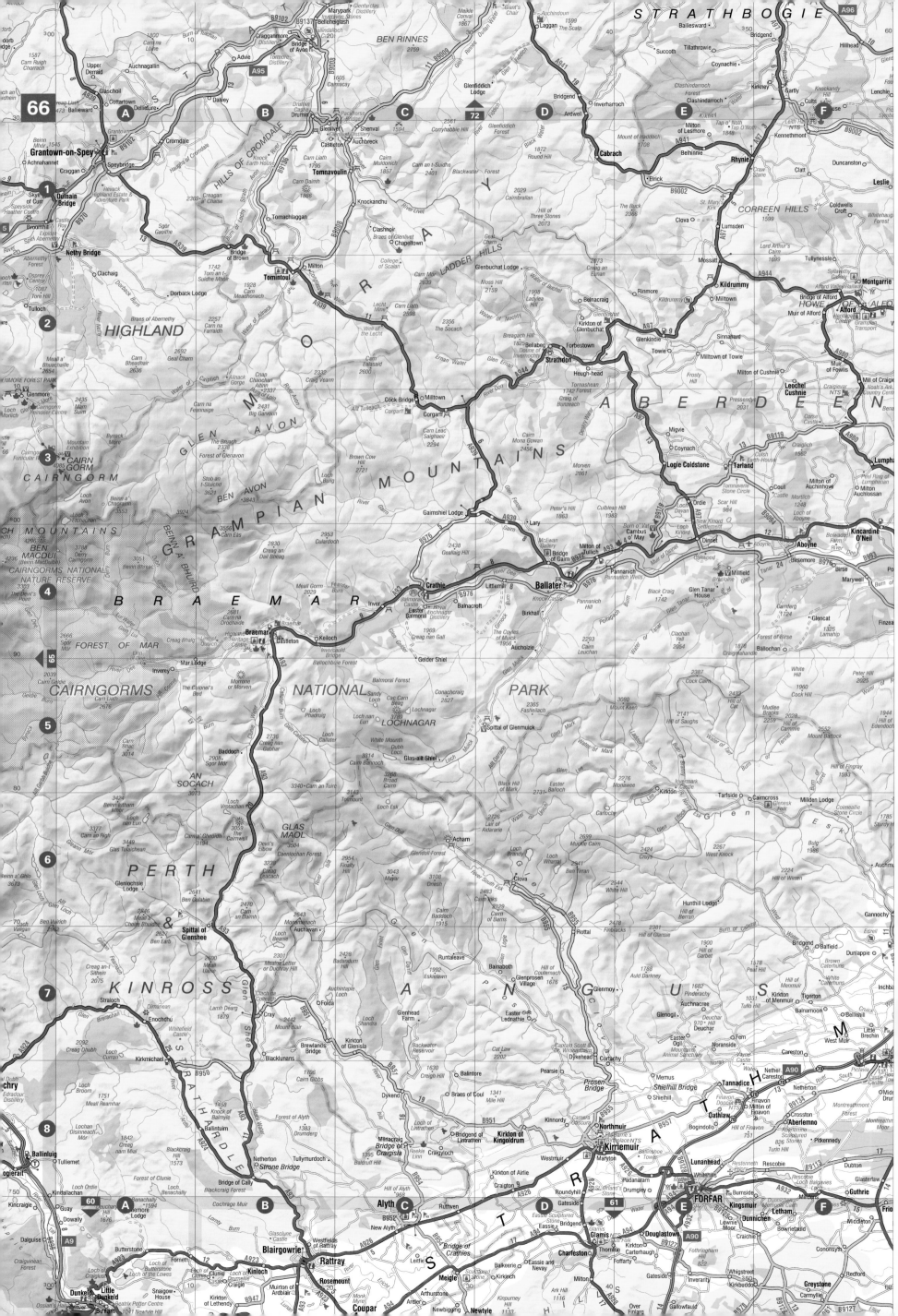

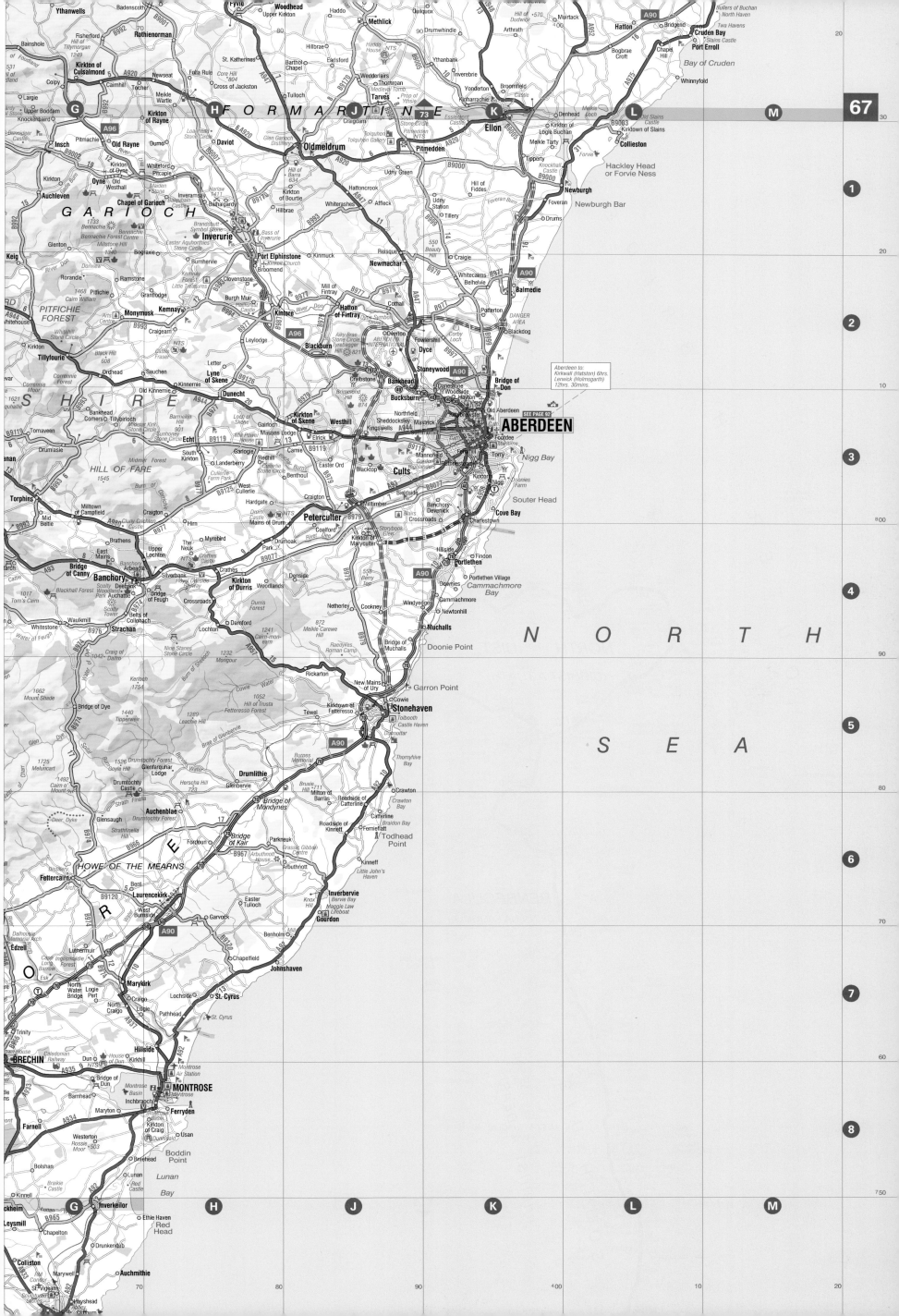

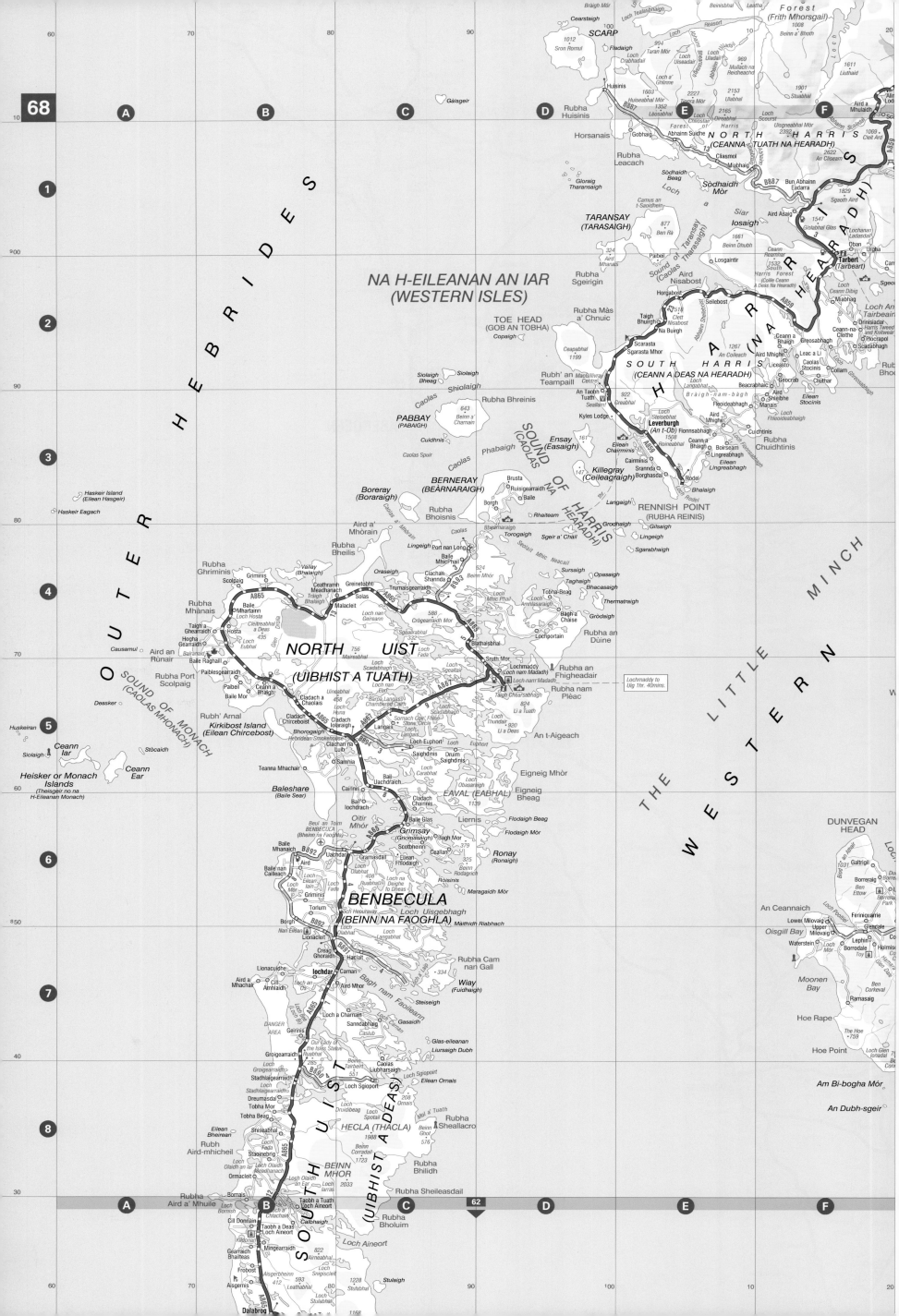

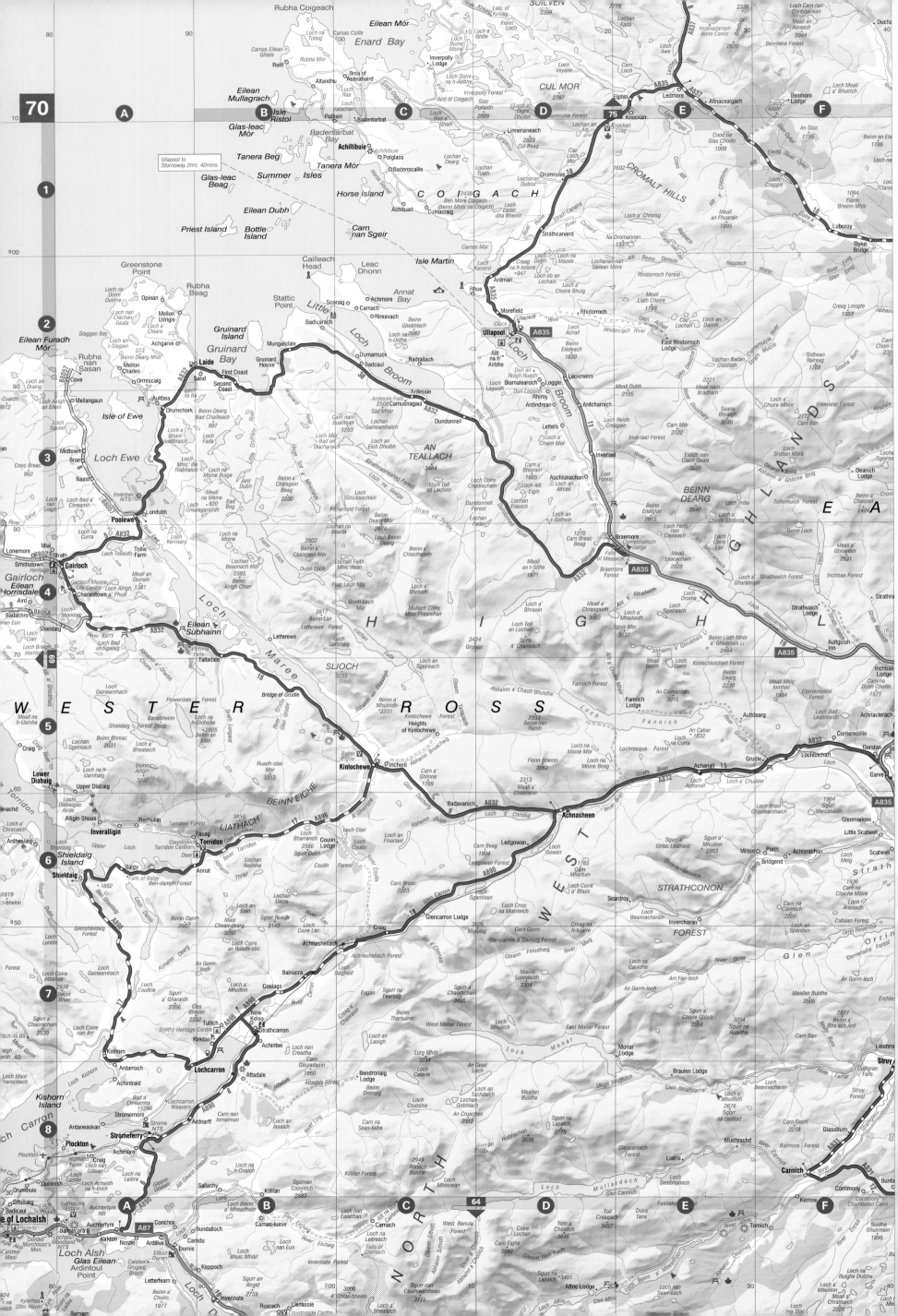

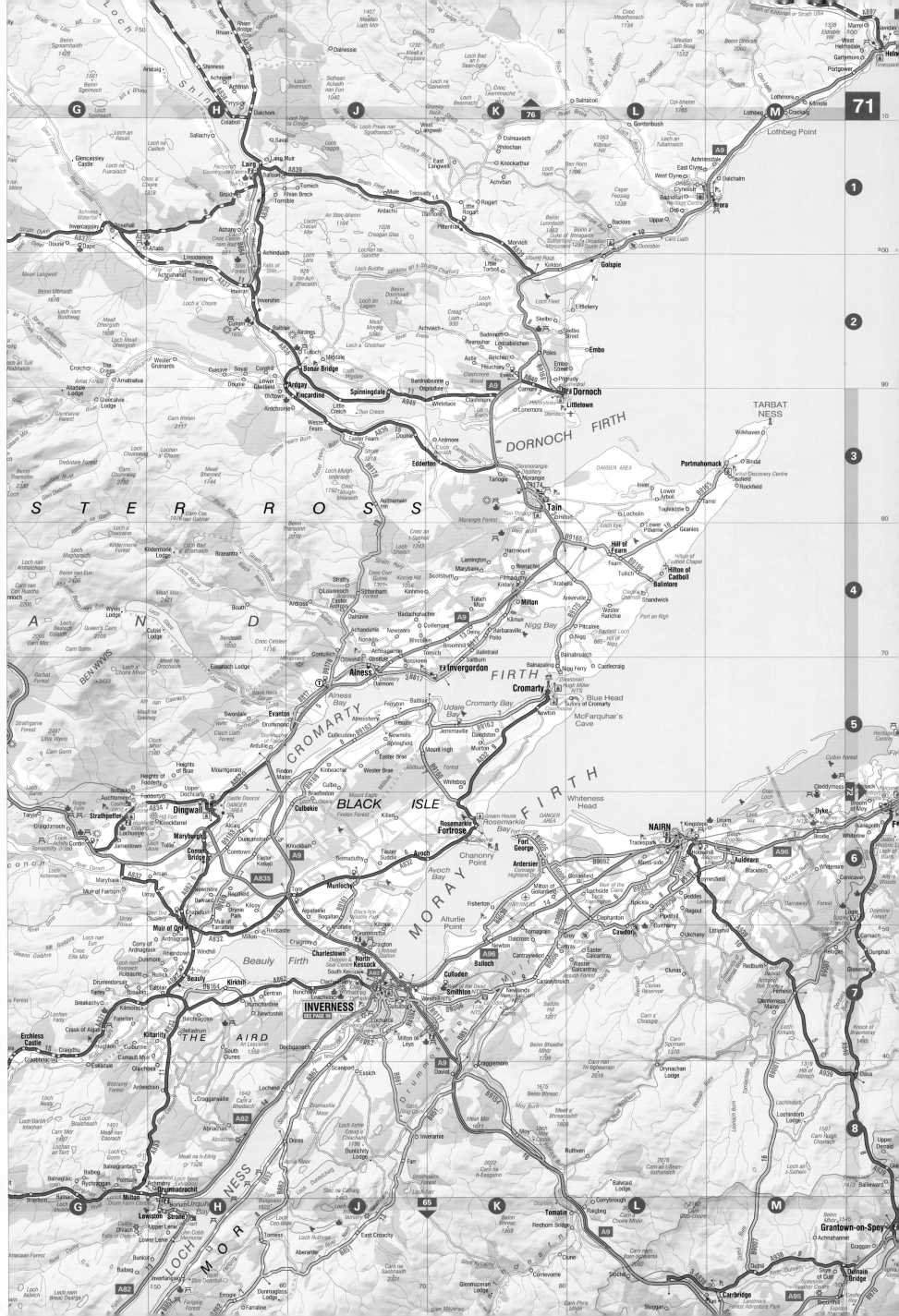

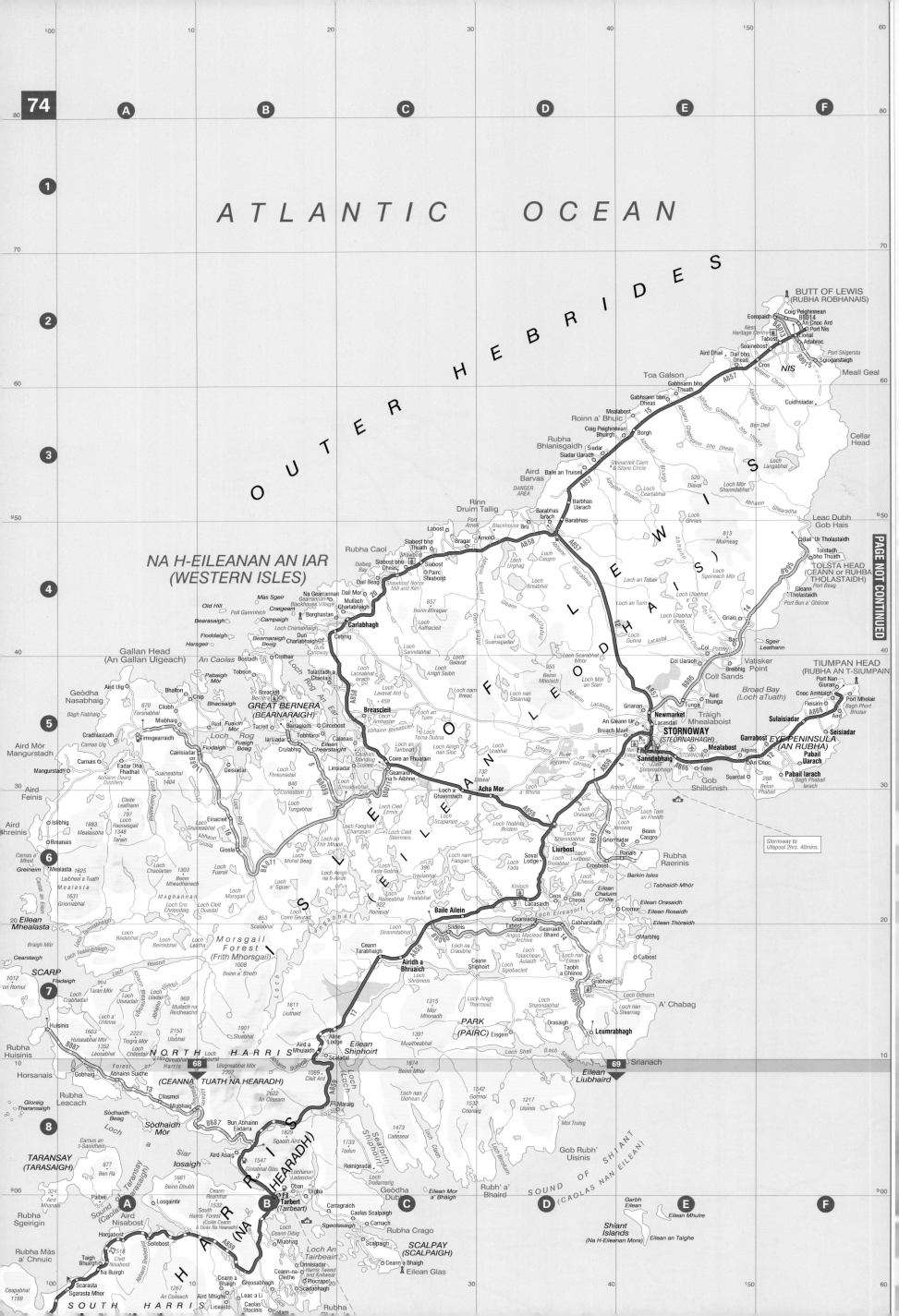

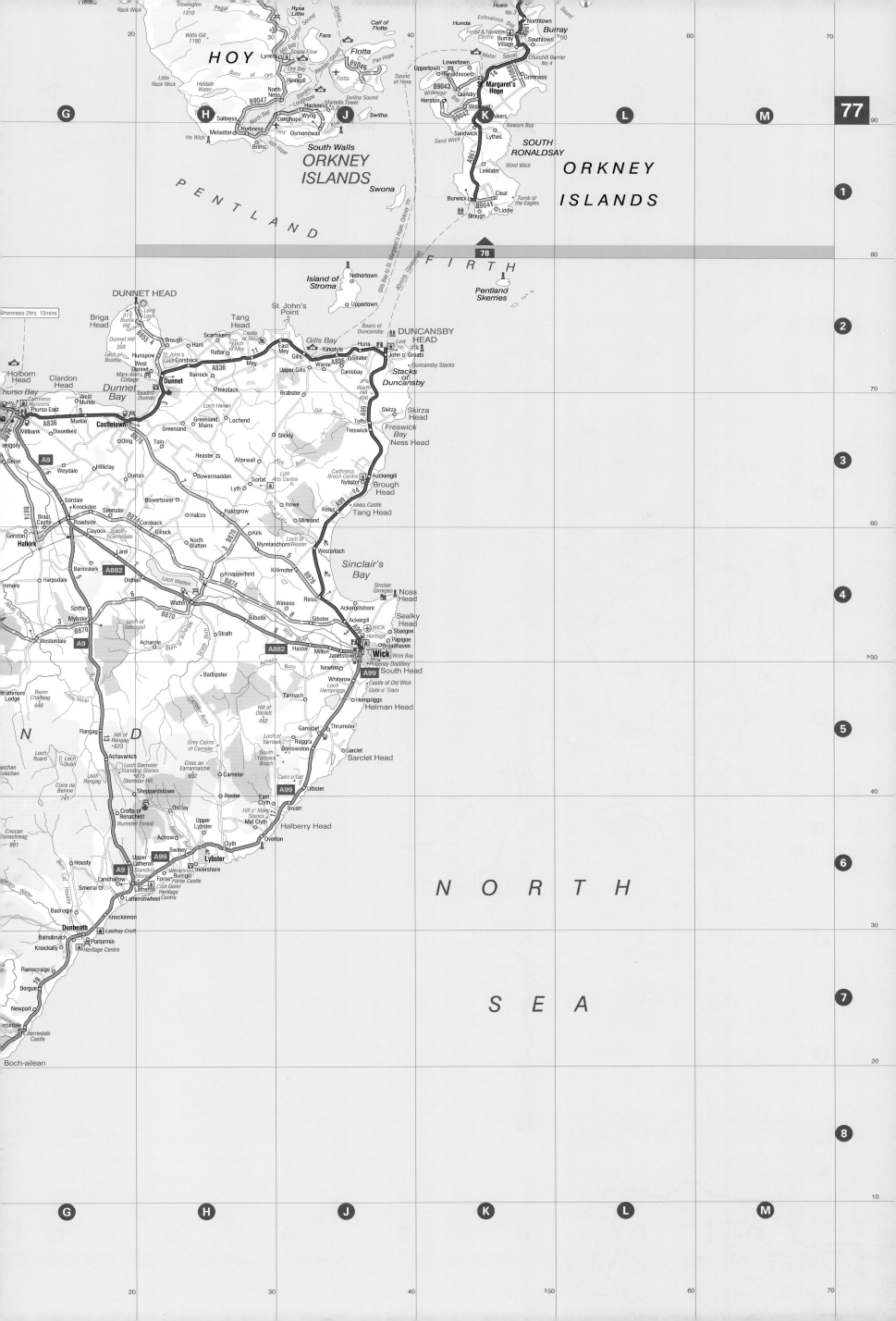

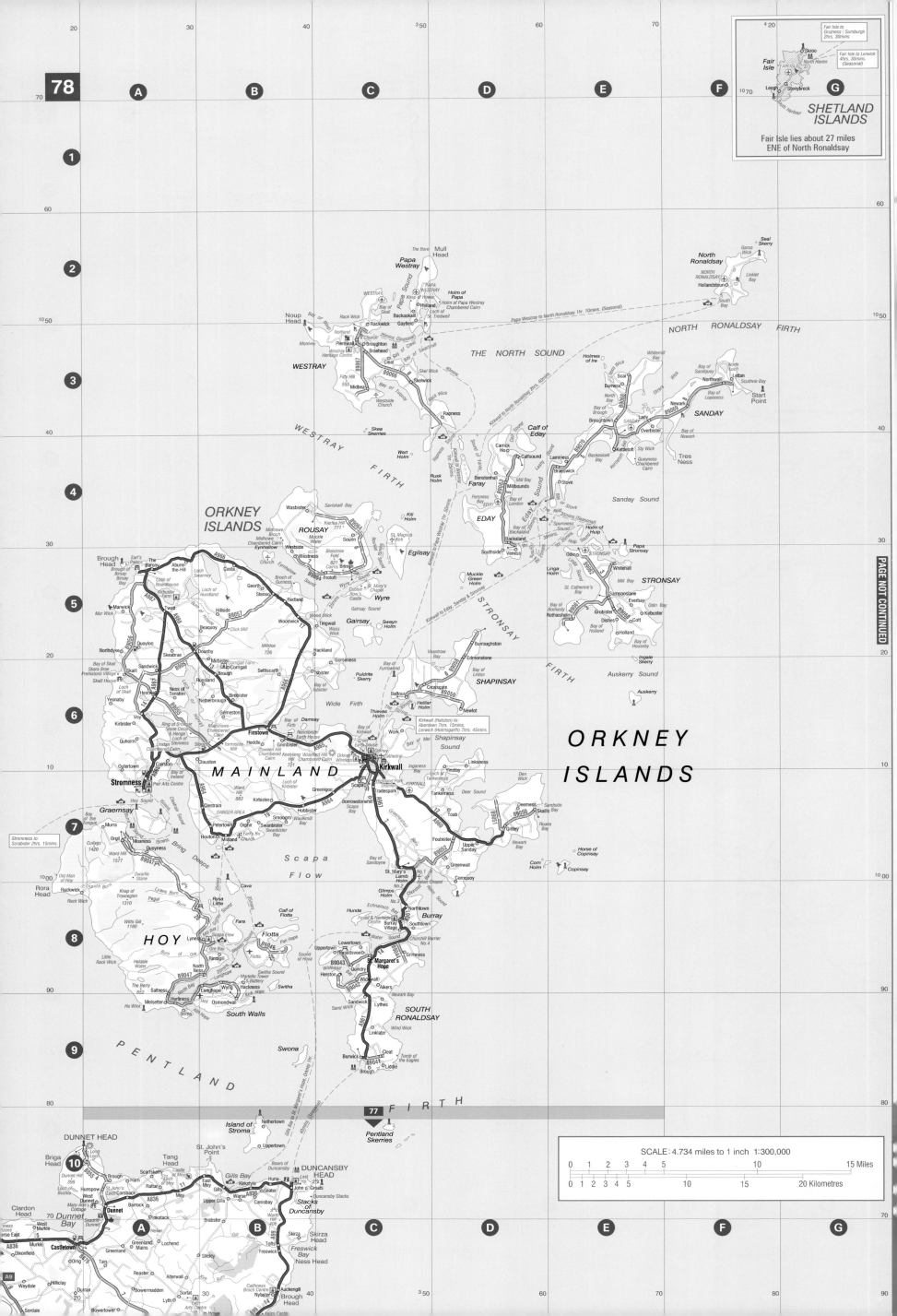

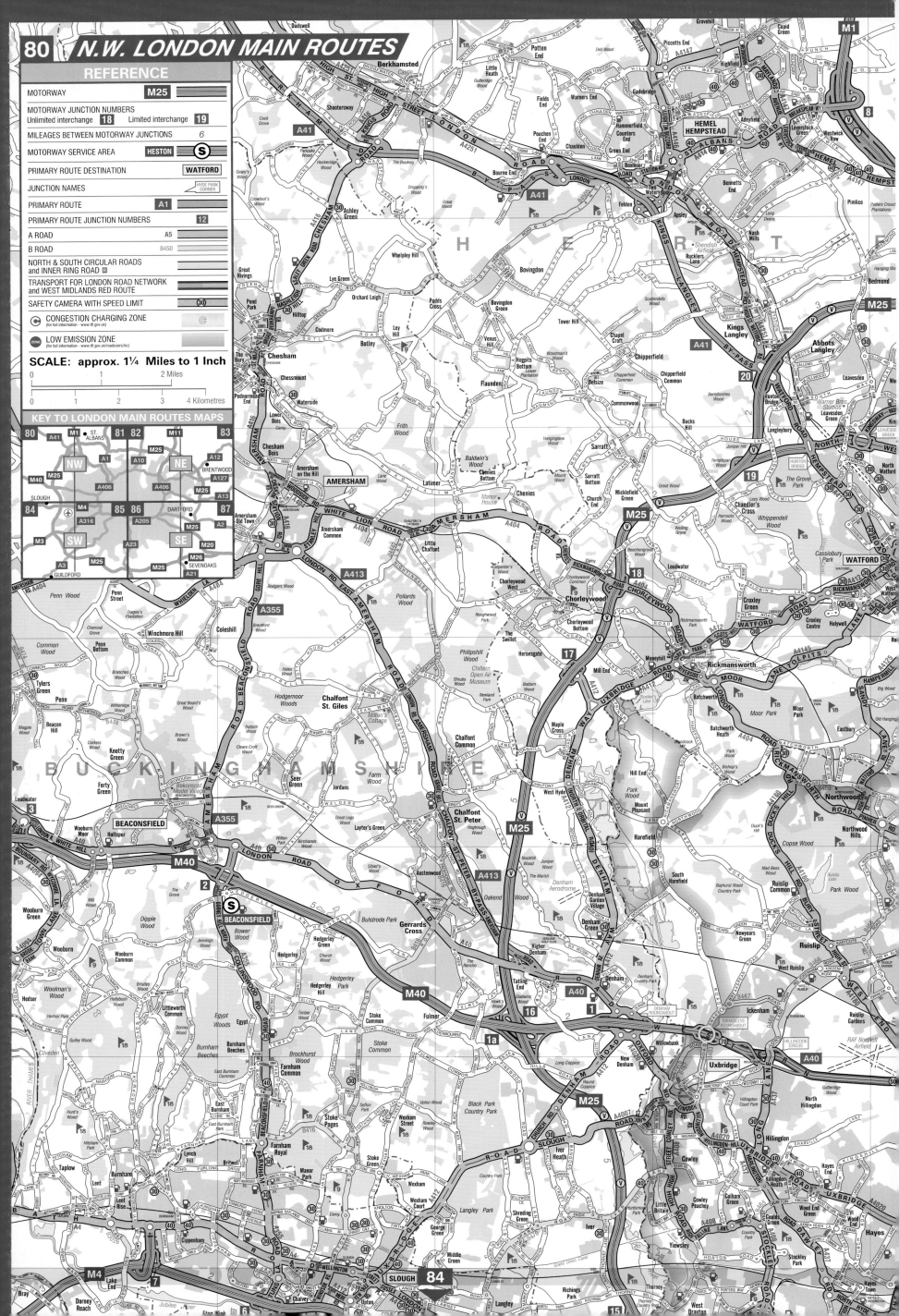

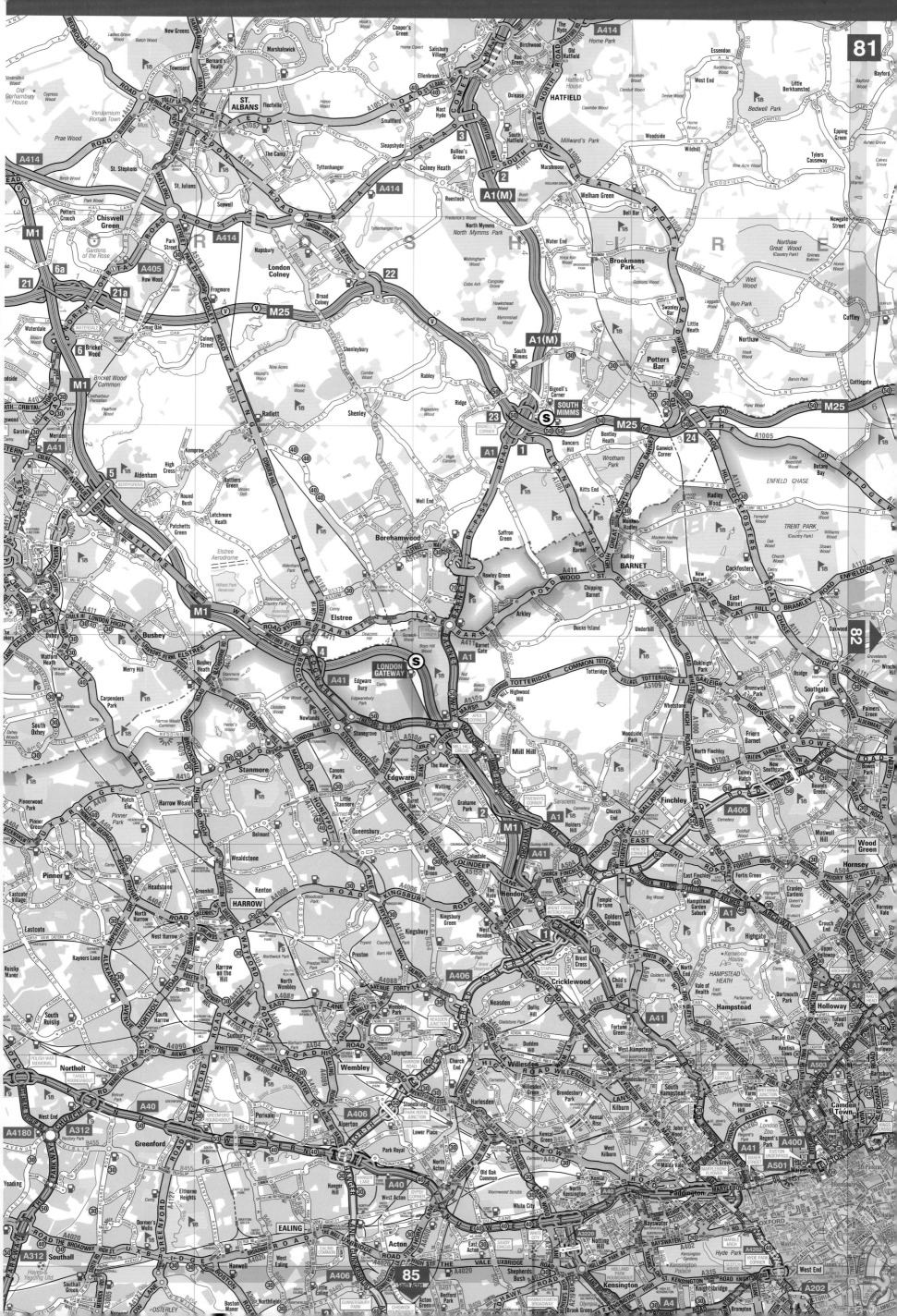

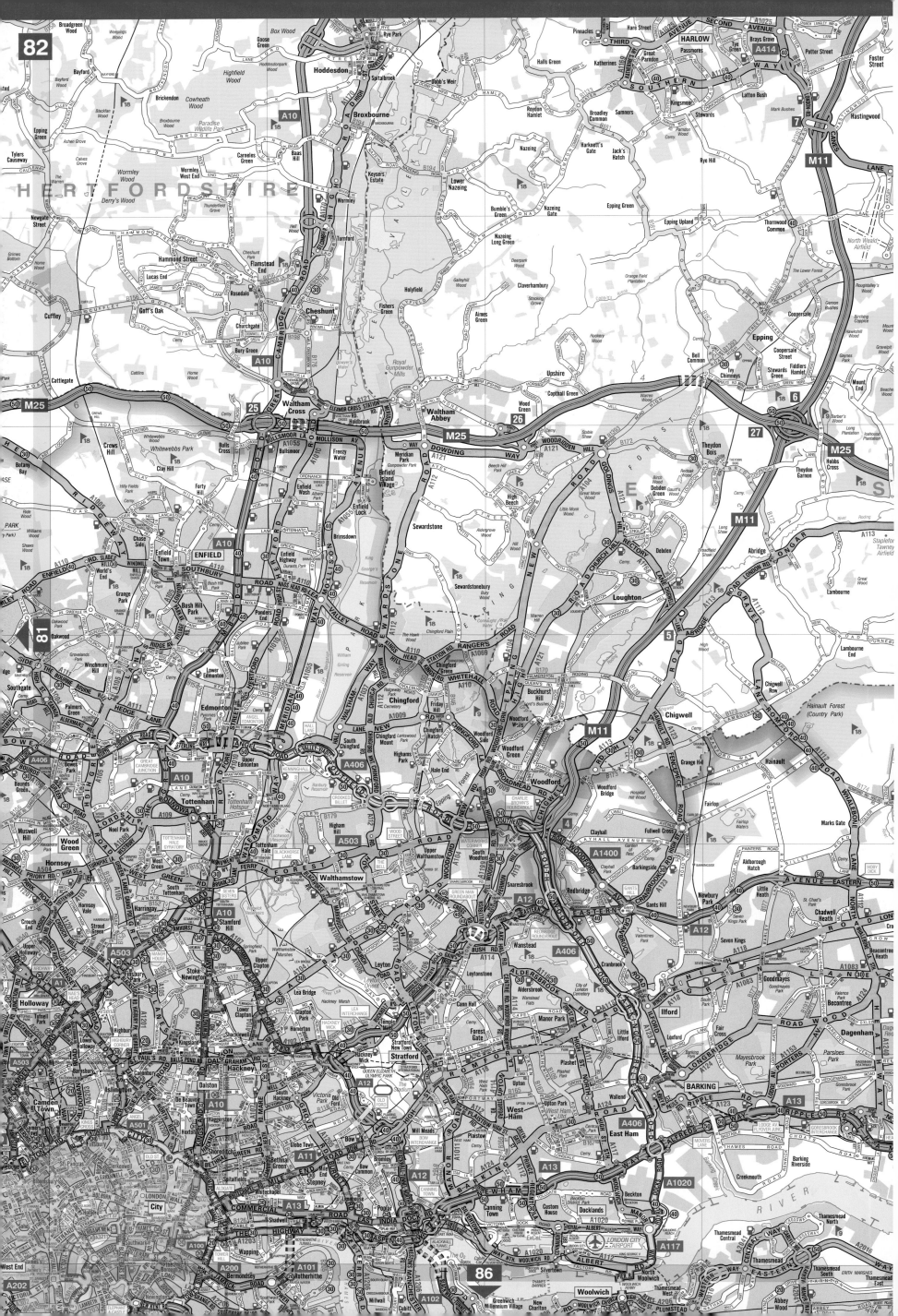

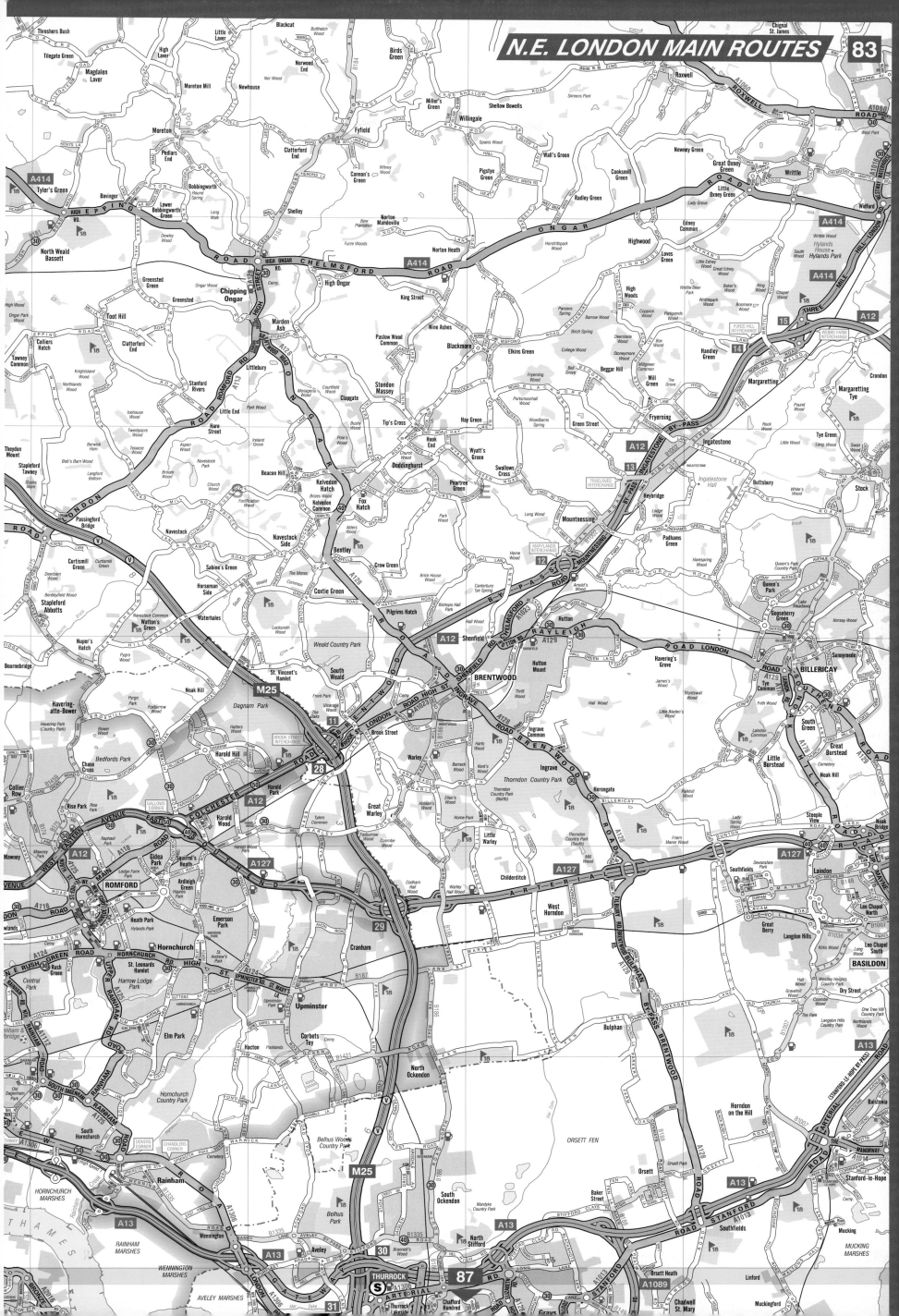

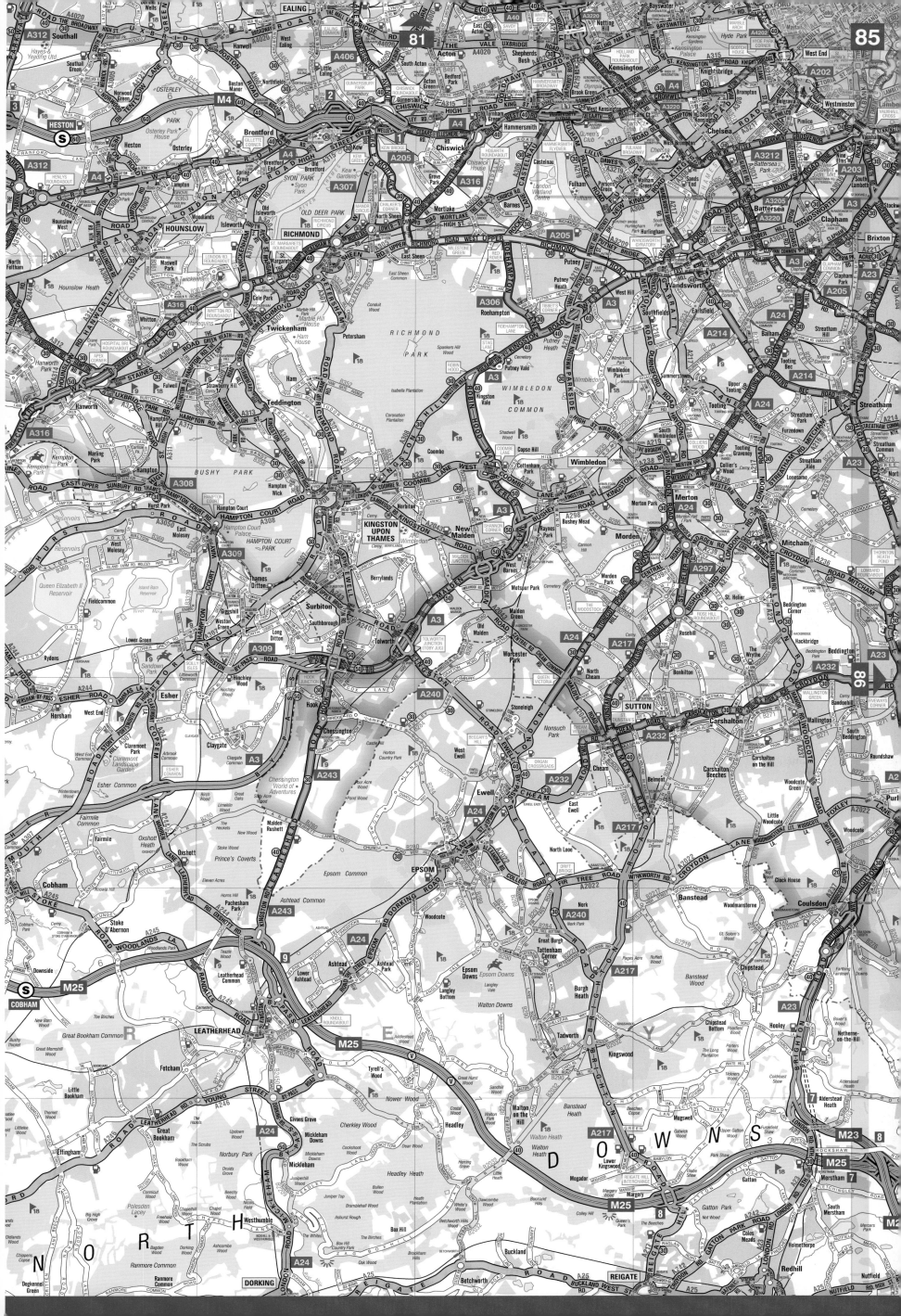

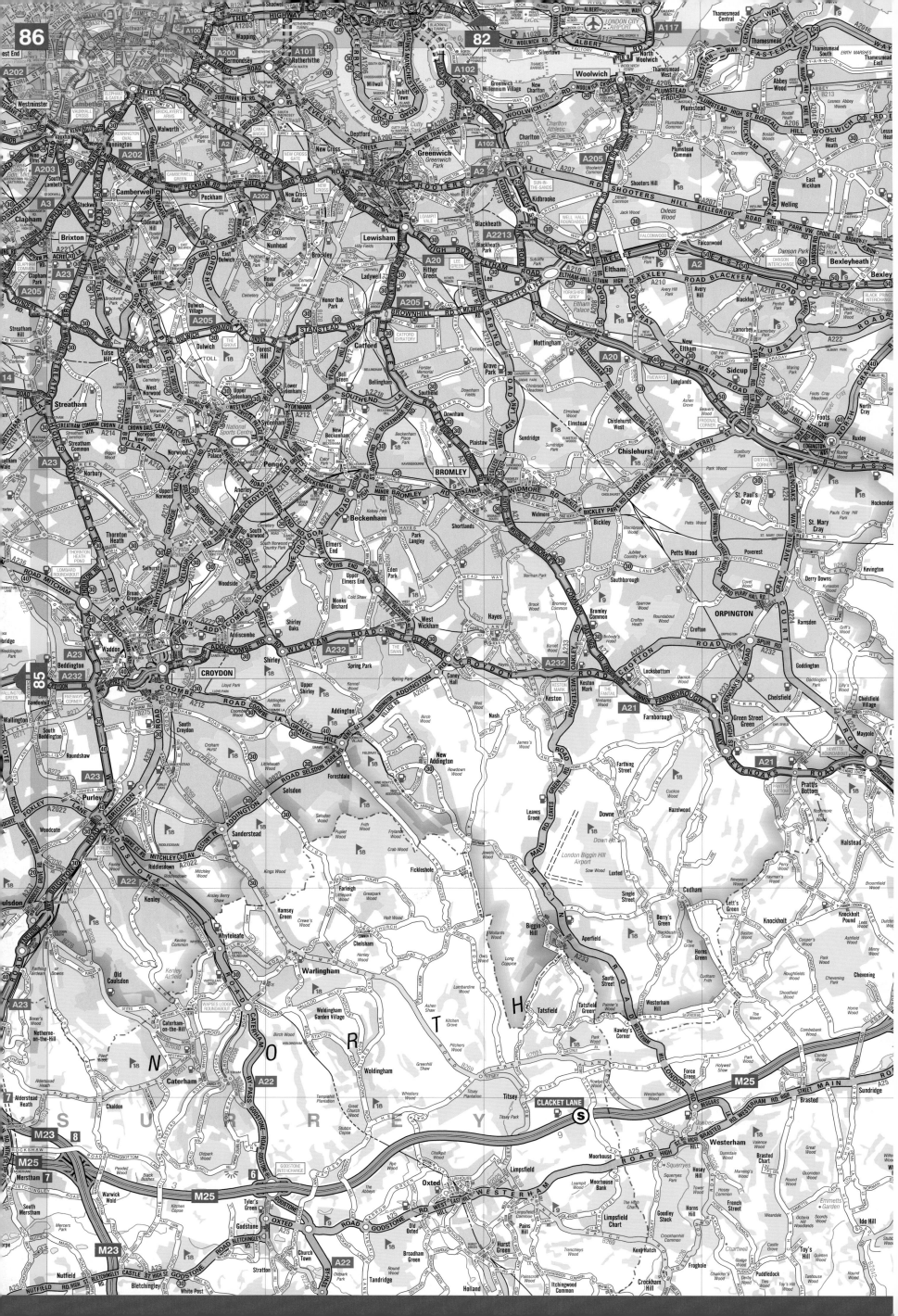

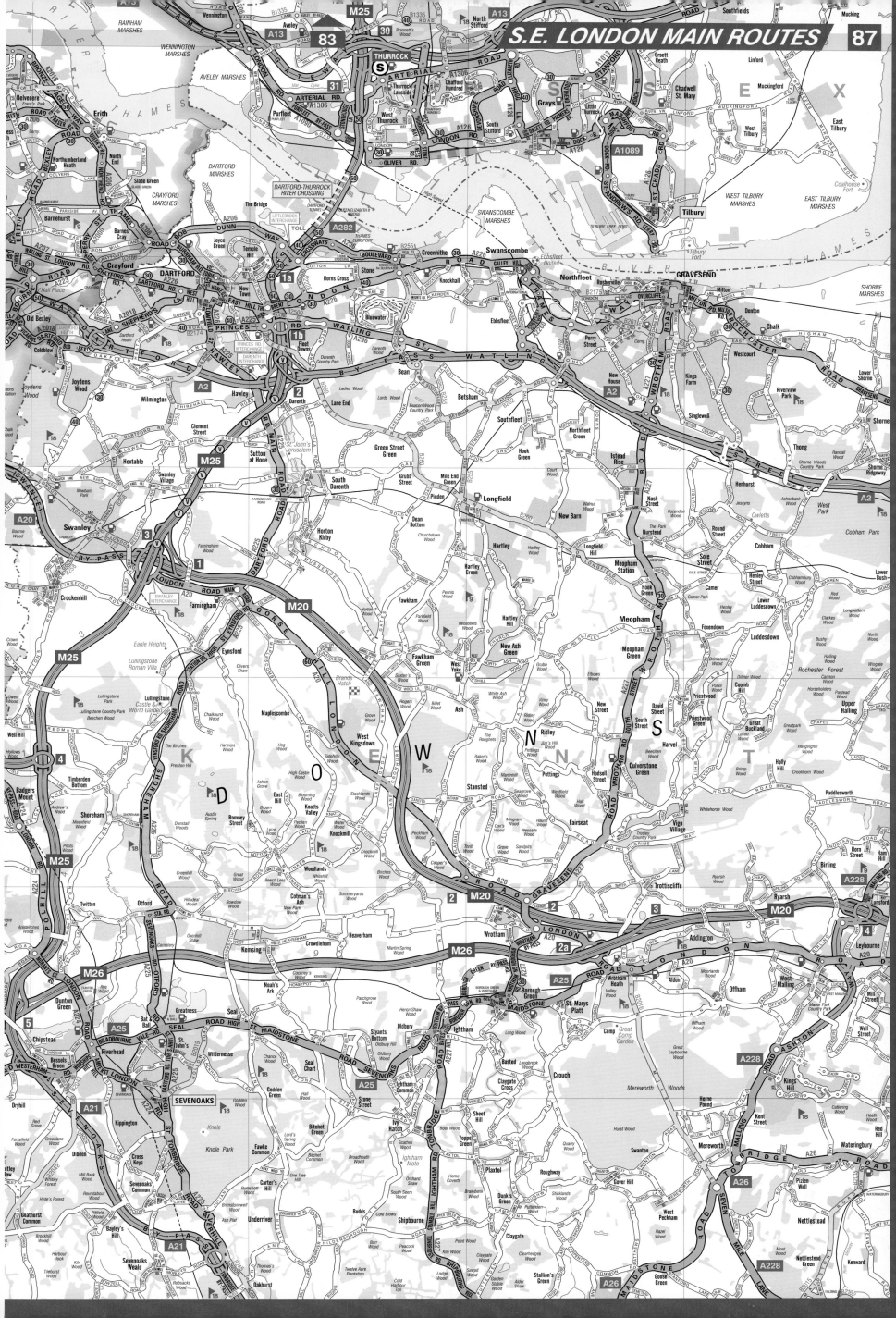

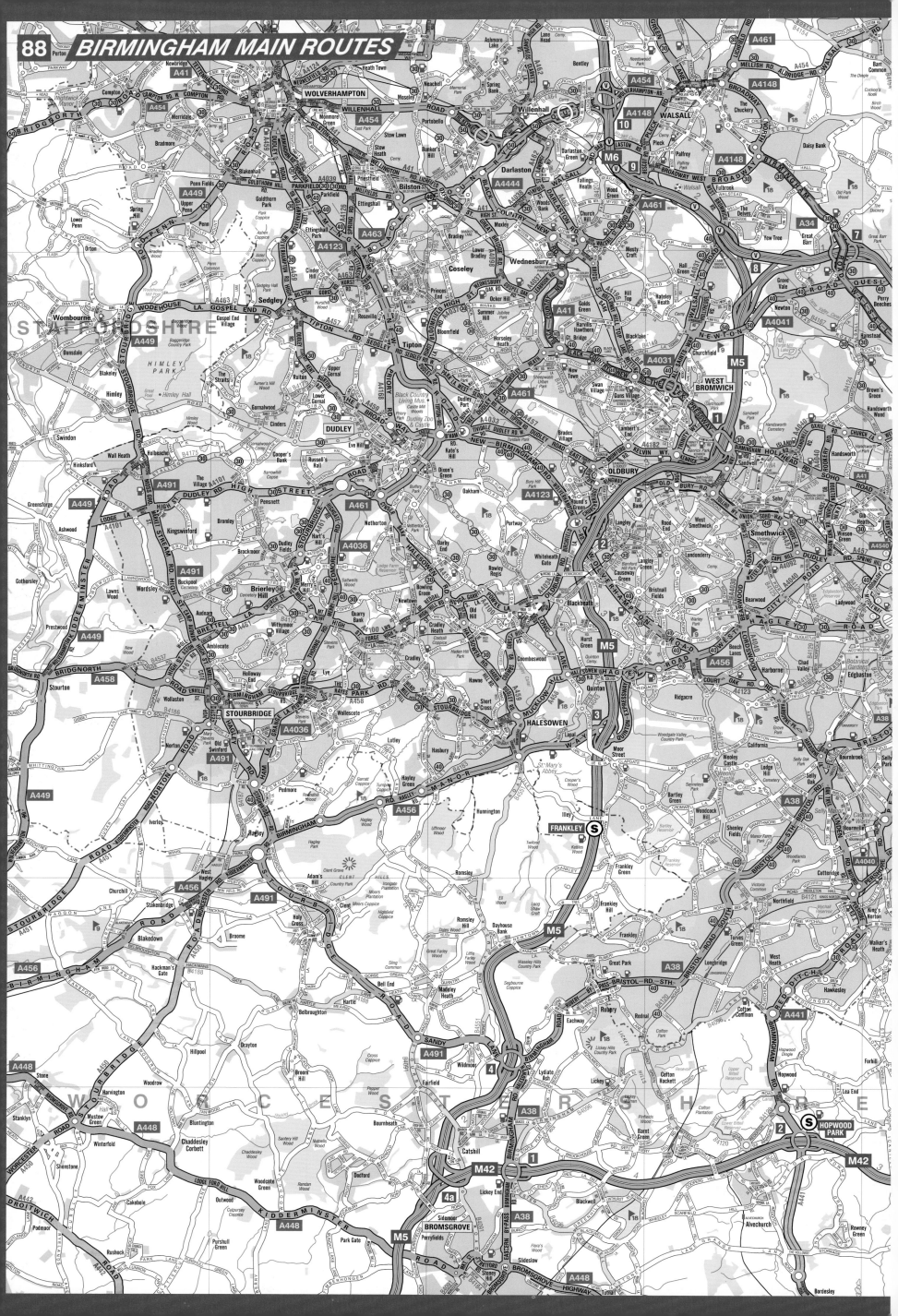

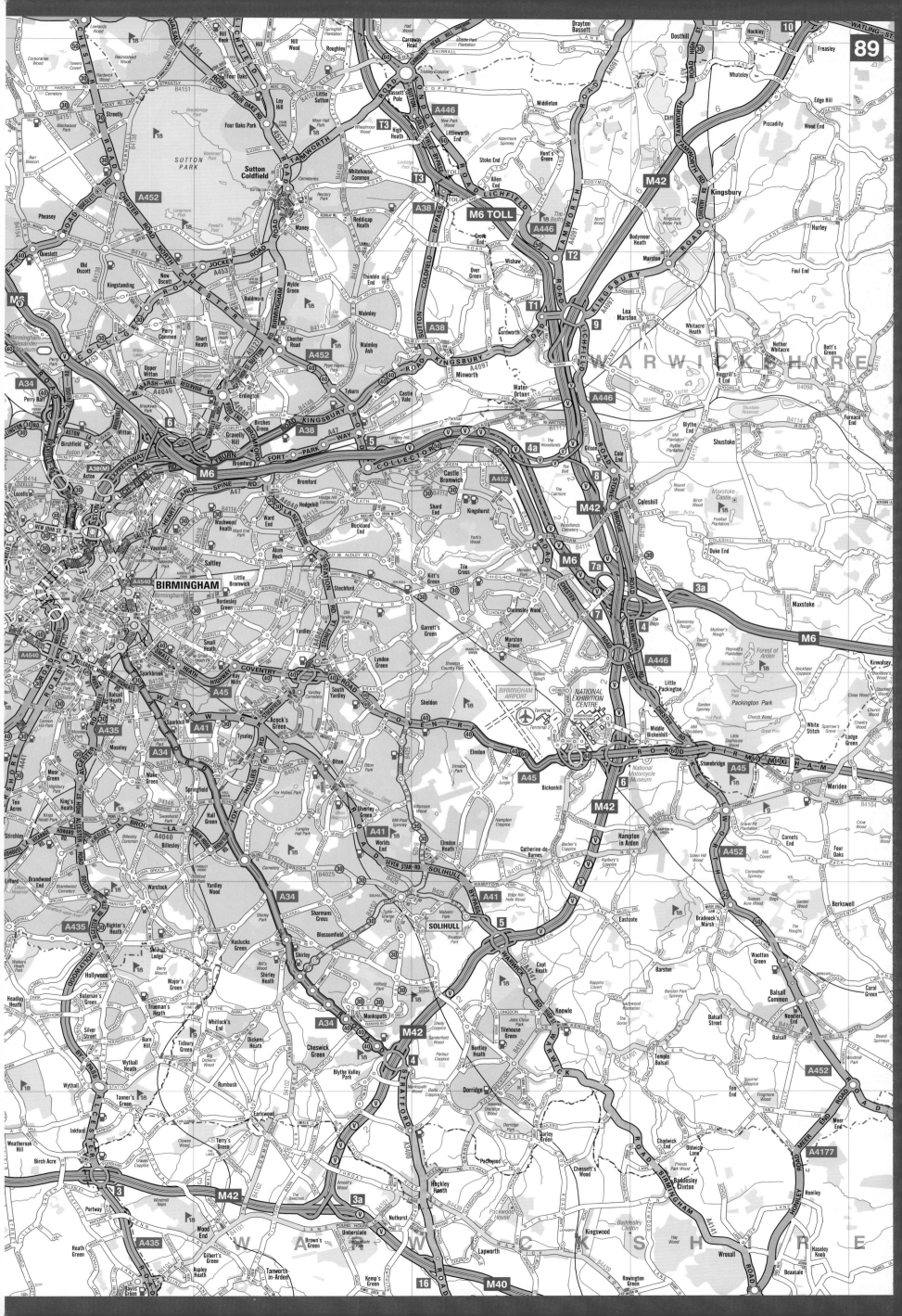

City & Town Centre Plans

Port Plans

Airport Plans

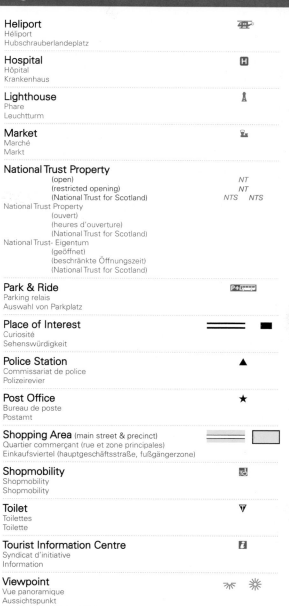

Reference Légende Zeichenerklärung

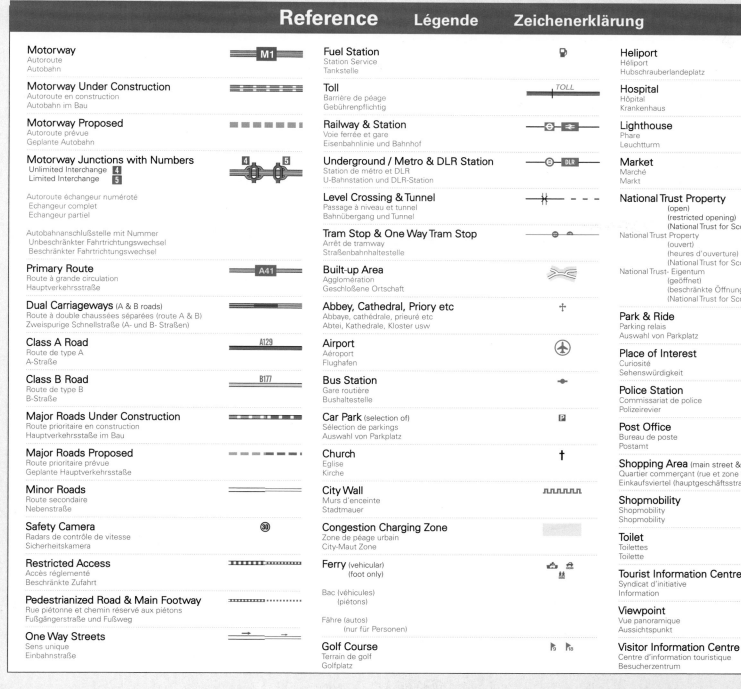

Motorway
Autoroute
Autobahn — M1

Motorway Under Construction
Autoroute en construction
Autobahn im Bau

Motorway Proposed
Autoroute prévue
Geplante Autobahn

Motorway Junctions with Numbers
Unlimited Interchange 4
Limited Interchange 5
Autoroute échangeur numéroté
Echangeur complet
Echangeur partiel
Autobahnanschlußstelle mit Nummer
Unbeschränkter Fahrtrichtungswechsel
Beschränkter Fahrtrichtungswechsel

Primary Route
Route à grande circulation
Hauptverkehrsstraße — A41

Dual Carriageways (A & B roads)
Route à double chaussées séparées (route A & B)
Zweispurige Schnellstraße (A- und B- Straßen)

Class A Road
Route de type A
A-Straße — A129

Class B Road
Route de type B
B-Straße — B177

Major Roads Under Construction
Route prioritaire en construction
Hauptverkehrsstaße im Bau

Major Roads Proposed
Route prioritaire prévue
Geplante Hauptverkehrsstraße

Minor Roads
Route secondaire
Nebenstraße

Safety Camera
Radars de contrôle de vitesse
Sicherheitskamera — 30

Restricted Access
Accès réglementé
Beschränkte Zufahrt

Pedestrianized Road & Main Footway
Rue piétonne et chemin réservé aux piétons
Fußgängerstraße und Fußweg

One Way Streets
Sens unique
Einbahnstraße

Fuel Station
Station Service
Tankstelle

Toll
Barrière de péage
Gebührenpflichtig — TOLL

Railway & Station
Voie ferrée et gare
Eisenbahnlinie und Bahnhof

Underground / Metro & DLR Station
Station de métro et DLR
U-Bahnstation und DLR-Station — DLR

Level Crossing & Tunnel
Passage à niveau et tunnel
Bahnübergang und Tunnel

Tram Stop & One Way Tram Stop
Arrêt de tramway
Straßenbahnhaltestelle

Built-up Area
Agglomération
Geschloßene Ortschaft

Abbey, Cathedral, Priory etc
Abbaye, cathédrale, prieuré etc
Abtei, Kathedrale, Kloster usw — †

Airport
Aéroport
Flughafen

Bus Station
Gare routière
Bushaltestelle

Car Park (selection of)
Sélection de parkings
Auswahl von Parkplatz — P

Church
Eglise
Kirche — †

City Wall
Murs d'enceinte
Stadtmauer

Congestion Charging Zone
Zone de péage urbain
City-Maut Zone

Ferry (vehicular)
(foot only)
Bac (véhicules)
(piétons)
Fähre (autos)
(nur für Personen)

Golf Course
Terrain de golf
Golfplatz

Heliport
Héliport
Hubschrauberlandeplatz

Hospital
Hôpital
Krankenhaus — H

Lighthouse
Phare
Leuchtturm

Market
Marché
Markt

National Trust Property
(open) — NT
(restricted opening) — NT
(National Trust for Scotland) — NTS
National Trust Property
(ouvert)
(heures d'ouverture)
(National Trust for Scotland)
National Trust- Eigentum
(geöffnet)
(beschränkte Öffnungszeit)
(National Trust for Scotland)

Park & Ride
Parking relais
Auswahl von Parkplatz

Place of Interest
Curiosité
Sehenswürdigkeit

Police Station
Commissariat de police
Polizeirevier — ▲

Post Office
Bureau de poste
Postamt — ★

Shopping Area (main street & precinct)
Quartier commerçant (rue et zone principales)
Einkaufsviertel (hauptgeschäftsstraße, fußgängerzone)

Shopmobility
Shopmobility
Shopmobility

Toilet
Toilettes
Toilette — ▽

Tourist Information Centre
Syndicat d'initiative
Information

Viewpoint
Vue panoramique
Aussichtspunkt

Visitor Information Centre
Centre d'information touristique
Besucherzentrum — V

ABERDEEN
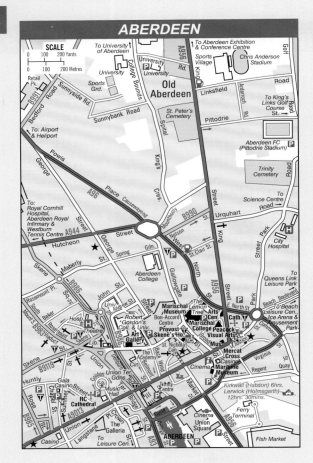

BATH
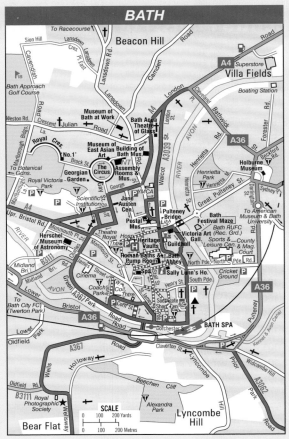

BLACKPOOL
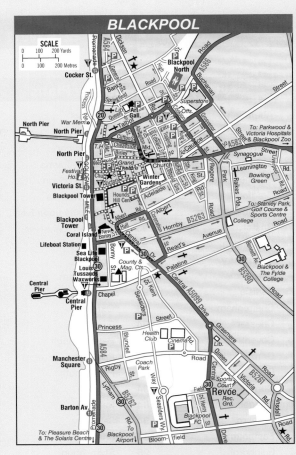

BIRMINGHAM (CITY CENTRE)
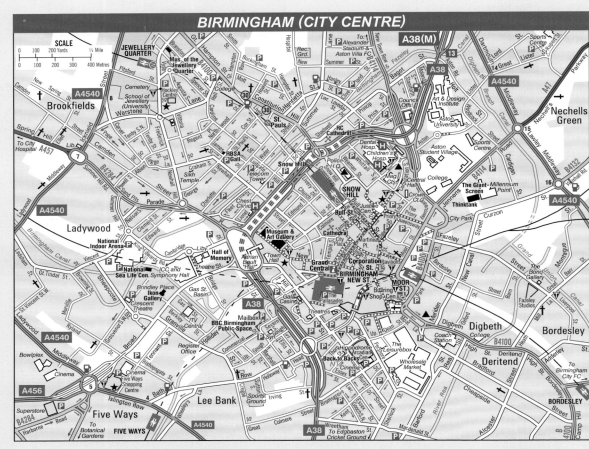

BOURNEMOUTH
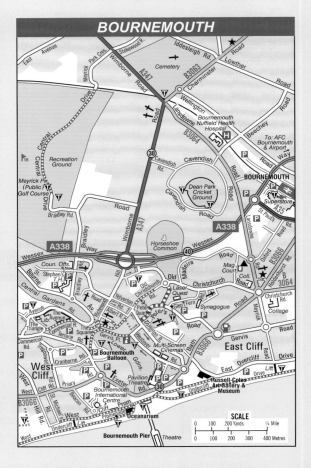

BRADFORD
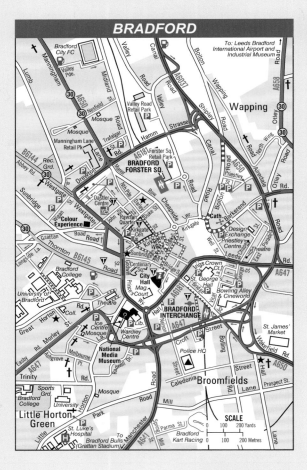

BRIGHTON and HOVE
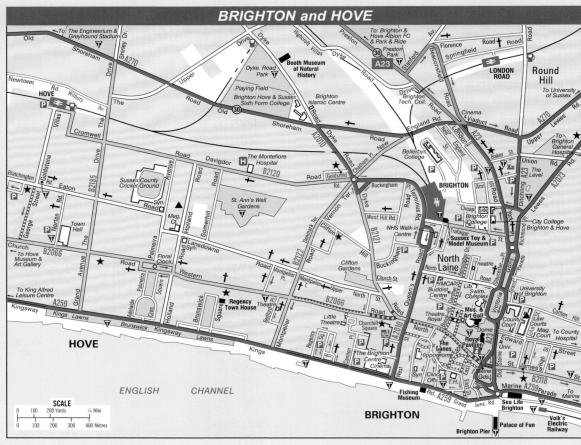

BRISTOL

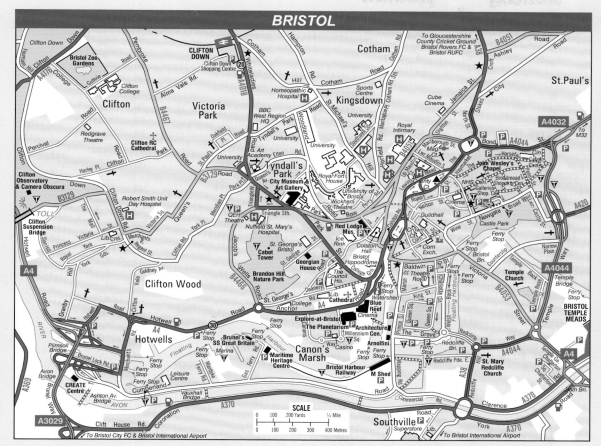

CANTERBURY

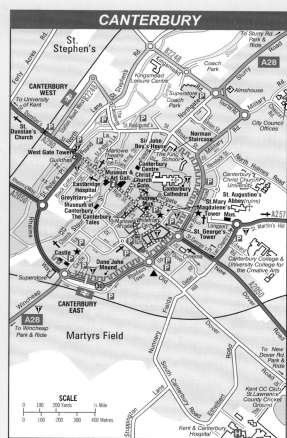

CAMBRIDGE

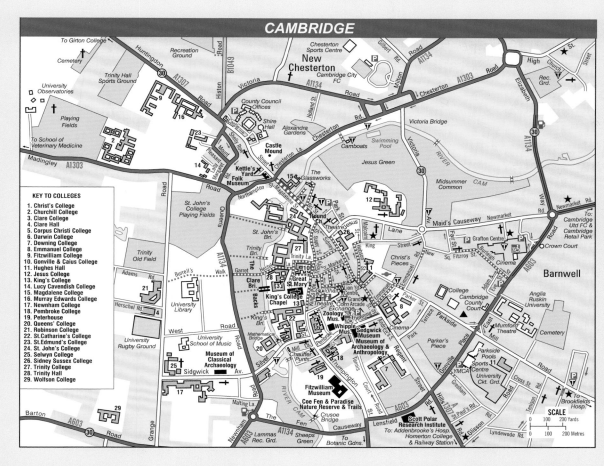

KEY TO COLLEGES
1. Christ's College
2. Churchill College
3. Clare College
4. Clare Hall
5. Corpus Christi College
6. Darwin College
7. Downing College
8. Emmanuel College
9. Fitzwilliam College
10. Gonville & Caius College
11. Hughes Hall
12. Jesus College
13. King's College
14. Lucy Cavendish College
15. Magdalene College
16. Murray Edwards College
17. Newnham College
18. Pembroke College
19. Peterhouse
20. Queens' College
21. Robinson College
22. St.Catharine's College
23. St.Edmund's College
24. St. John's College
25. Selwyn College
26. Sidney Sussex College
27. Trinity College
28. Trinity Hall
29. Wolfson College

CARLISLE

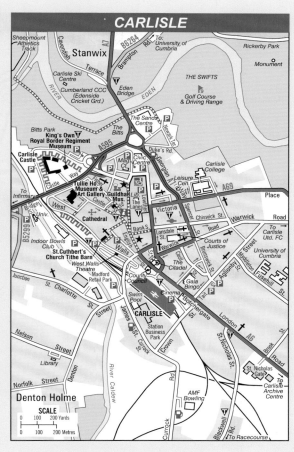

CARDIFF (CAERDYDD)

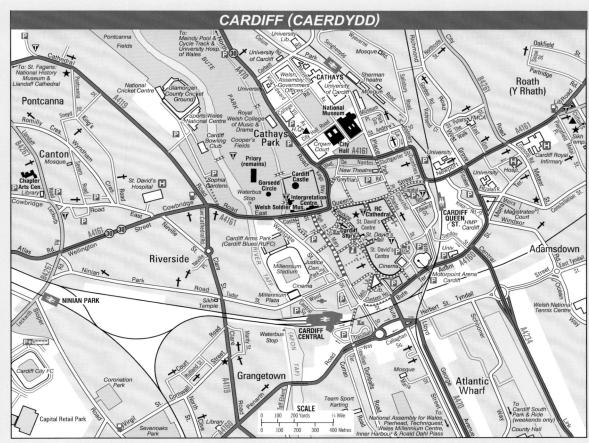

CHELTENHAM

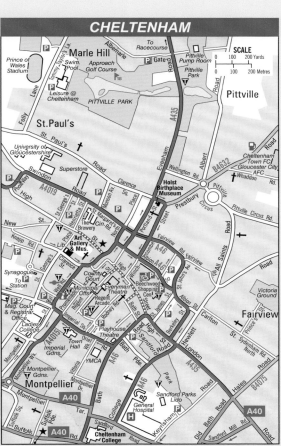

94

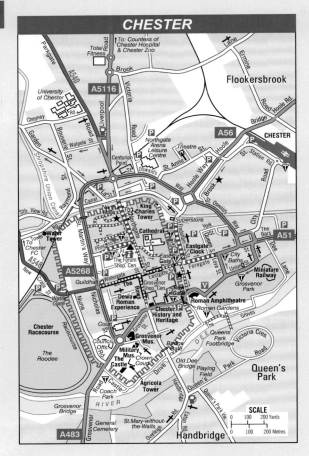
CHESTER

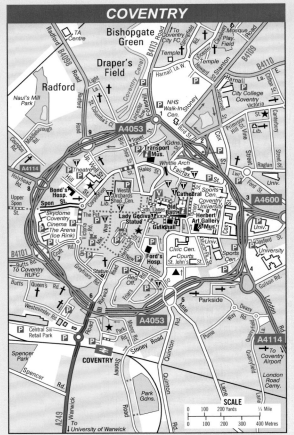
COVENTRY

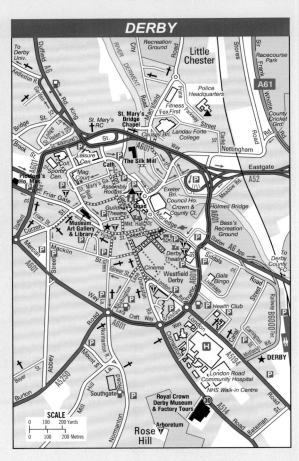
DERBY

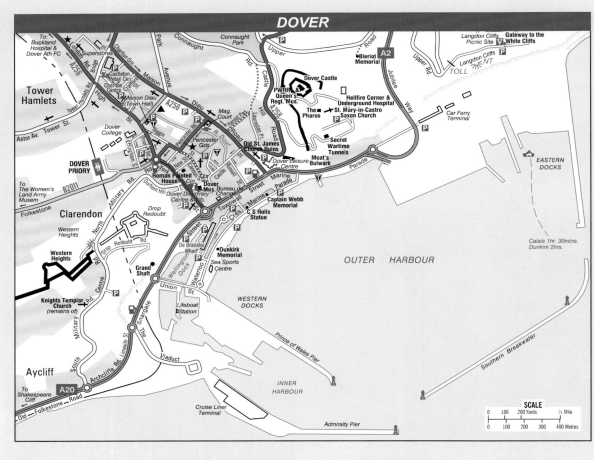
DOVER

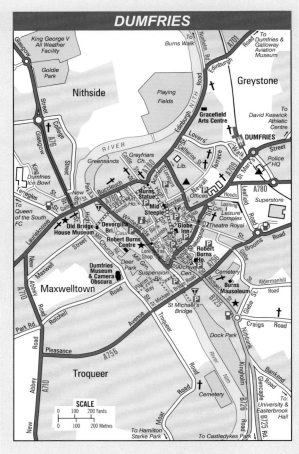
DUMFRIES

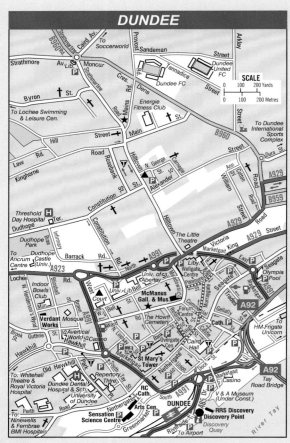
DUNDEE

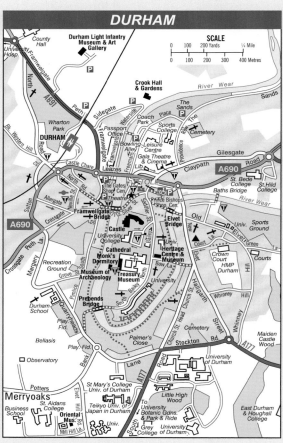
DURHAM

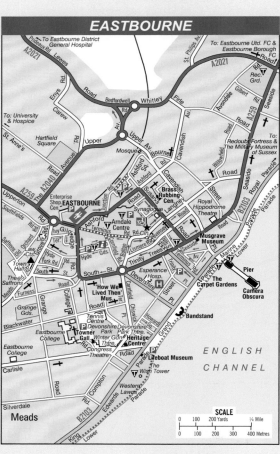
EASTBOURNE

EDINBURGH

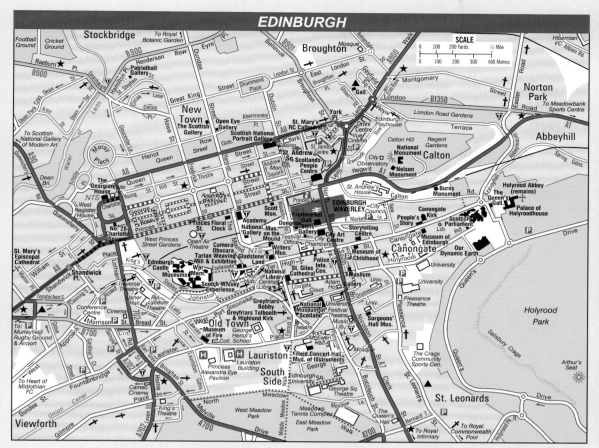

FOLKESTONE

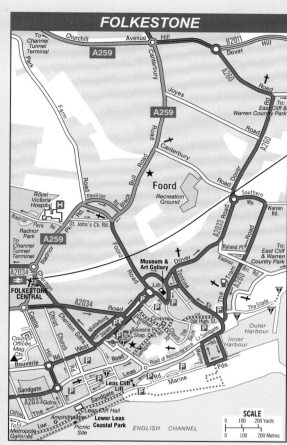

EXETER

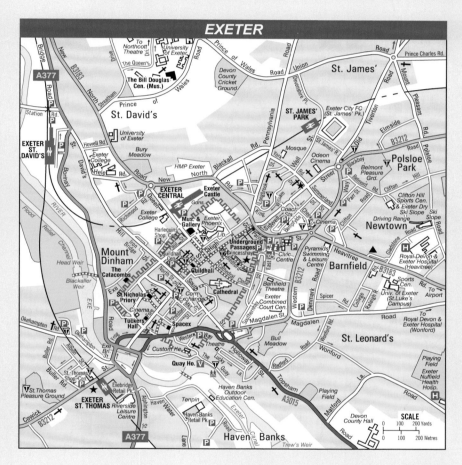

GUILDFORD

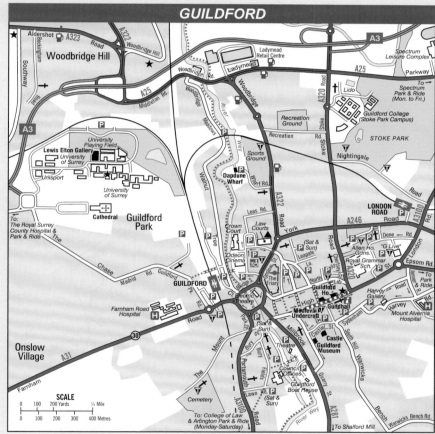

GLASGOW

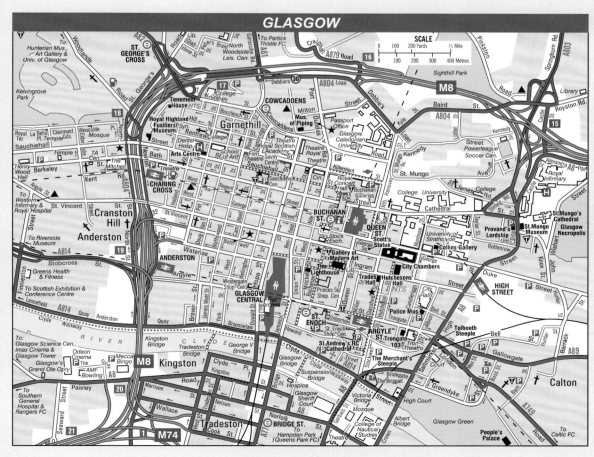

GLOUCESTER

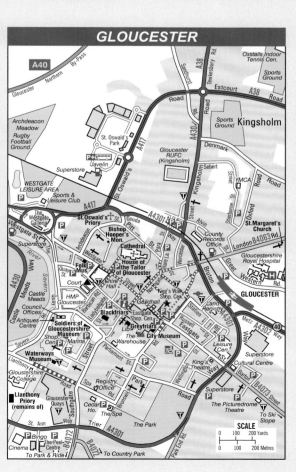

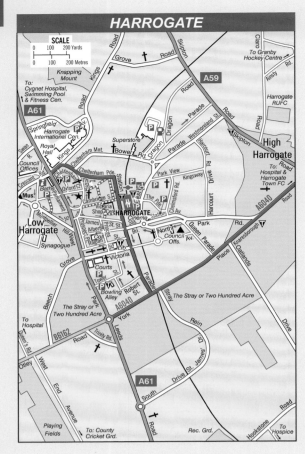

HARROGATE

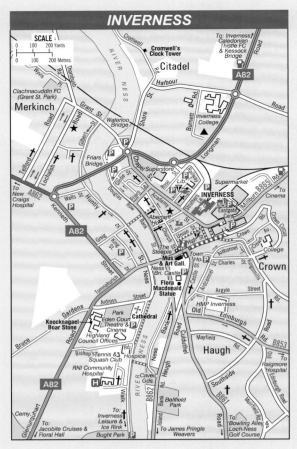

INVERNESS

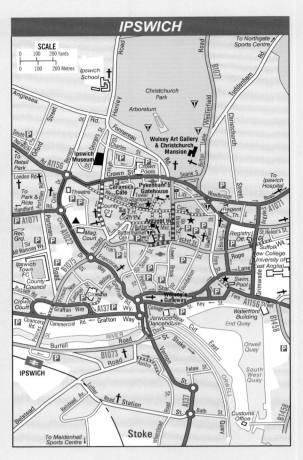

IPSWICH

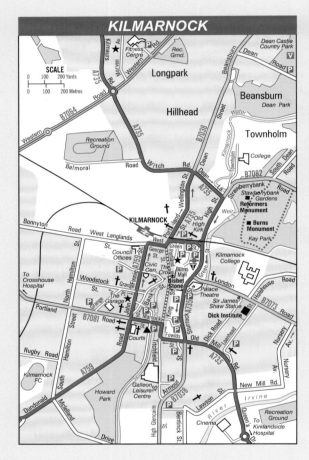

KILMARNOCK

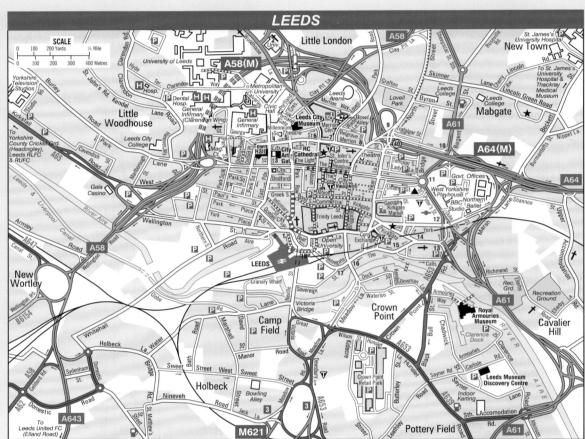

LEEDS

KINGSTON UPON HULL

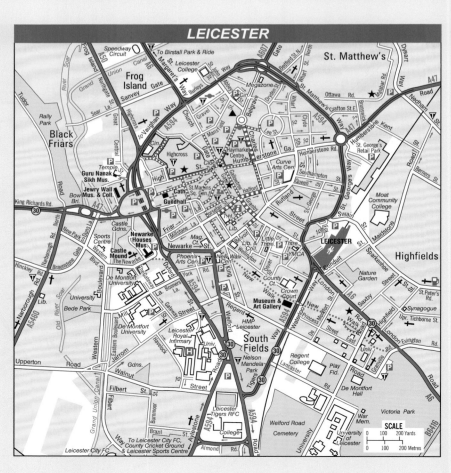

LEICESTER

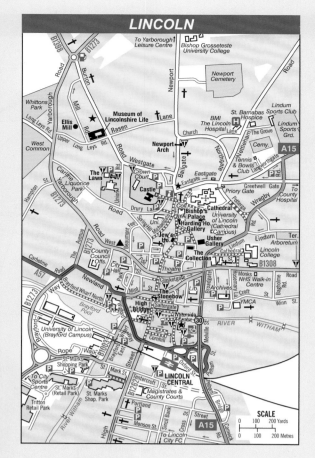

LINCOLN

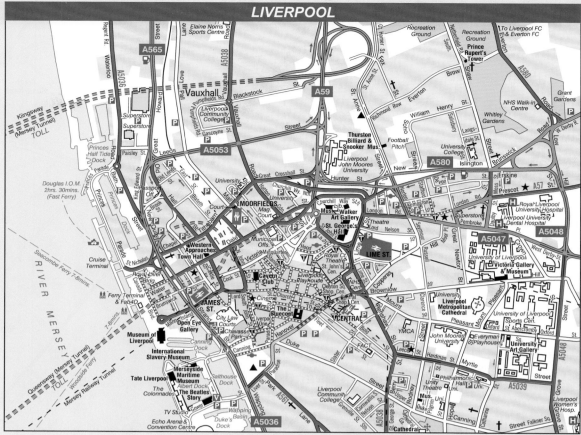

LIVERPOOL

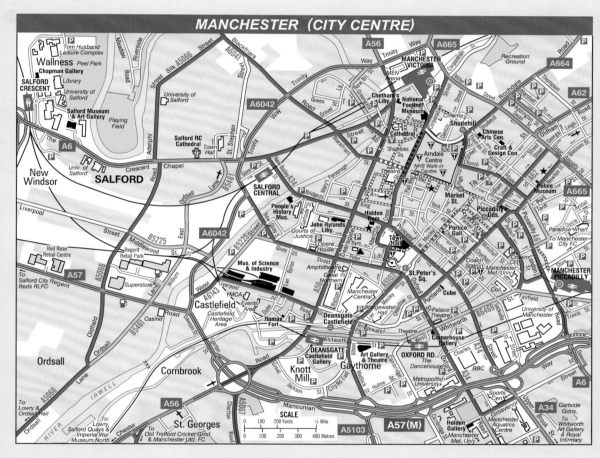

MANCHESTER (CITY CENTRE)

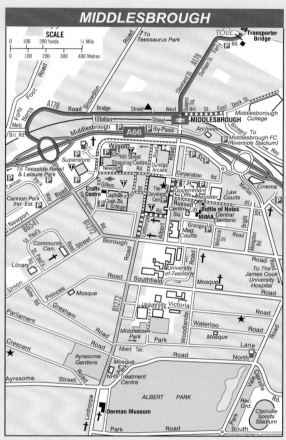

MIDDLESBROUGH

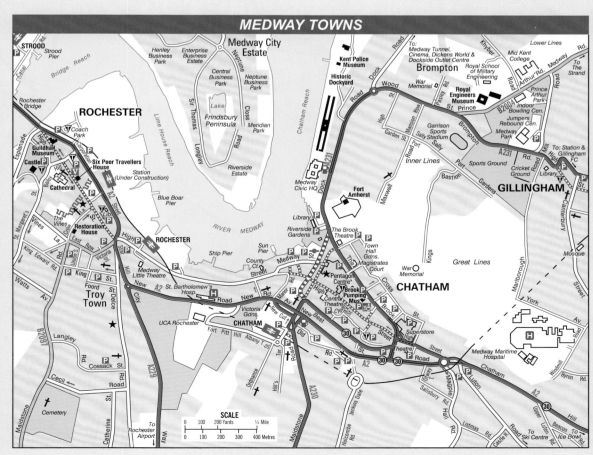

MEDWAY TOWNS

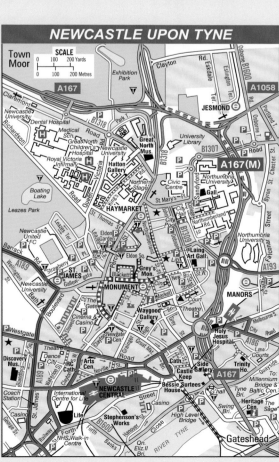

NEWCASTLE UPON TYNE

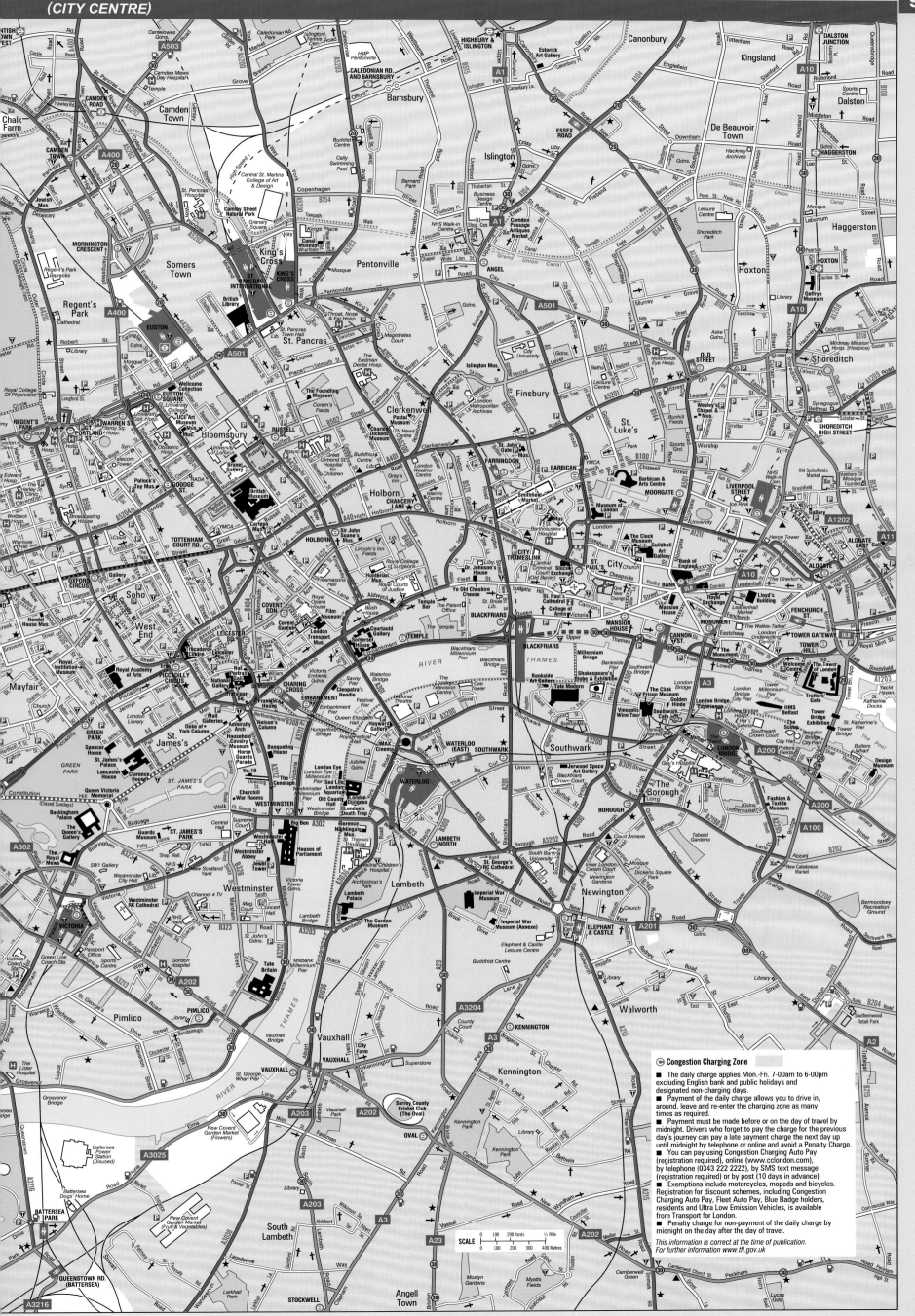

Congestion Charging Zone

■ The daily charge applies Mon.-Fri. 7-00am to 6-00pm excluding English bank and public holidays and designated non-charging days.

■ Payment of the daily charge allows you to drive in, around, leave and re-enter the charging zone as many times as required.

■ Payment must be made before or on the day of travel by midnight. Drivers who forget to pay the charge for the previous day's journey can pay a late payment charge the next day up until midnight by telephone or online and avoid a Penalty Charge.

■ You can pay using Congestion Charging Auto Pay (registration required), online (www.cclondon.com), by telephone (0343 222 2222), by SMS text message (registration required) or by post (10 days in advance).

■ Exemptions include motorcycles, mopeds and bicycles. Registration for discount schemes, including Congestion Charging Auto Pay, Fleet Auto Pay, Blue Badge holders, residents and Ultra Low Emission Vehicles, is available from Transport for London.

■ Penalty charge for non-payment of the daily charge by midnight on the day after the day of travel.

This information is correct at the time of publication. For further information www.tfl.gov.uk

SCALE

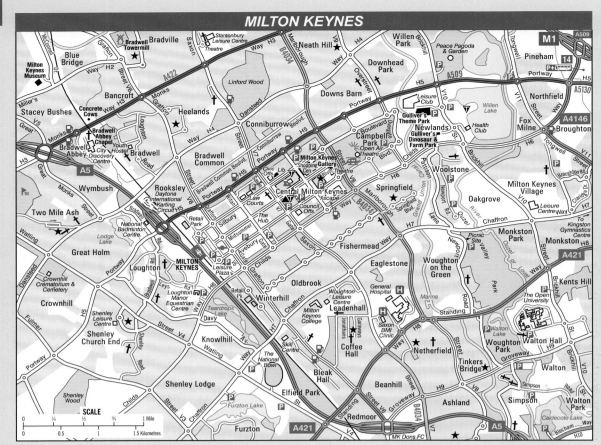

MILTON KEYNES

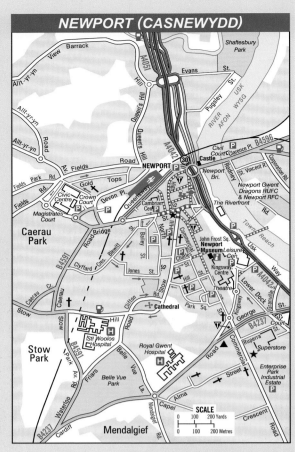

NEWPORT (CASNEWYDD)

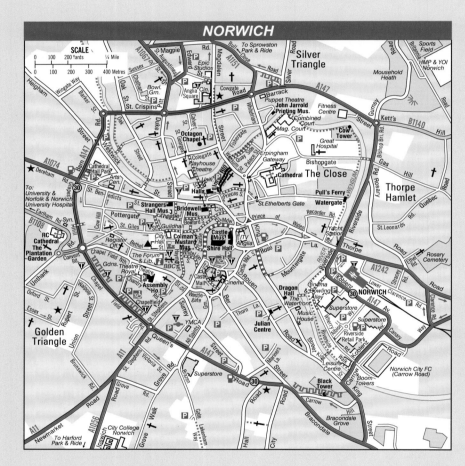

NORWICH

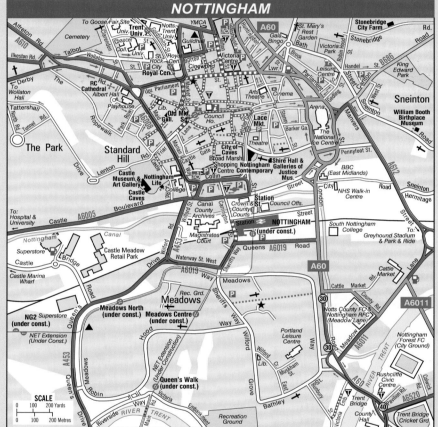

NOTTINGHAM

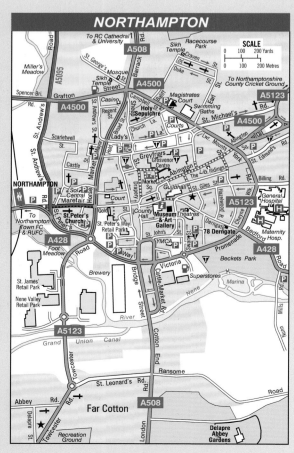

NORTHAMPTON

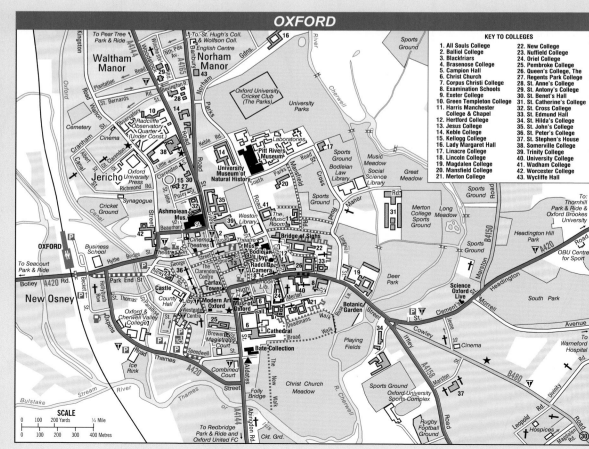

OXFORD

KEY TO COLLEGES

1. All Souls College
2. Balliol College
3. Blackfriars
4. Brasenose College
5. Campion Hall
6. Christ Church
7. Corpus Christi College
8. Examination Schools
9. Exeter College
10. Green Templeton College
11. Harris Manchester College & Chapel
12. Hertford College
13. Jesus College
14. Keble College
15. Kellogg College
16. Lady Margaret Hall
17. Linacre College
18. Lincoln College
19. Magdalen College
20. Mansfield College
21. Merton College
22. New College
23. Nuffield College
24. Oriel College
25. Pembroke College
26. Queen's College, The
27. Regents Park College
28. St. Anne's College
29. St. Antony's College
30. St. Benet's Hall
31. St. Catherine's College
32. St. Cross College
33. St. Edmund Hall
34. St. Hilda's College
35. St. John's College
36. St. Peter's College
37. St. Stephen's House
38. Somerville College
39. Trinity College
40. University College
41. Wadham College
42. Worcester College
43. Wycliffe Hall

OBAN

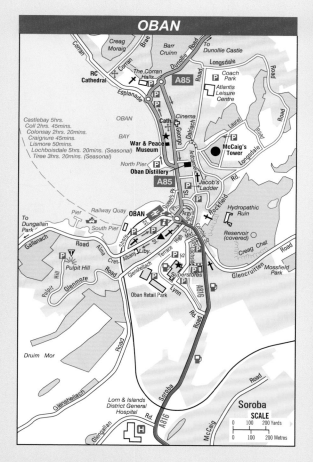

PERTH

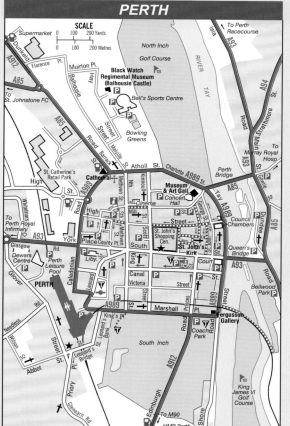

PETERBOROUGH

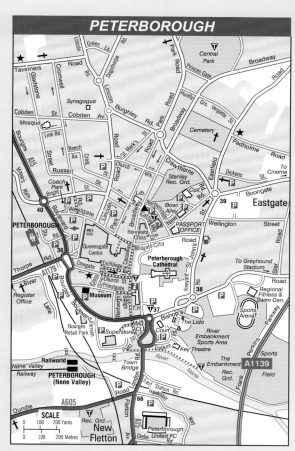

PLYMOUTH

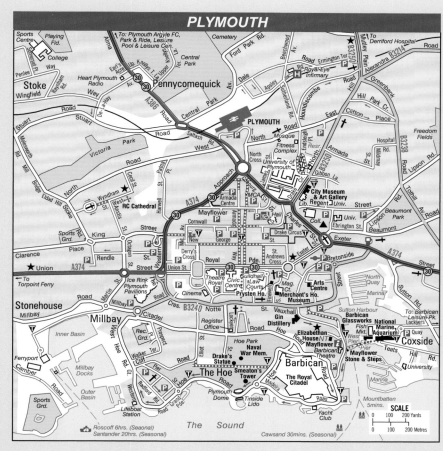

PORTSMOUTH

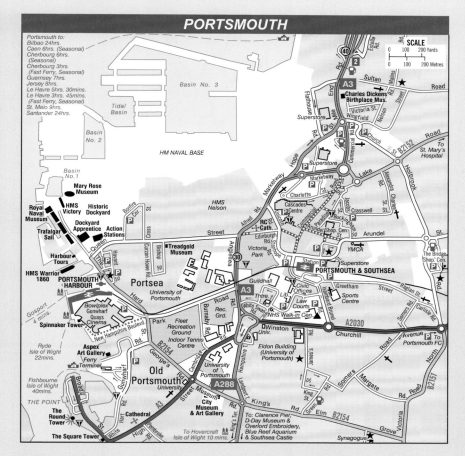

PRESTON

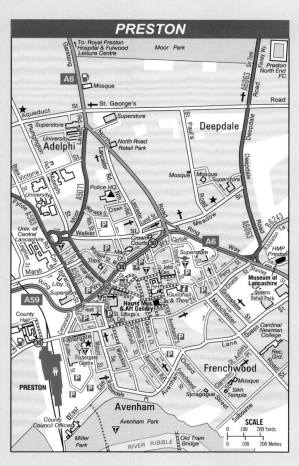

READING

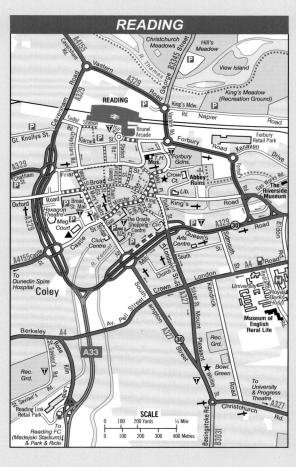

SALISBURY

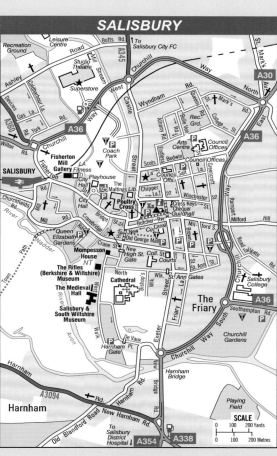

SHEFFIELD

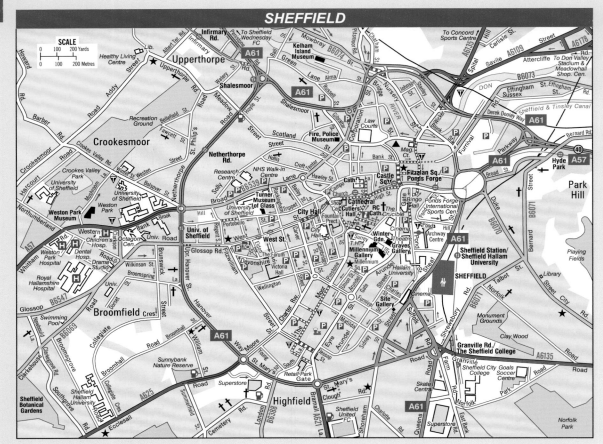

SHREWSBURY

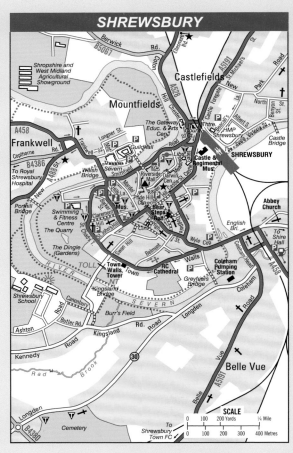

SOUTHAMPTON

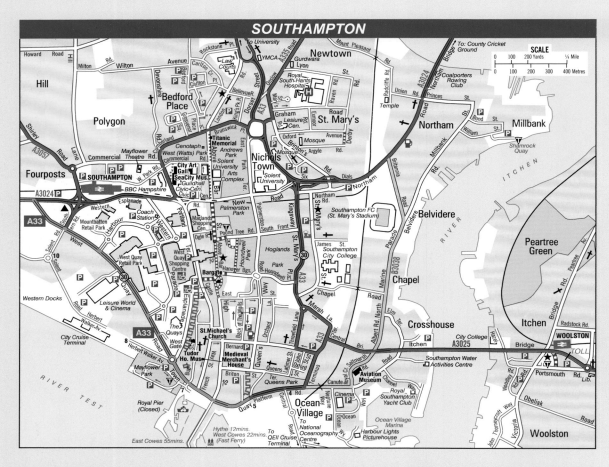

STIRLING

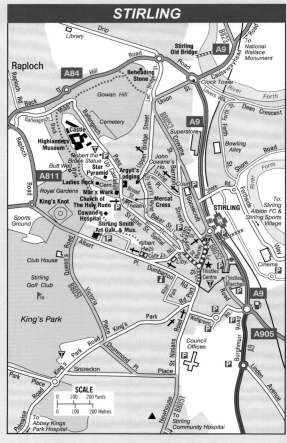

STOKE-ON-TRENT

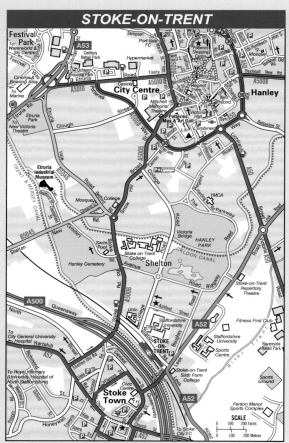

STRATFORD UPON AVON

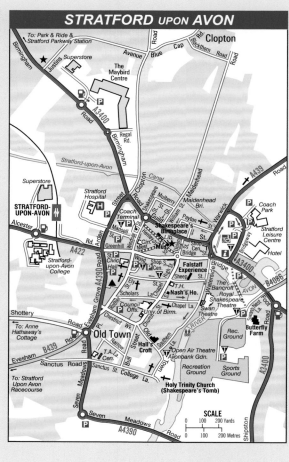

SUNDERLAND

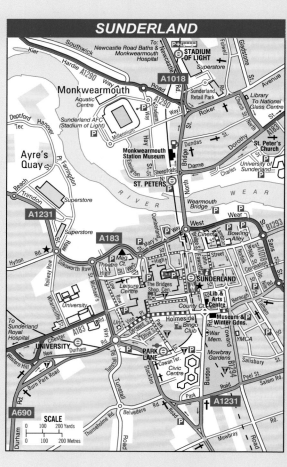

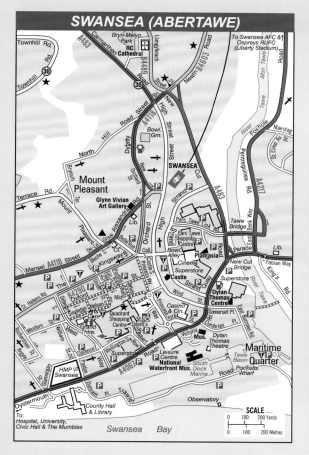

SWANSEA (ABERTAWE)

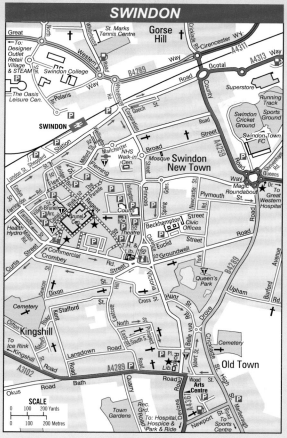

SWINDON

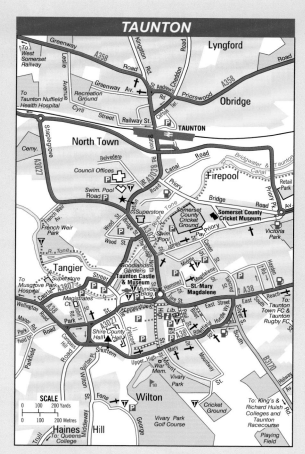

TAUNTON

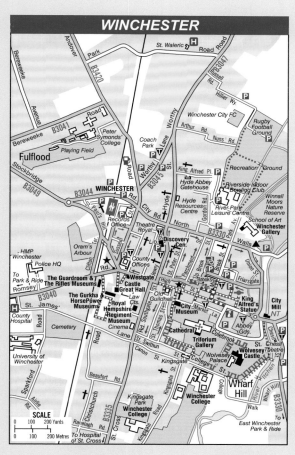

WINCHESTER

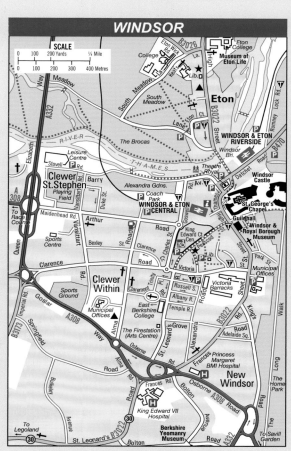

WINDSOR

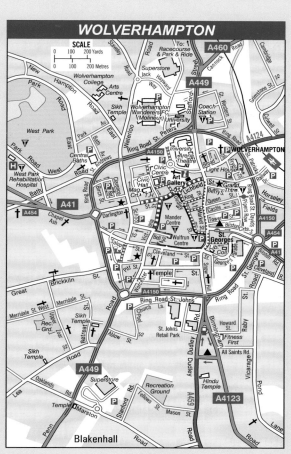

WOLVERHAMPTON

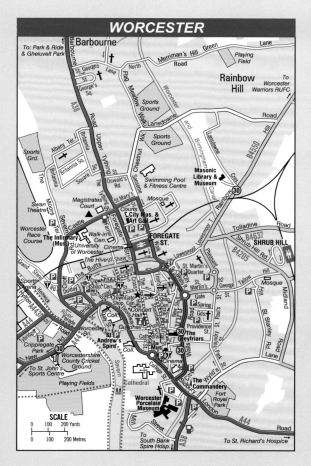

WORCESTER

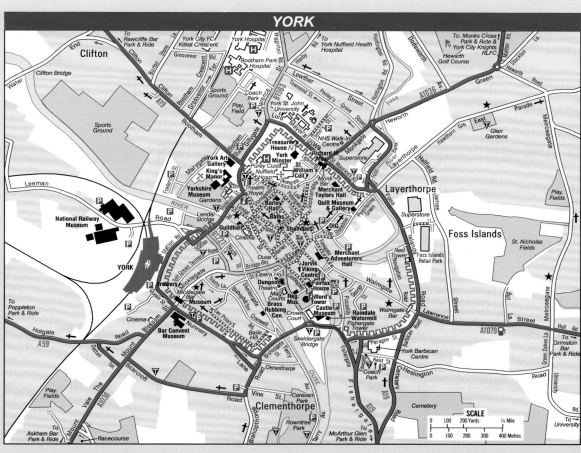

YORK

HARWICH

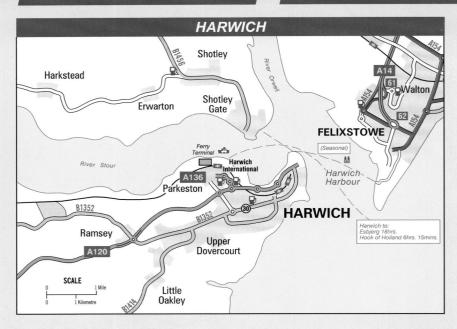

Harwich to:
Esbjerg 18hrs.
Hook of Holland 6hrs. 15mins.

KINGSTON UPON HULL

Hull to:
Rotterdam (Europoort) 10hrs.
Zeebrugge 12hrs. 30mins.

NEWCASTLE UPON TYNE

Newcastle to:
Amsterdam (IJmuiden) 15hrs.

NEWHAVEN

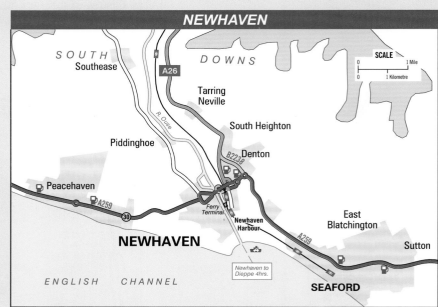

Newhaven to
Dieppe 4hrs.

PEMBROKE DOCK (DOC PENFRO)

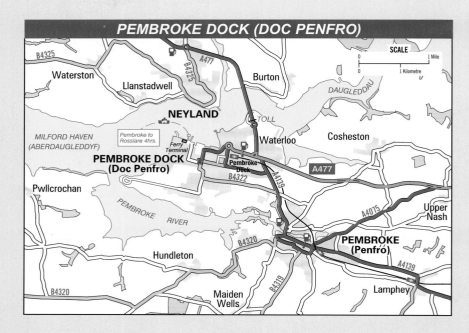

Pembroke to
Rosslare 4hrs.

POOLE

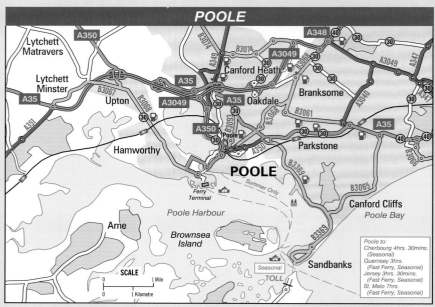

Poole to:
Cherbourg 4hrs. 30mins.
(Seasonal)
Guernsey 3hrs.
(Fast Ferry, Seasonal)
Jersey 3hrs. 30mins.
(Fast Ferry, Seasonal)
St. Malo 7hrs.
(Fast Ferry, Seasonal)

PORTSMOUTH

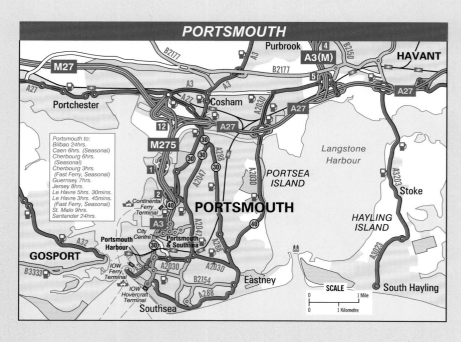

Portsmouth to:
Bilbao 24hrs.
Caen 6hrs. (Seasonal)
Cherbourg 6hrs.
(Seasonal)
Cherbourg 3hrs.
(Fast Ferry, Seasonal)
Guernsey 7hrs.
Jersey 8hrs.
Le Havre 5hrs. 30mins.
Le Havre 3hrs. 45mins.
(Fast Ferry, Seasonal)
St. Malo 9hrs.
Santander 24hrs.

WEYMOUTH

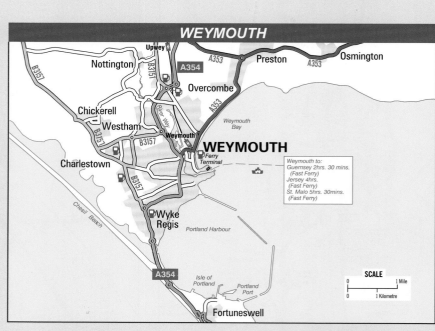

Weymouth to:
Guernsey 2hrs. 30 mins.
(Fast Ferry)
Jersey 4hrs.
(Fast Ferry)
St. Malo 5hrs. 30mins.
(Fast Ferry)

BIRMINGHAM

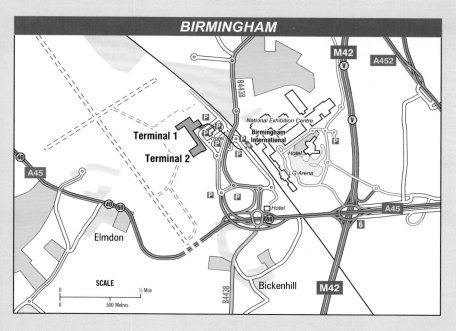

EAST MIDLANDS

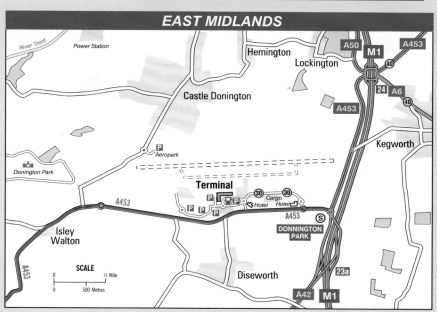

GLASGOW

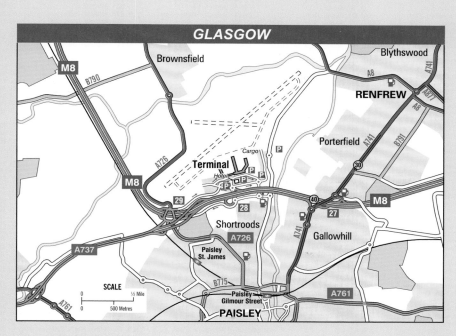

LONDON GATWICK

LONDON HEATHROW

LONDON LUTON

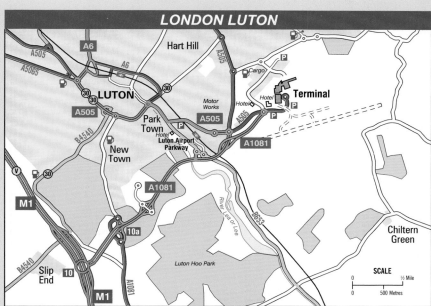

LONDON STANSTED

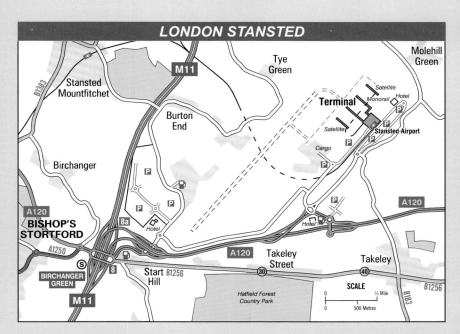

MANCHESTER INTERNATIONAL

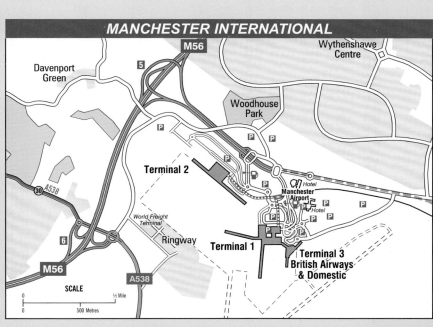

INDEX TO CITIES, TOWNS, VILLAGES, HAMLETS, LOCATIONS, AIRPORTS & PORTS

(1) A strict alphabetical order is used e.g. An Dùnan follows Andreas but precedes Andwell

(2) The map reference given refers to the actual map square in which the town spot or built-up area is located and not to the place name.

(3) Major towns and destinations are shown in bold, i.e. **Aberdeen.** *Aber* . . . .3K **67** & **92**
Where they appear on a Town Plan a second page reference is given.

(4) Where two or more places of the same name occur in the same County or Unitary Authority, the nearest large town is also given; e.g. Achiemore. *High* . . . .3L **75** (nr. Durness) indicates that Achiemore is located in square 3L on page **75** and is situated near Durness in the Unitary Authority of Highland.

(5) Only one reference is given although due to page overlaps the place may appear on more than one page.

COUNTIES and UNITARY AUTHORITIES with the abbreviations used in this index

Aberdeen : *Aber*
Aberdeenshire : *Abers*
Angus : *Ang*
Argyll & Bute : *Arg*
Bath & N E Somerset : *Bath*
Bedford : *Bed*
Blackburn with Darwen : *Bkbn*
Blackpool : *Bkpl*
Blaenau Gwent : *Blae*
Bournemouth : *Bour*
Bracknell Forest : *Brac*
Bridgend : *B'end*
Brighton & Hove : *Brig*
Bristol : *Bris*
Buckinghamshire : *Buck*
Caerphilly : *Cphy*
Cambridgeshire : *Cambs*
Cardiff : *Card*
Carmarthenshire : *Carm*
Central Bedfordshire : *C Beds*
Ceredigion : *Cdgn*
Cheshire East : *Ches E*
Cheshire West & Chester : *Ches W*
Clackmannanshire : *Clac*
Conwy : *Cnwy*
Cornwall : *Corn*
Cumbria : *Cumb*
Darlington : *Darl*
Denbighshire : *Den*
Derby : *Derb*
Derbyshire : *Derbs*
Devon : *Devn*
Dorset : *Dors*
Dumfries & Galloway : *Dum*
Dundee : *D'dee*
Durham : *Dur*
East Ayrshire : *E Ayr*
East Dunbartonshire : *E Dun*
East Lothian : *E Lot*
East Renfrewshire : *E Ren*
East Riding of Yorkshire : *E Yor*
East Sussex : *E Sus*
Edinburgh : *Edin*
Essex : *Essx*
Falkirk : *Falk*
Fife : *Fife*
Flintshire : *Flin*
Glasgow : *Glas*
Gloucestershire : *Glos*
Greater London : *G Lon*
Greater Manchester : *G Man*
Gwynedd : *Gwyn*
Halton : *Hal*
Hampshire : *Hants*
Hartlepool : *Hart*
Herefordshire : *Here*
Hertfordshire : *Herts*
Highland : *High*
Inverclyde : *Inv*
Isle of Anglesey : *IOA*
Isle of Man : *IOM*
Isle of Wight : *IOW*
Isles of Scilly : *IOS*
Kent : *Kent*
Kingston upon Hull : *Hull*
Lancashire : *Lanc*
Leicester : *Leic*
Leicestershire : *Leics*
Lincolnshire : *Linc*
Luton : *Lutn*
Medway : *Medw*
Merseyside : *Mers*
Merthyr Tydfil : *Mer T*
Middlesbrough : *Midd*
Midlothian : *Midl*
Milton Keynes : *Mil*
Monmouthshire : *Mon*
Moray : *Mor*
Neath Port Talbot : *Neat*
Newport : *Newp*
Norfolk : *Norf*
Northamptonshire : *Nptn*
North Ayrshire : *N Ayr*
North East Lincolnshire : *NE Lin*
North Lanarkshire : *N Lan*
North Lincolnshire : *N Lin*
North Somerset : *N Som*
Northumberland : *Nmbd*
North Yorkshire : *N Yor*
Nottingham : *Nott*
Nottinghamshire : *Notts*
Orkney : *Orkn*
Oxfordshire : *Oxon*
Pembrokeshire : *Pemb*
Perth & Kinross : *Per*
Peterborough : *Pet*
Plymouth : *Plym*
Poole : *Pool*
Portsmouth : *Port*
Powys : *Powy*
Reading : *Read*
Redcar & Cleveland : *Red C*
Renfrewshire : *Ren*
Rhondda Cynon Taff : *Rhon*
Rutland : *Rut*
Scottish Borders : *Bord*
Shetland : *Shet*
Shropshire : *Shrp*
Slough : *Slo*
Somerset : *Som*
Southampton : *Sotn*
South Ayrshire : *S Ayr*
Southend-on-Sea : *S'end*
South Gloucestershire : *S Glo*
South Lanarkshire : *S Lan*
South Yorkshire : *S Yor*
Staffordshire : *Staf*
Stirling : *Stir*
Stockton-on-Tees : *Stoc T*
Stoke-on-Trent : *Stoke*
Suffolk : *Suff*
Surrey : *Surr*
Swansea : *Swan*
Swindon : *Swin*
Telford & Wrekin : *Telf*
Thurrock : *Thur*
Torbay : *Torb*
Torfaen : *Torf*
Tyne & Wear : *Tyne*
Vale of Glamorgan, The : *V Glam*
Warrington : *Warr*
Warwickshire : *Warw*
West Berkshire : *W Ber*
West Dunbartonshire : *W Dun*
Western Isles : *W Isl*
West Lothian : *W Lot*
West Midlands : *W Mid*
West Sussex : *W Sus*
West Yorkshire : *W Yor*
Wiltshire : *Wilts*
Windsor & Maidenhead : *Wind*
Wokingham : *Wok*
Worcestershire : *Worc*
Wrexham : *Wrex*
York : *York*

INDEX

A

Abbas Combe. *Som* 3G 9
Abberley. *Worc* 5H 25
Abberley Common. *Worc* 5H 25
Abberton. *Essx* 2J 21
Abberton. *Worc* 6K 25
Abberwick. *Nmbd* 8L 57
Abbess Roding. *Essx* 2D 20
Abbey. *Devn* 4A 8
Abbey-cwm-hir. *Powy* 4A 24
Abbeydale. *S Yor* 7M 39
Abbeydale Park. *S Yor* 7M 39
Abbey Dore. *Here* 8D 24
Abbey Gate. *Devn* 6B 8
Abbey Hulton. *Stoke* 5G 33
Abbey St Bathans. *Bord* 3G 57
Abbeystead. *Lanc* 8G 43
Abbeytown. *Cumb* 6J 49
Abbey Village. *Lanc* 3E 38
Abbey Wood. *G Lon* 6C 20
Abbots Ann. *Hants* 1D 10
Abbots Bickington. *Devn* 4E 6
Abbots Bromley. *Staf* 7H 33
Abbotsbury. *Dors* 7E 8
Abbotsham. *Devn* 3F 6
Abbotskerswell. *Devn* 3K 5
Abbots Langley. *Herts* 3L 19
Abbots Leigh. *N Som* 6H 17
Abbotsley. *Cambs* 6L 27
Abbots Morton. *Worc* 6L 25
Abbots Ripton. *Cambs* 4L 27
Abbot's Salford. *Warw* 6L 25
Abbotstone. *Hants* 2F 10
Abbots Worthy. *Hants* 2E 10
Abcott. *Shrp* 4D 24
Abdon. *Shrp* 3F 24
Abenhall. *Glos* 2J 17
Aber. *Cdgn* 7G 23
Aberaeron. *Cdgn* 5G 23
Aberafan. *Neat* 4M 15
Aberaman. *Rhon* 3C 16
Aberangell. *Powy* 8H 31
Aberarad. *Carm* 8F 22
Aberarder. *High* 1J 65
Aberargie. *Per* 4G 61
Aberarth. *Cdgn* 5G 23
Aberavon. *Neat* 4M 15
Aber-banc. *Cdgn* 7F 22
Aberbargoed. *Cphy* 4D 16
Aberbechan. *Powy* 2B 24
Aberbeeg. *Blae* 3E 16
Aberbowlan. *Carm* 8J 23
Aberbran. *Powy* 1B 16
Abercanaid. *Mer T* 3C 16
Abercarn. *Cphy* 4E 16
Abercastle. *Pemb* 8A 22
Abercegir. *Powy* 1L 23
Aberchalder. *High* 3F 64
Aberchirder. *Abers* 4G 73
Abercorn. *W Lot* 2J 55
Abercraf. *Powy* 2A 16
Abercregan. *Neat* 4A 16
Abercrombie. *Fife* 5L 61
Abercwmboi. *Rhon* 4C 16
Abercych. *Pemb* 7E 22
Abercynon. *Rhon* 4C 16
Aber-Cywarch. *Gwyn* 8H 31
Aberdalgie. *Per* 3F 60
Aberdar. *Rhon* 3B 16
Aberdare. *Rhon* 3B 16
Aberdaron. *Gwyn* 7A 30
Aberdaugleddau. *Pemb* 3D 14
Aberdeen. *Aber* 3K 67 & 92
Aberdeen International Airport. *Aber* 2J 67
Aberdesach. *Gwyn* 4D 30
Aberdour. *Fife* 1K 55
Aberdovey. *Gwyn* 2J 23
Aberdulais. *Neat* 3M 15
Aberdyfi. *Gwyn* 2J 23
Aberedw. *Powy* 7A 24
Abereiddy. *Pemb* 1B 14
Abererch. *Gwyn* 6C 30
Aberfan. *Mer T* 3C 16
Aberfeldy. *Per* 1D 60
Aberffraw. *IOA* 3C 30
Aberffrwd. *Cdgn* 4J 23
Aberford. *W Yor* 2A 40
Aberfoyle. *Stir* 5A 60
Abergarw. *B'end* 5B 16
Abergarwed. *Neat* 3A 16
Abergavenny. *Mon* 2F 16
Abergele. *Cnwy* 2J 31
Aber-Giâr. *Carm* 7H 23
Abergorlech. *Carm* 8H 23
Abergwaun. *Pemb* 8B 22
Abergwesyn. *Powy* 6L 23
Abergwili. *Carm* 1J 15
Abergwynfi. *Neat* 4A 16
Abergwyngregyn. *Gwyn* 2F 30
Abergynolwyn. *Gwyn* 1J 23
Aberhafesp. *Powy* 2A 24
Aberhonddu. *Powy* 1C 16
Aberhosan. *Powy* 2L 23
Aberkenfig. *B'end* 5A 16
Aberlady. *E Lot* 2D 56
Aberlemno. *Ang* 8F 66
Aberllefenni. *Gwyn* 1K 23
Abermaw. *Gwyn* 8F 30
Abermeurig. *Cdgn* 6H 23
Aber-miwl. *Powy* 2B 24
Abermule. *Powy* 2B 24
Abernant. *Carm* 1H 15
Abernant. *Rhon* 3C 16
Abernethy. *Per* 4G 61
Abernyte. *Per* 2H 61
Aber-oer. *Wrex* 5M 31
Aberpennar. *Rhon* 4C 16
Aberporth. *Cdgn* 6E 22
Aberriw. *Powy* 1B 24
Abersoch. *Gwyn* 7C 30
Abersychan. *Torf* 3E 16
Abertawe. *Swan* 4L 15 & **Swansea** 103
Aberteifi. *Cdgn* 7D 22
Aberthin. *V Glam* 6C 16
Abertillery. *Blae* 3E 16
Abertridwr. *Cphy* 5D 16
Abertridwr. *Powy* 8K 31
Abertyleri. *Blae* 3E 16
Abertysswg. *Cphy* 3D 16
Aberuthven. *Per* 4E 60
Aber Village. *Powy* 1D 16
Aberwheeler. *Den* 3K 31
Aberyscir. *Powy* 1C 16
Aberystwyth. *Cdgn* 3H 23
Abhainn Suidhe. *W Isl* 1E 68
Abingdon-on-Thames. *Oxon* 4E 18
Abinger Common. *Surr* 1M 11
Abinger Hammer. *Surr* 1L 11
Abington. *S Lan* 7H 55
Abington Pigotts. *Cambs* 7M 27
Ab Kettleby. *Leics* 7D 34
Ab Lench. *Worc* 6L 25
Ablington. *Glos* 3B 18
Ablington. *Wilts* 1B 10
Abney. *Derbs* 8K 39
Aboyne. *Abers* 4F 66
Abram. *G Man* 5E 38
Abriachan. *High* 8H 71
Abridge. *Essx* 4C 20
Abronhill. *N Lan* 2F 54
Abson. *S Glo* 6K 17
Abthorpe. *Nptn* 7E 26
Abune-the-Hill. *Orkn* 5A 78
Aby. *Linc* 8L 41
Acairseid. *W Isl* 3B 62
Acaster Malbis. *York* 1B 40
Acaster Selby. *N Yor* 1B 40
Accott. *Devn* 2H 7
Accrington. *Lanc* 3F 38
Acha. *Arg* 8F 62
Achachork. *High* 7J 69
Achadh a' Chuirn. *High* 1L 63
Achahoish. *Arg* 2F 52
Achaleven. *Arg* 2G 59
Achallader. *Arg* 1L 59
Acha Mor. *W Isl* 6D 74
Achanalt. *High* 5E 70
Achandunie. *High* 4J 71
Ach' an Todhair. *High* 6C 64
Achany. *High* 1H 71
Achaphubuil. *High* 6C 64
Acharacle. *High* 7L 63
Acharn. *Ang* 6C 66
Acharn. *Per* 1C 60
Acharole. *High* 4H 77
Achateny. *High* 7K 63
Achavanich. *High* 5G 77
Achdalieu. *High* 6C 64
Achduart. *High* 1C 70
Achentoul. *High* 6D 76
Achfary. *High* 6K 75
Achfrish. *High* 8A 76
Achgarve. *High* 2A 70
Achiemore. *High* 3L 75 (nr. Durness)
Achiemore. *High* 4D 76 (nr. Thurso)
A' Chill. *High* 3G 63
Achiltibuie. *High* 1C 70
Achina. *High* 3C 76
Achinahuagh. *High* 3A 76
Achindarroch. *High* 8C 64
Achinduich. *High* 1H 71
Achinduin. *Arg* 2F 58
Achininver. *High* 3A 76
Achintee. *High* 7B 70
Achintraid. *High* 8A 70
Achleck. *Arg* 1B 58
Achlorachan. *High* 6F 70
Achluachrach. *High* 5E 64
Achlyness. *High* 4K 75
Achmelvich. *High* 7H 75
Achmony. *High* 8H 71
Achmore. *High* 8A 70 (nr. Stromeferry)
Achmore. *High* 2C 70 (nr. Ullapool)
Achnacarnin. *High* 6H 75
Achnacarry. *High* 5D 64
Achnaclerach. *High* 5G 71
Achnacloich. *High* 3K 63
Ach na Cloiche. *High* 3K 63
Achnaconeran. *High* 2G 65
Achnacroish. *Arg* 1F 58
Achnafalnich. *Arg* 3K 59
Achnagarron. *High* 4J 71
Achnagoul. *Arg* 5H 59
Achnaha. *High* 7J 63
Achnahanton Stokeat. *High* 2H 71
Achnahannet. *High* 1M 65
Achnairn. *High* 8A 76
Achnamara. *Arg* 1F 52
Achnanellan. *High* 5C 64
Achnasheen. *High* 6D 70
Achnashellach. *High* 7C 70
Achosnich. *High* 7J 63
Achow. *High* 6H 77
Achranich. *High* 1E 58
Achreamie. *High* 3F 76
Achriabhach. *High* 7D 64
Achriesgill. *High* 4K 75
Achrimsdale. *High* 1M 71
Achscrabster. *High* 3F 76
Achtoty. *High* 3B 76
Achurch. *Nptn* 3J 27
Achuvoldrach. *High* 4A 76
Achvaich. *High* 2K 71
Achvoan. *High* 1K 71
Ackenthwaite. *Cumb* 5G 43
Ackergill. *High* 4J 77
Ackergillshore. *High* 4J 77
Acklam. *Midd* 2D 44
Acklam. *N Yor* 7G 45
Ackleton. *Shrp* 2H 25
Acklington. *Nmbd* 1H 51
Ackton. *W Yor* 3A 40
Ackworth Moor Top. *W Yor* 4A 40
Acle. *Norf* 6L 37
Acocks Green. *W Mid* 3M 25
Acol. *Kent* 7M 21
Acomb. *Nmbd* 5E 50
Acomb. *York* 8E 44
Aconbury. *Here* 8F 24
Acre. *G Man* 5H 39
Acre. *Lanc* 3F 38
Acrefair. *Wrex* 5M 31
Acrise. *Kent* 3K 13
Acton. *Ches E* 4D 32
Acton. *Dors* 8J 9
Acton. *G Lon* 5M 19
Acton. *Shrp* 3D 24
Acton. *Staf* 5F 32
Acton. *Suff* 7E 28
Acton. *Worc* 5J 25
Acton. *Wrex* 4A 32
Acton Beauchamp. *Here* 6G 25
Acton Bridge. *Ches W* 8D 38
Acton Burnell. *Shrp* 1F 24
Acton Green. *Here* 6G 25
Acton Pigott. *Shrp* 1F 24
Acton Round. *Shrp* 2G 25
Acton Scott. *Shrp* 3E 24
Acton Trussell. *Staf* 8G 33
Acton Turville. *S Glo* 5L 17
Adabroc. *W Isl* 2F 74
Adam's Hill. *Worc* 4K 25
Adbaston. *Staf* 7E 32
Adber. *Dors* 3F 8
Adderbury. *Oxon* 8C 26
Adderley. *Shrp* 6D 32
Adderstone. *Nmbd* 6L 57
Addiewell. *W Lot* 3H 55
Addingham. *W Yor* 1J 39
Addington. *Buck* 1H 19
Addington. *G Lon* 7B 20
Addington. *Kent* 8E 20
Addinston. *Bord* 4E 56
Addiscombe. *G Lon* 7B 20
Addlestone. *Surr* 7L 19
Addlethorpe. *Linc* 3M 35
Adeney. *Telf* 8E 32
Adfa. *Powy* 1A 24
Adforton. *Here* 4E 24
Adgestone. *IOW* 7F 10
Adisham. *Kent* 8L 21
Adlestrop. *Glos* 1C 18
Adlingfleet. *E Yor* 3E 40
Adlington. *Ches E* 7H 39
Adlington. *Lanc* 4E 38
Admaston. *Staf* 7H 33
Admaston. *Telf* 8D 32
Admington. *Warw* 7M 25
Adpar. *Cdgn* 7F 22
Adsborough. *Som* 3B 8
Adstock. *Buck* 8F 26
Adstone. *Nptn* 6D 26
Adversane. *W Sus* 3L 11
Advie. *High* 6B 72
Adwalton. *W Yor* 3L 39
Adwell. *Oxon* 4G 19
Adwick le Street. *S Yor* 5B 40
Adwick upon Dearne. *S Yor* 5A 40
Adziel. *Abers* 4K 73
Ae. *Dum* 3G 49
Affleck. *Abers* 1J 67
Affpuddle. *Dors* 6H 9
Affric Lodge. *High* 1D 64
Afon-wen. *Flin* 2L 31
Agglethorpe. *N Yor* 5M 43
Aglionby. *Cumb* 6M 49
Aigburth. *Mers* 7B 38
Aiginis. *W Isl* 5E 74
Aike. *E Yor* 1G 41
Aikers. *Orkn* 8C 78
Aiketgate. *Cumb* 7M 49
Aikhead. *Cumb* 7K 49
Aikton. *Cumb* 6K 49
Ailey. *Here* 7D 24
Ailsworth. *Pet* 2K 27
Ainderby Quernhow. *N Yor* 5C 44
Ainderby Steeple. *N Yor* 4C 44
Aingers Green. *Essx* 1K 21
Ainsdale. *Mers* 4B 38
Ainsdale-on-Sea. *Mers* 4B 38
Ainstable. *Cumb* 7A 50
Ainsworth. *G Man* 4F 38
Ainthorpe. *N Yor* 3G 45
Aintree. *Mers* 6B 38
Aird. *Arg* 5E 58
Aird. *Dum* 5K 47
Aird. *High* 4M 69 (nr. Port Henderson)
Aird. *High* 3K 63 (nr. Tarskavaig)
Aird. *W Isl* 6B 68 (on Benbecula)
Aird. *W Isl* 5F 74 (on Isle of Lewis)
Àird a Bhasair. *High* 3L 63
Aird a Mhachair. *W Isl* 7B 68
Aird a Mhulaidh. *W Isl* 7B 74
Aird Asaig. *W Isl* 1F 68
Aird Dhail. *W Isl* 2E 74
Airdens. *High* 2J 71
Airdeny. *Arg* 3G 59
Aird Mhidhinis. *W Isl* 3B 62
Aird Mhighe. *W Isl* 2F 68 (nr. Ceann a Bhaigh)
Aird Mhighe. *W Isl* 3E 68 (nr. Fionnsabhagh)
Aird Mhor. *W Isl* 3B 62 (on Barra)
Aird Mhor. *W Isl* 7C 68 (on South Uist)
Airdrie. *N Lan* 3F 54
Aird Shleibhe. *W Isl* 3F 68
Aird, The. *High* 6J 69
Aird Thunga. *W Isl* 5E 74
Aird Uig. *W Isl* 5A 74
Airedale. *W Yor* 3A 40
Airidh a Bhruaich. *W Isl* 7C 74
Airies. *Dum* 5J 47
Airmyn. *E Yor* 3D 40
Airntully. *Per* 2F 60
Airor. *High* 3M 63
Airth. *Falk* 1H 55
Airton. *N Yor* 8L 43
Aisby. *Linc* 6E 40 (nr. Gainsborough)
Aisby. *Linc* 6G 35 (nr. Grantham)
Aisgernis. *W Isl* 1B 62
Aish. *Devn* 3H 5 (nr. Buckfastleigh)
Aish. *Devn* 4K 5 (nr. Totnes)
Aisholt. *Som* 2A 8
Aiskew. *N Yor* 5B 44
Aislaby. *N Yor* 5G 45 (nr. Pickering)
Aislaby. *N Yor* 3H 45 (nr. Whitby)
Aislaby. *Stoc T* 2D 44
Aisthorpe. *Linc* 7F 40
Aith. *Shet* 2G 79 (on Fetlar)
Aith. *Shet* 6D 79 (on Mainland)
Aithsetter. *Shet* 8E 79
Akeld. *Nmbd* 7J 57
Akeley. *Buck* 8F 26
Akenham. *Suff* 7H 29
Albaston. *Corn* 8F 6
Alberbury. *Shrp* 8A 32
Albert Town. *Pemb* 2D 14
Albert Village. *Leics* 8L 33
Albourne. *W Sus* 6A 12
Albrighton. *Shrp* 8B 32 (nr. Shrewsbury)
Albrighton. *Shrp* 1J 25 (nr. Telford)
Alburgh. *Norf* 3J 29
Albury. *Herts* 1C 20
Albury. *Surr* 1L 11
Albyfield. *Cumb* 6A 50
Alby Hill. *Norf* 4H 37
Alcaig. *High* 6H 71
Alcaston. *Shrp* 3E 24
Alcester. *Warw* 6L 25
Alciston. *E Sus* 7D 12
Alcombe. *Som* 1L 7
Alconbury. *Cambs* 4K 27
Alconbury Weston. *Cambs* 4K 27
Aldborough. *Norf* 4H 37
Aldborough. *N Yor* 7D 44
Aldbourne. *Wilts* 6C 18
Aldbrough. *E Yor* 2J 41
Aldbrough St John. *N Yor* 2B 44
Aldbury. *Herts* 2K 19
Aldcliffe. *Lanc* 7F 42
Aldclune. *Per* 7M 65
Aldeburgh. *Suff* 6L 29
Aldeby. *Norf* 2L 29
Aldenham. *Herts* 4M 19
Alderbury. *Wilts* 3B 10
Aldercar. *Derbs* 5A 34
Alderford. *Norf* 6H 37
Alderholt. *Dors* 4B 10
Alderley. *Glos* 4K 17
Alderley Edge. *Ches E* 8G 39
Aldermaston. *W Ber* 7F 18
Aldermaston Soke. *W Ber* 7G 19
Aldermaston Wharf. *W Ber* 7G 19
Alderminster. *Warw* 7A 26
Alder Moor. *Staf* 7K 33
Aldersey Green. *Ches W* 4B 32
Aldershot. *Hants* 8J 19
Alderton. *Glos* 8K 25
Alderton. *Nptn* 7F 26
Alderton. *Shrp* 7B 32
Alderton. *Suff* 7K 29
Alderton. *Wilts* 5L 17
Alderton Fields. *Glos* 8L 25
Alderwasley. *Derbs* 4L 33
Aldfield. *N Yor* 7B 44
Aldford. *Ches W* 4B 32
Aldgate. *Rut* 1H 27
Aldham. *Essx* 1H 21
Aldham. *Suff* 7G 29
Aldingbourne. *W Sus* 5K 11
Aldingham. *Cumb* 6D 42
Aldington. *Kent* 4J 13
Aldington. *Worc* 7L 25
Aldington Frith. *Kent* 4J 13
Aldochlay. *Arg* 6L 59
Aldon. *Shrp* 4E 24
Aldoth. *Cumb* 7J 49
Aldreth. *Cambs* 4A 28
Aldridge. *W Mid* 1L 25
Aldringham. *Suff* 5L 29
Aldsworth. *Glos* 2B 18
Aldsworth. *W Sus* 5H 11
Aldwark. *Derbs* 4K 33
Aldwark. *N Yor* 7D 44
Aldwick. *W Sus* 6K 11
Aldwincle. *Nptn* 3J 27
Aldworth. *W Ber* 6F 18
Alexandria. *W Dun* 1B 54
Aley. *Som* 2A 8
Aley Green. *C Beds* 2L 19
Alfardisworthy. *Devn* 4D 6
Alfington. *Devn* 6A 8
Alfold. *Surr* 2L 11
Alfold Bars. *W Sus* 2L 11
Alfold Crossways. *Surr* 2L 11
Alford. *Abers* 2F 66
Alford. *Linc* 8L 41
Alford. *Som* 2F 8
Alfreton. *Derbs* 4A 34
Alfrick. *Worc* 6H 25
Alfrick Pound. *Worc* 6H 25
Alfriston. *E Sus* 7D 12
Algarkirk. *Linc* 6J 35
Alhampton. *Som* 2F 8
Aline Lodge. *W Isl* 7B 74
Alkborough. *N Lin* 3E 40
Alkerton. *Oxon* 7B 26
Alkham. *Kent* 3L 13
Alkington. *Shrp* 6C 32
Alkmonton. *Derbs* 6J 33
Alladale Lodge. *High* 3G 71
Allaleigh. *Devn* 4K 5
Allanbank. *N Lan* 4G 55
Allanton. *N Lan* 4G 55
Allanton. *Bord* 4H 57
Allaston. *Glos* 3J 17
Allbrook. *Hants* 3E 10
All Cannings. *Wilts* 7A 18
Allendale Town. *Nmbd* 6D 50
Allen End. *Warw* 2M 25
Allenheads. *Nmbd* 7D 50
Allensford. *Dur* 7F 50
Allen's Green. *Herts* 2C 20
Allensmore. *Here* 8E 24
Allenton. *Derb* 6L 33
Aller. *Som* 3D 8
Allerby. *Cumb* 8H 49
Allercombe. *Devn* 6M 7
Allerford. *Som* 1L 7
Allerston. *N Yor* 5H 45
Allerthorpe. *E Yor* 1D 40
Allerton. *Mers* 7C 38
Allerton. *W Yor* 2K 39
Allerton Bywater. *W Yor* 3A 40
Allerton Mauleverer. *N Yor* 8D 44
Allesley. *W Mid* 3A 26
Allestree. *Derb* 6L 33
Allet. *Corn* 5E 3
Allexton. *Leics* 1G 27
Allgreave. *Ches E* 3G 33
Allhallows. *Medw* 6G 21
Allhallows-on-Sea. *Medw* 6G 21
Alligin Shuas. *High* 6A 70
Allimore Green. *Staf* 8F 32
Allington. *Kent* 8F 20
Allington. *Linc* 5E 34
Allington. *Wilts* 2C 10 (nr. Amesbury)
Allington. *Wilts* 7A 18 (nr. Devizes)
Allithwaite. *Cumb* 6E 42
Alloa. *Clac* 6D 60
Allonby. *Cumb* 7H 49
Allostock. *Ches W* 8F 38
Alloway. *S Ayr* 8B 54
Allowenshay. *Som* 4C 8
All Saints South Elmham. *Suff* 3K 29
Allscott. *Shrp* 2H 25
Allscott. *Telf* 8D 32
All Stretton. *Shrp* 2E 24
Allt. *Carm* 3K 15
Alltami. *Flin* 3M 31
Alltgobhlach. *N Ayr* 5G 53
Alltmawr. *Powy* 7A 24
Alltnacaillich. *High* 5M 75
Allt na h' Airbhe. *High* 2D 70
Alltour. *High* 5E 64
Alltsigh. *High* 2G 65
Alltwalis. *Carm* 8G 23
Alltwen. *Neat* 3M 15
Alltyblacca. *Cdgn* 7H 23
Allt-y-goed. *Pemb* 7D 22
Almeley. *Here* 6D 24
Almeley Wooton. *Here* 6D 24
Almer. *Dors* 6J 9
Almholme. *S Yor* 5B 40
Almington. *Staf* 6E 32
Alminstone Cross. *Devn* 3E 6
Almodington. *W Sus* 6J 11
Almondbank. *Per* 3F 60
Almondbury. *W Yor* 4K 39
Almondsbury. *S Glo* 5J 17
Alne. *N Yor* 7D 44
Alness. *High* 5J 71
Alnessferry. *High* 5J 71
Alnham. *Nmbd* 8J 57
Alnmouth. *Nmbd* 8M 57
Alnwick. *Nmbd* 8L 57
Alphamstone. *Essx* 8E 28
Alpheton. *Suff* 6E 28
Alphington. *Devn* 6L 7
Alpington. *Norf* 1J 29
Alport. *Derbs* 3K 33
Alport. *Powy* 2C 24
Alpraham. *Ches E* 4C 32
Alresford. *Essx* 1J 21
Alrewas. *Staf* 8J 33
Alsager. *Ches E* 4E 32
Alsagers Bank. *Staf* 5F 32
Alsop en le Dale. *Derbs* 4J 33
Alston. *Cumb* 7C 50
Alston. *Devn* 5C 8
Alstone. *Glos* 8K 25
Alstone. *Som* 1C 8
Alstonefield. *Staf* 4J 33
Alston Sutton. *Som* 8G 17
Alswear. *Devn* 3J 7
Altandhu. *High* 8G 75
Altanduin. *High* 7D 76
Altarnun. *Corn* 7D 6
Altass. *High* 1G 71
Alterwall. *High* 3H 77
Altgaltraig. *Arg* 2J 53
Altham. *Lanc* 2F 38
Althorne. *Essx* 4H 21
Althorpe. *N Lin* 5E 40
Altnabreac. *High* 5F 76
Altnacealgach. *High* 8K 75
Altnafeadh. *High* 8E 64
Altnaharra. *High* 6A 76
Altofts. *W Yor* 3M 39
Alton. *Derbs* 3L 33
Alton. *Hants* 2H 11
Alton. *Staf* 5H 33
Alton Barnes. *Wilts* 7B 18
Altonhill. *E Ayr* 6C 54
Alton Pancras. *Dors* 5G 9
Alton Priors. *Wilts* 7B 18
Altrincham. *G Man* 7F 38
Altrua. *High* 4E 64
Alva. *Clac* 6D 60
Alvanley. *Ches W* 8C 38
Alvaston. *Derb* 6L 33
Alvechurch. *Worc* 4L 25
Alvecote. *Warw* 1A 26
Alvediston. *Wilts* 3J 9
Alveley. *Shrp* 3H 25
Alverdiscott. *Devn* 3G 7
Alverstoke. *Hants* 6F 10
Alverstone. *IOW* 7F 10
Alverthorpe. *W Yor* 3M 39
Alverton. *Notts* 5D 34
Alves. *Mor* 3B 72
Alvescot. *Oxon* 3C 18
Alveston. *S Glo* 5J 17
Alveston. *Warw* 6A 26
Alvie. *High* 3L 65
Alvingham. *Linc* 6K 41
Alvington. *Glos* 3J 17
Alwalton. *Cambs* 2K 27
Alweston. *Dors* 4F 8
Alwington. *Devn* 3F 6
Alwinton. *Nmbd* 1E 50
Alwoodley. *W Yor* 1L 39
Alyth. *Per* 1H 61
Amatnatua. *High* 2G 71
Am Baile. *W Isl* 2B 62
Ambaston. *Derbs* 6A 34
Ambergate. *Derbs* 4L 33
Amber Hill. *Linc* 5J 35
Amberley. *Glos* 3L 17
Amberley. *W Sus* 4L 11
Amble. *Nmbd* 1H 51
Amblecote. *W Mid* 3J 25
Ambler Thorn. *W Yor* 3J 39
Ambleside. *Cumb* 3E 42
Ambleston. *Pemb* 1E 14
Ambrosden. *Oxon* 2G 19
Amcotts. *N Lin* 4E 40
Amersham. *Buck* 4K 19
Amerton. *Staf* 7G 33
Amesbury. *Wilts* 1B 10
Amisfield. *Dum* 3H 49
Amlwch. *IOA* 1D 30
Amlwch Port. *IOA* 1D 30
Ammanford. *Carm* 2L 15
Amotherby. *N Yor* 6G 45
Ampfield. *Hants* 3D 10
Ampleforth. *N Yor* 6E 44
Ampleforth College. *N Yor* 6E 44
Ampney Crucis. *Glos* 3A 18
Ampney St Mary. *Glos* 3A 18
Ampney St Peter. *Glos* 3A 18
Amport. *Hants* 1C 10
Ampthill. *C Beds* 8J 27
Ampton. *Suff* 4E 28
Amroth. *Pemb* 3F 14
Amulree. *Per* 2E 60
Amwell. *Herts* 2M 19
Anaheilt. *High* 7A 64
An Àird. *High* 3K 63
An Camus Darach. *High* 4L 63
Ancaster. *Linc* 5F 34
Anchor. *Shrp* 3B 24
Anchorsholme. *Bkpl* 1B 38
Anchor Street. *Norf* 5K 37
An Cnoc. *W Isl* 5E 74
An Cnoc Ard. *W Isl* 2F 74
An Coroghon. *High* 3G 63
Ancroft. *Nmbd* 5K 57
Ancrum. *Bord* 7F 56
Ancton. *W Sus* 5K 11
Anderby. *Linc* 8M 41
Anderby Creek. *Linc* 8M 41
Anderson. *Dors* 6H 9
Anderton. *Ches W* 8E 38
Andertons Mill. *Lanc* 4D 38
Andover. *Hants* 1D 10
Andover Down. *Hants* 1D 10
Andoversford. *Glos* 2A 18
Andreas. *IOM* 4E 46
An Dùnan. *High* 1K 63
Andwell. *Hants* 8G 19
Anelog. *Gwyn* 7A 30
Anfield. *Mers* 6B 38
Angarrack. *Corn* 6C 3
Angelbank. *Shrp* 4F 24
Angersleigh. *Som* 4B 8
Angerton. *Cumb* 6K 49
Angle. *Pemb* 3C 14
An Gleann Ur. *W Isl* 5E 74
Angmering. *W Sus* 5L 11
Angmering-on-Sea. *W Sus* 5L 11
Angram. *N Yor* 4K 43 (nr. Keld)
Angram. *N Yor* 1B 40 (nr. York)
Anick. *Nmbd* 5E 50
Ankerbold. *Derbs* 3L 33
Ankerville. *High* 4L 71
Anlaby. *E Yor* 3G 41
Anlaby Park. *Hull* 3G 41
An Leth Meadhanach. *W Isl* 2B 62
Anmer. *Norf* 5D 36
Anmore. *Hants* 4G 11
Annan. *Dum* 5K 49
Annaside. *Cumb* 5B 42
Annat. *Arg* 3H 59
Annat. *High* 6A 70
Annathill. *N Lan* 2F 54
Anna Valley. *Hants* 1D 10
Annbank. *S Ayr* 7C 54
Annesley. *Notts* 4B 34
Annesley Woodhouse. *Notts* 4B 34
Annfield Plain. *Dur* 6G 51
Annscroft. *Shrp* 1E 24
An Sailean. *High* 7L 63
Ansdell. *Lanc* 3B 38
Ansford. *Som* 2F 8
Ansley. *Warw* 2A 26
Anslow. *Staf* 7K 33
Anslow Gate. *Staf* 7J 33
Ansteadbrook. *Surr* 2K 11
Anstey. *Herts* 8A 28
Anstey. *Leics* 1D 26
Anston. *S Lan* 5J 55
Anstruther Easter. *Fife* 5L 61
Anstruther Wester. *Fife* 5L 61
Ansty. *Warw* 3B 26
Ansty. *W Sus* 5A 12
Ansty. *Wilts* 3J 9
An Taobh Tuath. *W Isl* 3D 68
An t-Aodann Ban. *High* 6H 69
An t Ath Leathann. *High* 1L 63
An Teanga. *High* 3L 63
Anthill Common. *Hants* 4G 11
Anthorn. *Cumb* 6J 49
Antingham. *Norf* 4J 37
An t-Òb. *W Isl* 3E 68
Anton's Gowt. *Linc* 5J 35
Antony. *Corn* 4F 4
An t-Òrd. *High* 2L 63
Antrobus. *Ches W* 8E 38
Anvil Corner. *Devn* 5E 6
Anwick. *Linc* 4H 35
Anwoth. *Dum* 6C 48
Apethorpe. *Nptn* 2J 27
Apeton. *Staf* 8F 32
Apley. *Linc* 8H 41
Apperknowle. *Derbs* 8M 39
Apperley. *Glos* 1L 17
Apperley Dene. *Nmbd* 6F 50
Appersett. *N Yor* 4K 43
Appin. *Arg* 1G 59
Appleby. *N Lin* 4F 40
Appleby-in-Westmorland. *Cumb* 1H 43
Appleby Magna. *Leics* 1B 26
Appleby Parva. *Leics* 1B 26
Applecross. *High* 7M 69
Appledore. *Devn* 2F 6 (nr. Bideford)
Appledore. *Devn* 4M 7 (nr. Tiverton)
Appledore. *Kent* 5H 13
Appledore Heath. *Kent* 4H 13
Appleford. *Oxon* 4F 18
Applegarthtown. *Dum* 3J 49
Applemore. *Hants* 5D 10
Appleshaw. *Hants* 1D 10
Applethwaite. *Cumb* 1D 42
Appleton. *Hal* 7D 38
Appleton. *Oxon* 3E 18
Appleton-le-Moors. *N Yor* 5G 45
Appleton-le-Street. *N Yor* 6G 45
Appleton Roebuck. *N Yor* 1B 40
Appleton Thorn. *Warr* 7E 38
Appleton Wiske. *N Yor* 3C 44
Appletree. *Nptn* 7C 26
Appletreehall. *Bord* 8E 56
Appletreewick. *N Yor* 7M 43
Appley. *Som* 3M 7
Appley Bridge. *Lanc* 5D 38
Apse Heath. *IOW* 7F 10
Apsley End. *C Beds* 8K 27
Apuldram. *W Sus* 5J 11
Arabella. *High* 4L 71
Arasaig. *High* 5L 63
Arbeadie. *Abers* 4G 67
Arberth. *Pemb* 2F 14
Arbirlot. *Ang* 1M 61
Arborfield. *Wok* 7H 19
Arborfield Cross. *Wok* 7H 19
Arborfield Garrison. *Wok* 7H 19
Arbourthorne. *S Yor* 7M 39
Arbroath. *Ang* 1M 61
Arbuthnott. *Abers* 6J 67
Arcan. *High* 6H 71
Archargary. *High* 4C 76
Archdeacon Newton. *Darl* 2B 44
Archiestown. *Mor* 5C 72
Arclid. *Ches E* 3E 32
Arclid Green. *Ches E* 3E 32
Ardachu. *High* 1J 71
Ardalanish. *Arg* 4A 58
Ardaneaskan. *High* 8A 70
Ardarroch. *High* 8A 70
Ardbeg. *Arg* 1K 53 (nr. Dunoon)
Ardbeg. *Arg* 5C 52 (on Islay)
Ardbeg. *Arg* 3J 53 (on Isle of Bute)
Ardcharnich. *High* 3D 70
Ardchiavaig. *Arg* 4A 58
Ardchonnell. *Arg* 4G 59
Ardchrishnish. *Arg* 3B 58
Ardchronie. *High* 3J 71
Ardchullarie. *Stir* 4A 60
Ardchyle. *Stir* 3A 60
Ard-dhubh. *High* 7M 69
Arddleen. *Powy* 8M 31
Arddlîn. *Powy* 8M 31
Ardechive. *High* 4D 64
Ardeley. *Herts* 1B 20
Ardelve. *High* 1A 64
Arden. *Arg* 1B 54
Ardendrain. *High* 8H 71
Arden Hall. *N Yor* 4E 44
Ardens Grafton. *Warw* 6M 25
Ardentinny. *Arg* 1K 53
Ardeonaig. *Stir* 2B 60
Ardersier. *High* 6K 71
Ardery. *High* 7M 63
Ardessie. *High* 3C 70
Ardfern. *Arg* 5F 58
Ardfernal. *Arg* 2D 52
Ardfin. *Arg* 3C 52
Ardgartan. *Arg* 5K 59
Ardgay. *High* 2H 71
Ardgour. *High* 7C 64
Ardheslaig. *High* 6M 69
Ardindrean. *High* 3D 70
Ardingly. *W Sus* 5B 12
Ardington. *Oxon* 5E 18
Ardlamont House. *Arg* 3H 53
Ardleigh. *Essx* 1J 21
Ardler. *Per* 1H 61
Ardley. *Oxon* 1F 18
Ardlui. *Arg* 4L 59
Ardlussa. *Arg* 1E 52
Ardmair. *High* 2D 70
Ardmay. *Arg* 5K 59
Ardminish. *Arg* 5E 52
Ardmolich. *High* 6M 63
Ardmore. *High* 4K 75 (nr. Kinlochbervie)
Ardmore. *High* 3K 71 (nr. Tain)
Ardnacross. *Arg* 1C 58
Ardnadam. *Arg* 1K 53
Ardnagrask. *High* 7H 71
Ardnamurach. *High* 4A 64
Ardnarff. *High* 8A 70
Ardnastang. *High* 7A 64
Ardoch. *Per* 2F 60
Ardochy House. *High* 3E 64
Ardpatrick. *Arg* 3F 52
Ardrishaig. *Arg* 1G 53
Ardroag. *High* 7G 69
Ardross. *High* 4J 71
Ardrossan. *N Ayr* 5A 54
Ardshealach. *High* 7L 63
Ardsley. *S Yor* 5M 39
Ardslignish. *High* 7K 63
Ardtalla. *Arg* 4C 52
Ardtalnaig. *Per* 2C 60
Ardtoe. *High* 6L 63
Arduaine. *Arg* 4E 58
Ardullie. *High* 5H 71
Ardvasar. *High* 3L 63
Ardvorlich. *Per* 3B 60
Ardwell. *Dum* 7L 47
Ardwell. *Mor* 6D 72
Arean. *High* 6L 63
Areley Common. *Worc* 4J 25
Areley Kings. *Worc* 4H 25
Arford. *Hants* 2J 11
Argoed. *Cphy* 4D 16
Argoed Mill. *Powy* 5M 23
Aridhglas. *Arg* 3A 58
Arinacrinachd. *High* 6M 69
Arinagour. *Arg* 8G 63
Arisaig. *High* 5L 63
Ariundle. *High* 7A 64
Arivegaig. *High* 7L 63
Arkendale. *N Yor* 7C 44
Arkesden. *Essx* 8A 28
Arkholme. *Lanc* 6G 43
Arkle Town. *N Yor* 3M 43
Arkley. *G Lon* 4A 20
Arksey. *S Yor* 5B 40
Arkwright Town. *Derbs* 8A 40
Arlecdon. *Cumb* 2B 42
Arlescote. *Warw* 7B 26
Arlesey. *C Beds* 8K 27
Arleston. *Telf* 8D 32
Arley. *Ches E* 7E 38
Arlingham. *Glos* 2K 17
Arlington. *Devn* 1H 7
Arlington. *E Sus* 7D 12
Arlington. *Glos* 3B 18
Arlington Beccott. *Devn* 1H 7
Armadail. *High* 3L 63
Armadale. *High* 3L 63 (nr. Isleornsay)
Armadale. *High* 3C 76 (nr. Strathy)
Armadale. *W Lot* 3H 55
Armathwaite. *Cumb* 7A 50
Arminghall. *Norf* 1J 29
Armitage. *Staf* 8H 33
Armitage Bridge. *W Yor* 4K 39
Armley. *W Yor* 2L 39
Armscote. *Warw* 7A 26
Arms, The. *Norf* 2E 28
Armston. *Nptn* 3J 27
Armthorpe. *S Yor* 5C 40
Arncliffe. *N Yor* 6L 43
Arncliffe Cote. *N Yor* 6L 43
Arncroach. *Fife* 5L 61
Arne. *Dors* 7J 9
Arnesby. *Leics* 2E 26
Arnicle. *Arg* 6F 52
Arnisdale. *High* 2A 64
Arnish. *High* 7K 69
Arniston. *Midl* 3M 55
Arnol. *W Isl* 4D 74
Arnold. *E Yor* 1H 41
Arnold. *Notts* 5B 34
Arnprior. *Stir* 6B 60
Arnside. *Cumb* 6F 42
Aros Mains. *Arg* 1C 58
Arpafeelie. *High* 6J 71
Arrad Foot. *Cumb* 5E 42
Arram. *E Yor* 1G 41
Arras. *E Yor* 1F 40
Arrathorne. *N Yor* 4A 44
Arreton. *IOW* 7F 10
Arrington. *Cambs* 6M 27
Arrochar. *Arg* 5K 59
Arrow. *Warw* 6L 25
Arscaig. *High* 8A 76
Artafallie. *High* 7J 71
Arthington. *W Yor* 1L 39
Arthingworth. *Nptn* 3F 26
Arthog. *Gwyn* 8F 30
Arthrath. *Abers* 6K 73
Arthurstone. *Per* 1H 61
Artington. *Surr* 1K 11
Arundel. *W Sus* 5L 11
Asby. *Cumb* 1B 42
Ascog. *Arg* 3K 53
Ascot. *Wind* 7K 19
Ascott-under-Wychwood. *Oxon* 2D 18
Asenby. *N Yor* 6C 44
Asfordby. *Leics* 8D 34
Asfordby Hill. *Leics* 8D 34
Asgarby. *Linc* 3K 35 (nr. Horncastle)
Asgarby. *Linc* 5H 35 (nr. Sleaford)
Ash. *Devn* 5K 5
Ash. *Dors* 4H 9
Ash. *Kent* 8L 21 (nr. Sandwich)
Ash. *Kent* 7E 20 (nr. Swanley)
Ash. *Som* 3D 8
Ash. *Surr* 8J 19
Ashampstead. *W Ber* 6F 18
Ashbocking. *Suff* 6H 29
Ashbourne. *Derbs* 5J 33
Ashbrittle. *Som* 3M 7
Ashbrook. *Shrp* 2E 24
Ashburton. *Devn* 3J 5
Ashbury. *Devn* 6G 7
Ashbury. *Oxon* 5C 18
Ashby. *N Lin* 5E 40
Ashby by Partney. *Linc* 3L 35
Ashby cum Fenby. *NE Lin* 5J 41
Ashby de la Launde. *Linc* 4G 35
Ashby-de-la-Zouch. *Leics* 8L 33
Ashby Folville. *Leics* 8D 34
Ashby Magna. *Leics* 2D 26
Ashby Parva. *Leics* 3D 26
Ashby Puerorum. *Linc* 8K 41
Ashby St Ledgars. *Nptn* 5D 26
Ashby St Mary. *Norf* 1K 29
Ashchurch. *Glos* 8K 25
Ashcombe. *Devn* 8L 7
Ashcott. *Som* 2D 8
Ashdon. *Essx* 7B 28
Ashe. *Hants* 8F 18
Asheldham. *Essx* 3H 21
Ashen. *Essx* 7D 28
Ashendon. *Buck* 2H 19
Ashey. *IOW* 7F 10
Ashfield. *Hants* 4D 10
Ashfield. *Here* 1H 17
Ashfield. *Shrp* 3F 24
Ashfield. *Stir* 5C 60
Ashfield. *Suff* 5J 29
Ashfield Green. *Suff* 4J 29
Ashfold Crossways. *W Sus* 5A 12
Ashford. *Devn* 2G 7 (nr. Barnstaple)
Ashford. *Devn* 5H 5 (nr. Kingsbridge)
Ashford. *Hants* 4B 10
Ashford. *Kent* 3J 13
Ashford. *Surr* 6L 19
Ashford Bowdler. *Shrp* 4F 24
Ashford Carbonel. *Shrp* 4F 24
Ashford Hill. *Hants* 7F 18
Ashford in the Water. *Derbs* 3J 33
Ashgill. *S Lan* 5F 54
Ash Green. *Warw* 3B 26
Ashgrove. *Mor* 3C 72
Ashill. *Devn* 4M 7
Ashill. *Norf* 1E 28
Ashill. *Som* 4C 8
Ashingdon. *Essx* 4G 21
Ashington. *Nmbd* 3H 51
Ashington. *W Sus* 4M 11
Ashkirk. *Bord* 7D 56
Ashlett. *Hants* 5E 10
Ashleworth. *Glos* 1L 17
Ashley. *Cambs* 5C 28
Ashley. *Ches E* 7F 38
Ashley. *Dors* 5B 10
Ashley. *Glos* 4M 17
Ashley. *Hants* 6C 10 (nr. New Milton)
Ashley. *Hants* 2D 10 (nr. Winchester)
Ashley. *Kent* 3M 13
Ashley. *Nptn* 2F 26
Ashley. *Staf* 6E 32
Ashley. *Wilts* 7L 17
Ashley Green. *Buck* 3K 19
Ashley Heath. *Dors* 5B 10
Ashley Heath. *Staf* 6E 32
Ashley Moor. *Here* 5E 24
Ash Magna. *Shrp* 6C 32
Ashmanhaugh. *Norf* 5K 37
Ashmansworth. *Hants* 8E 18
Ashmansworthy. *Devn* 4E 6
Ashmead Green. *Glos* 4K 17
Ashmill. *Devn* 6E 6 (nr. Holsworthy)
Ash Mill. *Devn* 3J 7 (nr. South Molton)
Ashmore. *Dors* 4J 9
Ashmore Green. *W Ber* 7F 18
Ashorne. *Warw* 6B 26
Ashover. *Derbs* 3L 33
Ashow. *Warw* 4B 26
Ash Parva. *Shrp* 6C 32
Ashperton. *Here* 7G 25
Ashprington. *Devn* 4K 5
Ash Priors. *Som* 3A 8
Ashreigney. *Devn* 4H 7
Ash Street. *Suff* 7G 29
Ashtead. *Surr* 8M 19
Ash Thomas. *Devn* 4M 7
Ashton. *Corn* 7D 3
Ashton. *Here* 5F 24
Ashton. *Inv* 2A 54
Ashton. *Nptn* 3J 27 (nr. Oundle)
Ashton. *Nptn* 7F 26 (nr. Roade)
Ashton. *Pet* 1K 27
Ashton Common. *Wilts* 8M 17
Ashton Hayes. *Ches W* 3C 32
Ashton-in-Makerfield. *G Man* 5D 38
Ashton Keynes. *Wilts* 4A 18
Ashton under Hill. *Worc* 8K 25
Ashton-under-Lyne. *G Man* 6H 39
Ashton upon Mersey. *G Man* 6F 38
Ashurst. *Hants* 4D 10
Ashurst. *Kent* 4D 12
Ashurst. *Lanc* 5C 38
Ashurst. *W Sus* 4M 11
Ashurst Wood. *W Sus* 4C 12
Ash Vale. *Surr* 8J 19
Ashwater. *Devn* 6E 6
Ashwell. *Herts* 8L 27
Ashwell. *Rut* 8E 34
Ashwellthorpe. *Norf* 2H 29
Ashwick. *Som* 1F 8
Ashwicken. *Norf* 6D 36
Ashwood. *Staf* 3J 25
Askam in Furness. *Cumb* 6D 42
Askern. *S Yor* 4B 40
Askerswell. *Dors* 6E 8
Askett. *Buck* 3J 19
Askham. *Cumb* 1G 43
Askham. *Notts* 8D 40
Askham Bryan. *York* 1B 40
Askham Richard. *York* 1B 40
Askrigg. *N Yor* 4L 43
Askwith. *N Yor* 1K 39
Aslackby. *Linc* 6G 35
Aslacton. *Norf* 2H 29
Aslockton. *Notts* 5D 34
Aspatria. *Cumb* 7J 49
Aspenden. *Herts* 1B 20
Asperton. *Linc* 6J 35
Aspley Guise. *C Beds* 8H 27
Aspley Heath. *C Beds* 8H 27
Aspull. *G Man* 5E 38
Asselby. *E Yor* 3D 40
Assington. *Suff* 8F 28
Assington Green. *Suff* 6D 28
Astbury. *Ches E* 3F 32
Astcote. *Nptn* 6E 26
Asterby. *Linc* 8J 41
Asterley. *Shrp* 1D 24
Asterton. *Shrp* 2D 24
Asthall. *Oxon* 2C 18
Asthall Leigh. *Oxon* 2D 18
Astle. *High* 2K 71
Astley. *G Man* 5F 38
Astley. *Shrp* 8C 32
Astley. *Warw* 3B 26
Astley. *Worc* 5H 25
Astley Abbotts. *Shrp* 2H 25

B

Bincombe—Broadsea

Bincombe. *Dors* 7F 8
Bindal. *High* 3M 71
Binegar. *Som* 1F 8
Bines Green. *W Sus* 4M 11
Binfield. *Brac* 6J 19
Binfield Heath. *Oxon* 6H 19
Bingfield. *Nmbd* 4E 50
Bingham. *Notts* 5D 34
Bingham's Melcombe. *Dors* 5G 9
Bingley. *W Yor* 2K 39
Bings Heath. *Shrp* 8C 32
Binham. *Norf* 4F 36
Binley. *Hants* 8E 18
Binley. *W Mid* 4B 26
Binnegar. *Dors* 7H 9
Binniehill. *Falk* 2G 55
Binsoe. *N Yor* 6B 44
Binstead. *IOW* 6F 10
Binstead. *W Sus* 5K 11
Binsted. *Hants* 1H 11
Binton. *Warw* 6M 25
Bintree. *Norf* 5G 37
Binweston. *Shrp* 1D 24
Birch. *Essx* 2H 21
Birchall. *Staf* 4G 33
Bircham Newton. *Norf* 4D 36
Bircham Tofts. *Norf* 4D 36
Birchanger. *Essx* 1D 20
Birchburn. *N Ayr* 7H 53
Birch Cross. *Staf* 6J 33
Bircher. *Here* 5E 24
Birch Green. *Essx* 2H 21
Birchgrove. *Card* 6D 16
Birchgrove. *Swan* 4M 15
Birch Heath. *Ches W* 3C 32
Birch Hill. *Ches W* 8D 38
Birchill. *Devn* 5C 8
Birchington. *Kent* 7L 21
Birch Langley. *G Man* 5G 39
Birchley Heath. *Warw* 2A 26
Birchmoor. *Warw* 1A 26
Birchmoor Green. *C Beds* 8H 27
Birchover. *Derbs* 3K 33
Birch Vale. *Derbs* 7J 39
Birchview. *Mor* 6B 72
Birchwood. *Linc* 3F 34
Birchwood. *Som* 4B 8
Birchwood. *Warr* 6E 38
Bircotes. *Notts* 6C 40
Birdbrook. *Essx* 7D 28
Birdham. *W Sus* 5J 11
Birdholme. *Derbs* 3L 33
Birdingbury. *Warw* 5C 26
Birdlip. *Glos* 2M 17
Birdsall. *N Yor* 7H 45
Birds Edge. *W Yor* 5L 39
Birds Green. *Essx* 3D 20
Birdsgreen. *Shrp* 3H 25
Birdsmoorgate. *Dors* 5C 8
Birdston. *E Dun* 2E 54
Birdwell. *S Yor* 5M 39
Birdwood. *Glos* 2K 17
Birgham. *Bord* 6G 57
Birichen. *High* 2K 71
Birkby. *Cumb* 8H 49
Birkby. *N Yor* 3C 44
Birkdale. *Mers* 4B 38
Birkenhead. *Mers* 7B 38
Birkenhills. *Abers* 5H 73
Birkenshaw. *N Lan* 3E 54
Birkenshaw. *W Yor* 3L 39
Birkhall. *Abers* 4D 66
Birkhill. *Ang* 2J 61
Birkholme. *Linc* 7F 34
Birkin. *N Yor* 3B 40
Birley. *Here* 6E 24
Birling. *Kent* 7E 20
Birling. *Nmbd* 1H 51
Birling Gap. *E Sus* 8D 12
Birlingham. *Worc* 7K 25
Birmingham. *W Mid* 3L 25 & 92
Birmingham Airport. *W Mid* 3M 25 & 105
Birnam. *Per* 1F 60
Birse. *Abers* 4F 66
Birsemore. *Abers* 4F 66
Birstall. *Leics* 1D 26
Birstall. *W Yor* 3L 39
Birstall Smithies. *W Yor* 3L 39
Birstwith. *N Yor* 8B 44
Birthorpe. *Linc* 6H 35
Birtle. *Lanc* 4G 39
Birtley. *Here* 5D 24
Birtley. *Nmbd* 4D 50
Birtley. *Tyne* 6H 51
Birtsmorton. *Worc* 8J 25
Birts Street. *Worc* 8H 25
Bisbrooke. *Rut* 2G 27
Bisham. *Wind* 5J 19
Bishampton. *Worc* 6K 25
Bish Mill. *Devn* 3J 7
Bishop Auckland. *Dur* 1B 44
Bishopbridge. *Linc* 6G 41
Bishopbriggs. *E Dun* 2E 54
Bishop Burton. *E Yor* 2F 40
Bishopdown. *Wilts* 2B 10
Bishop Middleham. *Dur* 8J 51
Bishopmill. *Mor* 3C 72
Bishop Monkton. *N Yor* 7C 44
Bishop Norton. *Linc* 6F 40
Bishopsbourne. *Kent* 8K 21
Bishops Cannings. *Wilts* 7A 18
Bishop's Castle. *Shrp* 3D 24
Bishop's Caundle. *Dors* 4F 8
Bishop's Cleeve. *Glos* 1M 17
Bishop's Down. *Dors* 4F 8
Bishop's Frome. *Here* 7G 25
Bishop's Green. *Essx* 2E 20
Bishop's Green. *Hants* 7F 18
Bishop's Hull. *Som* 3B 8
Bishop's Itchington. *Warw* 6B 26
Bishops Lydeard. *Som* 3A 8
Bishop's Norton. *Glos* 1L 17
Bishop's Nympton. *Devn* 3J 7
Bishop's Offley. *Staf* 7E 32
Bishop's Stortford. *Herts* 1C 20
Bishops Sutton. *Hants* 2G 11
Bishop's Tachbrook. *Warw* 5B 26
Bishop's Tawton. *Devn* 2G 7
Bishopsteignton. *Devn* 8L 7
Bishopstoke. *Hants* 4E 10
Bishopston. *Swan* 5K 15
Bishopstone. *Buck* 2J 19
Bishopstone. *E Sus* 7C 12
Bishopstone. *Here* 7E 24
Bishopstone. *Swin* 5C 18
Bishopstone. *Wilts* 3A 10
Bishopstrow. *Wilts* 1H 9
Bishop Sutton. *Bath* 8H 17
Bishop's Waltham. *Hants* 4F 10
Bishopswood. *Som* 4B 8
Bishops Wood. *Staf* 1J 25
Bishopsworth. *Bris* 7H 17
Bishop Thornton. *N Yor* 7B 44
Bishopthorpe. *York* 1B 40
Bishopton. *Darl* 1C 44
Bishopton. *Dum* 7B 48
Bishopton. *N Yor* 6C 44
Bishopton. *Ren* 2C 54
Bishopton. *Warw* 6M 25
Bishop Wilton. *E Yor* 8G 45
Bishton. *Newp* 5F 16
Bishton. *Staf* 7H 33
Bisley. *Glos* 3M 17
Bisley. *Surr* 8K 19
Bispham. *Bkpl* 1B 38
Bispham Green. *Lanc* 4C 38
Bissoe. *Corn* 5E 3
Bisterne. *Hants* 5B 10
Bisterne Close. *Hants* 5C 10
Bitchfield. *Linc* 7F 34
Bittadon. *Devn* 1G 7
Bittaford. *Devn* 4H 5
Bittering. *Norf* 6F 36
Bitterley. *Shrp* 4F 24
Bitterne. *Sotn* 4E 10
Bitteswell. *Leics* 3D 26
Bitton. *S Glo* 7J 17
Bix. *Oxon* 5H 19
Bixter. *Shet* 6D 79
Blaby. *Leics* 2D 26
Blackawton. *Devn* 4K 5
Black Bank. *Cambs* 3B 28
Black Barn. *Linc* 7L 35
Blackborough. *Devn* 5M 7
Blackborough. *Norf* 6C 36
Blackborough End. *Norf* 6C 36
Black Bourton. *Oxon* 3C 18
Blackboys. *E Sus* 5D 12
Blackbrook. *Derbs* 5L 33
Blackbrook. *Mers* 6D 38
Blackbrook. *Staf* 6E 32
Blackbrook. *Surr* 1M 11
Blackburn. *Abers* 2J 67
Blackburn. *Bkbn* 3E 38
Blackburn. *W Lot* 3H 55
Black Callerton. *Tyne* 5G 51
Black Carr. *Norf* 2G 29
Black Clauchrie. *S Ayr* 3M 47
Black Corries. *High* 8E 64
Black Crofts. *Arg* 2G 59
Black Cross. *Corn* 3A 4
Blackden Heath. *Ches E* 8F 38
Blackditch. *Oxon* 3E 18
Blackdog. *Abers* 2K 67
Black Dog. *Devn* 5K 7
Blackdown. *Dors* 5C 8
Blackdyke. *Cumb* 6J 49
Blacker Hill. *S Yor* 5M 39
Blackfen. *G Lon* 6C 20
Blackfield. *Hants* 5E 10
Blackford. *Cumb* 5L 49
Blackford. *Per* 5D 60
Blackford. *Shrp* 3F 24
Blackford. *Som* 1D 8
(nr. Burnham-on-Sea)
Blackford. *Som* 3F 8
(nr. Wincanton)
Blackfordby. *Leics* 8L 33
Blackgang. *IOW* 8E 10
Blackhall. *Edin* 2L 55
Blackhall. *Ren* 3C 54
Blackhall Colliery. *Dur* 8K 51
Blackhall Mill. *Tyne* 6G 51
Blackhall Rocks. *Dur* 8K 51
Blackham. *E Sus* 4C 12
Blackheath. *Essx* 1J 21
Blackheath. *G Lon* 6B 20
Blackheath. *Suff* 4L 29
Blackheath. *Surr* 1L 11
Blackheath. *W Mid* 3K 25
Black Heddon. *Nmbd* 4F 50
Blackhill. *Abers* 5L 73
Blackhill. *High* 6H 69
Black Hill. *Warw* 6A 26
Blackhills. *Abers* 3K 73
Blackhills. *High* 6M 71
Blackjack. *Linc* 6J 35
Blackland. *Wilts* 7A 18
Black Lane. *G Man* 5F 38
Blackleach. *Lanc* 2C 38
Blackley. *G Man* 5G 39
Blackley. *W Yor* 4K 39
Blacklunans. *Per* 7B 66
Blackmill. *B'end* 5B 16
Blackmoor. *G Man* 5E 38
Blackmoor. *Hants* 2H 11
Blackmoor Gate. *Devn* 1H 7
Blackmore. *Essx* 3E 20
Blackmore End. *Essx* 8D 28
Blackmore End. *Herts* 2M 19
Black Mount. *Arg* 1K 59
Blackness. *Falk* 2J 55
Blacknest. *Hants* 1H 11
Blackney. *Dors* 6D 8
Blacknoll. *Dors* 7H 9
Black Notley. *Essx* 1F 20
Blacko. *Lanc* 1G 39
Black Pill. *Swan* 5L 15
Blackpool. *Bkpl* 2B 38 & 92
Blackpool. *Devn* 5K 5
Blackpool Airport. *Lanc* 2B 38
Blackpool Corner. *Devn* 6C 8
Blackpool Gate. *Cumb* 4A 50
Blackridge. *W Lot* 3H 55
Blackrock. *Arg* 3B 52
Blackrock. *Mon* 2E 16
Blackrod. *G Man* 4E 38
Blackshaw. *Dum* 5H 49
Blackshaw Head. *W Yor* 3H 39
Blackshaw Moor. *Staf* 4H 33
Blacksmith's Green. *Suff* 5H 29
Blacksnape. *Bkbn* 3F 38
Blackstone. *W Sus* 6A 12
Black Street. *Suff* 3M 29
Black Tar. *Pemb* 3D 14
Blackthorn. *Oxon* 2G 19
Blackthorpe. *Suff* 5F 28
Blacktoft. *E Yor* 3E 40
Blacktop. *Aber* 3J 67
Black Torrington. *Devn* 5E 6
Blacktown. *Newp* 5E 16
Blackwall Tunnel. *G Lon* 5B 20
Blackwater. *Corn* 5E 3
Blackwater. *Hants* 8J 19
Blackwater. *IOW* 7F 10
Blackwater. *Som* 4B 8
Blackwaterfoot. *N Ayr* 7G 53
Blackwell. *Darl* 2B 44
Blackwell. *Derbs* 4A 34
(nr. Alfreton)
Blackwell. *Derbs* 8K 39
(nr. Buxton)
Blackwell. *Som* 3M 7
Blackwell. *Warw* 7A 26
Blackwell. *Worc* 4K 25
Blackwood. *Cphy* 4D 16
Blackwood. *Dum* 3G 49
Blackwood. *S Lan* 5F 54
Blackwood Hill. *Staf* 4G 33
Blacon. *Ches W* 3A 32
Bladnoch. *Dum* 6B 48
Bladon. *Oxon* 2E 18
Blaenannerch. *Cdgn* 7E 22
Blaenau Dolwyddelan. *Cnwy* 4F 30
Blaenau Ffestiniog. *Gwyn* 5G 31
Blaenavon. *Torf* 3E 16
Blaenawey. *Mon* 2E 16
Blaen Celyn. *Cdgn* 6F 22
Blaen Clydach. *Rhon* 4B 16
Blaencwm. *Rhon* 4B 16
Blaendulais. *Neat* 3A 16
Blaenffos. *Pemb* 8D 22
Blaengarw. *B'end* 4B 16
Blaen-geuffordd. *Cdgn* 3J 23
Blaengwrach. *Neat* 3A 16
Blaengwynfi. *Neat* 4A 16
Blaenllechau. *Rhon* 4C 16
Blaenpennal. *Cdgn* 5J 23
Blaenplwyf. *Cdgn* 4H 23
Blaenporth. *Cdgn* 7E 22
Blaenrhondda. *Rhon* 4B 16
Blaenwaun. *Carm* 1G 15
Blaen-y-coed. *Carm* 1H 15
Blagdon. *N Som* 8H 17
Blagdon. *Torb* 3K 5
Blagdon Hill. *Som* 4B 8
Blagill. *Cumb* 7C 50
Blaguegate. *Lanc* 5C 38
Blaich. *High* 6C 64
Blain. *High* 7L 63
Blaina. *Blae* 3E 16
Blair Atholl. *Per* 7L 65
Blair Drummond. *Stir* 6C 60
Blairgowrie. *Per* 1G 61
Blairhall. *Fife* 1J 55
Blairingone. *Per* 6E 60
Blairlogie. *Stir* 6D 60
Blairmore. *Abers* 6E 72
Blairmore. *Arg* 1K 53
Blairmore. *High* 4J 75
Blairquhanan. *W Dun* 1C 54
Blaisdon. *Glos* 2K 17
Blakebrook. *Worc* 4J 25
Blakedown. *Worc* 4J 25
Blake End. *Essx* 1F 20
Blakemere. *Here* 7D 24
Blakeney. *Glos* 3J 17
Blakeney. *Norf* 3G 37
Blakenhall. *Ches E* 5E 32
Blakenhall. *W Mid* 2J 25
Blakeshall. *Worc* 3J 25
Blakesley. *Nptn* 6E 26
Blanchland. *Nmbd* 6E 50
Blandford Camp. *Dors* 5J 9
Blandford Forum. *Dors* 5H 9
Blandford St Mary. *Dors* 5H 9
Bland Hill. *N Yor* 8B 44
Blandy. *High* 4B 76
Blanefield. *Stir* 2D 54
Blankney. *Linc* 3G 35
Blantyre. *S Lan* 4E 54
Blarmachfoldach. *High* 7C 64
Blarnalearoch. *High* 2D 70
Blashford. *Hants* 5B 10
Blaston. *Leics* 2G 27
Blatchbridge. *Som* 1G 9
Blathaisbhal. *W Isl* 4C 68
Blatherwycke. *Nptn* 2H 27
Blawith. *Cumb* 5D 42
Blaxhall. *Suff* 6K 29
Blaxton. *S Yor* 5C 40
Blaydon. *Tyne* 5G 51
Bleadney. *Som* 1D 8
Bleadon. *N Som* 8F 16
Blean. *Kent* 7K 21
Bleasby. *Linc* 7H 41
Bleasby. *Notts* 5D 34
Bleasby Moor. *Linc* 7H 41
Blebocraigs. *Fife* 4K 61
Bleddfa. *Powy* 5C 24
Bledington. *Glos* 1C 18
Bledlow. *Buck* 3H 19
Bledlow Ridge. *Buck* 4H 19
Blencarn. *Cumb* 8B 50
Blencogo. *Cumb* 7J 49
Blendworth. *Hants* 4H 11
Blenheim. *Oxon* 3F 18
Blennerhasset. *Cumb* 7J 49
Bletchingdon. *Oxon* 2F 18
Bletchingley. *Surr* 8B 20
Bletchley. *Mil* 8G 27
Bletchley. *Shrp* 6D 32
Bletherston. *Pemb* 1E 14
Bletsoe. *Bed* 6J 27
Blewbury. *Oxon* 5F 18
Blickling. *Norf* 5H 37
Blidworth. *Notts* 4B 34
Blindburn. *Nmbd* 8H 57
Blindcrake. *Cumb* 8J 49
Blindley Heath. *Surr* 3B 12
Blindmoor. *Som* 4B 8
Blisland. *Corn* 8B 6
Blissford. *Hants* 4B 10
Bliss Gate. *Worc* 4H 25
Blists Hill. *Telf* 1G 25
Blisworth. *Nptn* 6F 26
Blithbury. *Staf* 7H 33
Blitterlees. *Cumb* 6J 49
Blockley. *Glos* 8M 25
Blofield. *Norf* 1K 29
Blofield Heath. *Norf* 6K 37
Blo' Norton. *Norf* 4G 29
Bloomfield. *Bord* 7E 56
Blore. *Staf* 5J 33
Blount's Green. *Staf* 6H 33
Bloxham. *Oxon* 8C 26
Bloxholm. *Linc* 4G 35
Bloxwich. *W Mid* 1L 25
Bloxworth. *Dors* 6H 9
Blubberhouses. *N Yor* 8A 44
Blue Anchor. *Som* 1M 7
Blue Anchor. *Swan* 4K 15
Blue Bell Hill. *Kent* 7F 20
Blue Row. *Essx* 2J 21
Bluetown. *Kent* 8H 21
Blundeston. *Suff* 2M 29
Blunham. *C Beds* 6K 27
Blunsdon St Andrew. *Swin* 5B 18
Bluntington. *Worc* 4J 25
Bluntisham. *Cambs* 4M 27
Blunts. *Corn* 3E 4
Blurton. *Stoke* 5F 32
Blyborough. *Linc* 6F 40
Blyford. *Suff* 4L 29
Blymhill. *Staf* 8F 32
Blymhill Lawns. *Staf* 8F 32
Blyth. *Nmbd* 3J 51
Blyth. *Notts* 7C 40
Blyth. *Bord* 5K 55
Blyth Bank. *Bord* 5K 55
Blyth Bridge. *Bord* 5K 55
Blythburgh. *Suff* 4L 29
Blythe Bridge. *Staf* 5G 33
Blythe Marsh. *Staf* 5G 33
Blythe, The. *Staf* 7H 33
Blyton. *Linc* 6E 40
Boarhills. *Fife* 4L 61
Boarhunt. *Hants* 5G 11
Boarshead. *E Sus* 4D 12
Boar's Head. *G Man* 5D 38
Boars Hill. *Oxon* 3E 18
Boarstall. *Buck* 2G 19
Boasley Cross. *Devn* 6G 7
Boath. *High* 4H 71
Boat of Garten. *High* 2M 65
Bobbing. *Kent* 7G 21
Bobbington. *Staf* 2J 25
Bobbingworth. *Essx* 3D 20
Bocaddon. *Corn* 4C 4
Bocking. *Essx* 1F 20
Bocking Churchstreet. *Essx* 1F 20
Boddam. *Abers* 5M 73
Boddam. *Shet* 10D 79
Boddington. *Glos* 1L 17
Bodedern. *IOA* 1C 30
Bodelwyddan. *Den* 2K 31
Bodenham. *Here* 6F 24
Bodenham. *Wilts* 3B 10
Bodewryd. *IOA* 1C 30
Bodfari. *Den* 2K 31
Bodffordd. *IOA* 2D 30
Bodham. *Norf* 3H 37
Bodiam. *E Sus* 5F 12
Bodicote. *Oxon* 8C 26
Bodieve. *Corn* 8A 6
Bodinnick. *Corn* 4C 4
Bodle Street Green. *E Sus* 6E 12
Bodmin. *Corn* 3B 4
Bodnant. *Cnwy* 2H 31
Bodney. *Norf* 2E 28
Bodorgan. *IOA* 3C 30
Bodrane. *Corn* 3D 4
Bodsham. *Kent* 3K 13
Boduan. *Gwyn* 6C 30
Bodymoor Heath. *Warw* 2M 25
Bogallan. *High* 6J 71
Bogbrae Croft. *Abers* 6L 73
Bogend. *S Ayr* 6B 54
Boghall. *Midl* 3L 55
Boghall. *W Lot* 3H 55
Boghead. *S Lan* 5F 54
Bogindollo. *Ang* 8E 66
Bogmoor. *Mor* 3D 72
Bogniebrae. *Abers* 5F 72
Bognor Regis. *W Sus* 6K 11
Bograxie. *Abers* 2H 67
Bogside. *N Lan* 4G 55
Bog, The. *Shrp* 2D 24
Bogton. *Abers* 4G 73
Bogue. *Dum* 3D 48
Bohenie. *High* 5E 64
Bohortha. *Corn* 6F 3
Boirseam. *W Isl* 3E 68
Bokiddick. *Corn* 3B 4
Bolam. *Dur* 1A 44
Bolam. *Nmbd* 3F 50
Bolberry. *Devn* 6H 5
Bold Heath. *Mers* 7D 38
Boldon. *Tyne* 5J 51
Boldon Colliery. *Tyne* 5J 51
Boldre. *Hants* 6D 10
Boldron. *Dur* 2M 43
Bole. *Notts* 7D 40
Bolehall. *Staf* 1A 26
Bolehill. *Derbs* 4K 33
Bolenowe. *Corn* 6D 3
Boleside. *Bord* 6D 56
Bolham. *Devn* 4L 7
Bolham Water. *Devn* 4A 8
Bolingey. *Corn* 4E 3
Bollington. *Ches E* 8H 39
Bolney. *W Sus* 5A 12
Bolnhurst. *Bed* 6J 27
Bolshan. *Ang* 8G 67
Bolsover. *Derbs* 8A 40
Bolsterstone. *S Yor* 6L 39
Bolstone. *Here* 8F 24
Boltachan. *Per* 8L 65
Boltby. *N Yor* 5D 44
Bolton. *Cumb* 1H 43
Bolton. *E Lot* 2E 56
Bolton. *E Yor* 8G 45
Bolton. *G Man* 5F 38
Bolton. *Nmbd* 8L 57
Bolton Abbey. *N Yor* 8M 43
Bolton-by-Bowland. *Lanc* 1F 38
Boltonfellend. *Cumb* 5M 49
Boltongate. *Cumb* 7K 49
Bolton Green. *Lanc* 4D 38
Bolton-le-Sands. *Lanc* 7F 42
Bolton Low Houses. *Cumb* 7K 49
Bolton New Houses. *Cumb* 7K 49
Bolton-on-Swale. *N Yor* 4B 44
Bolton Percy. *N Yor* 1B 40
Bolton Town End. *Lanc* 7F 42
Bolton upon Dearne. *S Yor* 5A 40
Bolton Wood Lane. *Cumb* 7K 49
Bolventor. *Corn* 8C 6
Bomarsund. *Nmbd* 3H 51
Bomere Heath. *Shrp* 8B 32
Bonar Bridge. *High* 2J 71
Bonawe. *Arg* 2H 59
Bonby. *N Lin* 4G 41
Boncath. *Pemb* 8E 22
Bonchester Bridge. *Bord* 8E 56
Bonchurch. *IOW* 8F 10
Bond End. *Staf* 8J 33
Bondleigh. *Devn* 5H 7
Bonds. *Lanc* 1C 38
Bonehill. *Devn* 8J 7
Bonehill. *Staf* 1M 25
Bo'ness. *Falk* 1H 55
Boney Hay. *Staf* 8H 33
Bonham. *Wilts* 2G 9
Bonhill. *W Dun* 2B 54
Boningale. *Shrp* 1J 25
Bonjedward. *Bord* 7F 56
Bonkle. *N Lan* 4G 55
Bonnington. *Ang* 2L 61
Bonnington. *Edin* 3K 55
Bonnington. *Kent* 4J 13
Bonnybank. *Fife* 5J 61
Bonnybridge. *Falk* 1G 55
Bonnykelly. *Abers* 4J 73
Bonnyrigg. *Midl* 3M 55
Bonnyton. *Ang* 2J 61
Bonnytown. *Fife* 4L 61
Bonsall. *Derbs* 4K 33
Bont. *Mon* 2F 16
Bontddu. *Gwyn* 8F 30
Bont Dolgadfan. *Powy* 1L 23
Bontgoch. *Cdgn* 3J 23
Bonthorpe. *Linc* 8L 41
Bontnewydd. *Cdgn* 5J 23
Bont-newydd. *Cnwy* 2K 31
Bontnewydd. *Gwyn* 3D 30
(nr. Caernarfon)
Bont Newydd. *Gwyn* 5G 31
(nr. Llan Ffestiniog)
Bontuchel. *Den* 4K 31
Bonvilston. *V Glam* 6C 16
Bon-y-maen. *Swan* 4L 15
Booker. *Buck* 4J 19
Booley. *Shrp* 7C 32
Boorley Green. *Hants* 4F 10
Boosbeck. *Red C* 2F 44
Boot. *Cumb* 3C 42
Booth. *W Yor* 3J 39
Boothby Graffoe. *Linc* 4F 34
Boothby Pagnell. *Linc* 6F 34
Booth Green. *Ches E* 7H 39
Booth of Toft. *Shet* 4E 79
Boothstown. *G Man* 5F 38
Boothville. *Nptn* 5F 26
Booth Wood. *W Yor* 4J 39
Bootle. *Cumb* 5C 42
Bootle. *Mers* 6B 38
Booton. *Norf* 5H 37
Booze. *N Yor* 3M 43
Boquhan. *Stir* 1D 54
Boraston. *Shrp* 4G 25
Borden. *Kent* 7G 21
Borden. *W Sus* 3J 11
Bordlands. *Bord* 5K 55
Bordley. *N Yor* 7L 43
Bordon. *Hants* 2J 11
Boreham. *Essx* 3F 20
Boreham. *Wilts* 1H 9
Boreham Street. *E Sus* 6E 12
Borehamwood. *Herts* 4M 19
Boreland. *Dum* 2J 49
Boreston. *Devn* 4J 5
Borestone Brae. *Stir* 6D 60
Boreton. *Shrp* 1F 24
Borgh. *W Isl* 3A 62
(on Barra)
Borgh. *W Isl* 6B 68
(on Benbecula)
Borgh. *W Isl* 3D 68
(on Berneray)
Borgh. *W Isl* 3E 74
(on Isle of Lewis)
Borghasdal. *W Isl* 3E 68
Borghastan. *W Isl* 4B 74
Borgh na Sgiotaig. *High* 4H 69
Borgie. *High* 4B 76
Borgue. *Dum* 7D 48
Borgue. *High* 7G 77
Borley. *Essx* 7E 28
Borley Green. *Essx* 7E 28
Borley Green. *Suff* 5F 28
Borlum. *High* 1H 65
Bornais. *W Isl* 1B 62
Bornesketaig. *High* 4H 69
Boroughbridge. *N Yor* 7C 44
Borough Green. *Kent* 8E 20
Borras Head. *Wrex* 4A 32
Borreraig. *High* 6F 68
Borrobol Lodge. *High* 7D 76
Borrodale. *High* 7F 68
Borrowash. *Derb* 6A 34
Borrowby. *N Yor* 5D 44
(nr. Northallerton)
Borrowby. *N Yor* 2G 45
(nr. Whitby)
Borrowston. *High* 5J 77
Borrowstonehill. *Orkn* 7C 78
Borrowstoun. *Falk* 1H 55
Borstal. *Medw* 7F 20
Borth. *Cdgn* 3J 23
Borthwick. *Midl* 4M 55
Borth-y-Gest. *Gwyn* 6E 30
Borve. *High* 7J 69
Borwick. *Lanc* 6G 43
Bosbury. *Here* 7G 25
Boscastle. *Corn* 6B 6
Boscombe. *Bour* 6B 10
Boscombe. *Wilts* 2C 10
Boscoppa. *Corn* 4B 4
Bosham. *W Sus* 5J 11
Bosherston. *Pemb* 4D 14
Bosley. *Ches E* 3G 33
Bossall. *N Yor* 7G 45
Bossiney. *Corn* 7B 6
Bossingham. *Kent* 3K 13
Bossington. *Som* 1K 7
Bostadh. *W Isl* 4B 74
Bostock Green. *Ches W* 3D 32
Boston. *Linc* 5K 35
Boston Spa. *W Yor* 1A 40
Boswarthen. *Corn* 6B 3
Boswinger. *Corn* 5A 4
Botallack. *Corn* 6A 3
Botany Bay. *G Lon* 4A 20
Botcheston. *Leics* 1C 26
Botesdale. *Suff* 4G 29
Bothal. *Nmbd* 3H 51
Bothampstead. *W Ber* 6F 18
Bothamsall. *Notts* 8C 40
Bothel. *Cumb* 8J 49
Bothenhampton. *Dors* 6D 8
Bothwell. *S Lan* 4E 54
Botley. *Buck* 3K 19
Botley. *Hants* 4F 10
Botley. *Oxon* 3E 18
Botloe's Green. *Glos* 1K 17
Botolph Claydon. *Buck* 1H 19
Botolphs. *W Sus* 5M 11
Bottacks. *High* 5G 71
Bottesford. *Leics* 6E 34
Bottesford. *N Lin* 5E 40
Bottisham. *Cambs* 5B 28
Bottlesford. *Wilts* 8B 18
Bottomcraig. *Fife* 3J 61
Bottom o' th' Moor. *G Man* 4E 38
Botton. *N Yor* 3F 44
Botton Head. *Lanc* 7H 43
Bottreaux Mill. *Devn* 3K 7
Botus Fleming. *Corn* 3F 4
Botwnnog. *Gwyn* 6B 30
Bough Beech. *Kent* 3C 12
Boughrood. *Powy* 8B 24
Boughspring. *Glos* 4H 17
Boughton. *Norf* 1C 28
Boughton. *Nptn* 5F 26
Boughton. *Notts* 3C 34
Boughton Aluph. *Kent* 3J 13
Boughton Green. *Kent* 8F 20
Boughton Lees. *Kent* 3J 13
Boughton Malherbe. *Kent* 3G 13
Boughton Monchelsea. *Kent* 8F 20
Boughton under Blean. *Kent* 8J 21
Boulby. *Red C* 2G 45
Bouldnor. *IOW* 7D 10
Bouldon. *Shrp* 3F 24
Boulmer. *Nmbd* 8M 57
Boulston. *Pemb* 2D 14
Boultham. *Linc* 3F 34
Boulton. *Derb* 6L 33
Boundary. *Staf* 5G 33
Bounds. *Here* 8G 25
Bourn. *Cambs* 6M 27
Bournbrook. *W Mid* 3L 25
Bourne. *Linc* 7G 35
Bourne End. *Bed* 5J 27
Bourne End. *Buck* 5J 19
Bourne End. *C Beds* 7H 27
Bourne End. *Herts* 3L 19
Bournemouth. *Bour* 6A 10 & 92
Bournemouth Airport. *Dors* 6B 10
Bournes Green. *Glos* 3M 17
Bournes Green. *S'end* 5H 21
Bourne, The. *Surr* 1J 11
Bournheath. *Worc* 4K 25
Bournmoor. *Dur* 6J 51
Bournville. *W Mid* 3L 25
Bourton. *Dors* 2G 9
Bourton. *N Som* 7F 16
Bourton. *Oxon* 5C 18
Bourton. *Shrp* 2F 24
Bourton. *Wilts* 7A 18
Bourton on Dunsmore. *Warw* 4C 26
Bourton-on-the-Hill. *Glos* 8M 25
Bourton-on-the-Water. *Glos* 1B 18
Bousd. *Arg* 7G 63
Bousta. *Shet* 6C 79
Boustead Hill. *Cumb* 6K 49
Bouth. *Cumb* 5E 42
Bouthwaite. *N Yor* 6A 44
Boveney. *Buck* 6K 19
Boveridge. *Dors* 4A 10
Boverton. *V Glam* 7B 16
Bovey Tracey. *Devn* 8K 7
Bovingdon. *Herts* 3L 19
Bovingdon Green. *Buck* 5J 19
Bovinger. *Essx* 3D 20
Bovington Camp. *Dors* 7H 9
Bow. *Devn* 5J 7
Bowbank. *Dur* 1L 43
Bow Brickhill. *Mil* 8H 27
Bowbridge. *Glos* 3L 17
Bowburn. *Dur* 8J 51
Bowcombe. *IOW* 7E 10
Bowd. *Devn* 7A 8
Bowden. *Devn* 5K 5
Bowden. *Bord* 6E 56
Bowden Hill. *Wilts* 7M 17
Bowdens. *Som* 3D 8
Bowderdale. *Cumb* 3H 43
Bowdon. *G Man* 7F 38
Bower. *Nmbd* 3C 50
Bowerchalke. *Wilts* 3A 10
Bowerhill. *Wilts* 7M 17
Bower Hinton. *Som* 4D 8
Bowermadden. *High* 3H 77
Bowers. *Staf* 6F 32
Bowers Gifford. *Essx* 5F 20
Bowershall. *Fife* 6F 60
Bowertower. *High* 3H 77
Bowes. *Dur* 2L 43
Bowgreave. *Lanc* 1C 38
Bowhousebog. *N Lan* 4G 55
Bowithick. *Corn* 7C 6
Bowland Bridge. *Cumb* 5F 42
Bowlees. *Dur* 1L 43
Bowley. *Here* 6F 24
Bowlhead Green. *Surr* 2K 11
Bowling. *W Dun* 2C 54
Bowling. *W Yor* 2K 39
Bowling Bank. *Wrex* 5A 32
Bowling Green. *Worc* 6J 25
Bowlish. *Som* 1F 8
Bowmanstead. *Cumb* 4E 42
Bowmore. *Arg* 4B 52
Bowness-on-Solway. *Cumb* 5K 49
Bowness-on-Windermere. *Cumb* 4F 42
Bow of Fife. *Fife* 4J 61
Bowriefauld. *Ang* 1L 61
Bowscale. *Cumb* 8L 49
Bowsden. *Nmbd* 5J 57
Bowside Lodge. *High* 3D 76
Bowston. *Cumb* 4F 42
Bow Street. *Cdgn* 3J 23
Bowthorpe. *Norf* 1H 29
Box. *Glos* 3L 17
Box. *Wilts* 7L 17
Boxbush. *Glos* 1J 17
Box End. *Bed* 7J 27
Boxford. *Suff* 7F 28
Boxford. *W Ber* 6E 18
Boxgrove. *W Sus* 5K 11
Box Hill. *Wilts* 7L 17
Boxley. *Kent* 8F 20
Boxmoor. *Herts* 3L 19
Box's Shop. *Corn* 5D 6
Boxted. *Essx* 8F 28
Boxted. *Suff* 6E 28
Boxted Cross. *Essx* 8G 29
Boxworth. *Cambs* 5M 27
Boxworth End. *Cambs* 5M 27
Boyden End. *Suff* 6D 28
Boyden Gate. *Kent* 7L 21
Boylestone. *Derbs* 6J 33
Boylestonfield. *Derbs* 6J 33
Boyndie. *Abers* 3G 73
Boynton. *E Yor* 7L 45
Boys Hill. *Dors* 4F 8
Boythorpe. *Derbs* 3L 33
Boyton. *Corn* 6E 6
Boyton. *Suff* 7K 29
Boyton. *Wilts* 2J 9
Boyton Cross. *Essx* 3E 20
Boyton End. *Essx* 8C 28
Boyton End. *Suff* 7D 28
Bozeat. *Nptn* 6H 27
Braaid. *IOM* 6D 46
Braal Castle. *High* 3G 77
Brabling Green. *Suff* 5J 29
Brabourne. *Kent* 3K 13
Brabourne Lees. *Kent* 3J 13
Brabster. *High* 3J 77
Bracadale. *High* 8H 69
Bracara. *High* 4M 63
Braceborough. *Linc* 8G 35
Bracebridge. *Linc* 3F 34
Bracebridge Heath. *Linc* 3F 34
Braceby. *Linc* 6G 35
Bracewell. *Lanc* 1G 39
Brackenber. *Cumb* 2J 43
Brackenfield. *Derbs* 4L 33
Brackenlands. *Cumb* 7K 49
Brackenthwaite. *Cumb* 7K 49
Brackenthwaite. *N Yor* 8B 44
Brackla. *B'end* 6B 16
Brackla. *High* 6L 71
Bracklesham. *W Sus* 6J 11
Brackletter. *High* 5D 64
Brackley. *Nptn* 8D 26
Brackley Hatch. *Nptn* 7E 26
Brackloch. *High* 7J 75
Bracknell. *Brac* 7J 19
Braco. *Per* 5D 60
Bracobrae. *Mor* 4F 72
Bracon. *N Lin* 5D 40
Bracon Ash. *Norf* 2H 29
Bradbourne. *Derbs* 4K 33
Bradbury. *Dur* 1C 44
Bradda. *IOM* 6B 46
Bradden. *Nptn* 7E 26
Bradenham. *Buck* 4J 19
Bradenham. *Norf* 1F 28
Bradenstoke. *Wilts* 6A 18
Bradfield. *Essx* 8H 29
Bradfield. *Norf* 4J 37
Bradfield. *W Ber* 6G 19
Bradfield Combust. *Suff* 6E 28
Bradfield Green. *Ches E* 4D 32
Bradfield Heath. *Essx* 1K 21
Bradfield St Clare. *Suff* 6F 28
Bradfield St George. *Suff* 5F 28
Bradford. *Derbs* 3K 33
Bradford. *Devn* 5F 6
Bradford. *Nmbd* 6L 57
Bradford. *W Yor* 2K 39 & 92
Bradford Abbas. *Dors* 4E 8
Bradford Barton. *Devn* 4K 7
Bradford Leigh. *Wilts* 7L 17
Bradford-on-Avon. *Wilts* 7L 17
Bradford-on-Tone. *Som* 3A 8
Bradford Peverell. *Dors* 6F 8
Bradiford. *Devn* 2G 7
Brading. *IOW* 7G 11
Bradley. *Ches W* 8D 38
Bradley. *Derbs* 5K 33
Bradley. *Glos* 4K 17
Bradley. *Hants* 1G 11
Bradley. *NE Lin* 5J 41
Bradley. *N Yor* 5M 43
Bradley. *Staf* 8F 32
Bradley. *W Mid* 2K 25
Bradley. *W Yor* 3K 39
Bradley. *Wrex* 4A 32
Bradley Cross. *Som* 8G 17
Bradley Green. *Ches W* 5C 32
Bradley Green. *Som* 2B 8
Bradley Green. *Warw* 1A 26
Bradley Green. *Worc* 5K 25
Bradley in the Moors. *Staf* 5H 33
Bradley Mount. *Ches E* 8H 39
Bradley Stoke. *S Glo* 5J 17
Bradlow. *Here* 8H 25
Bradmore. *Notts* 6B 34
Bradmore. *W Mid* 2J 25
Bradninch. *Devn* 5M 7
Bradnop. *Staf* 4H 33
Bradpole. *Dors* 6D 8
Bradshaw. *G Man* 4F 38
Bradstone. *Devn* 7E 6
Bradwall Green. *Ches E* 3E 32
Bradway. *S Yor* 7M 39
Bradwell. *Derbs* 7K 39
Bradwell. *Essx* 1G 21
Bradwell. *Mil* 8G 27
Bradwell. *Norf* 1M 29
Bradwell-on-Sea. *Essx* 3J 21
Bradwell Waterside. *Essx* 3H 21
Bradworthy. *Devn* 4E 6
Brae. *High* 3A 70
Brae. *Shet* 5D 79
Braeantra. *High* 4H 71
Braefield. *High* 8G 71
Braefindon. *High* 6J 71
Braegrum. *Per* 3F 60
Braehead. *Ang* 8G 67
Braehead. *Dum* 6B 48
Braehead. *Mor* 5C 72
Braehead. *Orkn* 3C 78
Braehead. *S Lan* 6G 55
(nr. Coalburn)
Braehead. *S Lan* 4H 55
(nr. Forth)
Braehoulland. *Shet* 4C 79
Braemar. *Abers* 4B 66
Braemore. *High* 6F 76
(nr. Dunbeath)
Braemore. *High* 4D 70
(nr. Ullapool)
Brae of Achnahaird. *High* 8H 75
Brae Roy Lodge. *High* 4F 64
Braeside. *Abers* 6K 73
Braeside. *Inv* 2A 54
Braes of Coul. *Ang* 8C 66
Braeswick. *Orkn* 4E 78
Braetongue. *High* 4A 76
Braeval. *Stir* 5A 60
Braevallich. *Arg* 5G 59
Braewick. *Shet* 6D 79
Brafferton. *Darl* 1B 44
Brafferton. *N Yor* 6D 44
Brafield-on-the-Green. *Nptn* 6G 27
Bragar. *W Isl* 4C 74
Bragbury End. *Herts* 1A 20
Bragleenbeg. *Arg* 3G 59
Braichmelyn. *Gwyn* 3F 30
Braides. *Lanc* 8F 42
Braidwood. *S Lan* 5G 55
Braigo. *Arg* 3A 52
Brailsford. *Derbs* 5K 33
Braintree. *Essx* 1F 20
Braiseworth. *Suff* 4H 29
Braishfield. *Hants* 3D 10
Braithwaite. *Cumb* 1D 42
Braithwaite. *S Yor* 4C 40
Braithwaite. *W Yor* 1J 39
Braithwell. *S Yor* 6B 40
Brakefield Green. *Norf* 1G 29
Bramber. *W Sus* 4M 11
Brambledown. *Kent* 6H 21
Brambridge. *Hants* 3E 10
Bramcote. *Notts* 6B 34
Bramcote. *Warw* 3C 26
Bramdean. *Hants* 3G 11
Bramerton. *Norf* 1J 29
Bramfield. *Herts* 2A 20
Bramfield. *Suff* 4K 29
Bramford. *Suff* 7H 29
Bramhall. *G Man* 7G 39
Bramham. *W Yor* 1A 40
Bramhope. *W Yor* 1L 39
Bramley. *Hants* 8G 19
Bramley. *S Yor* 6A 40
Bramley. *Surr* 1L 11
Bramley. *W Yor* 2L 39
Bramley Green. *Hants* 8G 19
Bramley Head. *N Yor* 8A 44
Bramley Vale. *Derbs* 3A 34
Bramling. *Kent* 8L 21
Brampford Speke. *Devn* 6L 7
Brampton. *Cambs* 4L 27
Brampton. *Cumb* 1H 43
(nr. Appleby-in-Westmorland)
Brampton. *Cumb* 5A 50
(nr. Carlisle)
Brampton. *Linc* 8E 40
Brampton. *Norf* 5J 37
Brampton. *S Yor* 5A 40
Brampton. *Suff* 3L 29
Brampton Abbotts. *Here* 1J 17
Brampton Ash. *Nptn* 3F 26
Brampton Bryan. *Here* 4D 24
Brampton en le Morthen. *S Yor* 7A 40
Bramshall. *Staf* 6H 33
Bramshaw. *Hants* 4C 10
Bramshill. *Hants* 7H 19
Bramshott. *Hants* 2J 11
Branault. *High* 7K 63
Brancaster. *Norf* 3D 36
Brancaster Staithe. *Norf* 3D 36
Brancepeth. *Dur* 8H 51
Branch End. *Nmbd* 5F 50
Branchill. *Mor* 4A 72
Brand End. *Linc* 5K 35
Branderburgh. *Mor* 2C 72
Brandesburton. *E Yor* 1H 41
Brandeston. *Suff* 5J 29
Brand Green. *Glos* 1K 17
Brandhill. *Shrp* 4E 24
Brandis Corner. *Devn* 5F 6
Brandish Street. *Som* 1L 7
Brandiston. *Norf* 5H 37
Brandon. *Dur* 8H 51
Brandon. *Linc* 5F 34
Brandon. *Nmbd* 8K 57
Brandon. *Suff* 3D 28
Brandon. *Warw* 4C 26
Brandon Bank. *Cambs* 3C 28
Brandon Creek. *Norf* 2C 28
Brandon Parva. *Norf* 1G 29
Brandsby. *N Yor* 6E 44
Brandy Wharf. *Linc* 6G 41
Brane. *Corn* 7B 3
Bran End. *Essx* 1E 20
Branksome. *Pool* 6A 10
Bransbury. *Hants* 1E 10
Bransby. *Linc* 8F 40
Branscombe. *Devn* 7A 8
Bransford. *Worc* 6H 25
Bransgore. *Hants* 6B 10
Bransholme. *Hull* 2G 41
Bransley. *Shrp* 4G 25
Branston. *Leics* 7E 34
Branston. *Linc* 3G 35
Branston. *Staf* 7K 33
Branston Booths. *Linc* 3G 35
Branstone. *IOW* 7F 10
Bransty. *Cumb* 2A 42
Brant Broughton. *Linc* 4F 34
Brantham. *Suff* 8H 29
Branthwaite. *Cumb* 8K 49
(nr. Caldbeck)
Branthwaite. *Cumb* 1B 42
(nr. Workington)
Brantingham. *E Yor* 3F 40
Branton. *Nmbd* 8K 57
Branton. *S Yor* 5C 40
Branton Green. *N Yor* 7D 44
Branxholme. *Bord* 8D 56
Branxton. *Nmbd* 6H 57
Brassington. *Derbs* 4K 33
Brasted. *Kent* 8C 20
Brasted Chart. *Kent* 8C 20
Bratch, The. *Staf* 2J 25
Brathens. *Abers* 4G 67
Bratoft. *Linc* 3L 35
Brattleby. *Linc* 7F 40
Bratton. *Som* 1L 7
Bratton. *Telf* 8D 32
Bratton. *Wilts* 8M 17
Bratton Clovelly. *Devn* 6F 6
Bratton Fleming. *Devn* 2H 7
Bratton Seymour. *Som* 3F 8
Braughing. *Herts* 1B 20
Braulen Lodge. *High* 8E 70
Braunston. *Nptn* 5D 26
Braunstone Town. *Leic* 1D 26
Braunston-in-Rutland. *Rut* 1G 27
Braunton. *Devn* 2F 6
Brawby. *N Yor* 6G 45
Brawl. *High* 3D 76
Brawlbin. *High* 4F 76
Bray. *Wind* 6K 19
Braybrooke. *Nptn* 3F 26
Brayford. *Devn* 2H 7
Bray Shop. *Corn* 8E 6
Braystones. *Cumb* 3B 42
Brayton. *N Yor* 2C 40
Bray Wick. *Wind* 6J 19
Brazacott. *Corn* 6D 6
Brea. *Corn* 5D 3
Breach. *W Sus* 5H 11
Breachwood Green. *Herts* 1M 19
Breacleit. *W Isl* 5B 74
Breaden Heath. *Shrp* 6B 32
Breadsall. *Derbs* 5L 33
Breadstone. *Glos* 3K 17
Breage. *Corn* 7D 3
Breakachy. *High* 7G 71
Breakish. *High* 1L 63
Bream. *Glos* 3J 17
Breamore. *Hants* 4B 10
Bream's Meend. *Glos* 3J 17
Brean. *Som* 8E 16
Breanais. *W Isl* 6A 74
Brearton. *N Yor* 7C 44
Breascleit. *W Isl* 5C 74
Breaston. *Derbs* 6A 34
Brecais Àrd. *High* 1L 63
Brecais Iosal. *High* 1L 63
Brechfa. *Carm* 8H 23
Brechin. *Ang* 8G 67
Breckles. *Norf* 2F 28
Brecon. *Powy* 1C 16
Brecon Beacons. *Powy* 1B 16
Bredbury. *G Man* 6H 39
Brede. *E Sus* 6G 13
Bredenbury. *Here* 6G 25
Bredfield. *Suff* 6J 29
Bredgar. *Kent* 7G 21
Bredhurst. *Kent* 7F 20
Bredicot. *Worc* 6K 25
Bredon. *Worc* 8K 25
Bredon's Norton. *Worc* 8K 25
Bredwardine. *Here* 7D 24
Breedon on the Hill. *Leics* 7A 34
Breibhig. *W Isl* 4A 62
(on Barra)
Breibhig. *W Isl* 5E 74
(on Isle of Lewis)
Breich. *W Lot* 3H 55
Breightmet. *G Man* 4F 38
Breighton. *E Yor* 2D 40
Breinton. *Here* 8E 24
Breinton Common. *Here* 8E 24
Breiwick. *Shet* 7E 79
Brelston Green. *Here* 1H 17
Bremhill. *Wilts* 6M 17
Brenachie. *High* 4K 71
Brenchley. *Kent* 3E 12
Brendon. *Devn* 1J 7
Brent Cross. *G Lon* 5A 20
Brent Eleigh. *Suff* 7F 28
Brentford. *G Lon* 6M 19
Brentingby. *Leics* 8D 34
Brent Knoll. *Som* 8F 16
Brent Pelham. *Herts* 8A 28
Brentwood. *Essx* 4E 20
Brenzett. *Kent* 5J 13
Brereton. *Staf* 8H 33
Brereton Cross. *Staf* 8H 33
Brereton Green. *Ches E* 3E 32
Brereton Heath. *Ches E* 3F 32
Bressingham. *Norf* 3G 29
Bretby. *Derbs* 7K 33
Bretford. *Warw* 4C 26
Bretforton. *Worc* 7L 25
Bretherdale Head. *Cumb* 3G 43
Bretherton. *Lanc* 3C 38
Brettabister. *Shet* 6E 79
Brettenham. *Norf* 3F 28
Brettenham. *Suff* 6F 28
Bretton. *Flin* 3A 32
Bretton. *Pet* 1K 27
Brewer Street. *Surr* 8B 20
Brewlands Bridge. *Ang* 7B 66
Brewood. *Staf* 1J 25
Briantspuddle. *Dors* 6H 9
Bricket Wood. *Herts* 3M 19
Bricklehampton. *Worc* 7K 25
Bride. *IOM* 3E 46
Bridekirk. *Cumb* 8J 49
Bridell. *Pemb* 7D 22
Bridestowe. *Devn* 7G 7
Brideswell. *Abers* 6F 72
Bridford. *Devn* 7K 7
Bridge. *Corn* 5D 3
Bridge. *Kent* 8K 21
Bridge. *Som* 5C 8
Bridge End. *Bed* 6J 27
Bridge End. *Cumb* 4D 42
(nr. Broughton in Furness)
Bridge End. *Cumb* 7L 49
(nr. Dalston)
Bridge End. *Linc* 6H 35
Bridge End. *Shet* 8D 79
Bridgefoot. *Ang* 2J 61
Bridgefoot. *Cumb* 1B 42
Bridge Green. *Essx* 8A 28
Bridgehampton. *Som* 3E 8
Bridge Hewick. *N Yor* 6C 44
Bridgehill. *Dur* 6F 50
Bridgemary. *Hants* 5F 10
Bridgemere. *Ches E* 5E 32
Bridgemont. *Derbs* 7J 39
Bridgend. *Abers* 6F 72
(nr. Huntly)
Bridgend. *Abers* 6L 73
(nr. Peterhead)
Bridgend. *Ang* 7F 66
(nr. Brechin)
Bridgend. *Ang* 1J 61
(nr. Kirriemuir)
Bridgend. *Arg* 6F 58
(nr. Lochgilphead)
Bridgend. *Arg* 3B 52
(on Islay)
Bridgend. *B'end* 5B 16
Bridgend. *Cumb* 2F 42
Bridgend. *Devn* 5G 5
Bridgend. *Fife* 4J 61
Bridgend. *High* 6F 70
Bridgend. *Mor* 6D 72
Bridgend. *Per* 3G 61
Bridgend. *W Lot* 2J 55
Bridgend of Lintrathen. *Ang* 8C 66
Bridgeness. *Falk* 1J 55
Bridge of Alford. *Abers* 2F 66
Bridge of Allan. *Stir* 6C 60
Bridge of Avon. *Mor* 6B 72
Bridge of Awe. *Arg* 3H 59
Bridge of Balgie. *Per* 1A 60
Bridge of Brown. *High* 1B 66
Bridge of Cally. *Per* 8B 66
Bridge of Canny. *Abers* 4G 67
Bridge of Dee. *Dum* 5E 48
Bridge of Don. *Aber* 2K 67
Bridge of Dun. *Ang* 8G 67
Bridge of Dye. *Abers* 5G 67
Bridge of Earn. *Per* 4G 61
Bridge of Ericht. *Per* 8H 65
Bridge of Feugh. *Abers* 4H 67
Bridge of Gairn. *Abers* 4D 66
Bridge of Gaur. *Per* 8H 65
Bridge of Muchalls. *Abers* 4J 67
Bridge of Oich. *High* 3F 64
Bridge of Orchy. *Arg* 2L 59
Bridge of Walls. *Shet* 6C 79
Bridge of Weir. *Ren* 3B 54
Bridge Reeve. *Devn* 4H 7
Bridgerule. *Devn* 5D 6
Bridge Sollers. *Here* 7E 24
Bridge Street. *Suff* 7E 28
Bridgetown. *Devn* 3K 5
Bridgetown. *Som* 2L 7
Bridge Town. *Warw* 6A 26
Bridge Trafford. *Ches W* 8C 38
Bridgeyate. *S Glo* 6J 17
Bridgham. *Norf* 3F 28
Bridgnorth. *Shrp* 2H 25
Bridgtown. *Staf* 1K 25
Bridgwater. *Som* 2C 8
Bridlington. *E Yor* 7L 45
Bridport. *Dors* 6D 8
Bridstow. *Here* 1H 17
Brierfield. *Lanc* 2G 39
Brierley. *Glos* 2J 17
Brierley. *Here* 6E 24
Brierley. *S Yor* 4A 40
Brierley Hill. *W Mid* 3K 25
Brierton. *Hart* 8K 51
Briestfield. *W Yor* 4L 39
Brigg. *N Lin* 5G 41
Briggate. *Norf* 5K 37
Briggswath. *N Yor* 3H 45
Brigham. *Cumb* 8H 49
Brigham. *E Yor* 8K 45
Brighouse. *W Yor* 3K 39
Brighstone. *IOW* 7E 10
Brightgate. *Derbs* 4K 33
Brighthampton. *Oxon* 3D 18
Brightholmlee. *S Yor* 6L 39
Brightley. *Devn* 6H 7
Brightling. *E Sus* 5E 12
Brightlingsea. *Essx* 2J 21
Brighton. *Brig* 7B 12 & 92
Brighton. *Corn* 4A 4
Brighton Hill. *Hants* 1G 11
Brightons. *Falk* 2H 55
Brightwalton. *W Ber* 6E 18
Brightwalton Green. *W Ber* 6E 18
Brightwell. *Suff* 7J 29
Brightwell Baldwin. *Oxon* 4G 19
Brightwell-cum-Sotwell. *Oxon* 4F 18
Brigmerston. *Wilts* 1B 10
Brignall. *Dur* 2M 43
Brig o' Turk. *Stir* 5A 60
Brigsley. *NE Lin* 5J 41
Brigsteer. *Cumb* 5F 42
Brigstock. *Nptn* 3H 27
Brill. *Buck* 2G 19
Brill. *Corn* 7E 3
Brilley. *Here* 7C 24
Brimaston. *Pemb* 1D 14
Brimfield. *Here* 5F 24
Brimington. *Derbs* 8A 40
Brimley. *Devn* 8K 7
Brimpsfield. *Glos* 2M 17
Brimpton. *W Ber* 7F 18
Brims. *Orkn* 9A 78
Brimscombe. *Glos* 3L 17
Brimstage. *Mers* 7B 38
Brincliffe. *S Yor* 7M 39
Brind. *E Yor* 2D 40
Brindister. *Shet* 6C 79
(nr. West Burrafirth)
Brindister. *Shet* 8E 79
(nr. West Lerwick)
Brindle. *Lanc* 3E 38
Brindley. *Ches E* 4C 32
Brindley Ford. *Stoke* 4F 32
Brineton. *Staf* 8F 32
Bringhurst. *Leics* 2G 27
Bringsty Common. *Here* 6G 25
Brington. *Cambs* 4J 27
Brinian. *Orkn* 5C 78
Briningham. *Norf* 4G 37
Brinkhill. *Linc* 8K 41
Brinkley. *Cambs* 6C 28
Brinklow. *Warw* 4C 26
Brinkworth. *Wilts* 5A 18
Brinscall. *Lanc* 3E 38
Brinscombe. *Som* 8G 17
Brinsley. *Notts* 5A 34
Brinsworth. *S Yor* 7A 40
Brinton. *Norf* 4G 37
Brisco. *Cumb* 6M 49
Brisley. *Norf* 5F 36
Brislington. *Bris* 6J 17
Brissenden Green. *Kent* 4H 13
Bristol. *Bris* 6H 17 & 93
Bristol International Airport. *N Som* 7H 17
Briston. *Norf* 4G 37
Britannia. *Lanc* 3G 39
Britford. *Wilts* 3B 10
Brithdir. *Cphy* 3D 16
Brithdir. *Cdgn* 7F 22
Brithdir. *Gwyn* 8G 31
Briton Ferry. *Neat* 4M 15
Britwell Salome. *Oxon* 4G 19
Brixham. *Torb* 4L 5
Brixton. *Devn* 4G 5
Brixton. *G Lon* 6B 20
Brixton Deverill. *Wilts* 2H 9
Brixworth. *Nptn* 4F 26
Brize Norton. *Oxon* 3D 18
Broad Alley. *Worc* 5J 25
Broad Blunsdon. *Swin* 4B 18
Broadbottom. *G Man* 6H 39
Broadbridge. *W Sus* 5J 11
Broadbridge Heath. *W Sus* 2M 11
Broad Campden. *Glos* 8M 25
Broad Chalke. *Wilts* 3A 10
Broadclyst. *Devn* 6L 7
Broadfield. *Inv* 2B 54
Broadfield. *Pemb* 3F 14
Broadfield. *W Sus* 4A 12
Broadford. *High* 1L 63
Broadford Bridge. *W Sus* 3L 11
Broadgate. *Cumb* 5C 42
Broad Green. *Cambs* 6C 28
Broad Green. *C Beds* 7H 27
Broad Green. *Worc* 4K 25
(nr. Bromsgrove)
Broad Green. *Worc* 6H 25
(nr. Worcester)
Broadhaven. *High* 4J 77
Broad Haven. *Pemb* 2C 14
Broadheath. *G Man* 7F 38
Broad Heath. *Staf* 7F 32
Broadheath. *Worc* 5G 25
Broadhembury. *Devn* 5A 8
Broadhempston. *Devn* 3K 5
Broad Hill. *Cambs* 4B 28
Broad Hinton. *Wilts* 6B 18
Broadholm. *Derbs* 5L 33
Broadholme. *Linc* 8E 40
Broadlay. *Carm* 3H 15
Broad Laying. *Hants* 7E 18
Broadley. *Lanc* 4G 39
Broadley. *Mor* 3D 72
Broadley Common. *Essx* 3C 20
Broad Marston. *Worc* 7M 25
Broadmayne. *Dors* 7G 9
Broadmere. *Hants* 1G 11
Broadmoor. *Pemb* 3E 14
Broad Oak. *Carm* 1K 15
Broad Oak. *Cumb* 4C 42
Broad Oak. *Devn* 6M 7
Broadoak. *Dors* 6D 8
(nr. Bridport)
Broad Oak. *Dors* 4G 9
(nr. Sturminster Newton)
Broad Oak. *E Sus* 6G 13
(nr. Hastings)
Broad Oak. *E Sus* 5E 12
(nr. Heathfield)
Broadoak. *Glos* 2J 17
Broadoak. *Hants* 4E 10
Broad Oak. *Here* 1G 17
Broad Oak. *Kent* 7K 21
Broadrashes. *Mor* 4E 72
Broads. *Norf* 1L 29
Broadsea. *Abers* 3K 73

Broad's Green—Castlerigg

Broad's Green. Essx 2E 20
Broadshard. Som 4D 8
Broadstairs. Kent 7M 21
Broadstone. Pool 6A 10
Broadstone. Shrp 3F 24
Broad Street. E Sus 6G 13
Broad Street. Kent 3K 13
(nr. Ashford)
Broad Street. Kent 8G 21
(nr. Maidstone)
Broad Street Green. Essx 3G 21
Broad, The. Here 5E 24
Broad Town. Wilts 6A 18
Broadwas. Worc 6H 25
Broadwath. Cumb 6M 49
Broadway. Carm 3H 15
(nr. Kidwelly)
Broadway. Carm 2G 15
(nr. Laugharne)
Broadway. Pemb 2C 14
Broadway. Som 4C 8
Broadway. Suff 4K 29
Broadway. Worc 8M 25
Broadwell. Glos 2H 17
(nr. Cinderford)
Broadwell. Glos 1C 18
(nr. Stow-on-the-Wold)
Broadwell. Oxon 3C 18
Broadwell. Warw 5C 26
Broadwell House. Nmbd 6E 50
Broadwey. Dors 7F 8
Broadwindsor. Dors 5D 8
Broadwoodkelly. Devn 5H 7
Broadwoodwidger. Devn 7F 6
Broallan. High 7G 71
Brobury. Here 7D 24
Brochel. High 7K 69
Brockamin. Worc 6H 25
Brockbridge. Hants 4G 11
Brockdish. Norf 4J 29
Brockencote. Worc 4J 25
Brockenhurst. Hants 5C 10
Brocketsbrae. S Lan 6G 55
Brockford Street. Suff 5H 29
Brockhall. Nptn 5E 26
Brockham. Surr 1M 11
Brockhampton. Glos 1M 17
(nr. Bishop's Cleeve)
Brockhampton. Glos 1A 18
(nr. Sevenhampton)
Brockhampton. Here 8F 24
Brockhill. Bord 7M 55
Brockholes. W Yor 4K 39
Brockhurst. Hants 5F 10
Brocklesby. Linc 4H 41
Brockley. N Som 7G 17
Brockley Corner. Suff 4E 28
Brockley Green. Suff 7D 28
(nr. Bury St Edmunds)
Brockley Green. Suff 6E 28
(nr. Haverhill)
Brockleymoor. Cumb 8M 49
Brockmoor. W Mid 3J 25
Brockton. Shrp 3D 24
(nr. Bishop's Castle)
Brockton. Shrp 1H 25
(nr. Madeley)
Brockton. Shrp 2F 24
(nr. Much Wenlock)
Brockton. Shrp 1D 24
(nr. Pontesbury)
Brockton. Staf 6F 32
Brockton. Telf 8E 32
Brockweir. Glos 3H 17
Brockworth. Glos 2L 17
Brocton. Staf 8G 33
Brodick. N Ayr 6J 53
Brodie. Mor 6M 71
Brodiesord. Abers 4F 72
Brodsworth. S Yor 5B 40
Brogaig. High 5J 69
Brogborough. C Beds 8H 27
Brokenborough. Wilts 5M 17
Broken Cross. Ches E 8G 39
Bromborough. Mers 7B 38
Bromdon. Shrp 3G 25
Brome. Suff 4H 29
Brome Street. Suff 4H 29
Bromeswell. Suff 6K 29
Bromfield. Cumb 7J 49
Bromfield. Shrp 4E 24
Bromford. W Mid 2M 25
Bromham. Bed 6J 27
Bromham. Wilts 7M 17
Bromley. G Lon 7C 20
Bromley. Herts 1C 20
Bromley. Shrp 2H 25
Bromley Cross. G Man 4F 38
Bromley Green. Kent 4H 13
Bromley Wood. Staf 7J 33
Brompton. Medw 7F 20
Brompton. N Yor 4C 44
(nr. Northallerton)
Brompton. N Yor 5J 45
(nr. Scarborough)
Brompton. Shrp 1F 24
Brompton-on-Swale. N Yor 4B 44
Brompton Ralph. Som 2M 7
Brompton Regis. Som 2L 7
Bromsash. Here 1J 17
Bromsberrow. Glos 8H 25
Bromsberrow Heath. Glos 8H 25
Bromsgrove. Worc 4K 25
Bromstead Heath. Staf 8E 32
Bromyard. Here 6G 25
Bromyard Downs. Here 6G 25
Bronaber. Gwyn 6G 31
Broncroft. Shrp 3F 24
Brongest. Cdgn 7F 22
Brongwyn. Cdgn 7E 22
Bronington. Wrex 6B 32
Bronllys. Powy 8B 24
Bronnant. Cdgn 5J 23
Bronwydd Arms. Carm 1J 15
Bronydd. Powy 7C 24
Bronygarth. Shrp 6M 31
Brook. Carm 3G 15
Brook. Hants 4C 10
(nr. Cadnam)
Brook. Hants 3D 10
(nr. Romsey)
Brook. IOW 7D 10
Brook. Kent 3J 13
Brook. Surr 1L 11
(nr. Guildford)
Brook. Surr 2K 11
(nr. Haslemere)
Brooke. Norf 2J 29
Brooke. Rut 1G 27
Brookenby. Linc 6J 41
Brookend. Glos 3J 17
Brook End. Worc 7J 25
Brookfield. Lanc 2D 38
Brookfield. Ren 3C 54
Brookhouse. Lanc 7G 43
Brookhouse. S Yor 7B 40
Brookhouse Green. Ches E 3F 32
Brookhouses. Staf 5G 33
Brookhurst. Mers 7B 38
Brookland. Kent 5H 13
Brooklands. G Man 6F 38
Brooklands. Shrp 5C 32
Brookmans Park. Herts 3A 20
Brooks. Powy 2B 24
Brooksby. Leics 8C 34
Brooks Green. W Sus 3M 11
Brook Street. Essx 4D 20
Brook Street. Kent 4H 13
Brook Street. W Sus 5B 12
Brookthorpe. Glos 2L 17
Brookville. Norf 2D 28
Brookwood. Surr 8K 19
Broom. C Beds 7K 27
Broom. Fife 5J 61
Broom. Warw 6L 25
Broome. Norf 2K 29
Broome. Shrp 2F 24
(nr. Cardington)
Broome. Shrp 3E 24
(nr. Craven Arms)
Broome. Worc 4K 25
Broomedge. Warr 7F 38
Broomend. Abers 2H 67
Broome Park. Nmbd 8L 57
Broomer's Corner. W Sus 3M 11
Broomfield. Abers 6K 73
Broomfield. Essx 2F 20
Broomfield. Kent 7K 21
(nr. Herne Bay)
Broomfield. Kent 8G 21
(nr. Maidstone)
Broomfield. Som 2B 8
Broomfleet. E Yor 3E 40
Broom Green. Norf 5F 36
Broomhall. Ches E 5D 32
Broomhall. Wind 7K 19
Broomhaugh. Nmbd 5F 50
Broom Hill. Dors 5A 10
Broomhill. High 1M 65
(nr. Grantown-on-Spey)
Broomhill. High 4K 71
(nr. Invergordon)
Broomhill. Norf 1C 28
Broomhill. S Yor 5A 40
Broom Hill. Worc 4K 25
Broomhillbank. Dum 2J 49
Broomholm. Norf 4K 37
Broomlands. Dum 1H 49
Broomley. Nmbd 5F 50
Broom of Moy. Mor 4A 72
Broompark. Dur 7H 51
Broom's Green. Glos 8H 25
Brora. High 1M 71
Broseley. Shrp 1G 25
Brotherhouse Bar. Linc 8J 35
Brotheridge Green. Worc 7J 25
Brotherlee. Dur 8E 50
Brothertoft. Linc 5J 35
Brotherton. N Yor 3A 40
Brotton. Red C 1F 44
Broubster. High 3F 76
Brough. Cumb 2J 43
Brough. Derbs 7K 39
Brough. E Yor 3F 40
Brough. High 2H 77
Brough. Notts 4E 34
Brough. Orkn 6B 78
(nr. Finstown)
Brough. Orkn 9C 78
(nr. St Margaret's Hope)
Brough. Shet 6E 79
(nr. Benston)
Brough. Shet 4E 79
(nr. Booth of Toft)
Brough. Shet 7F 79
(on Bressay)
Brough. Shet 5F 79
(on Whalsay)
Broughall. Shrp 5C 32
Brougham. Cumb 1G 43
Brough Lodge. Shet 2F 79
Brough Sowerby. Cumb 2J 43
Broughton. Cambs 4L 27
Broughton. Flin 3A 32
Broughton. Hants 2D 10
Broughton. Lanc 2D 38
Broughton. Mil 8G 27
Broughton. Nptn 4G 27
Broughton. N Lin 5F 40
Broughton. N Yor 6G 45
(nr. Malton)
Broughton. N Yor 8L 43
(nr. Skipton)
Broughton. Orkn 3C 78
Broughton. Oxon 8C 26
Broughton. Bord 6K 55
Broughton. Staf 6E 32
Broughton. V Glam 6B 16
Broughton Astley. Leics 2D 26
Broughton Beck. Cumb 5D 42
Broughton Cross. Cumb 8H 49
Broughton Gifford. Wilts 7L 17
Broughton Green. Worc 5K 25
Broughton Hackett. Worc 6K 25
Broughton in Furness. Cumb 5D 42
Broughton Mills. Cumb 4D 42
Broughton Moor. Cumb 8H 49
Broughton Park. G Man 5G 39
Broughton Poggs. Oxon 3C 18
Broughtown. Orkn 3E 78
Broughty Ferry. D'dee 2K 61
Browland. Shet 6C 79
Brownbread Street. E Sus 6E 12
Brown Candover. Hants 2F 10
Brown Edge. Lanc 4B 38
Brown Edge. Staf 4G 33
Brownhill. Bkbn 2E 38
Brownhill. Shrp 7B 32
Brownhills. Shrp 6D 32
Brownhills. W Mid 1L 25
Brown Knowl. Ches W 4B 32
Brownlow. Ches E 3F 32
Brownlow Heath. Ches E 3F 32
Brown's Green. W Mid 2L 25
Brownshill. Glos 3L 17
Brownston. Devn 4H 5
Brownstone. Devn 5J 7
Browston Green. Norf 1L 29
Broxa. N Yor 4J 45
Broxbourne. Herts 3B 20
Broxburn. E Lot 2F 56
Broxburn. W Lot 2J 55
Broxholme. Linc 8F 40
Broxted. Essx 1D 20
Broxton. Ches W 4B 32
Broxwood. Here 6D 24
Broyle Side. E Sus 6C 12
Brù. W Isl 4D 74
Bruach Mairi. W Isl 5E 74
Bruairnis. W Isl 3B 62
Bruan. High 6J 77
Bruar Lodge. Per 6L 65
Brucehill. W Dun 2B 54
Brucklay. Abers 4K 73
Bruera. Ches W 3B 32
Bruern Abbey. Oxon 1C 18
Bruichladdich. Arg 3A 52
Bruisyard. Suff 5K 29
Bruisyard Street. Suff 5K 29
Brumby. N Lin 5E 40
Brund. Staf 3J 33
Brundall. Norf 1K 29
Brundish. Norf 2K 29
Brundish. Suff 5J 29
Brundish Street. Suff 4J 29
Brunery. High 6M 63
Brunswick Village. Tyne 4H 51
Brunthwaite. W Yor 1J 39
Bruntingthorpe. Leics 2E 26
Brunton. Fife 3J 61
Brunton. Nmbd 7M 57
Brunton. Wilts 8C 18
Brushford. Devn 5H 7
Brushford. Som 3L 7
Brusta. W Isl 3D 68
Bruton. Som 2F 8
Bryanston. Dors 5H 9
Bryant's Bottom. Buck 4J 19
Brydekirk. Dum 4J 49
Brymbo. Cnwy 2H 31
Brymbo. Wrex 4M 31
Brympton D'Evercy. Som 4E 8
Bryn. Carm 3K 15
Bryn. G Man 5D 38
Bryn. Neat 4A 16
Bryn. Shrp 3C 24
Brynamman. Carm 2M 15
Brynberian. Pemb 8D 22
Brynbryddan. Neat 4M 15
Bryncae. Rhon 5B 16
Bryncethin. B'end 5B 16
Bryncir. Gwyn 6D 30
Bryn-coch. Neat 4M 15
Bryncroes. Gwyn 6B 30
Bryncrug. Gwyn 1J 23
Bryn Du. IOA 2C 30
Bryn Eden. Gwyn 7G 31
Brynegllwys. Den 5L 31
Bryn Eglwys. Gwyn 3F 30
Brynford. Flin 2L 31
Bryn Gates. G Man 5D 38
Bryn Golau. Rhon 5C 16
Bryngwran. IOA 2C 30
Bryngwyn. Mon 3F 16
Bryngwyn. Powy 7B 24
Bryn-henllan. Pemb 8C 22
Brynhoffnant. Cdgn 6F 22
Bryn-llwyn. Flin 1K 31
Brynllywarch. Powy 3B 24
Brynmawr. Blae 2D 16
Bryn-mawr. Gwyn 6B 30
Brynmenyn. B'end 5B 16
Brynmill. Swan 4L 15
Brynna. Rhon 5B 16
Brynrefail. Gwyn 3E 30
Brynrefail. IOA 1D 30
Brynsadler. Rhon 5C 16
Bryn-Saith Marchog. Den 4K 31
Brynsiencyn. IOA 3D 30
Brynteg. IOA 1D 30
Brynteg. Wrex 4A 32
Brynygwenyn. Mon 2F 16
Bryn-y-maen. Cnwy 2H 31
Buaile nam Bodach. W Isl 3B 62
Bualintur. High 1J 63
Bubbenhall. Warw 4B 26
Bubwith. E Yor 2D 40
Buccleuch. Bord 8M 55
Buchanan Smithy. Stir 1C 54
Buchanhaven. Abers 5M 73
Buchanty. Per 3E 60
Buchany. Stir 5C 60
Buchley. E Dun 2D 54
Buchlyvie. Stir 6A 60
Buckabank. Cumb 7L 49
Buckden. Cambs 5K 27
Buckden. N Yor 6L 43
Buckenham. Norf 1K 29
Buckerell. Devn 5A 8
Buckfast. Devn 3J 5
Buckfastleigh. Devn 3J 5
Buckhaven. Fife 6J 61
Buckholm. Bord 6D 56
Buckholt. Here 2H 17
Buckhorn Weston. Dors 3G 9
Buckhurst Hill. Essx 4C 20
Buckie. Mor 3E 72
Buckingham. Buck 8E 26
Buckland. Buck 2J 19
Buckland. Glos 8L 25
Buckland. Here 6F 24
Buckland. Herts 8M 27
Buckland. Kent 3M 13
Buckland. Oxon 4D 18
Buckland. Surr 8A 20
Buckland Brewer. Devn 3F 6
Buckland Common. Buck 3K 19
Buckland Dinham. Som 8K 17
Buckland Filleigh. Devn 5F 6
Buckland in the Moor. Devn 8J 7
Buckland Monachorum. Devn 3F 4
Buckland Newton. Dors 5F 8
Buckland Ripers. Dors 7F 8
Buckland St Mary. Som 4B 8
Buckland-tout-Saints. Devn 5J 5
Bucklebury. W Ber 6F 18
Bucklegate. Linc 6K 35
Buckleigh. Devn 3F 6
Buckler's Hard. Hants 6E 10
Bucklesham. Suff 7J 29
Buckley. Flin 3M 31
Buckley Green. Warw 5M 25
Buckley Hill. Mers 6B 38
Bucklow Hill. Ches E 7F 38
Buckminster. Leics 7E 34
Bucknall. Linc 3H 35
Bucknall. Stoke 5G 33
Bucknell. Oxon 1F 18
Bucknell. Shrp 4D 24
Buckpool. Mor 3E 72
Bucksburn. Aber 3J 67
Buck's Cross. Devn 3E 6
Bucks Green. W Sus 2L 11
Buckshaw Village. Lanc 3D 38
Bucks Hill. Herts 3L 19
Bucks Horn Oak. Hants 1J 11
Buck's Mills. Devn 3E 6
Buckton. E Yor 6L 45
Buckton. Here 4D 24
Buckton. Nmbd 6K 57
Buckton Vale. G Man 5H 39
Buckworth. Cambs 4K 27
Budby. Notts 3C 34
Bude. Corn 5D 6
Budge's Shop. Corn 4E 4
Budlake. Devn 5L 7
Budle. Nmbd 6L 57
Budleigh Salterton. Devn 7M 7
Budock Water. Corn 6E 3
Buerton. Ches E 5D 32
Buffler's Holt. Buck 8E 26
Bugbrooke. Nptn 6E 26
Buglawton. Ches E 3F 32
Bugle. Corn 4B 4
Bugthorpe. E Yor 8G 45
Buildwas. Shrp 1G 25
Builth Road. Powy 6A 24
Builth Wells. Powy 6A 24
Bulbourne. Herts 2K 19
Bulby. Linc 7G 35
Bulcote. Notts 5C 34
Buldoo. High 3E 76
Bulford. Wilts 1B 10
Bulford Camp. Wilts 1B 10
Bulkeley. Ches E 4C 32
Bulkington. Warw 3B 26
Bulkington. Wilts 8M 17
Bulkworthy. Devn 4E 6
Bullamoor. N Yor 4C 44
Bull Bay. IOA 1D 30
Bullbridge. Derbs 4L 33
Bullgill. Cumb 8H 49
Bull Hill. Hants 6D 10
Bullinghope. Here 8F 24
Bull's Green. Herts 2A 20
Bullwood. Arg 2K 53
Bulmer. Essx 7E 28
Bulmer. N Yor 7F 44
Bulmer Tye. Essx 8E 28
Bulphan. Thur 5E 20
Bulverhythe. E Sus 7F 12
Bulwark. Abers 5K 73
Bulwell. Nott 5B 34
Bulwick. Nptn 2H 27
Bumble's Green. Essx 3C 20
Bun Abhainn Eadarra. W Isl 1F 68
Bunacaimb. High 5L 63
Bun a' Mhuillinn. W Isl 2B 62
Bunarkaig. High 5D 64
Bunbury. Ches E 4C 32
Bunchrew. High 7J 71
Bundalloch. High 1A 64
Buness. Shet 1G 79
Bunessan. Arg 3A 58
Bungay. Suff 3K 29
Bunkegivie. High 2H 65
Bunker's Hill. Cambs 1A 28
Bunker's Hill. Linc 4J 35
Bunker's Hill. Norf 1M 29
Bunloit. High 1H 65
Bunnahabhain. Arg 2C 52
Bunny. Notts 7B 34
Bunoich. High 3F 64
Bunree. High 7C 64
Bunroy. High 5E 64
Buntait. High 8F 70
Buntingford. Herts 1B 20
Buntings Green. Essx 8E 28
Bunwell. Norf 2H 29
Burbage. Derbs 8J 39
Burbage. Leics 2C 26
Burbage. Wilts 7C 18
Burcher. Here 5D 24
Burchett's Green. Wind 5J 19
Burcombe. Wilts 2A 10
Burcot. Oxon 4F 18
Burcot. Worc 4K 25
Burcote. Shrp 2H 25
Burcott. Buck 1J 19
Burcott. Som 1E 8
Burdale. N Yor 7H 45
Burdrop. Oxon 8B 26
Bures. Suff 8F 28
Burford. Oxon 2C 18
Burford. Shrp 5F 24
Burf, The. Worc 5J 25
Burg. Arg 1A 58
Burgate Great Green. Suff 4G 29
Burgate Little Green. Suff 4G 29
Burgess Hill. W Sus 6B 12
Burgh. Suff 6J 29
Burgh by Sands. Cumb 6L 49
Burgh Castle. Norf 1L 29
Burghclere. Hants 7E 18
Burghead. Mor 3B 72
Burghfield. W Ber 7G 19
Burghfield Common. W Ber 7G 19
Burghfield Hill. W Ber 7G 19
Burgh Heath. Surr 8A 20
Burghill. Here 7E 24
Burgh le Marsh. Linc 3M 35
Burgh Muir. Abers 2H 67
Burgh next Aylsham. Norf 5J 37
Burgh on Bain. Linc 7J 41
Burgh St Margaret. Norf 6L 37
Burgh St Peter. Norf 2L 29
Burghwallis. S Yor 4B 40
Burham. Kent 7F 20
Buriton. Hants 3H 11
Burland. Ches E 4D 32
Burland. Shet 8D 79
Burlawn. Corn 3A 4
Burleigh. Brac 6K 19
Burleigh. Glos 3L 17
Burlescombe. Devn 4M 7
Burleston. Dors 6G 9
Burlestone. Devn 5K 5
Burley. Hants 5C 10
Burley. Rut 8E 34
Burley. W Yor 2L 39
Burleydam. Ches E 5D 32
Burley Gate. Here 7F 24
Burley in Wharfedale. W Yor 1K 39
Burley Street. Hants 5C 10
Burley Woodhead. W Yor 1K 39
Burlingjobb. Powy 6C 24
Burlington. Shrp 8E 32
Burlton. Shrp 7B 32
Burmantofts. W Yor 2M 39
Burmarsh. Kent 4K 13
Burmington. Warw 8A 26
Burn. N Yor 3B 40
Burnage. G Man 6G 39
Burnaston. Derbs 6K 33
Burnbanks. Cumb 2G 43
Burnby. E Yor 1E 40
Burncross. S Yor 6M 39
Burneside. Cumb 4G 43
Burness. Orkn 3E 78
Burneston. N Yor 5C 44
Burnett. Bath 7J 17
Burnfoot. E Ayr 1B 48
Burnfoot. Per 5E 60
Burnfoot. Bord 8C 56
(nr. Hawick)
Burnfoot. Bord 8D 56
(nr. Roberton)
Burngreave. S Yor 7M 39
Burnham. Buck 5K 19
Burnham. N Lin 4G 41
Burnham Deepdale. Norf 3E 36
Burnham Green. Herts 2A 20
Burnham Market. Norf 3E 36
Burnham Norton. Norf 3E 36
Burnham-on-Crouch. Essx 4H 21
Burnham-on-Sea. Som 1C 8
Burnham Overy Staithe. Norf 3E 36
Burnham Overy Town. Norf 3E 36
Burnham Thorpe. Norf 3E 36
Burnhaven. Abers 5M 73
Burnhead. Dum 2F 48
Burnhervie. Abers 2H 67
Burnhill Green. Staf 1H 25
Burnhope. Dur 7G 51
Burnhouse. N Ayr 4B 54
Burniston. N Yor 4K 45
Burnlee. W Yor 5K 39
Burnley. Lanc 2G 39
Burnmouth. Bord 3J 57
Burn Naze. Lanc 1B 38
Burn of Cambus. Stir 5C 60
Burnopfield. Dur 6G 51
Burnsall. N Yor 7M 43
Burnside. Ang 8F 66
Burnside. E Ayr 8D 54
Burnside. Per 5G 61
Burnside. Shet 4C 79
Burnside. S Lan 4E 54
Burnside. W Lot 2J 55
(nr. Broxburn)
Burnside. W Lot 2J 55
(nr. Winchburgh)
Burntcommon. Surr 8L 19
Burntheath. Derbs 6K 33
Burnt Heath. Essx 1J 21
Burnt Hill. W Ber 6F 18
Burnt Houses. Dur 1A 44
Burntisland. Fife 1L 55
Burnt Oak. G Lon 4A 20
Burnton. E Ayr 1B 48
Burntstalk. Norf 4D 36
Burntwood. Staf 1L 25
Burntwood Green. Staf 1L 25
Burnt Yates. N Yor 7B 44
Burnwynd. Edin 3K 55
Burpham. Surr 8L 19
Burpham. W Sus 5L 11
Burradon. Nmbd 1E 50
Burradon. Tyne 4H 51
Burrafirth. Shet 1G 79
Burragarth. Shet 1F 79
Burras. Corn 6D 3
Burraton. Corn 4F 4
Burravoe. Shet 3D 79
(nr. North Roe)
Burravoe. Shet 5D 79
(on Mainland)
Burravoe. Shet 4F 79
(on Yell)
Burray Village. Orkn 8C 78
Burrells. Cumb 2H 43
Burrelton. Per 2G 61
Burridge. Devn 5C 8
Burridge. Hants 4F 10
Burrigill. High 6H 77
Burrill. N Yor 5B 44
Burringham. N Lin 5E 40
Burrington. Devn 4H 7
Burrington. Here 4E 24
Burrington. N Som 8G 17
Burrough End. Cambs 6C 28
Burrough Green. Cambs 6C 28
Burrough on the Hill. Leics 8D 34
Burroughston. Orkn 5D 78
Burrow. Devn 7M 7
Burrow. Som 1L 7
Burrowbridge. Som 3C 8
Burrowhill. Surr 7K 19
Burry. Swan 4J 15
Burry Green. Swan 4J 15
Burry Port. Carm 3J 15
Burscough. Lanc 4C 38
Burscough Bridge. Lanc 4C 38
Bursea. E Yor 2E 40
Burshill. E Yor 1G 41
Bursledon. Hants 5E 10
Burslem. Stoke 5F 32
Burstall. Suff 7G 29
Burstock. Dors 5D 8
Burston. Devn 5J 7
Burston. Norf 3H 29
Burston. Staf 6G 33
Burstow. Surr 3B 12
Burstwick. E Yor 3J 41
Burtersett. N Yor 5K 43
Burtholme. Cumb 5A 50
Burthorpe. Suff 5D 28
Burthwaite. Cumb 7M 49
Burtle. Som 1D 8
Burtoft. Linc 6J 35
Burton. Ches W 3C 32
(nr. Kelsall)
Burton. Ches W 8B 38
(nr. Neston)
Burton. Dors 6B 10
(nr. Christchurch)
Burton. Dors 6F 8
(nr. Dorchester)
Burton. Nmbd 6L 57
Burton. Pemb 3D 14
Burton. Som 1A 8
Burton. Wilts 6L 17
(nr. Chippenham)
Burton. Wilts 2H 9
(nr. Warminster)
Burton. Wrex 4A 32
Burton Agnes. E Yor 7L 45
Burton Bradstock. Dors 7D 8
Burton-by-Lincoln. Linc 8F 40
Burton Coggles. Linc 7F 34
Burton Constable. E Yor 2H 41
Burton Corner. Linc 5K 35
Burton End. Cambs 7C 28
Burton End. Essx 1D 20
Burton Fleming. E Yor 6K 45
Burton Green. W Mid 4A 26
Burton Green. Wrex 4A 32
Burton Hastings. Warw 3C 26
Burton-in-Kendal. Cumb 6G 43
Burton in Lonsdale. N Yor 6H 43
Burton Joyce. Notts 5C 34
Burton Latimer. Nptn 4H 27
Burton Lazars. Leics 8D 34
Burton Leonard. N Yor 7C 44
Burton on the Wolds. Leics 7B 34
Burton Overy. Leics 2E 26
Burton Pedwardine. Linc 5H 35
Burton Pidsea. E Yor 2J 41
Burton Salmon. N Yor 3A 40
Burton's Green. Essx 1G 21
Burton Stather. N Lin 4E 40
Burton upon Stather. N Lin 4E 40
Burton upon Trent. Staf 7K 33
Burton Wolds. Leics 7C 34
Burtonwood. Warr 6D 38
Burwardsley. Ches W 4C 32
Burwarton. Shrp 3G 25
Burwash. E Sus 5E 12
Burwash Common. E Sus 5E 12
Burwash Weald. E Sus 5E 12
Burwell. Cambs 5B 28
Burwell. Linc 8K 41
Burwen. IOA 1D 30
Burwick. Orkn 9C 78
Bury. Cambs 3L 27
Bury. G Man 4G 39
Bury. Som 3L 7
Bury. W Sus 4L 11
Burybank. Staf 6F 32
Bury End. Worc 8L 25
Bury Green. Herts 1C 20
Bury St Edmunds. Suff 5E 28
Burythorpe. N Yor 7G 45
Busbridge. Surr 1K 11
Busby. E Ren 4D 54
Busby. Per 3F 60
Buscot. Oxon 4C 18
Bush. Corn 5D 6
Bush Bank. Here 6E 24
Bushbury. W Mid 1K 25
Bushby. Leics 1E 26
Bushey. Dors 7J 9
Bushey. Herts 4M 19
Bushey Heath. Herts 4M 19
Bush Green. Norf 2G 29
(nr. Attleborough)
Bush Green. Norf 3J 29
(nr. Harleston)
Bush Green. Suff 6F 28
Bushley. Worc 8J 25
Bushley Green. Worc 8J 25
Bushmead. Bed 5K 27
Bushmoor. Shrp 3E 24
Bushton. Wilts 6A 18
Bushy Common. Norf 6F 36
Busk. Cumb 7B 50
Buslingthorpe. Linc 7G 41
Bussage. Glos 3L 17
Bussex. Som 2C 8
Busta. Shet 5D 79
Butcher's Cross. E Sus 5D 12
Butcombe. N Som 7H 17
Bute Town. Cphy 3D 16
Butleigh. Som 2D 8
Butleigh Wootton. Som 2E 8
Butlers Marston. Warw 6B 26
Butley. Suff 6K 29
Butley High Corner. Suff 7K 29
Butlocks Heath. Hants 5E 10
Butterburn. Cumb 4B 50
Buttercrambe. N Yor 8G 45
Butterknowle. Dur 1A 44
Butterleigh. Devn 5L 7
Buttermere. Cumb 2C 42
Buttermere. Wilts 7D 18
Buttershaw. W Yor 3K 39
Butterstone. Per 1F 60
Butterton. Staf 4H 33
(nr. Leek)
Butterton. Staf 5F 32
(nr. Stoke-on-Trent)
Butterwick. Dur 1C 44
Butterwick. Linc 5K 35
Butterwick. N Yor 6G 45
(nr. Malton)
Butterwick. N Yor 6J 45
(nr. Weaverthorpe)
Butteryhaugh. Nmbd 2B 50
Butt Green. Ches E 4D 32
Buttington. Powy 1C 24
Buttonbridge. Shrp 4H 25
Buttonoak. Shrp 4H 25
Buttsash. Hants 5E 10
Butt's Green. Essx 3F 20
Butt Yeats. Lanc 7G 43
Buxhall. Suff 6G 29
Buxted. E Sus 5C 12
Buxton. Derbs 8J 39
Buxton. Norf 5J 37
Buxworth. Derbs 7J 39
Bwcle. Flin 3M 31
Bwlch. Powy 1L 15
Bwlchderwin. Gwyn 5D 30
Bwlchgwyn. Wrex 4M 31
Bwlch-Llan. Cdgn 6H 23
Bwlchnewydd. Carm 1H 15
Bwlchtocyn. Gwyn 7C 30
Bwlch-y-cibau. Powy 8L 31
Bwlchyddar. Powy 7L 31
Bwlch-y-fadfa. Cdgn 7G 23
Bwlch-y-ffridd. Powy 2A 24
Bwlch y Garreg. Powy 2A 24
Bwlch-y-groes. Pemb 8E 22
Bwlch-y-sarnau. Powy 5A 24
Bybrook. Kent 3J 13
Byermoor. Tyne 6G 51
Byers Garth. Dur 7J 51
Byers Green. Dur 8H 51
Byfield. Nptn 6D 26
Byfleet. Surr 7L 19
Byford. Here 7D 24
Bygrave. Herts 8L 27
Byker. Tyne 5H 51
Byland Abbey. N Yor 6E 44
Bylchau. Cnwy 3J 31
Byley. Ches W 3E 32
Bynea. Carm 4K 15
Byram. N Yor 3A 40
Byrness. Nmbd 1C 50
Bystock. Devn 7M 7
Bythorn. Cambs 4J 27
Byton. Here 5D 24
Bywell. Nmbd 5F 50
Byworth. W Sus 3K 11

C

Cabharstadh. W Isl 7D 74
Cabourne. Linc 5H 41
Cabrach. Arg 3C 52
Cabrach. Mor 1D 66
Cabus. Lanc 1C 38
Cadbury. Devn 5L 7
Cadder. E Dun 2E 54
Caddington. C Beds 2L 19
Caddonfoot. Bord 6C 56
Cadeby. Leics 1C 26
Cadeby. S Yor 5B 40
Cadeleigh. Devn 5L 7
Cade Street. E Sus 5E 12
Cadgwith. Corn 8E 3
Cadham. Fife 5H 61
Cadishead. G Man 6F 38
Cadle. Swan 4L 15
Cadley. Lanc 2D 38
Cadley. Wilts 7C 18
(nr. Ludgershall)
Cadley. Wilts 7D 18
(nr. Marlborough)
Cadmore End. Buck 4H 19
Cadnam. Hants 4C 10
Cadney. N Lin 5G 41
Cadole. Flin 3M 31
Cadoxton-Juxta-Neath. Neat 4M 15
Cadwell. Herts 8K 27
Cadwst. Den 6K 31
Caeathro. Gwyn 3E 30
Caehopkin. Powy 3A 16
Caenby. Linc 7G 41
Caerau. B'end 4A 16
Caerau. Card 6D 16
Cae'r-bont. Powy 2A 16
Cae'r-bryn. Carm 2K 15
Caerdeon. Gwyn 8F 30
Caerdydd. Card 6D 16 & **Cardiff 93**
Caerfarchell. Pemb 1B 14
Caerffili. Cphy 5D 16
Caerfyrddin. Carm 2J 15
Caergeiliog. IOA 2C 30
Caergwrle. Flin 4A 32
Caergybi. IOA 1B 30
Caerlaverock. Per 4D 60
Caerleon. Newp 4F 16
Caerlleon. Carm 1G 15
Caerllion. Newp 4F 16
Caernarfon. Gwyn 3D 30
Caerphilly. Cphy 5D 16
Caersws. Powy 2A 24
Caerwedros. Cdgn 6F 22
Caerwent. Mon 4G 17
Caerwys. Flin 2L 31
Caim. IOA 1F 30
Caio. Carm 8J 23
Cairinis. W Isl 5C 68
Cairisiadar. W Isl 7B 74
Cairminis. W Isl 3E 68
Cairnbaan. Arg 6F 58
Cairnbulg. Abers 3L 73
Cairncross. Ang 6E 66
Cairndow. Arg 4J 59
Cairness. Abers 3L 73
Cairneyhill. Fife 1J 55
Cairngarroch. Dum 7F 46
Cairngorms. High 3M 65
Cairnhill. Abers 6G 73
Cairnie. Abers 5E 72
Cairnorrie. Abers 5J 73
Cairnryan. Dum 5K 47
Cairston. Orkn 6A 78
Caister-on-Sea. Norf 6M 37
Caistor. Linc 5H 41
Caistor St Edmund. Norf 1J 29
Caistron. Nmbd 1E 50
Cakebole. Worc 4J 25
Calais Street. Suff 7F 28
Calanais. W Isl 5C 74
Calbost. W Isl 7E 74
Calbourne. IOW 7E 10
Calceby. Linc 8K 41
Calcot. Glos 2A 18
Calcot Row. W Ber 6G 19
Calcott. Kent 7K 21
Calcott. Shrp 8B 32
Caldback. Shet 1G 79
Caldbeck. Cumb 8L 49
Caldbergh. N Yor 5M 43
Caldecote. Cambs 6M 27
(nr. Cambridge)
Caldecote. Cambs 3K 27
(nr. Peterborough)
Caldecote. Herts 8L 27
Caldecote. Nptn 6E 26
Caldecote. Warw 2B 26
Caldecott. Nptn 5H 27
Caldecott. Oxon 4E 18
Caldecott. Rut 2G 27
Calderbank. N Lan 3F 54
Calder Bridge. Cumb 3B 42
Calderbrook. G Man 4H 39
Caldercruix. N Lan 3G 55
Calder Grove. W Yor 4M 39
Calder Mains. High 4F 76
Caldermill. S Lan 5E 54
Calder Vale. Lanc 1D 38
Calderwood. S Lan 4E 54
Caldicot. Mon 5G 17
Caldwell. Derbs 8K 33
Caldwell. N Yor 2A 44
Caldy. Mers 7A 38
Calf Heath. Staf 1K 25
Calford Green. Suff 7C 28
Calfsound. Orkn 4D 78
Calgary. Arg 8H 63
Califer. Mor 4A 72
California. Cambs 3B 28
California. Falk 2H 55
California. Norf 6M 37
California. Suff 7H 29
Calke. Derbs 7L 33
Callakille. High 6L 69
Callaly. Nmbd 1F 50
Callander. Stir 5B 60
Callaughton. Shrp 2G 25
Callendoun. Arg 1B 54
Callestick. Corn 4E 3
Calligarry. High 3L 63
Callington. Corn 3E 4
Callingwood. Staf 7J 33
Callow. Here 8E 24
Callowell. Glos 3L 17
Callow End. Worc 7J 25
Callow Hill. Wilts 5A 18
Callow Hill. Worc 4H 25
(nr. Bewdley)
Callow Hill. Worc 5L 25
(nr. Redditch)
Calmore. Hants 4D 10
Calmsden. Glos 3A 18
Calne. Wilts 6M 17
Calow. Derbs 8A 40
Calshot. Hants 5E 10
Calstock. Corn 3F 4
Calstone Wellington. Wilts 7A 18
Calthorpe. Norf 4H 37
Calthorpe Street. Norf 5L 37
Calthwaite. Cumb 7M 49
Calton. N Yor 8L 43
Calton. Staf 4J 33
Calveley. Ches E 4C 32
Calver. Derbs 8L 39
Calverhall. Shrp 6D 32
Calverleigh. Devn 4L 7
Calverley. W Yor 2L 39
Calvert. Buck 1G 19
Calverton. Mil 8F 26
Calverton. Notts 5C 34
Calvine. Per 8L 65
Calvo. Cumb 6J 49
Cam. Glos 4K 17
Camaghael. High 6D 64
Camas-luinie. High 1B 64
Camasnacroise. High 8A 64
Camastianavaig. High 8K 69
Camasunary. High 2K 63
Camault Muir. High 7H 71
Camb. Shet 2F 79
Camber. E Sus 6H 13
Camberley. Surr 7J 19
Camberwell. G Lon 6B 20
Camblesforth. N Yor 3C 40
Cambo. Nmbd 3F 50
Cambois. Nmbd 3J 51
Camborne. Corn 6D 3
Cambourne. Cambs 6M 27
Cambridge. Cambs 6A 28 & 93
Cambridge. Glos 3K 17
Cambrose. Corn 5D 3
Cambus. Clac 6D 60
Cambusbarron. Stir 6C 60
Cambuskenneth. Stir 6D 60
Cambuslang. S Lan 3E 54
Cambusnethan. N Lan 4G 55
Cambus o' May. Abers 4E 66
Camden Town. G Lon 5A 20
Cameley. Bath 8J 17
Camelford. Corn 7C 6
Camelon. Falk 1G 55
Camelsdale. Surr 2K 11
Camer's Green. Worc 8H 25
Camerton. Bath 8J 17
Camerton. Cumb 8H 49
Camerton. E Yor 3J 41
Camghouran. Per 8H 65
Cammachmore. Abers 4K 67
Cammeringham. Linc 7F 40
Camore. High 2K 71
Campbelton. N Ayr 4K 53
Campbeltown. Arg 7F 52
Campbeltown Airport. Arg 7E 52
Cample. Dum 2G 49
Campmuir. Per 2H 61
Campsall. S Yor 4B 40
Campsea Ashe. Suff 6K 29
Camps End. Cambs 7C 28
Camp, The. Glos 3M 17
Campton. C Beds 8K 27
Camptoun. E Lot 2E 56
Camptown. Bord 8F 56
Camrose. Pemb 1D 14
Camserney. Per 1D 60
Camster. High 5H 77
Camus Croise. High 2L 63
Camuscross. High 2L 63
Camusdarach. High 4L 63
Camusnagaul. High 6C 64
(nr. Fort William)
Camusnagaul. High 3C 70
(nr. Little Loch Broom)
Camusteel. High 7M 69
Camusterrach. High 7M 69
Camusvrachan. Per 1B 60
Canada. Hants 4C 10
Canadia. E Sus 6F 12
Canaston Bridge. Pemb 2E 14
Candlesby. Linc 3L 35
Candle Street. Suff 4G 29
Candy Mill. S Lan 5J 55
Cane End. Oxon 6G 19
Canewdon. Essx 4G 21
Canford Cliffs. Pool 7A 10
Canford Heath. Pool 6A 10
Canford Magna. Pool 6A 10
Cangate. Norf 5K 37
Canham's Green. Suff 5G 29
Canholes. Derbs 8J 39
Canisbay. High 2J 77
Canley. W Mid 4B 26
Cann. Dors 3H 9
Cann Common. Dors 3H 9
Cannich. High 8F 70
Cannington. Som 2B 8
Cannock. Staf 8G 33
Cannock Wood. Staf 8H 33
Canonbie. Dum 4L 49
Canon Bridge. Here 7E 24
Canon Frome. Here 7G 25
Canon Pyon. Here 7E 24
Canons Ashby. Nptn 6D 26
Canonstown. Corn 6C 3
Canterbury. Kent 8K 21 & 93
Cantley. Norf 1K 29
Cantley. S Yor 5C 40
Cantlop. Shrp 1F 24
Canton. Card 6D 16
Cantray. High 7K 71
Cantraybruich. High 7K 71
Cantraywood. High 7K 71
Cantsdam. Fife 6G 61
Cantsfield. Lanc 6H 43
Canvey Island. Essx 5F 20
Canwick. Linc 3F 34
Canworthy Water. Corn 6D 6
Caol. High 6D 64
Caolas. Arg 8B 62
Caolas. W Isl 4A 62
Caolas Liubharsaigh. W Isl 7C 68
Caolas Scalpaigh. W Isl 2G 69
Caolas Stocinis. W Isl 3F 69
Caol Ila. Arg 3C 52
Caol Loch Ailse. High 1M 63
Caol Reatha. High 1M 63
Capel. Kent 3E 12
Capel. Surr 1M 11
Capel Bangor. Cdgn 3J 23
Capel Betws Lleucu. Cdgn 6J 23
Capel Coch. IOA 1D 30
Capel Curig. Cnwy 4G 31
Capel Cynon. Cdgn 7F 22
Capel Dewi. Carm 1J 15
Capel Dewi. Cdgn 3J 23
(nr. Aberystwyth)
Capel Dewi. Cdgn 7G 23
(nr. Llandysul)
Capel Garmon. Cnwy 4H 31
Capel Green. Suff 7K 29
Capel Gwyn. IOA 2C 30
Capel Gwynfe. Carm 1M 15
Capel Hendre. Carm 2K 15
Capel Isaac. Carm 1K 15
Capel Iwan. Carm 8E 22
Capel-le-Ferne. Kent 4L 13
Capel Llanilterne. Card 6C 16
Capel Mawr. IOA 2D 30
Capel Newydd. Pemb 8E 22
Capel St Andrew. Suff 7K 29
Capel St Mary. Suff 8G 29
Capel Seion. Carm 2K 15
Capel Seion. Cdgn 4J 23
Capel Uchaf. Gwyn 5D 30
Capel-y-ffin. Powy 8C 24
Capenhurst. Ches W 8B 38
Capernwray. Lanc 6G 43
Capheaton. Nmbd 3F 50
Cappercleuch. Bord 7L 55
Capplegill. Dum 1J 49
Capton. Devn 4K 5
Capton. Som 2M 7
Caputh. Per 2F 60
Caradon Town. Corn 8D 6
Carbis Bay. Corn 6C 3
Carbost. High 8H 69
(nr. Loch Harport)
Carbost. High 7J 69
(nr. Portree)
Carbrook. S Yor 7M 39
Carbrooke. Norf 1F 28
Carburton. Notts 8C 40
Carcluie. S Ayr 8B 54
Car Colston. Notts 5D 34
Carcroft. S Yor 4B 40
Cardenden. Fife 6H 61
Cardeston. Shrp 8A 32
Cardewlees. Cumb 6L 49
Cardiff. Card 6D 16 & 93
Cardiff International Airport. V Glam 7C 16
Cardigan. Cdgn 7D 22
Cardinal's Green. Cambs 7C 28
Cardington. Bed 7J 27
Cardington. Shrp 2F 24
Cardinham. Corn 3C 4
Cardno. Abers 3K 73
Cardow. Mor 5B 72
Cardross. Arg 2B 54
Cardurnock. Cumb 6J 49
Careby. Linc 8G 35
Careston. Ang 7F 66
Carew. Pemb 3E 14
Carew Cheriton. Pemb 3E 14
Carew Newton. Pemb 3E 14
Carey. Here 8F 24
Carfin. N Lan 4F 54
Carfrae. Bord 4E 56
Cargate Green. Norf 6K 37
Cargenbridge. Dum 4G 49
Cargill. Per 2G 61
Cargo. Cumb 6L 49
Cargreen. Corn 3F 4
Carham. Nmbd 6G 57
Carhampton. Som 1M 7
Carharrack. Corn 5E 3
Carie. Per 8J 65
(nr. Loch Rannah)
Carie. Per 2B 60
(nr. Loch Tay)
Carisbrooke. IOW 7E 10
Cark. Cumb 6E 42
Carkeel. Corn 3F 4
Carlabhagh. W Isl 4C 74
Carland Cross. Corn 4F 3
Carlbury. Darl 2B 44
Carlby. Linc 8G 35
Carlecotes. S Yor 5K 39
Carleen. Corn 7D 3
Carlesmoor. N Yor 6A 44
Carleton. Cumb 6M 49
(nr. Carlisle)
Carleton. Cumb 3B 42
(nr. Egremont)
Carleton. Cumb 1G 43
(nr. Penrith)
Carleton. Lanc 2B 38
Carleton. N Yor 1H 39
Carleton. W Yor 3A 40
Carleton Forehoe. Norf 1G 29
Carleton Rode. Norf 2H 29
Carleton St Peter. Norf 1K 29
Carlidnack. Corn 7E 3
Carlingcott. Bath 8J 17
Carlin How. Red C 2G 45
Carlisle. Cumb 6M 49 & 93
Carloonan. Arg 4H 59
Carlops. Bord 4K 55
Carlton. Bed 6H 27
Carlton. Cambs 6C 28
Carlton. Leics 1B 26
Carlton. N Yor 5F 44
(nr. Helmsley)
Carlton. N Yor 5M 43
(nr. Middleham)
Carlton. N Yor 3C 40
(nr. Selby)
Carlton. Notts 5C 34
Carlton. S Yor 4M 39
Carlton. Stoc T 1C 44
Carlton. Suff 5K 29
Carlton. W Yor 3M 39
Carlton Colville. Suff 2M 29
Carlton Curlieu. Leics 2E 26
Carlton Husthwaite. N Yor 6D 44
Carlton in Cleveland. N Yor 3E 44
Carlton in Lindrick. Notts 7B 40
Carlton-le-Moorland. Linc 4F 34
Carlton Miniott. N Yor 5C 44
Carlton-on-Trent. Notts 3E 34
Carlton Scroop. Linc 5F 34
Carluke. S Lan 4G 55
Carlyon Bay. Corn 4B 4
Carmarthen. Carm 2J 15
Carmel. Carm 2K 15
Carmel. Flin 2L 31
Carmel. Gwyn 4D 30
Carmel. IOA 1C 30
Carmichael. S Lan 6H 55
Carmunnock. Glas 4E 54
Carmyle. S Lan 3E 54
Carmyllie. Ang 1L 61
Carnaby. E Yor 7L 45
Carnach. High 1C 64
(nr. Lochcarron)
Carnach. High 2C 70
(nr. Ullapool)
Carnach. Mor 5A 72
Carnach. W Isl 2G 69
Carnachy. High 4C 76
Carnain. Arg 3B 52
Carnais. W Isl 5A 74
Carnan. Arg 8B 62
Carnan. W Isl 7B 68
Carnbee. Fife 5L 61
Carnbo. Per 5F 60
Carn Brea Village. Corn 5D 3
Carndu. High 1A 64
Carne. Corn 6A 4
Carnell. S Ayr 6C 54
Carnforth. Lanc 6G 43
Carn-gorm. High 1B 64
Carnhedryn. Pemb 1B 14
Carnhell Green. Corn 6D 3
Carnie. Abers 3J 67
Carnkie. Corn 6E 3
(nr. Falmouth)
Carnkie. Corn 6D 3
(nr. Redruth)
Carnkief. Corn 4E 3
Carno. Powy 2M 23
Carnock. Fife 1J 55
Carnon Downs. Corn 5E 3
Carnoustie. Ang 2L 61
Carntyne. Glas 3E 54
Carnwath. S Lan 5H 55
Carnyorth. Corn 6A 3
Carol Green. W Mid 4A 26
Carpalla. Corn 4A 4
Carperby. N Yor 5M 43
Carradale. Arg 6G 53
Carragraich. W Isl 2F 68
Carrbridge. High 1M 65
Carr Cross. Lanc 4B 38
Carreglefn. IOA 1C 30
Carrhouse. N Lin 5D 40
Carrick Castle. Arg 6J 59
Carrick Ho. Orkn 4D 78
Carriden. Falk 1J 55
Carrington. G Man 6F 38
Carrington. Linc 4K 35
Carrington. Midl 3M 55
Carrog. Cnwy 5G 31
Carrog. Den 5L 31
Carron. Falk 1G 55
Carron. Mor 5C 72
Carronbridge. Dum 2F 48
Carronshore. Falk 1G 55
Carrow Hill. Mon 4G 17
Carr Shield. Nmbd 7D 50
Carrutherstown. Dum 4J 49
Carr Vale. Derbs 3A 34
Carrville. Dur 7J 51
Carrycoats Hall. Nmbd 4E 50
Carsaig. Arg 3C 58
Carscreugh. Dum 5M 47
Carsegowan. Dum 6B 48
Carse House. Arg 3F 52
Carseriggan. Dum 5A 48
Carsethorn. Dum 6G 49
Carshalton. G Lon 7A 20
Carsington. Derbs 4K 33
Carskiey. Arg 8E 52
Carsluith. Dum 6B 48
Carsphairn. Dum 2C 48
Carstairs. S Lan 5H 55
Carstairs Junction. S Lan 5H 55
Cartbridge. Surr 8L 19
Carterhaugh. Ang 1K 61
Carter's Clay. Hants 3D 10
Carterton. Oxon 3C 18
Carterway Heads. Nmbd 6F 50
Carthew. Corn 4B 4
Carthorpe. N Yor 5C 44
Cartington. Nmbd 1F 50
Cartland. S Lan 5G 55
Cartmel. Cumb 6E 42
Cartmel Fell. Cumb 5F 42
Cartworth. W Yor 5K 39
Carwath. Cumb 7L 49
Carway. Carm 3J 15
Carwinley. Cumb 4M 49
Cascob. Powy 5C 24
Cas-gwent. Mon 4H 17
Cash Feus. Fife 5H 61
Cashlie. Per 1M 59
Cashmoor. Dors 4J 9
Cas-Mael. Pemb 1E 14
Casnewydd. Newp 5F 16 & **Newport 100**
Cassington. Oxon 2E 18
Cassop. Dur 8J 51
Castell. Cnwy 3G 31
Castell. Den 3L 31
Castell Hendre. Pemb 1E 14
Castell-nedd. Neat 4M 15
Castell Newydd Emlyn. Carm 7F 22
Castell-y-bwch. Torf 4E 16
Casterton. Cumb 6H 43
Castle. Som 1E 8
Castle Acre. Norf 6E 36
Castle Ashby. Nptn 6G 27
Castlebay. W Isl 4A 62
Castle Bolton. N Yor 4M 43
Castle Bromwich. W Mid 3M 25
Castle Bytham. Linc 8F 34
Castlebythe. Pemb 1E 14
Castle Caereinion. Powy 1B 24
Castle Camps. Cambs 7C 28
Castle Carrock. Cumb 6A 50
Castlecary. N Lan 2F 54
Castle Cary. Som 2F 8
Castle Combe. Wilts 6L 17
Castlecraig. High 5L 71
Castle Donington. Leics 7A 34
Castle Douglas. Dum 5E 48
Castle Eaton. Swin 4B 18
Castle Eden. Dur 8K 51
Castleford. W Yor 3A 40
Castle Frome. Here 7G 25
Castle Green. Surr 7K 19
Castle Green. Warw 4A 26
Castle Gresley. Derbs 8K 33
Castle Heaton. Nmbd 5J 57
Castle Hedingham. Essx 8D 28
Castle Hill. Kent 3E 12
Castlehill. Per 2H 61
Castlehill. S Lan 4G 55
Castle Hill. Suff 7H 29
Castlehill. W Dun 2B 54
Castle Kennedy. Dum 6L 47
Castle Lachlan. Arg 6H 59
Castlemartin. Pemb 4D 14
Castlemilk. Glas 4E 54
Castlemorris. Pemb 8B 22
Castlemorton. Worc 8H 25
Castle O'er. Dum 2K 49
Castle Park. N Yor 2H 45
Castlerigg. Cumb 1D 42

Castle Rising. *Norf* 5C **36**
Castleside. *Dur* 7F **50**
Castlethorpe. *Mil* 7F **26**
Castleton. *Abers* 4B **66**
Castleton. *Arg* 1G **53**
Castleton. *Derbs* 7K **39**
Castleton. *G Man* 3G **39**
Castleton. *Mor* 1B **66**
Castleton. *Newp* 5E **16**
Castleton. *N Yor* 3F **44**
Castleton. *Per* 4F **60**
Castletown. *Cumb* 8A **50**
Castletown. *Dors* 8F **8**
Castletown. *High* 3G **77**
Castletown. *IOM* 7C **46**
Castletown. *Tyne* 6J **51**
Castley. *N Yor* 1L **39**
Caston. *Norf* 2F **28**
Castor. *Pet* 2K **27**
Caswell. *Swan* 5K **15**
Catacol. *N Ayr* 5H **57**
Catbrook. *Mon* 3H **17**
Catchems End. *Worc* 4B **26**
Catchgate. *Dur* 6G **51**
Catcleugh. *Nmbd* 1C **50**
Catcliffe. *S Yor* 7A **40**
Catcott. *Som* 2C **8**
Caterham. *Surr* 8B **20**
Catfield. *Norf* 5K **37**
Catfield Common. *Norf* 5K **37**
Catfirth. *Shet* 6E **79**
Catford. *G Lon* 6B **20**
Catforth. *Lanc* 2C **38**
Cathcart. *Glas* 3D **54**
Cathedine. *Pow* 1D **16**

[index entries continue across columns]

Dawn—Edgefield

Dawn. Cnwy 2H 31
Daws Heath. Essx 5G 21
Dawshill. Worc 6J 25
Daw's House. Corn 7E 6
Dawsmere. Linc 6L 35
Dayhills. Staf 6G 33
Dayhouse Bank. Worc 4K 25
Daylesford. Glos 1C 18
Daywall. Shrp 6M 31
Ddol. Flin 2L 31
Ddol Cownwy. Powy 8K 31
Deadman's Cross. C Beds 7K 27
Deadwater. Nmbd 2B 50
Deaf Hill. Dur 8J 51
Deal. Kent 8M 21
Dean. Cumb 1B 42
Dean. Devn 1H 7
(nr. Combe Martin)
Dean. Devn 1J 7
(nr. Lynton)
Dean. Dors 4J 9
Dean. Hants 4F 10
(nr. Bishop's Waltham)
Dean. Hants 2E 10
(nr. Winchester)
Dean. Oxon 1D 18
Dean. Som 1F 8
Dean Bank. Dur 8H 51
Deanburnhaugh. Bord 8M 55
Dean Cross. Devn 1G 7
Deane. Hants 8F 18
Deanich Lodge. High 3F 70
Deanland. Dors 4J 9
Deanlane End. W Sus 4H 11
Dean Park. Shrp 5F 24
Dean Prior. Devn 3J 5
Dean Row. Ches E 7G 39
Deans. W Lot 3J 55
Deanscales. Cumb 1B 42
Deanshanger. Nptn 8F 26
Deanston. Stir 5C 60
Dearham. Cumb 8H 49
Dearne. S Yor 5A 40
Dearne Valley. S Yor 5M 39
Debach. Suff 6J 29
Debden. Essx 8B 28
Debden Green. Essx 4C 20
(nr. Loughton)
Debden Green. Essx 8B 28
(nr. Saffron Walden)
Debenham. Suff 5H 29
Dechmont. W Lot 2J 55
Deddington. Oxon 8C 26
Dedham. Essx 8G 29
Dedham Heath. Essx 8G 29
Deebank. Abers 4G 67
Deene. Nptn 2H 27
Deenethorpe. Nptn 2H 27
Deepcar. S Yor 6L 39
Deepcut. Surr 8K 19
Deepdale. Cumb 5J 43
Deepdale. N Lin 4G 41
Deepdale. N Yor 6K 43
Deeping Gate. Pet 1K 27
Deeping St James. Linc 1K 27
Deeping St Nicholas. Linc 8J 35
Deerhill. Mor 4E 72
Deerhurst. Glos 1L 17
Deerhurst Walton. Glos 1L 17
Deerness. Orkn 7D 78
Defford. Worc 7K 25
Defynnog. Powy 1B 16
Deganwy. Cnwy 2G 31
Deighton. N Yor 3C 44
Deighton. W Yor 4K 39
Deighton. York 1C 40
Deiniolen. Gwyn 3E 30
Delabole. Corn 7B 6
Delamere. Ches W 3C 32
Delfour. High 3L 65
Delliefure. High 6A 72
Dell, The. Suff 2L 29
Delly End. Oxon 2D 18
Delny. High 4K 71
Delph. G Man 5H 39
Delves. Dur 7G 51
Delves, The. W Mid 2L 25
Delvin End. Essx 8D 28
Dembleby. Linc 6G 35
Demelza. Corn 3A 4
Denaby Main. S Yor 6A 40
Denbeath. Fife 6J 61
Denbigh. Den 3K 31
Denbury. Devn 3K 5
Denby. Derbs 5L 33
Denby Common. Derbs 5A 34
Denby Dale. W Yor 5L 39
Denchworth. Oxon 4D 18
Dendron. Cumb 6D 42
Deneside. Dur 7K 51
Denford. Nptn 4H 27
Dengie. Essx 3H 21
Denham. Buck 5L 19
Denham. Suff 5D 28
(nr. Bury St Edmunds)
Denham. Suff 4H 29
(nr. Eye)
Denham Green. Buck 5L 19
Denham Street. Suff 4H 29
Denhead. Abers 6K 73
(nr. Ellon)
Denhead. Abers 4K 73
(nr. Strichen)
Denhead. Fife 4K 61
Denholm. Bord 8E 56
Denholme. W Yor 2J 39
Denholme Clough. W Yor 2J 39
Denholme Gate. W Yor 2J 39
Denio. Gwyn 6C 30
Denmead. Hants 4G 11
Dennington. Suff 5J 29
Denny. Falk 1G 55
Denny End. Cambs 5A 28
Dennyloanhead. Falk 1G 55
Den of Lindores. Fife 4H 61
Denshaw. G Man 4H 39
Denside. Abers 4J 67
Densole. Kent 3L 13
Denston. Suff 6D 28
Denstone. Staf 5J 33
Denstroude. Kent 7K 21
Dent. Cumb 5J 43
Den, The. N Ayr 4B 54
Denton. Cambs 3K 27
Denton. Darl 2B 44
Denton. E Sus 7C 12
Denton. G Man 6H 39
Denton. Kent 3L 13
Denton. Linc 6E 34
Denton. Norf 3J 29
Denton. Nptn 6G 27
Denton. N Yor 1K 39
Denton. Oxon 3F 18
Denver. Norf 1C 28
Denwick. Nmbd 8M 57
Deopham. Norf 1G 29
Deopham Green. Norf 2G 29
Depden. Suff 6D 28
Depden Green. Suff 6D 28
Deptford. G Lon 6B 20
Deptford. Wilts 2A 10
Derby. Derb 6L 33 & 94
Derbyhaven. IOM 7C 46
Derculich. Per 8L 65
Dereham. Norf 6F 36
Deri. Cphy 3D 16
Derril. Devn 5E 6
Derringstone. Kent 3L 13
Derrington. Shrp 2G 25
Derrington. Staf 7F 32
Derriton. Devn 5E 6
Derryguaig. Arg 2B 58
Derry Hill. Wilts 6M 17
Derrythorpe. N Lin 5E 40
Dersingham. Norf 4C 36
Dervaig. Arg 8J 63
Derwen. Den 4K 31
Derwen Gam. Cdgn 6G 23
Derwenlas. Powy 2K 23
Desborough. Nptn 3G 27
Desford. Leics 1C 26
Detchant. Nmbd 6K 57
Dethick. Derbs 4L 33
Detling. Kent 8F 20
Deuchar. Ang 7E 66
Deuddwr. Powy 8M 31
Devauden. Mon 4G 17
Devil's Bridge. Cdgn 4K 23
Devitts Green. Warw 2A 26
Devizes. Wilts 7A 18
Devonport. Plym 4F 4
Devonside. Clac 6E 60
Devoran. Corn 6E 3
Dewartown. Midl 3M 55
Dewlish. Dors 6G 9
Dewsall Court. Here 8E 24
Dewsbury. W Yor 3L 39
Dexbeer. Devn 5D 6
Dhoon. IOM 5E 46
Dhoor. IOM 4E 46
Dhowin. IOM 3E 46
Dial Green. W Sus 3K 11
Dial Post. W Sus 4M 11
Dibberford. Dors 5D 8
Dibden. Hants 5E 10
Dibden Purlieu. Hants 5E 10
Dickleburgh. Norf 3H 29
Didbrook. Glos 8L 25
Didcot. Oxon 4F 18
Diddington. Cambs 5K 27
Diddlebury. Shrp 3F 24
Didley. Here 8E 24
Didling. W Sus 4J 11
Didmarton. Glos 5L 17
Didsbury. G Man 6G 39
Didworthy. Devn 3H 5
Digby. Linc 4G 35
Digg. High 5J 69
Diggle. G Man 5J 39
Digmoor. Lanc 5C 38
Digswell. Herts 2A 20
Dihewyd. Cdgn 6G 23
Dilham. Norf 5K 37
Dilhorne. Staf 5G 33
Dillarburn. S Lan 5G 55
Dillington. Cambs 5K 27
Dilston. Nmbd 5E 50
Dilton Marsh. Wilts 1H 9
Dilwyn. Here 6E 24
Dimmer. Som 2F 8
Dimple. G Man 4F 38
Dinas. Carm 8E 22
Dinas. Gwyn 4D 30
(nr. Caernarfon)
Dinas. Gwyn 6B 30
(nr. Tudweiliog)
Dinas Cross. Pemb 8C 22
Dinas Dinlle. Gwyn 4D 30
Dinas Mawddwy. Gwyn 8H 31
Dinas Powys. V Glam 6D 16
Dinbych. Den 3K 31
Dinbych-y-Pysgod. Pemb 3F 14
Dinckley. Lanc 2E 38
Dinder. Som 1E 8
Dinedor. Here 8F 24
Dinedor Cross. Here 8F 24
Dingestow. Mon 2G 17
Dingle. Mers 7B 38
Dingleden. Kent 4G 13
Dingleton. Bord 6E 56
Dingley. Nptn 3F 26
Dingwall. High 6H 71
Dinmael. Cnwy 5K 31
Dinnet. Abers 4E 66
Dinnington. Som 4D 8
Dinnington. S Yor 7B 40
Dinnington. Tyne 4H 51
Dinorwig. Gwyn 3E 30
Dinton. Buck 2H 19
Dinton. Wilts 2A 10
Dinworthy. Devn 4E 6
Dipley. Hants 8H 19
Dippen. Arg 6F 52
Dippenhall. Surr 1J 11
Dippertown. Devn 7F 6
Dippin. N Ayr 7J 53
Dipple. S Ayr 1M 47
Diptford. Devn 4J 5
Dipton. Dur 6G 51
Dirleton. E Lot 1E 56
Dirt Pot. Nmbd 7D 50
Discoed. Powy 5C 24
Diseworth. Leics 7A 34
Dishes. Orkn 5E 78
Dishforth. N Yor 6C 44
Disley. Ches E 7H 39
Diss. Norf 4H 29
Disserth. Powy 6A 24
Distington. Cumb 1B 42
Ditchampton. Wilts 2A 10
Ditcheat. Som 2F 8
Ditchingham. Norf 2K 29
Ditchling. E Sus 6B 12
Ditteridge. Wilts 7L 17
Dittisham. Devn 4K 5
Ditton. Hal 7C 38
Ditton. Kent 8F 20
Ditton Green. Cambs 6C 28
Ditton Priors. Shrp 3G 25
Divach. High 1G 65
Dixonfield. High 3G 77
Dixton. Glos 8K 25
Dixton. Mon 2H 17
Dizzard. Corn 6C 6
Dobcross. G Man 5H 39
Dobs Hill. Flin 3A 32
Dobson's Bridge. Shrp 6B 32
Dobwalls. Corn 3D 4
Doccombe. Devn 7J 7
Dochgarroch. High 7J 71
Docking. Norf 4D 36
Docklow. Here 6F 24
Dockray. Cumb 1E 42
Doc Penfro. Pemb 3D 14 & 104
Dodbrooke. Devn 5J 5
Doddenham. Worc 6H 25
Doddinghurst. Essx 4D 20
Doddington. Cambs 2M 27
Doddington. Kent 8H 21
Doddington. Linc 3F 34
Doddington. Nmbd 6J 57
Doddington. Shrp 4G 25
Doddiscombsleigh. Devn 7K 7
Doddshill. Norf 4D 36
Dodford. Nptn 5E 26
Dodford. Worc 4K 25
Dodington. Som 1A 8
Dodington. S Glo 6K 17
Dodleston. Ches W 3A 32
Dods Leigh. Staf 6H 33
Dodworth. S Yor 5M 39
Doe Lea. Derbs 3A 34
Dogdyke. Linc 4J 35
Dogmersfield. Hants 8H 19
Dogsthorpe. Pet 1L 27
Dog Village. Devn 6L 7
Dolanog. Powy 8K 31
Dolau. Powy 5B 24
Dolau. Rhon 5C 16
Dolbenmaen. Gwyn 5E 30
Doley. Staf 7E 32
Dol-fâch. Powy 1M 23
(nr. Llanbrynmair)
Dolfach. Powy 4M 23
(nr. Llanidloes)
Dolfor. Powy 3B 24
Dolgarrog. Cnwy 3G 31
Dolgellau. Gwyn 8G 31
Dolgoch. Gwyn 1J 23
Dol-gran. Carm 8G 23
Dolhelfa. Powy 4M 23
Doll. High 1L 71
Dollar. Clac 6E 60
Dolley Green. Powy 5C 24
Dollwen. Cdgn 3J 23
Dolphin. Flin 2L 31
Dolphingstone. E Lot 2M 55
Dolphinholme. Lanc 8G 43
Dolphinton. S Lan 5K 55
Dolton. Devn 4G 7
Dolwen. Cnwy 2H 31
Dolwyddelan. Cnwy 4G 31
Dol-y-Bont. Cdgn 3J 23
Dolyhir. Powy 6C 24
Domgay. Powy 8M 31
Doncaster. S Yor 5B 40
Donhead St Andrew. Wilts 3J 9
Donhead St Mary. Wilts 3J 9
Doniford. Som 1M 7
Donington. Linc 6J 35
Donington. Shrp 1J 25
Donington Eaudike. Linc 6J 35
Donington le Heath. Leics 8A 34
Donington on Bain. Linc 7J 41
Donington South Ing. Linc 6J 35
Donisthorpe. Leics 8L 33
Donkey Street. Kent 4K 13
Donkey Town. Surr 7K 19
Donna Nook. Linc 6L 41
Donnington. Glos 1B 18
Donnington. Here 8H 25
Donnington. Shrp 1F 24
Donnington. Telf 8E 32
Donnington. W Ber 7E 18
Donnington. W Sus 5J 11
Donyatt. Som 4C 8
Doomsday Green. W Sus 2M 11
Doonfoot. S Ayr 8B 54
Doonholm. S Ayr 8B 54
Dorback Lodge. High 2A 66
Dorchester. Dors 6F 8
Dorchester on Thames. Oxon 4F 18
Dordon. Warw 1A 26
Dore. S Yor 7M 39
Dores. High 8H 71
Dorking. Surr 1M 11
Dorking Tye. Suff 8F 28
Dormansland. Surr 3C 12
Dormans Park. Surr 3B 12
Dormanstown. Red C 1E 44
Dormington. Here 7F 24
Dormston. Worc 6K 25
Dorn. Glos 8A 26
Dorney. Buck 6K 19
Dornie. High 1A 64
Dornoch. High 3K 71
Dornock. Dum 5K 49
Dorrery. High 4F 76
Dorridge. W Mid 4M 25
Dorrington. Linc 4G 35
Dorrington. Shrp 1E 24
Dorsington. Warw 7M 25
Dorstone. Here 7D 24
Dorton. Buck 2G 19
Dosthill. Staf 1A 26
Dotham. IOA 2C 30
Dottery. Dors 6D 8
Doublebois. Corn 3C 4
Dougarie. N Ayr 6G 53
Doughton. Glos 4L 17
Douglas. IOM 6D 46
Douglas. S Lan 6G 55
Douglastown. Ang 1K 61
Douglas Water. S Lan 6G 55
Doulting. Som 1F 8
Dounby. Orkn 5A 78
Doune. High 3L 65
(nr. Kingussie)
Doune. High 1G 71
(nr. Lairg)
Doune. Stir 5C 60
Dounie. High 2H 71
(nr. Bonar Bridge)
Dounie. High 3J 71
(nr. Tain)
Dounreay. High 3E 76
Doura. N Ayr 5B 54
Dousland. Devn 3G 5
Dovaston. Shrp 7A 32
Dove Holes. Derbs 8J 39
Dovenby. Cumb 8H 49
Dover. Kent 3M 13 & 94
Dovercourt. Essx 8J 29
Doverdale. Worc 5J 25
Doveridge. Derbs 6J 33
Doversgreen. Surr 3A 12
Dowally. Per 1F 60
Dowbridge. Lanc 2C 38
Dowdeswell. Glos 2A 18
Dowlais. Mer T 3C 16
Dowland. Devn 4G 7
Dowlands. Devn 6B 8
Dowles. Worc 4H 25
Dowlesgreen. Wok 7J 19
Dowlish Wake. Som 4C 8
Downall Green. Mers 5D 38
Down Ampney. Glos 4A 18
Downderry. Corn 4E 4
(nr. Looe)
Downderry. Corn 4A 4
(nr. St Austell)
Downe. G Lon 7C 20
Downend. IOW 7F 10
Downend. S Glo 6J 17
Downend. W Ber 6E 18
Down Field. Cambs 4C 28
Downfield. D'dee 2J 61
Downgate. Corn 8E 6
(nr. Kelly Bray)
Downgate. Corn 8D 6
(nr. Upton Cross)
Downham. Essx 4F 20
Downham. Lanc 1F 38
Downham. Nmbd 6H 57
Downham Market. Norf 1C 28
Down Hatherley. Glos 1L 17
Downhead. Som 1F 8
(nr. Frome)
Downhead. Som 3E 8
(nr. Yeovil)
Downholland Cross. Lanc 5B 38
Downholme. N Yor 4A 44
Downies. Abers 4K 67
Downley. Buck 4J 19
Down St Mary. Devn 5J 7
Downside. Som 8J 17
(nr. Chilcompton)
Downside. Som 1F 8
(nr. Shepton Mallet)
Downside. Surr 8M 19
Down, The. Shrp 2G 25
Down Thomas. Devn 4G 5
Downton. Hants 6C 10
Downton. Wilts 3B 10
Downton on the Rock. Here 4E 24
Dowsby. Linc 7H 35
Dowsdale. Linc 8J 35
Dowthwaitehead. Cumb 1E 42
Doxey. Staf 7G 33
Doxford. Nmbd 7L 57
Doynton. S Glo 6K 17
Drabblegate. Norf 5J 37
Draethen. Cphy 5E 16
Draffan. S Lan 5F 54
Dragonby. N Lin 4F 40
Dragons Green. W Sus 3M 11
Drakelow. Worc 3J 25
Drakemyre. N Ayr 4A 54
Drakes Broughton. Worc 7K 25
Drakes Cross. Worc 4L 25
Drakewalls. Corn 8F 6
Draughton. Nptn 4F 26
Draughton. N Yor 8M 43
Drax. N Yor 3C 40
Draycot. Oxon 3G 19
Draycote. Warw 5C 26
Draycot Foliat. Swin 6B 18
Draycott. Derbs 6A 34
Draycott. Glos 8M 25
Draycott. Shrp 2J 25
Draycott. Som 8G 17
(nr. Cheddar)
Draycott. Som 3E 8
(nr. Yeovil)
Draycott. Worc 7J 25
Draycott in the Clay. Staf 7J 33
Draycott in the Moors. Staf 5G 33
Drayford. Devn 4J 7
Drayton. Leics 2G 27
Drayton. Linc 6J 35
Drayton. Norf 6H 37
Drayton. Nptn 5D 26
Drayton. Oxon 4E 18
(nr. Abingdon)
Drayton. Oxon 7C 26
(nr. Banbury)
Drayton. Port 5G 11
Drayton. Som 3D 8
Drayton. Warw 6M 25
Drayton. Worc 4K 25
Drayton Bassett. Staf 1M 25
Drayton Beauchamp. Buck 2K 19
Drayton Parslow. Buck 1J 19
Drayton St Leonard. Oxon 4F 18
Drebley. N Yor 8M 43
Dreenhill. Pemb 2D 14
Drefach. Carm 2K 15
(nr. Meidrim)
Drefach. Carm 8F 22
(nr. Newcastle Emlyn)
Drefach. Carm 1G 15
(nr. Tumble)
Drefach. Cdgn 7G 23
Dreghorn. N Ayr 6B 54
Drellingore. Kent 3L 13
Drem. E Lot 2E 56
Dreumasdal. W Isl 8B 68
Drewsteignton. Devn 6J 7
Driby. Linc 8K 41
Driffield. E Yor 8K 45
Driffield. Glos 4A 18
Drift. Corn 7B 3
Drigg. Cumb 4B 42
Drighlington. W Yor 3L 39
Drimnin. High 8K 63
Drimpton. Dors 5D 8
Dringhoe. E Yor 8L 45
Drinisiadar. W Isl 2F 68
Drinkstone. Suff 5F 28
Drinkstone Green. Suff 5F 28
Drointon. Staf 7H 33
Droitwich Spa. Worc 5J 25
Droman. High 4J 75
Dron. Per 4G 61
Dronfield. Derbs 8M 39
Dronfield Woodhouse. Derbs 8M 39
Drongan. E Ayr 8C 54
Dronley. Ang 2J 61
Droop. Dors 5G 9
Drope. V Glam 6D 16
Droxford. Hants 4G 11
Droylsden. G Man 6G 39
Druggers End. Worc 8H 25
Druid. Den 5K 31
Druid's Heath. W Mid 1L 25
Druidston. Pemb 2C 14
Druim. High 6M 71
Druimarbin. High 6C 64
Druim Fhearna. High 2L 63
Druimindarroch. High 5L 63
Druim Saighdinis. W Isl 5C 68
Drum. Per 5F 60
Drumbeg. High 6J 75
Drumblade. Abers 5F 72
Drumbuie. Dum 3C 48
Drumbuie. High 8M 69
Drumburgh. Cumb 6K 49
Drumburn. Dum 5G 49
Drumchapel. Glas 2D 54
Drumchardine. High 7H 71
Drumchork. High 3A 70
Drumclog. S Lan 6E 54
Drumeldrie. Fife 5K 61
Drumelzier. Bord 6K 55
Drumfearn. High 2L 63
Drumgask. High 4J 65
Drumgelloch. N Lan 3F 54
Drumgley. Ang 8E 66
Drumguish. High 4K 65
Drumin. Mor 6B 72
Drumindorsair. High 7G 71
Drumlamford House. S Ayr 4M 47
Drumlasie. Abers 3G 67
Drumlemble. Arg 8E 52
Drumlithie. Abers 5H 67
Drummoddie. Dum 7A 48
Drummond. High 5J 71
Drummore. Dum 8L 47
Drummuir. Mor 5D 72
Drumnadrochit. High 8H 71
Drumnagorrach. Mor 4F 72
Drumoak. Abers 4H 67
Drumrunie. High 1D 70
Drumry. W Dun 2D 54
Drums. Abers 1K 67
Drumsleet. Dum 4G 49
Drumsmittal. High 7J 71
Drums of Park. Abers 4F 72
Drumsturdy. Ang 2K 61
Drumtochty Castle. Abers 5G 67
Drumuie. High 7J 69
Drumuillie. High 1M 65
Drumvaich. Stir 5B 60
Drumwhindle. Abers 6K 73
Drunkendub. Ang 1M 61
Drury. Flin 3M 31
Drury Square. Norf 6F 36
Drybeck. Cumb 2H 43
Drybridge. Mor 3E 72
Drybridge. N Ayr 6B 54
Drybrook. Glos 2J 17
Drybrook. Here 2H 17
Dryburgh. Bord 6E 56
Dry Doddington. Linc 5E 34
Dry Drayton. Cambs 5M 27
Drym. Corn 6D 3
Drymen. Stir 1C 54
Drymuir. Abers 5K 73
Drynachan Lodge. High 8L 71
Drynie Park. High 6H 71
Drynoch. High 8J 69
Dry Sandford. Oxon 3E 18
Dryslwyn. Carm 1K 15
Dry Street. Essx 5E 20
Dryton. Shrp 1F 24
Dubford. Abers 3H 73
Dubiton. Abers 4G 73
Dubton. Ang 8F 66
Duchally. High 8L 75
Duck End. Essx 1E 20
Duckington. Ches W 4B 32
Ducklington. Oxon 3D 18
Duckmanton. Derbs 8A 40
Duck Street. Hants 1D 10
Dudbridge. Glos 3L 17
Duddenhoe End. Essx 8A 28
Duddingston. Edin 2L 55
Duddington. Nptn 1H 27
Duddleswell. E Sus 5C 12
Duddo. Nmbd 5J 57
Duddon. Ches W 3C 32
Duddon Bridge. Cumb 5C 42
Dudleston. Shrp 6A 32
Dudleston Heath. Shrp 6A 32
Dudley. Tyne 4H 51
Dudley. W Mid 3K 25
Dudston. Shrp 2C 24
Dudwells. Pemb 1D 14
Duffield. Derbs 5L 33
Duffryn. Neat 4A 16
Dufftown. Mor 5D 72
Duffus. Mor 3B 72
Dufton. Cumb 1H 43
Duggleby. N Yor 7H 45
Duirinish. High 8M 69
Duisdalemore. High 2L 63
Duisdeil Mòr. High 2L 63
Duisky. High 6C 64
Dukesfield. Nmbd 6E 50
Dukestown. Blae 3D 16
Dukinfield. G Man 6H 39
Dulas. IOA 1D 30
Dulcote. Som 1E 8
Dulford. Devn 5M 7
Dull. Per 1D 60
Dullatur. N Lan 2F 54
Dullingham. Cambs 6C 28
Dullingham Ley. Cambs 6C 28
Dulnain Bridge. High 1M 65
Duloe. Bed 5K 27
Duloe. Corn 4D 4
Dulverton. Som 3L 7
Dulwich. G Lon 6B 20
Dumbarton. W Dun 2C 54
Dumbleton. Glos 8L 25
Dumfin. Arg 1B 54
Dumfries. Dum 4G 49 & 94
Dumgoyne. Stir 1D 54
Dummer. Hants 1F 10
Dumpford. W Sus 3J 11
Dun. Ang 7G 67
Dunagoil. Arg 4J 53
Dunalastair. Per 8K 65
Dunan. High 1K 63
Dunball. Som 1C 8
Dunbar. E Lot 2F 56
Dunbeath. High 7G 77
Dunbeg. Arg 2F 58
Dunblane. Stir 5C 60
Dunbog. Fife 4H 61
Dunbridge. Hants 3D 10
Duncanston. Abers 1F 66
Duncanston. High 6H 71
Dun Charlabhaigh. W Isl 4B 74
Dunchideock. Devn 7K 7
Dunchurch. Warw 4C 26
Duncote. Nptn 6E 26
Duncow. Dum 3G 49
Duncrievie. Per 5G 61
Duncton. W Sus 4K 11
Dundee. D'dee 2K 61 & 94
Dundee Airport. D'dee 3J 61
Dundon. Som 2D 8
Dundonald. S Ayr 6B 54
Dundonnell. High 3C 70
Dundraw. Cumb 7K 49
Dundreggan. High 2F 64
Dundrennan. Dum 7E 48
Dundridge. Hants 4F 10
Dundry. N Som 7H 17
Dunecht. Abers 3H 67
Dunfermline. Fife 1J 55
Dunford Bridge. S Yor 5K 39
Dungate. Kent 8H 21
Dunge. Wilts 8L 17
Dungeness. Kent 6J 13
Dungworth. S Yor 7L 39
Dunham-on-the-Hill. Ches W 8C 38
Dunham-on-Trent. Notts 8E 40
Dunhampton. Worc 5J 25
Dunham Town. G Man 7F 38
Dunham Woodhouses. G Man 7F 38
Dunholme. Linc 8G 41
Dunino. Fife 4L 61
Dunipace. Falk 1G 55
Dunira. Per 3C 60
Dunkeld. Per 1F 60
Dunkerton. Bath 8K 17
Dunkeswell. Devn 5A 8
Dunkeswick. N Yor 1M 39
Dunkirk. Kent 8J 21
Dunkirk. S Glo 5K 17
Dunkirk. Staf 4F 32
Dunkirk. Wilts 7M 17
Dunk's Green. Kent 8E 20
Dunlappie. Ang 7F 66
Dunley. Hants 8E 18
Dunley. Worc 5H 25
Dunlichity Lodge. High 8J 71
Dunlop. E Ayr 5C 54
Dunmaglass Lodge. High 1H 65
Dunmore. Arg 3F 52
Dunmore. Falk 1G 55
Dunmore. High 7H 71
Dunnet. High 2H 77
Dunnichen. Ang 1L 61
Dunning. Per 4F 60
Dunnington. E Yor 8L 45
Dunnington. Warw 6L 25
Dunnington. York 8F 44
Dunningwell. Cumb 5C 42
Dunnockshaw. Lanc 3G 39
Dunoon. Arg 2K 53
Dunphail. Mor 5A 72
Dunragit. Dum 6L 47
Dunrostan. Arg 1F 52
Duns. Bord 4G 57
Dunsby. Linc 7H 35
Dunscar. G Man 4F 38
Dunscore. Dum 3F 48
Dunscroft. S Yor 5C 40
Dunsdale. Red C 2F 44
Dunsden Green. Oxon 6H 19
Dunsfold. Surr 2L 11
Dunsford. Devn 7K 7
Dunshalt. Fife 4H 61
Dunshillock. Abers 5K 73
Dunsley. N Yor 2H 45
Dunsley. Staf 3J 25
Dunsmore. Buck 3J 19
Dunsop Bridge. Lanc 8H 43
Dunstable. C Beds 1L 19
Dunstal. Staf 7H 33
Dunstall. Staf 7J 33
Dunstall Green. Suff 5D 28
Dunstall Hill. W Mid 2K 25
Dunstan. Nmbd 8M 57
Dunster. Som 1L 7
Duns Tew. Oxon 1E 18
Dunston. Linc 3G 35
Dunston. Norf 1J 29
Dunston. Staf 8G 33
Dunston. Tyne 5H 51
Dunstone. Devn 4G 5
Dunston Heath. Staf 8G 33
Dunsville. S Yor 5C 40
Dunswell. E Yor 2G 41
Dunsyre. S Lan 5J 55
Dunterton. Devn 8E 6
Duntisbourne Abbots. Glos 3M 17
Duntisbourne Leer. Glos 3M 17
Duntisbourne Rouse. Glos 3M 17
Duntish. Dors 5F 8
Duntocher. W Dun 2C 54
Dunton. Buck 1J 19
Dunton. C Beds 7L 27
Dunton. Norf 4E 36
Dunton Bassett. Leics 2D 26
Dunton Green. Kent 8D 20
Dunton Patch. Norf 4E 36
Duntulm. High 4J 69
Dunure. S Ayr 8A 54
Dunvant. Swan 4K 15
Dunvegan. High 7G 69
Dunwich. Suff 4L 29
Dunwood. Staf 4G 33
Durdar. Cumb 6M 49
Durgates. E Sus 4E 12
Durham. Dur 7H 51 & 94
Durham Tees Valley Airport. Darl 2C 44
Durisdeer. Dum 1F 48
Durisdeermill. Dum 1F 48
Durkar. W Yor 4M 39
Durleigh. Som 2B 8
Durley. Hants 4F 10
Durley. Wilts 7C 18
Durley Street. Hants 4F 10
Durlow Common. Here 8G 25
Durnamuck. High 2C 70
Durness. High 3M 75
Durno. Abers 1H 67
Durns Town. Hants 6C 10
Duror. High 8B 64
Durran. Arg 5G 59
Durran. High 3G 77
Durrant Green. Kent 4G 13
Durrants. Hants 4H 11
Durrington. W Sus 5M 11
Durrington. Wilts 1B 10
Dursley. Glos 4K 17
Dursley Cross. Glos 2J 17
Durston. Som 3B 8
Durweston. Dors 5H 9
Dury. Shet 6E 79
Duston. Nptn 5F 26
Duthil. High 1M 65
Dutlas. Powy 4C 24
Duton Hill. Essx 1E 20
Dutson. Corn 7E 6
Dutton. Ches W 8D 38
Duxford. Cambs 7A 28
Duxford. Oxon 4D 18
Dwygyfylchi. Cnwy 2G 31
Dwyran. IOA 3D 30
Dyce. Aber 2J 67
Dyffryn. B'end 4A 16
Dyffryn. Carm 1H 15
Dyffryn. Pemb 8B 22
Dyffryn. V Glam 6C 16
Dyffryn Ardudwy. Gwyn 7E 30
Dyffryn Castell. Cdgn 3K 23
Dyffryn Ceidrych. Carm 1M 15
Dyffryn Cellwen. Neat 3A 16
Dyke. Linc 7H 35
Dyke. Mor 6M 71
Dykehead. Ang 7D 66
Dykehead. N Lan 3G 55
Dykehead. Stir 6A 60
Dykend. Ang 8C 66
Dykesfield. Cumb 6L 49
Dylife. Powy 2L 23
Dymchurch. Kent 5K 13
Dymock. Glos 8H 25
Dyrham. S Glo 6K 17
Dysart. Fife 6J 61
Dyserth. Den 2K 31

E

Eachwick. Nmbd 4G 51
Eadar Dha Fhadhail. W Isl 5A 74
Eagland Hill. Lanc 1C 38
Eagle. Linc 3E 34
Eagle Barnsdale. Linc 3E 34
Eagle Moor. Linc 3E 34
Eaglescliffe. Stoc T 2D 44
Eaglesfield. Cumb 1B 42
Eaglesfield. Dum 4K 49
Eaglesham. E Ren 4D 54
Eaglethorpe. Nptn 2J 27
Eagley. G Man 4F 38
Eairy. IOM 6C 46
Eakley Lanes. Mil 6G 27
Eakring. Notts 3C 34
Ealand. N Lin 4D 40
Ealing. G Lon 5M 19
Eallabus. Arg 3B 52
Eals. Nmbd 6B 50
Eamont Bridge. Cumb 1G 43
Earby. Lanc 1H 39
Earcroft. Bkbn 3E 38
Eardington. Shrp 2H 25
Eardisland. Here 6E 24
Eardisley. Here 7D 24
Eardiston. Shrp 7A 32
Eardiston. Worc 5G 25
Earith. Cambs 4M 27
Earlais. High 5H 69
Earle. Nmbd 7J 57
Earlesfield. Linc 6F 34
Earlestown. Mers 6D 38
Earley. Wok 6H 19
Earlham. Norf 1H 29
Earlish. High 5H 69
Earls Barton. Nptn 5G 27
Earls Colne. Essx 1G 21
Earls Common. Worc 6K 25
Earl's Croome. Worc 7J 25
Earlsdon. W Mid 4B 26
Earlsferry. Fife 5K 61
Earlsford. Abers 6J 73
Earl's Green. Suff 5G 29
Earlsheaton. W Yor 3L 39
Earl Shilton. Leics 2C 26
Earl Soham. Suff 5J 29
Earl Sterndale. Derbs 3H 33
Earlston. E Ayr 6C 54
Earlston. Bord 6E 56
Earl Stonham. Suff 6H 29
Earlstoun. Dum 3D 48
Earlswood. Mon 4G 17
Earlswood. Warw 4M 25
Earlyvale. Bord 4L 55
Earnley. W Sus 6J 11
Earsairidh. W Isl 4B 62
Earsdon. Tyne 4J 51
Earsham. Norf 3K 29
Earsham Street. Suff 4J 29
Earswick. York 8F 44
Eartham. W Sus 5K 11
Earthcott Green. S Glo 5J 17
Easby. N Yor 3E 44
(nr. Great Ayton)
Easby. N Yor 3A 44
(nr. Richmond)
Easdale. Arg 4E 58
Easebourne. W Sus 3J 11
Easenhall. Warw 4C 26
Eashing. Surr 1K 11
Easington. Buck 2G 19
Easington. Dur 7K 51
Easington. E Yor 4K 41
Easington. Nmbd 6L 57
Easington. Oxon 8C 26
(nr. Banbury)
Easington. Oxon 4G 19
(nr. Watlington)
Easington. Red C 2G 45
Easington Colliery. Dur 7K 51
Easington Lane. Tyne 7J 51
Easingwold. N Yor 7E 44
Eassie. Ang 1J 61
Eassie and Nevay. Ang 1J 61
East Aberthaw. V Glam 7C 16
Eastacombe. Devn 3G 7
Eastacott. Devn 3H 7
East Allington. Devn 5J 5
East Anstey. Devn 3K 7
East Anton. Hants 1D 10
East Appleton. N Yor 4B 44
East Ardsley. W Yor 3M 39
East Ashley. Devn 4H 7
East Ashling. W Sus 5J 11
East Aston. Hants 1E 10
East Ayton. N Yor 5J 45
East Barkwith. Linc 7H 41
East Barnby. N Yor 2H 45
East Barnet. G Lon 4A 20
East Barns. E Lot 2G 57
East Barsham. Norf 4F 36
East Beach. W Sus 6J 11
East Beckham. Norf 3H 37
East Bedfont. G Lon 6L 19
East Bennan. N Ayr 7H 53
East Bergholt. Suff 8G 29
East Bierley. W Yor 3K 39
East Bilney. Norf 6F 36
East Blatchington. E Sus 7C 12
East Bloxworth. Dors 6H 9
East Boldre. Hants 5D 10
East Bolton. Nmbd 8L 57
Eastbourne. Darl 2B 44
Eastbourne. E Sus 8E 12 & 94
East Brent. Som 8F 16
East Bridge. Suff 5L 29
East Bridgford. Notts 5C 34
East Briscoe. Dur 2L 43
East Buckland. Devn 2H 7
(nr. Barnstaple)
East Buckland. Devn 5H 5
(nr. Thurlestone)
East Budleigh. Devn 7M 7
Eastburn. W Yor 1J 39
East Burnham. Buck 5K 19
East Burrafirth. Shet 6D 79
East Burton. Dors 7H 9
Eastbury. Herts 4L 19
Eastbury. W Ber 6D 18
East Butsfield. Dur 7G 51
East Butterleigh. Devn 5L 7
East Butterwick. N Lin 5E 40
Eastby. N Yor 8M 43
East Calder. W Lot 3J 55
East Carleton. Norf 1H 29
East Carlton. Nptn 3G 27
East Carlton. W Yor 1L 39
East Chaldon. Dors 7G 9
East Challow. Oxon 5D 18
East Charleton. Devn 5J 5
East Chelborough. Dors 5E 8
East Chiltington. E Sus 6B 12
East Chinnock. Som 4D 8
East Chisenbury. Wilts 8B 18
Eastchurch. Kent 6H 21
East Clandon. Surr 8L 19
East Claydon. Buck 1H 19
East Clevedon. N Som 6G 17
East Clyne. High 1L 71
East Clyth. High 6H 77
East Coker. Som 4E 8
Eastcombe. Glos 3L 17
East Combe. Som 2A 8
East Common. N Yor 2C 40
East Compton. Som 1F 8
East Cornworthy. Devn 4K 5
Eastcote. G Lon 5M 19
Eastcote. Nptn 6E 26
Eastcote. W Mid 4M 25
Eastcott. Corn 4D 6
Eastcott. Wilts 8A 18
East Cottingwith. E Yor 1D 40
Eastcourt. Wilts 7C 18
(nr. Pewsey)
Eastcourt. Wilts 4M 17
(nr. Tetbury)
East Cowes. IOW 6F 10
East Cowick. E Yor 3C 40
East Cowton. N Yor 3C 44
East Cramlington. Nmbd 4H 51
East Cranmore. Som 1F 8
East Creech. Dors 7J 9
East Croachy. High 1J 65
East Dean. E Sus 8D 12
East Dean. Glos 1J 17
East Dean. Hants 3C 10
East Dean. W Sus 4K 11
East Down. Devn 1H 7
East Drayton. Notts 8D 40
East Dundry. N Som 7H 17
East Ella. Hull 3G 41
East End. Cambs 4M 27
East End. Dors 6J 9
East End. E Yor 8L 45
(nr. Ulrome)
East End. E Yor 3J 41
(nr. Withernsea)
East End. Hants 6D 10
(nr. Lymington)
East End. Hants 7E 18
(nr. Newbury)
East End. Herts 1C 20
East End. Kent 6H 21
(nr. Minster)
East End. Kent 4G 13
(nr. Tenterden)
East End. N Som 6G 17
East End. Oxon 2D 18
East End. Som 8H 17
East End. Suff 8H 29
Easter Ardross. High 4J 71
Easter Balgedie. Per 5G 61
Easter Balmoral. Abers 4C 66
Easter Brae. High 5J 71
Easter Buckieburn. Stir 1F 54
Easter Bush. Midl 3L 55
Easter Compton. S Glo 5H 17
Easter Fearn. High 3J 71
Easter Galcantray. High 7L 71
Eastergate. W Sus 5K 11
Easterhouse. Glas 3E 54
Easter Howgate. Midl 3L 55
Easter Kinkell. High 6H 71
Easter Lednathie. Ang 7D 66
Easter Ogil. Ang 7E 66
Easter Ord. Abers 3J 67
Easter Quarff. Shet 8E 79
Easter Rhynd. Per 4G 61
Easter Skeld. Shet 7D 79
Easter Suddie. High 6J 71
Easterton. Wilts 8A 18
Eastertown. Som 8F 16
Easter Tulloch. Abers 6H 67
East Everleigh. Wilts 8C 18
East Farleigh. Kent 8F 20
East Farndon. Nptn 3F 26
East Ferry. Linc 6E 40
Eastfield. N Lan 3G 55
(nr. Caldercruix)
Eastfield. N Lan 3G 55
(nr. Harthill)
Eastfield. N Yor 5K 45
Eastfield. S Lan 3E 54
Eastfield Hall. Nmbd 1H 51
East Fortune. E Lot 2E 56
East Garforth. W Yor 2A 40
East Garston. W Ber 6D 18
Eastgate. Dur 8E 50
Eastgate. Norf 5H 37
East Ginge. Oxon 5E 18
East Gores. Essx 1G 21
East Goscote. Leics 8C 34
East Grafton. Wilts 7C 18
East Green. Suff 6C 28
East Grimstead. Wilts 3C 10
East Grinstead. W Sus 4B 12
East Guldeford. E Sus 5H 13
East Haddon. Nptn 5E 26
East Hagbourne. Oxon 5F 18
East Halton. N Lin 3H 41
East Ham. G Lon 5C 20
Eastham. Mers 7B 38
Eastham. Worc 5G 25
Eastham Ferry. Mers 7B 38
Easthampstead. Brac 7J 19
Easthampton. Here 5E 24
East Hanney. Oxon 4E 18
East Hanningfield. Essx 3F 20
East Hardwick. W Yor 4A 40
East Harling. Norf 3F 28
East Harlsey. N Yor 4D 44
East Harnham. Wilts 3B 10
East Harptree. Bath 8H 17
East Hartford. Nmbd 4H 51
East Harting. W Sus 4J 11
East Hatch. Wilts 3J 9
East Hatley. Cambs 6L 27
Easthaugh. Norf 6G 37
East Hauxwell. N Yor 4A 44
East Haven. Ang 2L 61
Eastheath. Wok 7J 19
East Heckington. Linc 5H 35
East Hedleyhope. Dur 7G 51
East Helmsdale. High 8F 76
East Hendred. Oxon 5E 18
East Heslerton. N Yor 6J 45
East Hoathly. E Sus 6D 12
East Holme. Dors 7H 9
Easthope. Shrp 2F 24
Easthorpe. Essx 1H 21
Easthorpe. Leics 6E 34
East Horrington. Som 1E 8
East Horsley. Surr 8L 19
East Horton. Nmbd 6K 57
Easthouses. Midl 3M 55
East Howe. Bour 6A 10
East Huntspill. Som 1C 8
East Hyde. C Beds 2M 19
East Ilsley. W Ber 5E 18
Eastington. Devn 5J 7
Eastington. Glos 2B 18
(nr. Northleach)
Eastington. Glos 3K 17
(nr. Stonehouse)
East Keal. Linc 3K 35
East Kennett. Wilts 7B 18
East Keswick. W Yor 1M 39
East Kilbride. S Lan 4E 54
East Kirkby. Linc 3K 35
East Knapton. N Yor 6H 45
East Knighton. Dors 7H 9
East Knowstone. Devn 3K 7
East Knoyle. Wilts 2H 9
East Kyloe. Nmbd 6K 57
East Lambrook. Som 4D 8
East Langdon. Kent 3M 13
East Langton. Leics 2F 26
East Langwell. High 1K 71
East Lavant. W Sus 5J 11
East Lavington. W Sus 4K 11
East Layton. N Yor 3A 44
Eastleach Martin. Glos 3C 18
Eastleach Turville. Glos 3B 18
East Leake. Notts 7B 34
East Learmouth. Nmbd 6H 57
Eastleigh. Devn 3F 6
(nr. Bideford)
East Leigh. Devn 5J 7
(nr. Crediton)
East Leigh. Devn 4H 5
(nr. Modbury)
Eastleigh. Hants 4E 10
East Lexham. Norf 6E 36
East Lilburn. Nmbd 7K 57
Eastling. Kent 8H 21
East Linton. E Lot 2E 56
East Liss. Hants 3H 11
East Lockinge. Oxon 5E 18
East Looe. Corn 4D 4
East Lound. N Lin 6D 40
East Lulworth. Dors 7H 9
East Lutton. N Yor 7J 45
East Lydford. Som 2E 8
East Lyng. Som 3C 8
East Mains. Abers 4G 67
East Malling. Kent 8F 20
East Marden. W Sus 4J 11
East Markham. Notts 8D 40
East Marton. N Yor 8L 43
East Meon. Hants 3G 11
East Mersea. Essx 2J 21
East Mey. High 2J 77
East Midlands Airport. Leics 7A 34 & 105
East Molesey. Surr 7M 19
Eastmoor. Norf 1D 28
East Morden. Dors 6J 9
East Morton. W Yor 1K 39
East Ness. N Yor 6F 44
East Newton. E Yor 2J 41
East Newton. N Yor 6F 44
Eastney. Port 6G 11
Eastnor. Here 8H 25
East Norton. Leics 1F 26
East Nynehead. Som 3A 8
East Oakley. Hants 8F 18
Eastoft. N Lin 4E 40
East Ogwell. Devn 8K 7
Easton. Cambs 4K 27
Easton. Cumb 6K 49
(nr. Burgh by Sands)
Easton. Cumb 4M 49
(nr. Longtown)
Easton. Devn 7J 7
Easton. Dors 8F 8
Easton. Hants 2F 10
Easton. Linc 7F 34
Easton. Norf 6H 37
Easton. Som 1E 8
Easton. Suff 6J 29
Easton. Wilts 6L 17
Easton Grey. Wilts 5L 17
Easton-in-Gordano. N Som 6H 17
Easton Maudit. Nptn 6G 27
Easton on the Hill. Nptn 1J 27
Easton Royal. Wilts 7C 18
East Orchard. Dors 4H 9
East Ord. Nmbd 4J 57
East Panson. Devn 6E 6
East Peckham. Kent 3E 12
East Pennard. Som 2E 8
East Perry. Cambs 5K 27
East Pitcorthie. Fife 5L 61
East Portlemouth. Devn 6J 5
East Prawle. Devn 6J 5
East Preston. W Sus 5L 11
East Putford. Devn 4E 6
East Quantoxhead. Som 1A 8
East Rainton. Tyne 7J 51
East Ravendale. NE Lin 6J 41
East Raynham. Norf 5E 36
Eastrea. Cambs 2L 27
East Rhidorroch Lodge. High 2E 70
Eastriggs. Dum 5K 49
East Rigton. W Yor 1M 39
Eastrington. E Yor 2D 40
East Rounton. N Yor 3D 44
East Row. N Yor 2H 45
East Rudham. Norf 5E 36
East Runton. Norf 3H 37
East Ruston. Norf 5K 37
Eastry. Kent 8M 21
East Saltoun. E Lot 3D 56
East Shaws. Dur 2M 43
East Shefford. W Ber 6D 18
Eastshore. Shet 10D 79
East Sleekburn. Nmbd 3H 51
East Somerton. Norf 6L 37
East Stockwith. Linc 6D 40
East Stoke. Dors 7H 9
East Stoke. Notts 5D 34
East Stoke. Som 4D 8
East Stour. Dors 3H 9
East Stourmouth. Kent 7L 21
East Stowford. Devn 3H 7
East Stratton. Hants 1F 10
East Studdal. Kent 3M 13
East Taphouse. Corn 3C 4
East-the-Water. Devn 3F 6
East Thirston. Nmbd 2G 51
East Tilbury. Thur 6E 20
East Tisted. Hants 2H 11
East Torrington. Linc 7H 41
East Tuddenham. Norf 6G 37
East Tytherley. Hants 3C 10
East Tytherton. Wilts 6M 17
East Village. Devn 5K 7
Eastville. Linc 4L 35
East Wall. Shrp 2F 24
East Walton. Norf 6D 36
East Week. Devn 6H 7
Eastwell. Leics 7D 34
East Wellow. Hants 3D 10
East Wemyss. Fife 6J 61
East Whitburn. W Lot 3H 55
Eastwick. Herts 2C 20
Eastwick. Shet 4D 79
East Williamston. Pemb 3E 14
East Winch. Norf 6C 36
East Winterslow. Wilts 2C 10
East Wittering. W Sus 6H 11
East Witton. N Yor 5A 44
Eastwood. Notts 5A 34
Eastwood. S'end 5G 21
East Woodburn. Nmbd 3E 50
Eastwood End. Cambs 2A 28
East Woodhay. Hants 7E 18
East Woodlands. Som 1G 9
East Worldham. Hants 2H 11
East Worlington. Devn 4J 7
East Wretham. Norf 2F 28
East Youlstone. Devn 4D 6
Eathorpe. Warw 5B 26
Eaton. Ches E 3F 32
Eaton. Ches W 3C 32
Eaton. Leics 7D 34
Eaton. Norf 4C 36
(nr. Heacham)
Eaton. Norf 1J 29
(nr. Norwich)
Eaton. Notts 8D 40
Eaton. Oxon 3E 18
Eaton. Shrp 3D 24
(nr. Bishop's Castle)
Eaton. Shrp 2F 24
(nr. Church Stretton)
Eaton Bishop. Here 8E 24
Eaton Bray. C Beds 1K 19
Eaton Constantine. Shrp 1F 24
Eaton Hastings. Oxon 4C 18
Eaton Socon. Cambs 6K 27
Eaton upon Tern. Shrp 7D 32
Eau Brink. Norf 8M 35
Eaves Green. W Mid 3A 26
Ebberley Hill. Devn 4G 7
Ebberston. N Yor 5H 45
Ebbesbourne Wake. Wilts 3J 9
Ebblake. Dors 5B 10
Ebbsfleet. Kent 6E 20
Ebbw Vale. Blae 3D 16
Ebchester. Dur 6G 51
Ebernoe. W Sus 3K 11
Ebford. Devn 7L 7
Ebley. Glos 3L 17
Ebnal. Ches W 5B 32
Ebrington. Glos 7M 25
Ecchinswell. Hants 8F 18
Ecclefechan. Dum 4J 49
Eccles. G Man 6F 38
Eccles. Kent 7F 20
Eccles. Bord 5G 57
Ecclesall. S Yor 7M 39
Ecclesfield. S Yor 6M 39
Eccles Green. Here 7D 24
Eccleshall. Staf 7F 32
Eccleshill. W Yor 2K 39
Ecclesmachan. W Lot 2J 55
Eccles on Sea. Norf 5L 37
Eccles Road. Norf 2G 29
Eccleston. Ches W 3B 32
Eccleston. Lanc 4D 38
Eccleston. Mers 6C 38
Eccup. W Yor 1L 39
Echt. Abers 3H 67
Eckford. Bord 7G 57
Eckington. Derbs 8A 40
Eckington. Worc 7K 25
Ecton. Nptn 5G 27
Edale. Derbs 7K 39
Eday Airport. Orkn 4D 78
Edburton. W Sus 6A 12
Edderside. Cumb 7J 49
Edderton. High 3K 71
Eddington. Kent 7K 21
Eddington. W Ber 7D 18
Eddleston. Bord 5L 55
Eddlewood. S Lan 4F 54
Edenbridge. Kent 3C 12
Edendonich. Arg 3J 59
Edenfield. Lanc 4G 39
Edenhall. Cumb 8A 50
Edenham. Linc 7G 35
Edensor. Derbs 3K 33
Edentaggart. Arg 6L 59
Edenthorpe. S Yor 5C 40
Eden Vale. Dur 8K 51
Edern. Gwyn 6B 30
Edgarley. Som 2E 8
Edgbaston. W Mid 3L 25
Edgcott. Buck 1G 19
Edgcott. Som 2K 7
Edge. Glos 3L 17
Edge. Shrp 1D 24
Edgebolton. Shrp 7C 32
Edge End. Glos 2H 17
Edgefield. Norf 4G 37

Edgefield Street—Fromes Hill

Edgefield Street. Norf 4G 37
Edge Green. Ches W 4B 32
Edgehead. Midl 3M 55
Edgeley. Shrp 5C 32
Edgeside. Lanc 3G 39
Edgeworth. Glos 3M 17
Edgiock. Worc 5L 25
Edgmond. Telf 8E 32
Edgmond Marsh. Telf 7E 32
Edgton. Shrp 3D 24
Edgware. G Lon 4M 19
Edgworth. Bkbn 4F 38
Edinbane. High 6H 69
Edinburgh. Edin 2L 55 & 95
Edinburgh Airport. Edin 2K 55
Edingale. Staf 8K 33
Edingley. Notts 4C 34
Edingthorpe. Norf 4K 37
Edington. Som 2C 8
Edington. Wilts 8M 17
Edingworth. Som 8F 16
Edistone. Devn 3D 6
Edithmead. Som 1C 8
Edith Weston. Rut 1H 27
Edlaston. Derbs 5J 33
Edlesborough. Buck 2K 19
Edlingham. Nmbd 1G 51
Edlington. Linc 8J 41
Edmondsham. Dors 4A 10
Edmondsley. Dur 7H 51
Edmondthorpe. Leics 8E 34
Edmonstone. Orkn 5D 78
Edmonton. Corn 8A 6
Edmonton. G Lon 4B 20
Edmundbyers. Dur 6F 50
Ednam. Bord 6G 57
Ednaston. Derbs 5K 33
Edney Common. Essx 3E 20
Edrom. Bord 4H 57
Edstaston. Shrp 6C 32
Edstone. Warw 5M 25
Edwalton. Notts 6C 34
Edwardstone. Suff 7F 28
Edwardsville. Mer T 4C 16
Edwinsford. Carm 8J 23
Edwinstowe. Notts 3C 34
Edworth. C Beds 7L 27
Edwyn Ralph. Here 6G 25
Edzell. Ang 7G 67
Efail-fach. Neat 4M 15
Efail Isaf. Rhon 5C 16
Efailnewydd. Gwyn 6C 30
Efail-rhyd. Powy 7L 31
Efailwen. Carm 1F 14
Efenechtyd. Den 4L 31
Effingham. Surr 8M 19
Effingham Common. Surr 8M 19
Effirth. Shet 6D 79
Efflinch. Staf 8J 33
Efford. Devn 5K 7
Efstigarth. Shet 2E 79
Egbury. Hants 8E 18
Egdon. Worc 6K 25
Egerton. G Man 4F 38
Egerton. Kent 3H 13
Egerton Forstal. Kent 3G 13
Eggborough. N Yor 3B 40
Eggbuckland. Plym 4F 4
Eggesford. Devn 4H 7
Eggington. C Beds 1K 19
Egginton. Derbs 7K 33
Egglescliffe. Stoc T 2D 44
Eggleston. Dur 1L 43
Egham. Surr 6L 19
Egham Hythe. Surr 6L 19
Egleton. Rut 1G 27
Eglingham. Nmbd 8L 57
Egloshayle. Corn 8B 6
Egloskerry. Corn 7D 6
Eglwysbach. Cnwy 2H 31
Eglwys-Brewis. V Glam 7C 16
Eglwys Fach. Cdgn 2J 23
Eglwyswrw. Pemb 8D 22
Egmanton. Notts 3D 34
Egmere. Norf 4F 36
Egremont. Cumb 2B 42
Egremont. Mers 6B 38
Egton. N Yor 3H 45
Egton Bridge. N Yor 3H 45
Egypt. Buck 5K 19
Egypt. Hants 1E 10
Eight Ash Green. Essx 1H 21
Eight Mile Burn. Midl 4K 55
Eignaig. High 1E 58
Eilanreach. High 2A 64
Eildon. Bord 6E 56
Eileanach Lodge. High 5H 71
Eilean Fhlodaigh. W Isl 6C 68
Eilean Iarmain. High 2M 63
Einacleit. W Isl 6B 74
Eisgein. W Isl 7D 74
Eisingrug. Gwyn 6F 30
Elan Village. Powy 5M 23
Elberton. S Glo 5J 17
Elbridge. W Sus 5K 11
Elburton. Plym 4G 5
Elcho. Per 3G 61
Elcombe. Swin 5B 18
Elcot. W Ber 7D 18
Eldernell. Cambs 2M 27
Eldersfield. Worc 8J 25
Elderslie. Ren 3C 54
Elder Street. Essx 8B 28
Eldon. Dur 1B 44
Eldroth. N Yor 7J 43
Eldwick. W Yor 1K 39
Elfhowe. Cumb 4F 42
Elford. Nmbd 6L 57
Elford. Staf 8J 33
Elford Closes. Cambs 4A 28
Elgin. Mor 3C 72
Elgol. High 2K 63
Elham. Kent 3K 13
Elie. Fife 5K 61
Eling. Hants 4D 10
Eling. W Ber 6F 18
Elishaw. Nmbd 2D 50
Elizafield. Dum 4H 49
Elkesley. Notts 8C 40
Elkington. Nptn 4E 26
Elkins Green. Essx 3E 20
Elkstone. Glos 2M 17
Ellan. High 1L 65
Elland. W Yor 3K 39
Ellary. Arg 2F 52
Ellastone. Staf 5J 33
Ellbridge. Corn 3F 4
Ellel. Lanc 8F 42
Ellemford. Bord 3G 57
Ellenabeich. Arg 4E 58
Ellenborough. Cumb 8H 49
Ellenbrook. Herts 3A 20
Ellenhall. Staf 7F 32
Ellen's Green. Surr 2L 11
Ellerbeck. N Yor 4D 44
Ellerburn. N Yor 5H 45
Ellerby. N Yor 2G 45
Ellerdine. Telf 7D 32
Ellerdine Heath. Telf 7D 32
Ellerhayes. Devn 5L 7
Elleric. Arg 1H 59
Ellerker. E Yor 3F 40
Ellerton. E Yor 2D 40
Ellerton. N Yor 4B 44
Ellerton. Shrp 7E 32
Ellesborough. Buck 3J 19
Ellesmere. Shrp 6A 32
Ellesmere Port. Ches W 8C 38
Ellingham. Hants 5B 10
Ellingham. Norf 2K 29
Ellingham. Nmbd 7L 57
Ellingstring. N Yor 5A 44
Ellington. Cambs 4K 27
Ellington. Nmbd 2H 51
Ellington Thorpe. Cambs 4K 27
Elliot. Ang 2M 61
Ellisfield. Hants 1G 11
Ellishadder. High 5K 69
Ellistown. Leics 8A 34
Ellon. Abers 6K 73
Ellonby. Cumb 8M 49
Ellough. Suff 3L 29
Elloughton. E Yor 3F 40
Ellwood. Glos 3H 17
Elm. Cambs 1A 28
Elmbridge. Glos 2L 17
Elmbridge. Worc 5K 25
Elmdon. Essx 8A 28
Elmdon. W Mid 3M 25
Elmdon Heath. W Mid 3M 25
Elmesthorpe. Leics 2C 26
Elmfield. IOW 6F 10
Elm Hill. Dors 3H 9
Elmhurst. Staf 8J 33
Elmley Castle. Worc 7K 25
Elmley Lovett. Worc 5J 25
Elmore. Glos 2K 17
Elmore Back. Glos 2K 17
Elm Park. G Lon 5D 20
Elmscott. Devn 3D 6
Elmsett. Suff 7G 29
Elmstead. Essx 1J 21
Elmstead Heath. Essx 1J 21
Elmstead Market. Essx 1J 21
Elmsted. Kent 3K 13
Elmstone. Kent 7L 21
Elmstone Hardwicke. Glos 1M 17
Elmswell. E Yor 8J 45
Elmswell. Suff 5F 28
Elmton. Derbs 8B 40
Elphin. High 8K 75
Elphinstone. E Lot 2M 55
Elrick. Abers 3J 67
Elrick. Mor 1E 66
Elrig. Dum 7A 48
Elsdon. Nmbd 2E 50
Elsecar. S Yor 6M 39
Elsenham. Essx 1D 20
Elsfield. Oxon 2F 18
Elsham. N Lin 4G 41
Elsing. Norf 6G 37
Elslack. N Yor 1H 39
Elsrickle. S Lan 5J 55
Elstead. Surr 1K 11
Elsted. W Sus 4J 11
Elsted Marsh. W Sus 3J 11
Elsthorpe. Linc 7G 35
Elstob. Dur 1C 44
Elston. Devn 5J 7
Elston. Lanc 2E 38
Elston. Notts 5D 34
Elston. Wilts 1A 10
Elstone. Devn 4H 7
Elstow. Bed 7J 27
Elstree. Herts 4M 19
Elstronwick. E Yor 2J 41
Elswick. Lanc 2C 38
Elswick. Tyne 5H 51
Elsworth. Cambs 5M 27
Elterwater. Cumb 3E 42
Eltham. G Lon 6C 20
Eltisley. Cambs 6L 27
Elton. Cambs 2J 27
Elton. Ches W 8C 38
Elton. Derbs 3K 33
Elton. Glos 2K 17
Elton. G Man 4F 38
Elton. Here 4E 24
Elton. Notts 6D 34
Elton. Stoc T 2D 44
Elton Green. Ches W 8C 38
Eltringham. Nmbd 5F 50
Elvanfoot. S Lan 8H 55
Elvaston. Derbs 6A 34
Elveden. Suff 4E 28
Elvetham Heath. Hants 8H 19
Elvingston. E Lot 2D 56
Elvington. Kent 8L 21
Elvington. York 1D 40
Elwick. Hart 8K 51
Elwick. Nmbd 6L 57
Elworth. Ches E 3E 32
Elworth. Dors 7E 8
Elworthy. Som 2M 7
Ely. Cambs 3B 28
Ely. Card 6D 16
Emberton. Mil 7G 27
Embleton. Cumb 8J 49
Embleton. Dur 1D 44
Embleton. Nmbd 7M 57
Embo. High 2L 71
Emborough. Som 8J 17
Embo Street. High 2L 71
Embsay. N Yor 8M 43
Emery Down. Hants 5C 10
Emley. W Yor 4L 39
Emmbrook. Wok 7H 19
Emmer Green. Read 6H 19
Emmington. Oxon 3H 19
Emneth. Norf 1A 28
Emneth Hungate. Norf 1B 28
Empingham. Rut 1H 27
Empshott. Hants 2H 11
Emsworth. Hants 5H 11
Enborne. W Ber 7E 18
Enborne Row. W Ber 7E 18
Enchmarsh. Shrp 2F 24
Enderby. Leics 2D 26
Endmoor. Cumb 5G 43
Endon. Staf 4G 33
Endon Bank. Staf 4G 33
Enfield. G Lon 4B 20
Enfield Wash. G Lon 4B 20
Enford. Wilts 8B 18
Engine Common. S Glo 5J 17
Englefield. W Ber 6G 19
Englefield Green. Surr 6K 19
Englesea-brook. Ches E 4E 32
English Bicknor. Glos 2H 17
Englishcombe. Bath 7K 17
English Frankton. Shrp 7B 32
Enham Alamein. Hants 1D 10
Enmore. Som 2B 8
Ennerdale Bridge. Cumb 2B 42
Enniscaven. Corn 4A 4
Enoch. Dum 1F 48
Enochdhu. Per 7A 66
Ensay. Arg 1A 58
Ensbury. Bour 6A 10
Ensdon. Shrp 8B 32
Ensis. Devn 3G 7
Enson. Staf 7G 33
Enstone. Oxon 1D 18
Enterkinfoot. Dum 1F 48
Enville. Staf 3J 25
Eolaigearraidh. W Isl 3B 62
Eorabus. Arg 3A 58
Eoropaidh. W Isl 2F 74
Epney. Glos 2K 17
Epperstone. Notts 5C 34
Epping. Essx 3C 20
Epping Green. Essx 3C 20
Epping Green. Herts 3A 20
Epping Upland. Essx 3C 20
Eppleby. N Yor 2A 44
Eppleworth. E Yor 2G 41
Epsom. Surr 7A 20
Epwell. Oxon 7B 26
Epworth. N Lin 5D 40
Epworth Turbary. N Lin 5D 40
Erbistock. Wrex 5A 32
Erbusaig. High 1M 63
Erchless Castle. High 7G 71
Erdington. W Mid 2M 25
Eredine. Arg 5G 59
Eriboll. High 4M 75
Ericstane. Dum 8J 55
Eridge Green. E Sus 4D 12
Erines. Arg 2G 53
Eriswell. Suff 4D 28
Erith. G Lon 6D 20
Erlestoke. Wilts 8M 17
Ermine. Linc 8F 40
Ermington. Devn 4H 5
Ernesettle. Plym 4F 4
Erpingham. Norf 4H 37
Erriottwood. Kent 8H 21
Errogie. High 1H 65
Errol. Per 3H 61
Errol Station. Per 3H 61
Erskine. Ren 2C 54
Erskine Bridge. Ren 2C 54
Ervie. Dum 5K 47
Erwarton. Suff 8J 29
Erwood. Powy 7A 24
Eryholme. N Yor 3C 44
Eryrys. Den 4M 31
Escalls. Corn 7A 3
Escomb. Dur 8G 51
Escrick. N Yor 1C 40
Esgair. Carm 1H 15
(nr. Carmarthen)
Esgair. Carm 2G 15
(nr. St Clears)
Esgairgeiliog. Powy 1K 23
Esh. Dur 7G 51
Esher. Surr 7M 19
Esholt. W Yor 1K 39
Eshott. Nmbd 2H 51
Eshton. N Yor 8L 43
Esh Winning. Dur 7G 51
Eskadale. High 8G 71
Eskbank. Midl 3M 55
Eskdale Green. Cumb 3C 42
Eskdalemuir. Dum 2K 49
Eskham. Linc 6K 41
Esknish. Arg 3B 52
Esk Valley. N Yor 3H 45
Eslington Hall. Nmbd 8K 57
Espley Hall. Nmbd 2G 51
Esprick. Lanc 2C 38
Essendine. Rut 8G 35
Essendon. Herts 3A 20
Essich. High 8J 71
Essington. Staf 1K 25
Eston. Red C 2E 44
Estover. Plym 4G 5
Eswick. Shet 6E 79
Etal. Nmbd 6J 57
Etchilhampton. Wilts 7A 18
Etchingham. E Sus 5F 12
Etchinghill. Kent 4K 13
Etchinghill. Staf 8H 33
Etherley Dene. Dur 1A 44
Ethie Haven. Ang 1M 61
Etling Green. Norf 6G 37
Etloe. Glos 3J 17
Eton. Wind 6K 19
Eton Wick. Wind 6K 19
Etteridge. High 4J 65
Ettersgill. Dur 1K 43
Ettiley Heath. Ches E 3E 32
Ettington. Warw 7A 26
Etton. E Yor 1F 40
Etton. Pet 1K 27
Ettrick. Bord 8L 55
Ettrickbridge. Bord 7M 55
Etwall. Derbs 6K 33
Eudon Burnell. Shrp 3H 25
Eudon George. Shrp 3G 25
Euston. Suff 4E 28
Euxton. Lanc 4D 38
Evanstown. B'end 5B 16
Evanton. High 5J 71
Evedon. Linc 5G 35
Evelix. High 2K 71
Evendine. Here 7H 25
Evenjobb. Powy 5C 24
Evenley. Nptn 8D 26
Evenlode. Glos 1C 18
Even Swindon. Swin 5B 18
Evenwood. Dur 1A 44
Evenwood Gate. Dur 1A 44
Everbay. Orkn 5E 78
Evercreech. Som 2F 8
Everdon. Nptn 6D 26
Everingham. E Yor 1E 40
Everleigh. Wilts 8C 18
Everley. N Yor 5J 45
Eversholt. C Beds 8H 27
Evershot. Dors 5E 8
Eversley. Hants 7H 19
Eversley Centre. Hants 7H 19
Eversley Cross. Hants 7H 19
Everthorpe. E Yor 2F 40
Everton. C Beds 6L 27
Everton. Hants 6C 10
Everton. Mers 6B 38
Everton. Notts 6C 40
Evertown. Dum 4L 49
Evesbatch. Here 7G 25
Evesham. Worc 7L 25
Evington. Leic 1E 26
Ewden Village. S Yor 6L 39
Ewdness. Shrp 2H 25
Ewell. Surr 7A 20
Ewell Minnis. Kent 3L 13
Ewelme. Oxon 4G 19
Ewen. Glos 4A 18
Ewenny. V Glam 6B 16
Ewerby. Linc 5H 35
Ewes. Dum 2L 49
Ewesley. Nmbd 2F 50
Ewhurst. Surr 1L 11
Ewhurst Green. E Sus 5F 12
Ewhurst Green. Surr 2L 11
Ewlo. Flin 3A 32
Ewloe. Flin 3A 32
Ewood Bridge. Lanc 3F 38
Eworthy. Devn 6F 6
Ewshot. Hants 8J 19
Ewyas Harold. Here 1F 16
Exbourne. Devn 5H 7
Exbury. Hants 5E 10
Exceat. E Sus 8D 12
Exebridge. Som 3L 7
Exelby. N Yor 5B 44
Exeter. Devn 6L 7 & 95
Exeter International Airport. Devn 6M 7
Exford. Som 2K 7
Exfords Green. Shrp 1E 24
Exhall. Warw 6M 25
Exlade Street. Oxon 5G 19
Exminster. Devn 7L 7
Exmoor. Som 2K 7
Exmouth. Devn 7M 7
Exnaboe. Shet 10D 79
Exning. Suff 5C 28
Exton. Devn 7L 7
Exton. Hants 3G 11
Exton. Rut 8F 34
Exton. Som 2L 7
Exwick. Devn 6L 7
Eyam. Derbs 8L 39
Eydon. Nptn 6D 26
Eye. Here 5E 24
Eye. Pet 1L 27
Eye. Suff 4H 29
Eye Green. Pet 1L 27
Eyemouth. Bord 3J 57
Eyeworth. C Beds 7L 27
Eyhorne Street. Kent 8G 21
Eyke. Suff 6K 29
Eynesbury. Cambs 6K 27
Eynort. High 1H 63
Eynsford. Kent 7D 20
Eynsham. Oxon 3E 18
Eyre. High 6J 69
(on Isle of Skye)
Eyre. High 8K 69
(on Raasay)
Eythorne. Kent 3L 13
Eyton. Here 5E 24
Eyton. Shrp 3D 24
(nr. Bishop's Castle)
Eyton. Shrp 8A 32
(nr. Shrewsbury)
Eyton. Wrex 5A 32
Eyton on Severn. Shrp 1F 24
Eyton upon the Weald Moors. Telf 8D 32

F

Faccombe. Hants 8D 18
Faceby. N Yor 3D 44
Faddiley. Ches E 4C 32
Fadmoor. N Yor 5F 44
Fagwyr. Swan 3L 15
Faichem. High 3E 64
Faifley. W Dun 2D 54
Fail. S Ayr 7C 54
Failand. N Som 6H 17
Failford. S Ayr 7C 54
Failsworth. G Man 5H 39
Fairbourne. Gwyn 8F 30
Fairbourne Heath. Kent 8G 21
Fairburn. N Yor 3A 40
Fairfield. Derbs 8J 39
Fairfield. Kent 5H 13
Fairfield. Worc 4K 25
(nr. Bromsgrove)
Fairfield. Worc 7L 25
(nr. Evesham)
Fairford. Glos 3B 18
Fair Green. Norf 6C 36
Fair Hill. Cumb 8A 50
Fairhill. S Lan 4F 54
Fair Isle Airport. Shet 1G 78
Fairlands. Surr 8K 19
Fairlie. N Ayr 4A 54
Fairlight. E Sus 6G 13
Fairlight Cove. E Sus 6G 13
Fairmile. Devn 6M 7
Fairmile. Surr 7M 19
Fairmilehead. Edin 3L 55
Fair Oak. Devn 4M 7
Fair Oak. Hants 4E 10
(nr. Eastleigh)
Fair Oak. Hants 7F 18
(nr. Kingsclere)
Fairoak. Staf 6E 32
Fair Oak Green. Hants 7G 19
Fairseat. Kent 7E 20
Fairstead. Essx 2F 20
Fairstead. Norf 6C 36
Fairwarp. E Sus 5C 12
Fairwater. Card 6D 16
Fairy Cross. Devn 3F 6
Fakenham. Norf 5F 36
Fakenham Magna. Suff 4F 28
Fala. Midl 3D 56
Fala Dam. Midl 3D 56
Falcon. Here 8G 25
Faldingworth. Linc 7G 41
Falfield. S Glo 4J 17
Falkenham. Suff 8J 29
Falkirk. Falk 2G 55
Falkland. Fife 5H 61
Fallin. Stir 6D 60
Fallowfield. G Man 6G 39
Falmer. E Sus 7B 12
Falmouth. Corn 6F 3
Falsgrave. N Yor 5K 45
Falstone. Nmbd 3C 50
Fanagmore. High 5J 75
Fancott. C Beds 1L 19
Fanellan. High 7G 71
Fangdale Beck. N Yor 4E 44
Fangfoss. E Yor 8G 45
Fankerton. Falk 1F 54
Fanmore. Arg 1B 58
Fanner's Green. Essx 2E 20
Fannich Lodge. High 5E 70
Fans. Bord 5F 56
Farcet. Cambs 2L 27
Far Cotton. Nptn 6F 26
Fareham. Hants 5F 10
Farewell. Staf 8H 33
Far Forest. Worc 4H 25
Farforth. Linc 8K 41
Far Green. Glos 3K 17
Far Hoarcross. Staf 7J 33
Faringdon. Oxon 4C 18
Farington. Lanc 3D 38
Farlam. Cumb 6A 50
Farleigh. N Som 7G 17
Farleigh. Surr 7B 20
Farleigh Hungerford. Som 8L 17
Farleigh Wallop. Hants 1G 11
Farleigh Wick. Wilts 7L 17
Farlesthorpe. Linc 8L 41
Farleton. Cumb 5G 43
Farleton. Lanc 7G 43
Farley. High 7G 71
Farley. N Som 6G 17
Farley. Shrp 1D 24
(nr. Shrewsbury)
Farley. Shrp 1G 25
(nr. Telford)
Farley. Staf 5H 33
Farley. Wilts 3C 10
Farley Green. Suff 6D 28
Farley Green. Surr 1L 11
Farley Hill. Wok 7H 19
Farley's End. Glos 2K 17
Farlington. N Yor 7F 44
Farlington. Port 5G 11
Farlow. Shrp 3G 25
Farmborough. Bath 7J 17
Farmcote. Glos 1A 18
Farmcote. Shrp 2H 25
Farmington. Glos 2B 18
Far Moor. G Man 5D 38
Farmoor. Oxon 3E 18
Farmtown. Mor 4F 72
Farnah Green. Derbs 5L 33
Farnborough. G Lon 7C 20
Farnborough. Hants 8J 19
Farnborough. Warw 7C 26
Farnborough. W Ber 5E 18
Farncombe. Surr 1K 11
Farndish. Bed 5H 27
Farndon. Ches W 4B 32
Farndon. Notts 4D 34
Farnell. Ang 8G 67
Farnham. Dors 4J 9
Farnham. Essx 1C 20
Farnham. N Yor 7C 44
Farnham. Suff 5K 29
Farnham. Surr 1J 11
Farnham Common. Buck 5K 19
Farnham Green. Essx 1C 20
Farnham Royal. Buck 5K 19
Farnhill. N Yor 1J 39
Farningham. Kent 7D 20
Farnley. N Yor 1L 39
Farnley Tyas. W Yor 4K 39
Farnsfield. Notts 4C 34
Farnworth. G Man 5F 38
Farnworth. Hal 7D 38
Far Oakridge. Glos 3M 17
Farr. High 3C 76
(nr. Bettyhill)
Farr. High 8J 71
(nr. Inverness)
Farr. High 3L 65
(nr. Kingussie)
Farraline. High 1H 65
Farringdon. Devn 6M 7
Farrington. Dors 4H 9
Farrington Gurney. Bath 8J 17
Far Sawrey. Cumb 4E 42
Farsley. W Yor 2L 39
Farthinghoe. Nptn 8D 26
Farthingstone. Nptn 6E 26
Farthorpe. Linc 8J 41
Fartown. W Yor 4K 39
Farway. Devn 6A 8
Fasag. High 6A 70
Fascadale. High 6K 63
Fasnacloich. Arg 1H 59
Fassfern. High 6C 64
Fatfield. Tyne 6J 51
Faugh. Cumb 6A 50
Fauld. Staf 7J 33
Fauldhouse. W Lot 3H 55
Faulkbourne. Essx 2F 20
Faulkland. Som 8K 17
Fauls. Shrp 6C 32
Faverdale. Darl 2B 44
Faversham. Kent 7J 21
Fawdington. N Yor 6D 44
Fawfieldhead. Staf 3H 33
Fawkham Green. Kent 7D 20
Fawler. Oxon 2D 18
Fawley. Buck 5H 19
Fawley. Hants 5E 10
Fawley. W Ber 5D 18
Fawley Chapel. Here 1H 17
Fawton. Corn 3C 4
Faxfleet. E Yor 3E 40
Faygate. W Sus 4A 12
Fazakerley. Mers 6B 38
Fazeley. Staf 1M 25
Feagour. High 4H 65
Fearann Dhomhnaill. High 3L 63
Fearby. N Yor 5A 44
Fearn. High 4L 71
Fearnan. Per 1C 60
Fearnbeg. High 6M 69
Fearnhead. Warr 6E 38
Fearnmore. High 5M 69
Featherstone. Staf 1K 25
Featherstone. W Yor 3A 40
Featherstone Castle. Nmbd 5B 50
Feckenham. Worc 5L 25
Feering. Essx 1G 21
Feetham. N Yor 4L 43
Feizor. N Yor 7J 43
Felbridge. Surr 4B 12
Felbrigg. Norf 4J 37
Felcourt. Surr 3B 12
Felden. Herts 3L 19
Felhampton. Shrp 3E 24
Felindre. Carm 1K 15
(nr. Llandeilo)
Felindre. Carm 8J 23
(nr. Llandovery)
Felindre. Carm 8F 22
(nr. Newcastle Emlyn)
Felindre. Powy 3B 24
Felindre. Swan 3L 15
Felindre Farchog. Pemb 8D 22
Felinfach. Cdgn 6H 23
Felinfach. Powy 8A 24
Felinfoel. Carm 3K 15
Felingwmisaf. Carm 1K 15
Felingwmuchaf. Carm 1K 15
Felin Newydd. Powy 1A 24
(nr. Newtown)
Felin Newydd. Powy 7M 31
(nr. Oswestry)
Felin Wnda. Cdgn 7F 22
Felinwynt. Cdgn 6E 22
Felixkirk. N Yor 5D 44
Felixstowe. Suff 8J 29
Felixstowe Ferry. Suff 8K 29
Felkington. Nmbd 5J 57
Fell End. Cumb 4J 43
Felling. Tyne 5H 51
Fell Side. Cumb 8L 49
Felmersham. Bed 6H 27
Felmingham. Norf 5J 37
Felpham. W Sus 6K 11
Felsham. Suff 6F 28
Felsted. Essx 1E 20
Feltham. G Lon 6M 19
Felthamhill. Surr 6L 19
Felthorpe. Norf 6H 37
Felton. Here 7F 24
Felton. N Som 7H 17
Felton. Nmbd 1G 51
Felton Butler. Shrp 8A 32
Feltwell. Norf 2D 28
Fenay Bridge. W Yor 4K 39
Fence. Lanc 2G 39
Fence Houses. Tyne 6J 51
Fencott. Oxon 2F 18
Fen Ditton. Cambs 5A 28
Fen Drayton. Cambs 5M 27
Fen End. Linc 7J 35
Fen End. W Mid 4A 26
Fenham. Nmbd 5K 57
Fenham. Tyne 5H 51
Fenhouses. Linc 5J 35
Feniscowles. Bkbn 3E 38
Feniton. Devn 6M 7
Fenn Green. Shrp 3H 25
Fenn's Bank. Wrex 6C 32
Fenn Street. Medw 6F 20
Fenny Bentley. Derbs 4J 33
Fenny Bridges. Devn 6A 8
Fenny Compton. Warw 6C 26
Fenny Drayton. Leics 2B 26
Fenny Stratford. Mil 8G 27
Fenrother. Nmbd 2G 51
Fenstanton. Cambs 5M 27
Fen Street. Norf 2G 29
Fenton. Cambs 4M 27
Fenton. Cumb 6A 50
Fenton. Linc 4E 34
(nr. Caythorpe)
Fenton. Linc 8E 40
(nr. Saxilby)
Fenton. Nmbd 6J 57
Fenton. Notts 7D 40
Fenton. Stoke 5F 32
Fentonadle. Corn 8B 6
Fenton Barns. E Lot 1E 56
Fenwick. E Ayr 5C 54
Fenwick. Nmbd 5K 57
(nr. Berwick-upon-Tweed)
Fenwick. Nmbd 4F 50
(nr. Hexham)
Fenwick. S Yor 4B 40
Feochaig. Arg 8F 52
Feock. Corn 6F 3
Feolin Ferry. Arg 3C 52
Feorlan. Arg 8E 52
Ferindonald. High 3L 63
Feriniquarrie. High 6F 68
Fern. Ang 7E 66
Ferndale. Rhon 4B 16
Ferndown. Dors 5A 10
Ferness. High 7M 71
Fernham. Oxon 4C 18
Fernhill. W Sus 3A 12
Fernhill Heath. Worc 6J 25
Fernhurst. W Sus 3J 11
Fernieflatt. Abers 6J 67
Ferniegair. S Lan 4F 54
Fernilea. High 8H 69
Fernilee. Derbs 8J 39
Ferrensby. N Yor 7C 44
Ferriby Sluice. N Lin 3F 40
Ferring. W Sus 5M 11
Ferrybridge. W Yor 3A 40
Ferryden. Ang 8H 67
Ferryhill. Aber 3K 67
Ferry Hill. Cambs 3M 27
Ferryhill. Dur 8H 51
Ferryhill Station. Dur 8H 51
Ferryside. Carm 2H 15
Ferryton. High 5J 71
Fersfield. Norf 3G 29
Fersit. High 6F 64
Feshiebridge. High 3L 65
Fetcham. Surr 8M 19
Fetterangus. Abers 4K 73
Fettercairn. Abers 6G 67
Fewcott. Oxon 1F 18
Fewston. N Yor 8A 44
Ffairfach. Carm 1L 15
Ffair Rhos. Cdgn 5K 23
Ffaldybrenin. Carm 7J 23
Ffarmers. Carm 7J 23
Ffawyddog. Powy 2E 16
Ffodun. Powy 1C 24
Ffont-y-gari. V Glam 7C 16
Fforest. Carm 3K 15
Fforest-fach. Swan 4L 15
Fforest Goch. Neat 3M 15
Ffostrasol. Cdgn 7F 22
Ffos-y-ffin. Cdgn 5G 23
Ffrith. Flin 4M 31
Ffwl-y-mwn. V Glam 7C 16
Ffynnon-ddrain. Carm 1J 15
Ffynnongroyw. Flin 1L 31
Ffynnon Gynydd. Powy 7B 24
Ffynnon-oer. Cdgn 6H 23
Fiag Lodge. High 7M 75
Fidden. Arg 3A 58
Fiddington. Glos 8K 25
Fiddington. Som 1B 8
Fiddleford. Dors 4H 9
Fiddlers Hamlet. Essx 3C 20
Field. Staf 6H 33
Field Assarts. Oxon 2D 18
Field Broughton. Cumb 5E 42
Field Dalling. Norf 4G 37
Fieldhead. Cumb 8M 49
Field Head. Leics 1C 26
Fifehead Magdalen. Dors 3G 9
Fifehead Neville. Dors 4G 9
Fifehead St Quintin. Dors 4G 9
Fife Keith. Mor 4E 72
Fifield. Oxon 2C 18
Fifield. Wilts 8B 18
Fifield. Wind 6K 19
Fifield Bavant. Wilts 3A 10
Figheldean. Wilts 1B 10
Filby. Norf 6L 37
Filey. N Yor 5L 45
Filford. Dors 6D 8
Filgrave. Mil 7G 27
Filkins. Oxon 3C 18
Filleigh. Devn 4J 7
(nr. Crediton)
Filleigh. Devn 3H 7
(nr. South Molton)
Fillingham. Linc 7F 40
Fillongley. Warw 3A 26
Filton. S Glo 6J 17
Fimber. E Yor 7H 45
Finavon. Ang 8E 66
Fincham. Norf 1C 28
Finchampstead. Wok 7H 19
Fincharn. Arg 5G 59
Finchdean. Hants 4H 11
Finchingfield. Essx 8C 28
Finchley. G Lon 4A 20
Findern. Derbs 6L 33
Findhorn. Mor 3A 72
Findhorn Bridge. High 1L 65
Findochty. Mor 3E 72
Findo Gask. Per 3F 60
Findon. Abers 4K 67
Findon. W Sus 5M 11
Findon Mains. High 5J 71
Findon Valley. W Sus 5M 11
Finedon. Nptn 4H 27
Fingal Street. Suff 4J 29
Fingest. Buck 4H 19
Finghall. N Yor 5A 44
Fingland. Cumb 6K 49
Fingland. Dum 8F 54
Finglesham. Kent 8M 21
Fingringhoe. Essx 1J 21
Finiskaig. High 4A 64
Finmere. Oxon 8E 26
Finnart. Per 8H 65
Finningham. Suff 5G 29
Finningley. S Yor 6C 40
Finnygaud. Abers 4G 73
Finsbury. G Lon 5B 20
Finstall. Worc 4K 25
Finsthwaite. Cumb 5E 42
Finstock. Oxon 2D 18
Finstown. Orkn 6B 78
Fintry. Abers 4H 73
Fintry. D'dee 2K 61
Fintry. Stir 1E 54
Finwood. Warw 5M 25
Finzean. Abers 4G 67
Fionnphort. Arg 3A 58
Fionnsabhagh. W Isl 3E 68
Firbeck. S Yor 7B 40
Firby. N Yor 5B 44
(nr. Bedale)
Firby. N Yor 7G 45
(nr. Malton)
Firgrove. G Man 4H 39
Firle. E Sus 7C 12
Firsby. Linc 3L 35
Firsdown. Wilts 2C 10
First Coast. High 2B 70
Firth. Shet 4E 79
Fir Tree. Dur 8G 51
Fishbourne. IOW 6F 10
Fishbourne. W Sus 5J 11
Fishburn. Dur 8J 51
Fishcross. Clac 6E 60
Fisherford. Abers 6G 73
Fisherrow. E Lot 2M 55
Fisher's Pond. Hants 3E 10
Fisher's Row. Lanc 1C 38
Fisherstreet. W Sus 2K 11
Fisherton. High 6K 71
Fisherton. S Ayr 8A 54
Fisherton de la Mere. Wilts 2J 9
Fishguard. Pemb 8B 22
Fishlake. S Yor 4C 40
Fishley. Norf 6L 37
Fishnish. Arg 1D 58
Fishpond Bottom. Dors 6C 8
Fishponds. Bris 6J 17
Fishpool. Glos 1J 17
Fishpool. G Man 5G 39
Fishpools. Powy 5B 24
Fishtoft. Linc 5K 35
Fishtoft Drove. Linc 5K 35
Fishwick. Bord 4J 57
Fiskavaig. High 8H 69
Fiskerton. Linc 8G 41
Fiskerton. Notts 4D 34
Fitch. Shet 7D 79
Fitling. E Yor 2J 41
Fittleton. Wilts 1B 10
Fittleworth. W Sus 4L 11
Fitton End. Cambs 8L 35
Fitz. Shrp 8B 32
Fitzhead. Som 3A 8
Fitzwilliam. W Yor 4A 40
Fiunary. High 1D 58
Five Ash Down. E Sus 5C 12
Five Ashes. E Sus 5D 12
Five Bells. Som 1M 7
Five Bridges. Here 7G 25
Fivehead. Som 3C 8
Five Lane Ends. Lanc 8G 43
Fivelanes. Corn 7D 6
Five Oak Green. Kent 3E 12
Five Oaks. W Sus 3L 11
Five Roads. Carm 3J 15
Five Ways. Warw 4A 26
Flack's Green. Essx 2F 20
Flackwell Heath. Buck 5J 19
Fladbury. Worc 7K 25
Fladda. Shet 3D 79
Fladdabister. Shet 8E 79
Flagg. Derbs 3J 33
Flamborough. E Yor 6M 45
Flamstead. Herts 2L 19
Flansham. W Sus 5K 11
Flasby. N Yor 8L 43
Flash. Staf 3H 33
Flashader. High 6H 69
Flatt, The. Cumb 4A 50
Flaunden. Herts 3L 19
Flawborough. Notts 5D 34
Flawith. N Yor 7D 44
Flax Bourton. N Som 7H 17
Flaxby. N Yor 8C 44
Flaxholme. Derbs 5L 33
Flaxley. Glos 2J 17
Flaxley Green. Staf 8H 33
Flaxpool. Som 2A 8
Flaxton. N Yor 7F 44
Fleck. Shet 10D 79
Fleckney. Leics 2E 26
Flecknoe. Warw 5D 26
Fledborough. Notts 8E 40
Fleet. Dors 7F 8
Fleet. Hants 8J 19
(nr. Farnborough)
Fleet. Hants 5H 11
(nr. South Hayling)
Fleet. Linc 7K 35
Fleet Hargate. Linc 7K 35
Fleetville. Herts 3M 19
Fleetwood. Lanc 1B 38
Fleggburgh. Norf 6L 37
Fleisirin. W Isl 5F 74
Flemingston. V Glam 6C 16
Flemington. S Lan 3E 54
(nr. Glasgow)
Flemington. S Lan 5F 54
(nr. Strathaven)
Flempton. Suff 5E 28
Fleoideabhagh. W Isl 3E 68
Fletcher's Green. Kent 3D 12
Fletchertown. Cumb 7K 49
Fletching. E Sus 5C 12
Fleuchary. High 2K 71
Flexbury. Corn 5D 6
Flexford. Surr 8K 19
Flimby. Cumb 8H 49
Flimwell. E Sus 4F 12
Flint. Flin 8A 38
Flintham. Notts 5D 34
Flint Mountain. Flin 8A 38
Flinton. E Yor 2J 41
Flintsham. Here 6D 24
Flishinghurst. Kent 4F 12
Flitcham. Norf 5D 36
Flitton. C Beds 8J 27
Flitwick. C Beds 8J 27
Flixborough. N Lin 4E 40
Flixton. G Man 6F 38
Flixton. N Yor 6K 45
Flixton. Suff 3K 29
Flockton. W Yor 4L 39
Flodden. Nmbd 6J 57
Flodigarry. High 4J 69
Flood's Ferry. Cambs 2M 27
Flookburgh. Cumb 6E 42
Flordon. Norf 2H 29
Flore. Nptn 5E 26
Flotterton. Nmbd 1F 50
Flowton. Suff 7G 29
Flushing. Abers 5L 73
Flushing. Corn 6F 3
Fluxton. Devn 6M 7
Flyford Flavell. Worc 6K 25
Fobbing. Thur 5F 20
Fochabers. Mor 4D 72
Fochriw. Cphy 3D 16
Fockerby. N Lin 4E 40
Fodderty. High 6H 71
Foddington. Som 3E 8
Foel. Powy 8J 31
Foffarty. Ang 1K 61
Foggathorpe. E Yor 2D 40
Fogo. Bord 5G 57
Fogorig. Bord 5G 57
Foindle. High 5J 75
Folda. Ang 7B 66
Fole. Staf 6H 33
Foleshill. W Mid 3B 26
Foley Park. Worc 4J 25
Folke. Dors 4F 8
Folkestone. Kent 4L 13 & 95
Folkingham. Linc 6G 35
Folkington. E Sus 7D 12
Folksworth. Cambs 2K 27
Folkton. N Yor 6K 45
Folla Rule. Abers 6H 73
Follifoot. N Yor 8C 44
Folly Cross. Devn 5F 6
Folly Gate. Devn 6G 7
Folly, The. Herts 2M 19
Folly, The. W Ber 7E 18
Fonmon. V Glam 7C 16
Fonthill Bishop. Wilts 2J 9
Fonthill Gifford. Wilts 2J 9
Fontmell Magna. Dors 4H 9
Fontwell. W Sus 5K 11
Font-y-gary. V Glam 7C 16
Foodieash. Fife 4J 61
Foolow. Derbs 8K 39
Footdee. Aber 3K 67
Footherley. Staf 1M 25
Foots Cray. G Lon 6C 20
Forbestown. Abers 2D 66
Force Forge. Cumb 4E 42
Force Mills. Cumb 4E 42
Forcett. N Yor 2A 44
Ford. Arg 5F 58
Ford. Buck 3H 19
Ford. Derbs 7A 40
Ford. Devn 3F 6
(nr. Bideford)
Ford. Devn 4H 5
(nr. Holbeton)
Ford. Devn 5J 5
(nr. Salcombe)
Ford. Glos 1A 18
Ford. Nmbd 6J 57
Ford. Plym 4F 4
Ford. Shrp 8B 32
Ford. Som 8H 17
(nr. Wells)
Ford. Som 3M 7
(nr. Wiveliscombe)
Ford. Staf 4H 33
Ford. W Sus 5L 11
Ford. Wilts 6L 17
(nr. Chippenham)
Ford. Wilts 2B 10
(nr. Salisbury)
Forda. Devn 2F 6
Ford Barton. Devn 4L 7
Fordcombe. Kent 3D 12
Fordell. Fife 1K 55
Forden. Powy 1C 24
Ford End. Essx 2E 20
Forder Green. Devn 3J 5
Ford Green. Lanc 1C 38
Fordham. Cambs 4C 28
Fordham. Essx 1H 21
Fordham. Norf 2C 28
Fordham Heath. Essx 1H 21
Ford Heath. Shrp 8B 32
Fordhouses. W Mid 1K 25
Fordie. Per 3C 60
Fordingbridge. Hants 4B 10
Fordington. Linc 8L 41
Fordon. E Yor 6K 45
Fordoun. Abers 6H 67
Ford Street. Essx 1H 21
Ford Street. Som 4A 8
Fordton. Devn 6K 7
Fordwells. Oxon 2D 18
Fordwich. Kent 8K 21
Fordyce. Abers 3F 72
Forebridge. Staf 7G 33
Foremark. Derbs 7L 33
Forest. N Yor 3B 44
Forestburn Gate. Nmbd 2F 50
Foresterseat. Mor 4B 72
Forest Green. Glos 4L 17
Forest Green. Surr 1M 11
Forest Hall. Cumb 3G 43
Forest Head. Cumb 6A 50
Forest Hill. Oxon 3F 18
Forest-in-Teesdale. Dur 1K 43
Forest Lodge. Per 6M 65
Forest Mill. Clac 6E 60
Forest Row. E Sus 4C 12
Forestside. W Sus 4H 11
Forest Town. Notts 3B 34
Forfar. Ang 8E 66
Forgandenny. Per 4F 60
Forge. Powy 2K 23
Forge Side. Torf 3E 16
Forge, The. Here 6D 24
Forgewood. N Lan 4F 54
Forgie. Mor 4D 72
Forgue. Abers 5G 73
Formby. Mers 5A 38
Forncett End. Norf 2H 29
Forncett St Mary. Norf 2H 29
Forncett St Peter. Norf 2H 29
Forneth. Per 1F 60
Fornham All Saints. Suff 5E 28
Fornham St Martin. Suff 5E 28
Forres. Mor 4A 72
Forrestfield. N Lan 3G 55
Forrest Lodge. Dum 3C 48
Forsbrook. Staf 5G 33
Forse. High 6H 77
Forsinard. High 5D 76
Forss. High 3F 76
Forstal, The. Kent 4J 13
Forston. Dors 6F 8
Fort Augustus. High 3F 64
Forteviot. Per 4F 60
Fort George. High 6K 71
Forth. S Lan 4H 55
Forthampton. Glos 8J 25
Forthay. Glos 4K 17
Forth Road Bridge. Fife 2K 55
Fortingall. Per 1C 60
Fort Matilda. Inv 2A 54
Forton. Hants 1E 10
Forton. Lanc 8F 42
Forton. Shrp 8B 32
Forton. Som 5C 8
Forton. Staf 7E 32
Forton Heath. Shrp 8B 32
Fortrie. Abers 5G 73
Fortrose. High 6K 71
Fortuneswell. Dors 8F 8
Fort William. High 6D 64
Forty Green. Buck 4K 19
Forty Hill. G Lon 4B 20
Forward Green. Suff 6G 29
Fosbury. Wilts 8D 18
Foscot. Oxon 1C 18
Fosdyke. Linc 6K 35
Foss. Per 8K 65
Fossebridge. Glos 2A 18
Foster Street. Essx 3C 20
Foston. Derbs 6J 33
Foston. Leics 2E 26
Foston. Linc 5E 34
Foston. N Yor 7F 44
Foston on the Wolds. E Yor 8L 45
Fotherby. Linc 6K 41
Fothergill. Cumb 8H 49
Fotheringhay. Nptn 2J 27
Foubister. Orkn 7D 78
Foula Airport. Shet 9B 79
Foul Anchor. Cambs 8L 35
Foulbridge. Cumb 7M 49
Foulden. Norf 2D 28
Foulden. Bord 4J 57
Foul Mile. E Sus 6E 12
Foulridge. Lanc 1G 39
Foulsham. Norf 5G 37
Fountainhall. Bord 5D 56
Four Alls, The. Shrp 6D 32
Four Ashes. Staf 1K 25
(nr. Cannock)
Four Ashes. Staf 3J 25
(nr. Kinver)
Four Ashes. Suff 4G 29
Four Crosses. Powy 1A 24
(nr. Llanerfyl)
Four Crosses. Powy 8M 31
(nr. Llanymynech)
Four Crosses. Staf 1K 25
Four Elms. Kent 3C 12
Four Forks. Som 2B 8
Four Gotes. Cambs 8L 35
Four Lane End. S Yor 5L 39
Four Lane Ends. Lanc 8G 43
Four Lanes. Corn 6D 3
Fourlanes End. Ches E 4E 32
Four Marks. Hants 2G 11
Four Mile Bridge. IOA 2B 30
Four Oaks. E Sus 5G 13
Four Oaks. Glos 1J 17
Four Oaks. W Mid 3A 26
Four Roads. Carm 3J 15
Four Roads. IOM 7C 46
Fourstones. Nmbd 5D 50
Four Throws. Kent 5F 12
Fovant. Wilts 3A 10
Foveran. Abers 1K 67
Fowey. Corn 4C 4
Fowlershill. Abers 2K 67
Fowley Common. Warr 6E 38
Fowlis. Ang 2J 61
Fowlis Wester. Per 3E 60
Fowlmere. Cambs 7A 28
Fownhope. Here 8F 24
Foxcombe Hill. Oxon 3E 18
Fox Corner. Surr 8K 19
Foxcote. Glos 2A 18
Foxcote. Som 8K 17
Foxdale. IOM 6C 46
Foxearth. Essx 7E 28
Foxfield. Cumb 5D 42
Foxham. Wilts 6M 17
Fox Hatch. Essx 4D 20
Foxhole. Corn 4A 4
Foxholes. N Yor 6K 45
Foxhunt Green. E Sus 6D 12
Fox Lane. Hants 8J 19
Foxley. Norf 5G 37
Foxley. Nptn 6E 26
Foxley. Wilts 5L 17
Foxlydiate. Worc 5L 25
Fox Street. Essx 1J 21
Foxt. Staf 5H 33
Foxton. Cambs 7A 28
Foxton. Dur 1C 44
Foxton. Leics 3E 26
Foxton. N Yor 4D 44
Foxup. N Yor 6K 43
Foxwist Green. Ches W 3D 32
Foxwood. Shrp 4G 25
Foy. Here 1H 17
Foyers. High 1G 65
Foynesfield. High 6L 71
Fraddam. Corn 6C 3
Fraddon. Corn 4A 4
Fradley. Staf 8J 33
Fradley South. Staf 8J 33
Fradswell. Staf 6G 33
Fraisthorpe. E Yor 7L 45
Framfield. E Sus 5C 12
Framingham Earl. Norf 1J 29
Framingham Pigot. Norf 1J 29
Framlingham. Suff 5J 29
Frampton. Dors 6F 8
Frampton. Linc 6K 35
Frampton Cotterell. S Glo 5J 17
Frampton Mansell. Glos 3M 17
Frampton on Severn. Glos 3K 17
Frampton West End. Linc 5J 35
Framsden. Suff 6H 29
Framwellgate Moor. Dur 7H 51
Franche. Worc 4J 25
Frandley. Ches W 8E 38
Frankby. Mers 7A 38
Frankfort. Norf 5K 37
Frankley. Worc 3K 25
Frank's Bridge. Powy 6B 24
Frankton. Warw 4C 26
Frankwell. Shrp 8B 32
Frant. E Sus 4D 12
Fraserburgh. Abers 3K 73
Frating Green. Essx 1J 21
Fratton. Port 5G 11
Freathy. Corn 4F 4
Freckenham. Suff 4C 28
Freckleton. Lanc 3C 38
Freeby. Leics 7E 34
Freefolk Priors. Hants 1E 10
Freehay. Staf 5H 33
Freeland. Oxon 2E 18
Freester. Shet 6E 79
Freethorpe. Norf 1L 29
Freiston. Linc 5K 35
Freiston Shore. Linc 5K 35
Fremington. Devn 2G 7
Fremington. N Yor 4M 43
Frenchay. Bris 6J 17
Frenchbeer. Devn 7H 7
French Street. Kent 8C 20
Frenich. Stir 5M 59
Frensham. Surr 1J 11
Frenze. Norf 3H 29
Fresgoe. High 3E 76
Freshfield. Mers 5A 38
Freshford. Bath 7K 17
Freshwater. IOW 7D 10
Freshwater Bay. IOW 7D 10
Freshwater East. Pemb 4E 14
Fressingfield. Suff 4J 29
Freston. Suff 8H 29
Freswick. High 3J 77
Fretherne. Glos 3K 17
Frettenham. Norf 6J 37
Freuchie. Fife 5H 61
Freystrop. Pemb 2D 14
Friar's Gate. E Sus 4C 12
Friar Waddon. Dors 7F 8
Friday Bridge. Cambs 1A 28
Friday Street. E Sus 7E 12
Friday Street. Surr 1M 11
Fridaythorpe. E Yor 8H 45
Friden. Derbs 3J 33
Friern Barnet. G Lon 4A 20
Friesthorpe. Linc 7G 41
Frieston. Linc 5F 34
Frieth. Buck 4H 19
Friezeland. Notts 4A 34
Frilford. Oxon 4E 18
Frilsham. W Ber 6F 18
Frimley. Surr 8J 19
Frimley Green. Surr 8J 19
Frindsbury. Medw 7F 20
Fring. Norf 4D 36
Fringford. Oxon 1G 19
Frinsted. Kent 8G 21
Frinton-on-Sea. Essx 2L 21
Friockheim. Ang 1L 61
Friog. Gwyn 8F 30
Frisby. Leics 1F 26
Frisby on the Wreake. Leics 8C 34
Friskney. Linc 4L 35
Friskney Eaudyke. Linc 4L 35
Friston. E Sus 8D 12
Friston. Suff 5L 29
Fritchley. Derbs 4L 33
Fritham. Hants 4C 10
Frith Bank. Linc 5K 35
Frith Common. Worc 5G 25
Frithelstock. Devn 4F 6
Frithelstock Stone. Devn 4F 6
Frithsden. Herts 3L 19
Frithville. Linc 4K 35
Frittenden. Kent 3G 13
Frittiscombe. Devn 5K 5
Fritton. Norf 1L 29
(nr. Great Yarmouth)
Fritton. Norf 2J 29
(nr. Long Stratton)
Fritwell. Oxon 1F 18
Frizinghall. W Yor 2K 39
Frizington. Cumb 2B 42
Frobost. W Isl 1B 62
Frocester. Glos 3K 17
Frochas. Powy 1B 24
Frodesley. Shrp 1F 24
Frodingham. N Lin 4F 40
Frodsham. Ches W 8D 38
Froggatt. Derbs 8L 39
Froghall. Staf 5H 33
Frogham. Hants 4B 10
Frogham. Kent 8L 21
Frogmore. Devn 5J 5
Frogmore. Hants 7J 19
Frogmore. Herts 3M 19
Frognall. Linc 8H 35
Frogshall. Norf 4J 37
Frogwell. Corn 3E 4
Frolesworth. Leics 2D 26
Frome. Som 1G 9
Fromefield. Som 1G 9
Frome St Quintin. Dors 5E 8
Fromes Hill. Here 7G 25

Fron—Guiseley

Fron. *Gwyn* 6C **30**
Fron. *Powy* 5A **24**
(nr. Llandrindod Wells)
Fron. *Powy* 2B **24**
(nr. Newtown)
Fron. *Powy* 1C **24**
(nr. Welshpool)
Froncysyllte. *Wrex* 5M **31**
Frongoch. *Gwyn* 6J **31**
Fron Isaf. *Wrex* 5M **31**
Fronoleu. *Gwyn* 6G **31**
Frosterley. *Dur* 8F **50**
Frotoft. *Orkn* 5C **78**
Froxfield. *C Beds* 8H **27**
Froxfield. *Wilts* 7C **18**
Froxfield Green. *Hants* 3H **11**
Fryern Hill. *Hants* 3E **10**
Fryerning. *Essx* 3E **20**
Fryton. *N Yor* 6F **44**
Fugglestone St Peter. *Wilts* 2B **10**
Fulbeck. *Linc* 4F **34**
Fulbourn. *Cambs* 6B **28**
Fulbrook. *Oxon* 2C **18**
Fulflood. *Hants* 2E **10**
Fulford. *Som* 3B **8**
Fulford. *Staf* 6G **33**
Fulford. *York* 1C **40**
Fulham. *G Lon* 6A **20**
Fulking. *W Sus* 6A **12**
Fuller's Moor. *Ches W* 4B **32**
Fuller Street. *Essx* 2F **20**
Fullerton. *Hants* 2D **10**
Fulletby. *Linc* 8J **41**
Full Sutton. *E Yor* 8G **45**
Fullwood. *E Ayr* 4C **54**
Fulmer. *Buck* 5K **19**
Fulmodestone. *Norf* 4F **36**
Fulnetby. *Linc* 8G **41**
Fulney. *Linc* 7J **35**
Fulstow. *Linc* 6K **41**
Fulthorpe. *Stoc T* 1D **44**
Fulwell. *Tyne* 6J **51**
Fulwood. *Lanc* 2D **38**
Fulwood. *Notts* 4A **34**
Fulwood. *Som* 4B **8**
Fulwood. *S Yor* 7L **39**
Fundenhall. *Norf* 2H **29**
Funtington. *W Sus* 5J **11**
Funtley. *Hants* 5F **10**
Funzie. *Shet* 2G **79**
Furley. *Devn* 5B **8**
Furnace. *Arg* 5H **59**
Furnace. *Carm* 3K **15**
Furnace. *Cdgn* 2J **23**
Furner's Green. *E Sus* 5C **12**
Furness Vale. *Derbs* 7J **39**
Furneux Pelham. *Herts* 1C **20**
Furzebrook. *Dors* 7J **9**
Furzehill. *Devn* 1J **7**
Furzehill. *Dors* 5A **10**
Furzeley Corner. *Hants* 4G **11**
Furzey Lodge. *Hants* 5D **10**
Furzley. *Hants* 4C **10**
Fyfield. *Essx* 3D **20**
Fyfield. *Glos* 3C **18**
Fyfield. *Hants* 1C **10**
Fyfield. *Oxon* 4E **18**
Fyfield. *Wilts* 7B **18**
Fylde, The. *Lanc* 2B **38**
Fylingthorpe. *N Yor* 3J **45**
Fyning. *W Sus* 3J **11**
Fyvie. *Abers* 6H **73**

G

Gabhsann bho Dheas. *W Isl* 3E **74**
Gabhsann bho Thuath. *W Isl* 3E **74**
Gabroc Hill. *E Ayr* 4C **54**
Gadbrook. *Surr* 3A **12**
Gaddesby. *Leics* 8C **34**
Gadfa. *IOA* 1D **30**
Gadgirth. *S Ayr* 7C **54**
Gaer. *Powy* 1D **16**
Gaerwen. *IOA* 2D **30**
Gagingwell. *Oxon* 1E **18**
Gaick Lodge. *High* 5K **65**
Gailey. *Staf* 8G **33**
Gainford. *Dur* 2A **44**
Gainsborough. *Linc* 6E **40**
Gainsborough. *Suff* 7H **29**
Gainsford End. *Essx* 8D **28**
Gairletter. *Arg* 1K **53**
Gairloch. *Abers* 3H **67**
Gairloch. *High* 4A **70**
Gairlochy. *High* 5D **64**
Gairney Bank. *Per* 6G **61**
Gairnshiel Lodge. *Abers* 3C **66**
Gaisgill. *Cumb* 3H **43**
Gaitsgill. *Cumb* 7L **49**
Galashiels. *Bord* 6D **56**
Galgate. *Lanc* 8F **42**
Galhampton. *Som* 3F **8**
Gallatown. *Fife* 6H **61**
Galley Common. *Warw* 2B **26**
Galleyend. *Essx* 3F **20**
Galleywood. *Essx* 3F **20**
Gallin. *Per* 1A **60**
Gallowfauld. *Ang* 1K **61**
Gallowhill. *E Dun* 2E **54**
Gallowhill. *Per* 2G **61**
Gallowhill. *Ren* 3C **54**
Gallowhills. *Abers* 4L **73**
Gallows Green. *Staf* 5H **33**
Gallows Green. *Worc* 5K **25**
Gallowstree Common. *Oxon* 5G **19**
Galltair. *High* 1A **64**
Gallt Melyd. *Den* 1K **31**
Galmington. *Som* 3B **8**
Galmisdale. *High* 5J **63**
Galmpton. *Devn* 5H **5**
Galmpton. *Torb* 4K **5**
Galmpton Warborough. *Torb* 4K **5**
Galphay. *N Yor* 6B **44**
Galston. *E Ayr* 6C **54**
Galton. *Dors* 7G **9**
Galtrigill. *High* 6F **68**
Gamblesby. *Cumb* 8B **50**
Gamelsby. *Cumb* 6K **49**
Gamesley. *Derbs* 6J **39**
Gamlingay. *Cambs* 6L **27**
Gamlingay Cinques. *Cambs* 6L **27**
Gamlingay Great Heath. *C Beds* 6L **27**
Gammaton. *Devn* 3F **6**
Gammersgill. *N Yor* 5M **43**
Gamston. *Notts* 6C **34**
(nr. Nottingham)
Gamston. *Notts* 8D **40**
(nr. Retford)
Ganarew. *Here* 2H **17**
Ganavan. *Arg* 2F **58**
Ganborough. *Glos* 1B **18**
Gang. *Corn* 3E **4**
Ganllwyd. *Gwyn* 7G **31**
Gannochy. *Ang* 6F **66**
Gannochy. *Per* 3G **61**
Gansclet. *High* 5J **77**
Ganstead. *E Yor* 2H **41**
Ganthorpe. *N Yor* 6F **44**
Ganton. *N Yor* 6J **45**
Gants Hill. *G Lon* 5C **20**
Gappah. *Devn* 8K **7**
Garafad. *High* 5J **69**
Garboldisham. *Norf* 3G **29**
Garden City. *Flin* 3A **32**
Gardeners Green. *Wok* 7J **19**
Gardenstown. *Abers* 3J **73**
Garden Village. *S Yor* 6L **39**
Garden Village. *Swan* 4K **15**
Garderhouse. *Shet* 7D **79**
Gardham. *E Yor* 1F **40**
Gardie. *Shet* 5B **79**
(on Papa Stour)
Gardie. *Shet* 1G **79**
(on Unst)
Gardie Ho. *Shet* 7E **79**
Gare Hill. *Som* 1G **9**
Garelochhead. *Arg* 6K **59**
Garford. *Oxon* 4E **18**
Garforth. *W Yor* 2A **40**
Gargrave. *N Yor* 8L **43**
Gargunnock. *Stir* 6C **60**
Garleffin. *S Ayr* 3K **47**
Garlieston. *Dum* 7B **48**
Garlinge Green. *Kent* 8K **21**
Garlogie. *Abers* 3H **67**
Garmelow. *Staf* 7E **32**
Garmond. *Abers* 4J **73**
Garmondsway. *Dur* 8J **51**
Garmony. *Arg* 1D **58**
Garmouth. *Mor* 3D **72**
Garmston. *Shrp* 1G **25**
Garnant. *Carm* 2L **15**
Garndiffaith. *Torf* 3E **16**
Garndolbenmaen. *Gwyn* 5D **30**
Garnett Bridge. *Cumb* 4G **43**
Garnfadryn. *Gwyn* 6B **30**
Garnkirk. *N Lan* 3E **54**
Garnlydan. *Blae* 2D **16**
Garnsgate. *Linc* 7L **35**
Garnswllt. *Swan* 3L **15**
Garn-yr-erw. *Torf* 2E **16**
Garrabost. *W Isl* 5F **74**
Garrallan. *E Ayr* 8D **54**
Garras. *Corn* 7E **3**
Garreg. *Gwyn* 5F **30**
Garrigill. *Cumb* 7C **50**
Garriston. *N Yor* 4A **44**
Garrogie Lodge. *High* 2H **65**
Garros. *High* 5J **69**
Garrow. *Per* 1D **60**
Garsdale. *Cumb* 5J **43**
Garsdale Head. *Cumb* 4J **43**
Garsdon. *Wilts* 5M **17**
Garshall Green. *Staf* 6G **33**
Garsington. *Oxon* 3F **18**
Garstang. *Lanc* 1C **38**
Garston. *Mers* 7C **38**
Garswood. *Mers* 6D **38**
Gartcosh. *N Lan* 3E **54**
Garth. *B'end* 4A **16**
Garth. *Cdgn* 3J **23**
Garth. *Gwyn* 6E **30**
Garth. *IOM* 6D **46**
Garth. *Powy* 7M **23**
(nr. Builth Wells)
Garth. *Powy* 4C **24**
(nr. Knighton)
Garth. *Shet* 6C **79**
(nr. Sandness)
Garth. *Shet* 6E **79**
(nr. Skellister)
Garth. *Wrex* 5M **31**
Garthamlock. *Glas* 3E **54**
Garthbrengy. *Powy* 8A **24**
Gartheli. *Cdgn* 6H **23**
Garthmyl. *Powy* 2B **24**
Garthorpe. *Leics* 7E **34**
Garthorpe. *N Lin* 4E **40**
Garth Owen. *Powy* 2B **24**
Garth Row. *Cumb* 4G **43**
Gartly. *Abers* 6F **72**
Gartmore. *Stir* 6A **60**
Gartness. *N Lan* 3F **54**
Gartness. *Stir* 1D **54**
Gartocharn. *W Dun* 1C **54**
Garton. *E Yor* 2J **41**
Garton-on-the-Wolds. *E Yor* 8J **45**
Gartsherrie. *N Lan* 3F **54**
Gartymore. *High* 8F **76**
Garvald. *E Lot* 2E **56**
Garvamore. *High* 4H **65**
Garvard. *Arg* 6A **58**
Garvault. *High* 6C **76**
Garve. *High* 5F **70**
Garvestone. *Norf* 1G **29**
Garvie. *Arg* 6H **59**
Garvock. *Abers* 6H **67**
Garvock. *Inv* 2A **54**
Garway. *Here* 1G **17**
Garway Common. *Here* 1G **17**
Garway Hill. *Here* 1G **17**
Garwick. *Linc* 5H **35**
Gaskan. *High* 6A **64**
Gasper. *Wilts* 2G **9**
Gastard. *Wilts* 7L **17**
Gasthorpe. *Norf* 3F **28**
Gatcombe. *IOW* 7E **10**
Gateacre. *Mers* 7C **38**
Gatebeck. *Cumb* 5G **43**
Gate Burton. *Linc* 7E **40**
Gateforth. *N Yor* 3B **40**
Gatehead. *E Ayr* 6B **54**
Gate Helmsley. *N Yor* 8F **44**
Gatehouse. *Nmbd* 3C **50**
Gatehouse of Fleet. *Dum* 6D **48**
Gatelawbridge. *Dum* 2G **49**
Gateley. *Norf* 5F **36**
Gatenby. *N Yor* 5C **44**
Gatesgarth. *Cumb* 2C **42**
Gateshead. *Tyne* 5H **51**
Gatesheath. *Ches W* 3B **32**
Gateside. *Ang* 1K **61**
(nr. Forfar)
Gateside. *Ang* 1J **61**
(nr. Kirriemuir)
Gateside. *Fife* 5G **61**
Gateside. *N Ayr* 4B **54**
Gathurst. *G Man* 5D **38**
Gatley. *G Man* 7G **39**
Gatton. *Surr* 8A **20**
Gattonside. *Bord* 6E **56**
Gatwick (London) Airport. *W Sus* 3A **12** & **105**
Gaufron. *Powy* 5M **23**
Gaulby. *Leics* 1E **26**
Gauldry. *Fife* 3J **61**
Gaultree. *Norf* 1A **28**
Gaunt's Common. *Dors* 5A **10**
Gaunt's Earthcott. *S Glo* 5J **17**
Gautby. *Linc* 8H **41**
Gavinton. *Bord* 4G **57**
Gawber. *S Yor* 5M **39**
Gawcott. *Buck* 8E **26**
Gawsworth. *Ches E* 3F **32**
Gawthorpe. *W Yor* 3L **39**
Gawthrop. *Cumb* 5H **43**
Gawthwaite. *Cumb* 5D **42**
Gay Bowers. *Essx* 3F **20**
Gaydon. *Warw* 6B **26**
Gayfield. *Orkn* 2C **78**
Gayhurst. *Mil* 7G **27**
Gayle. *N Yor* 5K **43**
Gayles. *N Yor* 3A **44**
Gay Street. *W Sus* 3L **11**
Gayton. *Mers* 7A **38**
Gayton. *Norf* 6D **36**
Gayton. *Nptn* 6F **26**
Gayton. *Staf* 7G **33**
Gayton le Marsh. *Linc* 7L **41**
Gayton le Wold. *Linc* 7J **41**
Gayton Thorpe. *Norf* 6D **36**
Gaywood. *Norf* 5C **36**
Gazeley. *Suff* 5D **28**
Geanies. *High* 4L **71**
Gearraidh Bhailteas. *W Isl* 1B **62**
Gearraidh Bhaird. *W Isl* 7D **74**
Gearraidh ma Monadh. *W Isl* 2B **62**
Gearraidh na h-Aibhne. *W Isl* 5C **74**
Geary. *High* 5G **69**
Geddes. *High* 6L **71**
Gedding. *Suff* 6F **28**
Geddington. *Nptn* 3G **27**
Gedintailor. *High* 8K **69**
Gedling. *Notts* 5C **34**
Gedney. *Linc* 7L **35**
Gedney Broadgate. *Linc* 7L **35**
Gedney Drove End. *Linc* 7L **35**
Gedney Dyke. *Linc* 7L **35**
Gedney Hill. *Linc* 8K **35**
Gee Cross. *G Man* 6H **39**
Geeston. *Rut* 1H **27**
Geilston. *Arg* 2B **54**
Geirinis. *W Isl* 7B **68**
Geise. *High* 3G **77**
Geisiadar. *W Isl* 5B **74**
Gelder Shiel. *Abers* 5C **66**
Geldeston. *Norf* 2K **29**
Gell. *Cnwy* 3H **31**
Gelli. *Pemb* 2E **14**
Gelli. *Rhon* 4B **16**
Gellifor. *Den* 3L **31**
Gelligaer. *Cphy* 4D **16**
Gellilydan. *Gwyn* 6F **30**
Gellinudd. *Neat* 3M **15**
Gellyburn. *Per* 2F **60**
Gellywen. *Carm* 1G **15**
Gelston. *Dum* 6E **48**
Gelston. *Linc* 5F **34**
Gembling. *E Yor* 8L **45**
Geneva. *Cdgn* 6G **23**
Gentleshaw. *Staf* 8H **33**
Geocrab. *W Isl* 2F **68**
George Green. *Buck* 5K **19**
Georgeham. *Devn* 2F **6**
George Nympton. *Devn* 3J **7**
Georgetown. *Blae* 3D **16**
Georgetown. *Ren* 3C **54**
Georth. *Orkn* 5B **78**
Gerlan. *Gwyn* 3F **30**
Germansweek. *Devn* 6F **6**
Germoe. *Corn* 7C **3**
Gerrans. *Corn* 6F **3**
Gerrard's Bromley. *Staf* 6E **32**
Gerrards Cross. *Buck* 5K **19**
Gerston. *High* 4G **77**
Gestingthorpe. *Essx* 8E **28**
Gethsemane. *Pemb* 7C **22**
Geuffordd. *Powy* 8M **31**
Gibraltar. *Buck* 2H **19**
Gibraltar. *Linc* 4M **35**
Gibraltar. *Suff* 6H **29**
Gibsmere. *Notts* 5D **34**
Giddeahall. *Wilts* 6L **17**
Gidea Park. *G Lon* 5D **20**
Gidleigh. *Devn* 7H **7**
Giffnock. *E Ren* 4D **54**
Gifford. *E Lot* 3E **56**
Giffordtown. *Fife* 4H **61**
Giggetty. *Staf* 2J **25**
Giggleswick. *N Yor* 7K **43**
Gignog. *Pemb* 1C **14**
Gilberdyke. *E Yor* 3E **40**
Gilbert's End. *Worc* 7J **25**
Gilbert's Green. *Warw* 4M **25**
Gilchriston. *E Lot* 3D **56**
Gilcrux. *Cumb* 8J **49**
Gildersome. *W Yor* 3L **39**
Gildingwells. *S Yor* 7B **40**
Gilesgate Moor. *Dur* 7H **51**
Gileston. *V Glam* 7C **16**
Gilfach. *Cphy* 4D **16**
Gilfach Goch. *Rhon* 5B **16**
Gilfachreda. *Cdgn* 6G **23**
Gilgarran. *Cumb* 1B **42**
Gillamoor. *N Yor* 4F **44**
Gillan. *Corn* 7E **3**
Gillar's Green. *Mers* 6C **38**
Gillen. *High* 6G **69**
Gilling East. *N Yor* 6F **44**
Gillingham. *Dors* 3H **9**
Gillingham. *Medw* 7F **20** & **Medway 97**
Gillingham. *Norf* 2L **29**
Gilling West. *N Yor* 3A **44**
Gillock. *High* 4H **77**
Gillow Heath. *Staf* 4F **32**
Gills. *High* 2J **77**
Gill's Green. *Kent* 4F **12**
Gilmanscleuch. *Bord* 7M **55**
Gilmerton. *Edin* 3L **55**
Gilmerton. *Per* 3D **60**
Gilmonby. *Dur* 2L **43**
Gilmorton. *Leics* 3D **26**
Gilsland. *Nmbd* 5B **50**
Gilsland Spa. *Cumb* 5B **50**
Gilston. *Midl* 4D **56**
Giltbrook. *Notts* 5A **34**
Gilwern. *Mon* 2E **16**
Gimingham. *Norf* 4J **37**
Giosla. *W Isl* 6B **74**
Gipping. *Suff* 5G **29**
Gipsey Bridge. *Linc* 5J **35**
Gipton. *W Yor* 2M **39**
Girdle Toll. *N Ayr* 5B **54**
Girlsta. *Shet* 6E **79**
Girsby. *N Yor* 3C **44**
Girthon. *Dum* 6D **48**
Girton. *Cambs* 5A **28**
Girton. *Notts* 3E **34**
Girvan. *S Ayr* 2L **47**
Gisburn. *Lanc* 1G **39**
Gisleham. *Suff* 3M **29**
Gislingham. *Suff* 4G **29**
Gissing. *Norf* 3H **29**
Gittisham. *Devn* 6A **8**
Gladestry. *Powy* 6C **24**
Gladsmuir. *E Lot* 2D **56**
Glaichbea. *High* 8H **71**
Glais. *Swan* 3M **15**
Glaisdale. *N Yor* 3G **45**
Glame. *High* 7K **69**
Glamis. *Ang* 1J **61**
Glanaman. *Carm* 2L **15**
Glan-Conwy. *Cnwy* 4H **31**
Glandford. *Norf* 3G **37**
Glan Duar. *Carm* 7H **23**
Glandwr. *Blae* 3E **16**
Glandwr. *Pemb* 1F **14**
Glan-Dwyfach. *Gwyn* 5D **30**
Glandy Cross. *Carm* 1F **14**
Glandyfi. *Cdgn* 2J **23**
Glangrwyney. *Powy* 2E **16**
Glanmule. *Powy* 2B **24**
Glanrhyd. *Gwyn* 6B **30**
Glanrhyd. *Pemb* 7D **22**
(nr. Cardigan)
Glan-rhyd. *Pemb* 8D **22**
(nr. Crymych)
Glan-rhyd. *Powy* 3M **15**
Glanton. *Nmbd* 8K **57**
Glanton Pyke. *Nmbd* 8K **57**
Glanvilles Wootton. *Dors* 5F **8**
Glan-y-don. *Flin* 2L **31**
Glan-y-nant. *Powy* 3M **23**
Glan-yr-afon. *Gwyn* 5K **31**
Glan-yr-afon. *IOA* 2F **30**
Glan-yr-afon. *Powy* 1A **24**
Glan-y-wern. *Gwyn* 7F **30**
Glapthorn. *Nptn* 2J **27**
Glapwell. *Derbs* 3A **34**
Glas Aird. *Arg* 6A **58**
Glas-allt Shiel. *Abers* 5C **66**
Glasbury. *Powy* 8B **24**
Glaschoil. *High* 6A **72**
Glascoed. *Den* 2J **31**
Glascoed. *Mon* 3F **16**
Glascote. *Staf* 1A **26**
Glascwm. *Powy* 6B **24**
Glasfryn. *Cnwy* 4J **31**
Glasgow. *Glas* 3D **54** & **95**
Glasgow Airport. *Ren* 3C **54** & **105**
Glasgow Prestwick Airport. *S Ayr* 7B **54**
Glashvin. *High* 5J **69**
Glasinfryn. *Gwyn* 3E **30**
Glas na Cardaich. *High* 4L **63**
Glasnacardoch. *High* 4L **63**
Glasnakille. *High* 2K **63**
Glaspwll. *Cdgn* 2K **23**
Glassburn. *High* 8F **70**
Glassenbury. *Kent* 4F **12**
Glasserton. *Dum* 8B **48**
Glassford. *S Lan* 5F **54**
Glassgreen. *Mor* 3C **72**
Glasshouse. *Glos* 1K **17**
Glasshouses. *N Yor* 7A **44**
Glasson. *Cumb* 5K **49**
Glasson. *Lanc* 8F **42**
Glassonby. *Cumb* 8A **50**
Glasterlaw. *Ang* 8F **66**
Glaston. *Rut* 1G **27**
Glastonbury. *Som* 2D **8**
Glatton. *Cambs* 3K **27**
Glazebrook. *Warr* 6E **38**
Glazebury. *Warr* 6E **38**
Glazeley. *Shrp* 3H **25**
Gleadless. *S Yor* 7M **39**
Gleadsmoss. *Ches E* 3F **32**
Gleann Dail bho Dheas. *W Isl* 2B **62**
Gleann Tholastaidh. *W Isl* 4F **74**
Gleann Uige. *High* 6L **63**
Gleaston. *Cumb* 6D **42**
Glecknabae. *Arg* 3J **53**
Gledrid. *Shrp* 6M **31**
Gleiniant. *Powy* 2M **23**
Glemsford. *Suff* 7E **28**
Glen. *Dum* 6C **48**
Glenancross. *High* 4L **63**
Glen Auldyn. *IOM* 4E **46**
Glenbarr. *Arg* 6E **52**
Glenbeg. *High* 7K **63**
Glen Bernisdale. *High* 7J **69**
Glenbervie. *Abers* 5H **67**
Glenboig. *N Lan* 3F **54**
Glenborrodale. *High* 7L **63**
Glenbranter. *Arg* 6J **59**
Glenbreck. *Bord* 7J **55**
Glenbrein Lodge. *High* 2G **65**
Glenbrittle. *High* 1J **63**
Glenbuchat Lodge. *Abers* 2D **66**
Glenbuck. *E Ayr* 7F **54**
Glenburn. *Ren* 3C **54**
Glencalvie Lodge. *High* 3J **71**
Glencaple. *Dum* 5G **49**
Glencarron Lodge. *High* 6C **70**
Glencarse. *Per* 3G **61**
Glencassley Castle. *High* 1G **71**
Glencat. *Abers* 4F **66**
Glencoe. *High* 8D **64**
Glen Cottage. *High* 5L **63**
Glencraig. *Fife* 6G **61**
Glendale. *High* 7F **68**
Glendevon. *Per* 5E **60**
Glendoebeg. *High* 4F **64**
Glendoick. *Per* 3H **61**
Glendoune. *S Ayr* 2L **47**
Glenduckie. *Fife* 4H **61**
Gleneagles. *Per* 5E **60**
Glenegedale. *Arg* 4B **52**
Glenegedale Lots. *Arg* 4B **52**
Glenelg. *High* 2A **64**
Glenernie. *Mor* 5A **72**
Glenesslin. *Dum* 3F **48**
Glenfarg. *Per* 4G **61**
Glenfarquhar Lodge. *Abers* 5H **67**
Glenferness Mains. *High* 7M **71**
Glenfeshie Lodge. *High* 4L **65**
Glenfiddich Lodge. *Mor* 6D **72**
Glenfield. *Leics* 1D **26**
Glenfinnan. *High* 5B **64**
Glenfintaig Lodge. *High* 5E **64**
Glenfoot. *Per* 4G **61**
Glenfyne Lodge. *Arg* 4K **59**
Glengap. *Dum* 6D **48**
Glengarnock. *N Ayr* 4B **54**
Glengolly. *High* 3G **77**
Glengorm Castle. *Arg* 8J **63**
Glengrasco. *High* 7J **69**
Glenhead Farm. *Ang* 7C **66**
Glenholm. *Bord* 6K **55**
Glen House. *Bord* 6L **55**
Glenhurich. *High* 7A **64**
Glenkerry. *Bord* 8L **55**
Glenkiln. *Dum* 4F **48**
Glenkindie. *Abers* 2E **66**
Glenkinglass Lodge. *Arg* 2J **59**
Glenkirk. *Bord* 7J **55**
Glenlean. *Arg* 1J **53**
Glenlee. *Dum* 3D **48**
Glenleraig. *High* 6J **75**
Glenlichorn. *Per* 4C **60**
Glenlivet. *Mor* 1B **66**
Glenlochar. *Dum* 5E **48**
Glenlochsie Lodge. *Per* 6A **66**
Glenluce. *Dum* 6L **47**
Glenmarksie. *High* 6F **70**
Glenmassan. *Arg* 1K **53**
Glenmavis. *N Lan* 3F **54**
Glen Maye. *IOM* 6C **46**
Glenmazeran Lodge. *High* 1K **65**
Glenmidge. *Dum* 3F **48**
Glen Mona. *IOM* 5E **46**
Glenmore. *High* 7K **63**
(nr. Glenborrodale)
Glenmore. *High* 3M **65**
(nr. Kingussie)
Glenmore. *High* 7J **69**
(on Isle of Skye)
Glenmoy. *Ang* 7E **66**
Glennoe. *Arg* 2H **59**
Glen of Coachford. *Abers* 5E **72**
Glenogil. *Ang* 7E **66**
Glen Parva. *Leics* 2D **26**
Glenprosen Village. *Ang* 7D **66**
Glenree. *N Ayr* 7H **53**
Glenridding. *Cumb* 2E **42**
Glenrosa. *N Ayr* 6J **53**
Glenrothes. *Fife* 5H **61**
Glensanda. *High* 1F **58**
Glensaugh. *Abers* 6G **67**
Glenshero Lodge. *High* 4H **65**
Glensluain. *Arg* 6H **59**
Glenstockadale. *Dum* 5K **47**
Glenstriven. *Arg* 2J **53**
Glen Tanar House. *Abers* 4E **66**
Glentham. *Linc* 6G **41**
Glenton. *Abers* 1G **67**
Glentress. *Bord* 6L **55**
Glentromie Lodge. *High* 4K **65**
Glentrool Lodge. *Dum* 3B **48**
Glentrool Village. *Dum* 4A **48**
Glentruim House. *High* 4J **65**
Glentworth. *Linc* 7F **40**
Glenuig. *High* 6L **63**
Glen Village. *Falk* 2G **55**
Glen Vine. *IOM* 6D **46**
Glenwhilly. *Dum* 4L **47**
Glenzierfoot. *Dum* 4L **49**
Glespin. *S Lan* 7G **55**
Gletness. *Shet* 6E **79**
Glewstone. *Here* 1H **17**
Glib Cheois. *W Isl* 6D **74**
Glinton. *Pet* 1K **27**
Glooston. *Leics* 2F **26**
Glossop. *Derbs* 6J **39**
Gloster Hill. *Nmbd* 1H **51**
Gloucester. *Glos* 2L **17** & **95**
Gloucestershire Airport. *Glos* 1L **17**
Gloup. *Shet* 1F **79**
Glusburn. *N Yor* 1J **39**
Glutt Lodge. *High* 6E **76**
Glutton Bridge. *Staf* 3H **33**
Gluvian. *Corn* 3A **4**
Glympton. *Oxon* 1E **18**
Glyn. *Cnwy* 2H **31**
Glynarthen. *Cdgn* 7F **22**
Glynbrochan. *Powy* 3M **23**
Glyn Ceiriog. *Wrex* 6M **31**
Glyncoch. *Rhon* 4C **16**
Glyncorrwg. *Neat* 4A **16**
Glynde. *E Sus* 7C **12**
Glyndebourne. *E Sus* 6C **12**
Glyndyfrdwy. *Den* 5L **31**
Glyn Ebwy. *Blae* 3D **16**
Glynllan. *B'end* 5B **16**
Glyn-neath. *Neat* 3A **16**
Glynogwr. *B'end* 5B **16**
Glyntaff. *Rhon* 5C **16**
Glyntawe. *Powy* 2A **16**
Glynteg. *Carm* 8F **22**
Gnosall. *Staf* 7F **32**
Gnosall Heath. *Staf* 7F **32**
Goadby. *Leics* 2F **26**
Goadby Marwood. *Leics* 7D **34**
Goatacre. *Wilts* 6A **18**
Goathill. *Dors* 4F **8**
Goathland. *N Yor* 3H **45**
Goathurst. *Som* 2B **8**
Goathurst Common. *Kent* 8C **20**
Goat Lees. *Kent* 3J **13**
Gobernuisgach Lodge. *High* 5M **75**
Gobernuisgeach. *High* 6E **76**
Gobhaig. *W Isl* 1E **68**
Gobowen. *Shrp* 6A **32**
Godalming. *Surr* 1K **11**
Goddard's Corner. *Suff* 5J **29**
Goddard's Green. *Kent* 4G **13**
(nr. Benenden)
Goddard's Green. *Kent* 4F **12**
(nr. Cranbrook)
Goddards Green. *W Sus* 5A **12**
Godford Cross. *Devn* 5A **8**
Godleybrook. *Staf* 5G **33**
Godmanchester. *Cambs* 4L **27**
Godmanstone. *Dors* 6F **8**
Godmersham. *Kent* 8J **21**
Godolphin Cross. *Corn* 6D **3**
Godre'r-graig. *Neat* 3M **15**
Godshill. *Hants* 4B **10**
Godshill. *IOW* 7F **10**
Godstone. *Staf* 6H **33**
Godstone. *Surr* 8B **20**
Goetre. *Mon* 3F **16**
Goff's Oak. *Herts* 3B **20**
Gogar. *Edin* 2K **55**
Goginan. *Cdgn* 3J **23**
Golan. *Gwyn* 5E **30**
Golant. *Corn* 4C **4**
Golberdon. *Corn* 8E **6**
Golborne. *G Man* 6E **38**
Golcar. *W Yor* 4J **39**
Goldcliff. *Newp* 5F **16**
Golden Cross. *E Sus* 6D **12**
Golden Green. *Kent* 3E **12**
Golden Grove. *Carm* 2K **15**
Golden Grove. *N Yor* 3H **45**
Golden Hill. *Pemb* 1D **14**
Goldenhill. *Stoke* 4F **32**
Golden Pot. *Hants* 1H **11**
Golden Valley. *Glos* 1M **17**
Golders Green. *G Lon* 5A **20**
Goldhanger. *Essx* 3H **21**
Gold Hill. *Norf* 2B **28**
Golding. *Shrp* 1F **24**
Goldington. *Bed* 6J **27**
Goldsborough. *N Yor* 8C **44**
(nr. Harrogate)
Goldsborough. *N Yor* 2H **45**
(nr. Whitby)
Goldsithney. *Corn* 6C **3**
Goldstone. *Kent* 7L **21**
Goldstone. *Shrp* 7E **32**
Goldthorpe. *S Yor* 5A **40**
Goldworthy. *Devn* 3E **6**
Golfa. *Powy* 7L **31**
Gollanfield. *High* 6L **71**
Gollinglith Foot. *N Yor* 5A **44**
Golsoncott. *Som* 2M **7**
Golspie. *High* 2L **71**
Gomeldon. *Wilts* 2B **10**
Gomersal. *W Yor* 3L **39**
Gometra House. *Arg* 1A **58**
Gomshall. *Surr* 1L **11**
Gonalston. *Notts* 5C **34**
Gonerby Hill Foot. *Linc* 6F **34**
Gonfirth. *Shet* 5D **79**
Good Easter. *Essx* 2E **20**
Gooderstone. *Norf* 1D **28**
Goodleigh. *Devn* 2H **7**
Goodmanham. *E Yor* 1E **40**
Goodmayes. *G Lon* 5C **20**
Goodnestone. *Kent* 8L **21**
(nr. Aylesham)
Goodnestone. *Kent* 7J **21**
(nr. Faversham)
Goodrich. *Here* 2H **17**
Goodrington. *Torb* 4K **5**
Goodshaw. *Lanc* 3G **39**
Goodshaw Fold. *Lanc* 3G **39**
Goodstone. *Devn* 8J **7**
Goodwick. *Pemb* 8B **22**
Goodworth Clatford. *Hants* 1D **10**
Goole. *E Yor* 3D **40**
Goom's Hill. *Worc* 6L **25**
Goonabarn. *Corn* 4A **4**
Goonbell. *Corn* 5E **3**
Goonhavern. *Corn* 4E **3**
Goonvrea. *Corn* 5E **3**
Goose Green. *Cumb* 5G **43**
Goose Green. *S Glo* 5K **17**
Gooseham. *Corn* 4D **6**
Goosewell. *Plym* 4G **5**
Goosey. *Oxon* 4D **18**
Goosnargh. *Lanc* 2D **38**
Goostrey. *Ches E* 8F **38**
Gorcott Hill. *Warw* 5L **25**
Gord. *Shet* 9E **79**
Gordon. *Bord* 5F **56**
Gordonbush. *High* 1L **71**
Gordonstown. *Abers* 4F **72**
(nr. Cornhill)
Gordonstown. *Abers* 6H **73**
(nr. Fyvie)
Gorebridge. *Midl* 3M **55**
Gorefield. *Cambs* 8L **35**
Gores. *Wilts* 8B **18**
Gorgie. *Edin* 2L **55**
Goring. *Oxon* 5G **19**
Goring-by-Sea. *W Sus* 5M **11**
Goring Heath. *Oxon* 6G **19**
Gorleston-on-Sea. *Norf* 1M **29**
Gornalwood. *W Mid* 2K **25**
Gorran Churchtown. *Corn* 5A **4**
Gorran Haven. *Corn* 5B **4**
Gorran High Lanes. *Corn* 5A **4**
Gors. *Cdgn* 4J **23**
Gorsedd. *Flin* 2L **31**
Gorseinon. *Swan* 4K **15**
Gorseness. *Orkn* 6C **78**
Gorseybank. *Derbs* 4K **33**
Gorsgoch. *Cdgn* 6G **23**
Gorslas. *Carm* 2K **15**
Gorsley. *Glos* 1J **17**
Gorsley Common. *Here* 1J **17**
Gorstan. *High* 5F **70**
Gorstella. *Ches W* 3A **32**
Gorsty Common. *Here* 8E **24**
Gorsty Hill. *Staf* 7H **33**
Gortantaoid. *Arg* 2B **52**
Gorteneorn. *High* 7L **63**
Gortenfern. *High* 7L **63**
Gorton. *G Man* 6G **39**
Gosbeck. *Suff* 6H **29**
Gosberton. *Linc* 6J **35**
Gosberton Cheal. *Linc* 7J **35**
Gosberton Clough. *Linc* 7H **35**
Goseley Dale. *Derbs* 7L **33**
Gosfield. *Essx* 1F **20**
Gosford. *Oxon* 2F **18**
Gosforth. *Cumb* 3B **42**
Gosforth. *Tyne* 5H **51**
Gosmore. *Herts* 1M **19**
Gospel End Village. *Staf* 2J **25**
Gosport. *Hants* 5G **11**
Gossabrough. *Shet* 3F **79**
Gossington. *Glos* 3K **17**
Gossops Green. *W Sus* 4A **12**
Goswick. *Nmbd* 5K **57**
Gotham. *Notts* 6B **34**
Gotherington. *Glos* 1M **17**
Gott. *Arg* 8B **62**
Gott. *Shet* 7E **79**
Goudhurst. *Kent* 4F **12**
Goulceby. *Linc* 8J **41**
Gourdon. *Abers* 6J **67**
Gourock. *Inv* 2A **54**
Govan. *Glas* 3D **54**
Govanhill. *Glas* 3D **54**
Goverton. *Notts* 5D **34**
Goveton. *Devn* 5J **5**
Govilon. *Mon* 2E **16**
Gowanhill. *Abers* 3L **73**
Gowdall. *E Yor* 3C **40**
Gowerton. *Swan* 4K **15**
Gowkhall. *Fife* 1J **55**
Gowthorpe. *E Yor* 8G **45**
Goxhill. *E Yor* 1H **41**
Goxhill. *N Lin* 3H **41**
Goxhill Haven. *N Lin* 3H **41**
Goytre. *Neat* 5M **15**
Grabhair. *W Isl* 7D **74**
Graby. *Linc* 7G **35**
Graffham. *W Sus* 4K **11**
Grafham. *Cambs* 5K **27**
Grafham. *Surr* 1L **11**
Grafton. *Here* 8E **24**
Grafton. *N Yor* 7D **44**
Grafton. *Oxon* 3C **18**
Grafton. *Shrp* 8B **32**
Grafton. *Worc* 8K **25**
(nr. Evesham)
Grafton. *Worc* 5F **24**
(nr. Leominster)
Grafton Flyford. *Worc* 6K **25**
Grafton Regis. *Nptn* 7F **26**
Grafton Underwood. *Nptn* 3H **27**
Grafty Green. *Kent* 3G **13**
Graianrhyd. *Den* 4M **31**
Graig. *Carm* 3J **15**
Graig. *Cnwy* 2H **31**
Graig. *Den* 2K **31**
Graig-fechan. *Den* 4L **31**
Graig Penllyn. *V Glam* 6B **16**
Grain. *Medw* 6G **21**
Grainsby. *Linc* 6J **41**
Grainthorpe. *Linc* 6K **41**
Grainthorpe Fen. *Linc* 6K **41**
Graiselound. *N Lin* 6D **40**
Gramasdail. *W Isl* 6C **68**
Grampound. *Corn* 5A **4**
Grampound Road. *Corn* 4A **4**
Granborough. *Buck* 1H **19**
Granby. *Notts* 6D **34**
Grandborough. *Warw* 5C **26**
Grandpont. *Oxon* 3F **18**
Grandtully. *Per* 8M **65**
Grange. *Cumb* 2D **42**
Grange. *E Ayr* 6C **54**
Grange. *Here* 4E **24**
Grange. *Mers* 7A **38**
Grange. *Per* 3H **61**
Grange Crossroads. *Mor* 4E **72**
Grange Hill. *G Lon* 4C **20**
Grangemill. *Derbs* 4K **33**
Grange Moor. *W Yor* 4L **39**
Grangemouth. *Falk* 1H **55**
Grange of Lindores. *Fife* 4H **61**
Grange-over-Sands. *Cumb* 6F **42**
Grangepans. *Falk* 1J **55**
Grange, The. *N Yor* 4E **44**
Grangetown. *Card* 6D **16**
Grangetown. *Red C* 1E **44**
Grange Villa. *Dur* 6H **51**
Granish. *High* 2L **65**
Gransmoor. *E Yor* 8L **45**
Granston. *Pemb* 8A **22**
Grantchester. *Cambs* 6A **28**
Grantham. *Linc* 6F **34**
Grantley. *N Yor* 7B **44**
Grantlodge. *Abers* 2H **67**
Granton. *Edin* 2L **55**
Grantown-on-Spey. *High* 1A **66**
Grantshouse. *Bord* 3H **57**
Grappenhall. *Warr* 7E **38**
Grasby. *Linc* 5G **41**
Grasmere. *Cumb* 3E **42**
Grasscroft. *G Man* 5H **39**
Grassendale. *Mers* 7B **38**
Grassgarth. *Cumb* 7L **49**
Grassholme. *Dur* 1L **43**
Grassington. *N Yor* 7M **43**
Grassmoor. *Derbs* 3A **34**
Grassthorpe. *Notts* 3D **34**
Grateley. *Hants* 1C **10**
Gratton. *Devn* 4E **6**
Gratton. *Staf* 4G **33**
Gratwich. *Staf* 6H **33**
Graveley. *Cambs* 5L **27**
Graveley. *Herts* 1A **20**
Gravelhill. *Shrp* 8B **32**
Gravel Hole. *G Man* 5H **39**
Gravelly Hill. *W Mid* 2M **25**
Graven. *Shet* 4E **79**
Graveney. *Kent* 7J **21**
Gravesend. *Kent* 6E **20**
Grayingham. *Linc* 6F **40**
Grayrigg. *Cumb* 4G **43**
Grays. *Thur* 6E **20**
Grayshott. *Hants* 2J **11**
Grayson Green. *Cumb* 1A **42**
Grayswood. *Surr* 2K **11**
Graythorp. *Hart* 1E **44**
Grazeley. *Wok* 7G **19**
Grealin. *High* 5K **69**
Greasbrough. *S Yor* 6A **40**
Greasby. *Mers* 7A **38**
Great Abington. *Cambs* 7B **28**
Great Addington. *Nptn* 4H **27**
Great Alne. *Warw* 6M **25**
Great Altcar. *Lanc* 5B **38**
Great Amwell. *Herts* 2B **20**
Great Asby. *Cumb* 2H **43**
Great Ashfield. *Suff* 5F **28**
Great Ayton. *N Yor* 2E **44**
Great Baddow. *Essx* 3F **20**
Great Bardfield. *Essx* 8C **28**
Great Barford. *Bed* 6K **27**
Great Barr. *W Mid* 2L **25**
Great Barrington. *Glos* 2C **18**
Great Barrow. *Ches W* 3B **32**
Great Barton. *Suff* 5E **28**
Great Barugh. *N Yor* 6G **45**
Great Bavington. *Nmbd* 3E **50**
Great Bealings. *Suff* 7J **29**
Great Bedwyn. *Wilts* 7C **18**
Great Bentley. *Essx* 1K **21**
Great Billing. *Nptn* 5G **27**
Great Bircham. *Norf* 4D **36**
Great Blakenham. *Suff* 6H **29**
Great Blencow. *Cumb* 8M **49**
Great Bolas. *Telf* 7D **32**
Great Bookham. *Surr* 8M **19**
Great Bosullow. *Corn* 6B **3**
Great Bourton. *Oxon* 7C **26**
Great Bowden. *Leics* 3F **26**
Great Bradley. *Suff* 6C **28**
Great Braxted. *Essx* 2G **21**
Great Bricett. *Suff* 6G **29**
Great Brickhill. *Buck* 8H **27**
Great Bridgeford. *Staf* 7F **32**
Great Brington. *Nptn* 5E **26**
Great Bromley. *Essx* 1J **21**
Great Broughton. *Cumb* 8H **49**
Great Broughton. *N Yor* 3E **44**
Great Budworth. *Ches W* 8E **38**
Great Burdon. *Darl* 2C **44**
Great Burstead. *Essx* 4E **20**
Great Busby. *N Yor* 3E **44**
Great Canfield. *Essx* 2D **20**
Great Carlton. *Linc* 7L **41**
Great Casterton. *Rut* 1J **27**
Great Chalfield. *Wilts* 7L **17**
Great Chart. *Kent* 3H **13**
Great Chatwell. *Staf* 8E **32**
Great Chesterford. *Essx* 7B **28**
Great Cheverell. *Wilts* 8M **17**
Great Chilton. *Dur* 8H **51**
Great Chishill. *Cambs* 8A **28**
Great Clacton. *Essx* 2K **21**
Great Cliff. *W Yor* 4M **39**
Great Clifton. *Cumb* 1B **42**
Great Coates. *NE Lin* 4J **41**
Great Comberton. *Worc* 7K **25**
Great Corby. *Cumb* 6M **49**
Great Cornard. *Suff* 7E **28**
Great Cowden. *E Yor* 1J **41**
Great Coxwell. *Oxon* 4C **18**
Great Crakehall. *N Yor* 5B **44**
Great Cransley. *Nptn* 4G **27**
Great Cressingham. *Norf* 1E **28**
Great Crosby. *Mers* 6B **38**
Great Cubley. *Derbs* 6J **33**
Great Dalby. *Leics* 8D **34**
Great Doddington. *Nptn* 5G **27**
Great Doward. *Here* 2H **17**
Great Dunham. *Norf* 6E **36**
Great Dunmow. *Essx* 1E **20**
Great Durnford. *Wilts* 2B **10**
Great Easton. *Essx* 1E **20**
Great Easton. *Leics* 2G **27**
Great Eccleston. *Lanc* 1C **38**
Great Edstone. *N Yor* 5G **45**
Great Ellingham. *Norf* 2G **29**
Great Elm. *Som* 1G **9**
Great Eppleton. *Tyne* 7J **51**
Great Eversden. *Cambs* 6M **27**
Great Fencote. *N Yor* 4B **44**
Great Finborough. *Suff* 6G **29**
Greatford. *Linc* 8G **35**
Great Fransham. *Norf* 6E **36**
Great Gaddesden. *Herts* 2L **19**
Great Gate. *Staf* 5H **33**
Great Gidding. *Cambs* 3K **27**
Great Givendale. *E Yor* 8H **45**
Great Glemham. *Suff* 5K **29**
Great Glen. *Leics* 2E **26**
Great Gonerby. *Linc* 6F **34**
Great Gransden. *Cambs* 6L **27**
Great Green. *Norf* 3J **29**
Great Green. *Suff* 6F **28**
(nr. Lavenham)
Great Green. *Suff* 4H **29**
(nr. Palgrave)
Great Habton. *N Yor* 6G **45**
Great Hale. *Linc* 5H **35**
Great Hallingbury. *Essx* 2D **20**
Greatham. *Hants* 2H **11**
Greatham. *Hart* 1D **44**
Greatham. *W Sus* 4L **11**
Great Hampden. *Buck* 3J **19**
Great Harrowden. *Nptn* 4G **27**
Great Harwood. *Lanc* 2F **38**
Great Haseley. *Oxon* 3G **19**
Great Hatfield. *E Yor* 1H **41**
Great Haywood. *Staf* 7G **33**
Great Heath. *W Mid* 3B **26**
Great Heck. *N Yor* 3B **40**
Great Henny. *Essx* 8E **28**
Great Hinton. *Wilts* 8M **17**
Great Hockham. *Norf* 2F **28**
Great Holland. *Essx* 2L **21**
Great Horkesley. *Essx* 8F **28**
Great Hormead. *Herts* 8A **28**
Great Horton. *W Yor* 2K **39**
Great Horwood. *Buck* 8F **26**
Great Houghton. *Nptn* 6F **26**
Great Houghton. *S Yor* 5A **40**
Great Hucklow. *Derbs* 8K **39**
Great Kelk. *E Yor* 8L **45**
Great Kendale. *E Yor* 7K **45**
Great Kimble. *Buck* 3J **19**
Great Kingshill. *Buck* 4J **19**
Great Langdale. *Cumb* 3D **42**
Great Langton. *N Yor* 4B **44**
Great Leighs. *Essx* 2F **20**
Great Limber. *Linc* 5H **41**
Great Linford. *Mil* 7G **27**
Great Livermere. *Suff* 4E **28**
Great Longstone. *Derbs* 8L **39**
Great Lumley. *Dur* 7H **51**
Great Lyth. *Shrp* 1E **24**
Great Malvern. *Worc* 7H **25**
Great Maplestead. *Essx* 8E **28**
Great Marton. *Bkpl* 2B **38**
Great Massingham. *Norf* 5D **36**
Great Melton. *Norf* 1H **29**
Great Milton. *Oxon* 3G **19**
Great Missenden. *Buck* 3J **19**
Great Mitton. *Lanc* 2F **38**
Great Mongeham. *Kent* 8M **21**
Great Moulton. *Norf* 2H **29**
Great Munden. *Herts* 1B **20**
Great Musgrave. *Cumb* 2J **43**
Great Ness. *Shrp* 8A **32**
Great Notley. *Essx* 1F **20**
Great Oak. *Mon* 3F **16**
Great Oakley. *Essx* 1K **21**
Great Oakley. *Nptn* 3G **27**
Great Offley. *Herts* 1M **19**
Great Ormside. *Cumb* 2J **43**
Great Orton. *Cumb* 6L **49**
Great Ouseburn. *N Yor* 7D **44**
Great Oxendon. *Nptn* 3F **26**
Great Oxney Green. *Essx* 3E **20**
Great Parndon. *Essx* 3C **20**
Great Paxton. *Cambs* 5L **27**
Great Plumpton. *Lanc* 2B **38**
Great Plumstead. *Norf* 6K **37**
Great Ponton. *Linc* 6F **34**
Great Potheridge. *Devn* 4G **7**
Great Preston. *W Yor* 3A **40**
Great Raveley. *Cambs* 3L **27**
Great Rissington. *Glos* 2B **18**
Great Rollright. *Oxon* 8B **26**
Great Ryburgh. *Norf* 5F **36**
Great Ryle. *Nmbd* 8K **57**
Great Ryton. *Shrp* 1E **24**
Great Saling. *Essx* 1E **20**
Great Salkeld. *Cumb* 8A **50**
Great Sampford. *Essx* 8C **28**
Great Sankey. *Warr* 7D **38**
Great Saredon. *Staf* 1K **25**
Great Saxham. *Suff* 5D **28**
Great Shefford. *W Ber* 6D **18**
Great Shelford. *Cambs* 6A **28**
Great Shoddesden. *Hants* 1C **10**
Great Smeaton. *N Yor* 3C **44**
Great Snoring. *Norf* 4F **36**
Great Somerford. *Wilts* 5M **17**
Great Stainton. *Darl* 1C **44**
Great Stambridge. *Essx* 4G **21**
Great Staughton. *Cambs* 5K **27**
Great Steeping. *Linc* 3L **35**
Great Stonar. *Kent* 8M **21**
Greatstone-on-Sea. *Kent* 5J **13**
Great Strickland. *Cumb* 1G **43**
Great Stukeley. *Cambs* 4L **27**
Great Sturton. *Linc* 8J **41**
Great Sutton. *Ches W* 8B **38**
Great Sutton. *Shrp* 3F **24**
Great Swinburne. *Nmbd* 4E **50**
Great Tew. *Oxon* 1D **18**
Great Tey. *Essx* 1G **21**
Great Thirkleby. *N Yor* 6D **44**
Great Thorness. *IOW* 6E **10**
Great Thurlow. *Suff* 6C **28**
Great Torr. *Devn* 5H **5**
Great Torrington. *Devn* 4F **6**
Great Tosson. *Nmbd* 1F **50**
Great Totham North. *Essx* 2G **21**
Great Totham South. *Essx* 2G **21**
Great Tows. *Linc* 6J **41**
Great Urswick. *Cumb* 6D **42**
Great Wakering. *Essx* 5H **21**
Great Waldingfield. *Suff* 7F **28**
Great Walsingham. *Norf* 4F **36**
Great Waltham. *Essx* 2E **20**
Great Warley. *Essx* 4D **20**
Great Washbourne. *Glos* 8K **25**
Great Wenham. *Suff* 8G **29**
Great Whelnetham. *Suff* 6E **28**
Great Whittington. *Nmbd* 4F **50**
Great Wigborough. *Essx* 2H **21**
Great Wilbraham. *Cambs* 6B **28**
Great Wilne. *Derbs* 6A **34**
Great Wishford. *Wilts* 2A **10**
Great Witchingham. *Norf* 5H **37**
Great Witcombe. *Glos* 2M **17**
Great Witley. *Worc* 5H **25**
Great Wolford. *Warw* 8A **26**
Greatworth. *Nptn* 7D **26**
Great Wratting. *Suff* 7C **28**
Great Wymondley. *Herts* 1A **20**
Great Wyrley. *Staf* 1K **25**
Great Wytheford. *Shrp* 8C **32**
Great Yarmouth. *Norf* 1M **29**
Great Yeldham. *Essx* 8D **28**
Grebby. *Linc* 3L **35**
Greeba Castle. *IOM* 5D **46**
Greenbank. *Shet* 1F **79**
Greenbottom. *Corn* 5E **3**
Greenburn. *W Lot* 3H **55**
Greencroft. *Dur* 6G **51**
Greencroft Park. *Dur* 7G **51**
Greendown. *Som* 8H **17**
Greendykes. *Nmbd* 7K **57**
Green End. *Bed* 7J **27**
(nr. Bedford)
Green End. *Bed* 5K **27**
(nr. St Neots)
Green End. *Herts* 8M **27**
(nr. Buntingford)
Green End. *Herts* 1B **20**
(nr. Stevenage)
Green End. *N Yor* 3H **45**
Green End. *Warw* 3A **26**
Greenfield. *Arg* 6K **59**
Greenfield. *C Beds* 8J **27**
Greenfield. *Flin* 2L **31**
Greenfield. *G Man* 5H **39**
Greenfield. *Oxon* 4H **19**
Greenfoot. *N Lan* 3F **54**
Greenford. *G Lon* 5M **19**
Greengairs. *N Lan* 2F **54**
Greengate. *Norf* 6G **37**
Greengill. *Cumb* 8J **49**
Greenhalgh. *Lanc* 2C **38**
Greenham. *Dors* 5D **8**
Greenham. *Som* 3M **7**
Greenham. *W Ber* 7E **18**
Green Hammerton. *N Yor* 8D **44**
Greenhaugh. *Nmbd* 3C **50**
Greenhead. *Nmbd* 5B **50**
Green Heath. *Staf* 8G **33**
Greenhill. *Dum* 4J **49**
Greenhill. *Falk* 2G **55**
Greenhill. *Kent* 7K **21**
Greenhill. *S Yor* 7M **39**
Greenhill. *Worc* 4J **25**
Greenhills. *N Ayr* 4B **54**
Greenhithe. *Kent* 6D **20**
Greenholm. *E Ayr* 6D **54**
Greenhow Hill. *N Yor* 7A **44**
Greenigoe. *Orkn* 7C **78**
Greenland. *High* 3H **77**
Greenland Mains. *High* 3H **77**
Greenlands. *Worc* 5L **25**
Green Lane. *Shrp* 7D **32**
Green Lane. *Warw* 5L **25**
Greenlaw. *Bord* 5G **57**
Greenlea. *Dum* 4H **49**
Greenloaning. *Per* 5D **60**
Greenmount. *G Man* 4F **38**
Greenmow. *Shet* 9E **79**
Greenock. *Inv* 2A **54**
Greenock Mains. *E Ayr* 7E **54**
Greenodd. *Cumb* 5E **42**
Green Ore. *Som* 8H **17**
Greenrow. *Cumb* 6J **49**
Greens. *Abers* 5J **73**
Greensgate. *Norf* 6H **37**
Greenside. *Tyne* 5G **51**
Greensidehill. *Nmbd* 8J **57**
Greens Norton. *Nptn* 7E **26**
Greenstead Green. *Essx* 1G **21**
Greensted Green. *Essx* 3D **20**
Green Street. *Herts* 4M **19**
Green Street. *Suff* 4H **29**
Green Street Green. *G Lon* 7C **20**
Green Street Green. *Kent* 6D **20**
Greenstreet Green. *Suff* 7G **29**
Green, The. *Cumb* 5C **42**
Green, The. *Wilts* 2H **9**
Green Tye. *Herts* 2C **20**
Greenwall. *Orkn* 7D **78**
Greenway. *Pemb* 1E **14**
Greenway. *V Glam* 6C **16**
Greenwell. *Cumb* 6A **50**
Greenwich. *G Lon* 6B **20**
Greet. *Glos* 8L **25**
Greete. *Shrp* 4F **24**
Greetham. *Linc* 8K **41**
Greetham. *Rut* 8F **34**
Greetland. *W Yor* 3J **39**
Gregson Lane. *Lanc* 3D **38**
Grein. *W Isl* 3A **62**
Greinetobht. *W Isl* 4C **68**
Greinton. *Som* 2D **8**
Gremista. *Shet* 7E **79**
Grenaby. *IOM* 6C **46**
Grendon. *Nptn* 5G **27**
Grendon. *Warw* 2A **26**
Grendon Common. *Warw* 2A **26**
Grendon Green. *Here* 6F **24**
Grendon Underwood. *Buck* 1G **19**
Grenofen. *Devn* 8F **6**
Grenoside. *S Yor* 6M **39**
Greosabhagh. *W Isl* 2F **68**
Gresford. *Wrex* 4A **32**
Gresham. *Norf* 4H **37**
Greshornish. *High* 6H **69**
Gressenhall. *Norf* 6F **36**
Gressingham. *Lanc* 6G **43**
Greta Bridge. *Dur* 2M **43**
Gretna. *Dum* 5L **49**
Gretna Green. *Dum* 5L **49**
Gretton. *Glos* 8L **25**
Gretton. *Nptn* 2H **27**
Gretton. *Shrp* 2F **24**
Grewelthorpe. *N Yor* 6B **44**
Greygarth. *N Yor* 6A **44**
Grey Green. *N Lin* 5D **40**
Greylake. *Som* 2C **8**
Greysouthen. *Cumb* 1B **42**
Greystoke. *Cumb* 8M **49**
Greystoke Gill. *Cumb* 1F **42**
Greystone. *Ang* 1L **61**
Greystones. *S Yor* 7M **39**
Greywell. *Hants* 8H **19**
Griais. *W Isl* 4E **74**
Grianan. *W Isl* 5E **74**
Gribthorpe. *E Yor* 2D **40**
Gribun. *Arg* 2B **58**
Griff. *Warw* 3B **26**
Griffithstown. *Torf* 4E **16**
Griffydam. *Leics* 8A **34**
Griggs Green. *Hants* 2J **11**
Grimbister. *Orkn* 6B **78**
Grimeford Village. *Lanc* 4E **38**
Grimeston. *Orkn* 6B **78**
Grimethorpe. *S Yor* 5A **40**
Griminis. *W Isl* 6B **68**
(on Benbecula)
Griminis. *W Isl* 4B **68**
(on North Uist)
Grimister. *Shet* 2E **79**
Grimley. *Worc* 5J **25**
Grimness. *Orkn* 8C **78**
Grimoldby. *Linc* 7K **41**
Grimpo. *Shrp* 7A **32**
Grimsargh. *Lanc* 2D **38**
Grimsbury. *Oxon* 7C **26**
Grimsby. *NE Lin* 4J **41**
Grimscote. *Nptn* 6E **26**
Grimscott. *Corn* 5D **6**
Grimshaw. *Bkbn* 3F **38**
Grimshaw Green. *Lanc* 4C **38**
Grimsthorpe. *Linc* 7G **35**
Grimston. *E Yor* 2J **41**
Grimston. *Leics* 7C **34**
Grimston. *Norf* 5D **36**
Grimston. *York* 8F **44**
Grimstone. *Dors* 6F **8**
Grimstone End. *Suff* 5F **28**
Grinacombe Moor. *Devn* 6F **6**
Grindale. *E Yor* 6L **45**
Grindhill. *Devn* 6F **6**
Grindiscol. *Shet* 8E **79**
Grindle. *Shrp* 1H **25**
Grindleford. *Derbs* 8L **39**
Grindleton. *Lanc* 1F **38**
Grindley. *Staf* 7H **33**
Grindley Brook. *Shrp* 5C **32**
Grindlow. *Derbs* 8K **39**
Grindon. *Nmbd* 5J **57**
Grindon. *Staf* 4H **33**
Gringley on the Hill. *Notts* 6D **40**
Grinsdale. *Cumb* 6L **49**
Grinshill. *Shrp* 7C **32**
Grinton. *N Yor* 4M **43**
Griomsidar. *W Isl* 6E **74**
Grishipoll. *Arg* 8F **62**
Grisling Common. *E Sus* 5C **12**
Gristhorpe. *N Yor* 5K **45**
Griston. *Norf* 2F **28**
Gritley. *Orkn* 7D **78**
Grittenham. *Wilts* 5A **18**
Grittleton. *Wilts* 6L **17**
Grizebeck. *Cumb* 5D **42**
Grizedale. *Cumb* 4E **42**
Grobister. *Orkn* 5E **78**
Grobsness. *Shet* 5D **79**
Groby. *Leics* 1D **26**
Groes. *Cnwy* 3K **31**
Groes. *Neat* 5M **15**
Groes-faen. *Rhon* 5C **16**
Groesffordd. *Gwyn* 6B **30**
Groesffordd. *Powy* 1C **16**
Groeslon. *Gwyn* 4D **30**
Groes-lwyd. *Powy* 8M **31**
Groes-wen. *Cphy* 5D **16**
Grogport. *Arg* 5G **53**
Groigearraidh. *W Isl* 7B **68**
Gromford. *Suff* 6K **29**
Gronant. *Flin* 1K **31**
Groombridge. *E Sus* 4D **12**
Grosmont. *Mon* 1G **17**
Grosmont. *N Yor* 3H **45**
Groton. *Suff* 7F **28**
Grove. *Dors* 8G **9**
Grove. *Kent* 7L **21**
Grove. *Notts* 8D **40**
Grove. *Oxon* 4D **18**
Grovehill. *E Yor* 2G **41**
Grove Park. *G Lon* 6C **20**
Grovesend. *Swan* 3K **15**
Grove, The. *Dum* 4G **49**
Grove, The. *Worc* 7J **25**
Grub Street. *Staf* 7E **32**
Grudie. *High* 5F **70**
Gruids. *High* 1H **71**
Gruinard House. *High* 2B **70**
Gruinart. *Arg* 3A **52**
Grulinbeg. *Arg* 3A **52**
Gruline. *Arg* 1C **58**
Grummore. *High* 6B **76**
Grundisburgh. *Suff* 6J **29**
Gruting. *Shet* 7C **79**
Grutness. *Shet* 10E **79**
Gualachulain. *High* 1J **59**
Gualin House. *High* 4L **75**
Guardbridge. *Fife* 4K **61**
Guarlford. *Worc* 7J **25**
Guay. *Per* 1F **60**
Gubblecote. *Herts* 2K **19**
Guestling Green. *E Sus* 6G **13**
Guestling Thorn. *E Sus* 6G **13**
Guestwick. *Norf* 5G **37**
Guestwick Green. *Norf* 5G **37**
Guide. *Bkbn* 3F **38**
Guide Post. *Nmbd* 3H **51**
Guilden Down. *Shrp* 3D **24**
Guilden Morden. *Cambs* 7L **27**
Guilden Sutton. *Ches W* 3B **32**
Guildford. *Surr* 1K **11** & **95**
Guildtown. *Per* 2G **61**
Guilsborough. *Nptn* 4E **26**
Guilsfield. *Powy* 8M **31**
Guineaford. *Devn* 2G **7**
Guisborough. *Red C* 2F **44**
Guiseley. *W Yor* 1K **39**

Guist—Highwood

Guist. *Norf* 5F **36**
Guiting Power. *Glos* 1A **18**
Gulberwick. *Shet* 8E **79**
Gullane. *E Lot* 1D **56**
Gulling Green. *Suff* 6E **28**
Gulval. *Corn* 6B **3**
Gumfreston. *Pemb* 3F **14**
Gumley. *Leics* 2E **26**
Gunby. *E Yor* 2D **40**
Gunby. *Linc* 7F **34**
Gundleton. *Hants* 2G **11**
Gun Green. *Kent* 4F **12**
Gun Hill. *E Sus* 6D **12**
Gunn. *Devn* 2H **7**
Gunnerside. *N Yor* 4L **43**
Gunnerton. *Nmbd* 4E **50**
Gunness. *N Lin* 4E **40**
Gunnislake. *Corn* 8F **6**
Gunnista. *Shet* 7E **79**
Gunsgreenhill. *Bord* 3J **57**
Gunstone. *Staf* 1J **25**
Gunthorpe. *Norf* 4G **37**
Gunthorpe. *N Lin* 6E **40**
Gunthorpe. *Notts* 5C **34**
Gunthorpe. *Pet* 1K **27**
Gunville. *IOW* 7E **10**
Gupworthy. *Som* 2L **7**
Gurnard. *IOW* 6E **10**
Gurney Slade. *Som* 1F **8**
Gurnos. *Powy* 3M **15**
Gussage All Saints. *Dors* 4A **10**
Gussage St Andrew. *Dors* 4J **9**
Gussage St Michael. *Dors* 4J **9**
Guston. *Kent* 3M **13**
Gutcher. *Shet* 2F **79**
Guthram Gowt. *Linc* 7H **35**
Guthrie. *Ang* 8F **66**
Guyhirn. *Cambs* 1A **28**
Guyhirn Gull. *Cambs* 1M **27**
Guy's Head. *Linc* 7L **35**
Guy's Marsh. *Dors* 3H **9**
Guyzance. *Nmbd* 1H **51**
Gwaelod-y-garth. *Card* 5D **16**
Gwaenynog Bach. *Den* 3K **31**
Gwaenysgor. *Flin* 1K **31**
Gwalchmai. *IOA* 2C **30**
Gwastad. *Pemb* 1E **14**
Gwaun-Cae-Gurwen. *Neat* 2M **15**
Gwaun-y-bara. *Cphy* 5D **16**
Gwbert. *Cdgn* 7D **22**
Gweek. *Corn* 7E **3**
Gwehelog. *Mon* 3F **16**
Gwenddwr. *Powy* 7A **24**
Gwennap. *Corn* 5E **3**
Gwenter. *Corn* 8E **3**
Gwernaffield. *Flin* 3M **31**
Gwernesney. *Mon* 3G **17**
Gwernogle. *Carm* 8H **23**
Gwern-y-go. *Powy* 2C **24**
Gwernymynydd. *Flin* 3M **31**
Gwersyllt. *Wrex* 4A **32**
Gwespyr. *Flin* 1L **31**
Gwinear. *Corn* 6C **3**
Gwithian. *Corn* 5C **3**
Gwredog. *IOA* 1D **30**
Gwyddelwern. *Den* 5K **31**
Gwyddgrug. *Carm* 8G **23**
Gwynfryn. *Wrex* 4M **31**
Gwystre. *Powy* 5A **24**
Gwytherin. *Cnwy* 3H **31**
Gyfelia. *Wrex* 5A **32**
Gyffin. *Cnwy* 2G **31**

H

Haa of Houlland. *Shet* 1F **79**
Habberley. *Shrp* 1D **24**
Habblesthorpe. *Notts* 7D **40**
Habergham. *Lanc* 2G **39**
Habin. *W Sus* 3J **11**
Habrough. *NE Lin* 4H **41**
Haceby. *Linc* 6G **35**
Hacheston. *Suff* 6K **29**
Hackenthorpe. *S Yor* 7A **40**
Hackford. *Norf* 1G **29**
Hackforth. *N Yor* 4B **44**
Hackland. *Orkn* 5B **78**
Hackleton. *Nptn* 6G **27**
Hackman's Gate. *Worc* 4J **25**
Hackness. *N Yor* 4J **45**
Hackness. *Orkn* 8B **78**
Hackney. *G Lon* 5B **20**
Hackthorn. *Linc* 7F **40**
Hackthorpe. *Cumb* 1G **43**
Haclait. *W Isl* 7C **68**
Haconby. *Linc* 7H **35**
Hadden. *Bord* 6G **57**
Haddenham. *Buck* 3H **19**
Haddenham. *Cambs* 4A **28**
Haddenham End. *Cambs* 4A **28**
Haddington. *E Lot* 2E **56**
Haddington. *Linc* 3F **34**
Haddiscoe. *Norf* 2L **29**
Haddo. *Abers* 6J **73**
Haddon. *Cambs* 2K **27**
Hademore. *Staf* 1M **25**
Hadfield. *Derbs* 6J **39**
Hadham Cross. *Herts* 2C **20**
Hadham Ford. *Herts* 1C **20**
Hadleigh. *Essx* 5G **21**
Hadleigh. *Suff* 7G **29**
Hadleigh Heath. *Suff* 7F **28**
Hadley. *Telf* 8D **32**
Hadley. *Worc* 5J **25**
Hadley End. *Staf* 7J **33**
Hadley Wood. *G Lon* 4A **20**
Hadlow. *Kent* 3E **12**
Hadlow Down. *E Sus* 5D **12**
Hadnall. *Shrp* 7C **32**
Hadstock. *Essx* 7B **28**
Hadston. *Nmbd* 2H **51**
Hady. *Derbs* 8M **39**
Hadzor. *Worc* 5K **25**
Haffenden Quarter. *Kent* 3G **13**
Haggate. *Lanc* 2G **39**
Haggbeck. *Cumb* 4M **49**
Haggersta. *Shet* 7D **79**
Haggerston. *Nmbd* 5K **57**
Haggrister. *Shet* 4D **79**
Hagley. *Here* 7F **24**
Hagley. *Worc* 3K **25**
Hagnaby. *Linc* 3K **35**
Hagworthingham. *Linc* 3K **35**
Haigh. *G Man* 5E **38**
Haigh Moor. *W Yor* 3L **39**
Haighton Green. *Lanc* 2D **38**
Haile. *Cumb* 3B **42**
Hailes. *Glos* 8L **25**
Hailey. *Herts* 2B **20**
Hailey. *Oxon* 2D **18**
Hailsham. *E Sus* 7D **12**
Hail Weston. *Cambs* 5K **27**
Hainault. *G Lon* 4C **20**
Hainford. *Norf* 6J **37**
Hainton. *Linc* 7H **41**
Hainworth. *W Yor* 2J **39**
Haisthorpe. *E Yor* 7L **45**
Hakin. *Pemb* 3C **14**
Halam. *Notts* 4C **34**
Halbeath. *Fife* 1K **55**
Halberton. *Devn* 4M **7**
Halcro. *High* 3H **77**
Hale. *Cumb* 6G **43**
Hale. *G Man* 7F **38**
Hale. *Hal* 7C **38**
Hale. *Hants* 4B **10**
Hale. *Surr* 1J **11**
Hale Bank. *Hal* 7C **38**
Halebarns. *G Man* 7F **38**
Hales. *Norf* 2K **29**
Hales. *Staf* 6E **32**
Halesgate. *Linc* 7K **35**
Hales Green. *Derbs* 5J **33**
Halesowen. *W Mid* 3K **25**
Hale Street. *Kent* 3E **12**
Halesworth. *Suff* 4K **29**
Halewood. *Mers* 7C **38**
Halford. *Shrp* 3E **24**
Halford. *Warw* 7A **26**
Halfpenny. *Cumb* 5G **43**
Halfpenny Furze. *Carm* 2G **15**
Halfpenny Green. *Shrp* 2J **25**
Halfway. *Carm* 8J **23**
Halfway. *Powy* 8L **23**
Halfway. *S Yor* 7A **40**
Halfway. *W Ber* 7E **18**
Halfway House. *Shrp* 8A **32**
Halfway Houses. *Kent* 6H **21**
Halgabron. *Corn* 7B **6**
Halifax. *W Yor* 3J **39**
Halistra. *High* 6G **69**
Halket. *E Ayr* 4C **54**
Halkirk. *High* 4G **77**
Halkyn. *Flin* 8A **38**
Hall. *E Ren* 4C **54**
Hallam Fields. *Derbs* 5A **34**
Halland. *E Sus* 6D **12**
Hallands, The. *N Lin* 3G **41**
Hallaton. *Leics* 2F **26**
Hallatrow. *Bath* 8J **17**
Hallbank. *Cumb* 4H **43**
Hallbankgate. *Cumb* 6A **50**
Hall Dunnerdale. *Cumb* 4D **42**
Hallen. *S Glo* 5H **17**
Hall End. *Bed* 7J **27**
Hallgarth. *Dur* 7J **51**
Hall Green. *Ches E* 4F **32**
Hall Green. *Norf* 3H **29**
Hall Green. *W Mid* 3M **25**
Hall Green. *W Yor* 4M **39**
Hall Green. *Wrex* 5B **32**
Halliburton. *Bord* 5F **56**
Hallin. *High* 6G **69**
Halling. *Medw* 7F **20**
Hallington. *Linc* 7K **41**
Hallington. *Nmbd* 4E **50**
Halloughton. *Notts* 4C **34**
Hallow. *Worc* 6J **25**
Hallow Heath. *Worc* 6J **25**
Hallowsgate. *Ches W* 3C **32**
Hallsands. *Devn* 6K **5**
Hall's Green. *Herts* 1A **20**
Hallspill. *Devn* 3F **6**
Hallthwaites. *Cumb* 5C **42**
Hall Waberthwaite. *Cumb* 4C **42**
Hallwood Green. *Glos* 8G **25**
Hallworthy. *Corn* 7C **6**
Hallyne. *Bord* 5K **55**
Halmer End. *Staf* 5F **32**
Halmond's Frome. *Here* 7G **25**
Halmore. *Glos* 3J **17**
Halnaker. *W Sus* 5K **11**
Halsall. *Lanc* 4B **38**
Halse. *Nptn* 7D **26**
Halse. *Som* 3A **8**
Halsetown. *Corn* 6C **3**
Halsham. *E Yor* 3J **41**
Halsinger. *Devn* 2G **7**
Halstead. *Essx* 8E **28**
Halstead. *Kent* 7C **20**
Halstead. *Leics* 1F **26**
Halstock. *Dors* 5E **8**
Halsway. *Som* 2A **8**
Haltcliff Bridge. *Cumb* 8L **49**
Haltham. *Linc* 3J **35**
Haltoft End. *Linc* 5K **35**
Halton. *Buck* 3J **19**
Halton. *Hal* 7D **38**
Halton. *Lanc* 7G **43**
Halton. *Nmbd* 5E **50**
Halton. *W Yor* 2M **39**
Halton. *Wrex* 6A **32**
Halton East. *N Yor* 8M **43**
Halton Fenside. *Linc* 3L **35**
Halton Gill. *N Yor* 6K **43**
Halton Holegate. *Linc* 3L **35**
Halton Lea Gate. *Nmbd* 6B **50**
Halton Moor. *W Yor* 2M **39**
Halton Shields. *Nmbd* 5F **50**
Halton West. *N Yor* 8K **43**
Haltwhistle. *Nmbd* 5C **50**
Halvergate. *Norf* 1L **29**
Halwell. *Devn* 4J **5**
Halwill. *Devn* 6F **6**
Halwill Junction. *Devn* 6F **6**
Ham. *Devn* 5B **8**
Ham. *Glos* 4J **17**
Ham. *G Lon* 6M **19**
Ham. *High* 2H **77**
Ham. *Kent* 8M **21**
Ham. *Plym* 4F **4**
Ham. *Shet* 9B **79**
Ham. *Som* 4B **8**
(nr. Ilminster)
Ham. *Som* 3B **8**
(nr. Taunton)
Ham. *Som* 3A **8**
(nr. Wellington)
Ham. *Wilts* 7D **18**
Hambleden. *Buck* 5H **19**
Hambledon. *Hants* 4G **11**
Hambledon. *Surr* 2K **11**
Hamble-le-Rice. *Hants* 5E **10**
Hambleton. *Lanc* 1B **38**
Hambleton. *N Yor* 2B **40**
Hambridge. *Som* 3C **8**
Hambrook. *S Glo* 6J **17**
Hambrook. *W Sus* 5H **11**
Ham Common. *Dors* 3H **9**
Hameringham. *Linc* 3K **35**
Hamerton. *Cambs* 4K **27**
Ham Green. *Here* 7H **25**
Ham Green. *Kent* 7G **21**
Ham Green. *N Som* 6H **17**
Ham Green. *Worc* 5L **25**
Ham Hill. *Kent* 7E **20**
Hamilton. *Leics* 1E **26**
Hamilton. *S Lan* 4F **54**
Hamister. *Shet* 5F **79**
Hammer. *W Sus* 2J **11**
Hammersmith. *G Lon* 6A **20**
Hammerwich. *Staf* 1L **25**
Hammerwood. *E Sus* 4C **12**
Hammill. *Kent* 8L **21**
Hammond Street. *Herts* 3B **20**
Hammoon. *Dors* 4H **9**
Hamnavoe. *Shet* 3C **79**
(nr. Braehoulland)
Hamnavoe. *Shet* 8D **79**
(nr. Burland)
Hamnavoe. *Shet* 4E **79**
(nr. Lunna)
Hamnavoe. *Shet* 3E **79**
(on Yell)
Hamp. *Som* 2C **8**
Hampden Park. *E Sus* 7E **12**
Hampen. *Glos* 1A **18**
Hamperden End. *Essx* 8B **28**
Hamperley. *Shrp* 3E **24**
Hampnett. *Glos* 2A **18**
Hampole. *S Yor* 4B **40**
Hampreston. *Dors* 6A **10**
Hampstead. *G Lon* 5A **20**
Hampstead Norreys.
W Ber 6F **18**
Hampsthwaite. *N Yor* 8B **44**
Hampton. *Devn* 6B **8**
Hampton. *G Lon* 6M **19**
Hampton. *Kent* 7K **21**
Hampton. *Shrp* 3H **25**
Hampton. *Swin* 4B **18**
Hampton. *Worc* 7L **25**
Hampton Bishop. *Here* 8F **24**
Hampton Fields. *Glos* 4L **17**
Hampton Hargate. *Pet* 2K **27**
Hampton Heath. *Ches W* 5C **32**
Hampton in Arden. *W Mid* 3A **26**
Hampton Loade. *Shrp* 3H **25**
Hampton Lovett. *Worc* 5J **25**
Hampton Lucy. *Warw* 6A **26**
Hampton Magna. *Warw* 5A **26**
Hampton on the Hill.
Warw 5A **26**
Hampton Poyle. *Oxon* 2F **18**
Hampton Wick. *G Lon* 7M **19**
Hamptworth. *Wilts* 4C **10**
Hamrow. *Norf* 5F **36**
Hamsey. *E Sus* 6C **12**
Hamsey Green. *Surr* 8B **20**
Hamstall Ridware. *Staf* 8J **33**
Hamstead. *IOW* 6E **10**
Hamstead. *W Mid* 2L **25**
Hamstead Marshall. *W Ber* 7E **18**
Hamsterley. *Dur* 6G **51**
(nr. Consett)
Hamsterley. *Dur* 8G **51**
(nr. Wolsingham)
Hamsterley Mill. *Dur* 6G **51**
Hamstreet. *Kent* 4J **13**
Ham Street. *Som* 2E **8**
Hamworthy. *Pool* 6J **9**
Hanbury. *Staf* 7J **33**
Hanbury. *Worc* 5K **25**
Hanbury Woodend. *Staf* 7J **33**
Hanby. *Linc* 6G **35**
Hanchurch. *Staf* 5F **32**
Hand and Pen. *Devn* 6M **7**
Handbridge. *Ches W* 3B **32**
Handcross. *W Sus* 5A **12**
Handforth. *Ches E* 7G **39**
Handley. *Ches W* 4B **32**
Handley. *Derbs* 3L **33**
Handsacre. *Staf* 8H **33**
Handsworth. *S Yor* 7A **40**
Handsworth. *W Mid* 2L **25**
Handy Cross. *Buck* 4J **19**
Hanford. *Dors* 4H **9**
Hanford. *Stoke* 5F **32**
Hangersley. *Hants* 5B **10**
Hanging Houghton.
Nptn 4F **26**
Hanging Langford.
Wilts 2A **10**
Hangleton. *Brig* 7A **12**
Hangleton. *W Sus* 5L **11**
Hanham. *S Glo* 6J **17**
Hanham Green. *S Glo* 6J **17**
Hankelow. *Ches E* 5D **32**
Hankerton. *Wilts* 4M **17**
Hankham. *E Sus* 7E **12**
Hanley.
Stoke 5F **32** & **Stoke 102**
Hanley Castle. *Worc* 7J **25**
Hanley Childe. *Worc* 5G **25**
Hanley Swan. *Worc* 7J **25**
Hanley William. *Worc* 5G **25**
Hanlith. *N Yor* 7L **43**
Hanmer. *Wrex* 6B **32**
Hannaborough. *Devn* 5G **7**
Hannaford. *Devn* 3H **7**
Hannah. *Linc* 8M **41**
Hannington. *Hants* 8F **18**
Hannington. *Nptn* 4G **27**
Hannington. *Swin* 4B **18**
Hannington Wick. *Swin* 4B **18**
Hanscombe End.
C Beds 8K **27**
Hanslope. *Mil* 7G **27**
Hanthorpe. *Linc* 7G **35**
Hanwell. *G Lon* 5M **19**
Hanwell. *Oxon* 7C **26**
Hanwood. *Shrp* 1E **24**
Hanworth. *G Lon* 6M **19**
Hanworth. *Norf* 4H **37**
Happas. *Ang* 1K **61**
Happendon. *S Lan* 6G **55**
Happisburgh. *Norf* 4K **37**
Happisburgh Common.
Norf 5K **37**
Hapsford. *Ches W* 8C **38**
Hapton. *Lanc* 2F **38**
Hapton. *Norf* 2H **29**
Harberton. *Devn* 4J **5**
Harbertonford. *Devn* 4J **5**
Harbledown. *Kent* 8K **21**
Harborne. *W Mid* 3L **25**
Harborough Magna. *Warw* 4C **26**
Harbottle. *Nmbd* 1E **50**
Harbourneford. *Devn* 3J **5**
Harbours Hill. *Worc* 5K **25**
Harbridge. *Hants* 4B **10**
Harbury. *Warw* 5B **26**
Harby. *Leics* 6D **34**
Harby. *Notts* 8E **40**
Harcombe. *Devn* 6A **8**
Harcombe Bottom. *Devn* 6C **8**
Harcourt. *Corn* 6F **3**
Harden. *W Yor* 2J **39**
Hardenhuish. *Wilts* 6M **17**
Hardgate. *Abers* 3H **67**
Hardgate. *Dum* 5F **48**
Hardham. *W Sus* 4L **11**
Hardingham. *Norf* 1G **29**
Hardingstone. *Nptn* 6F **26**
Hardings Wood. *Ches E* 4F **32**
Hardington. *Som* 8K **17**
Hardington Mandeville.
Som 4E **8**
Hardington Marsh. *Som* 5E **8**
Hardington Moor. *Som* 4E **8**
Hardley. *Hants* 5E **10**
Hardley Street. *Norf* 1K **29**
Hardmead. *Mil* 7H **27**
Hardraw. *N Yor* 4K **43**
Hardstoft. *Derbs* 3A **34**
Hardway. *Hants* 5G **11**
Hardway. *Som* 2G **9**
Hardwick. *Buck* 2J **19**
Hardwick. *Cambs* 6M **27**
Hardwick. *Norf* 3J **29**
Hardwick. *Nptn* 5G **27**
Hardwick. *Oxon* 1F **18**
(nr. Bicester)
Hardwick. *Oxon* 3D **18**
(nr. Witney)
Hardwick. *Shrp* 2D **24**
Hardwick. *S Yor* 7A **40**
Hardwick. *Stoc T* 1D **44**
Hardwick. *W Mid* 2L **25**
Hardwicke. *Glos* 1M **17**
(nr. Cheltenham)
Hardwicke. *Glos* 2K **17**
(nr. Gloucester)
Hardwicke. *Here* 7C **24**
Hardwick Village. *Notts* 8C **40**
Hardy's Green. *Essx* 1H **21**
Hare. *Som* 4B **8**
Hareby. *Linc* 3K **35**
Hareden. *Lanc* 8H **43**
Harefield. *G Lon* 4L **19**
Hare Green. *Essx* 1J **21**
Hare Hatch. *Wok* 6J **19**
Harehill. *Derbs* 6J **33**
Harehills. *W Yor* 2M **39**
Harehope. *Nmbd* 7K **57**
Harelaw. *Dum* 4M **49**
Harelaw. *Dur* 6G **51**
Hareplain. *Kent* 4G **13**
Haresceugh. *Cumb* 7B **50**
Harescombe. *Glos* 2L **17**
Haresfield. *Glos* 2L **17**
Haresfinch. *Mers* 6D **38**
Hareshaw. *N Lan* 3G **55**
Hare Street. *Essx* 3C **20**
Hare Street. *Herts* 1B **20**
Harewood. *W Yor* 1M **39**
Harewood End. *Here* 1H **17**
Harford. *Devn* 4H **5**
Hargate. *Norf* 2H **29**
Hargatewall. *Derbs* 8K **39**
Hargrave. *Ches W* 3B **32**
Hargrave. *Nptn* 4J **27**
Hargrave. *Suff* 6D **28**
Harker. *Cumb* 5L **49**
Harkland. *Shet* 3E **79**
Harkstead. *Suff* 8H **29**
Harlaston. *Staf* 8K **33**
Harlaxton. *Linc* 6E **34**
Harlech. *Gwyn* 6E **30**
Harlequin. *Notts* 6C **34**
Harlescott. *Shrp* 8C **32**
Harleston. *Devn* 5J **5**
Harleston. *Norf* 3J **29**
Harleston. *Suff* 5G **29**
Harlestone. *Nptn* 5F **26**
Harley. *Shrp* 1F **24**
Harley. *S Yor* 6M **39**
Harling Road. *Norf* 3F **28**
Harlington. *C Beds* 8J **27**
Harlington. *G Lon* 6L **19**
Harlington. *S Yor* 5A **40**
Harlosh. *High* 7G **69**
Harlow. *Essx* 2C **20**
Harlow Hill. *Nmbd* 5F **50**
Harlsey Castle. *N Yor* 4D **44**
Harlthorpe. *E Yor* 2D **40**
Harlton. *Cambs* 6M **27**
Harlyn Bay. *Corn* 2F **3**
Harman's Cross. *Dors* 7J **9**
Harmby. *N Yor* 5A **44**
Harmer Green. *Herts* 2A **20**
Harmer Hill. *Shrp* 7B **32**
Harmondsworth. *G Lon* 6L **19**
Harmston. *Linc* 3F **34**
Harnage. *Shrp* 1F **24**
Harnham. *Nmbd* 3F **50**
Harnhill. *Glos* 3A **18**
Harold Hill. *G Lon* 4D **20**
Haroldston West. *Pemb* 2C **14**
Haroldswick. *Shet* 1G **79**
Harold Wood. *G Lon* 4D **20**
Harome. *N Yor* 5F **44**
Harpenden. *Herts* 2M **19**
Harpford. *Devn* 6M **7**
Harpham. *E Yor* 7K **45**
Harpley. *Norf* 5D **36**
Harpley. *Worc* 5G **25**
Harpole. *Nptn* 5E **26**
Harpsdale. *High* 4G **77**
Harpsden. *Oxon* 5H **19**
Harpswell. *Linc* 7F **40**
Harpurhey. *G Man* 5G **39**
Harpur Hill. *Derbs* 8J **39**
Harraby. *Cumb* 6M **49**
Harracott. *Devn* 3G **7**
Harrapool. *High* 1L **63**
Harrapul. *High* 1L **63**
Harrietfield. *Per* 3E **60**
Harrietsham. *Kent* 8G **21**
Harrington. *Cumb* 1A **42**
Harrington. *Linc* 8K **41**
Harrington. *Nptn* 3F **26**
Harringworth. *Nptn* 2H **27**
Harriseahead. *Staf* 4F **32**
Harriston. *Cumb* 7J **49**
Harrogate. *N Yor* 8C **44** & **96**
Harrold. *Bed* 6H **27**
Harrop Dale. *G Man* 5J **39**
Harrow. *G Lon* 5M **19**
Harrowbarrow. *Corn* 3E **4**
Harrowden. *Bed* 7J **27**
Harrowgate Hill. *Darl* 2B **44**
Harrow on the Hill.
G Lon 5M **19**
Harrow Weald. *G Lon* 4M **19**
Harry Stoke. *S Glo* 6J **17**
Harston. *Cambs* 6A **28**
Harston. *Leics* 6E **34**
Harswell. *E Yor* 1E **40**
Hart. *Hart* 8K **51**
Hartburn. *Nmbd* 3F **50**
Hartburn. *Stoc T* 2D **44**
Hartest. *Suff* 6E **28**
Hartfield. *E Sus* 4C **12**
Hartford. *Cambs* 4L **27**
Hartford. *Ches W* 8E **38**
Hartford. *Som* 3L **7**
Hartfordbridge. *Hants* 8H **19**
Hartford End. *Essx* 2E **20**
Harthill. *Ches W* 4C **32**
Harthill. *N Lan* 3H **55**
Harthill. *S Yor* 7A **40**
Hartington. *Derbs* 3J **33**
Hartland. *Devn* 3D **6**
Hartland Quay. *Devn* 3D **6**
Hartle. *Worc* 4K **25**
Hartlebury. *Worc* 4J **25**
Hartlepool. *Hart* 8L **51**
Hartley. *Cumb* 3J **43**
Hartley. *Kent* 4F **12**
(nr. Cranbrook)
Hartley. *Kent* 7E **20**
(nr. Dartford)
Hartley. *Nmbd* 4J **51**
Hartley Green. *Staf* 6G **33**
Hartley Mauditt. *Hants* 2H **11**
Hartley Wespall. *Hants* 8G **19**
Hartley Wintney. *Hants* 8H **19**
Hartlip. *Kent* 7G **21**
Hartmount. *High* 4K **71**
Hartoft End. *N Yor* 4G **45**
Harton. *N Yor* 7G **45**
Harton. *Shrp* 3E **24**
Harton. *Tyne* 5J **51**
Hartpury. *Glos* 1K **17**
Hartshead. *W Yor* 3K **39**
Hartshill. *Warw* 2B **26**
Hartshorne. *Derbs* 7L **33**
Hartsop. *Cumb* 2F **42**
Hart Station. *Hart* 8K **51**
Hartswell. *Som* 3M **7**
Hartwell. *Nptn* 6F **26**
Hartwood. *Lanc* 4D **38**
Hartwood. *N Lan* 4G **55**
Harvel. *Kent* 7E **20**
Harvington. *Worc* 7L **25**
(nr. Evesham)
Harvington. *Worc* 4J **25**
(nr. Kidderminster)
Harwell. *Oxon* 5E **18**
Harwich. *Essx* 8J **29** & **104**
Harwood. *Dur* 8D **50**
Harwood. *G Man* 4F **38**
Harwood Dale. *N Yor* 4J **45**
Harworth. *Notts* 6C **40**
Hascombe. *Surr* 2K **11**
Haselbech. *Nptn* 4F **26**
Haselbury Plucknett. *Som* 4D **8**
Haseley. *Warw* 5A **26**
Haselor. *Warw* 6M **25**
Hasfield. *Glos* 1L **17**
Hasguard. *Pemb* 3C **14**
Haskayne. *Lanc* 5B **38**
Hasketon. *Suff* 6J **29**
Hasland. *Derbs* 3L **33**
Haslemere. *Surr* 2K **11**
Haslingden. *Lanc* 3F **38**
Haslingden Grane. *Lanc* 3F **38**
Haslingfield. *Cambs* 6A **28**
Haslington. *Ches E* 4E **32**
Hassall. *Ches E* 4E **32**
Hassall Green. *Ches E* 4E **32**
Hassell Street. *Kent* 3J **13**
Hassendean. *Bord* 7E **56**
Hassingham. *Norf* 1K **29**
Hassocks. *W Sus* 6B **12**
Hassop. *Derbs* 8L **39**
Haster. *High* 4J **77**
Hasthorpe. *Linc* 3L **35**
Hastigrow. *High* 3H **77**
Hastingleigh. *Kent* 3J **13**
Hastings. *E Sus* 7G **13**
Hastingwood. *Essx* 3C **20**
Hastoe. *Herts* 3K **19**
Haston. *Shrp* 7C **32**
Haswell. *Dur* 7J **51**
Haswell Plough. *Dur* 7J **51**
Hatch. *C Beds* 7K **27**
Hatch Beauchamp. *Som* 3C **8**
Hatch End. *G Lon* 4M **19**
Hatch Green. *Som* 4C **8**
Hatching Green. *Herts* 2M **19**
Hatchmere. *Ches W* 8D **38**
Hatch Warren. *Hants* 1G **11**
Hatcliffe. *NE Lin* 5J **41**
Hatfield. *Here* 6F **24**
Hatfield. *Herts* 3A **20**
Hatfield. *S Yor* 5C **40**
Hatfield. *Worc* 6J **25**
Hatfield Broad Oak. *Essx* 2D **20**
Hatfield Garden Village.
Herts 3A **20**
Hatfield Heath. *Essx* 2D **20**
Hatfield Hyde. *Herts* 2A **20**
Hatfield Peverel. *Essx* 2F **20**
Hatfield Woodhouse.
S Yor 5C **40**
Hatford. *Oxon* 4D **18**
Hatherden. *Hants* 8D **18**
Hatherleigh. *Devn* 5G **7**
Hathern. *Leics* 7B **34**
Hatherop. *Glos* 3B **18**
Hathersage. *Derbs* 7L **39**
Hathersage Booths. *Derbs* 7L **39**
Hatherton. *Ches E* 5D **32**
Hatherton. *Staf* 8G **33**
Hatley St George. *Cambs* 6L **27**
Hatt. *Corn* 3E **4**
Hattersley. *G Man* 6H **39**
Hattingley. *Hants* 2G **11**
Hatton. *Abers* 6L **73**
Hatton. *Derbs* 6K **33**
Hatton. *G Lon* 6L **19**
Hatton. *Linc* 8H **41**
Hatton. *Shrp* 2E **24**
Hatton. *Warr* 7D **38**
Hatton. *Warw* 5A **26**
Hattoncrook. *Abers* 1J **67**
Hatton Heath. *Ches W* 3B **32**
Hatton of Fintray. *Abers* 2J **67**
Haugh. *E Ayr* 7C **54**
Haugh. *Linc* 8L **41**
Haugham. *Linc* 7K **41**
Haugh Head. *Nmbd* 7K **57**
Haughley. *Suff* 5G **29**
Haughley Green. *Suff* 5G **29**
Haugh of Ballechin. *Per* 8M **65**
Haugh of Glass. *Mor* 6E **72**
Haugh of Urr. *Dum* 5F **48**
Haughton. *Ches E* 4C **32**
Haughton. *Notts* 8C **40**
Haughton. *Shrp* 2G **25**
(nr. Bridgnorth)
Haughton. *Shrp* 7A **32**
(nr. Oswestry)
Haughton. *Shrp* 1H **25**
(nr. Shifnal)
Haughton. *Shrp* 8C **32**
(nr. Shrewsbury)
Haughton. *Staf* 7F **32**
Haughton Green. *G Man* 6H **39**
Haughton le Skerne. *Darl* 2C **44**
Haultwick. *Herts* 1B **20**
Haunn. *Arg* 1A **58**
Haunn. *W Isl* 2B **62**
Haunton. *Staf* 8K **33**
Hauxton. *Cambs* 6A **28**
Havannah. *Ches E* 3F **32**
Havant. *Hants* 5H **11**
Haven. *Here* 6E **24**
Haven Bank. *Linc* 4J **35**
Havenside. *E Yor* 3H **41**
Havenstreet. *IOW* 6F **10**
Haven, The. *W Sus* 2L **11**
Havercroft. *W Yor* 4M **39**
Haverfordwest. *Pemb* 2D **14**
Haverhill. *Suff* 7C **28**
Haverigg. *Cumb* 6C **42**
Havering-atte-Bower.
G Lon 4D **20**
Havering's Grove. *Essx* 4E **20**
Haversham. *Mil* 7G **27**
Haverthwaite. *Cumb* 5E **42**
Haverton Hill. *Stoc T* 1D **44**
Havyatt. *Som* 2E **8**
Hawarden. *Flin* 3A **32**
Hawbridge. *Worc* 7K **25**
Hawcoat. *Cumb* 6D **42**
Hawcross. *Glos* 8H **25**
Hawen. *Cdgn* 7F **22**
Hawes. *N Yor* 5K **43**
Hawes Green. *Norf* 2J **29**
Hawick. *Bord* 8E **56**
Hawkchurch. *Devn* 5C **8**
Hawkedon. *Suff* 6D **28**
Hawkenbury. *Kent* 3G **13**
Hawkeridge. *Wilts* 8L **17**
Hawkerland. *Devn* 7M **7**
Hawkesbury. *S Glo* 5K **17**
Hawkesbury. *W Mid* 3B **26**
Hawkesbury Upton. *S Glo* 5K **17**
Hawkes End. *W Mid* 3A **26**
Hawk Green. *G Man* 7H **39**
Hawkhurst. *Kent* 4F **12**
Hawkhurst Common.
E Sus 6D **12**
Hawkinge. *Kent* 3L **13**
Hawkley. *Hants* 3H **11**
Hawkridge. *Som* 2K **7**
Hawksdale. *Cumb* 7L **49**
Hawkshaw. *G Man* 4F **38**
Hawkshead. *Cumb* 4E **42**
Hawkshead Hill. *Cumb* 4E **42**
Hawkswick. *N Yor* 6L **43**
Hawksworth. *Notts* 5D **34**
Hawksworth. *W Yor* 1K **39**
Hawkwell. *Essx* 4G **21**
Hawley. *Hants* 8J **19**
Hawley. *Kent* 6D **20**
Hawling. *Glos* 1A **18**
Hawnby. *N Yor* 5E **44**
Haworth. *W Yor* 2J **39**
Hawstead. *Suff* 6E **28**
Hawthorn. *Dur* 7K **51**
Hawthorn Hill. *Brac* 6J **19**
Hawthorn Hill. *Linc* 4J **35**
Hawthorpe. *Linc* 7G **35**
Hawton. *Notts* 4D **34**
Haxby. *York* 8F **44**
Haxey. *N Lin* 6D **40**
Haybridge. *Shrp* 4G **25**
Haybridge. *Som* 1E **8**
Haydock. *Mers* 6D **38**
Haydon. *Bath* 8J **17**
Haydon. *Dors* 4F **8**
Haydon. *Som* 3B **8**
Haydon Bridge. *Nmbd* 5D **50**
Haydon Wick. *Swin* 5B **18**
Haye. *Corn* 3E **4**
Hayes. *G Lon* 7C **20**
(nr. Bromley)
Hayes. *G Lon* 5L **19**
(nr. Uxbridge)
Hayfield. *Derbs* 7J **39**
Hay Green. *Norf* 8M **35**
Hayhill. *E Ayr* 8C **54**
Haylands. *IOW* 6F **10**
Hayle. *Corn* 6C **3**
Hayley Green. *W Mid* 3K **25**
Hayling Island. *Hants* 6H **11**
Hayne. *Devn* 5K **7**
Haynes. *C Beds* 7J **27**
Haynes West End. *C Beds* 7J **27**
Hay-on-Wye. *Powy* 7C **24**
Hayscastle. *Pemb* 1C **14**
Hayscastle Cross. *Pemb* 1D **14**
Haysden. *Kent* 3D **12**
Hayshead. *Ang* 1M **61**
Hay Street. *Herts* 1B **20**
Hayton. *Aber* 3K **67**
Hayton. *Cumb* 7J **49**
(nr. Aspatria)
Hayton. *Cumb* 6A **50**
(nr. Brampton)
Hayton. *E Yor* 1E **40**
Hayton. *Notts* 7D **40**
Hayton's Bent. *Shrp* 3F **24**
Haytor Vale. *Devn* 8J **7**
Haytown. *Devn* 4E **6**
Haywards Heath. *W Sus* 5B **12**
Haywood. *S Lan* 4H **55**
Hazelbank. *S Lan* 5G **55**
Hazelbury Bryan. *Dors* 5G **9**
Hazeleigh. *Essx* 3G **21**
Hazeley. *Hants* 8H **19**
Hazel Grove. *G Man* 7H **39**
Hazelhead. *S Yor* 5K **39**
Hazelslade. *Staf* 8H **33**
Hazel Street. *Kent* 4E **12**
Hazelton Walls. *Fife* 3J **61**
Hazelwood. *Derbs* 5L **33**
Hazlemere. *Buck* 4J **19**
Hazler. *Shrp* 2E **24**
Hazlerigg. *Tyne* 4H **51**
Hazles. *Staf* 5H **33**
Hazleton. *Glos* 2A **18**
Hazon. *Nmbd* 1G **51**
Heacham. *Norf* 4C **36**
Headbourne Worthy. *Hants* 2E **10**
Headcorn. *Kent* 3G **13**
Headingley. *W Yor* 2L **39**
Headington. *Oxon* 3F **18**
Headlam. *Dur* 2A **44**
Headless Cross. *Worc* 5L **25**
Headley. *Hants* 2J **11**
(nr. Haslemere)
Headley. *Hants* 7F **18**
(nr. Kingsclere)
Headley. *Surr* 8A **20**
Headley Down. *Hants* 2J **11**
Headley Heath. *Worc* 4L **25**
Headley Park. *Bris* 7H **17**
Head of Muir. *Falk* 1G **55**
Headon. *Notts* 8D **40**
Heads Nook. *Cumb* 6M **49**
Heage. *Derbs* 4L **33**
Healaugh. *N Yor* 4M **43**
(nr. Grinton)
Healaugh. *N Yor* 1B **40**
(nr. York)
Heald Green. *G Man* 7G **39**
Heale. *Devn* 1H **7**
Healey. *G Man* 4G **39**
Healey. *Nmbd* 6F **50**
Healey. *N Yor* 5A **44**
Healeyfield. *Dur* 7F **50**
Healey Hall. *Nmbd* 6F **50**
Healing. *NE Lin* 4J **41**
Heamoor. *Corn* 6B **3**
Heanish. *Arg* 8B **62**
Heanor. *Derbs* 5A **34**
Heanton Punchardon. *Devn* 2G **7**
Heapham. *Linc* 7E **40**
Heartsease. *Powy* 5B **24**
Heasley Mill. *Devn* 2J **7**
Heaste. *High* 2L **63**
Heath. *Derbs* 3A **34**
Heath and Reach. *C Beds* 1K **19**
Heath Common. *W Sus* 4M **11**
Heathcote. *Derbs* 3J **33**
Heath Cross. *Devn* 6J **7**
Heathencote. *Nptn* 7F **26**
Heath End. *Derbs* 7L **33**
Heath End. *Hants* 7F **18**
Heath End. *W Mid* 1L **25**
Heather. *Leics* 8L **33**
Heatherfield. *High* 7J **69**
Heatherton. *Derb* 6L **33**
Heathfield. *Cambs* 7A **28**
Heathfield. *Cumb* 7J **49**
Heathfield. *Devn* 8K **7**
Heathfield. *E Sus* 5D **12**
Heathfield. *Ren* 3B **54**
Heathfield. *Som* 2A **8**
(nr. Lydeard St Lawrence)
Heathfield. *Som* 3A **8**
(nr. Norton Fitzwarren)
Heath Green. *Worc* 4L **25**
Heathhall. *Dum* 4G **49**
Heath Hayes. *Staf* 8H **33**
Heath Hill. *Shrp* 8E **32**
Heath House. *Som* 1D **8**
Heathrow (London) Airport.
G Lon 6L **19** & **105**
Heathstock. *Devn* 5B **8**
Heath, The. *Norf* 5J **37**
(nr. Buxton)
Heath, The. *Norf* 5F **36**
(nr. Fakenham)
Heath, The. *Norf* 5H **37**
(nr. Hevingham)
Heath, The. *Staf* 6H **33**
Heath, The. *Suff* 8H **29**
Heathton. *Shrp* 2J **25**
Heathtop. *Derbs* 6J **33**
Heath Town. *W Mid* 2K **25**
Heatley. *G Man* 7F **38**
Heatley. *Staf* 7H **33**
Heaton. *Lanc* 7F **42**
Heaton. *Staf* 3G **33**
Heaton. *Tyne* 5H **51**
Heaton. *W Yor* 2K **39**
Heaton Moor. *G Man* 6G **39**
Heaton's Bridge. *Lanc* 4C **38**
Heaverham. *Kent* 8D **20**
Heavitree. *Devn* 6L **7**
Hebburn. *Tyne* 5J **51**
Hebden. *N Yor* 7M **43**
Hebden Bridge. *W Yor* 3H **39**
Hebden Green. *Ches W* 3D **32**
Hebing End. *Herts* 1B **20**
Hebron. *Carm* 1F **14**
Hebron. *Nmbd* 3G **51**
Heck. *Dum* 3H **49**
Heckdyke. *Notts* 6D **40**
Heckfield. *Hants* 7H **19**
Heckfield Green. *Suff* 4H **29**
Heckfordbridge. *Essx* 1H **21**
Heckington. *Linc* 5H **35**
Heckmondwike. *W Yor* 3L **39**
Heddington. *Wilts* 7M **17**
Heddle. *Orkn* 6B **78**
Heddon. *Devn* 3H **7**
Heddon-on-the-Wall.
Nmbd 5G **51**
Hedenham. *Norf* 2K **29**
Hedge End. *Hants* 4E **10**
Hedgerley. *Buck* 5K **19**
Hedging. *Som* 3C **8**
Hedley on the Hill. *Nmbd* 6F **50**
Hednesford. *Staf* 8H **33**
Hedon. *E Yor* 3H **41**
Hegdon Hill. *Here* 6F **24**
Heglibister. *Shet* 6D **79**
Heighington. *Darl* 1B **44**
Heighington. *Linc* 3G **35**
Heightington. *Worc* 4H **25**
Heights of Brae. *High* 5H **71**
Heights of Fodderty. *High* 5H **71**
Heights of Kinlochewe.
High 5C **70**
Heiton. *Bord* 6G **57**
Hele. *Devn* 5L **7**
(nr. Exeter)
Hele. *Devn* 6E **6**
(nr. Holsworthy)
Hele. *Devn* 1G **7**
(nr. Ilfracombe)
Hele. *Torb* 3L **5**
Helensburgh. *Arg* 1A **54**
Helford. *Corn* 7E **3**
Helhoughton. *Norf* 5E **36**
Helions Bumpstead. *Essx* 7C **28**
Helland. *Corn* 8B **6**
Helland. *Som* 3C **8**
Hellandbridge. *Corn* 8B **6**
Hellesdon. *Norf* 6J **37**
Hellesveor. *Corn* 5C **3**
Hellidon. *Nptn* 6D **26**
Hellifield. *N Yor* 8K **43**
Hellingly. *E Sus* 6D **12**
Hellington. *Norf* 1K **29**
Hellister. *Shet* 7D **79**
Helmdon. *Nptn* 7D **26**
Helmingham. *Suff* 6H **29**
Helmington Row. *Dur* 8G **51**
Helmsdale. *High* 8F **76**
Helmshore. *Lanc* 3F **38**
Helmsley. *N Yor* 5F **44**
Helperby. *N Yor* 7D **44**
Helperthorpe. *N Yor* 6J **45**
Helpringham. *Linc* 5H **35**
Helpston. *Pet* 1K **27**
Helsby. *Ches W* 8C **38**
Helsey. *Linc* 8M **41**
Helston. *Corn* 7D **3**
Helstone. *Corn* 7B **6**
Helton. *Cumb* 1G **43**
Helwith. *N Yor* 3M **43**
Helwith Bridge. *N Yor* 7K **43**
Helygain. *Flin* 8A **38**
Hemblington. *Norf* 6K **37**
Hemel Hempstead. *Herts* 3L **19**
Hemerdon. *Devn* 4G **5**
Hemingbrough. *N Yor* 2C **40**
Hemingby. *Linc* 8J **41**
Hemingfield. *S Yor* 5M **39**
Hemingford Abbots.
Cambs 4L **27**
Hemingford Grey. *Cambs* 4L **27**
Hemingstone. *Suff* 6H **29**
Hemington. *Leics* 7A **34**
Hemington. *Nptn* 3J **27**
Hemington. *Som* 8K **17**
Hemley. *Suff* 7J **29**
Hemlington. *Midd* 2D **44**
Hempholme. *E Yor* 8K **45**
Hempnall. *Norf* 2J **29**
Hempnall Green. *Norf* 2J **29**
Hempriggs. *High* 5J **77**
Hemp's Green. *Essx* 1H **21**
Hempstead. *Essx* 8C **28**
Hempstead. *Medw* 7F **20**
Hempstead. *Norf* 4H **37**
(nr. Holt)
Hempstead. *Norf* 5L **37**
(nr. Stalham)
Hempsted. *Glos* 2L **17**
Hempton. *Norf* 5F **36**
Hempton. *Oxon* 8C **26**
Hemsby. *Norf* 6L **37**
Hemswell. *Linc* 6F **40**
Hemswell Cliff. *Linc* 7F **40**
Hemsworth. *Dors* 5J **9**
Hemsworth. *W Yor* 4A **40**
Hem, The. *Shrp* 1H **25**
Hemyock. *Devn* 4A **8**
Henallt. *Carm* 1J **15**
Henbury. *Bris* 6H **17**
Henbury. *Ches E* 8G **39**
Hendomen. *Powy* 2C **24**
Hendon. *G Lon* 5A **20**
Hendon. *Tyne* 6K **51**
Hendra. *Corn* 4A **4**
Hendre. *B'end* 5B **16**
Hendreforgan. *Rhon* 5B **16**
Hendy. *Carm* 3K **15**
Heneglwys. *IOA* 2D **30**
Henfeddau Fawr. *Pemb* 8E **22**
Henfield. *S Glo* 6J **17**
Henfield. *W Sus* 6A **12**
Henford. *Devn* 6E **6**
Hengoed. *Cphy* 4D **16**
Hengoed. *Shrp* 6M **31**
Hengrave. *Suff* 5E **28**
Henham. *Essx* 1D **20**
Heniarth. *Powy* 1B **24**
Henlade. *Som* 3B **8**
Henley. *Dors* 5F **8**
Henley. *Shrp* 3E **24**
(nr. Church Stretton)
Henley. *Shrp* 4F **24**
(nr. Ludlow)
Henley. *Som* 2D **8**
Henley. *Suff* 6H **29**
Henley. *W Sus* 3J **11**
Henley-in-Arden. *Warw* 5M **25**
Henley-on-Thames. *Oxon* 5H **19**
Henley's Down. *E Sus* 6F **12**
Henley Street. *Kent* 7E **20**
Henllan. *Cdgn* 7F **22**
Henllan. *Den* 3K **31**
Henllan. *Mon* 1E **16**
Henllan Amgoed. *Carm* 2F **14**
Henllys. *Torf* 4E **16**
Henlow. *C Beds* 8K **27**
Hennock. *Devn* 7K **7**
Henny Street. *Essx* 8E **28**
Henryd. *Cnwy* 2G **31**
Henry's Moat. *Pemb* 1E **14**
Hensall. *N Yor* 3B **40**
Henshaw. *Nmbd* 5C **50**
Hensingham. *Cumb* 2A **42**
Henstead. *Suff* 3L **29**
Hensting. *Hants* 3E **10**
Henstridge. *Som* 4G **9**
Henstridge Ash. *Som* 3G **9**
Henstridge Bowden. *Som* 3F **8**
Henstridge Marsh. *Som* 3G **9**
Henton. *Oxon* 3H **19**
Henton. *Som* 1D **8**
Henwood. *Corn* 8D **6**
Heogan. *Shet* 7E **79**
Heol Senni. *Powy* 1B **16**
Heol-y-Cyw. *B'end* 5B **16**
Hepburn. *Nmbd* 7K **57**
Hepple. *Nmbd* 1E **50**
Hepscott. *Nmbd* 3H **51**
Heptonstall. *W Yor* 3H **39**
Hepworth. *Suff* 4F **28**
Hepworth. *W Yor* 5K **39**
Herbrandston. *Pemb* 3C **14**
Hereford. *Here* 8F **24**
Heribusta. *High* 4J **69**
Heriot. *Bord* 4D **56**
Hermiston. *Edin* 2K **55**
Hermitage. *Dors* 5F **8**
Hermitage. *Bord* 2A **50**
Hermitage. *W Ber* 6F **18**
Hermitage. *W Sus* 5H **11**
Hermon. *Carm* 1L **15**
(nr. Llandeilo)
Hermon. *Carm* 8F **22**
(nr. Newcastle Emlyn)
Hermon. *IOA* 3C **30**
Hermon. *Pemb* 8E **22**
Herne. *Kent* 7K **21**
Herne Bay. *Kent* 7K **21**
Herne Common. *Kent* 7K **21**
Herne Pound. *Kent* 8E **20**
Herner. *Devn* 3G **7**
Hernhill. *Kent* 7J **21**
Herodsfoot. *Corn* 3D **4**
Heronden. *Kent* 8L **21**
Herongate. *Essx* 4E **20**
Heronsford. *S Ayr* 3L **47**
Heronsgate. *Herts* 4L **19**
Heron's Ghyll. *E Sus* 5C **12**
Herra. *Shet* 2G **79**
Herriard. *Hants* 1G **11**
Herringfleet. *Suff* 2L **29**
Herringswell. *Suff* 5D **28**
Herrington. *Tyne* 6J **51**
Hersden. *Kent* 7L **21**
Hersham. *Corn* 5D **6**
Hersham. *Surr* 7M **19**
Herstmonceux. *E Sus* 6E **12**
Herston. *Dors* 8A **10**
Herston. *Orkn* 8C **78**
Hertford. *Herts* 2B **20**
Hertford Heath. *Herts* 2B **20**
Hertingfordbury. *Herts* 2B **20**
Hesketh. *Lanc* 3C **38**
Hesketh Bank. *Lanc* 3C **38**
Hesketh Lane. *Lanc* 1E **38**
Hesket Newmarket. *Cumb* 8L **49**
Heskin Green. *Lanc* 4D **38**
Hesleden. *Dur* 8K **51**
Hesleyside. *Nmbd* 3D **50**
Heslington. *York* 8F **44**
Hessay. *York* 8E **44**
Hessenford. *Corn* 4E **4**
Hessett. *Suff* 5F **28**
Hessilhead. *N Ayr* 4B **54**
Hessle. *Hull* 3G **41**
Hestaford. *Shet* 6C **79**
Hest Bank. *Lanc* 7F **42**
Hester's Way. *Glos* 1M **17**
Hestinsetter. *Shet* 7C **79**
Heston. *G Lon* 6M **19**
Hestwall. *Orkn* 6A **78**
Heswall. *Mers* 7A **38**
Hethe. *Oxon* 1F **18**
Hethelpit Cross. *Glos* 1K **17**
Hethersett. *Norf* 1H **29**
Hethersgill. *Cumb* 5M **49**
Hetherside. *Cumb* 5M **49**
Hethpool. *Nmbd* 7H **57**
Hett. *Dur* 8H **51**
Hetton. *N Yor* 8L **43**
Hetton-le-Hole. *Tyne* 7J **51**
Hetton Steads. *Nmbd* 6K **57**
Heugh. *Nmbd* 4F **50**
Heugh-head. *Abers* 2D **66**
Heveningham. *Suff* 4K **29**
Hever. *Kent* 3C **12**
Heversham. *Cumb* 5F **42**
Hevingham. *Norf* 5H **37**
Hewas Water. *Corn* 5A **4**
Hewelsfield. *Glos* 3H **17**
Hewish. *N Som* 7F **16**
Hewish. *Som* 5D **8**
Hewood. *Dors* 5C **8**
Heworth. *York* 8F **44**
Hexham. *Nmbd* 5E **50**
Hextable. *Kent* 6D **20**
Hexton. *Herts* 8K **27**
Hexworthy. *Devn* 8H **7**
Heybridge. *Essx* 4E **20**
(nr. Brentwood)
Heybridge. *Essx* 3G **21**
(nr. Maldon)
Heybridge Basin. *Essx* 3G **21**
Heybrook Bay. *Devn* 5F **4**
Heydon. *Cambs* 7A **28**
Heydon. *Norf* 5H **37**
Heydour. *Linc* 6G **35**
Heylipol. *Arg* 8A **62**
Heyop. *Powy* 4C **24**
Heysham. *Lanc* 7F **42**
Heyshott. *W Sus* 4J **11**
Heytesbury. *Wilts* 1J **9**
Heythrop. *Oxon* 1D **18**
Heywood. *G Man* 4G **39**
Heywood. *Wilts* 8L **17**
Hibaldstow. *N Lin* 5F **40**
Hickleton. *S Yor* 5A **40**
Hickling. *Norf* 5L **37**
Hickling. *Notts* 7C **34**
Hickling Green. *Norf* 5L **37**
Hickling Heath. *Norf* 5L **37**
Hickstead. *W Sus* 5A **12**
Hidcote Bartrim. *Glos* 7M **25**
Hidcote Boyce. *Glos* 7M **25**
Higford. *Shrp* 1H **25**
High Ackworth. *W Yor* 4A **40**
Higham. *Derbs* 4L **33**
Higham. *Kent* 6F **20**
Higham. *Lanc* 2G **39**
Higham. *S Yor* 5M **39**
Higham. *Suff* 8G **29**
(nr. Ipswich)
Higham. *Suff* 5D **28**
(nr. Newmarket)
Higham Dykes. *Nmbd* 4G **51**
Higham Ferrers. *Nptn* 5H **27**
Higham Gobion. *C Beds* 8K **27**
Higham on the Hill. *Leics* 2B **26**
Highampton. *Devn* 5F **6**
Higham Wood. *Kent* 3D **12**
High Angerton. *Nmbd* 3F **50**
High Auldgirth. *Dum* 3G **49**
High Bankhill. *Cumb* 7A **50**
High Banton. *N Lan* 1F **54**
High Barnet. *G Lon* 4A **20**
High Beech. *Essx* 4C **20**
High Bentham. *N Yor* 7H **43**
High Bickington. *Devn* 3H **7**
High Biggins. *Cumb* 6H **43**
High Birkwith. *N Yor* 6K **43**
High Blantyre. *S Lan* 4E **54**
High Bonnybridge. *Falk* 2G **55**
High Borrans. *Cumb* 3F **42**
High Bradfield. *S Yor* 6L **39**
High Bray. *Devn* 2H **7**
Highbridge. *Cumb* 7L **49**
Highbridge. *High* 5D **64**
Highbridge. *Som* 1C **8**
Highbrook. *W Sus* 4B **12**
High Brooms. *Kent* 3D **12**
High Bullen. *Devn* 3G **7**
Highburton. *W Yor* 4K **39**
Highbury. *Som* 1F **8**
High Buston. *Nmbd* 1H **51**
High Callerton. *Nmbd* 4G **51**
High Carlingill. *Cumb* 3H **43**
High Catton. *E Yor* 8G **45**
High Church. *Nmbd* 3G **51**
Highclere. *Hants* 7E **18**
Highcliffe. *Dors* 6C **10**
High Cogges. *Oxon* 3D **18**
High Common. *Norf* 1F **28**
High Coniscliffe. *Darl* 2B **44**
High Crosby. *Cumb* 6M **49**
High Cross. *Hants* 3H **11**
High Cross. *Herts* 2B **20**
High Easter. *Essx* 2E **20**
High Eggborough. *N Yor* 3B **40**
High Ellington. *N Yor* 5A **44**
Higher Alham. *Som* 1F **8**
Higher Ansty. *Dors* 5G **9**
Higher Ashton. *Devn* 7K **7**
Higher Ballam. *Lanc* 2B **38**
Higher Bartle. *Lanc* 2D **38**
Higher Bockhampton. *Dors* 6G **9**
Higher Bojewyan. *Corn* 6A **3**
High Ercall. *Telf* 8C **32**
Higher Cheriton. *Devn* 5A **8**
Higher Clovelly. *Devn* 3E **6**
Higher Compton. *Plym* 4F **4**
Higher Dean. *Devn* 3J **5**
Higher Dinting. *Derbs* 6J **39**
Higher Dunstone. *Devn* 8J **7**
Higher End. *G Man* 5D **38**
Higherford. *Lanc* 1G **39**
Higher Gabwell. *Devn* 3L **5**
Higher Halstock Leigh. *Dors* 5E **8**
Higher Heysham. *Lanc* 7F **42**
Higher Hurdsfield. *Ches E* 8H **39**
Higher Kingcombe. *Dors* 6E **8**
Higher Kinnerton. *Flin* 3A **32**
Higher Melcombe. *Dors* 5G **9**
Higher Penwortham. *Lanc* 3D **38**
Higher Porthpean. *Corn* 4B **4**
Higher Poynton. *Ches E* 7H **39**
Higher Shotton. *Flin* 3A **32**
Higher Shurlach. *Ches W* 8E **38**
Higher Slade. *Devn* 1G **7**
Higher Tale. *Devn* 5M **7**
Highertown. *Corn* 5F **3**
Higher Town. *IOS* 2C **3**
Higher Town. *Som* 1L **7**
Higher Vexford. *Som* 2A **8**
Higher Walton. *Lanc* 3D **38**
Higher Walton. *Warr* 7D **38**
Higher Whatcombe. *Dors* 5H **9**
Higher Wheelton. *Lanc* 3E **38**
Higher Whiteleigh. *Corn* 6D **6**
Higher Whitley. *Ches W* 8E **38**
Higher Wincham. *Ches W* 8E **38**
Higher Wraxall. *Dors* 5E **8**
Higher Wych. *Wrex* 5B **32**
Higher Yalberton. *Torb* 4K **5**
High Etherley. *Dur* 1A **44**
High Ferry. *Linc* 5K **35**
Highfield. *E Yor* 2D **40**
Highfield. *N Ayr* 4B **54**
Highfield. *Tyne* 6G **51**
Highfields Caldecote.
Cambs 6M **27**
High Garrett. *Essx* 1F **20**
Highgate. *G Lon* 5A **20**
Highgate. *N Ayr* 4B **54**
Highgate. *Powy* 2B **24**
High Grange. *Dur* 8G **51**
High Green. *Cumb* 3F **42**
High Green. *Norf* 1H **29**
High Green. *Shrp* 3H **25**
High Green. *S Yor* 6M **39**
High Green. *W Yor* 4K **39**
High Green. *Worc* 7J **25**
Highgreen Manor. *Nmbd* 2D **50**
High Halden. *Kent* 4G **13**
High Halstow. *Medw* 6F **20**
High Ham. *Som* 2D **8**
High Harrington. *Cumb* 1B **42**
High Haswell. *Dur* 7J **51**
High Hatton. *Shrp* 7D **32**
High Hawsker. *N Yor* 3J **45**
High Hesket. *Cumb* 7M **49**
High Hesleden. *Dur* 8K **51**
High Hoyland. *S Yor* 4L **39**
High Hunsley. *E Yor* 2F **40**
High Hurstwood. *E Sus* 5C **12**
High Hutton. *N Yor* 7G **45**
High Ireby. *Cumb* 8K **49**
High Keil. *Arg* 8E **52**
High Kelling. *Norf* 3H **37**
High Kilburn. *N Yor* 6E **44**
High Knipe. *Cumb* 2G **43**
High Lands. *Dur* 1A **44**
Highlands, The. *Shrp* 3G **25**
Highlane. *Ches E* 3F **32**
Highlane. *Derbs* 7A **40**
High Lane. *G Man* 7H **39**
High Lane. *Here* 5G **25**
High Laver. *Essx* 3D **20**
Highlaws. *Cumb* 7J **49**
Highleadon. *Glos* 1K **17**
High Legh. *Ches E* 7E **38**
Highleigh. *W Sus* 6J **11**
High Leven. *Stoc T* 2D **44**
Highley. *Shrp* 3H **25**
High Littleton. *Bath* 8J **17**
High Longthwaite. *Cumb* 7K **49**
High Lorton. *Cumb* 1C **42**
High Marishes. *N Yor* 6H **45**
High Marnham. *Notts* 8E **40**
High Melton. *S Yor* 5B **40**
High Mickley. *Nmbd* 5F **50**
Highmoor. *Cumb* 7K **49**
High Moor. *Lanc* 4D **38**
Highmoor. *Oxon* 5H **19**
Highmoor Cross. *Oxon* 5H **19**
Highmoor Hill. *Mon* 5G **17**
High Mowthorpe. *N Yor* 7H **45**
Highnam. *Glos* 2K **17**
High Newport. *Tyne* 6J **51**
High Newton. *Cumb* 5F **42**
High Newton-by-the-Sea.
Nmbd 7M **57**
High Nibthwaite. *Cumb* 5D **42**
High Offley. *Staf* 7E **32**
High Ongar. *Essx* 3D **20**
High Onn. *Staf* 8F **32**
High Orchard. *Glos* 2L **17**
High Park. *Mers* 4B **38**
High Roding. *Essx* 2E **20**
High Row. *Cumb* 8L **49**
High Salvington. *W Sus* 5M **11**
High Scales. *Cumb* 7J **49**
High Shaw. *N Yor* 4K **43**
High Shincliffe. *Dur* 7H **51**
High Side. *Cumb* 8K **49**
High Spen. *Tyne* 5G **51**
Highsted. *Kent* 7H **21**
High Stoop. *Dur* 7G **51**
High Street. *Corn* 4A **4**
High Street. *Suff* 6L **29**
(nr. Aldeburgh)
High Street. *Suff* 3K **29**
(nr. Bungay)
High Street. *Suff* 4L **29**
(nr. Yoxford)
Highstreet Green. *Essx* 8D **28**
High Street Green. *Suff* 6G **29**
Highstreet Green. *Surr* 2K **11**
Hightae. *Dum* 4H **49**
High Throston. *Hart* 8K **51**
Hightown. *Ches E* 3F **32**
Hightown. *Mers* 5A **38**
High Town. *Staf* 8G **33**
Hightown Green. *Suff* 6F **28**
High Toynton. *Linc* 3J **35**
High Trewhitt. *Nmbd* 1F **50**
High Valleyfield. *Fife* 1J **55**
Highway. *Here* 7E **24**
Highweek. *Devn* 8K **7**
High Westwood. *Dur* 6G **51**
Highwood. *Staf* 6H **33**
Highwood. *Worc* 5G **25**

High Worsall—Kemsley

High Worsall. *N Yor* 3C 44
Highworth. *Swin* 4C 18
High Wray. *Cumb* 4E 42
High Wych. *Herts* 2C 20
High Wycombe. *Buck* 4J 19
Hilborough. *Norf* 1E 28
Hilcott. *Wilts* 8B 18
Hildenborough. *Kent* 3D 12
Hildersham. *Cambs* 7B 28
Hilderstone. *Staf* 6G 33
Hilderthorpe. *E Yor* 7L 45
Hilfield. *Dors* 5F 8
Hilgay. *Norf* 2C 28
Hill. *S Glo* 4J 17
Hill. *Warw* 5C 26
Hill. *Worc* 7K 25
Hillam. *N Yor* 3B 40
Hillbeck. *Cumb* 2J 43
Hillberry. *IOM* 6D 46
Hillborough. *Kent* 7L 21
Hillbourne. *Pool* 6A 10
Hillbrae. *Abers* 5G 73
(nr. Aberchirder)
Hillbrae. *Abers* 1H 67
(nr. Inverurie)
Hillbrae. *Abers* 6J 73
(nr. Methlick)
Hill Brow. *Hants* 3H 11
Hillbutts. *Dors* 5J 9
Hillcliffane. *Derbs* 5K 33
Hillcommon. *Som* 3A 8
Hill Deverill. *Wilts* 1H 9
Hilldyke. *Linc* 5K 35
Hill End. *Dur* 8F 50
Hillend. *Fife* 1K 55
(nr. Inverkeithing)
Hill End. *Fife* 6F 60
(nr. Saline)
Hillend. *N Lan* 3G 55
Hill End. *N Yor* 8M 43
Hillend. *Shrp* 2J 25
Hillend. *Swan* 4J 15
Hillersland. *Glos* 2H 17
Hillerton. *Devn* 6J 7
Hillesden. *Buck* 1G 19
Hillesley. *Glos* 5K 17
Hillfarrance. *Som* 3A 8
Hill Furze. *Worc* 7K 25
Hill Gate. *Here* 1G 17
Hill Green. *Essx* 8A 28
Hillgreen. *W Ber* 6E 18
Hillhead. *Abers* 6F 72
Hill Head. *Hants* 5F 10
Hillhead. *S Ayr* 8C 54
Hillhead. *Torb* 4L 5
Hillhead of Auchentumb.
Abers 4K 73
Hilliard's Cross. *Staf* 8J 33
Hilliclay. *High* 3G 77
Hillingdon. *G Lon* 5L 19
Hillington. *Norf* 5D 36
Hillington. *Ren* 3D 54
Hillmorton. *Warw* 4D 26
Hill of Beath. *Fife* 6G 61
Hill of Fearn. *High* 4L 71
Hill of Fiddes. *Abers* 1K 67
Hill of Keillor. *Ang* 1H 61
Hill of Overbrae. *Abers* 3J 73
Hill Ridware. *Staf* 8H 33
Hillsborough. *S Yor* 6M 39
Hillside. *Abers* 4K 67
Hillside. *Ang* 7H 67
Hillside. *Devn* 3J 5
Hillside. *Mers* 4B 38
Hillside. *Orkn* 5B 78
Hillside. *Shet* 5E 79
Hillside. *Shrp* 3G 25
Hill Side. *W Yor* 4K 39
Hillside. *Worc* 5H 25
Hillside of Prieston. *Ang* 2J 61
Hill Somersal. *Derbs* 6J 33
Hillstown. *Derbs* 3A 34
Hillstreet. *Hants* 4D 10
Hillswick. *Shet* 4C 79
Hill, The. *Cumb* 5C 42
Hill Top. *Dur* 1L 43
(nr. Barnard Castle)
Hill Top. *Dur* 7H 51
(nr. Durham)
Hill Top. *Dur* 6G 51
(nr. Stanley)
Hill View. *Dors* 6J 9
Hillwell. *Shet* 10D 79
Hill Wootton. *Warw* 5B 26
Hillyland. *Per* 3F 60
Hilmarton. *Wilts* 6A 18
Hilperton. *Wilts* 8L 17
Hilperton Marsh. *Wilts* 8L 17
Hilsea. *Port* 5G 11
Hilston. *E Yor* 2J 41
Hiltingbury. *Hants* 3E 10
Hilton. *Cambs* 5L 27
Hilton. *Cumb* 1J 43
Hilton. *Derbs* 6K 33
Hilton. *Dors* 5G 9
Hilton. *Dur* 1A 44
Hilton. *High* 3K 71
Hilton. *Shrp* 2H 25
Hilton. *Staf* 1L 25
Hilton. *Stoc T* 2D 44
Hilton of Cadboll. *High* 4L 71
Himbleton. *Worc* 6K 25
Himley. *Staf* 2J 25
Hincaster. *Cumb* 5G 43
Hinchcliffe Mill. *W Yor* 5K 39
Hinchwick. *Glos* 8M 25
Hinckley. *Leics* 2C 26
Hinderclay. *Suff* 4G 29
Hinderwell. *N Yor* 2G 45
Hindford. *Shrp* 6A 32
Hindhead. *Surr* 2J 11
Hindley. *G Man* 5E 38
Hindley. *Nmbd* 6F 50
Hindley Green. *G Man* 5E 38
Hindlip. *Worc* 6J 25
Hindolveston. *Norf* 5G 37
Hindon. *Wilts* 2J 9
Hindringham. *Norf* 4F 36
Hingham. *Norf* 1G 29
Hinksford. *Staf* 3J 25
Hinstock. *Shrp* 7D 32
Hintlesham. *Suff* 7G 29
Hinton. *Hants* 6C 10
Hinton. *Here* 8D 24
Hinton. *Nptn* 6D 26
Hinton. *Shrp* 1E 24
Hinton. *S Glo* 6K 17
Hinton Ampner. *Hants* 3F 10
Hinton Blewett. *Bath* 8H 17
Hinton Charterhouse. *Bath* 8K 17
Hinton-in-the-Hedges.
Nptn 8D 26
Hinton Martell. *Dors* 5A 10
Hinton on the Green. *Worc* 7L 25
Hinton Parva. *Swin* 5C 18
Hinton St George. *Som* 4D 8
Hinton St Mary. *Dors* 4G 9
Hinton Waldrist. *Oxon* 4D 18
Hints. *Shrp* 4G 25
Hints. *Staf* 1M 25
Hinwick. *Bed* 5H 27
Hinxhill. *Kent* 3J 13
Hinxton. *Cambs* 7A 28
Hinxworth. *Herts* 7L 27
Hipley. *Hants* 4G 11
Hipperholme. *W Yor* 3K 39
Hipsburn. *Nmbd* 8M 57
Hipswell. *N Yor* 4A 44
Hiraeth. *Carm* 1F 14
Hirn. *Abers* 3H 67
Hirnant. *Powy* 7K 31
Hirst. *N Lan* 3G 55
Hirst. *Nmbd* 3H 51
Hirst Courtney. *N Yor* 3C 40
Hirwaen. *Den* 3L 31
Hirwaun. *Rhon* 3B 16
Hiscott. *Devn* 3G 7
Histon. *Cambs* 5A 28
Hitcham. *Suff* 6F 28
Hitchin. *Herts* 1M 19
Hittisleigh. *Devn* 6J 7
Hittisleigh Barton. *Devn* 6J 7
Hive. *E Yor* 2E 40
Hixon. *Staf* 7H 33
Hoaden. *Kent* 8L 21
Hoar Cross. *Staf* 7J 33
Hoarwithy. *Here* 1H 17
Hoath. *Kent* 7L 21
Hobarris. *Shrp* 4D 24
Hobbister. *Orkn* 7B 78
Hobbles Green. *Suff* 6D 28
Hobbs Cross. *Essx* 4C 20
Hobkirk. *Bord* 8E 56
Hobson. *Dur* 6G 51
Hoby. *Leics* 8C 34
Hockering. *Norf* 6G 37
Hockering Heath. *Norf* 6G 37
Hockerton. *Notts* 4D 34
Hockley. *Essx* 4G 21
Hockley. *Staf* 1A 26
Hockley. *W Mid* 4A 26
Hockley Heath. *W Mid* 4M 25
Hockliffe. *C Beds* 1K 19
Hockwold cum Wilton.
Norf 3D 28
Hockworthy. *Devn* 4M 7
Hoddesdon. *Herts* 3B 20
Hoddlesden. *Bkbn* 3F 38
Hoddomcross. *Dum* 4J 49
Hodgeston. *Pemb* 4E 14
Hodley. *Powy* 2B 24
Hodnet. *Shrp* 7D 32
Hodsoll Street. *Kent* 7E 20
Hodson. *Swin* 5B 18
Hodthorpe. *Derbs* 8B 40
Hoe. *Norf* 6F 36
Hoe Gate. *Hants* 4G 11
Hoe, The. *Plym* 4F 4
Hoff. *Cumb* 2H 43
Hoffleet Stow. *Linc* 6J 35
Hogaland. *Shet* 4D 79
Hogben's Hill. *Kent* 8J 21
Hoggard's Green. *Suff* 6E 28
Hoggeston. *Buck* 1J 19
Hoggrill's End. *Warw* 2A 26
Hogha Gearraidh. *W Isl* 4B 68
Hoghton. *Lanc* 3E 38
Hoghton Bottoms. *Lanc* 3E 38
Hognaston. *Derbs* 4K 33
Hogsthorpe. *Linc* 8M 41
Hogstock. *Dors* 5J 9
Holbeach. *Linc* 7K 35
Holbeach Bank. *Linc* 7K 35
Holbeach Clough. *Linc* 7K 35
Holbeach Drove. *Linc* 8K 35
Holbeach Hurn. *Linc* 7K 35
Holbeach St Johns. *Linc* 8K 35
Holbeach St Marks. *Linc* 6K 35
Holbeach St Matthew. *Linc* 6L 35
Holbeck. *Notts* 8B 40
Holbeck. *W Yor* 2L 39
Holbeck Woodhouse.
Notts 8B 40
Holberrow Green. *Worc* 6L 25
Holbeton. *Devn* 4H 5
Holborn. *G Lon* 5B 20
Holbrook. *Derbs* 5L 33
Holbrook. *S Yor* 7A 40
Holbrook. *Suff* 8H 29
Holburn. *Nmbd* 6K 57
Holbury. *Hants* 5E 10
Holcombe. *Devn* 8L 7
Holcombe. *G Man* 4F 38
Holcombe. *Som* 1F 8
Holcombe Brook. *G Man* 4F 38
Holcombe Rogus. *Devn* 4M 7
Holcot. *Nptn* 5F 26
Holden. *Lanc* 1F 38
Holdenby. *Nptn* 5E 26
Holder's Green. *Essx* 1E 20
Holdgate. *Shrp* 3F 24
Holdingham. *Linc* 5G 35
Holditch. *Dors* 5C 8
Holemoor. *Devn* 5F 6
Hole Street. *W Sus* 4M 11
Holford. *Som* 1A 8
Holker. *Cumb* 6E 42
Holkham. *Norf* 3E 36
Hollacombe. *Devn* 5E 6
Holland. *Orkn* 2C 78
(on Papa Westray)
Holland. *Orkn* 5E 78
(on Stronsay)
Holland Fen. *Linc* 5J 35
Holland Lees. *Lanc* 5D 38
Holland-on-Sea. *Essx* 2L 21
Holland Park. *W Mid* 1L 25
Hollandstoun. *Orkn* 2F 78
Hollesley. *Suff* 7K 29
Hollinfare. *Warr* 6E 38
Hollingbourne. *Kent* 8G 21
Hollingbury. *Brig* 7B 12
Hollingdon. *Buck* 1J 19
Hollingrove. *E Sus* 5E 12
Hollington. *Derbs* 5K 33
Hollington. *E Sus* 6F 12
Hollington. *Staf* 6H 33
Hollington Grove. *Derbs* 6K 33
Hollingworth. *G Man* 6J 39
Hollins. *Derbs* 8M 39
Hollins. *G Man* 5G 39
(nr. Bury)
Hollins. *G Man* 5G 39
(nr. Middleton)
Hollinsclough. *Staf* 3H 33
Hollinswood. *Telf* 1G 25
Hollinthorpe. *W Yor* 2M 39
Hollinwood. *G Man* 5H 39
Hollinwood. *Shrp* 6C 32
Hollocombe. *Devn* 4H 7
Holloway. *Derbs* 4L 33
Hollow Court. *Worc* 6K 25
Hollowell. *Nptn* 4E 26
Hollow Meadows. *S Yor* 7L 39
Hollows. *Dum* 4L 49
Hollybush. *Cphy* 3D 16
Hollybush. *E Ayr* 8B 54
Hollybush. *Worc* 8H 25
Holly End. *Norf* 1A 28
Holly Hill. *N Yor* 3A 44
Hollyhurst. *Ches E* 5C 32
Hollym. *E Yor* 3K 41
Hollywood. *Worc* 4L 25
Holmacott. *Devn* 3G 7
Holmbridge. *W Yor* 5K 39
Holmbury St Mary. *Surr* 1M 11
Holmbush. *Corn* 4B 4
Holmcroft. *Staf* 7G 33
Holme. *Cambs* 3K 27
Holme. *Cumb* 6G 43
Holme. *N Lin* 5F 40
Holme. *N Yor* 5C 44
Holme. *Notts* 4E 34
Holme. *W Yor* 5K 39
Holmebridge. *Dors* 7H 9
Holme Chapel. *Lanc* 3G 39
Holme Hale. *Norf* 1E 28
Holme Lacy. *Here* 8F 24
Holme Marsh. *Here* 6D 24
Holmend. *Dum* 1H 49
Holme next the Sea. *Norf* 3D 36
Holme-on-Spalding-Moor.
E Yor 2E 40
Holme on the Wolds. *E Yor* 1F 40
Holme Pierrepont. *Notts* 6C 34
Holmer. *Here* 7F 24
Holmer Green. *Buck* 4K 19
Holmes. *Lanc* 4C 38
Holme St Cuthbert. *Cumb* 7J 49
Holmes Chapel. *Ches E* 3E 32
Holmesfield. *Derbs* 8M 39
Holmeswood. *Lanc* 4C 38
Holmewood. *Derbs* 3A 34
Holmfirth. *W Yor* 5K 39
Holmhead. *E Ayr* 7D 54
Holmisdale. *High* 7F 68
Holm of Drumlanrig. *Dum* 2F 48
Holmpton. *E Yor* 3K 41
Holmrook. *Cumb* 4B 42
Holmsgarth. *Shet* 7E 79
Holmside. *Dur* 7H 51
Holmwrangle. *Cumb* 7A 50
Holne. *Devn* 3J 5
Holsworthy. *Devn* 5E 6
Holsworthy Beacon. *Devn* 5E 6
Holt. *Dors* 5A 10
Holt. *Norf* 4G 37
Holt. *Wilts* 7L 17
Holt. *Worc* 5J 25
Holt. *Wrex* 4B 32
Holtby. *York* 8F 44
Holt End. *Hants* 2G 11
Holt End. *Worc* 5L 25
Holt Fleet. *Worc* 5J 25
Holt Green. *Lanc* 5B 38
Holt Heath. *Dors* 5A 10
Holt Heath. *Worc* 5J 25
Holton. *Oxon* 3G 19
Holton. *Som* 3F 8
Holton. *Suff* 4K 29
Holton cum Beckering.
Linc 7H 41
Holton Heath. *Dors* 6J 9
Holton le Clay. *Linc* 5J 41
Holton le Moor. *Linc* 6G 41
Holton St Mary. *Suff* 8G 29
Holt Pound. *Hants* 1J 11
Holtsmere End. *Herts* 2L 19
Holtye. *E Sus* 4C 12
Holwell. *Dors* 4G 9
Holwell. *Herts* 8K 27
Holwell. *Leics* 7D 34
Holwell. *Oxon* 3C 18
Holwell. *Som* 1G 9
Holwick. *Dur* 1L 43
Holworth. *Dors* 7G 9
Holybourne. *Hants* 1H 11
Holy City. *Devn* 5C 8
Holy Cross. *Worc* 4K 25
Holyfield. *Essx* 3B 20
Holyhead. *IOA* 1B 30
Holy Island. *Nmbd* 5L 57
Holymoorside. *Derbs* 3L 33
Holyport. *Wind* 6J 19
Holystone. *Nmbd* 1E 50
Holytown. *N Lan* 3F 54
Holywell. *Cambs* 4M 27
Holywell. *Dors* 5E 8
Holywell. *Flin* 2L 31
Holywell. *Glos* 4K 17
Holywell. *Nmbd* 4J 51
Holywell. *Warw* 5M 25
Holywell Bay. *Corn* 4E 3
Holywell Green. *W Yor* 4J 39
Holywell Lake. *Som* 3A 8
Holywell Row. *Suff* 4D 28
Holywood. *Dum* 3G 49
Homer. *Shrp* 1G 25
Homer Green. *Mers* 5B 38
Homersfield. *Suff* 3J 29
Hom Green. *Here* 1H 17
Homington. *Wilts* 3B 10
Honeyborough. *Pemb* 3D 14
Honeybourne. *Worc* 7M 25
Honeychurch. *Devn* 5H 7
Honeydon. *Bed* 6K 27
Honey Hill. *Kent* 7K 21
Honey Street. *Wilts* 7B 18
Honey Tye. *Suff* 8F 28
Honeywick. *C Beds* 1K 19
Honiley. *Warw* 4A 26
Honing. *Norf* 5K 37
Honingham. *Norf* 6H 37
Honington. *Linc* 5F 34
Honington. *Suff* 4F 28
Honington. *Warw* 7A 26
Honiton. *Devn* 5A 8
Honley. *W Yor* 4K 39
Honnington. *Telf* 8E 32
Hoo. *Suff* 6J 29
Hoobrook. *Worc* 4J 25
Hood Green. *S Yor* 5M 39
Hooe. *E Sus* 7E 12
Hooe. *Plym* 4G 5
Hooe Common. *E Sus* 6E 12
Hoo Green. *Ches E* 7F 38
Hoohill. *Bkpl* 2B 38
Hook. *Cambs* 2A 28
Hook. *E Yor* 3D 40
Hook. *G Lon* 7M 19
Hook. *Hants* 8H 19
(nr. Basingstoke)
Hook. *Hants* 5F 10
(nr. Fareham)
Hook. *Pemb* 2D 14
Hook. *Wilts* 5A 18
Hook-a-Gate. *Shrp* 1E 24
Hook Bank. *Worc* 7J 25
Hooke. *Dors* 5E 8
Hooker Gate. *Tyne* 6G 51
Hookgate. *Staf* 6E 32
Hook Green. *Kent* 4E 12
(nr. Lamberhurst)
Hook Green. *Kent* 6E 20
(nr. Longfield)
Hook Green. *Kent* 7E 20
(nr. Meopham)
Hook Norton. *Oxon* 8B 26
Hook's Cross. *Herts* 1A 20
Hook Street. *Glos* 4J 17
Hookway. *Devn* 6K 7
Hookwood. *Surr* 3A 12
Hoole. *Ches W* 3B 32
Hooley. *Surr* 8A 20
Hooley Bridge. *G Man* 4G 39
Hooley Brow. *G Man* 4G 39
Hoo St Werburgh. *Medw* 6F 20
Hooton. *Ches W* 8B 38
Hooton Levitt. *S Yor* 6B 40
Hooton Pagnell. *S Yor* 5A 40
Hooton Roberts. *S Yor* 6A 40
Hoove. *Shet* 7D 79
Hope. *Derbs* 7K 39
Hope. *Flin* 4A 32
Hope. *High* 3M 75
Hope. *Powy* 1C 24
Hope. *Shrp* 1D 24
Hope. *Staf* 4J 33
Hope Bagot. *Shrp* 4F 24
Hope Bowdler. *Shrp* 2E 24
Hopedale. *Staf* 4J 33
Hope Green. *Ches E* 7H 39
Hopeman. *Mor* 3B 72
Hope Mansell. *Here* 2J 17
Hopesay. *Shrp* 3D 24
Hope's Green. *Essx* 5F 20
Hopetown. *W Yor* 3M 39
Hope under Dinmore. *Here* 6F 24
Hopley's Green. *Here* 6D 24
Hopperton. *N Yor* 8D 44
Hop Pole. *Linc* 8H 35
Hopstone. *Shrp* 2H 25
Hopton. *Derbs* 4K 33
Hopton. *Powy* 2C 24
Hopton. *Shrp* 7A 32
(nr. Oswestry)
Hopton. *Shrp* 7C 32
(nr. Wem)
Hopton. *Staf* 7G 33
Hopton. *Suff* 4F 28
Hopton Cangeford. *Shrp* 3F 24
Hopton Castle. *Shrp* 4D 24
Hoptonheath. *Shrp* 4D 24
Hopton Heath. *Staf* 7G 33
Hopton on Sea. *Norf* 1M 29
Hopton Wafers. *Shrp* 4G 25
Hopwas. *Staf* 1M 25
Hopwood. *Worc* 4L 25
Horam. *E Sus* 6D 12
Horbling. *Linc* 6H 35
Horbury. *W Yor* 4L 39
Horcott. *Glos* 3B 18
Horden. *Dur* 7K 51
Horderley. *Shrp* 3E 24
Hordle. *Hants* 6C 10
Hordley. *Shrp* 6A 32
Horeb. *Carm* 1K 15
(nr. Brechfa)
Horeb. *Carm* 3J 15
(nr. Llanelli)
Horeb. *Cdgn* 7F 22
Horfield. *Bris* 6J 17
Horgabost. *W Isl* 2E 68
Horham. *Suff* 4J 29
Horkesley Heath. *Essx* 1H 21
Horkstow. *N Lin* 4F 40
Horley. *Oxon* 7C 26
Horley. *Surr* 3A 12
Horn Ash. *Dors* 5C 8
Hornblotton Green. *Som* 2E 8
Hornby. *Lanc* 7G 43
Hornby. *N Yor* 3C 44
(nr. Appleton Wiske)
Hornby. *N Yor* 4B 44
(nr. Catterick Garrison)
Horncastle. *Linc* 3J 35
Hornchurch. *G Lon* 5D 20
Horncliffe. *Nmbd* 5J 57
Horndean. *Hants* 4G 11
Horndean. *Bord* 5H 57
Horndon. *Devn* 7G 7
Horndon on the Hill. *Thur* 5E 20
Horne. *Surr* 3B 12
Horner. *Som* 1L 7
Horning. *Norf* 6K 37
Horninghold. *Leics* 2G 27
Horninglow. *Staf* 7K 33
Horningsea. *Cambs* 5A 28
Horningsham. *Wilts* 1H 9
Horningtoft. *Norf* 5F 36
Hornsbury. *Som* 4C 8
Hornsby. *Cumb* 6A 50
Hornsbygate. *Cumb* 6A 50
Horns Corner. *Kent* 5F 12
Horns Cross. *Devn* 3E 6
Hornsea. *E Yor* 1J 41
Hornsea Burton. *E Yor* 1J 41
Hornsey. *G Lon* 5B 20
Hornton. *Oxon* 7B 26
Horpit. *Swin* 5C 18
Horrabridge. *Devn* 3G 5
Horringer. *Suff* 5E 28
Horringford. *IOW* 7F 10
Horrocks Fold. *G Man* 4F 38
Horrocksford. *Lanc* 1F 38
Horsbrugh Ford. *Bord* 6L 55
Horsebridge. *Devn* 8F 6
Horsebridge. *E Sus* 6D 12
Horsebridge. *Hants* 2D 10
Horse Bridge. *Staf* 4G 33
Horsebrook. *Staf* 8F 32
Horsecastle. *N Som* 7G 17
Horsehay. *Telf* 1G 25
Horseheath. *Cambs* 7C 28
Horsehouse. *N Yor* 5M 43
Horsell. *Surr* 8K 19
Horseman's Green. *Wrex* 5B 32
Horsenden. *Buck* 3H 19
Horseway. *Cambs* 3A 28
Horsey. *Norf* 5L 37
Horsey. *Som* 2C 8
Horsford. *Norf* 6H 37
Horsforth. *W Yor* 2L 39
Horsham. *W Sus* 2M 11
Horsham. *Worc* 6H 25
Horsham St Faith. *Norf* 6J 37
Horsington. *Linc* 3H 35
Horsington. *Som* 3G 9
Horsley. *Derbs* 5L 33
Horsley. *Glos* 4L 17
Horsley. *Nmbd* 5F 50
(nr. Prudhoe)
Horsley. *Nmbd* 2D 50
(nr. Rochester)
Horsley Cross. *Essx* 1K 21
Horsleycross Street. *Essx* 1K 21
Horsleyhill. *Bord* 8E 56
Horsleyhope. *Dur* 7F 50
Horsley Woodhouse.
Derbs 5L 33
Horsmonden. *Kent* 3E 12
Horspath. *Oxon* 3F 18
Horstead. *Norf* 6J 37
Horsted Keynes. *W Sus* 5B 12
Horton. *Buck* 2K 19
Horton. *Dors* 5A 10
Horton. *Lanc* 8K 43
Horton. *Nptn* 6G 27
Horton. *Shrp* 6B 32
Horton. *Som* 4C 8
Horton. *S Glo* 5K 17
Horton. *Staf* 4G 33
Horton. *Swan* 5J 15
Horton. *Wilts* 7A 18
Horton. *Wind* 6L 19
Horton Cross. *Som* 4C 8
Horton-cum-Studley. *Oxon* 2F 18
Horton Grange. *Nmbd* 4H 51
Horton Green. *Ches W* 5B 32
Horton Heath. *Hants* 4E 10
Horton in Ribblesdale.
N Yor 6K 43
Horton Kirby. *Kent* 7D 20
Hortonwood. *Telf* 8D 32
Horwich. *G Man* 4E 38
Horwich End. *Derbs* 7J 39
Horwood. *Devn* 3G 7
Hoscar. *Lanc* 4C 38
Hose. *Leics* 7D 34
Hosh. *Per* 3D 60
Hosta. *W Isl* 4B 68
Hoswick. *Shet* 9E 79
Hotham. *E Yor* 2E 40
Hothfield. *Kent* 3H 13
Hoton. *Leics* 7B 34
Houbie. *Shet* 2G 79
Hough. *Arg* 8A 62
Hough. *Ches E* 4E 32
(nr. Crewe)
Hough. *Ches E* 8G 39
(nr. Wilmslow)
Hougham. *Linc* 5E 34
Hough Green. *Hal* 7C 38
Hough-on-the-Hill. *Linc* 5F 34
Houghton. *Cambs* 4L 27
Houghton. *Cumb* 6M 49
Houghton. *Hants* 2D 10
Houghton. *Nmbd* 5G 51
Houghton. *Pemb* 3D 14
Houghton. *W Sus* 4L 11
Houghton Bank. *Darl* 1B 44
Houghton Conquest.
C Beds 7J 27
Houghton Green. *E Sus* 5H 13
Houghton-le-Side. *Darl* 1B 44
Houghton-le-Spring. *Tyne* 7J 51
Houghton on the Hill.
Leics 1E 26
Houghton Regis. *C Beds* 1L 19
Houghton St Giles. *Norf* 4F 36
Houlland. *Shet* 6D 79
(on Mainland)
Houlland. *Shet* 4F 79
(on Yell)
Houlsyke. *N Yor* 3G 45
Hound. *Hants* 5E 10
Hound Green. *Hants* 8H 19
Houndslow. *Bord* 5F 56
Houndsmoor. *Som* 3A 8
Houndwood. *Bord* 3H 57
Hounsdown. *Hants* 4D 10
Hounslow. *G Lon* 6M 19
Housabister. *Shet* 6E 79
Housay. *Shet* 4G 79
Househill. *High* 6L 71
Housetter. *Shet* 3D 79
Houss. *Shet* 8D 79
Houston. *Ren* 3C 54
Housty. *High* 6G 77
Houton. *Orkn* 7B 78
Hove. *Brig* 7A 12 & 92
Hoveringham. *Notts* 5D 34
Hoveton. *Norf* 6K 37
Hovingham. *N Yor* 6F 44
How. *Cumb* 6A 50
How Caple. *Here* 8G 25
Howden. *E Yor* 3D 40
Howden-le-Wear. *Dur* 8G 51
Howe. *High* 3J 77
Howe. *Norf* 1J 29
Howe. *N Yor* 5C 44
Howe Green. *Essx* 3F 20
(nr. Chelmsford)
Howegreen. *Essx* 3G 21
(nr. Maldon)
Howe Green. *Warw* 3B 26
Howell. *Linc* 5H 35
How End. *C Beds* 7J 27
Howe of Teuchar. *Abers* 5H 73
Howes. *Dum* 5J 49
Howe Street. *Essx* 2E 20
(nr. Chelmsford)
Howe Street. *Essx* 8C 28
(nr. Finchingfield)
Howe, The. *Cumb* 5F 42
Howe, The. *IOM* 7B 46
Howey. *Powy* 6A 24
Howgate. *Midl* 4L 55
Howgill. *Lanc* 1G 39
Howgill. *N Yor* 8M 43
How Green. *Kent* 3C 12
How Hill. *Norf* 6K 37
Howick. *Nmbd* 8M 57
Howle. *Telf* 7D 32
Howle Hill. *Here* 1J 17
Howleigh. *Som* 4B 8
Howlett End. *Essx* 8B 28
Howley. *Som* 5B 8
Howley. *Warr* 7E 38
Hownam. *Bord* 8G 57
Howsham. *N Lin* 5G 41
Howsham. *N Yor* 7G 45
Howtel. *Nmbd* 6H 57
Howt Green. *Kent* 7G 21
Howton. *Here* 1G 17
Howwood. *Ren* 3B 54
Hoxne. *Suff* 4H 29
Hoylake. *Mers* 7A 38
Hoyland. *S Yor* 5M 39
Hoylandswaine. *S Yor* 5L 39
Hoyle. *W Sus* 4K 11
Hubberholme. *N Yor* 6L 43
Hubberston. *Pemb* 3C 14
Hubbert's Bridge. *Linc* 5J 35
Huby. *N Yor* 1L 39
(nr. Harrogate)
Huby. *N Yor* 7E 44
(nr. York)
Hucclecote. *Glos* 2L 17
Hucking. *Kent* 8G 21
Hucknall. *Notts* 5B 34
Huddersfield. *W Yor* 4K 39
Huddington. *Worc* 6K 25
Huddlesford. *Staf* 1M 25
Hudswell. *N Yor* 3A 44
Huggate. *E Yor* 8H 45
Hugglescote. *Leics* 8A 34
Hughenden Valley. *Buck* 4J 19
Hughley. *Shrp* 2F 24
Hughton. *High* 7G 71
Hugh Town. *IOS* 2C 3
Hugus. *Corn* 5E 3
Huish. *Devn* 4G 7
Huish. *Wilts* 7B 18
Huish Champflower. *Som* 3M 7
Huish Episcopi. *Som* 3D 8
Huisinis. *W Isl* 1D 68
Hulcote. *Nptn* 6F 26
Hulcott. *Buck* 2J 19
Hulham. *Devn* 7M 7
Hull. *Hull* 3G 41 & 96
Hulland. *Derbs* 5K 33
Hulland Moss. *Derbs* 5K 33
Hulland Ward. *Derbs* 5K 33
Hullavington. *Wilts* 5L 17
Hullbridge. *Essx* 4G 21
Hulme. *G Man* 6G 39
Hulme. *Staf* 5G 33
Hulme End. *Staf* 4J 33
Hulme Walfield. *Ches E* 3F 32
Hulverstone. *IOW* 7D 10
Hulver Street. *Suff* 3L 29
Humber. *Devn* 8L 7
Humber. *Here* 6F 24
Humber Bridge. *N Lin* 3G 41
Humberside International Airport.
N Lin 4G 41
Humberston. *NE Lin* 5K 41
Humberstone. *Leic* 1E 26
Humbie. *E Lot* 3D 56
Humbleton. *E Yor* 2J 41
Humbleton. *Nmbd* 7J 57
Humby. *Linc* 6G 35
Hume. *Bord* 5G 57
Humshaugh. *Nmbd* 4E 50
Huna. *High* 2J 77
Huncoat. *Lanc* 2F 38
Huncote. *Leics* 2D 26
Hundall. *Derbs* 8M 39
Hunderthwaite. *Dur* 1L 43
Hundleby. *Linc* 3K 35
Hundle Houses. *Linc* 4J 35
Hundleton. *Pemb* 3D 14
Hundon. *Suff* 7D 28
Hundred Acres. *Hants* 4F 10
Hundred House. *Powy* 6B 24
Hundred, The. *Here* 5F 24
Hungarton. *Leics* 1E 26
Hungerford. *Hants* 4B 10
Hungerford. *Shrp* 3F 24
Hungerford. *Som* 1M 7
Hungerford. *W Ber* 7D 18
Hungerford Newtown.
W Ber 6D 18
Hunger Hill. *G Man* 5E 38
Hungerton. *Linc* 6E 34
Hungladder. *High* 4H 69
Hungryhatton. *Shrp* 7D 32
Hunmanby. *N Yor* 6K 45
Hunmanby Sands. *N Yor* 6L 45
Hunningham. *Warw* 5B 26
Hunnington. *Worc* 3K 25
Hunny Hill. *IOW* 7E 10
Hunsdon. *Herts* 2C 20
Hunsdonbury. *Herts* 2C 20
Hunsingore. *N Yor* 8D 44
Hunslet. *W Yor* 2M 39
Hunslet Carr. *W Yor* 3M 39
Hunsonby. *Cumb* 8A 50
Hunspow. *High* 2H 77
Hunstanton. *Norf* 3C 36
Hunstanworth. *Dur* 7E 50
Hunston. *Suff* 5F 28
Hunston. *W Sus* 5J 11
Hunstrete. *Bath* 7J 17
Hunt End. *Worc* 5L 25
Hunterfield. *Midl* 3M 55
Hunters Forstal. *Kent* 7K 21
Hunter's Quay. *Arg* 2K 53
Huntham. *Som* 3C 8
Hunthill Lodge. *Ang* 6E 66
Huntingdon. *Cambs* 4L 27
Huntingfield. *Suff* 4K 29
Huntingford. *Wilts* 2H 9
Huntington. *Ches W* 3B 32
Huntington. *E Lot* 2D 56
Huntington. *Here* 6C 24
Huntington. *Staf* 8G 33
Huntington. *Telf* 1G 25
Huntington. *York* 8F 44
Huntingtower. *Per* 3F 60
Huntley. *Glos* 2K 17
Huntley. *Staf* 5H 33
Huntly. *Abers* 5F 72
Huntlywood. *Bord* 5F 56
Hunton. *Hants* 2E 10
Hunton. *Kent* 3F 12
Hunton. *N Yor* 4A 44
Hunton Bridge. *Herts* 3L 19
Hunt's Corner. *Norf* 3G 29
Huntscott. *Som* 1L 7
Hunt's Cross. *Mers* 7C 38
Hunts Green. *Warw* 2M 25
Huntsham. *Devn* 3M 7
Huntshaw. *Devn* 3G 7
Huntspill. *Som* 1C 8
Huntstile. *Som* 2B 8
Huntworth. *Som* 2C 8
Hunwick. *Dur* 8G 51
Hunworth. *Norf* 4G 37
Hurcott. *Som* 4C 8
(nr. Ilminster)
Hurcott. *Som* 3E 8
(nr. Somerton)
Hurdcott. *Wilts* 2B 10
Hurdley. *Powy* 2C 24
Hurdsfield. *Ches E* 8H 39
Hurlet. *Glas* 3D 54
Hurley. *Warw* 2A 26
Hurley. *Wind* 5J 19
Hurlford. *E Ayr* 6C 54
Hurliness. *Orkn* 9A 78
Hurlston Green. *Lanc* 4B 38
Hurn. *Dors* 6B 10
Hursey. *Dors* 5D 8
Hursley. *Hants* 3E 10
Hurst. *G Man* 5H 39
Hurst. *N Yor* 3M 43
Hurst. *Som* 4D 8
Hurst. *Wok* 6H 19
Hurstbourne Priors. *Hants* 1E 10
Hurstbourne Tarrant.
Hants 8D 18
Hurst Green. *Ches E* 5C 32
Hurst Green. *E Sus* 5F 12
Hurst Green. *Essx* 2J 21
Hurst Green. *Lanc* 2E 38
Hurst Green. *Surr* 8B 20
Hurstley. *Here* 7D 24
Hurstpierpoint. *W Sus* 6A 12
Hurstway Common. *Here* 7C 24
Hurst Wickham. *W Sus* 6A 12
Hurstwood. *Lanc* 2G 39
Hurtmore. *Surr* 1K 11
Hurworth-on-Tees. *Darl* 2C 44
Hurworth Place. *Darl* 2B 44
Hury. *Dur* 2L 43
Husbands Bosworth. *Leics* 3E 26
Husborne Crawley. *C Beds* 8H 27
Husthwaite. *N Yor* 6E 44
Hutcherleigh. *Devn* 4J 5
Hut Green. *N Yor* 3B 40
Huthwaite. *Notts* 4A 34
Huttoft. *Linc* 8M 41
Hutton. *Cumb* 1F 42
Hutton. *E Yor* 8K 45
Hutton. *Essx* 4E 20
Hutton. *Lanc* 3C 38
Hutton. *N Som* 8F 16
Hutton. *Bord* 4J 57
Hutton Bonville. *N Yor* 3C 44
Hutton Buscel. *N Yor* 5J 45
Hutton Conyers. *N Yor* 6C 44
Hutton Cranswick. *E Yor* 8K 45
Hutton End. *Cumb* 8M 49
Hutton Gate. *Red C* 2E 44
Hutton Henry. *Dur* 8K 51
Hutton-le-Hole. *N Yor* 5G 45
Hutton Magna. *Dur* 2A 44
Hutton Mulgrave. *N Yor* 3H 45
Hutton Roof. *Cumb* 6G 43
(nr. Kirkby Lonsdale)
Hutton Roof. *Cumb* 8L 49
(nr. Penrith)
Hutton Rudby. *N Yor* 3D 44
Huttons Ambo. *N Yor* 7G 45
Hutton Sessay. *N Yor* 6D 44
Hutton Village. *Red C* 2F 44
Hutton Wandesley. *N Yor* 8E 44
Huxham. *Devn* 6L 7
Huxham Green. *Som* 2E 8
Huxley. *Ches W* 3C 32
Huxter. *Shet* 6B 79
(on Mainland)
Huxter. *Shet* 5F 79
(on Whalsay)
Huyton. *Mers* 6C 38
Hwlffordd. *Pemb* 2D 14
Hycemoor. *Cumb* 5B 42
Hyde. *Glos* 3L 17
(nr. Stroud)
Hyde. *Glos* 1A 18
(nr. Winchcombe)
Hyde. *G Man* 6H 39
Hyde Heath. *Buck* 3K 19
Hyde Lea. *Staf* 7G 33
Hyde Park. *S Yor* 5B 40
Hydestile. *Surr* 1K 11
Hyndford Bridge. *S Lan* 5H 55
Hynish. *Arg* 9A 62
Hyssington. *Powy* 2D 24
Hythe. *Hants* 5E 10
Hythe. *Kent* 4K 13
Hythe End. *Wind* 6L 19
Hythie. *Abers* 4L 73
Hyton. *Cumb* 5B 42

I

Ianstown. *Mor* 3E 72
Iarsiadar. *W Isl* 5B 74
Ibberton. *Dors* 5G 9
Ible. *Derbs* 4K 33
Ibrox. *Glas* 3D 54
Ibsley. *Hants* 5B 10
Ibstock. *Leics* 8A 34
Ibstone. *Buck* 4H 19
Ibthorpe. *Hants* 8D 18
Iburndale. *N Yor* 3H 45
Ibworth. *Hants* 8F 18
Icelton. *N Som* 7F 16
Ichrachan. *Arg* 2H 59
Ickburgh. *Norf* 2E 28
Ickenham. *G Lon* 5L 19
Ickenthwaite. *Cumb* 5E 42
Ickford. *Buck* 3G 19
Ickham. *Kent* 8L 21
Ickleford. *Herts* 8K 27
Icklesham. *E Sus* 6G 13
Ickleton. *Cambs* 7A 28
Icklingham. *Suff* 4D 28
Ickwell. *C Beds* 7K 27
Icomb. *Glos* 1C 18
Idbury. *Oxon* 1C 18
Iddesleigh. *Devn* 5G 7
Ide. *Devn* 6K 7
Ideford. *Devn* 8K 7
Ide Hill. *Kent* 8C 20
Iden. *E Sus* 5H 13
Iden Green. *Kent* 4G 13
(nr. Benenden)
Iden Green. *Kent* 4F 12
(nr. Goudhurst)
Idle. *W Yor* 2K 39
Idless. *Corn* 5F 3
Idlicote. *Warw* 7A 26
Idmiston. *Wilts* 2B 10
Idole. *Carm* 2J 15
Idridgehay. *Derbs* 5K 33
Idrigill. *High* 5H 69
Idstone. *Oxon* 5C 18
Iffley. *Oxon* 3F 18
Ifield. *W Sus* 4A 12
Ifieldwood. *W Sus* 4A 12
Ifold. *W Sus* 2L 11
Iford. *E Sus* 7C 12
Ifton Heath. *Shrp* 6A 32
Ightfield. *Shrp* 6C 32
Ightham. *Kent* 8D 20
Iken. *Suff* 6L 29
Ilam. *Staf* 4J 33
Ilchester. *Som* 3E 8
Ilderton. *Nmbd* 7K 57
Ilford. *G Lon* 5C 20
Ilford. *Som* 4C 8
Ilfracombe. *Devn* 1G 7
Ilkeston. *Derbs* 5A 34
Ilketshall St Andrew. *Suff* 3K 29
Ilketshall St Lawrence.
Suff 3K 29
Ilketshall St Margaret. *Suff* 3K 29
Ilkley. *W Yor* 1K 39
Illand. *Corn* 8D 6
Illey. *W Mid* 3K 25
Illidge Green. *Ches E* 3E 32
Illington. *Norf* 3F 28
Illingworth. *W Yor* 3J 39
Illogan. *Corn* 5D 3
Illogan Highway. *Corn* 5D 3
Illston on the Hill. *Leics* 2F 26
Ilmer. *Buck* 3H 19
Ilmington. *Warw* 7A 26
Ilminster. *Som* 4C 8
Ilsington. *Devn* 8J 7
Ilsington. *Dors* 6G 9
Ilston. *Swan* 4K 15
Ilton. *N Yor* 6A 44
Ilton. *Som* 4C 8
Imachar. *N Ayr* 5G 53
Imber. *Wilts* 1J 9
Immingham. *NE Lin* 4H 41
Immingham Dock. *NE Lin* 4H 41
Impington. *Cambs* 5A 28
Ince. *Ches W* 8C 38
Ince Blundell. *Mers* 5B 38
Ince-in-Makerfield.
G Man 5D 38
Inchbae Lodge. *High* 5G 71
Inchbare. *Ang* 7G 67
Inchberry. *Mor* 4D 72
Inchbraoch. *Ang* 8H 67
Inchbrook. *Glos* 3L 17
Incheril. *High* 5C 70
Inchinnan. *Ren* 3C 54
Inchlaggan. *High* 3D 64
Inchmichael. *Per* 3H 61
Inchnadamph. *High* 7K 75
Inchree. *High* 7C 64
Inchture. *Per* 3H 61
Inchyra. *Per* 3G 61
Indian Queens. *Corn* 4A 4
Ingatestone. *Essx* 4E 20
Ingbirchworth. *S Yor* 5L 39
Ingestre. *Staf* 7G 33
Ingham. *Linc* 7F 40
Ingham. *Norf* 5K 37
Ingham. *Suff* 4E 28
Ingham Corner. *Norf* 5K 37
Ingleborough. *Norf* 8L 35
Ingleby. *Derbs* 7L 33
Ingleby Arncliffe. *N Yor* 3D 44
Ingleby Barwick. *Stoc T* 2D 44
Ingleby Greenhow. *N Yor* 3E 44
Ingleigh Green. *Devn* 5H 7
Inglemire. *Hull* 2G 41
Inglesbatch. *Bath* 7K 17
Ingleton. *Dur* 1A 44
Ingleton. *N Yor* 6H 43
Inglewhite. *Lanc* 1D 38
Ingoe. *Nmbd* 4F 50
Ingol. *Lanc* 2D 38
Ingoldisthorpe. *Norf* 4C 36
Ingoldmells. *Linc* 3M 35
Ingoldsby. *Linc* 6G 35
Ingon. *Warw* 6A 26
Ingram. *Nmbd* 8K 57
Ingrave. *Essx* 4E 20
Ingrow. *W Yor* 2J 39
Ings. *Cumb* 4F 42
Ingst. *S Glo* 5H 17
Ingthorpe. *Rut* 1H 27
Ingworth. *Norf* 5H 37
Inkberrow. *Worc* 6L 25
Inkford. *Worc* 4L 25
Inkpen. *W Ber* 7D 18
Inkstack. *High* 2H 77
Innellan. *Arg* 3K 53
Inner Hope. *Devn* 6H 5
Innerleith. *Fife* 4H 61
Innerleithen. *Bord* 6M 55
Innerleven. *Fife* 5J 61
Innermessan. *Dum* 5K 47
Innerwick. *E Lot* 2G 57
Innerwick. *Per* 1A 60
Innsworth. *Glos* 1L 17
Insch. *Abers* 1G 67
Insh. *High* 3L 65
Inshegra. *High* 4K 75
Inshore. *High* 2L 75
Inskip. *Lanc* 2C 38
Instow. *Devn* 2F 6
Intwood. *Norf* 1H 29
Inver. *Abers* 4C 66
Inver. *High* 3L 71
Inver. *Per* 1F 60
Inverailort. *High* 5M 63
Inveralligin. *High* 6A 70
Inverallochy. *Abers* 3L 73
Inveramsay. *Abers* 1H 67
Inveran. *High* 2H 71
Inveraray. *Arg* 5H 59
Inverarish. *High* 8K 69
Inverarity. *Ang* 1K 61
Inverarnan. *Arg* 4L 59
Inverarnie. *High* 8J 71
Inverbeg. *Arg* 6L 59
Inverbervie. *Abers* 6J 67
Inverboyndie. *Abers* 3G 73
Invercassley. *High* 1G 71
Invercharnan. *High* 1J 59
Inverchoran. *High* 6E 70
Invercreran. *Arg* 1H 59
Inverdruie. *High* 2M 65
Inverebrie. *Abers* 6K 73
Invereck. *Arg* 1K 53
Inveresk. *E Lot* 2M 55
Inveresragan. *Arg* 2G 59
Inverey. *Abers* 5A 66
Inverfarigaig. *High* 1H 65
Invergarry. *High* 3F 64
Invergeldie. *Per* 3C 60
Invergordon. *High* 5K 71
Invergowrie. *Per* 2J 61
Inverguseran. *High* 3M 63
Inverharroch. *Mor* 6D 72
Inverie. *High* 3M 63
Inverinan. *Arg* 4G 59
Inverinate. *High* 1B 64
Inverkeilor. *Ang* 1M 61
Inverkeithing. *Fife* 1K 55
Inverkeithny. *Abers* 5G 73
Inverkip. *Inv* 2A 54
Inverkirkaig. *High* 8H 75
Inverlael. *High* 3D 70
Inverliever Lodge. *Arg* 5F 58
Inverliver. *Arg* 2H 59
Inverlochlarig. *Stir* 4M 59
Inverlochy. *High* 6D 64
Inverlussa. *Arg* 1E 52
Inver Mallie. *High* 5D 64
Invermarkie. *Abers* 6E 72
Invermoriston. *High* 2G 65
Invernaver. *High* 3C 76
Inverneil House. *Arg* 1G 53
Inverness. *High* 7J 71 & 96
Inverness Airport. *High* 6K 71
Invernettie. *Abers* 5M 73
Inverpolly Lodge. *High* 8H 75
Inverquhomery. *Abers* 5L 73
Inverroy. *High* 5E 64
Inversanda. *High* 8B 64
Invershiel. *High* 2B 64
Invershin. *High* 2H 71
Invershore. *High* 6H 77
Inversnaid. *Stir* 5L 59
Inverugie. *Abers* 5M 73
Inveruglas. *Arg* 5L 59
Inverurie. *Abers* 1H 67
Invervar. *Per* 1B 60
Inverythan. *Abers* 5H 73
Inwardleigh. *Devn* 6G 7
Inworth. *Essx* 2G 21
Iochdar. *W Isl* 7B 68
Iping. *W Sus* 3J 11
Ipplepen. *Devn* 3K 5
Ipsden. *Oxon* 5G 19
Ipstones. *Staf* 5H 33
Ipswich. *Suff* 7H 29 & 96
Irby. *Mers* 7A 38
Irby in the Marsh. *Linc* 3L 35
Irby upon Humber. *NE Lin* 5H 41
Irchester. *Nptn* 5H 27
Ireby. *Cumb* 8K 49
Ireby. *Lanc* 6H 43
Ireland. *Shet* 9D 79
Ireleth. *Cumb* 6D 42
Ireshopeburn. *Dur* 8D 50
Ireton Wood. *Derbs* 5K 33
Irlam. *G Man* 6F 38
Irnham. *Linc* 7G 35
Iron Acton. *S Glo* 5J 17
Iron Bridge. *Cambs* 2A 28
Ironbridge. *Telf* 1G 25
Iron Cross. *Warw* 6L 25
Ironville. *Derbs* 4A 34
Irstead. *Norf* 5K 37
Irthington. *Cumb* 5M 49
Irthlingborough. *Nptn* 4H 27
Irton. *N Yor* 5K 45
Irvine. *N Ayr* 6B 54
Irvine Mains. *N Ayr* 6B 54
Isabella Pit. *Nmbd* 3J 51
Isauld. *High* 3E 76
Isbister. *Orkn* 6B 78
Isbister. *Shet* 2D 79
(on Mainland)
Isbister. *Shet* 5F 79
(on Whalsay)
Isfield. *E Sus* 6C 12
Isham. *Nptn* 4G 27
Island Carr. *N Lin* 5F 40
Islay Airport. *Arg* 4B 52
Isle Abbotts. *Som* 3C 8
Isle Brewers. *Som* 3C 8
Isleham. *Cambs* 4C 28
Isle of Man Airport. *IOM* 7C 46
Isle of Thanet. *Kent* 7M 21
Isle of Whithorn. *Dum* 8B 48
Isleornsay. *High* 2M 63
Islesburgh. *Shet* 5D 79
Isles of Scilly (St Mary's) Airport.
IOS 2C 3
Islesteps. *Dum* 4G 49
Isleworth. *G Lon* 6M 19
Isley Walton. *Leics* 7A 34
Islibhig. *W Isl* 6A 74
Islington. *G Lon* 5B 20
Islington. *Telf* 7E 32
Islip. *Nptn* 4H 27
Islip. *Oxon* 2F 18
Islwyn. *Cphy* 4E 16
Isombridge. *Telf* 8D 32
Istead Rise. *Kent* 7E 20
Itchen. *Sotn* 4E 10
Itchen Abbas. *Hants* 2F 10
Itchen Stoke. *Hants* 2F 10
Itchingfield. *W Sus* 3M 11
Itchington. *S Glo* 5J 17
Itlaw. *Abers* 4G 73
Itteringham. *Norf* 4H 37
Itteringham Common.
Norf 5H 37
Itton. *Devn* 6H 7
Itton Common. *Mon* 4G 17
Ivegill. *Cumb* 7M 49
Ivelet. *N Yor* 4L 43
Iverchaolain. *Arg* 2J 53
Iver Heath. *Buck* 5L 19
Iveston. *Dur* 6G 51
Ivetsey Bank. *Staf* 8F 32
Ivinghoe. *Buck* 2K 19
Ivinghoe Aston. *Buck* 2K 19
Ivington. *Here* 6E 24
Ivington Green. *Here* 6E 24
Ivybridge. *Devn* 4H 5
Ivychurch. *Kent* 5J 13
Ivy Hatch. *Kent* 8D 20
Ivy Todd. *Norf* 1E 28
Iwade. *Kent* 7H 21
Iwerne Courtney. *Dors* 4H 9
Iwerne Minster. *Dors* 4H 9
Ixworth. *Suff* 4F 28
Ixworth Thorpe. *Suff* 4F 28

J

Jackfield. *Shrp* 1G 25
Jack Hill. *N Yor* 8B 44
Jacksdale. *Notts* 4A 34
Jackton. *S Lan* 4D 54
Jacobstow. *Corn* 6C 6
Jacobstowe. *Devn* 5G 7
Jacobswell. *Surr* 8K 19
Jameston. *Pemb* 4E 14
Jamestown. *Dum* 2L 49
Jamestown. *Fife* 1K 55
Jamestown. *High* 6G 71
Jamestown. *W Dun* 1B 54
Janetstown. *High* 3F 76
(nr. Thurso)
Janetstown. *High* 4J 77
(nr. Wick)
Jarrow. *Tyne* 5J 51
Jarvis Brook. *E Sus* 5D 12
Jasper's Green. *Essx* 1F 20
Jaywick. *Essx* 2K 21
Jedburgh. *Bord* 7F 56
Jeffreyston. *Pemb* 3E 14
Jemimaville. *High* 5K 71
Jenkins Park. *High* 3F 64
Jersey Marine. *Neat* 4M 15
Jesmond. *Tyne* 5H 51
Jevington. *E Sus* 7D 12
Jingle Street. *Mon* 2G 17
Jockey End. *Herts* 2L 19
Jodrell Bank. *Ches E* 8F 38
Johnby. *Cumb* 8M 49
John o' Gaunts. *W Yor* 3M 39
John o' Groats. *High* 2J 77
John's Cross. *E Sus* 5F 12
Johnshaven. *Abers* 7H 67
Johnson Street. *Norf* 6K 37
Johnston. *Pemb* 2D 14
Johnstone. *Ren* 3C 54
Johnstonebridge. *Dum* 2H 49
Johnstown. *Carm* 2H 15
Johnstown. *Wrex* 5A 32
Joppa. *Edin* 2M 55
Joppa. *S Ayr* 8C 54
Jordan Green. *Norf* 5G 37
Jordans. *Buck* 4K 19
Jordanston. *Pemb* 8B 22
Jump. *S Yor* 5M 39
Jumpers Common. *Dors* 6B 10
Juniper. *Nmbd* 6E 50
Juniper Green. *Edin* 3K 55
Jurby East. *IOM* 4D 46
Jurby West. *IOM* 4D 46
Jury's Gap. *E Sus* 6H 13

K

Kaber. *Cumb* 2J 43
Kaimend. *S Lan* 5H 55
Kaimes. *Edin* 3L 55
Kaimrig End. *Bord* 5J 55
Kames. *Arg* 2H 53
Kames. *E Ayr* 7E 54
Kea. *Corn* 5F 3
Keadby. *N Lin* 4E 40
Keal Cotes. *Linc* 3K 35
Kearsley. *G Man* 5F 38
Kearsney. *Kent* 3L 13
Kearstwick. *Cumb* 5H 43
Kearton. *N Yor* 4L 43
Kearvaig. *High* 2K 75
Keasden. *N Yor* 7J 43
Keason. *Corn* 3E 4
Keckwick. *Hal* 7D 38
Keddington. *Linc* 7K 41
Keddington Corner. *Linc* 7K 41
Kedington. *Suff* 7D 28
Kedleston. *Derbs* 5L 33
Kedlock Feus. *Fife* 4J 61
Keekle. *Cumb* 2B 42
Keelby. *Linc* 4H 41
Keele. *Staf* 5F 32
Keeley Green. *Bed* 7J 27
Keeston. *Pemb* 2D 14
Keevil. *Wilts* 8M 17
Kegworth. *Leics* 7A 34
Kehelland. *Corn* 5D 3
Keig. *Abers* 2G 67
Keighley. *W Yor* 1J 39
Keilarsbrae. *Clac* 6D 60
Keillmore. *Arg* 1E 52
Keillor. *Per* 1H 61
Keillour. *Per* 3E 60
Keills. *Arg* 3C 52
Keiloch. *Abers* 4B 66
Keils. *Arg* 3D 52
Keinton Mandeville. *Som* 2E 8
Keir Mill. *Dum* 2F 48
Keirsleywell Row. *Nmbd* 6C 50
Keisby. *Linc* 7G 35
Keisley. *Cumb* 1J 43
Keiss. *High* 3J 77
Keith. *Mor* 4E 72
Keith Inch. *Abers* 5M 73
Kelbrook. *Lanc* 1H 39
Kelby. *Linc* 5G 35
Keld. *Cumb* 2G 43
Keld. *N Yor* 3K 43
Keldholme. *N Yor* 5G 45
Kelfield. *N Lin* 5E 40
Kelfield. *N Yor* 2B 40
Kelham. *Notts* 4D 34
Kellacott. *Devn* 7F 6
Kellan. *Arg* 1C 58
Kellas. *Ang* 2K 61
Kellas. *Mor* 4B 72
Kellaton. *Devn* 6K 5
Kelleth. *Cumb* 3H 43
Kelling. *Norf* 3G 37
Kellingley. *N Yor* 3B 40
Kellington. *N Yor* 3B 40
Kelloe. *Dur* 8J 51
Kelloholm. *Dum* 8F 54
Kells. *Cumb* 2A 42
Kelly. *Devn* 7E 6
Kelly Bray. *Corn* 8E 6
Kelmarsh. *Nptn* 4F 26
Kelmscott. *Oxon* 4C 18
Kelsale. *Suff* 5K 29
Kelsall. *Ches W* 3C 32
Kelshall. *Herts* 8M 27
Kelsick. *Cumb* 6J 49
Kelso. *Bord* 6G 57
Kelstedge. *Derbs* 3L 33
Kelstern. *Linc* 6J 41
Kelsterton. *Flin* 8A 38
Kelston. *Bath* 7K 17
Keltneyburn. *Per* 1C 60
Kelton. *Dum* 4G 49
Kelton Hill. *Dum* 6E 48
Kelty. *Fife* 6G 61
Kelvedon. *Essx* 2G 21
Kelvedon Hatch. *Essx* 4D 20
Kelvinside. *Glas* 3D 54
Kelynack. *Corn* 6A 3
Kemback. *Fife* 4K 61
Kemberton. *Shrp* 1H 25
Kemble. *Glos* 4M 17
Kemerton. *Worc* 8K 25
Kemeys Commander. *Mon* 3F 16
Kemnay. *Abers* 2H 67
Kempe's Corner. *Kent* 3J 13
Kempley. *Glos* 1J 17
Kempley Green. *Glos* 1J 17
Kempsey. *Worc* 7J 25
Kempsford. *Glos* 4B 18
Kemps Green. *Warw* 4M 25
Kempshott. *Hants* 8G 19
Kempston. *Bed* 7J 27
Kempston Hardwick. *Bed* 7J 27
Kempton. *Shrp* 3D 24
Kemp Town. *Brig* 7B 12
Kemsing. *Kent* 8D 20
Kemsley. *Kent* 7H 21

Kenardington—Lemmington Hall

Kenardington. Kent 4H 13
Kenchester. Here 7E 24
Kencot. Oxon 3C 18
Kendal. Cumb 4G 43
Kendleshire. S Glo 6J 17
Kendray. S Yor 5M 39
Kenfig. B'end 5A 16
Kenfig Hill. B'end 5A 16
Kengharair. Arg 1B 58
Kenilworth. Warw 4A 26
Kenknock. Stir 2M 59
Kenley. G Lon 8B 20
Kenley. Shrp 1F 24
Kenmore. High 6M 69
Kenmore. Per 1C 60
Kenn. Devn 7L 7
Kenn. N Som 7G 17
Kennacraig. Arg 3G 53
Kenneggy Downs. C
orn 7C 3
Kennerleigh. Devn 5K 7
Kennet. Clac 6E 60
Kennethmont. Abers 1F 66
Kennett. Cambs 5D 28
Kennford. Devn 7L 7
Kenninghall. Norf 3G 29
Kennington. Kent 3J 13
Kennington. Oxon 3F 18
Kennoway. Fife 5J 61
Kennyhill. Suff 4C 28
Kennythorpe. N Yor 7G 45
Kenovay. Arg 8A 62
Kensaleyre. High 6J 69
Kensington. G Lon 6A 20
Kenstone. Shrp 7C 32
Kensworth. C Beds 2L 19
Kensworth Common.
C Beds 2L 19
Kentallen. High 8C 64
Kentchurch. Here 1G 17
Kentford. Suff 5D 28
Kent International Airport.
Kent 7M 21
Kentisbeare. Devn 5M 7
Kentisbury. Devn 1H 7
Kentisbury Ford. Devn 1H 7
Kentmere. Cumb 3F 42
Kenton. Devn 7L 7
Kenton. G Lon 5M 19
Kenton. Suff 5H 29
Kenton Bankfoot. Tyne 5H 51
Kentra. High 7L 63
Kentrigg. Cumb 4G 43
Kents Bank. Cumb 6E 42
Kent's Green. Glos 1K 17
Kent's Oak. Hants 3D 10
Kent Street. E Sus 6F 12
Kent Street. Kent 8E 20
Kent Street. W Sus 5A 12
Kenwick. Shrp 6B 32
Kenwyn. Corn 5F 3
Kenyon. Warr 6E 38
Keoldale. High 3L 75
Keppoch. High 1B 64
Kepwick. N Yor 4D 44
Keresley. W Mid 3B 26
Keresley Newland. Warw 3B 26
Keristal. IOM 6D 46
Kerne Bridge. Here 2H 17
Kerridge. Ches E 8H 39
Kerris. Corn 7B 3
Kerrow. High 8F 70
Kerry. Powy 3B 24
Kerrycroy. Arg 3K 53
Kerry's Gate. Here 8D 24
Kersall. Notts 3D 34
Kersbrook. Devn 7M 7
Kerse. Ren 4B 54
Kersey. Suff 7G 29
Kershopefoot. Cumb 3M 49
Kersoe. Worc 8K 25
Kerswell. Devn 5M 7
Kerswell Green. Worc 7J 25
Kesgrave. Suff 7J 29
Kessingland. Suff 3M 29
Kessingland Beach. Suff 3M 29
Kestle. Corn 5A 4
Kestle Mill. Corn 4F 3
Keston. G Lon 7C 20
Keswick. Cumb 1D 42
Keswick. Norf 4K 37
(nr. North Walsham)
Keswick. Norf 1J 29
(nr. Norwich)
Ketsby. Linc 8K 41
Kettering. Nptn 4G 27
Ketteringham. Norf 1H 29
Kettins. Per 2H 61
Kettlebaston. Suff 6F 28
Kettlebridge. Fife 5J 61
Kettlebrook. Staf 1A 26
Kettleburgh. Suff 5J 29
Kettleholm. Dum 4J 49
Kettleness. N Yor 2H 45
Kettleshulme. Ches E 8H 39
Kettlesing. N Yor 8B 44
Kettlesing Bottom. N Yor 8B 44
Kettlestone. Norf 4F 36
Kettlethorpe. Linc 8E 40
Kettletoft. Orkn 4E 78
Kettlewell. N Yor 6L 43
Ketton. Rut 1H 27
Kew. G Lon 6M 19
Kewaigue. IOM 6D 46
Kewstoke. N Som 7F 16
Kexbrough. S Yor 5M 39
Kexby. Linc 7E 40
Kexby. York 8G 45
Keyford. Som 1G 9
Key Green. Ches E 3F 32
Key Green. N Yor 3H 45
Keyham. Leics 1E 26
Keyhaven. Hants 6D 10
Keyhead. Abers 4L 73
Keyingham. E Yor 3J 41
Keymer. W Sus 6B 12
Keynsham. Bath 7J 17
Keysoe. Bed 5J 27
Keysoe Row. Bed 5J 27
Key's Toft. Linc 4L 35
Keyston. Cambs 4J 27
Key Street. Kent 7G 21
Keyworth. Notts 6C 34
Kibblesworth. Tyne 6H 51
Kibworth Beauchamp.
Leics 2E 26
Kibworth Harcourt. Leics 2E 26
Kidbrooke. G Lon 6C 20
Kidburngill. Cumb 1B 42
Kiddemore Green. Staf 1J 25
Kidderminster. Worc 4J 25
Kiddington. Oxon 1E 18
Kidd's Moor. Norf 1H 29
Kidlington. Oxon 2E 18
Kidmore End. Oxon 6G 19
Kidnal. Ches W 5B 32
Kidsgrove. Staf 4F 32
Kidstones. N Yor 5L 43
Kidwelly. Carm 3J 15
Kiel Crofts. Arg 2G 59
Kielder. Nmbd 2B 50
Kilbagie. Fife 6E 60
Kilbarchan. Ren 3C 54
Kilbeg. High 3L 63
Kilberry. Arg 3F 52
Kilbirnie. N Ayr 4B 54
Kilbride. Arg 3F 58
Kilbride. High 1K 63
Kilbucho Place. Bord 6J 55
Kilburn. Derbs 5L 33
Kilburn. G Lon 5A 20
Kilburn. N Yor 6E 44
Kilby. Leics 2E 26
Kilchattan. Arg 6A 58
Kilchattan Bay. Arg 4K 53
Kilchenzie. Arg 7E 52
Kilcheran. Arg 2F 58
Kilchiaran. Arg 3A 52
Kilchoan. High 4M 63
(nr. Inverie)
Kilchoan. High 7J 63
(nr. Tobermory)
Kilchoman. Arg 3A 52
Kilchrenan. Arg 3H 59
Kilconquhar. Fife 5K 61
Kilcot. Glos 1J 17
Kilcoy. High 6H 71
Kilcreggan. Arg 1A 54
Kildale. N Yor 3F 44
Kildary. High 4K 71
Kildermorie Lodge. High 4H 71
Kildonan. Dum 6K 47
Kildonan. High 7E 76
(nr. Helmsdale)
Kildonan. High 6H 69
(on Isle of Skye)
Kildonan. N Ayr 7J 53
Kildonnan. High 5J 63
Kildrummy. Abers 2E 66
Kildwick. N Yor 1J 39
Kilfillan. Dum 6M 47
Kilfinan. Arg 2H 53
Kilfinnan. High 4E 64
Kilgetty. Pemb 3F 14
Kilgour. Fife 5H 61
Kilgrammie. S Ayr 1M 47
Kilham. E Yor 7K 45
Kilham. Nmbd 6H 57
Kilkenneth. Arg 8A 62
Kilkhampton. Corn 4D 6
Killamarsh. Derbs 7A 40
Killandrist. Arg 1F 58
Killay. Swan 4L 15
Killean. Arg 5E 52
Killearn. Stir 1D 54
Killellan. Arg 8E 52
Killen. High 6J 71
Killerby. Darl 2A 44
Killichonan. Per 8H 65
Killiechronan. Arg 1C 58
Killiecrankie. Per 7M 65
Killilan. High 8B 70
Killimster. High 4J 77
Killin. Stir 2A 60
Killinghall. N Yor 8B 44
Killington. Cumb 5H 43
Killingworth. Tyne 4H 51
Killin Lodge. High 3H 65
Killinochonoch. Arg 6F 58
Killochyett. Bord 5D 56
Killundine. High 1C 58
Kilmacolm. Inv 3B 54
Kilmahog. Stir 5B 60
Kilmahumaig. Arg 6E 58
Kilmalieu. High 8A 64
Kilmaluag. High 4J 69
Kilmany. Fife 3J 61
Kilmarie. High 2K 63
Kilmarnock. E Ayr 6C 54 & 96
Kilmaron. Fife 4J 61
Kilmartin. Arg 6F 58
Kilmaurs. E Ayr 5C 54
Kilmelford. Arg 4F 58
Kilmeny. Arg 3B 52
Kilmersdon. Som 8J 17
Kilmeston. Hants 3F 10
Kilmichael Glassary. Arg 6F 58
Kilmichael of Inverlussa.
Arg 1F 52
Kilmington. Devn 6B 8
Kilmington. Wilts 2G 9
Kilmoluaig. Arg 8A 62
Kilmorack. High 7G 71
Kilmore. Arg 3F 58
Kilmore. High 3L 63
Kilmory. Arg 2F 52
Kilmory. High 6K 63
(nr. Kilchoan)
Kilmory. High 3H 63
(on Rùm)
Kilmory. N Ayr 7H 53
Kilmory Lodge. Arg 5E 58
Kilmote. High 8E 76
Kilmuir. High 7G 69
(nr. Dunvegan)
Kilmuir. High 4K 71
(nr. Invergordon)
Kilmuir. High 7J 71
(nr. Inverness)
Kilmuir. High 4H 69
(nr. Uig)
Kilmun. Arg 1K 53
Kilnave. Arg 2A 52
Kilncadzow. S Lan 5G 55
Kilndown. Kent 4F 12
Kiln Green. Here 2J 17
Kiln Green. Wind 6J 19
Kilnhill. Cumb 8K 49
Kilnhurst. S Yor 6A 40
Kilninian. Arg 1A 58
Kilninver. Arg 3F 58
Kiln Pit Hill. Nmbd 6F 50
Kilnsea. E Yor 4L 41
Kilnsey. N Yor 7L 43
Kilnwick. E Yor 1F 40
Kiloran. Arg 6A 58
Kilpatrick. N Ayr 7H 53
Kilpeck. Here 8E 24
Kilpin. E Yor 3D 40
Kilpin Pike. E Yor 3D 40
Kilrenny. Fife 5L 61
Kilsby. Nptn 4D 26
Kilspindie. Per 3H 61
Kilsyth. N Lan 2F 54
Kiltarlity. High 7H 71
Kilton. Som 1A 8
Kilton Thorpe. Red C 2F 44
Kilvaxter. High 5H 69
Kilve. Som 1A 8
Kilvington. Notts 5E 34
Kilwinning. N Ayr 5A 54
Kimberley. Norf 1G 29
Kimberley. Notts 5A 34
Kimblesworth. Dur 7H 51
Kimble Wick. Buck 3J 19
Kimbolton. Cambs 5J 27
Kimbolton. Here 5F 24
Kimcote. Leics 3D 26
Kimmeridge. Dors 8J 9
Kimmerston. Nmbd 6J 57
Kimpton. Hants 1C 10
Kimpton. Herts 2M 19
Kinbeachie. High 5J 71
Kinbrace. High 6D 76
Kinbuck. Stir 5C 60
Kincaple. Fife 4K 61
Kincardine. Fife 1H 55
Kincardine. High 3J 71
Kincardine Bridge. Fife 1H 55
Kincardine O'Neil. Abers 4F 66
Kinchrackine. Arg 3J 59
Kincorth. Aber 3K 67
Kincraig. High 3L 65
Kincraigie. Per 1E 60
Kindallachan. Per 8M 65
Kineton. Glos 1A 18
Kineton. Warw 6B 26
Kinfauns. Per 3G 61
Kingairloch. High 8A 64
Kingarth. Arg 4J 53
Kingcoed. Mon 3G 17
King Edward. Abers 4H 73
Kingerby. Linc 6G 41
Kingham. Oxon 1C 18
Kingholm Quay. Dum 4G 49
Kinghorn. Fife 1L 55
Kingie. High 3D 64
Kinglassie. Fife 6H 61
Kingledores. Bord 7K 55
Kingodie. Per 3J 61
King o' Muirs. Clac 6D 60
King's Acre. Here 7E 24
Kingsand. Corn 4F 4
Kingsash. Buck 3J 19
Kingsbarns. Fife 4L 61
Kingsbridge. Devn 5J 5
Kingsbridge. Som 2L 7
King's Bromley. Staf 8J 33
Kingsburgh. High 6H 69
Kingsbury. G Lon 5M 19
Kingsbury. Warw 2A 26
Kingsbury Episcopi. Som 3D 8
Kings Caple. Here 1H 17
Kingscavil. W Lot 2J 55
Kingsclere. Hants 8F 18
King's Cliffe. Nptn 2J 27
Kings Clipstone. Notts 3C 34
Kingscote. Glos 4L 17
Kingscott. Devn 4G 7
Kings Coughton. Warw 6L 25
Kingscross. N Ayr 7J 53
Kingsdon. Som 3E 8
Kingsdown. Kent 3M 13
Kingsdown. Swin 5B 18
Kingsdown. Wilts 7L 17
Kingseat. Fife 6G 61
Kingsey. Buck 3H 19
Kingsfold. Lanc 3D 38
Kingsfold. W Sus 2M 11
Kingsford. E Ayr 5C 54
Kingsford. Worc 3J 25
Kingsforth. N Lin 4G 41
Kingsgate. Kent 6M 21
King's Green. Glos 8H 25
Kingshall Street. Suff 5F 28
Kingsheanton. Devn 2G 7
King's Heath. W Mid 3L 25
Kings Hill. Kent 8E 20
Kingsholm. Glos 2L 17
Kingshouse. High 8E 64
Kingshouse. Stir 3A 60
Kingshurst. W Mid 3M 25
Kingskerswell. Devn 3K 5
Kingskettle. Fife 5J 61
Kingsland. Here 5E 24
Kingsland. IOA 1B 30
Kings Langley. Herts 3L 19
Kingsley. Ches W 8D 38
Kingsley. Hants 2H 11
Kingsley. Staf 5H 33
Kingsley Green. W Sus 2J 11
Kingsley Holt. Staf 5H 33
King's Lynn. Norf 5C 36
King's Meaburn. Cumb 1H 43
Kings Moss. Mers 5D 38
Kingsmuir. Ang 1K 61
Kingsmuir. Fife 5L 61
Kings Muir. Bord 6L 55
King's Newnham. Warw 4C 26
Kings Newton. Derbs 7L 33
Kingsnorth. Kent 4J 13
Kingsnorth. Medw 6G 21
King's Norton. Leics 1E 26
King's Norton. W Mid 4L 25
King's Nympton. Devn 4H 7
King's Pyon. Here 6E 24
Kings Ripton. Cambs 4L 27
King's Somborne. Hants 2D 10
King's Stag. Dors 4G 9
King's Stanley. Glos 3L 17
King's Sutton. Nptn 8C 26
Kingstanding. W Mid 2L 25
Kingsteignton. Devn 8K 7
Kingsteps. High 6M 71
King Sterndale. Derbs 8J 39
King's Thorn. Here 8F 24
Kingsthorpe. Nptn 5F 26
Kingston. Cambs 6M 27
Kingston. Devn 5H 5
Kingston. Dors 5G 9
(nr. Sturminster Newton)
Kingston. Dors 8J 9
(nr. Swanage)
Kingston. E Lot 1E 56
Kingston. Hants 5B 10
Kingston. IOW 7E 10
Kingston. Kent 8K 21
Kingston. Mor 3D 72
Kingston. W Sus 5L 11
Kingston Bagpuize. Oxon 4E 18
Kingston Blount. Oxon 4H 19
Kingston by Sea. W Sus 7A 12
Kingston Deverill. Wilts 2H 9
Kingstone. Here 8E 24
Kingstone. Som 4C 8
Kingstone. Staf 7H 33
Kingston Lisle. Oxon 5D 18
Kingston Maurward. Dors 6G 9
Kingston near Lewes.
E Sus 7B 12
Kingston on Soar. Notts 7B 34
Kingston Russell. Dors 6E 8
Kingston St Mary. Som 3B 8
Kingston Seymour. N Som 7G 17
Kingston Stert. Oxon 3H 19
Kingston upon Hull.
Hull 3G 41 & 96
Kingston upon Thames.
G Lon 7M 19
King's Walden. Herts 1M 19
Kingswear. Devn 4K 5
Kingswells. Aber 3J 67
Kingswinford. W Mid 3J 25
Kingswood. Buck 2G 19
Kingswood. Glos 4K 17
Kingswood. Here 6C 24
Kingswood. Kent 8G 21
Kingswood. Per 2F 60
Kingswood. Powy 1C 24
Kingswood. Som 2A 8
Kingswood. S Glo 6J 17
Kingswood. Surr 8A 20
Kingswood. Warw 4M 25
Kingswood Common. Staf 1J 25
Kings Worthy. Hants 2E 10
Kingthorpe. Linc 8H 41
Kington. Here 6D 24
Kington. S Glo 4J 17
Kington. Worc 6K 25
Kington Langley. Wilts 6M 17
Kington Magna. Dors 3G 9
Kington St Michael. Wilts 6M 17
Kingussie. High 3K 65
Kingweston. Som 2E 8
Kinharrachie. Abers 6K 73
Kinhrive. High 4K 71
Kinkell Bridge. Per 4E 60
Kinknockie. Abers 5L 73
Kinkry Hill. Cumb 4A 50
Kinlet. Shrp 3H 25
Kinloch. High 6L 75
(nr. Loch More)
Kinloch. High 8L 63
(nr. Lochaline)
Kinloch. High 4J 63
(on Rùm)
Kinloch. Per 1G 61
Kinlochard. Stir 5M 59
Kinlochbervie. High 4K 75
Kinlocheil. High 6B 64
Kinlochewe. High 5C 70
Kinloch Hourn. High 3B 64
Kinloch Laggan. High 5H 65
Kinlochleven. High 7D 64
Kinloch Lodge. High 4A 76
Kinlochmoidart. High 6M 63
Kinlochmore. High 7D 64
Kinloch Rannoch. Per 8J 65
Kinlochspelve. Arg 3D 58
Kinloid. High 5L 63
Kinloss. Mor 3A 72
Kinmel Bay. Cnwy 1J 31
Kinmuck. Abers 2J 67
Kinnadie. Abers 5K 73
Kinnaird. Per 3H 61
Kinneff. Abers 6J 67
Kinnelhead. Dum 1H 49
Kinnell. Ang 8G 67
Kinnerley. Shrp 7A 32
Kinnernie. Abers 2H 67
Kinnersley. Here 7D 24
Kinnersley. Worc 7J 25
Kinnerton. Powy 5C 24
Kinnerton. Shrp 2D 24
Kinnesswood. Per 5G 61
Kinninvie. Dur 1M 43
Kinnordy. Ang 8D 66
Kinoulton. Notts 6C 34
Kinross. Per 5G 61
Kinrossie. Per 2G 61
Kinsbourne Green. Herts 2M 19
Kinsey Heath. Ches E 5D 32
Kinsham. Here 5D 24
Kinsham. Worc 8K 25
Kinsley. W Yor 4A 40
Kinson. Bour 6A 10
Kintbury. W Ber 7D 18
Kintessack. Mor 3A 72
Kintillo. Per 4G 61
Kinton. Here 4E 24
Kinton. Shrp 8A 32
Kintore. Abers 2H 67
Kintour. Arg 4C 52
Kintra. Arg 3A 58
Kintraw. Arg 5F 58
Kinveachy. High 2M 65
Kinver. Staf 3J 25
Kinwarton. Warw 6M 25
Kiplingcotes. E Yor 1F 40
Kippax. W Yor 2A 40
Kippen. Stir 6B 60
Kippford. Dum 6F 48
Kipping's Cross. Kent 3E 12
Kirbister. Orkn 7B 78
(nr. Hobbister)
Kirbister. Orkn 6A 78
(nr. Quholm)
Kirbuster. Orkn 5E 78
Kirby Bedon. Norf 1J 29
Kirby Bellars. Leics 8D 34
Kirby Cane. Norf 2K 29
Kirby Cross. Essx 1L 21
Kirby Fields. Leics 1D 26
Kirby Green. Norf 2K 29
Kirby Grindalythe. N Yor 7J 45
Kirby Hill. N Yor 3A 44
(nr. Richmond)
Kirby Hill. N Yor 7C 44
(nr. Ripon)
Kirby Knowle. N Yor 5D 44
Kirby-le-Soken. Essx 1L 21
Kirby Misperton. N Yor 6G 45
Kirby Muxloe. Leics 1D 26
Kirby Sigston. N Yor 4D 44
Kirby Underdale. E Yor 8H 45
Kirby Wiske. N Yor 5C 44
Kirdford. W Sus 3L 11
Kirk. High 4H 77
Kirkabister. Shet 8E 79
(on Bressay)
Kirkabister. Shet 6E 79
(on Mainland)
Kirkandrews. Dum 7D 48
Kirkandrews-on-Eden.
Cumb 6L 49
Kirkapol. Arg 8B 62
Kirkbampton. Cumb 6L 49
Kirkbean. Dum 6G 49
Kirk Bramwith. S Yor 4C 40
Kirkbride. Cumb 6K 49
Kirkbridge. N Yor 4B 44
Kirkbuddo. Ang 1L 61
Kirkburn. E Yor 8J 45
Kirkburton. W Yor 4K 39
Kirkby. Linc 6G 41
Kirkby. Mers 6C 38
Kirkby. N Yor 3E 44
Kirkby Fenside. Linc 3K 35
Kirkby Fleetham. N Yor 4B 44
Kirkby Green. Linc 4G 35
Kirkby-in-Ashfield.
Notts 4B 34
Kirkby-in-Furness. Cumb 5D 42
Kirkby la Thorpe. Linc 5H 35
Kirkby Lonsdale. Cumb 6H 43
Kirkby Malham. N Yor 7K 43
Kirkby Mallory. Leics 1C 26
Kirkby Malzeard. N Yor 6B 44
Kirkby Mills. N Yor 5G 45
Kirkbymoorside. N Yor 5F 44
Kirkby on Bain. Linc 3J 35
Kirkby Overblow. N Yor 1M 39
Kirkby Stephen. Cumb 3J 43
Kirkby Thore. Cumb 1H 43
Kirkby Underwood. Linc 7G 35
Kirkby Wharfe. N Yor 1B 40
Kirkcaldy. Fife 6H 61
Kirkcambeck. Cumb 5A 50
Kirkcolm. Dum 5K 47
Kirkconnel. Dum 8F 54
Kirkconnell. Dum 5G 49
Kirkcowan. Dum 5A 48
Kirkcudbright. Dum 6D 48
Kirkdale. Mers 6B 38
Kirk Deighton. N Yor 8C 44
Kirk Ella. E Yor 3G 41
Kirkfieldbank. S Lan 5G 55
Kirkforthar Feus. Fife 5H 61
Kirkgunzeon. Dum 5F 48
Kirk Hallam. Derbs 5A 34
Kirkham. Lanc 2C 38
Kirkham. N Yor 7G 45
Kirkhamgate. W Yor 3L 39
Kirk Hammerton. N Yor 8D 44
Kirkharle. Nmbd 3F 50
Kirkheaton. Nmbd 4F 50
Kirkheaton. W Yor 4K 39
Kirkhill. Ang 7G 67
Kirkhill. High 7H 71
Kirkhope. S Lan 1G 49
Kirkhouse. Bord 6M 55
Kirkibost. High 2K 63
Kirkinch. Ang 1J 61
Kirkinner. Dum 6B 48
Kirkintilloch. E Dun 2E 54
Kirk Ireton. Derbs 4K 33
Kirkland. Cumb 2B 42
(nr. Cleator Moor)
Kirkland. Cumb 8B 50
(nr. Penrith)
Kirkland. Cumb 7K 49
(nr. Wigton)
Kirkland. Dum 8F 54
(nr. Kirkconnel)
Kirkland. Dum 2F 48
(nr. Moniaive)
Kirkland Guards. Cumb 7J 49
Kirk Langley. Derbs 6K 33
Kirklauchline. Dum 6K 47
Kirkleatham. Red C 1E 44
Kirklevington. Stoc T 3D 44
Kirkley. Suff 2M 29
Kirklington. N Yor 5C 44
Kirklington. Notts 4C 34
Kirklinton. Cumb 5M 49
Kirkliston. Edin 2K 55
Kirkmabreck. Dum 6B 48
Kirkmaiden. Dum 8L 47
Kirk Merrington. Dur 8H 51
Kirk Michael. IOM 4D 46
Kirkmichael. Per 7A 66
Kirkmichael. S Ayr 1A 48
Kirkmuirhill. S Lan 5F 54
Kirknewton. Nmbd 6J 57
Kirknewton. W Lot 3K 55
Kirkney. Abers 6F 72
Kirk of Shotts. N Lan 3G 55
Kirkoswald. Cumb 7A 50
Kirkoswald. S Ayr 1M 47
Kirkpatrick. Dum 2G 49
Kirkpatrick Durham. Dum 4E 48
Kirkpatrick-Fleming. Dum 4K 49
Kirk Sandall. S Yor 5C 40
Kirksanton. Cumb 5C 42
Kirk Smeaton. N Yor 4B 40
Kirkstall. W Yor 2L 39
Kirkstile. Dum 2L 49
Kirkstyle. High 2J 77
Kirkthorpe. W Yor 3M 39
Kirkton. Abers 2G 67
(nr. Alford)
Kirkton. Abers 1G 67
(nr. Insch)
Kirkton. Abers 5J 73
(nr. Turriff)
Kirkton. Ang 2K 61
(nr. Dundee)
Kirkton. Ang 1K 61
(nr. Forfar)
Kirkton. Ang 5E 66
(nr. Tarfside)
Kirkton. Dum 3G 49
Kirkton. Fife 3J 61
Kirkton. High 2K 71
(nr. Golspie)
Kirkton. High 1A 64
(nr. Kyle of Lochalsh)
Kirkton. High 7B 70
(nr. Lochcarron)
Kirkton. Bord 8E 56
Kirkton. S Lan 7H 55
Kirktonhill. W Dun 2B 54
Kirkton Manor. Bord 6L 55
Kirkton of Airlie. Ang 8D 66
Kirkton of Auchterhouse.
Ang 2J 61
Kirkton of Bourtie. Abers 1J 67
Kirkton of Collace. Per 2G 61
Kirkton of Craig. Ang 8H 67
Kirkton of Culsalmond.
Abers 6G 73
Kirkton of Durris. Abers 4H 67
Kirkton of Glenbuchat.
Abers 2D 66
Kirkton of Glenisla. Ang 7C 66
Kirkton of Kingoldrum.
Ang 8D 66
Kirkton of Largo. Fife 5K 61
Kirkton of Lethendy.
Per 1G 61
Kirkton of Logie Buchan.
Abers 1K 67
Kirkton of Maryculter.
Abers 4J 67
Kirkton of Menmuir. Ang 7F 66
Kirkton of Monikie. Ang 2L 61
Kirkton of Oyne. Abers 1G 67
Kirkton of Rayne. Abers 6G 73
Kirkton of Skene. Abers 3J 67
Kirktown. Abers 3K 73
(nr. Fraserburgh)
Kirktown. Abers 4L 73
(nr. Peterhead)
Kirktown of Alvah. Abers 3G 73
Kirktown of Auchterless.
Abers 5H 73
Kirktown of Deskford. Mor 3F 72
Kirktown of Fetteresso.
Abers 5J 67
Kirktown of Mortlach.
Mor 6D 72
Kirktown of Slains. Abers 1L 67
Kirkurd. Bord 5K 55
Kirkwall. Orkn 6C 78
Kirkwall Airport. Orkn 7C 78
Kirkwhelpington. Nmbd 3E 50
Kirk Yetholm. Bord 7H 57
Kirmington. N Lin 4H 41
Kirmond le Mire. Linc 6H 41
Kirn. Arg 2K 53
Kirriemuir. Ang 8D 66
Kirstead Green. Norf 2J 29
Kirtlebridge. Dum 4K 49
Kirtleton. Dum 4K 49
Kirtling. Cambs 6C 28
Kirtling Green. Cambs 6C 28
Kirtlington. Oxon 2F 18
Kirtomy. High 3C 76
Kirton. Linc 6K 35
Kirton. Notts 3C 34
Kirton. Suff 8J 29
Kirton End. Linc 5J 35
Kirton Holme. Linc 5J 35
Kirton in Lindsey. N Lin 6F 40
Kishorn. High 7A 70
Kislingbury. Nptn 6E 26
Kite Hill. IOW 6F 10
Kites Hardwick. Warw 5C 26
Kittisford. Som 3M 7
Kittle. Swan 5K 15
Kittybrewster. Aber 3K 67
Kitwood. Hants 2G 11
Kivernoll. Here 8E 24
Kiveton Park. S Yor 7A 40
Knaith. Linc 7E 40
Knaith Park. Linc 7E 40
Knaphill. Surr 8K 19
Knapp. Hants 3E 10
Knapp. Per 2H 61
Knapp. Som 3C 8
Knapperfield. High 4H 77
Knapton. Norf 4K 37
Knapton. York 8E 44
Knapton Green. Here 6E 24
Knapwell. Cambs 5M 27
Knaresborough. N Yor 8C 44
Knarsdale. Nmbd 6B 50
Knatts Valley. Kent 7D 20
Knaven. Abers 5J 73
Knayton. N Yor 5D 44
Knebworth. Herts 1A 20
Knedlington. E Yor 3D 40
Kneesall. Notts 3D 34
Kneesworth. Cambs 7M 27
Kneeton. Notts 5D 34
Knelston. Swan 5J 15
Knenhall. Staf 6G 33
Knightacott. Devn 2H 7
Knightcote. Warw 6C 26
Knightcott. N Som 8F 16
Knightley. Staf 7F 32
Knightley Dale. Staf 7F 32
Knightlow Hill. Warw 4C 26
Knighton. Devn 5G 5
Knighton. Dors 4F 8
Knighton. Leic 1E 26
Knighton. Powy 4C 24
Knighton. Som 1A 8
Knighton. Staf 7E 32
(nr. Eccleshall)
Knighton. Staf 5E 32
(nr. Woore)
Knighton. Wilts 6C 18
Knighton. Worc 6L 25
Knighton Common. Worc 4G 25
Knight's End. Cambs 2A 28
Knightswood. Glas 3D 54
Knightwick. Worc 6H 25
Knill. Here 5C 24
Knipton. Leics 6E 34
Knitsley. Dur 7G 51
Kniveton. Derbs 4K 33
Knock. Arg 2C 58
Knock. Cumb 1H 43
Knock. Mor 4F 72
Knockally. High 7G 77
Knockan. Arg 3B 58
Knockan. High 8K 75
Knockandhu. Mor 1C 66
Knockando. Mor 5B 72
Knockarthur. High 1K 71
Knockbain. High 6J 71
Knockbreck. High 5G 69
Knockdee. High 3G 77
Knockdolian. S Ayr 3L 47
Knockdon. S Ayr 8B 54
Knockdown. Glos 5L 17
Knockenbaird. Abers 1G 67
Knockenkelly. N Ayr 7J 53
Knockentiber. E Ayr 6B 54
Knockfarrel. High 6H 71
Knockglass. High 3F 76
Knockholt. Kent 8C 20
Knockholt Pound. Kent 8C 20
Knockie Lodge. High 2G 65
Knockin. Shrp 7A 32
Knockinlaw. E Ayr 6C 54
Knockinnon. High 6G 77
Knockrome. Arg 2D 52
Knocksharry. IOM 5C 46
Knockshinnoch. E Ayr 8C 54
Knockvennie. Dum 4E 48
Knockvologan. Arg 4A 58
Knodishall. Suff 5L 29
Knole. Som 3D 8
Knollbury. Mon 5G 17
Knolls Green. Ches E 8G 39
Knolton. Wrex 6A 32
Knook. Wilts 1J 9
Knossington. Leics 1G 27
Knott. High 6H 69
Knott End-on-Sea. Lanc 1B 38
Knotting. Bed 5J 27
Knotting Green. Bed 5J 27
Knottingley. W Yor 3A 40
Knotts. Cumb 1F 42
Knotty Ash. Mers 6C 38
Knotty Green. Buck 4K 19
Knowbury. Shrp 4F 24
Knowe. Dum 4A 48
Knowefield. Cumb 6M 49
Knowehead. Dum 2D 48
Knowes. E Lot 2F 56
Knowesgate. Nmbd 3E 50
Knoweside. S Ayr 8A 54
Knowes of Elrick. Abers 4G 73
Knowle. Bris 6H 17
Knowle. Devn 2F 6
(nr. Braunton)
Knowle. Devn 7M 7
(nr. Budleigh Salterton)
Knowle. Devn 5J 7
(nr. Crediton)
Knowle. Shrp 4F 24
Knowle. W Mid 4M 25
Knowle Green. Lanc 2E 38
Knowle St Giles. Som 4C 8
Knowlesands. Shrp 2H 25
Knowle Village. Hants 5F 10
Knowl Hill. Wind 6J 19
Knowlton. Kent 8L 21
Knowsley. Mers 6C 38
Knowstone. Devn 3K 7
Knucklas. Powy 4C 24
Knuston. Nptn 5H 27
Knutsford. Ches E 8F 38
Knypersley. Staf 4F 32
Krumlin. W Yor 4J 39
Kuggar. Corn 8E 3
Kyleakin. High 1M 63
Kyle of Lochalsh. High 1M 63
Kylerhea. High 1M 63
Kylesku. High 6K 75
Kyles Lodge. W Isl 3D 68
Kylesmorar. High 4A 64
Kylestrome. High 6K 75
Kymin. Mon 2H 17
Kynaston. Here 8G 25
Kynaston. Shrp 7A 32
Kynnersley. Telf 8D 32
Kyre Green. Worc 5G 25
Kyre Park. Worc 5G 25
Kyrewood. Worc 5G 25

L

Labost. W Isl 4C 74
Lacasaidh. W Isl 6D 74
Lacasdail. W Isl 5E 74
Laceby. NE Lin 5J 41
Lacey Green. Buck 3J 19
Lach Dennis. Ches W 8F 38
Lache. Ches W 3A 32
Lackford. Suff 4D 28
Lacock. Wilts 7M 17
Ladbroke. Warw 6C 26
Laddingford. Kent 3E 12
Lade Bank. Linc 4K 35
Ladock. Corn 4F 3
Lady. Orkn 3E 78
Ladybank. Fife 4J 61
Ladycross. Corn 7E 6
Lady Green. Mers 5B 38
Lady Hall. Cumb 5C 42
Ladykirk. Bord 5H 57
Ladysford. Abers 3K 73
Ladywood. W Mid 3L 25
Ladywood. Worc 5J 25
Laga. High 7L 63
Lagavulin. Arg 5C 52
Lagg. Arg 2D 52
Lagg. N Ayr 7H 53
Laggan. Arg 4A 52
Laggan. High 4E 64
(nr. Fort Augustus)
Laggan. High 4J 65
(nr. Newtonmore)
Laggan. Mor 6D 72
Lagganlia. High 3L 65
Lagganulva. Arg 1B 58
Laglingarten. Arg 5J 59
Lagness. W Sus 5J 11
Laid. High 4M 75
Laide. High 2B 70
Laigh Fenwick. E Ayr 5C 54
Laindon. Essx 5E 20
Lairg. High 1H 71
Lairg Muir. High 1H 71
Laithes. Cumb 8M 49
Laithkirk. Dur 1L 43
Lake. Devn 2G 7
Lake. IOW 7F 10
Lake. Wilts 2B 10
Lake District. Cumb 2E 42
Lakenham. Norf 1J 29
Lakenheath. Suff 3D 28
Lakesend. Norf 2B 28
Lakeside. Cumb 5E 42
Laleham. Surr 7L 19
Laleston. B'end 5A 16
Lamancha. Bord 4L 55
Lamarsh. Essx 8E 28
Lamas. Norf 5J 37
Lamb Corner. Essx 8G 29
Lambden. Bord 5G 57
Lamberhead Green.
G Man 5D 38
Lamberhurst. Kent 4E 12
Lamberhurst Quarter. Kent 4E 12
Lamberton. Bord 4J 57
Lambeth. G Lon 6B 20
Lambfell Moar. IOM 5C 46
Lambhill. Glas 3D 54
Lambley. Nmbd 6B 50
Lambley. Notts 5C 34
Lambourn. W Ber 6D 18
Lambourne End. Essx 4C 20
Lambourn Woodlands.
W Ber 6D 18
Lambrook. Som 3B 8
Lambs Green. Dors 6J 9
Lambs Green. W Sus 4A 12
Lambston. Pemb 2D 14
Lamellion. Corn 3D 4
Lamerton. Devn 8F 6
Lamesley. Tyne 6H 51
Laminess. Orkn 4E 78
Lamington. High 4K 71
Lamington. S Lan 6H 55
Lamlash. N Ayr 6J 53
Lamonby. Cumb 8M 49
Lamorick. Corn 3B 4
Lamorna. Corn 7B 3
Lamorran. Corn 5F 3
Lampeter. Cdgn 7H 23
Lampeter Velfrey. Pemb 2F 14
Lamphey. Pemb 3E 14
Lamplugh. Cumb 1B 42
Lamport. Nptn 4F 26
Lamyatt. Som 2F 8
Lana. Devn 6E 6
(nr. Ashwater)
Lana. Devn 5E 6
(nr. Holsworthy)
Lanark. S Lan 5G 55
Lanarth. Corn 7E 3
Lancaster. Lanc 7F 42
Lanchester. Dur 7G 51
Lancing. W Sus 5M 11
Landbeach. Cambs 5A 28
Landcross. Devn 3F 6
Landerberry. Abers 3H 67
Landford. Wilts 4C 10
Land Gate. G Man 5D 38
Landhallow. High 6G 77
Landimore. Swan 4J 15
Landkey. Devn 2G 7
Landkey Newland. Devn 2G 7
Landore. Swan 4L 15
Landport. Port 5G 11
Landrake. Corn 3E 4
Landscove. Devn 3J 5
Land's End (St Just) Airport.
Corn 7A 3
Landshipping. Pemb 2E 14
Landulph. Corn 3F 4
Landywood. Staf 1K 25
Lane. Corn 3F 3
Laneast. Corn 7D 6
Lane Bottom. Lanc 2G 39
Lane End. Buck 4J 19
Lane End. Hants 3F 10
Lane End. IOW 7G 11
Lane End. Wilts 1H 9
Lane Ends. Derbs 6K 33
Lane Ends. Dur 8G 51
Lane Ends. Lanc 8J 43
Laneham. Notts 8E 40
Lanehead. Dur 7D 50
(nr. Cowshill)
Lane Head. Dur 2A 44
(nr. Hutton Magna)
Lane Head. Dur 1M 43
(nr. Woodland)
Lane Head. G Man 6E 38
Lanehead. Nmbd 3C 50
Lane Head. W Yor 5K 39
Lane Heads. Lanc 2C 38
Lanercost. Cumb 5A 50
Laneshaw Bridge. Lanc 1H 39
Laney Green. Staf 1K 25
Langais. W Isl 5C 68
Langal. High 7M 63
Langar. Notts 6D 34
Langbank. Ren 2B 54
Langbar. N Yor 8M 43
Langburnshiels. Bord 1A 50
Langcliffe. N Yor 7K 43
Langdale End. N Yor 4J 45
Langdon. Corn 6D 6
Langdon Beck. Dur 8D 50
Langdon Cross. Corn 7E 6
Langdon Hills. Essx 5E 20
Langdown. Hants 5E 10
Langdyke. Fife 5J 61
Langenhoe. Essx 2J 21
Langford. C Beds 7K 27
Langford. Devn 5M 7
Langford. Essx 3G 21
Langford. Notts 4E 34
Langford. Oxon 3C 18
Langford. Som 3B 8
Langford Budville. Som 3A 8
Langham. Dors 3G 9
Langham. Essx 8G 29
Langham. Norf 3G 37
Langham. Rut 8E 34
Langham. Suff 5F 28
Langho. Lanc 2F 38
Langholm. Dum 3L 49
Langland. Swan 5L 15
Langleeford. Nmbd 7J 57
Langley. Ches E 8H 39
Langley. Derbs 5A 34
Langley. Essx 8A 28
Langley. Glos 1A 18
Langley. Hants 5E 10
Langley. Herts 1A 20
Langley. Kent 8G 21
Langley. Nmbd 5D 50
Langley. Slo 6L 19
Langley. Som 3M 7
Langley. Warw 5M 25
Langley. W Sus 3J 11
Langley Burrell. Wilts 6M 17
Langleybury. Herts 3L 19
Langley Common. Derbs 6K 33
Langley Green. Derbs 6K 33
Langley Green. Norf 1K 29
Langley Green. Warw 5M 25
Langley Green. W Sus 4A 12
Langley Heath. Kent 8G 21
Langley Marsh. Som 3M 7
Langley Moor. Dur 7H 51
Langley Park. Dur 7H 51
Langley Street. Norf 1K 29
Langney. E Sus 7E 12
Langold. Notts 7B 40
Langore. Corn 7E 6
Langport. Som 3D 8
Langrick. Linc 5J 35
Langridge. Bath 7K 17
Langridgeford. Devn 3G 7
Langrigg. Cumb 7J 49
Langrish. Hants 3H 11
Langsett. S Yor 5L 39
Langshaw. Bord 6E 56
Langstone. Hants 5H 11
Langthorne. N Yor 4B 44
Langthorpe. N Yor 7C 44
Langthwaite. N Yor 3M 43
Langtoft. E Yor 7K 45
Langtoft. Linc 8H 35
Langton. Dur 2A 44
Langton. Linc 3J 35
(nr. Horncastle)
Langton. Linc 8K 41
(nr. Spilsby)
Langton. N Yor 7G 45
Langton by Wragby. Linc 8H 41
Langton Green. Kent 4D 12
Langton Herring. Dors 7F 8
Langton Long Blandford.
Dors 5J 9
Langton Matravers. Dors 8A 10
Langtree. Devn 4F 6
Langwathby. Cumb 8A 50
Langwith. Derbs 3B 34
Langworth. Linc 8G 41
Lanivet. Corn 3B 4
Lanjeth. Corn 4A 4
Lank. Corn 8B 6
Lanlivery. Corn 4B 4
Lanner. Corn 6E 3
Lanreath. Corn 4C 4
Lansallos. Corn 4C 4
Lansdown. Bath 7K 17
Lansdown. Glos 1M 17
Lanteglos Highway. Corn 4C 4
Lanton. Nmbd 6J 57
Lanton. Bord 7F 56
Lapford. Devn 5J 7
Lapford Cross. Devn 5J 7
Laphroaig. Arg 5B 52
Lapley. Staf 8F 32
Lapworth. Warw 4M 25
Larachbeg. High 1D 58
Larbert. Falk 1G 55
Larden Green. Ches E 4C 32
Larel. High 4G 77
Largie. Abers 6G 73
Largiemore. Arg 1H 53
Largoward. Fife 5K 61
Largs. N Ayr 4A 54
Largue. Abers 5G 73
Largybeg. N Ayr 7J 53
Largymeanoch. N Ayr 7J 53
Largymore. N Ayr 7J 53
Larkfield. Inv 2A 54
Larkfield. Kent 8E 20
Larkhall. Bath 7K 17
Larkhall. S Lan 4F 54
Larkhill. Wilts 1B 10
Larling. Norf 3F 28
Larport. Here 8F 24
Lartington. Dur 2M 43
Lary. Abers 3D 66
Lasham. Hants 1G 11
Lashenden. Kent 3G 13
Lassodie. Fife 6G 61
Lasswade. Midl 3M 55
Lastingham. N Yor 4G 45
Latchford. Herts 1B 20
Latchford. Oxon 3G 19
Latchingdon. Essx 3G 21
Latchley. Corn 8F 6
Latchmere Green. Hants 7G 19
Lathbury. Mil 7G 27
Latheron. High 6G 77
Latheronwheel. High 6G 77
Lathom. Lanc 5C 38
Lathones. Fife 5K 61
Latimer. Buck 4L 19
Latteridge. S Glo 5J 17
Lattiford. Som 3F 8
Latton. Wilts 4A 18
Laudale House. High 8M 63
Lauder. Bord 5E 56
Laugharne. Carm 2H 15
Laughterton. Linc 8E 40
Laughton. E Sus 6D 12
Laughton. Leics 3E 26
Laughton. Linc 6E 40
(nr. Gainsborough)
Laughton. Linc 6G 35
(nr. Grantham)
Laughton Common. S Yor 7B 40
Laughton en le Morthen.
S Yor 7B 40
Launcells. Corn 5D 6
Launceston. Corn 7E 6
Launcherley. Som 1E 8
Launton. Oxon 1G 19
Laurencekirk. Abers 6H 67
Laurieston. Dum 5D 48
Laurieston. Falk 2H 55
Lavendon. Mil 6H 27
Lavenham. Suff 7F 28
Laverhay. Dum 2J 49
Laversdale. Cumb 5M 49
Laverstock. Wilts 2B 10
Laverstoke. Hants 1E 10
Laverton. Glos 8L 25
Laverton. N Yor 6B 44
Laverton. Som 8K 17
Lavister. Wrex 4A 32
Law. S Lan 4G 55
Lawers. Per 2B 60
Lawford. Essx 8G 29
Lawhitton. Corn 7E 6
Lawkland. N Yor 7J 43
Lawley. Telf 1G 25
Lawnhead. Staf 7F 32
Lawrenny. Pemb 3E 14
Lawshall. Suff 6E 28
Lawton. Here 6E 24
Laxey. IOM 5E 46
Laxfield. Suff 4J 29
Laxfirth. Shet 6E 79
Laxo. Shet 5E 79
Laxton. E Yor 3D 40
Laxton. Nptn 2H 27
Laxton. Notts 3D 34
Laycock. W Yor 1J 39
Layer Breton. Essx 2H 21
Layer-de-la-Haye. Essx 1H 21
Layer Marney. Essx 2H 21
Layland's Green. W Ber 7D 18
Laymore. Dors 5C 8
Laysters Pole. Here 5F 24
Layter's Green. Buck 4K 19
Laytham. E Yor 2D 40
Lazenby. Red C 2E 44
Lazonby. Cumb 8A 50
Lea. Derbs 4L 33
Lea. Here 1J 17
Lea. Linc 7E 40
Lea. Shrp 3D 24
(nr. Bishop's Castle)
Lea. Shrp 1E 24
(nr. Shrewsbury)
Lea. Wilts 5M 17
Leabrooks. Derbs 4A 34
Leac a Li. W Isl 2F 68
Leachd. Arg 6H 59
Leachkin. High 7J 71
Leachpool. Pemb 2D 14
Leadburn. Midl 4L 55
Leadenham. Linc 4F 34
Leaden Roding. Essx 2D 20
Leaderfoot. Bord 6E 56
Leadgate. Cumb 7C 50
Leadgate. Dur 6G 51
Leadgate. Nmbd 6G 51
Leadhills. S Lan 8G 55
Leadingcross Green. Kent 8G 21
Lea End. Worc 4L 25
Leafield. Oxon 2D 18
Leagrave. Lutn 1L 19
Lea Hall. W Mid 3M 25
Lea Heath. Staf 7H 33
Leake. N Yor 4D 44
Leake Common Side. Linc 4K 35
Leake Fold Hill. Linc 4L 35
Leake Hurn's End. Linc 5L 35
Lealholm. N Yor 3G 45
Lealt. Arg 6D 58
Lealt. High 5K 69
Leam. Derbs 8L 39
Lea Marston. Warw 2A 26
Leamington Hastings.
Warw 5C 26
Leamington Spa, Royal.
Warw 5B 26
Leamonsley. Staf 1M 25
Leamside. Dur 7J 51
Leargybreck. Arg 2D 52
Lease Rigg. N Yor 3H 45
Leasgill. Cumb 5F 42
Leasingham. Linc 5G 35
Leasingthorne. Dur 8H 51
Leasowe. Mers 6A 38
Leatherhead. Surr 8M 19
Leathley. N Yor 1L 39
Leaths. Dum 5E 48
Leaton. Shrp 8B 32
Leaton. Telf 8D 32
Lea Town. Lanc 2C 38
Leaveland. Kent 8J 21
Leavenheath. Suff 8F 28
Leavening. N Yor 7G 45
Leaves Green. G Lon 7C 20
Lea Yeat. Cumb 5J 43
Leazes. Dur 6G 51
Lebberston. N Yor 5K 45
Lechlade on Thames. Glos 4C 18
Leck. Lanc 6H 43
Leckford. Hants 2D 10
Leckfurin. High 4C 76
Leckgruinart. Arg 3A 52
Leckhampstead. Buck 8F 26
Leckhampstead. W Ber 6E 18
Leckhampstead Street.
W Ber 6E 18
Leckhampton. Glos 2M 17
Leckmelm. High 2D 70
Leckwith. V Glam 6D 16
Leconfield. E Yor 1G 41
Ledaig. Arg 2G 59
Ledburn. Buck 1K 19
Ledbury. Here 8H 25
Ledgemoor. Here 6E 24
Ledgowan. High 6D 70
Ledicot. Here 5E 24
Ledmore. High 8K 75
Lednabirichen. High 2K 71
Lednagullin. High 3D 76
Ledsham. Ches W 8B 38
Ledsham. W Yor 3A 40
Ledston. W Yor 3A 40
Ledstone. Devn 5J 5
Ledwell. Oxon 1E 18
Lee. Devn 1F 6
(nr. Ilfracombe)
Lee. Devn 3K 7
(nr. South Molton)
Lee. G Lon 6C 20
Lee. Hants 4D 10
Lee. Lanc 8G 43
Lee. Shrp 6B 32
Leeans. Shet 7D 79
Leebotten. Shet 9E 79
Leebotwood. Shrp 2E 24
Lee Brockhurst. Shrp 7C 32
Leece. Cumb 7D 42
Leechpool. Mon 5H 17
Lee Clump. Buck 3K 19
Leeds. Kent 8G 21
Leeds. W Yor 2L 39 & 96
Leeds Bradford
International Airport.
W Yor 1L 39
Leedstown. Corn 6D 3
Leegomery. Telf 8D 32
Lee Head. Derbs 6J 39
Leek. Staf 4G 33
Leekbrook. Staf 4G 33
Leek Wootton. Warw 5A 26
Lee Mill. Devn 4G 5
Leeming. N Yor 5B 44
Leeming Bar. N Yor 4B 44
Lee Moor. Devn 3G 5
Lee Moor. W Yor 3M 39
Lee-on-the-Solent. Hants 5F 10
Lees. Derbs 6K 33
Lees. G Man 5H 39
Lees. W Yor 2J 39
Lees, The. Kent 8J 21
Leeswood. Flin 3M 31
Lee, The. Buck 3K 19
Leetown. Per 3H 61
Leftwich. Ches W 8E 38
Legbourne. Linc 7K 41
Legburthwaite. Cumb 2E 42
Legerwood. Bord 5E 56
Legsby. Linc 7H 41
Leicester. Leic 1D 26 & 96
Leicester Forest East.
Leics 1D 26
Leigh. Dors 5F 8
Leigh. G Man 5E 38
Leigh. Kent 3D 12
Leigh. Shrp 1D 24
Leigh. Surr 3A 12
Leigh. Wilts 4A 18
Leigh. Worc 6H 25
Leigham. Plym 4G 5
Leigh Beck. Essx 5G 21
Leigh Common. Som 3G 9
Leigh Delamere. Wilts 6L 17
Leigh Green. Kent 4H 13
Leighland Chapel. Som 2M 7
Leigh-on-Sea. S'end 5G 21
Leigh Park. Hants 5H 11
Leigh Sinton. Worc 6H 25
Leighterton. Glos 4L 17
Leigh, The. Glos 1L 17
Leighton. N Yor 6A 44
Leighton. Powy 1C 24
Leighton. Shrp 1G 25
Leighton. Som 1G 9
Leighton Bromswold.
Cambs 4K 27
Leighton Buzzard. C Beds 1K 19
Leigh-upon-Mendip. Som 1F 8
Leinthall Earls. Here 5E 24
Leinthall Starkes. Here 5E 24
Leintwardine. Here 4E 24
Leire. Leics 2D 26
Leirinmore. High 3M 75
Leishmore. High 7G 71
Leiston. Suff 5L 29
Leitfie. Per 1H 61
Leith. Edin 2L 55
Leitholm. Bord 5G 57
Lelant. Corn 6C 3
Lelant Downs. Corn 6C 3
Lelley. E Yor 2J 41
Lem Hill. Worc 4H 25
Lemington. Tyne 5G 51
Lemmington Hall. Nmbd 8L 57

Millthorpe. Linc	6H 35	Moaness. Orkn	7A 78	Moreton. Mers	6A 38	Mountsorrel. Leics	8B 35	Nantgaredig. Carm	1J 15
Millthrop. Cumb	4H 43	Moarfield. Shet	1F 79	Moreton. Oxon	3G 19	Mount Stuart. Arg	4K 53	Nantgarw. Rhon	5D 16
Milltimber. Aber	3J 67	Moat. Cumb	4M 49	Moreton. Staf	8E 32	Mousehole. Corn	7B 3	Nant Glas. Powy	5M 23
Milltown. Abers	3C 66	Mobberley. Ches E	8F 38	Moreton Corbet. Shrp	7C 32	Mouswald. Dum	4H 49	Nantglyn. Cnwy	3K 31
(nr. Corgarff)		Moberley. Staf	5H 33	Moretonhampstead. Devn	7J 7	Mow Cop. Ches E	4F 32	Nantgwyn. Powy	4M 23
Milltown. Abers	2E 66	Moccas. Here	7D 24	Moreton-in-Marsh. Glos	8A 26	Mowden. Darl	2B 44	Nantle. Gwyn	4E 30
(nr. Lumsden)		Mochdre. Cnwy	2H 31	Moreton Jeffries. Here	7G 25	Mowhaugh. Bord	7H 57	Nantmawr. Shrp	7M 31
Milltown. Corn	4C 4	Mochdre. Powy	3A 24	Moreton Morrell. Warw	6B 26	Mowsley. Leics	3E 26	Nantmel. Powy	5A 24
Milltown. Derbs	3L 33	Mochrum. Dum	7A 48	Moreton on Lugg. Here	7F 24	Moy. High	8K 71	Nantmor. Gwyn	5F 30
Milltown. Devn	2G 7	Mockbeggar. Hants	5B 10	Moreton Pinkney. Nptn	7D 26	Moy Lodge. High	7D 22	Nant Peris. Gwyn	4F 30
Milltown. Dum	4L 49	Mockerkin. Cumb	1B 42	Moreton Say. Shrp	6E 32	Moylgrove. Pemb	7D 22	Nant-y-bai. Carm	2D 16
Milltown of Aberdalgie.		Moddershall. Staf	6G 33	Moreton Valence. Glos	3F 17	Muasdale. Arg	5E 52	Nant-y-bwch. Blae	3M 16
Per	3F 60	Modsarie. High	3B 76	Morfa. Cdgn	4A 22	Muchalls. Abers	4K 67	Nant-y-derry. Mon	3F 16
Milltown of Auchindoun.		Moelfre. Cdgn	2J 31	Morfa Bach. Carm	2H 15	Much Birch. Here	8F 24	Nant-y-dugoed. Powy	8J 31
Mor	5D 72	Moelfre. IOA	1E 30	Morfa Bychan. Gwyn	6E 30	Much Cowarne. Here	7G 25	Nant-y-felin. Cnwy	2F 30
Milltown of Campdell.		Moelfre. Powy	7L 31	Morfa Glas. Neat	3A 16	Much Dewchurch. Here	8E 24	Nantyffyllon. B'end	4A 16
Abers	3G 67	Moffat. Dum	1H 49	Morfa Nefyn. Gwyn	5B 30	Muchelney. Som	3D 8	Nantyglo. Blae	2D 16
Milltown of Edinvillie. Mor	5C 72	Moggerhanger. C Beds	7K 27	Morganstown. Card	5D 16	Muchelney Ham. Som	3D 8	Nant-y-meichiaid. Powy	8L 31
Milltown of Rothiemay.		Mogworthy. Devn	4K 7	Morgan's Vale. Wilts	3B 10	Much Hadham. Herts	1M 19	Nant-y-moel. B'end	4B 16
Mor	5F 72	Moira. Leics	8L 33	Moriah. Cdgn	4J 23	Much Hoole. Lanc	3C 38	Nant-y-Pandy. Cnwy	2F 30
Milltown of Towie. Abers	2E 66	Molash. Kent	8G 39	Morland. Cumb	1G 43	Much Marcle. Here	8G 25	Naphill. Buck	4J 19
Milnacraig. Ang	8C 66	Mol-chlach. High	2J 63	Morley. Ches E	7G 39	Much Wenlock. Shrp	2G 25	Nappa. Lanc	8K 43
Milnathort. Per	5G 61	Mold. Flin	3M 31	Morley. Derbs	5L 33	Muchrachd. High	8E 70	Napton on the Hill. Warw	5C 26
Milngavie. E Dun	2D 54	Molehill Green. Essx	1D 20	Morley. Dur	1A 44	Much Wenlock. Shrp	2G 25	Narberth. Pemb	2F 14
Milnholm. Stir	1F 54	Molescroft. E Yor	1G 41	Morley. W Yor	3L 39	Mucking. Thur	5D 20	Narberth Bridge. Pemb	2F 14
Milnrow. G Man	4H 39	Molesden. Nmbd	3G 51	Morley St Botolph. Norf	2G 29	Muckle Breck. Shet	5F 79	Narborough. Leics	2C 26
Milnthorpe. Cumb	5F 42	Molesworth. Cambs	4J 27	Morningside. N Lan	4G 55	Muckleford. Dors	6E 8	Narborough. Norf	1D 28
Milnthorpe. W Yor	4M 39	Moll. High	2K 69	Morningside. Edin	2L 55	Mucklestone. Staf	6F 32	Narkurs. Corn	6E 4
Milson. Shrp	4G 25	Molland. Devn	3K 7	Morningthorpe. Norf	2J 29	Muckleton. Staf	4E 36	Narth, The. Mon	3H 17
Milstead. Kent	8J 21	Mollington. Ches W	8B 38	Morpeth. Nmbd	3H 51	Muckleton. Shrp	7C 32	Narthwaite. Cumb	4J 43
Milston. Wilts	1A 10	Mollington. Oxon	7C 26	Morrey. Staf	8J 33	Muckley Corner. Staf	1L 25	Naseby. Nptn	4E 26
Milthorpe. Nptn	7D 28	Mollinsburn. N Lan	2F 54	Morridge Side. Staf	4H 33	Muckton. Linc	7K 41	Nash. Here	5D 24
Milton. Ang	1J 61	Monachty. Cdgn	5H 23	Morridge Top. Staf	3H 33	Mudale. High	6A 76	Nash. Buck	1E 20
Milton. Cambs	5A 28	Monachyle. Stir	4M 59	Morrington. Dum	3F 48	Muddiford. Devn	2G 7	Nash. Newp	5E 16
Milton. Cumb	5A 50	Monaughty. Powy	5C 24	Morriston. Swan	4L 15	Mudeford. Dors	6B 10	Nash. Shrp	4G 25
(nr. Brampton)		Monewden. Suff	6J 29	Morston. Norf	3G 37	Mudford. Som	4E 8	Nash Lee. Buck	3J 19
Milton. Cumb	5G 43	Moneyrow Green. Wind	5G 31	Mortehoe. Devn	1F 6	Mudgley. Som	1D 8	Nassington. Nptn	2J 27
(nr. Crooklands)		Moniaive. Dum	2E 48	Morthen. S Yor	7A 40	Mugdock. Stir	2D 54	Nasty. Herts	1B 20
Milton. Derbs	7L 33	Monifieth. Ang	2L 61	Mortimer. W Ber	7G 19	Mugeary. High	8J 69	Natcott. Devn	3D 6
Milton. Dum	4F 48	Monikie. Ang	1L 61	Mortimer's Cross. Here	5E 24	Muggington. Derbs	5K 33	Nateby. Cumb	4F 42
(nr. Crocketford)		Monimail. Fife	4H 61	Mortimer West End. Hants	7G 19	Muggintonlane End. Derbs	5K 33	Nateby. Lanc	1C 38
Milton. Dum	6M 47	Monington. Pemb	7D 22	Mortomley. S Yor	6M 39	Muggleswick. Dur	6D 50	Nately Scures. Hants	8H 19
(nr. Glenluce)		Monk Bretton. S Yor	5M 39	Morton. Cumb	6J 49	Muirden. Aber	8G 73	Natland. Cumb	5G 43
Milton. E Ayr	7C 54	Monken Hadley. G Lon	4A 20	(nr. Caldbeck)		Muirdrum. Ang	2L 61	Naughton. Suff	7G 29
Milton. Glas	4C 58	Monk Fryston. N Yor	3B 40	Morton. Cumb	6L 49	Muiredge. Per	2H 61	Naunton. Glos	1K 18
Milton. High	8H 21	Monk Hesleden. Dur	8K 51	(nr. Carlisle)		Muirend. Glas	3D 54	Naunton. Worc	8G 25
(nr. Achnasheen)		Monkhide. Here	7G 25	Morton. Derbs	3A 34	Muirhead. Ang	2J 61	Naunton Beauchamp.	
Milton. High	7M 69	Monkhill. Cumb	6L 49	Morton. Linc	7G 35	Muirhead. Fife	5J 61	Worc	6K 25
(nr. Applecross)		Monkhopton. Shrp	2G 25	(nr. Bourne)		Muirhead. N Lan	3F 54	Navenby. Linc	4F 34
Milton. High	8G 71	Monkland. Here	6C 24	Morton. Linc	6E 40	Muirhouses. Falk	1J 55	Navestock Heath. Essx	4D 20
(nr. Drumnadrochit)		Monkleigh. Devn	3F 6	(nr. Gainsborough)		Muirkirk. E Ayr	7E 54	Navestock Side. Essx	4D 20
Milton. High	4H 71	Monknash. V Glam	8B 16	Morton. Linc	3E 34	Muir of Alford. Abers	2F 66	Navidale. High	8F 76
(nr. Invergordon)		Monkokehampton. Devn	5G 7	(nr. Lincoln)		Muir of Fairburn. Abers	6G 71	Nawton. N Yor	5F 44
Milton. High	4J 77	Monkseaton. Tyne	4J 51	Morton. Norf	1H 37	Muir of Fowlis. Abers	2F 66	Nayland. Suff	8F 28
(nr. Wick)		Monk's Gate. W Sus	5A 12	Morton. Notts	4D 34	Muir of Miltonduff. Mor	4B 72	Nazeing. Essx	3C 20
Milton. Mor	3F 72	Monk's Heath. Ches E	8G 39	Morton. Shrp	7M 31	Muir of Ord. High	6H 71	Neacroft. Hants	6B 10
(nr. Cullen)		Monk Sherborne. Hants	5H 19	Morton. S Glo	4J 17	Muir of Tarradale. High	5H 71	(nr. Penrith)	
Milton. Mor	2B 66	Monksilver. Som	8M 49	Morton Bagot. Warw	5M 25	Muirshearlich. High	5D 64	Neal's Green. W Mid	4B 42
(nr. Tomintoul)		Monks Kirby. Warw	3C 26	Morton Mill. Shrp	7D 32	Muirtack. Abers	4H 73	Neap House. N Lin	7F 42
Milton. N Som	7C 16	Monk Soham. Suff	5J 29	Morton-on-Swale. N Yor	4C 44	Muirton. Per	2E 60	(nr. Seascale)	
Milton. Notts	3D 40	Monk Soham Green. Suff	5J 29	Morton Tinmouth. Dur	1A 44	Muirton. Per	3G 61	Near Sawrey. Cumb	7G 51
Milton. Oxon	8C 26	Monks Risborough. Buck	3J 19	Morvah. Corn	5H 3	Muirton of Ardblair. Per	1G 61	Neap House. Darl	1L 43
(nr. Bloxham)		Monksthorpe. Linc	3L 35	Morval. Corn	4D 4	Muirtown. Per	4C 60	Neasham. Darl	2C 44
Milton. Oxon	4E 18	Monk Street. Essx	1E 20	Morvich. High	1K 71	Muiryfold. Abers	8G 73	Neath. Neat	4M 15
(nr. Didcot)		Monkswood. Mon	3H 16	(nr. Golspie)		Muker. N Yor	4L 43	Neath Abbey. Neat	4M 15
Milton. Pemb	3E 14	Monkton. Devn	5A 8	Morvich. High	4M 25	Mulbarton. Norf	1H 29	Neatham. Hants	2H 11
Milton. Port	6G 11	Monkton. Kent	7L 21	(nr. Shiel Bridge)		Mulben. Mor	4H 31	Neatishead. Norf	7K 37
Milton. Som	3D 8	Monkton. N Ayr	3B 10	Morvil. Pemb	8C 27	Mulindry. Arg	4B 52	Nebo. Cdgn	5H 23
Milton. Stir	5A 60	Monkton. S Ayr	7B 54	Morville. Shrp	2G 25	Mullach Charlabhaigh.		Nebo. Cnwy	4H 31
(nr. Aberfoyle)		Monkton Combe. Bath	7H 17	Morwenstow. Corn	4D 6	W Isl	4C 74	Nebo. Gwyn	5L 43
Milton. Stir	4M 59	Monkton Deverill. Wilts	2H 9	Morwick Hall. Nmbd	1H 51	Mullacott. Devn	1F 6	Nebo. IOA	1D 30
(nr. Drymen)		Monkton Farleigh. Wilts	7H 17	Mosborough. S Yor	7A 40	Mullion. Corn	8K 3	Necton. Norf	1E 28
Milton. Stoke	4G 33	Monkton Heathfield. Som	3A 8	Moscow. E Ayr	5C 54	Mullion Cove. Corn	8D 3	Nedd. High	6A 76
Milton. W Dun	2C 54	Monktonhill. S Ayr	7B 54	Mose. Shrp	2H 25	Mumbles. Swan	5L 15	Nedderton. Nmbd	3G 51
Milton Abbas. Dors	5H 9	Monkton Up Wimborne.		Mosedale. Cumb	8J 49	Mumby. Linc	8M 41	Nedging. Suff	7G 29
Milton Abbot. Devn	8C 6	Dors	4A 10	Moseley. W Mid	1J 25	Munderfield Row. Here	6G 25	Nedging Tye. Suff	7G 29
Milton Auchlossan. Abers	3F 66	Monkwearmouth. Tyne	6D 8	(nr. Birmingham)		Munderfield Stocks. Here	6G 25	Needham. Norf	3J 29
Milton Bridge. Midl	3L 55	Monkwood. Dors	5D 8	Moseley. W Mid	3H 25	Mundesley. Norf	4K 37	Needham Market. Suff	6G 29
Milton Bryan. C Beds	8H 27	Monkwood. Hants	2G 11	(nr. Wolverhampton)		Mundford. Norf	2D 28	Needham Street. Suff	5D 28
Milton Clevedon. Som	2E 8	Monmarsh. Here	7F 24	Moseley. Worc	6J 25	Mundham. Norf	2K 29	Needingworth. Cambs	4M 27
Milton Coldwells. Abers	6K 73	Monmouth. Mon	2H 17	Moss. Arg	8A 62	Mundon. Essx	3G 21	Needwood. Staf	7J 33
Milton Combe. Devn	5G 7	Monnington on Wye. Here	7D 24	Moss. High	7L 63	Munerigie. High	3E 64	Neen Savage. Shrp	4G 25
Milton Common. Oxon	3G 19	Monreith. Dum	7A 48	Moss. S Yor	5C 40	Muness. Shet	1G 79	Neen Sollars. Shrp	4G 25
Milton Damerel. Devn	4E 6	Montacute. Som	4D 8	Moss. Wrex	4A 32	Mungasdale. Cumb	8L 49	Neenton. Shrp	3G 25
Miltonduff. Mor	3B 72	Montford. Arg	3J 53	Mossat. Abers	2E 66	Mungrisdale. Cumb	8L 49	Nefyn. Gwyn	5C 30
Milton End. Glos	3B 18	Montford. Shrp	8C 32	Moss Bank. Mers	6D 38	Munlochy. High	6J 71	Neilston. E Ren	4C 54
Milton Ernest. Bed	6J 27	Montford Bridge. Shrp	8B 32	Mossblown. S Ayr	7C 54	Munsley. Here	7G 25	Neithrop. Oxon	7C 26
Milton Green. Ches W	4B 32	Montgarrie. Abers	2F 66	Mossbrow. G Man	7F 38	Munslow. Shrp	3F 24	Nelly Andrews Green.	
Milton Hill. Devn	8L 7	Montgarswood. E Ayr	7D 54	Mossburnford. Bord	8F 56	Murcheston. Shrp	7H 7	Powy	1C 24
Milton Hill. Oxon	4E 18	Montgomery. Powy	2A 24	Mossdale. Dum	4D 48	Murcott. Worc	7L 25	Nelson. Cphy	5L 39
Milton Keynes. Mil	8G 27 & 100	Montgreenan. N Ayr	5B 54	Moss Edge. Lanc	1C 38	Murcott. Oxon	2F 18	Nelson. Lanc	2G 39
Milton Keynes Village. Mil	8G 27	Montrave. Fife	5J 61	Mossend. N Lan	3F 54	Murdishaw. Hal	7D 38	Nelson Village. Nmbd	4H 51
Milton Lilbourne. Wilts	7B 18	Montrose. Ang	8H 67	Mossgate. Staf	6G 33	Murkle. High	3G 77	Nemphlar. S Lan	5G 55
Milton Malsor. Nptn	6E 26	Monxton. Hants	1D 10	Moss Lane. Ches E	8H 39	Murlaggan. High	4C 64	Nempnett Thrubwell. Bath	7H 17
Milton Morenish. Per	2B 60	Monyash. Derbs	3J 33	Mosspaul. Bord	2M 49	Murra. Orkn	7A 78	Nene Terrace. Linc	1L 27
Milton of Auchinhove.		Monymusk. Abers	2G 67	Moss Side. Cumb	6J 49	Murrayfield. Edin	2L 55	Nenthall. Cumb	7L 27
Abers	3F 66	Monzie. Per	3D 60	Moss Side. G Man	8G 39	Murray, The. S Lan	4E 54	Nenthead. Cumb	7C 50
Milton of Balgonie. Fife	5J 61	Moodiesburn. N Lan	2E 54	Moss-side. High	6L 71	Murrell Green. Hants	8H 19	Nenthorn. Bord	6E 56
Milton of Barras. Abers	8L 67	Moon's Green. Kent	5G 13	Moss-side. Lanc	4B 38	Murroes. Ang	2K 61	Nesbit. Nmbd	6G 57
Milton of Campsie. E Dun	2E 54	Moonzie. Fife	4J 61	(nr. Blackpool)		Murrow. Cambs	1M 27	Nesfield. N Yor	1J 39
Milton of Cultoquhey. Per	3D 60	Moor. Som	3C 8	Moss Side. Lanc	4C 38	Mursley. Buck	1J 19	Ness. Ches W	8B 38
Milton of Cushnie. Abers	2F 66	Moor Allerton. W Yor	2L 39	(nr. Preston)		Murthly. Per	1C 60	Nesscliffe. Shrp	8B 32
Milton of Finavon. Ang	8F 66	Moorbath. Dors	6C 8	Moss Side. Mers	5B 38	Murton. Cumb	5K 17	Ness of Tenston. Orkn	6A 78
Milton of Gollanfield. High	6K 71	Moorbrae. Shet	4J 79	Moss-side of Cairness.		Murton. Dur	7G 51	Neston. Ches W	8A 38
Milton of Lesmore. Abers	1E 66	Moorby. Linc	3J 35	Abers	3L 73	Murton. Nmbd	5G 57	Neston. Wilts	7H 17
Milton of Leys. High	1J 71	Moorcot. Here	6D 24	Mosstodloch. Mor	3D 72	Murton. Swan	5K 15	Nethanfoot. S Lan	5G 55
Milton of Tullich. Abers	4D 66	Moor Crichel. Dors	5J 9	Mosswood. Nmbd	5F 50	Murton. York	8F 44	Nether Alderley. Ches E	2F 38
Milton on Stour. Dors	3G 9	Moor Cross. Devn	6H 7	Mossy Lea. Lanc	6D 38	Musbury. Devn	6B 8	Netheravon. Wilts	1B 10
Milton Regis. Kent	7E 21	Moordown. Bour	6J 9	Mosterton. Dors	5D 8	Muscoates. N Yor	5F 44	Nether Blainslie. Bord	5B 56
Milton Street. E Sus	5B 12	Moore. Hal	7D 38	Moston. Shrp	7C 32	Muscott. Nptn	5D 26	Nether Broughton. Leics	7D 34
Milton-under-Wychwood.		Moorend. Dum	4K 49	Moston Green. Ches E	3E 32	Musselburgh. E Lot	2M 55	Netherburn. S Lan	5G 55
Oxon	2C 18	Moor End. E Yor	2E 40	Mostyn. Flin	1L 31	Muston. Leics	6E 34	Nether Burrow. Lanc	5E 42
Milverton. Som	3A 8	Moorend. Glos	3K 17	Mostyn Quay. Flin	1L 31	Muston. N Yor	6K 45	Netherbury. Dors	6D 8
Milverton. Warw	5B 26	(nr. Dursley)		Motcombe. Dors	3H 9	Mustow Green. Worc	4J 25	Netherby. Cumb	3J 49
Milwich. Staf	6G 33	Moorend. Glos	2F 18	Mothecombe. Devn	7H 7	Muswell Hill. G Lon	4L 21	Nether Careston. Ang	8F 66
Mimbridge. Surr	7H 19	(nr. Gloucester)		Motherby. Cumb	1F 42	Mutehill. Dum	7A 48	Nether Cerne. Dors	5F 8
Minard. Arg	6G 59	Moorgate. S Yor	6A 40	Motherwell. N Lan	4F 54	Muthill. Per	3D 60	Nether Compton. Dors	4E 8
Minchington. Dors	4J 9	Moorgreen. Hants	4C 10	Mottingham. G Lon	6M 21	Mutterton. Devn	5M 7	Nethercote. Glos	1D 18
Minchinhampton. Glos	3G 18	Moorgreen. Notts	5B 34	Mottisfont. Hants	3D 10	Muxton. Telf	8F 32	Nethercote. Warw	5C 26
Mindrum. Nmbd	6H 57	Moorhaigh. Notts	3B 34	Mottistone. IOW	7B 10	Mwmbwls. Swan	5L 15	Nethercott. Devn	2F 6
Minehead. Som	1L 7	Moorhampton. Here	7D 24	Mottram in Longdendale.		Mybster. High	4D 77	Nethercott. Oxon	1B 18
Minera. Wrex	4A 18	Moorhouse. Cumb	6J 49	G Man	8H 39	Myddfai. Carm	2D 16	Nether Dallachy. Mor	3D 72
Minety. Wilts	4J 18	(nr. Carlisle)		Mottram St Andrew.		Mydroilyn. Cdgn	6G 23	Nether Durdie. Per	3H 61
Minffordd. Gwyn	6E 30	Moorhouse. Cumb	6G 49	Ches E	3G 39	Myerscough. Lanc	2C 38	Nether End. Derbs	3H 17
Mingarrypark. High	1T 63	(nr. Wigton)		Mott's Mill. E Sus	4D 12	Mylor Bridge. Corn	6F 3	Netherend. Glos	3E 44
Mingary. High	1L 63	Moorhouse. Notts	3D 34	Mouldsworth. Ches W	8D 38	Mylor Churchtown. Corn	6F 3	Nether Exe. Devn	5M 7
Mingearraidh. W Isl	1B 62	Moorhouse. Surr	8M 21	Moulin. Per	1C 60	Mynachlog-ddu. Pemb	5G 34	Netherfield. E Sus	4D 12
Miningsby. Linc	3K 35	Moorhouses. Linc	3K 35	Moulsecoomb. Brig	7B 12	Mynydd-bach. Mon	4G 17	Netherfield. Notts	5C 34
Minions. Corn	8B 6	Moorland. Som	2C 8	Moulsford. Oxon	5D 18	Mynydd Isa. Flin	3M 31	Nethergate. Norf	6G 37
Minishant. S Ayr	8B 50	Moorlinch. Som	2D 8	Moulsoe. Mil	7G 33	Mynyddislwyn. Cphy	4D 16	Netherhampton. Wilts	3K 9
Minllyn. Gwyn	5B 48	Moor Monkton. N Yor	8E 44	Moulton. Ches W	3E 32	Mynydd Llandegai. Gwyn	4F 30	Nether Handley. Derbs	2B 40
Minngaff. Dum	5B 48	Moor of Granary. Mor	4A 72	Moulton. Linc	7K 35	Mynydd Mechell. IOA	1C 30	Nether Haugh. S Yor	7B 40
Minorca. IOM	6D 44	Moor Row. Cumb	3K 49	Moulton. Nptn	5F 26	Mynyddygarreg. Carm	5L 15	Nether Heage. Derbs	4A 34
Minskip. N Yor	7C 44	(nr. Whitehaven)		Moulton. N Yor	5L 43	Mynytho. Gwyn	6C 30	Nether Heyford. Nptn	6D 26
Minstead. Hants	4C 10	Moor Row. Cumb	7K 49	Moulton. Suff	5C 28	Myrebird. Abers	4H 67	Netherhouses. Cumb	7A 42
Minsted. W Sus	3J 11	(nr. Wigton)		Moulton. V Glam	8K 15	Myrelandhorn. High	4H 77	Nether Howcleugh. Dum	8J 55
Minster. Kent	7H 21	Moorsholm. Red C	4E 44	Moulton Chapel. Linc	8J 35	Mytchett. Surr	8H 9	Nether Kellet. Lanc	5E 42
(nr. Ramsgate)		Moorside. Dors	4G 9	Moulton Eaugate. Linc	1K 29	Mythe, The. Glos	8H 25	Nether Kinmundy. Abers	5L 73
Minster. Kent	6H 21	Moorside. G Man	5H 39	Moulton St Mary. Norf	1K 29	Mytholm. W Yor	5J 39	Netherland Green. Staf	6J 33
(nr. Sheerness)		Moor, The. Kent	5E 9	Moulton Seas End. Linc	7K 35	Mytholmroyd. W Yor	5J 39	Netherlaw. Dum	8A 48
Minsteracres. Nmbd	6F 50	Moortown. Devn	7E 6	Mount. Corn	2C 4	Myton-on-Swale. N Yor	7D 44	Netherley. Abers	4H 67
Minsterley. Shrp	1D 24	Moortown. Hants	5B 10	(nr. Bodmin)		Mytton. Shrp	8C 32	Nethermill. Dum	3F 48
Minster Lovell. Oxon	2D 18	Moortown. IOW	7B 10	Mount. Corn	4E 3			Nethermills. Mor	4F 72
Minsterworth. Glos	2F 18	Moortown. Linc	8J 21	(nr. Newquay)		**N**		Nether Moor. Derbs	3L 33
Minterne Magna. Dors	5F 8	Moortown. Telf	8D 32	Mountain Ash. Rhon	4C 16			Netherplace. E Ren	4D 54
Minterne Parva. Dors	5F 8	Moortown. W Yor	2L 39	Mountain Cross. Bord	5K 55	Naast. High	3A 70	Nether Padley. Derbs	2L 33
Minting. Linc	3H 41	Morangie. High	3K 71	Mountain Street. Kent	8G 39	Na Buirgh. W Isl	2E 68	Netherplace. E Ren	3M 23
Mintlaw. Abers	5L 73	Moranpie. High	3K 71	Mountain Water. Pemb	1D 14	Nab Wood. W Yor	1B 40	Netherseal. Derbs	8K 33
Minto. Bord	7E 56	Morar. High	1G 63	Mount Ambrose. Corn	4L 3	Nab Wood. W Yor	1B 40	Nether Silton. N Yor	4D 41
Minton. Shrp	2E 24	Morborne. Cambs	2J 27	Mount Bures. Essx	8F 28	Nackington. Kent	8H 21	Nether Stowey. Som	2A 8
Minwear. Pemb	5G 15	Morchard Bishop. Devn	5J 7	Mountfield. E Sus	4D 12	Nacton. Suff	7J 29	Netherstreet. Wilts	7J 17
Minworth. W Mid	2M 25	Morcombelake. Dors	6C 8	Mountgerald. High	5H 71	Nafferton. E Yor	1H 41	Netherthird. E Ayr	8D 54
Miodar. Arg	8B 62	Morcott. Rut	1H 27	Mount Hawke. Corn	4L 3	Na Gearrannan. W Isl	3C 74	Netherthong. W Yor	5K 39
Mirbister. Orkn	5B 78	Morda. Shrp	7M 31	Mount High. High	5J 71	Nailbridge. Glos	2E 17	Netherton. Ang	1J 61
Mireland. High	5C 78	Morden. G Lon	7K 20	Mountjoy. Corn	3F 3	Nailsbourne. Som	3A 8	Netherton. Cumb	8E 48
Mirfield. W Yor	4L 39	More. Shrp	2C 24	Mount Lothian. Midl	4L 55	Nailsea. N Som	6C 16	Netherton. Devn	8L 7
Miserden. Glos	3H 18	Morebath. Devn	3J 7	Mountnessing. Essx	4D 20	Nailstone. Leics	1B 26	Netherton. Hants	8D 18
Miskin. Rhon	5C 16	Morebattle. Bord	7G 57	Mounton. Mon	4D 16	Nailsworth. Glos	4G 17	Netherton. Here	8E 24
Misson. Notts	6C 40	Morecambe. Lanc	7K 17	Mount Pleasant. Buck	8E 26	Nairn. High	6L 71	Netherton. Mers	6B 38
Misterton. Leics	3D 26	Morefield. High	2D 70	Mount Pleasant. Ches E	4F 32	Nalderswick. Cumb	2D 38	Netherton. N Lan	4F 54
Misterton. Notts	6D 8	Moreleigh. Devn	6K 7	(nr. Derby)		Nancegollan. Corn	6D 3	Netherton. Nptn	3H 27
Misterton. Som	5D 8	Morenish. Per	2B 60	Mount Pleasant. Derbs	8K 33	Nancledra. Corn	5H 3	Netherton. Nmbd	1D 50
Mistley. Essx	8H 29	Moresby Parks. Cumb	2A 42	(nr. Swadlincote)		Nanhyfer. Pemb	7D 22	Netherton. Oxon	3B 18
Mistley Heath. Essx	8H 29	Morestead. Hants	3C 10	Mount Pleasant. Derbs	4A 34	Nannerch. Flin	3L 31	Netherton. Per	1C 60
Mitcham. G Lon	7K 20	Moreton. Dors	7H 9	(nr. Derby)		Nanpantan. Leics	8B 34	Netherton. Shrp	3H 25
Mitcheldean. Glos	2J 17	Moreton. Essx	3C 20	Mount Pleasant. E Sus	4B 12	Nanpean. Corn	6B 4	Netherton. Stir	2C 54
Mitchell. Corn	4F 3	Moreton. Here	5E 24	Mount Pleasant. Fife	6C 10	Nanstallon. Corn	5C 4	Netherton. W Mid	3H 25
Mitcheltroy Common.		Moreton. Here	5F 24	Mount Pleasant. Hants	6C 10	Nant-ddu. Powy	2C 16	Netherton. W Yor	5K 39
Mon	3G 17	Moreton. Mers	6A 38	Mount Skippett. Oxon	2B 18	Nanternis. Cdgn	6F 22	(nr. Horbury)	
Mitford. Nmbd	3G 51							Netherton. W Yor	5L 39
Mithian. Corn	4E 9							(nr. Huddersfield)	
Mitton. Staf	4F 8							Netherton. Worc	7H 25
Mixbury. Oxon	8E 26								
Mixenden. W Yor	4K 39								
Mixon. Staf	4H 33								

Nethertown. Cumb	3A 42	New Earswick. York	8F 44	Newstead. Bord	6E 56	
Nethertown. High	2J 77	New Edlington. S Yor	6B 40	New Stevenston. N Lan	4F 54	
Nether Urquhart. Fife	5G 61	New Elgin. Mor	3C 72	New Street. Here	6D 24	
Nether Wallop. Hants	2D 10	New Ellerby. E Yor	2H 41	New Swanage. Dors	7A 10	
Nether Wasdale. Cumb	3C 42	Newell Green. Brac	5J 20	New Swannington. Leics	8A 34	
Nether Welton. Cumb	7L 49	New Eltham. G Lon	6C 20	Newthorpe. Notts	5A 34	
Nether Whitacre. Warw	2A 26	New End. Warw	5M 25	Newton. Arg	6A 16	
Nether Winchendon. Buck	2H 19	New End. Worc	6L 25	Newton. B'end	7A 28	
Netherwitton. Nmbd	2E 50	Newenden. Kent	5G 13	Newton. Cambs	8L 35	
Nether Worton. Oxon	8C 26	New England. Essx	7D 28	(nr. Cambridge)		
Nethy Bridge. High	4J 66	New England. Pet	1K 27	Newton. Cambs	1K 27	
Netley. Hants	5E 10	New Ferry. Mers	7B 38	(nr. Wisbech)		
Netley Marsh. Hants	4C 10	Newfield. Dur	8F 51	Newton. Ches W	3B 32	
Nettacott. Devn	5H 19	(nr. Chester-le-Street)		(nr. Chester)		
Nettlebed. Oxon	5H 19	Newfield. Dur	8H 51	Newton. Ches W	4C 32	
Nettlebridge. Som	6E 8	(nr. Willington)		(nr. Tattenhall)		
Nettlecombe. IOW	8E 10	New Forest. Hants	4C 10	Newton. Cumb	6D 42	
Nettleden. Herts	2L 19	Newfound. Hants	8F 18	Newton. Derbs	4A 34	
Nettleham. Linc	8G 41	New Fryston. W Yor	3A 40	Newton. Dors	4G 9	
Nettlestead. Kent	8E 20	Newgale. Pemb	1C 14	Newton. Dum	2J 49	
Nettlestead Green. Kent	8E 20	New Galloway. Dum	4D 48	(nr. Annan)		
Nettlestone. IOW	6G 11	Newgate. Norf	3G 37	Newton. Dum	2J 49	
Nettlesworth. Dur	5H 41	Newgate Street. Herts	3B 20	(nr. Moffat)		
Nettleton. Linc	6J 37	New Greens. Herts	3M 19	Newton. G Man	6H 39	
Nettleton. Wilts	5D 23	New Grimsby. IOS	2B 3	Newton. Here	6J 37	
Netton. Devn	5G 5	New Hainford. Norf	6J 37	(nr. Ewyas Harold)		
Netton. Wilts	2B 10	Newhall. Ches E	5D 32	Newton. Here	6F 24	
Neuadd. Powy	1J 24	Newhall. Staf	7K 33	(nr. Leominster)		
Neuk, The. Abers	4H 67	New Hartley. Nmbd	4J 51	Newton. High	5K 71	
Nevendon. Essx	4F 20	Newhaven. E Sus	7C 12 & 104	(nr. Cromarty)		
Nevern. Pemb	2L 55	Newhaven. Edin	2L 55	Newton. High	1H 43	
New Abbey. Dum	5G 49	Newhey. G Man	4H 39	(nr. Inverness)		
New Aberdour. Abers	3J 73	New Hedges. Pemb	3F 14	Newton. High	5J 77	
New Addington. G Lon	7B 20	New Herrington. Tyne	6J 51	(nr. Kylestrome)		
Newall. W Yor	1K 39	New Holkham. Norf	4E 36	Newton. High	5J 77	
New Alresford. Hants	2F 10	New Holland. N Lin	3G 41	(nr. Wick)		
New Alyth. Per	1H 61	Newholm. N Yor	4F 44	Newton. Lanc	2B 38	
Newark. Orkn	3F 78	New Houghton. Derbs	3B 34	(nr. Blackpool)		
Newark. Pet	1K 27	New Houghton. Norf	5D 36	Newton. Lanc	6G 43	
Newark-on-Trent. Notts	4D 34	Newhouse. N Lan	3F 54	(nr. Carnforth)		
New Arley. Warw	3A 26	New Houses. N Yor	6G 43	Newton. Lanc	8H 43	
Newarthill. N Lan	4F 54	New Hutton. Cumb	4G 43	(nr. Clitheroe)		
New Ash Green. Kent	7E 20	New Hythe. Kent	8E 20	Newton. Linc	6G 35	
New Balderton. Notts	4E 34	Newick. E Sus	5C 12	Newton. Mers	7A 38	
New Barnetby. N Lin	4G 41	Newingreen. Kent	4K 13	Newton. Mor	3B 72	
New Barnetby. N Lin	4G 41	Newington. Edin	2L 55	Newton. Nmbd	6E 36	
New Barnet. G Lon	4L 21	Newington. Kent	4K 13	Newton. Nptn	5F 50	
Newbattle. Midl	3M 55	(nr. Folkestone)		Newton. Notts	5D 34	
Newbie. Dum	5J 49	Newington. Kent	7G 21	Newton. Bord	7F 56	
Newbiggin. Cumb	5J 49	(nr. Sittingbourne)		Newton. Shet	8D 79	
(nr. Appleby)		Newington. Notts	6C 40	Newton. Shrp	2H 25	
Newbiggin. Cumb	8E 42	Newington Bagpath. Glos	4L 17	(nr. Bridgnorth)		
(nr. Barrow-in-Furness)		New Inn. Carm	5J 23	Newton. Shrp	6B 32	
Newbiggin. Cumb	6L 49	New Inn. Mon	3G 17	(nr. Wem)		
(nr. Cumrew)		New Inn. N Yor	8G 43	Newton. Som	3E 54	
Newbiggin. Cumb	1F 42	New Inn. Torf	4A 16	Newton. S Lan	6H 55	
(nr. Penrith)		New Invention. Shrp	4C 24	(nr. Glasgow)		
Newbiggin. Dur	7G 51	New Kelso. High	8B 70	Newton. S Lan	7H 33	
(nr. Consett)		New Lanark. S Lan	5G 55	Newton. Staf	7F 28	
Newbiggin. Dur	1L 43	Newland. Glos	3H 17	Newton. Suff	5L 15	
(nr. Holwick)		Newland. Hull	4D 26	Newton. Swan	4D 26	
Newbiggin. Dur	8E 42	Newland. N Som	2G 41	Newton. Warw	4D 26	
(nr. Askrigg)		Newland. Som	2L 7	Newton. Wilts	3C 10	
Newbiggin. N Yor	1F 28	Newland. Worc	7G 25	**Newton Abbot. Devn**	8K 7	
Newbiggin. N Yor	5L 45	Newlandrig. Midl	3M 55	Newtonairds. Dum	3F 48	
(nr. Filey)		Newlands. Cumb	6K 49	**Newton Arlosh. Cumb**	6J 49	
Newbiggin. Nmbd	6F 50	Newlands. Essx	5G 21	**Newton Aycliffe. Dur**	1B 44	
Newbiggin. Staf	7H 33	Newlands. Nmbd	6F 50	Newton Bewley. Hart	1C 44	
Newbiggin-by-the-Sea.		Newlands. Staf	7H 33	Newton Blossomville. Mil	6H 27	
Nmbd	3J 51	Newlands of Geise. High	3F 76	Newton Bromswold. Bed	5H 27	
Newbigging. Ang	2K 61	Newlands of Tynet. Mor	3D 72	Newton Burgoland. Leics	1B 26	
Newbigging. Ang	2K 61	Newlands Park. IOA	1B 30	Newton Ferrers. Devn	5G 5	
(nr. Monikie)		New Lane. Lanc	6C 38	Newton Flotman. Norf	2J 29	
Newbigging. S Lan	5J 55	New Lane End. Warr	6E 38	Newtongrange. Midl	3M 55	
Newbigging. Edin	2K 55	New Langholm. Dum	3L 49	Newton Green. Mon	4H 17	
Newbiggin. S Lan	3J 43	New Leake. Linc	4L 35	Newton Hall. Dur	7H 51	
Newbold. Derbs	8M 39	New Leeds. Abers	4K 73	Newton Hall. Nmbd	5F 50	
Newbold. Leics	8A 34	New Lenton. Notts	6B 34	Newton Harcourt. Leics	2E 26	
Newbold on Avon. Warw	4C 26	New Longton. Lanc	3D 38	Newton Heath. G Man	6H 39	
Newbold on Stour. Warw	7A 26	Newloot. Orkn	6D 78	Newtonhill. Abers	4K 67	
Newbold Pacey. Warw	6A 26	New Luce. Dum	5L 47	Newtonhill. High	7H 71	
Newbold Verdon. Leics	1C 26	Newlyn. Corn	7B 3	Newton Ketton. Darl	1C 44	
New Bolingbroke. Linc	4L 35	Newmachar. Abers	2H 67	Newton Kyme. N Yor	2A 40	
Newborough. IOA	4D 30	Newmains. N Lan	4G 55	Newton-le-Willows. Mers	6D 38	
Newborough. Pet	1L 27	New Malden. G Lon	7A 20	**Newton-le-Willows. N Yor**	5B 44	
Newborough. Staf	7K 33	Newmarket. Suff	5C 28	Newton Longville. Buck	8G 27	
New Boultham. Linc	8F 40	Newmarket. W Isl	5C 74	Newton Mearns. E Ren	4D 54	
Newbourne. Suff	7J 29	New Marske. Red C	1F 44	Newton Morrell. N Yor	3B 44	
New Brancepeth. Dur	7F 51	New Marton. Shrp	6A 32	Newton Mulgrave. N Yor	2G 45	
Newbridge. Cphy	4M 16	New Mill. Corn	6B 3	Newton-on-Ouse. N Yor	8E 44	
Newbridge. Cphy	4M 16	New Mill. Herts	2K 19	Newton-on-Rawcliffe.		
Newbridge. Corn	6B 3	New Mill. W Yor	6K 39	N Yor	4H 45	
Newbridge. Edin	2K 55	Newmill. Mor	4E 72	Newton on the Hill. Shrp	7C 32	
Newbridge. Hants	4C 10	Newmillerdam. W Yor	4M 39	Newton-on-the-Moor.		
Newbridge. IOW	7B 10	Newmill of Inshewan. Ang	4F 3	Nmbd	1G 51	
Newbridge. N Yor	6G 45	Newmills. Fife	1J 55	Newton on Trent. Linc	8E 40	
Newbridge. Pemb	2E 14	Newmill on Teifi. Dum	7E 22	Newton Poppleford. Devn	7M 7	
Newbridge. Wrex	5M 31	Newmilns. E Ayr	6D 54	Newton Purcell. Oxon	8E 26	
Newbridge Green. Worc	8G 25	New Mills. Corn	3F 3	Newton Regis. Warw	1A 26	
Newbridge-on-Usk. Mon	4B 16	New Mills. Derbs	1J 33	Newton Reigny. Cumb	8K 49	
Newbridge on Wye. Powy	6A 24	New Mills. Mon	3D 16	Newton St Cyres. Devn	6K 7	
New Brighton. Flin	3M 31	New Mills. Powy	2K 23	Newton St Faith. Norf	7J 37	
New Brighton. Hants	5G 11	Newmiln. Per	1D 60	Newton St Loe. Bath	7H 17	
New Brighton. Mers	6B 38	Newmilns. E Ayr	8H 29	Newton St Petrock. Devn	4F 6	
New Brinsley. Notts	4B 34	New Milton. Hants	6C 10	Newton Solney. Derbs	7K 33	
New Broughton. Wrex	4A 32	New Mistley. Essx	8H 29	Newton Stacey. Hants	1E 10	
New Buckenham. Norf	2G 29	New Moat. Pemb	1F 14	Newton Stewart. Dum	5B 48	
Newbuildings. Devn	5J 7	Newnham. Cambs	7M 27	Newton Toney. Wilts	1C 10	
Newburgh. Abers	1K 67	Newnham. Glos	2E 17	Newton Tony. Wilts	1C 10	
Newburgh. Fife	4H 61	Newnham. Hants	8H 19	Newton Tracey. Devn	3G 7	
Newburgh. Lanc	6D 38	Newnham. Herts	8K 27	Newton under Roseberry.		
Newburn. Tyne	5G 51	Newnham. Kent	8J 21	Red C	2E 44	
Newbury. W Ber	7E 18	Newnham. Nptn	6D 26	Newton Unthank. Leics	1C 26	
Newbury. Wilts	1H 9	Newnham Bridge. Worc	5G 25	Newton upon Ayr. S Ayr	7B 54	
Newby. Cumb	1G 43	New Ollerton. Notts	3C 34	Newton upon Derwent.		
Newby. N Yor	6G 43	New Oscott. W Mid	2K 25	E Yor	1D 40	
(nr. Ingleton)		Newpark. Fife	6H 61	Newton Valence. Hants	2H 11	
Newby. N Yor	6E 44	New Park. N Yor	8B 44	Newton-with-Scales. Lanc	2C 38	
(nr. Scarborough)		New Pitsligo. Abers	4J 73	Newtown. Abers	3H 33	
Newby. N Yor	2E 44	New Polzeath. Corn	8A 6	Newtown. Cambs	4A 28	
(nr. Stokesley)		Newport. Corn	7C 6	Newtown. Corn	8D 6	
Newby Bridge. Cumb	5E 42	Newport. Devn	2G 7	Newtown. Cumb	4G 9	
Newby Cote. N Yor	6G 43	Newport. E Yor	2E 40	(nr. Aspatria)		
Newby East. Cumb	6M 49	Newport. Essx	8B 28	Newtown. Cumb	5A 50	
Newby Head. Cumb	2G 43	Newport. Glos	4E 44	(nr. Brampton)		
Newby West. Cumb	6J 49	Newport. High	1F 77	Newtown. Derbs	1H 39	
Newby Wiske. N Yor	5C 44	Newport. IOW	7C 10	Newtown. Devn	3H 7	
Newcastle. B'end	5B 16	**Newport. Newp**	5B 16 & 100	Newtown. Dors	5D 8	
Newcastle. Mon	2D 16	Newport. Norf	8M 37	Newtown. Falk	1H 55	
Newcastle. Shrp	3B 24	Newport. Pemb	6D 22	Newtown. Glos	3E 44	
Newcastle Emlyn. Carm	7F 22	Newport. Som	3C 8	Newtown. Glos	5D 8	
Newcastle International Airport.		Newport. Telf	8F 32	Newtown. Derbs	7H 39	
Tyne	4G 51	Newport-on-Tay. Fife	5J 61	Newtown. Dors	5D 8	
Newcastleton. Bord	3M 49	**Newport Pagnell. Mil**	7G 27	(nr. Beaminster)		
Newcastle-under-Lyme.		Newpound Common.		New Town. Dors	4J 9	
Staf	5F 32	W Sus	3L 11	(nr. Sixpenny Handley)		
Newcastle Upon Tyne.		New Prestwick. S Ayr	1H 55	New Town. E Lot	2C 55	
Tyne	5H 51 & 97	New Quay. Cdgn	6F 22	Newtown. Falk	1H 55	
Newchapel. Pemb	5J 39	**Newquay. Corn**	3F 3	Newtown. Glos	6J 17	
Newchapel. Powy	3M 23	Newquay Cornwall Airport.		(nr. Lydney)		
Newchapel. Staf	4F 32	Corn	3F 3	Newtown. Glos	6F 22	
Newchapel. Surr	8L 19	New Rackheath. Norf	5C 4	(nr. Tewkesbury)		
Newchurch. Carm	2H 15	New Radnor. Powy	6C 24	Newtown. Hants	4D 10	
Newchurch. Here	6C 24	New Rent. Cumb	8M 49	(nr. Bishop's Waltham)		
Newchurch. IOW	7C 10	New Ridley. Nmbd	6E 50	Newtown. Hants	2J 11	
Newchurch. Kent	4G 13	New Romney. Kent	5G 13	(nr. Liphook)		
Newchurch. Lanc	2G 39	New Rossington. S Yor	6C 40	Newtown. Hants	3K 9	
Newchurch. Mon	4F 16	New Row. Cdgn	4K 23	(nr. Lyndhurst)		
Newchurch. Powy	7C 30	New Row. Lanc	2E 38	New Town. Hants	7J 17	
Newchurch. Staf	7K 33	New Sauchie. Clac	8B 60	(nr. Newbury)		
Newchurch in Pendle. Lanc	2G 39	Newsbank. Ches E	3F 32	Newtown. Here	7F 24	
Newcott. Devn	5A 8	Newseat. Abers	2D 66	(nr. Little Dewchurch)		
New Costessey. Norf	6H 37	Newsham. Lanc	2D 38	Newtown. IOM	6C 44	
New Cowper. Cumb	7J 49	Newsham. Nmbd	4J 51	Newtown. IOW	6B 10	
Newcraighall. Edin	2M 55	Newsham. N Yor	4L 43	Newtown. Lanc	6D 38	
New Crofton. W Yor	5A 40	(nr. Richmond)		Newtown. Nmbd	7H 57	
New Cross. Cdgn	5F 22	Newsham. N Yor	5C 44	(nr. Wooler)		
New Cross. Som	4D 8	(nr. Thirsk)		Newtown. Nmbd	1E 50	
New Cumnock. E Ayr	8E 54	New Sharlston. W Yor	5A 40	(nr. Rothbury)		
New Deer. Abers	5J 73	Newsholme. E Yor	5D 40	Newtown. Pemb	4G 15	
New Denham. Buck	5H 19	Newsholme. Lanc	1G 39	Newtown. **Powy**	3L 23	
New Duston. Nptn	5E 26	New Shoreston. Nmbd	6J 57	Newtown. Rhon	5K 16	
New Town. Lutn	1L 19	New Springs. G Man	6D 38			
		Newstead. Notts	4B 34			

Newtown—Pendoylan

Newtown. *Nmbd* 1F 50
(nr. Rothbury)
Newtown. *Nmbd* 7K 57
(nr. Wooler)
Newtown. *Pool* 6A 10
Newtown. *Powy* 2B 24
Newtown. *Rhon* 4C 16
Newtown. *Shet* 3E 79
Newtown. *Shrp* 6B 32
Newtown. *Som* 4B 8
Newtown. *Staf* 3G 33
(nr. Biddulph)
Newtown. *Staf* 1K 25
(nr. Cannock)
Newtown. *Staf* 3H 33
(nr. Longnor)
New Town. *W Yor* 3A 40
Newtown. *Wilts* 3J 9
Newtown-in-St Martin. *Corn* 7E 3
Newtown Linford. *Leics* 8B 34
Newtown St Boswells. *Bord* 6E 56
New Tredegar. *Cphy* 3D 16
Newtyle. *Ang* 1H 61
New Village. *E Yor* 2G 41
New Village. *S Yor* 5B 40
New Walsoken. *Cambs* 1A 28
New Waltham. *NE Lin* 5J 41
New Winton. *E Lot* 2D 56
New World. *Cambs* 2M 27
New Yatt. *Oxon* 2D 18
Newyears Green. *G Lon* 5L 19
New York. *Linc* 4J 35
New York. *Tyne* 4J 51
Nextend. *Here* 6D 24
Neyland. *Pemb* 3D 14
Nib Heath. *Shrp* 8B 32
Nicholashayne. *Devn* 4A 8
Nicholaston. *Swan* 5K 15
Nidd. *N Yor* 7C 44
Niddrie. *Edin* 2L 55
Niddry. *Edin* 2J 55
Nigg. *Aber* 3K 67
Nigg. *High* 4L 71
Nigg Ferry. *High* 5K 71
Nightcott. *Som* 3K 7
Nimmer. *Som* 4C 8
Nine Ashes. *Essx* 3D 20
Ninebanks. *Nmbd* 6C 50
Nine Elms. *Swin* 5B 18
Ninemile Bar. *Dum* 4F 48
Nine Mile Burn. *Midl* 4K 55
Ninfield. *E Sus* 6F 12
Ningwood. *IOW* 7E 10
Nisbet. *Bord* 7F 56
Nisbet Hill. *Bord* 4G 57
Niton. *IOW* 8F 10
Nitshill. *E Ren* 4D 54
Niwbwrch. *IOA* 3D 30
Noak Hill. *G Lon* 4D 20
Nobold. *Shrp* 8B 32
Nobottle. *Nptn* 5E 26
Nocton. *Linc* 3G 35
Nogdam End. *Norf* 1K 29
Noke. *Oxon* 2F 18
Nolton. *Pemb* 2C 14
Nolton Haven. *Pemb* 2C 14
No Man's Heath. *Ches W* 5C 32
No Man's Heath. *Warw* 1A 26
Nomansland. *Devn* 4K 7
Nomansland. *Wilts* 4C 10
Noneley. *Shrp* 7B 32
Noness. *Shet* 9E 79
Nonikiln. *High* 4J 71
Nonington. *Kent* 8L 21
Nook. *Cumb* 4M 49
(nr. Longtown)
Nook. *Cumb* 5G 43
(nr. Milnthorpe)
Noranside. *Ang* 7E 66
Norbreck. *Bkpl* 1B 38
Norbridge. *Here* 7H 25
Norbury. *Ches E* 5C 32
Norbury. *Derbs* 5J 33
Norbury. *Shrp* 2D 24
Norbury. *Staf* 7E 32
Norby. *N Yor* 5D 44
Norby. *Shet* 6B 79
Norcross. *Lanc* 1B 38
Nordelph. *Norf* 1B 28
Norden. *G Man* 4G 39
Nordley. *Shrp* 2G 25
Norfolk Broads. *Norf* 1L 29
Norham. *Nmbd* 5J 57
Norland Town. *W Yor* 3J 39
Norley. *Ches W* 8D 38
Norleywood. *Hants* 6D 10
Normanby. *N Lin* 4E 40
Normanby. *N Yor* 5G 45
Normanby. *Red C* 2E 44
Normanby-by-Spital. *Linc* 7G 41
Normanby le Wold. *Linc* 6H 41
Norman Cross. *Cambs* 2K 27
Normandy. *Surr* 8K 19
Norman's Bay. *E Sus* 7E 12
Norman's Green. *Devn* 5M 7
Normanton. *Derb* 6L 33
Normanton. *Leics* 5E 34
Normanton. *Linc* 5F 34
Normanton. *Notts* 4D 34
Normanton. *W Yor* 3M 39
Normanton le Heath. *Leics* 8L 33
Normanton on Soar. *Notts* 7B 34
Normanton-on-the-Wolds. *Notts* 6C 34
Normanton on Trent. *Notts* 3D 34
Normoss. *Lanc* 2B 38
Norrington Common. *Wilts* 7L 17
Norris Green. *Mers* 6B 38
Norris Hill. *Leics* 8L 33
Norristhorpe. *W Yor* 3L 39
Northacre. *Norf* 2F 28
Northall. *Buck* 1K 19
Northallerton. *N Yor* 4C 44
Northam. *Devn* 3F 6
Northam. *Sotn* 4E 10
Northampton. *Nptn* 5F 26 & 100
North Anston. *S Yor* 7B 40
North Ascot. *Brac* 7K 19
North Aston. *Oxon* 1E 18
Northaw. *Herts* 3A 20
Northay. *Som* 4B 8
North Baddesley. *Hants* 3D 10
North Balfern. *Dum* 6B 48
North Ballachulish. *High* 7C 64
North Barrow. *Som* 3F 8
North Barsham. *Norf* 4F 36
Northbeck. *Linc* 5G 35
North Benfleet. *Essx* 5F 20
North Bersted. *W Sus* 5K 11
North Berwick. *E Lot* 1E 56
North Bitchburn. *Dur* 8G 51
North Blyth. *Nmbd* 3J 51
North Boarhunt. *Hants* 4G 11
North Bockhampton. *Dors* 6B 10
Northborough. *Pet* 1K 27
Northbourne. *Kent* 8M 21
Northbourne. *Oxon* 5F 18
North Bovey. *Devn* 7J 7
North Bowood. *Dors* 6D 8
North Bradley. *Wilts* 8L 17
North Brentor. *Devn* 7F 6
North Brewham. *Som* 2G 9
Northbrook. *Oxon* 1E 18
North Brook End. *Cambs* 7L 27
North Broomhill. *Nmbd* 1H 51
North Buckland. *Devn* 1F 6
North Burlingham. *Norf* 6K 37
North Cadbury. *Som* 3F 8
North Carlton. *Linc* 8F 40
North Cave. *E Yor* 2E 40
North Cerney. *Glos* 3A 18
North Chailey. *E Sus* 5B 12
Northchapel. *W Sus* 3K 11
North Charford. *Hants* 4B 10
North Charlton. *Nmbd* 7L 57
North Cheriton. *Som* 3F 8
North Chideock. *Dors* 6D 8
Northchurch. *Herts* 3K 19
North Cliffe. *E Yor* 2E 40
North Clifton. *Notts* 8E 40
North Close. *Dur* 8H 51
North Cockerington. *Linc* 6K 41
North Coker. *Som* 4E 8
North Collafirth. *Shet* 3D 79
North Common. *E Sus* 5B 12
North Commonty. *Abers* 5J 73
North Coombe. *Devn* 4K 7
North Cornelly. *B'end* 5A 16
North Cotes. *Linc* 5K 41
Northcott. *Devn* 6E 6
(nr. Boyton)
Northcott. *Devn* 4M 7
(nr. Culmstock)
Northcourt. *Oxon* 4F 18
North Cove. *Suff* 3L 29
North Cowton. *N Yor* 3B 44
North Craigo. *Ang* 7G 67
North Crawley. *Mil* 7H 27
North Cray. *G Lon* 6C 20
North Creake. *Norf* 4E 36
North Curry. *Som* 3C 8
North Dalton. *E Yor* 8J 45
North Deighton. *N Yor* 8C 44
North Dronley. *Ang* 2J 61
North Duffield. *N Yor* 2C 40
Northdyke. *Orkn* 5A 78
Northedge. *Derbs* 3L 33
North Elkington. *Linc* 6J 41
North Elmham. *Norf* 5F 36
North Elmsall. *W Yor* 4A 40
Northend. *Buck* 4H 19
North End. *E Yor* 2J 41
North End. *Essx* 2E 20
(nr. Great Dunmow)
North End. *Essx* 8D 28
(nr. Great Yeldham)
North End. *Hants* 7E 18
North End. *Leics* 8B 34
North End. *Linc* 5J 35
North End. *Norf* 2F 28
North End. *N Som* 7G 17
North End. *Port* 5G 11
Northend. *Warw* 6B 26
North End. *W Sus* 5M 11
North End. *Wilts* 4A 18
North Erradale. *High* 3M 69
North Evington. *Leic* 1E 26
North Fambridge. *Essx* 4G 21
North Fearns. *High* 8K 69
North Featherstone. *W Yor* 3A 40
North Feorline. *N Ayr* 7H 53
North Ferriby. *E Yor* 3F 40
Northfield. *Aber* 3J 67
Northfield. *Hull* 3G 41
Northfield. *Som* 2B 8
Northfield. *W Mid* 4L 25
Northfleet. *Kent* 6E 20
North Frodingham. *E Yor* 8L 45
Northgate. *Linc* 7H 35
North Gluss. *Shet* 4D 79
North Gorley. *Hants* 4B 10
North Green. *Norf* 3J 29
North Green. *Suff* 5K 29
(nr. Framlingham)
North Green. *Suff* 4K 29
(nr. Halesworth)
North Green. *Suff* 5K 29
(nr. Saxmundham)
North Greetwell. *Linc* 8G 41
North Grimston. *N Yor* 7H 45
North Halling. *Medw* 7F 20
North Hayling. *Hants* 5H 11
North Hazelrigg. *Nmbd* 6K 57
North Heasley. *Devn* 2J 7
North Heath. *W Sus* 3L 11
North Hill. *Corn* 8D 6
North Hinksey Village. *Oxon* 3E 18
North Holmwood. *Surr* 1M 11
North Huish. *Devn* 4J 5
North Hykeham. *Linc* 3F 34
Northiam. *E Sus* 5G 13
Northill. *C Beds* 7K 27
Northington. *Hants* 2F 10
North Kelsey. *Linc* 5G 41
North Kelsey Moor. *Linc* 5G 41
North Kessock. *High* 7J 71
North Killingholme. *N Lin* 4H 41
North Kilvington. *N Yor* 5D 44
North Kilworth. *Leics* 3E 26
North Kyme. *Linc* 4H 35
North Lancing. *W Sus* 5M 11
Northlands. *Linc* 4K 35
Northleach. *Glos* 2B 18
North Lee. *Buck* 3J 19
North Lees. *N Yor* 6B 44
Northleigh. *Devn* 2H 7
(nr. Barnstaple)
Northleigh. *Devn* 6A 8
(nr. Honiton)
North Leigh. *Kent* 3K 13
North Leigh. *Oxon* 2D 18
North Leverton. *Notts* 7D 40
Northlew. *Devn* 6G 7
North Littleton. *Worc* 7L 25
North Lopham. *Norf* 3G 29
North Luffenham. *Rut* 1H 27
North Marden. *W Sus* 4J 11
North Marston. *Buck* 1H 19
North Middleton. *Midl* 4M 55
North Middleton. *Nmbd* 7K 57
North Molton. *Devn* 3J 7
North Moor. *N Yor* 5J 45
Northmoor. *Oxon* 3E 18
Northmoor Green. *Som* 2C 8
North Moreton. *Oxon* 5F 18
Northmuir. *Ang* 8D 66
North Mundham. *W Sus* 5J 11
North Murie. *Per* 3H 61
North Muskham. *Notts* 4D 34
North Ness. *Orkn* 8B 78
North Newbald. *E Yor* 2F 40
North Newington. *Oxon* 8C 26
North Newnton. *Wilts* 8B 18
North Newton. *Som* 2B 8
Northney. *Hants* 5H 11
North Nibley. *Glos* 4K 17
North Oakley. *Hants* 8F 18
North Ockendon. *G Lon* 5D 20
Northolt. *G Lon* 5M 19
Northop. *Flin* 3M 31
Northop Hall. *Flin* 3M 31
North Ormesby. *Midd* 2E 44
North Ormsby. *Linc* 6J 41
Northorpe. *Linc* 8G 35
(nr. Bourne)
Northorpe. *Linc* 6J 35
(nr. Donington)
Northorpe. *Linc* 6E 40
(nr. Gainsborough)
North Otterington. *N Yor* 5C 44
Northover. *Som* 2D 8
(nr. Glastonbury)
Northover. *Som* 3E 8
(nr. Yeovil)
North Owersby. *Linc* 6G 41
Northowram. *W Yor* 3K 39
North Perrott. *Som* 5D 8
North Petherton. *Som* 2B 8
North Petherwin. *Corn* 7D 6
North Pickenham. *Norf* 1E 28
North Piddle. *Worc* 6K 25
North Poorton. *Dors* 6E 8
North Port. *Arg* 3H 59
Northport. *Dors* 7J 9
North Queensferry. *Fife* 1K 55
North Radworthy. *Devn* 2J 7
North Rauceby. *Linc* 5G 35
Northrepps. *Norf* 4J 37
North Rigton. *N Yor* 1L 39
North Rode. *Ches E* 3F 32
North Roe. *Shet* 3D 79
North Ronaldsay Airport. *Orkn* 2F 78
North Row. *Cumb* 8K 49
North Runcton. *Norf* 6C 36
North Sannox. *N Ayr* 5J 53
North Scale. *Cumb* 6C 42
North Scarle. *Linc* 3E 34
North Seaton. *Nmbd* 3H 51
North Seaton Colliery. *Nmbd* 3H 51
North Sheen. *G Lon* 6M 19
North Shian. *Arg* 1G 59
North Shields. *Tyne* 5J 51
North Shoebury. *S'end* 5H 21
North Shore. *Bkpl* 2B 38
North Side. *Cumb* 1B 42
North Skelton. *Red C* 2F 44
North Somercotes. *Linc* 6L 41
North Stainley. *N Yor* 6B 44
North Stainmore. *Cumb* 2K 43
North Stifford. *Thur* 5E 20
North Stoke. *Bath* 7K 17
North Stoke. *Oxon* 5G 19
North Stoke. *W Sus* 4L 11
Northstowe. *Cambs* 5A 28
North Street. *Hants* 2G 11
North Street. *Kent* 8J 21
North Street. *Medw* 6G 21
North Street. *W Ber* 6G 19
North Sunderland. *Nmbd* 6M 57
North Tamerton. *Corn* 6E 6
North Tawton. *Devn* 5H 7
North Thoresby. *Linc* 6J 41
North Tidworth. *Wilts* 1C 10
North Town. *Devn* 5G 7
Northtown. *Orkn* 8C 78
North Town. *Shet* 10D 79
North Tuddenham. *Norf* 6G 37
North Walbottle. *Tyne* 5G 51
Northwall. *Orkn* 3F 78
North Walney. *Cumb* 7C 42
North Walsham. *Norf* 4J 37
North Waltham. *Hants* 1F 10
North Warnborough. *Hants* 8H 19
North Water Bridge. *Ang* 7G 67
North Watten. *High* 4H 77
Northway. *Glos* 8K 25
Northway. *Swan* 5K 15
North Weald Bassett. *Essx* 3D 20
North Weston. *N Som* 6G 17
North Weston. *Oxon* 3G 19
North Wheatley. *Notts* 7D 40
North Whilborough. *Devn* 3K 5
Northwich. *Ches W* 8E 38
North Wick. *Bath* 7H 17
Northwick. *Som* 1C 8
Northwick. *S Glo* 5H 17
North Widcombe. *Bath* 8H 17
North Willingham. *Linc* 7H 41
North Wingfield. *Derbs* 3A 34
North Witham. *Linc* 7F 34
Northwold. *Norf* 2D 28
Northwood. *Derbs* 3K 33
Northwood. *G Lon* 4L 19
Northwood. *IOW* 6E 10
Northwood. *Kent* 7M 21
Northwood. *Shrp* 6B 32
Northwood. *Stoke* 5F 32
Northwood Green. *Glos* 2K 17
North Wootton. *Dors* 4F 8
North Wootton. *Norf* 5C 36
North Wootton. *Som* 1E 8
North Wraxall. *Wilts* 6L 17
North Wroughton. *Swin* 5B 18
North Yardhope. *Nmbd* 1E 50
North York Moors. *N Yor* 4F 44
Norton. *Devn* 4K 5
Norton. *Glos* 1L 17
Norton. *Hal* 7D 38
Norton. *Herts* 8L 27
Norton. *IOW* 7D 10
Norton. *Mon* 1G 17
Norton. *Nptn* 5E 26
Norton. *Notts* 8B 40
Norton. *Powy* 5D 24
Norton. *Shrp* 3E 24
(nr. Ludlow)
Norton. *Shrp* 1H 25
(nr. Madeley)
Norton. *Shrp* 1F 24
(nr. Shrewsbury)
Norton. *S Yor* 4B 40
(nr. Askern)
Norton. *S Yor* 7M 39
(nr. Sheffield)
Norton. *Stoc T* 1D 44
Norton. *Suff* 5F 28
Norton. *Swan* 5L 15
Norton. *W Sus* 5K 11
(nr. Arundel)
Norton. *W Sus* 6J 11
(nr. Selsey)
Norton. *Wilts* 5L 17
Norton. *Worc* 7L 25
(nr. Evesham)
Norton. *Worc* 6J 25
(nr. Worcester)
Norton Bavant. *Wilts* 1J 9
Norton Bridge. *Staf* 6F 32
Norton Canes. *Staf* 1L 25
Norton Canon. *Here* 7D 24
Norton Corner. *Norf* 5G 37
Norton Disney. *Linc* 4E 34
Norton East. *Staf* 1L 25
Norton Ferris. *Wilts* 2G 9
Norton Fitzwarren. *Som* 3B 8
Norton Green. *IOW* 7D 10
Norton Green. *Stoke* 4G 33
Norton Hawkfield. *Bath* 7H 17
Norton Heath. *Essx* 3E 20
Norton in Hales. *Shrp* 6E 32
Norton in the Moors. *Stoke* 4F 32
Norton-Juxta-Twycross. *Leics* 1B 26
Norton-le-Clay. *N Yor* 6D 44
Norton Lindsey. *Warw* 5A 26
Norton Little Green. *Suff* 5F 28
Norton Malreward. *Bath* 7J 17
Norton Mandeville. *Essx* 3D 20
Norton-on-Derwent. *N Yor* 6G 45
Norton St Philip. *Som* 8K 17
Norton Subcourse. *Norf* 2L 29
Norton sub Hamdon. *Som* 4D 8
Norton Woodseats. *S Yor* 7M 39
Norwell. *Notts* 3D 34
Norwell Woodhouse. *Notts* 3D 34
Norwich. *Norf* 1J 29 & 100
Norwich International Airport. *Norf* 6J 37
Norwick. *Shet* 1G 79
Norwood. *Derbs* 7A 40
Norwood Green. *W Yor* 3K 39
Norwood Hill. *Surr* 3A 12
Norwood Park. *Som* 2E 8
Norwoodside. *Cambs* 2A 28
Noseley. *Leics* 2F 26
Noss. *Shet* 10D 79
Noss Mayo. *Devn* 5G 5
Nosterfield. *N Yor* 5B 44
Nostie. *High* 1A 64
Notgrove. *Glos* 1B 18
Nottage. *B'end* 6A 16
Nottingham. *Nott* 5B 34 & 100
Nottington. *Dors* 7F 8
Notton. *Dors* 6F 8
Notton. *W Yor* 4M 39
Notton. *Wilts* 7M 17
Nounsley. *Essx* 2F 20
Noutard's Green. *Worc* 5H 25
Nox. *Shrp* 8B 32
Noyadd Trefawr. *Cdgn* 7E 22
Nuffield. *Oxon* 5G 19
Nunburnholme. *E Yor* 1E 40
Nuncargate. *Notts* 4A 34
Nunclose. *Cumb* 7M 49
Nuneaton. *Warw* 2B 26
Nuneham Courtenay. *Oxon* 4F 18
Nun Monkton. *N Yor* 8E 44
Nunnerie. *S Lan* 8H 55
Nunney. *Som* 1G 9
Nunnington. *N Yor* 6F 44
Nunnykirk. *Nmbd* 2F 50
Nunsthorpe. *NE Lin* 5J 41
Nunthorpe. *Red C* 2E 44
Nunthorpe. *York* 1B 40
Nunton. *Wilts* 3B 10
Nunwick. *Nmbd* 4D 50
Nunwick. *N Yor* 6C 44
Nupend. *Glos* 3K 17
Nursling. *Hants* 4D 10
Nursted. *W Sus* 3H 11
Nursteed. *Wilts* 7A 18
Nurston. *V Glam* 7C 16
Nutbourne. *W Sus* 5H 11
(nr. Chichester)
Nutbourne. *W Sus* 4L 11
(nr. Pulborough)
Nutfield. *Surr* 8B 20
Nuthall. *Notts* 5B 34
Nuthampstead. *Herts* 8A 28
Nuthurst. *Warw* 4M 25
Nuthurst. *W Sus* 3M 11
Nutley. *E Sus* 5C 12
Nuttall. *G Man* 4F 38
Nutwell. *S Yor* 5C 40
Nybster. *High* 3J 77
Nyetimber. *W Sus* 6J 11
Nyewood. *W Sus* 3J 11
Nymet Rowland. *Devn* 5J 7
Nymet Tracey. *Devn* 5J 7
Nympsfield. *Glos* 3L 17
Nynehead. *Som* 3A 8
Nyton. *W Sus* 5K 11

O

Oadby. *Leics* 1E 26
Oad Street. *Kent* 7G 21
Oakamoor. *Staf* 5H 33
Oakbank. *Arg* 2E 58
Oakbank. *W Lot* 3J 55
Oakdale. *Cphy* 4D 16
Oakdale. *Pool* 6A 10
Oake. *Som* 3A 8
Oaken. *Staf* 1J 25
Oakenclough. *Lanc* 1D 38
Oakengates. *Telf* 8E 32
Oakenholt. *Flin* 8A 38
Oakenshaw. *Dur* 8H 51
Oakenshaw. *W Yor* 3K 39
Oakerthorpe. *Derbs* 4L 33
Oakford. *Cdgn* 6G 23
Oakford. *Devn* 3L 7
Oakfordbridge. *Devn* 3L 7
Oakgrove. *Ches E* 3G 33
Oakham. *Rut* 1G 27
Oakhanger. *Ches E* 4E 32
Oakhanger. *Hants* 2H 11
Oakhill. *Som* 1F 8
Oakington. *Cambs* 5A 28
Oaklands. *Powy* 6A 24
Oakle Street. *Glos* 2K 17
Oakley. *Bed* 6J 27
Oakley. *Buck* 2G 19
Oakley. *Fife* 1J 55
Oakley. *Hants* 8F 18
Oakley. *Suff* 4H 29
Oakley Green. *Wind* 6K 19
Oakley Park. *Powy* 3M 23
Oakmere. *Ches W* 3C 32
Oakridge. *Glos* 3M 17
Oaks. *Shrp* 1E 24
Oaksey. *Wilts* 4M 17
Oaks Green. *Derbs* 6J 33
Oakshaw Ford. *Cumb* 4A 50
Oakshott. *Hants* 3H 11
Oakthorpe. *Leics* 8L 33
Oak Tree. *Darl* 2C 44
Oakwood. *Derb* 6L 33
Oakwood. *W Yor* 2M 39
Oakwoodhill. *Surr* 2M 11
Oakworth. *W Yor* 2J 39
Oape. *High* 1G 71
Oare. *Kent* 7J 21
Oare. *Som* 1K 7
Oare. *W Ber* 6F 18
Oare. *Wilts* 7B 18
Oareford. *Som* 1K 7
Oasby. *Linc* 6G 35
Oath. *Som* 3C 8
Oathlaw. *Ang* 8E 66
Oatlands. *N Yor* 8C 44
Oban. *Arg* 3F 58 & 101
Oban. *W Isl* 1F 68
Oborne. *Dors* 4F 8
Obsdale. *High* 5J 71
Obthorpe. *Linc* 8G 35
Occlestone Green. *Ches W* 3D 32
Occold. *Suff* 4H 29
Ochiltree. *E Ayr* 7D 54
Ochtermuthill. *Per* 4D 60
Ochtertyre. *Per* 3D 60
Ockbrook. *Derbs* 6A 34
Ockeridge. *Worc* 5H 25
Ockham. *Surr* 8L 19
Ockle. *High* 6K 63
Ockley. *Surr* 1M 11
Ocle Pychard. *Here* 7F 24
Octofad. *Arg* 4A 52
Octomore. *Arg* 4A 52
Octon. *E Yor* 7K 45
Odcombe. *Som* 4E 8
Odd Down. *Bath* 7K 17
Oddingley. *Worc* 6K 25
Oddington. *Oxon* 2F 18
Oddsta. *Shet* 2F 79
Odell. *Bed* 6H 27
Odie. *Orkn* 5E 78
Odiham. *Hants* 8H 19
Odsey. *Cambs* 8L 27
Odstock. *Wilts* 3B 10
Odstone. *Leics* 1B 26
Offchurch. *Warw* 5B 26
Offenham. *Worc* 7L 25
Offenham Cross. *Worc* 7L 25
Offerton. *G Man* 7H 39
Offerton. *Tyne* 6J 51
Offham. *E Sus* 6C 12
Offham. *Kent* 8E 20
Offham. *W Sus* 5L 11
Offleyhay. *Staf* 7F 32
Offley Hoo. *Herts* 1M 19
Offleymarsh. *Staf* 7E 32
Offord Cluny. *Cambs* 5L 27
Offord D'Arcy. *Cambs* 5L 27
Offton. *Suff* 7G 29
Offwell. *Devn* 6A 8
Ogbourne Maizey. *Wilts* 6B 18
Ogbourne St Andrew. *Wilts* 6B 18
Ogbourne St George. *Wilts* 6C 18
Ogden. *G Man* 4H 39
Ogle. *Nmbd* 4G 51
Ogmore. *V Glam* 6A 16
Ogmore-by-Sea. *V Glam* 6A 16
Ogmore Vale. *B'end* 4B 16
Okeford Fitzpaine. *Dors* 4H 9
Okehampton. *Devn* 6G 7
Okehampton Camp. *Devn* 6G 7
Okraquoy. *Shet* 8E 79
Okus. *Swin* 5B 18
Old. *Nptn* 4F 26
Old Aberdeen. *Aber* 3K 67
Old Alresford. *Hants* 2F 10
Oldany. *High* 6J 75
Old Arley. *Warw* 2A 26
Old Basford. *Nott* 5B 34
Old Basing. *Hants* 8G 19
Oldberrow. *Warw* 5M 25
Old Bewick. *Nmbd* 7K 57
Old Bexley. *G Lon* 6C 20
Old Blair. *Per* 7L 65
Old Bolingbroke. *Linc* 3K 35
Oldborough. *Devn* 5J 7
Old Brampton. *Derbs* 8M 39
Old Bridge of Tilt. *Per* 7L 65
Old Bridge of Urr. *Dum* 5E 48
Old Buckenham. *Norf* 2G 29
Old Burghclere. *Hants* 8E 18
Oldbury. *Shrp* 2H 25
Oldbury. *Warw* 2B 26
Oldbury. *W Mid* 3K 25
Oldbury-on-Severn. *S Glo* 4J 17
Oldbury on the Hill. *Glos* 5L 17
Old Byland. *N Yor* 5E 44
Old Cassop. *Dur* 8J 51
Oldcastle. *Mon* 1F 16
Oldcastle Heath. *Ches W* 5B 32
Old Catton. *Norf* 6J 37
Old Clee. *NE Lin* 5J 41
Old Cleeve. *Som* 1M 7
Old Colwyn. *Cnwy* 2H 31
Oldcotes. *Notts* 7B 40
Old Coulsdon. *G Lon* 8B 20
Old Dailly. *S Ayr* 2M 47
Old Dalby. *Leics* 7C 34
Old Dam. *Derbs* 8K 39
Old Deer. *Abers* 5K 73
Old Dilton. *Wilts* 1H 9
Old Down. *S Glo* 5J 17
Oldeamere. *Cambs* 2M 27
Old Edlington. *S Yor* 6B 40
Old Eldon. *Dur* 1B 44
Old Ellerby. *E Yor* 2H 41
Old Fallings. *W Mid* 1K 25
Oldfallow. *Staf* 8G 33
Old Felixstowe. *Suff* 8K 29
Oldfield. *Shrp* 3G 25
Oldfield. *Worc* 5J 25
Old Fletton. *Pet* 2K 27
Oldford. *Som* 8K 17
Old Forge. *Here* 2H 17
Old Glossop. *Derbs* 6J 39
Old Goole. *E Yor* 3D 40
Old Gore. *Here* 1J 17
Old Graitney. *Dum* 5L 49
Old Grimsby. *IOS* 2B 3
Oldhall. *High* 4H 77
Old Hall Street. *Norf* 4K 37
Oldham. *G Man* 5H 39
Oldhamstocks. *E Lot* 2G 57
Old Heathfield. *E Sus* 5D 12
Old Hill. *W Mid* 3K 25
Old Hunstanton. *Norf* 3C 36
Oldhurst. *Cambs* 4L 27
Old Hutton. *Cumb* 5G 43
Old Kea. *Corn* 5F 3
Old Kilpatrick. *W Dun* 2C 54
Old Kinnernie. *Abers* 3H 67
Old Knebworth. *Herts* 1A 20
Oldland. *S Glo* 6J 17
Old Laxey. *IOM* 5E 46
Old Leake. *Linc* 4L 35
Old Lenton. *Nott* 6B 34
Old Llanberis. *Gwyn* 4F 30
Old Malton. *N Yor* 6G 45
Oldmeldrum. *Abers* 1J 67
Old Micklefield. *W Yor* 2A 40
Old Mill. *Corn* 8E 6
Oldmixon. *N Som* 8F 16
Old Monkland. *N Lan* 3F 54
Old Newton. *Suff* 5G 29
Old Park. *Telf* 1G 25
Old Pentland. *Midl* 3L 55
Old Philpstoun. *W Lot* 2J 55
Old Quarrington. *Dur* 8J 51
Old Radnor. *Powy* 6C 24
Old Rayne. *Abers* 1G 67
Oldridge. *Devn* 6K 7
Old Romney. *Kent* 5J 13
Old Scone. *Per* 3G 61
Oldshore Beg. *High* 4J 75
Oldshoremore. *High* 4K 75
Old Snydale. *W Yor* 3A 40
Old Sodbury. *S Glo* 5K 17
Old Somerby. *Linc* 6F 34
Old Spital. *Dur* 2L 43
Oldstead. *N Yor* 5E 44
Old Stratford. *Nptn* 7F 26
Old Swan. *Mers* 6B 38
Old Swarland. *Nmbd* 1G 51
Old Tebay. *Cumb* 3H 43
Old Town. *Cumb* 7M 49
Old Town. *E Sus* 8D 12
Oldtown. *High* 3H 71
Old Town. *IOS* 2C 3
Old Town. *Nmbd* 2D 50
Old Trafford. *G Man* 6G 39
Old Tupton. *Derbs* 3L 33
Oldwall. *Cumb* 5M 49
Oldwalls. *Swan* 4J 15
Old Warden. *C Beds* 7K 27
Oldways End. *Som* 3K 7
Old Westhall. *Abers* 1G 67
Old Weston. *Cambs* 4J 27
Oldwhat. *Abers* 4J 73
Old Windsor. *Wind* 6K 19
Old Wives Lees. *Kent* 8J 21
Old Woking. *Surr* 8L 19
Oldwood Common. *Worc* 5F 24
Old Woodstock. *Oxon* 2E 18
Olgrinmore. *High* 4F 76
Oliver's Battery. *Hants* 3E 10
Ollaberry. *Shet* 3D 79
Ollerton. *Ches E* 8F 38
Ollerton. *Notts* 3C 34
Ollerton. *Shrp* 7D 32
Olmarch. *Cdgn* 6J 23
Olmstead Green. *Cambs* 7C 28
Olney. *Mil* 6G 27
Olrig. *High* 3G 77
Olton. *W Mid* 3M 25
Olveston. *S Glo* 5J 17
Ombersley. *Worc* 5J 25
Ompton. *Notts* 3C 34
Omunsgarth. *Shet* 7D 79
Onchan. *IOM* 6E 46
Onecote. *Staf* 4H 33
Onehouse. *Suff* 6G 29
Onen. *Mon* 2G 17
Ongar Hill. *Norf* 7M 35
Ongar Street. *Here* 5D 24
Onibury. *Shrp* 4E 24
Onich. *High* 7C 64
Onllwyn. *Neat* 2A 16
Onneley. *Shrp* 5E 32
Onslow Green. *Essx* 2E 20
Onslow Village. *Surr* 1K 11
Onthank. *E Ayr* 6C 54
Openwoodgate. *Derbs* 5L 33
Opinan. *High* 4M 69
(nr. Gairloch)
Opinan. *High* 2A 70
(nr. Laide)
Orasaigh. *W Isl* 7D 74
Orbost. *High* 7G 69
Orby. *Linc* 3L 35
Orchard Hill. *Devn* 3F 6
Orchard Portman. *Som* 3B 8
Orcheston. *Wilts* 1A 10
Orcop. *Here* 1G 17
Orcop Hill. *Here* 1G 17
Ord. *High* 2L 63
Ordale. *Shet* 1G 79
Ordhead. *Abers* 2G 67
Ordie. *Abers* 3E 66
Ordiquish. *Mor* 4D 72
Ordley. *Nmbd* 6E 50
Ordsall. *Notts* 8D 40
Ore. *E Sus* 6G 13
Oreham Common. *W Sus* 6A 12
Oreton. *Shrp* 3G 25
Orford. *Suff* 7L 29
Orford. *Warr* 6E 38
Organford. *Dors* 6J 9
Orgil. *Orkn* 7A 78
Orgreave. *Staf* 8J 33
Oridge Street. *Glos* 1K 17
Orlestone. *Kent* 4H 13
Orleton. *Here* 5E 24
Orleton. *Worc* 5G 25
Orleton Common. *Here* 5E 24
Orlingbury. *Nptn* 4G 27
Ormacleit. *W Isl* 8B 68
Ormathwaite. *Cumb* 1D 42
Ormesby. *Midd* 2E 44
Ormesby St Margaret. *Norf* 6L 37
Ormesby St Michael. *Norf* 6L 37
Ormiscaig. *High* 2A 70
Ormiston. *E Lot* 3D 56
Ormsaigbeg. *High* 7J 63
Ormsaigmore. *High* 7J 63
Ormsary. *Arg* 2F 52
Ormsgill. *Cumb* 6C 42
Ormskirk. *Lanc* 5C 38
Orphir. *Orkn* 7B 78
Orpington. *G Lon* 7C 20
Orrell. *Lanc* 5D 38
Orrell. *Mers* 6B 38
Orrisdale. *IOM* 4D 46
Orsett. *Thur* 5E 20
Orslow. *Staf* 8F 32
Orston. *Notts* 5D 34
Orthwaite. *Cumb* 8K 49
Orton. *Cumb* 3H 43
Orton. *Mor* 4D 72
Orton. *Nptn* 4G 27
Orton. *Staf* 2J 25
Orton Longueville. *Pet* 2K 27
Orton-on-the-Hill. *Leics* 1B 26
Orton Waterville. *Pet* 2K 27
Orton Wistow. *Pet* 2K 27
Orwell. *Cambs* 6M 27
Osbaldeston. *Lanc* 2E 38
Osbaldwick. *York* 8F 44
Osbaston. *Leics* 1C 26
Osbaston. *Shrp* 7A 32
Osbournby. *Linc* 6G 35
Osclay. *High* 6H 77
Oscroft. *Ches W* 3C 32
Ose. *High* 7H 69
Osgathorpe. *Leics* 8A 34
Osgodby. *Linc* 6G 41
Osgodby. *N Yor* 5K 45
(nr. Scarborough)
Osgodby. *N Yor* 2C 40
(nr. Selby)
Oskaig. *High* 8K 69
Oskamull. *Arg* 1B 58
Osleston. *Derbs* 6K 33
Osmaston. *Derb* 6L 33
Osmaston. *Derbs* 5K 33
Osmington. *Dors* 7G 9
Osmington Mills. *Dors* 7G 9
Osmondthorpe. *W Yor* 2M 39
Osmondwall. *Orkn* 9B 78
Osmotherley. *N Yor* 4D 44
Osnaburgh. *Fife* 4K 61
Ospisdale. *High* 3K 71
Ospringe. *Kent* 7J 21
Ossett. *W Yor* 3L 39
Ossington. *Notts* 3D 34
Ostend. *Essx* 4H 21
Ostend. *Norf* 4K 37
Osterley. *G Lon* 6M 19
Oswaldkirk. *N Yor* 6F 44
Oswaldtwistle. *Lanc* 3F 38
Oswestry. *Shrp* 7M 31
Otby. *Linc* 6H 41
Otford. *Kent* 8D 20
Otham. *Kent* 8F 20
Otherton. *Staf* 8G 33
Othery. *Som* 2C 8
Otley. *Suff* 6J 29
Otley. *W Yor* 1L 39
Otterbourne. *Hants* 3E 10
Otterburn. *Nmbd* 2D 50
Otterburn. *N Yor* 8K 43
Otterburn Camp. *Nmbd* 2D 50
Otterburn Hall. *Nmbd* 2D 50
Otter Ferry. *Arg* 1H 53
Otterford. *Som* 4B 8
Otterham. *Corn* 6C 6
Otterhampton. *Som* 1B 8
Otterham Quay. *Kent* 7G 21
Ottershaw. *Surr* 7L 19
Otterspool. *Mers* 7B 38
Otterswick. *Shet* 3F 79
Otterton. *Devn* 7M 7
Otterwood. *Hants* 5E 10
Ottery St Mary. *Devn* 6A 8
Ottinge. *Kent* 3K 13
Ottringham. *E Yor* 3J 41
Oughterby. *Cumb* 6K 49
Oughtershaw. *N Yor* 5K 43
Oughterside. *Cumb* 7J 49
Oughtibridge. *S Yor* 6M 39
Oughtrington. *Warr* 7E 38
Oulston. *N Yor* 6E 44
Oulton. *Cumb* 6K 49
Oulton. *Norf* 5H 37
Oulton. *Staf* 7E 32
(nr. Gnosall Heath)
Oulton. *Staf* 6G 33
(nr. Stone)
Oulton. *Suff* 2M 29
Oulton. *W Yor* 3M 39
Oulton Broad. *Suff* 2M 29
Oulton Street. *Norf* 5H 37
Oundle. *Nptn* 3J 27
Ousby. *Cumb* 8B 50
Ousdale. *High* 7F 76
Ousden. *Suff* 6D 28
Ousefleet. *E Yor* 3E 40
Ouston. *Dur* 6H 51
Ouston. *Nmbd* 6C 50
(nr. Bearsbridge)
Ouston. *Nmbd* 4F 50
(nr. Stamfordham)
Outer Hope. *Devn* 5H 5
Outertown. *Orkn* 6A 78
Outgate. *Cumb* 4E 42
Outhgill. *Cumb* 3J 43
Outlands. *Staf* 6E 32
Outlane. *W Yor* 4J 39
Out Newton. *E Yor* 3K 41
Out Rawcliffe. *Lanc* 1C 38
Outwell. *Norf* 1B 28
Outwick. *Hants* 4B 10
Outwood. *Surr* 3B 12
Outwood. *W Yor* 3M 39
Outwood. *Worc* 4K 25
Outwoods. *Leics* 8A 34
Outwoods. *Staf* 8E 32
Ouzlewell Green. *W Yor* 3M 39
Ovenden. *W Yor* 3J 39
Over. *Cambs* 4M 27
Over. *Ches W* 3D 32
Over. *Glos* 2L 17
Over. *S Glo* 5H 17
Overbister. *Orkn* 3E 78
Over Burrows. *Derbs* 6K 33
Overbury. *Worc* 8K 25
Overcombe. *Dors* 7F 8
Over Compton. *Dors* 4E 8
Over End. *Cambs* 2J 27
Over Finlarg. *Ang* 1K 61
Overgreen. *Derbs* 8M 39
Over Green. *W Mid* 2M 25
Over Haddon. *Derbs* 3K 33
Over Hulton. *G Man* 5E 38
Over Kellet. *Lanc* 6G 43
Over Kiddington. *Oxon* 1E 18
Overleigh. *Som* 2D 8
Overley. *Staf* 8J 33
Over Monnow. *Mon* 2H 17
Over Norton. *Oxon* 1D 18
Over Peover. *Ches E* 8F 38
Overpool. *Ches W* 8B 38
Overscaig. *High* 7M 75
Overseal. *Derbs* 8K 33
Over Silton. *N Yor* 4D 44
Oversland. *Kent* 8J 21
Overstone. *Nptn* 5G 27
Over Stowey. *Som* 2A 8
Overstrand. *Norf* 3J 37
Over Stratton. *Som* 4D 8
Over Street. *Wilts* 2A 10
Overthorpe. *Nptn* 7C 26
Overton. *Aber* 2J 67
Overton. *Ches W* 8D 38
Overton. *Hants* 1F 10
Overton. *High* 6H 77
Overton. *Lanc* 8F 42
Overton. *N Yor* 8E 44
Overton. *Shrp* 3G 25
(nr. Bridgnorth)
Overton. *Shrp* 4F 24
(nr. Ludlow)
Overton. *Swan* 5J 15
Overton. *W Yor* 4L 39
Overton. *Wrex* 5A 32
Overtown. *Lanc* 6H 43
Overtown. *N Lan* 4G 55
Overtown. *Swin* 6B 18
Over Wallop. *Hants* 2C 10
Over Whitacre. *Warw* 2A 26
Over Worton. *Oxon* 1E 18
Oving. *Buck* 1H 19
Oving. *W Sus* 5K 11
Ovingdean. *Brig* 7B 12
Ovingham. *Nmbd* 5F 50
Ovington. *Dur* 2A 44
Ovington. *Essx* 7D 28
Ovington. *Hants* 2F 10
Ovington. *Norf* 1F 28
Ovington. *Nmbd* 5F 50
Owen's Bank. *Staf* 7K 33
Ower. *Hants* 5E 10
(nr. Holbury)
Ower. *Hants* 4D 10
(nr. Totton)
Owermoigne. *Dors* 7G 9
Owlbury. *Shrp* 2D 24
Owler Bar. *Derbs* 8L 39
Owlerton. *S Yor* 7M 39
Owlsmoor. *Brac* 7J 19
Owlswick. *Buck* 3H 19
Owmby. *Linc* 5G 41
Owmby-by-Spital. *Linc* 7G 41
Ownham. *W Ber* 6E 18
Owrytn. *Wrex* 5A 32
Owslebury. *Hants* 3F 10
Owston. *Leics* 1F 26
Owston. *S Yor* 4B 40
Owston Ferry. *N Lin* 5E 40
Owstwick. *E Yor* 2J 41
Owthorne. *E Yor* 3K 41
Owthorpe. *Notts* 6C 34
Owton Manor. *Hart* 1D 44
Oxborough. *Norf* 1D 28
Oxbridge. *Dors* 6D 8
Oxcombe. *Linc* 8K 41
Oxen End. *Essx* 1E 20
Oxenhall. *Glos* 1K 17
Oxenholme. *Cumb* 4G 43
Oxenhope. *W Yor* 2J 39
Oxen Park. *Cumb* 5E 42
Oxenpill. *Som* 1D 8
Oxenton. *Glos* 8K 25
Oxenwood. *Wilts* 8D 18
Oxford. *Oxon* 3F 18 & 100
Oxgangs. *Edin* 3L 55
Oxhey. *Herts* 4M 19
Oxhill. *Warw* 7B 26
Oxley. *W Mid* 1J 25
Oxley Green. *Essx* 2H 21
Oxley's Green. *E Sus* 5E 12
Oxlode. *Cambs* 3A 28
Oxnam. *Bord* 8G 57
Oxshott. *Surr* 7M 19
Oxspring. *S Yor* 5L 39
Oxted. *Surr* 8B 20
Oxton. *Mers* 7A 38
Oxton. *N Yor* 1B 40
Oxton. *Notts* 4C 34
Oxton. *Bord* 4D 56
Oxwich. *Swan* 5J 15
Oxwich Green. *Swan* 5J 15
Oxwick. *Norf* 5F 36
Oykel Bridge. *High* 1F 70
Oyne. *Abers* 1G 67
Oystermouth. *Swan* 5L 15
Ozleworth. *Glos* 4K 17

P

Pabail Iarach. *W Isl* 5F 74
Pabail Uarach. *W Isl* 5F 74
Pachesham. *Surr* 8M 19
Packers Hill. *Dors* 4G 9
Packington. *Leics* 8L 33
Packmoor. *Stoke* 4F 32
Packmores. *Warw* 5A 26
Packwood. *W Mid* 4M 25
Packwood Gullett. *W Mid* 4M 25
Padanaram. *Ang* 8E 66
Padbury. *Buck* 8F 26
Paddington. *G Lon* 5A 20
Paddington. *Warr* 7E 38
Paddlesworth. *Kent* 4K 13
Paddock. *Kent* 8H 21
Paddockhole. *Dum* 3K 49
Paddock Wood. *Kent* 3E 12
Paddolgreen. *Shrp* 6C 32
Padeswood. *Flin* 3M 31
Padiham. *Lanc* 2F 38
Padside. *N Yor* 8A 44
Padson. *Devn* 6G 7
Padstow. *Corn* 8A 6
Padworth. *W Ber* 7G 19
Page Bank. *Dur* 8H 51
Pagham. *W Sus* 6J 11
Paglesham Churchend. *Essx* 4H 21
Paglesham Eastend. *Essx* 4H 21
Paibeil. *W Isl* 5B 68
(on North Uist)
Paibeil. *W Isl* 2E 68
(on Taransay)
Paiblesgearraidh. *W Isl* 5B 68
Paignton. *Torb* 3K 5
Pailton. *Warw* 3C 26
Paine's Corner. *E Sus* 5E 12
Painleyhill. *Staf* 6H 33
Painscastle. *Powy* 7B 24
Painshawfield. *Nmbd* 5F 50
Painsthorpe. *E Yor* 8H 45
Painswick. *Glos* 3L 17
Painter's Forstal. *Kent* 8H 21
Painthorpe. *W Yor* 4M 39
Pairc Shiaboist. *W Isl* 4C 74
Paisley. *Ren* 3C 54
Pakefield. *Suff* 2M 29
Pakenham. *Suff* 5F 28
Pale. *Gwyn* 6J 31
Palehouse Common. *E Sus* 6C 12
Palestine. *Hants* 1C 10
Paley Street. *Wind* 6J 19
Palgowan. *Dum* 3A 48
Palgrave. *Suff* 4H 29
Pallington. *Dors* 6G 9
Palmarsh. *Kent* 4K 13
Palmer Moor. *Derbs* 6J 33
Palmers Cross. *W Mid* 1J 25
Palmerstown. *V Glam* 7D 16
Palnackie. *Dum* 6F 48
Palnure. *Dum* 5B 48
Palterton. *Derbs* 3A 34
Pamber End. *Hants* 8G 19
Pamber Green. *Hants* 8G 19
Pamber Heath. *Hants* 7G 19
Pamington. *Glos* 8K 25
Pamphill. *Dors* 5J 9
Pampisford. *Cambs* 7A 28
Panborough. *Som* 1D 8
Panbride. *Ang* 2L 61
Pancakehill. *Glos* 2A 18
Pancrasweek. *Devn* 5D 6
Pandy. *Gwyn* 7H 31
(nr. Bala)
Pandy. *Gwyn* 1J 23
(nr. Tywyn)
Pandy. *Mon* 1F 16
Pandy. *Powy* 1M 23
Pandy. *Wrex* 6L 31
Pandy Tudur. *Cnwy* 3H 31
Panfield. *Essx* 1F 20
Pangbourne. *W Ber* 6G 19
Pannal. *N Yor* 8C 44
Pannal Ash. *N Yor* 8B 44
Pannanich. *Abers* 4D 66
Pant. *Shrp* 7M 31
Pant. *Wrex* 5A 32
Pantasaph. *Flin* 2L 31
Pant Glas. *Gwyn* 5D 30
Pant-glas. *Shrp* 6M 31
Pantgwyn. *Carm* 1K 15
Pantgwyn. *Cdgn* 7E 22
Pant-lasau. *Swan* 4L 15
Panton. *Linc* 8H 41
Pant-pastynog. *Den* 3K 31
Pantperthog. *Gwyn* 1K 23
Pant-teg. *Carm* 1J 15
Pant-y-Caws. *Carm* 1F 14
Pant-y-dwr. *Powy* 4M 23
Pant-y-ffridd. *Powy* 1B 24
Pantyffynnon. *Carm* 2L 15
Pantygasseg. *Torf* 3E 16
Pant-y-llyn. *Carm* 2L 15
Pant-yr-awel. *B'end* 5B 16
Pant y Wacco. *Flin* 2L 31
Panxworth. *Norf* 6K 37
Papa Stour Airport. *Shet* 6B 79
Papa Westray Airport. *Orkn* 2C 78
Papcastle. *Cumb* 8J 49
Papigoe. *High* 4J 77
Papil. *Shet* 8D 79
Papple. *E Lot* 2E 56
Papplewick. *Notts* 4B 34
Papworth Everard. *Cambs* 5L 27
Papworth St Agnes. *Cambs* 5L 27
Par. *Corn* 4B 4
Paramour Street. *Kent* 7L 21
Parbold. *Lanc* 4C 38
Parbrook. *Som* 2E 8
Parbrook. *W Sus* 3L 11
Parc. *Gwyn* 6H 31
Parcllyn. *Cdgn* 6E 22
Parc-Seymour. *Newp* 4G 17
Pardown. *Hants* 1F 10
Pardshaw. *Cumb* 1B 42
Parham. *Suff* 5K 29
Park. *Abers* 4H 67
Park. *Arg* 1G 59
Park. *Dum* 2G 49
Park Bottom. *Corn* 5D 3
Parkburn. *Abers* 6H 73
Park Corner. *E Sus* 4D 12
Park Corner. *Oxon* 5G 19
Parkend. *Glos* 3J 17
Park End. *Nmbd* 4D 50
Parkeston. *Essx* 8J 29
Parkfield. *Corn* 3E 4
Parkgate. *Ches W* 8A 38
Parkgate. *Cumb* 7K 49
Parkgate. *Dum* 3H 49
Park Gate. *Hants* 5F 10
Parkgate. *Surr* 3A 12
Park Gate. *Worc* 4K 25
Parkhall. *W Dun* 2C 54
Parkham. *Devn* 3E 6
Parkham Ash. *Devn* 3E 6
Parkhead. *Cumb* 7L 49
Parkhead. *Glas* 3E 54
Park Hill. *Mers* 5C 38
Parkhouse. *Mon* 3G 17
Parkhurst. *IOW* 6E 10
Park Lane. *G Man* 5F 38
Park Lane. *Staf* 1J 25
Parkmill. *Swan* 5K 15
Park Mill. *W Yor* 4L 39
Parkneuk. *Abers* 6H 67
Parkside. *N Lan* 4G 55
Parkstone. *Pool* 6A 10
Park Street. *Herts* 3M 19
Park Street. *W Sus* 2M 11
Park Town. *Oxon* 3F 18
Park Village. *Nmbd* 5B 50
Parkway. *Here* 8H 25
Parley Cross. *Dors* 6A 10
Parmoor. *Buck* 5H 19
Parr. *Mers* 6D 38
Parracombe. *Devn* 1H 7
Parrog. *Pemb* 8C 22
Parsonage Green. *Essx* 2F 20
Parsonby. *Cumb* 8J 49
Parson Cross. *S Yor* 6M 39
Parson Drove. *Cambs* 1M 27
Partick. *Glas* 3D 54
Partington. *G Man* 6F 38
Partney. *Linc* 3L 35
Parton. *Cumb* 1A 42
(nr. Whitehaven)
Parton. *Cumb* 6K 49
(nr. Wigton)
Parton. *Dum* 4D 48
Partridge Green. *W Sus* 4M 11
Parwich. *Derbs* 4J 33
Passenham. *Nptn* 8F 26
Passfield. *Hants* 2J 11
Passingford Bridge. *Essx* 4D 20
Paston. *Norf* 4K 37
Pasturefields. *Staf* 7G 33
Patchacott. *Devn* 6F 6
Patcham. *Brig* 7B 12
Patchetts Green. *Herts* 4M 19
Patching. *W Sus* 5L 11
Patchole. *Devn* 1H 7
Patchway. *S Glo* 5J 17
Pateley Bridge. *N Yor* 7A 44
Pathe. *Som* 2C 8
Pathfinder Village. *Devn* 6K 7
Pathhead. *Abers* 7H 67
Pathhead. *E Ayr* 8E 54
Pathhead. *Fife* 6H 61
Pathhead. *Midl* 3M 55
Pathlow. *Warw* 6M 25
Path of Condie. *Per* 4F 60
Pathstruie. *Per* 4F 60
Patmore Heath. *Herts* 1C 20
Patna. *E Ayr* 8C 54
Patney. *Wilts* 8A 18
Patrick. *IOM* 5C 46
Patrick Brompton. *N Yor* 4B 44
Patrington. *E Yor* 3K 41
Patrington Haven. *E Yor* 3K 41
Patrixbourne. *Kent* 8K 21
Patterdale. *Cumb* 2E 42
Pattiesmuir. *Fife* 1J 55
Pattingham. *Staf* 2J 25
Pattishall. *Nptn* 6E 26
Pattiswick. *Essx* 1G 21
Patton Bridge. *Cumb* 4G 43
Paul. *Corn* 7B 3
Paulerspury. *Nptn* 7F 26
Paull. *E Yor* 3H 41
Paulton. *Bath* 8J 17
Pauperhaugh. *Nmbd* 2G 51
Pave Lane. *Telf* 8E 32
Pavenham. *Bed* 6H 27
Pawlett. *Som* 1C 8
Pawston. *Nmbd* 6H 57
Paxford. *Glos* 8M 25
Paxton. *Bord* 4J 57
Payhembury. *Devn* 5M 7
Paythorne. *Lanc* 8K 43
Payton. *Som* 3A 8
Peacehaven. *E Sus* 7C 12
Peak Dale. *Derbs* 8J 39
Peak District. *Derbs* 7K 39
Peak Forest. *Derbs* 8K 39
Peak Hill. *Linc* 8J 35
Peakirk. *Pet* 1K 27
Pearsie. *Ang* 8D 66
Peasedown St John. *Bath* 8K 17
Peaseland Green. *Norf* 6G 37
Peasemore. *W Ber* 6E 18
Peasenhall. *Suff* 5K 29
Pease Pottage. *W Sus* 4A 12
Peaslake. *Surr* 1L 11
Peasley Cross. *Mers* 6D 38
Peasmarsh. *E Sus* 5G 13
Peasmarsh. *Som* 4C 8
Peasmarsh. *Surr* 1K 11
Peaston. *E Lot* 3D 56
Peastonbank. *E Lot* 3D 56
Peathill. *Abers* 3K 73
Peat Inn. *Fife* 5K 61
Peatling Magna. *Leics* 2D 26
Peatling Parva. *Leics* 3D 26
Peaton. *Arg* 1A 54
Peaton. *Shrp* 3F 24
Peats Corner. *Suff* 5H 29
Pebmarsh. *Essx* 8E 28
Pebworth. *Worc* 7M 25
Pecket Well. *W Yor* 3H 39
Peckforton. *Ches E* 4C 32
Peckham Bush. *Kent* 8E 20
Peckleton. *Leics* 1C 26
Pedair-ffordd. *Powy* 7L 31
Pedham. *Norf* 6K 37
Pedlinge. *Kent* 4K 13
Pedmore. *W Mid* 3K 25
Pedwell. *Som* 2D 8
Peebles. *Bord* 5L 55
Peel. *IOM* 5C 46
Peel. *Bord* 6D 56
Peel Common. *Hants* 5F 10
Peening Quarter. *Kent* 5G 13
Peggs Green. *Leics* 8A 34
Pegsdon. *C Beds* 8K 27
Pegswood. *Nmbd* 3H 51
Peinchorran. *High* 8K 69
Peinlich. *High* 6J 69
Pelaw. *Tyne* 5J 51
Pelcomb Bridge. *Pemb* 2D 14
Pelcomb Cross. *Pemb* 2D 14
Peldon. *Essx* 2H 21
Pelsall. *W Mid* 1L 25
Pelton. *Dur* 6H 51
Pelutho. *Cumb* 7J 49
Pelynt. *Corn* 4D 4
Pemberton. *Carm* 3K 15
Pembrey. *Carm* 3J 15
Pembridge. *Here* 6D 24
Pembroke. *Pemb* 3D 14
Pembroke Dock. *Pemb* 3D 14 & 104
Pembroke Ferry. *Pemb* 3D 14
Pembury. *Kent* 3E 12
Penallt. *Mon* 2H 17
Penally. *Pemb* 4F 14
Penalt. *Here* 1H 17
Penalum. *Pemb* 4F 14
Penare. *Corn* 5A 4
Penarth. *V Glam* 6D 16
Penbeagle. *Corn* 6C 3
Penberth. *Corn* 7B 3
Pen-bont Rhydybeddau. *Cdgn* 3J 23
Penbryn. *Cdgn* 6E 22
Pencader. *Carm* 8G 23
Pen-cae. *Cdgn* 6G 23
Pencaenewydd. *Gwyn* 5D 30
Pencaerau. *Neat* 4M 15
Pencaitland. *E Lot* 3D 56
Pencarnisiog. *IOA* 2C 30
Pencarreg. *Carm* 7H 23
Pencarrow. *Corn* 7C 6
Pencelli. *Powy* 1C 16
Pen-clawdd. *Swan* 4K 15
Pencoed. *B'end* 5B 16
Pencombe. *Here* 6F 24
Pencraig. *Here* 1H 17
Pencraig. *Powy* 7K 31
Pendeen. *Corn* 6A 3
Pendeford. *W Mid* 1K 25
Penderyn. *Rhon* 3B 16
Pendine. *Carm* 3G 15
Pendlebury. *G Man* 5F 38
Pendleton. *G Man* 6G 39
Pendleton. *Lanc* 2F 38
Pendock. *Worc* 8H 25
Pendoggett. *Corn* 8B 6
Pendomer. *Som* 4E 8
Pendoylan. *V Glam* 6C 16

Redmarshall—Scorborough

Redmarshall. Stoc T 1C 44
Redmile. Leics 6D 34
Redmire. N Yor 4M 43
Rednal. Shrp 7A 32
Redpath. Bord 6E 56
Redpoint. High 5M 69
Red Post. Corn 5D 6
Red Rock. G Man 5D 38
Red Roses. Carm 2G 15
Red Row. Nmbd 2H 51
Redruth. Corn 5E 3
Red Street. Staf 4F 32
Redvales. G Man 5F 38
Red Wharf Bay. IOA 1E 30
Redwick. Newp 5G 17
Redwick. S Glo 5H 17
Redworth. Darl 1B 44
Reed. Herts 8M 27
Reed End. Herts 8M 27
Reedham. Linc 4J 35
Reedham. Norf 1L 29
Reedness. E Yor 3E 40
Reeds Beck. Linc 3J 35
Reemshill. Abers 5H 73
Reepham. Linc 8G 41
Reepham. Norf 5G 37
Reeth. N Yor 4M 43
Regaby. IOM 4E 46
Regil. N Som 7H 17
Regoul. High 6L 71
Reiff. High 8G 75
Reigate. Surr 8A 20
Reighton. N Yor 6L 45
Reilth. Shrp 3C 24
Reinigeadal. W Isl 1G 69
Reisque. Abers 1J 67
Reiss. High 4J 77
Rejerrah. Corn 4E 3
Releath. Corn 6D 3
Relubbus. Corn 6C 3
Relugas. Mor 7M 71
Remenham. Wok 5H 19
Remenham Hill. Wok 5H 19
Rempstone. Notts 7B 34
Rendcomb. Glos 3A 18
Rendham. Suff 5K 29
Rendlesham. Suff 6K 29
Renfrew. Ren 3D 54
Renhold. Bed 6J 27
Renishaw. Derbs 8A 40
Rennington. Nmbd 8M 57
Renton. W Dun 2B 54
Renwick. Cumb 7A 50
Repps. Norf 6L 37
Repton. Derbs 7L 33
Rescassa. Corn 5A 4
Rescobie. Ang 8F 66
Rescorla. Corn 4B 4 (nr. Rosevean)
Rescorla. Corn 5A 4 (nr. St Ewe)
Resipole. High 7M 63
Resolfen. Neat 3A 16
Resolis. High 5J 71
Resolven. Neat 3A 16
Rest and be thankful. Arg 5K 59
Reston. Bord 3H 57
Restrop. Wilts 5A 18
Retford. Notts 7D 40
Retire. Corn 3B 4
Rettendon. Essx 4F 20
Revesby. Linc 3K 35
Rew. Devn 6J 5
Rewe. Devn 6L 7
Rew Street. IOW 6E 10
Rexon. Devn 7F 6
Reybridge. Wilts 7M 17
Reydon. Suff 4M 29
Reymerston. Norf 1G 29
Reynalton. Pemb 3E 14
Reynoldston. Swan 5J 15
Rezare. Corn 8E 6
Rhadyr. Mon 3F 16
Rhaeadr Gwy. Powy 5M 23
Rhandirmwyn. Carm 7K 23
Rhayader. Powy 5M 23
Rheindown. High 7H 71
Rhemore. High 8K 63
Rhenetra. High 6J 69
Rhewl. Den 5L 31 (nr. Llangollen)
Rhewl. Den 3L 31 (nr. Ruthin)
Rhewl. Shrp 6A 32
Rhewl-Mostyn. Flin 2L 31
Rhian. High 8A 76
Rhian Breck. High 1H 71
Rhicarn. High 7H 75
Rhiconich. High 4K 75
Rhicullen. High 4J 71
Rhidorroch. High 2D 70
Rhifail. High 5C 76
Rhigos. Rhon 3B 16
Rhilochan. High 1K 71
Rhiroy. High 3D 70
Rhitongue. High 4B 76
Rhiw. Gwyn 7B 30
Rhiwabon. Wrex 5A 32
Rhiwbina. Card 5D 16
Rhiwbryfdir. Gwyn 5F 30
Rhiwderin. Newp 5E 16
Rhiwlas. Gwyn 6J 31 (nr. Bala)
Rhiwlas. Gwyn 3E 30 (nr. Bangor)
Rhiwlas. Powy 6L 31
Rhodes. G Man 5G 39
Rhodesia. Notts 7B 40
Rhodes Minnis. Kent 3K 13
Rhodiad-y-Brenin. Pemb 1B 14
Rhondda. Rhon 4B 16
Rhonehouse. Dum 6E 48
Rhoose. V Glam 7C 16
Rhos. Carm 8F 22
Rhos. Neat 3M 15
Rhosaman. Carm 2M 15
Rhoscefnhir. IOA 2E 30
Rhoscolyn. IOA 2B 30
Rhos Common. Powy 8M 31
Rhoscrowther. Pemb 3D 14
Rhos-ddu. Gwyn 6B 30
Rhosdylluan. Gwyn 7H 31
Rhosesmor. Flin 3M 31
Rhos-fawr. Gwyn 6C 30
Rhosgadfan. Gwyn 4E 30
Rhosgoch. IOA 1D 30
Rhosgoch. Powy 7B 24
Rhos Haminiog. Cdgn 5H 23
Rhos-hill. Pemb 7D 22
Rhoshirwaun. Gwyn 7A 30
Rhoslan. Gwyn 5D 30
Rhoslefain. Gwyn 1H 23
Rhosllanerchrugog. Wrex 5M 31
Rhôs Lligwy. IOA 1D 30
Rhosmaen. Carm 1L 15
Rhosmeirch. IOA 2D 30
Rhosneigr. IOA 2C 30
Rhos-on-Sea. Cnwy 1H 31
Rhossili. Swan 5J 15
Rhosson. Pemb 1B 14
Rhos, The. Pemb 2E 14
Rhostrenwfa. IOA 2D 30
Rhostryfan. Gwyn 4D 30
Rhostyllen. Wrex 5A 32
Rhoswiel. Shrp 6M 31
Rhosybol. IOA 1D 30
Rhos-y-brithdir. Powy 7L 31
Rhos-y-garth. Cdgn 4J 23
Rhos-y-gwaliau. Gwyn 6J 31
Rhos-y-llan. Gwyn 6B 30
Rhos-y-meirch. Powy 5C 24
Rhu. Arg 1A 54
Rhuallt. Den 2K 31
Rhubha Stoer. High 6H 75
Rhubodach. Arg 2J 53
Rhuddall Heath. Ches W 3C 32
Rhuddlan. Cdgn 7G 23
Rhuddlan. Den 2K 31
Rhue. High 2C 70
Rhulen. Powy 7B 24
Rhunahaorine. Arg 5F 52
Rhuthun. Den 4L 31
Rhuvoult. High 4K 75
Rhyd. Gwyn 5F 30
Rhydaman. Carm 2L 15
Rhydargaeau. Carm 1J 15
Rhydcymerau. Carm 8H 23
Rhydd. Worc 7J 25
Rhyd-Ddu. Gwyn 4E 30
Rhydding. Neat 4M 15
Rhydfudr. Cdgn 5H 23
Rhydlanfair. Cnwy 4H 31
Rhydlewis. Cdgn 7F 22
Rhydlios. Gwyn 6A 30
Rhydlydan. Cnwy 4H 31
Rhyd-meirionydd. Cdgn 3J 23
Rhydowen. Cdgn 7G 23
Rhyd-Rosser. Cdgn 5H 23
Rhydspence. Powy 7C 24
Rhydtalog. Flin 4M 31
Rhyd-uchaf. Gwyn 6J 31
Rhydwyn. IOA 1C 30
Rhyd-y-clafdy. Gwyn 6C 30
Rhydycroesau. Shrp 6M 31
Rhydyfelin. Cdgn 4H 23
Rhydyfelin. Rhon 5D 16
Rhyd-y-foel. Cnwy 2J 31
Rhyd-y-fro. Neat 3M 15
Rhydymain. Gwyn 7H 31
Rhyd-y-meudwy. Den 4L 31
Rhydymwyn. Flin 3M 31
Rhyd-yr-onen. Gwyn 1J 23
Rhyd-y-sarn. Gwyn 5F 30
Rhyl. Den 1K 31
Rhymney. Cphy 3D 16
Rhymni. Cphy 3D 16
Rhynd. Per 3G 61
Rhynie. Abers 1E 66
Ribbesford. Worc 4H 25
Ribbleton. Lanc 2D 38
Ribby. Lanc 2C 38
Ribchester. Lanc 2E 38
Riber. Derbs 4L 33
Ribigill. High 4A 76
Riby. Linc 5H 41
Riccall. N Yor 2C 40
Riccarton. E Ayr 6C 54
Richards Castle. Here 5E 24
Richborough Port. Kent 7M 21
Richings Park. Buck 6L 19
Richmond. G Lon 6M 19
Richmond. N Yor 3A 44
Rickarton. Abers 5J 67
Rickerby. Cumb 6M 49
Rickerscote. Staf 7G 33
Rickford. N Som 8G 17
Rickham. Devn 6J 5
Rickinghall. Suff 4G 29
Rickleton. Tyne 6H 51
Rickling. Essx 8A 28
Rickling Green. Essx 1D 20
Rickmansworth. Herts 4L 19
Riddings. Derbs 4A 34
Riddlecombe. Devn 4H 7
Riddlesden. W Yor 1J 39
Ridge. Dors 7J 9
Ridge. Herts 3A 20
Ridge. Wilts 2J 9
Ridgebourne. Powy 5A 24
Ridge Lane. Warw 2A 26
Ridgeway. Derbs 4L 33 (nr. Alfreton)
Ridgeway. Derbs 7A 40 (nr. Sheffield)
Ridgeway. Staf 4F 32
Ridgeway Cross. Here 7H 25
Ridgeway Moor. Derbs 7A 40
Ridgewell. Essx 7D 28
Ridgewood. E Sus 5C 12
Ridgmont. C Beds 8H 27
Ridgwardine. Shrp 6D 32
Riding Mill. Nmbd 5F 50
Ridley. Kent 7E 20
Ridley. Nmbd 5C 50
Ridlington. Norf 4K 37
Ridlington. Rut 1G 27
Ridsdale. Nmbd 3E 50
Riemore Lodge. Per 1F 60
Rievaulx. N Yor 5E 44
Rift House. Hart 8K 51
Rigg. Dum 5K 49
Riggend. N Lan 2F 54
Rigsby. Linc 8L 41
Rigside. S Lan 6G 55
Riley Green. Lanc 3E 38
Rileyhill. Staf 8J 33
Rilla Mill. Corn 8D 6
Rillington. N Yor 6H 45
Rimington. Lanc 1G 39
Rimpton. Som 3F 8
Rimsdale. High 5C 76
Rimswell. E Yor 3K 41
Ringasta. Shet 10D 79
Ringford. Dum 6D 48
Ringing Hill. Leics 8A 34
Ringinglow. S Yor 7L 39
Ringland. Norf 6H 37
Ringlestone. Kent 8G 21
Ringmer. E Sus 6C 12
Ringmore. Devn 5H 5 (nr. Kingsbridge)
Ringmore. Devn 8L 7 (nr. Teignmouth)
Ring o' Bells. Lanc 4C 38
Ring's End. Cambs 1M 27
Ringsfield. Suff 3L 29
Ringsfield Corner. Suff 3L 29
Ringshall. Buck 2K 19
Ringshall. Suff 6G 29
Ringshall Stocks. Suff 6G 29
Ringstead. Norf 3D 36
Ringstead. Nptn 4H 27
Ringwood. Hants 5B 10
Ringwould. Kent 3M 13
Rinmore. Abers 2E 66
Rinnigill. Orkn 8B 78
Rinsey. Corn 7C 3
Riof. W Isl 5B 74
Ripe. E Sus 6D 12
Ripley. Derbs 5A 34
Ripley. Hants 6B 10
Ripley. N Yor 7B 44
Ripley. Surr 8L 19
Riplingham. E Yor 2F 40
Riplington. Hants 3G 11
Ripon. N Yor 6C 44
Rippingale. Linc 7G 35
Ripple. Kent 3M 13
Ripple. Worc 8J 25
Ripponden. W Yor 4J 39
Rireavach. High 2C 70
Risabus. Arg 5B 52
Risbury. Here 6F 24
Risby. E Yor 2G 41
Risby. N Lin 4F 40
Risby. Suff 5D 28
Risca. Cphy 4E 16
Rise. E Yor 1H 41
Riseden. E Sus 4E 12
Riseden. Kent 4F 12
Rise End. Derbs 4K 33
Risegate. Linc 6J 35
Riseholme. Linc 8F 40
Riseley. Bed 5J 27
Riseley. Wok 7H 19
Rishangles. Suff 5H 29
Rishton. Lanc 2F 38
Rishworth. W Yor 4J 39
Risley. Derbs 6A 34
Risley. Warr 6E 38
Risplith. N Yor 7B 44
Rispond. High 3M 75
Rivar. Wilts 7D 18
Rivenhall. Essx 2G 21
Rivenhall End. Essx 2G 21
River. Kent 3L 13
River. W Sus 3K 11
River Bank. Cambs 5B 28
Riverhead. Kent 8D 20
Rivington. Lanc 4E 38
Roach Bridge. Lanc 3D 38
Roachill. Devn 3K 7
Roade. Nptn 6F 26
Road Green. Norf 2J 29
Roadhead. Cumb 4A 50
Roadmeetings. S Lan 5G 55
Roadside. High 3G 77
Roadside of Catterline. Abers 6J 67
Roadside of Kinneff. Abers 6J 67
Roadwater. Som 2M 7
Road Weedon. Nptn 6E 26
Roag. High 7G 69
Roa Island. Cumb 7D 42
Roath. Card 6D 16
Roberton. Bord 8D 56
Roberton. S Lan 7H 55
Robertsbridge. E Sus 5F 12
Robertstown. Mor 5C 72
Robertstown. Rhon 3B 16
Roberttown. W Yor 3K 39
Robeston Back. Pemb 2E 14
Robeston Wathen. Pemb 2E 14
Robeston West. Pemb 3C 14
Robin Hood. Lanc 4D 38
Robin Hood. W Yor 3M 39
Robin Hood Airport Doncaster Sheffield. S Yor 6C 40
Robinhood End. Essx 8D 28
Robin Hood's Bay. N Yor 3J 45
Roborough. Devn 4G 7 (nr. Great Torrington)
Roborough. Devn 3G 5 (nr. Plymouth)
Rob Roy's House. Arg 4J 59
Roby Mill. Lanc 5D 38
Rocester. Staf 6J 33
Roch. Pemb 1C 14
Rochdale. G Man 4G 39
Roche. Corn 3A 4
Rochester. Medw 7F 20 & **Medway 97**
Rochester. Nmbd 2D 50
Rochford. Essx 4G 21
Rock. Corn 8A 6
Rock. Nmbd 7M 57
Rock. W Sus 4M 11
Rock. Worc 4H 25
Rockbeare. Devn 6M 7
Rockbourne. Hants 4B 10
Rockcliffe. Cumb 5L 49
Rockcliffe. Dum 6F 48
Rockcliffe Cross. Cumb 5L 49
Rock Ferry. Mers 7B 38
Rockfield. High 3M 71
Rockfield. Mon 2G 17
Rockford. Hants 5B 10
Rockgreen. Shrp 4F 24
Rockhampton. S Glo 4J 17
Rockhead. Corn 7B 6
Rockingham. Nptn 2G 27
Rockland All Saints. Norf 2F 28
Rockland St Mary. Norf 1K 29
Rockland St Peter. Norf 2F 28
Rockley. Wilts 6B 18
Rockwell End. Buck 5H 19
Rockwell Green. Som 4A 8
Rodborough. Glos 3L 17
Rodbourne. Wilts 5M 17
Rodd. Here 5D 24
Roddam. Nmbd 7K 57
Rodden. Dors 7F 8
Roddenloft. E Ayr 7C 54
Roddymoor. Dur 8G 51
Rode. Som 8L 17
Rodeheath. Ches E 3F 32 (nr. Congleton)
Rode Heath. Ches E 4F 32 (nr. Kidsgrove)
Rodel. W Isl 3E 68
Roden. Telf 8C 32
Rodhuish. Som 2M 7
Rodington. Telf 8C 32
Rodington Heath. Telf 8C 32
Rodley. Glos 2K 17
Rodmarton. Glos 4M 17
Rodmell. E Sus 7C 12
Rodmersham. Kent 7H 21
Rodmersham Green. Kent 7H 21
Rodney Stoke. Som 1D 8
Rodsley. Derbs 5K 33
Rodway. Som 1B 8
Rodway. Telf 8D 32
Rodwell. Dors 8F 8
Roecliffe. N Yor 7C 44
Roe Green. Herts 8M 27
Roehampton. G Lon 6A 20
Roesound. Shet 5D 79
Roffey. W Sus 2M 11
Rogart. High 1K 71
Rogate. W Sus 3J 11
Roger Ground. Cumb 4E 42
Rogerstone. Newp 5E 16
Rogiet. Mon 5G 17
Rogue's Alley. Cambs 1M 27
Roke. Oxon 4G 19
Rokemarsh. Oxon 4G 19
Roker. Tyne 6K 51
Rollesby. Norf 6L 37
Rolleston. Leics 1F 26
Rolleston. Notts 4D 34
Rolleston on Dove. Staf 7K 33
Rolston. E Yor 1J 41
Rolvenden. Kent 4G 13
Rolvenden Layne. Kent 4G 13
Romaldkirk. Dur 1L 43
Roman Bank. Shrp 2F 24
Romanby. N Yor 4C 44
Roman Camp. W Lot 2J 55
Romannobridge. Bord 5K 55
Romansleigh. Devn 3J 7
Romers Common. Worc 5F 24
Romesdal. High 6J 69
Romford. Dors 5A 10
Romford. G Lon 5D 20
Romiley. G Man 6H 39
Romsey. Hants 3D 10
Romsley. Shrp 3H 25
Romsley. Worc 4K 25
Ronague. IOM 6C 46
Ronaldsvoe. Orkn 8C 78
Rookby. Cumb 2K 43
Rookhope. Dur 7E 50
Rooking. Cumb 2F 42
Rookley. IOW 7F 10
Rooks Bridge. Som 8F 16
Rooksey Green. Suff 6F 28
Rook's Nest. Som 2M 7
Rookwood. W Sus 6H 11
Roos. E Yor 2J 41
Roosebeck. Cumb 7D 42
Roosecote. Cumb 7D 42
Rootfield. High 6H 71
Rootham's Green. Bed 6K 27
Rootpark. S Lan 4H 55
Ropley. Hants 2G 11
Ropley Dean. Hants 2G 11
Ropsley. Linc 6F 34
Rora. Abers 4L 73
Rorandle. Abers 2G 67
Rorrington. Shrp 1D 24
Rose. Corn 4E 3
Roseacre. Lanc 2C 38
Rose Ash. Devn 3J 7
Rosebank. S Lan 5G 55
Rosebush. Pemb 1E 14
Rosedale Abbey. N Yor 4G 45
Roseden. Nmbd 7K 57
Rose Green. Essx 1H 21
Rose Green. Suff 7F 28
Rosehall. High 1G 71
Rosehearty. Abers 3K 73
Rose Hill. E Sus 6C 12
Rose Hill. Lanc 2G 39
Rosehill. Shrp 6D 32 (nr. Market Drayton)
Rosehill. Shrp 8B 32 (nr. Shrewsbury)
Roseisle. Mor 3B 72
Rosemarket. Pemb 3D 14
Rosemarkie. High 6K 71
Rosemary Lane. Devn 4A 8
Rosemount. Per 1G 61
Rosenannon. Corn 3A 4
Roser's Cross. E Sus 5D 12
Rosevean. Corn 4B 4
Rosewell. Midl 3L 55
Roseworth. Stoc T 1D 44
Roseworthy. Corn 6D 3
Rosgill. Cumb 2G 43
Roshven. High 6M 63
Roskhill. High 7G 69
Roskorwell. Corn 7E 3
Rosley. Cumb 7L 49
Roslin. Midl 3L 55
Rosliston. Derbs 8K 33
Rosneath. Arg 1A 54
Ross. Dum 7D 48
Ross. Nmbd 6L 57
Ross. Per 3C 60
Ross. Bord 3J 57
Rossendale. Lanc 3F 38
Rossett. Wrex 4A 32
Rossington. S Yor 6C 40
Rosskeen. High 5J 71
Rossland. Ren 2C 54
Ross-on-Wye. Here 1J 17
Roster. High 5H 77
Rostherne. Ches E 7F 38
Rostholme. S Yor 5B 40
Rosthwaite. Cumb 2D 42
Roston. Derbs 5J 33
Rosudgeon. Corn 7C 3
Rosyth. Fife 1K 55
Rothbury. Nmbd 1F 50
Rotherby. Leics 8C 34
Rotherfield. E Sus 5D 12
Rotherfield Greys. Oxon 5H 19
Rotherfield Peppard. Oxon 5H 19
Rotherham. S Yor 6A 40
Rothersthorpe. Nptn 6F 26
Rotherwick. Hants 8H 19
Rothes. Mor 5C 72
Rothesay. Arg 3J 53
Rothienorman. Abers 6H 73
Rothiesholm. Orkn 5E 78
Rothley. Leics 8B 34
Rothley. Nmbd 3F 50
Rothwell. Linc 6H 41
Rothwell. Nptn 3G 27
Rothwell. W Yor 3M 39
Rotsea. E Yor 8K 45
Rottal. Ang 7D 66
Rotten End. Suff 5K 29
Rotten Row. Norf 6G 37
Rotten Row. W Ber 6F 18
Rotten Row. W Mid 4M 25
Rottingdean. Brig 7B 12
Rottington. Cumb 2A 42
Roud. IOW 7F 10
Rougham. Norf 5E 36
Rougham. Suff 5F 28
Rough Close. Staf 6G 33
Rough Common. Kent 8K 21
Roughcote. Staf 5G 33
Rough Haugh. High 5C 76
Rough Hay. Staf 7K 33
Roughlee. Lanc 1G 39
Roughley. W Mid 2M 25
Roughsike. Cumb 4A 50
Roughton. Linc 3J 35
Roughton. Norf 4J 37
Roughton. Shrp 2H 25
Roundbush Green. Essx 2D 20
Roundham. Som 5D 8
Roundhay. W Yor 2M 39
Round Hill. Torb 3L 5
Roundhurst. W Sus 2K 11
Round Maple. Suff 7F 28
Round Oak. Shrp 3D 24
Roundstreet Common. W Sus 3L 11
Roundthwaite. Cumb 3H 43
Roundway. Wilts 7A 18
Roundyhill. Ang 8D 66
Rousdon. Devn 6B 8
Rousham. Oxon 1E 18
Rous Lench. Worc 6L 25
Routh. E Yor 1G 41
Rout's Green. Buck 4H 19
Row. Corn 8B 6
Row. Cumb 5F 42 (nr. Kendal)
Row. Cumb 8B 50 (nr. Penrith)
Rowanburn. Dum 4M 49
Rowanhill. Abers 4L 73
Rowardennan. Stir 6L 59
Rowarth. Derbs 7J 39
Row Ash. Hants 4F 10
Rowberrow. Som 8G 17
Rowde. Wilts 7M 17
Rowden. Devn 6H 7
Rowen. Cnwy 2G 31
Rowfoot. Nmbd 5B 50
Row Green. Essx 1F 20
Row Heath. Essx 2K 21
Rowhedge. Essx 1J 21
Rowhook. W Sus 2M 11
Rowington. Warw 5A 26
Rowland. Derbs 8L 39
Rowland's Castle. Hants 4H 11
Rowlands Gill. Tyne 6G 51
Rowledge. Surr 1J 11
Rowley. Dur 7F 50
Rowley. E Yor 2F 40
Rowley. Shrp 1D 24
Rowley Hill. W Yor 4K 39
Rowley Regis. W Mid 3K 25
Rowlstone. Here 1F 16
Rowly. Surr 1L 11
Rowner. Hants 5F 10
Rowney Green. Worc 4L 25
Rownhams. Hants 4D 10
Rowrah. Cumb 2B 42
Rowsham. Buck 2J 19
Rowsley. Derbs 3K 33
Rowstock. Oxon 5E 18
Rowston. Linc 4G 35
Row, The. Lanc 6F 42
Rowthorne. Derbs 3A 34
Rowton. Ches W 3B 32
Rowton. Shrp 3E 24 (nr. Ludlow)
Rowton. Shrp 8A 32 (nr. Shrewsbury)
Rowton. Telf 8D 32
Row Town. Surr 7L 19
Roxburgh. Bord 6G 57
Roxby. N Lin 4F 40
Roxby. N Yor 2G 45
Roxton. Bed 6K 27
Roxwell. Essx 3E 20
Royal Leamington Spa. Warw 5B 26
Royal Oak. Darl 1B 44
Royal Oak. Lanc 5C 38
Royal Oak. N Yor 6L 45
Royal's Green. Ches E 5D 32
Royal Tunbridge Wells. Kent 4D 12
Royal Wootton Bassett. Wilts 5A 18
Roybridge. High 5E 64
Roydon. Essx 2C 20
Roydon. Norf 3G 29 (nr. Diss)
Roydon. Norf 5D 36 (nr. King's Lynn)
Roydon Hamlet. Essx 3C 20
Royston. Herts 7M 27
Royston. S Yor 4M 39
Royston Water. Som 4B 8
Royton. G Man 5H 39
Ruabon. Wrex 5A 32
Ruaig. Arg 8B 62
Ruan High Lanes. Corn 6A 4
Ruan Lanihorne. Corn 5F 3
Ruan Major. Corn 8E 3
Ruan Minor. Corn 8E 3
Ruarach. High 1B 64
Ruardean. Glos 2J 17
Ruardean Hill. Glos 2J 17
Ruardean Woodside. Glos 2J 17
Rubery. W Mid 4K 25
Ruchazie. Glas 3E 54
Ruckcroft. Cumb 7A 50
Ruckinge. Kent 4J 13
Ruckland. Linc 8K 41
Rucklers Lane. Herts 3L 19
Ruckley. Shrp 1F 24
Rudbaxton. Pemb 1D 14
Rudby. N Yor 3D 44
Ruddington. Notts 6B 34
Rudford. Glos 1K 17
Rudge. Shrp 2J 25
Rudge. Wilts 8L 17
Rudge Heath. Shrp 2H 25
Rudgeway. S Glo 5J 17
Rudgwick. W Sus 2L 11
Rudhall. Here 1J 17
Rudheath. Ches W 8E 38
Rudley Green. Essx 3G 21
Rudloe. Wilts 6L 17
Rudry. Cphy 5D 16
Rudston. E Yor 7K 45
Rudyard. Staf 4G 33
Rufford. Lanc 4C 38
Rufforth. York 8E 44
Rugby. Warw 4D 26
Rugeley. Staf 8H 33
Ruglen. S Ayr 1M 47
Ruilick. High 7H 71
Ruisaurie. High 7G 71
Ruishton. Som 3B 8
Ruisigearraidh. W Isl 3D 68
Ruislip. G Lon 5L 19
Ruislip Common. G Lon 5L 19
Rumbling Bridge. Per 6F 60
Rumburgh. Suff 3K 29
Rumford. Corn 2F 3
Rumford. Falk 2H 55
Rumney. Card 6E 16
Rumwell. Som 3A 8
Runcorn. Hal 7D 38
Runcton. W Sus 5J 11
Runcton Holme. Norf 1C 28
Rundlestone. Devn 8G 7
Runfold. Surr 1J 11
Runhall. Norf 1G 29
Runham. Norf 6L 37
Runnington. Som 3A 8
Runshaw Moor. Lanc 4D 38
Runswick. N Yor 2H 45
Runtaleave. Ang 7C 66
Runwell. Essx 4F 20
Ruscombe. Wok 6H 19
Rushall. Here 8G 25
Rushall. Norf 3H 29
Rushall. W Mid 1L 25
Rushall. Wilts 8B 18
Rushbrooke. Suff 5E 28
Rushbury. Shrp 2F 24
Rushden. Herts 8M 27
Rushden. Nptn 5H 27
Rushenden. Kent 6H 21
Rushford. Devn 8F 6
Rushford. Suff 3F 28
Rush Green. Herts 1A 20
Rushlake Green. E Sus 6E 12
Rushmere. Suff 3L 29
Rushmere St Andrew. Suff 7H 29
Rushmoor. Surr 1J 11
Rushock. Worc 4J 25
Rusholme. G Man 6G 39
Rushton. Ches W 3C 32
Rushton. Nptn 3G 27
Rushton. Shrp 1G 25
Rushton Spencer. Staf 3G 33
Rushwick. Worc 6J 25
Rushyford. Dur 1B 44
Ruskie. Stir 5B 60
Ruskington. Linc 4G 35
Rusland. Cumb 5E 42
Rusper. W Sus 4A 12
Ruspidge. Glos 2J 17
Russell's Water. Oxon 5H 19
Russel's Green. Suff 4J 29
Russ Hill. Surr 3A 12
Russland. Orkn 6B 78
Rusthall. Kent 4D 12
Rustington. W Sus 5L 11
Ruston. N Yor 5J 45
Ruston Parva. E Yor 7K 45
Ruswarp. N Yor 3H 45
Rutherglen. S Lan 3E 54
Ruthernbridge. Corn 3B 4
Ruthin. Den 4L 31
Ruthin. V Glam 6B 16
Ruthrieston. Aber 3K 67
Ruthven. Abers 5F 72
Ruthven. Ang 1H 61
Ruthven. High 8L 71 (nr. Inverness)
Ruthven. High 4K 65 (nr. Kingussie)
Ruthvoes. Corn 3A 4
Ruthwaite. Cumb 8K 49
Ruthwell. Dum 5J 49
Ruxton Green. Here 2H 17
Ruyton-XI-Towns. Shrp 7A 32
Ryal. Nmbd 4F 50
Ryall. Dors 6D 8
Ryall. Worc 7J 25
Ryarsh. Kent 8E 20
Rychraggan. High 8G 71
Rydal. Cumb 3E 42
Ryde. IOW 6F 10
Rye. E Sus 5H 13
Ryecroft Gate. Staf 3G 33
Ryeford. Here 1J 17
Rye Foreign. E Sus 5H 13
Rye Harbour. E Sus 6H 13
Ryehill. E Yor 3J 41
Rye Street. Worc 8H 25
Ryhall. Rut 8G 35
Ryhill. W Yor 4M 39
Ryhope. Tyne 6K 51
Ryhope Colliery. Tyne 6K 51
Rylands. Notts 6B 34
Rylstone. N Yor 8L 43
Ryme Intrinseca. Dors 4E 8
Ryther. N Yor 2B 40
Ryton. Glos 8H 25
Ryton. N Yor 6G 45
Ryton. Shrp 1H 25
Ryton. Tyne 5G 51
Ryton. Warw 3B 26
Ryton-on-Dunsmore. Warw 4B 26
Ryton Woodside. Tyne 5G 51

S

Saasaig. High 3L 63
Sabden. Lanc 2F 38
Sacombe. Herts 2B 20
Sacriston. Dur 7H 51
Sadberge. Darl 2C 44
Saddell. Arg 6F 52
Saddington. Leics 2E 26
Saddle Bow. Norf 6C 36
Saddlescombe. W Sus 6A 12
Saddleworth. G Man 5H 39
Sadgill. Cumb 3F 42
Saffron Walden. Essx 8B 28
Sageston. Pemb 3E 14
Saham Hills. Norf 1F 28
Saham Toney. Norf 1E 28
Saighdinis. W Isl 5C 68
Saighton. Ches W 3B 32
Sain Dunwyd. V Glam 7B 16
Sain Hilari. V Glam 6C 16
St Abbs. Bord 3J 57
St Agnes. Corn 4E 3
St Albans. Herts 3M 19
St Allen. Corn 4F 3
St Andrews. Fife 4L 61
St Andrews Major. V Glam 6D 16
St Anne's. Lanc 3B 38
St Ann's. Dum 2H 49
St Ann's Chapel. Corn 8F 6
St Ann's Chapel. Devn 5H 5
St Anthony. Corn 6F 3
St Anthony-in-Meneage. Corn 7E 3
St Arvans. Mon 4H 17
St Asaph. Den 2K 31
St Athan. V Glam 7C 16
Sain Tathan. V Glam 7C 16
St Austell. Corn 4B 4
St Bartholomew's Hill. Wilts 3J 9
St Bees. Cumb 2A 42
St Blazey. Corn 4B 4
St Blazey Gate. Corn 4B 4
St Boswells. Bord 6F 56
St Breock. Corn 8A 6
St Breward. Corn 8B 6
St Briavels. Glos 3H 17
St Brides. Pemb 2B 14
St Bride's Major. V Glam 6A 16
St Bride's Netherwent. Mon 5G 17
St Bride's-super-Ely. V Glam 6C 16
St Brides Wentlooge. Newp 5E 16
St Budeaux. Plym 4F 4
Saintbury. Glos 8M 25
St Buryan. Corn 7B 3
St Catherine. Bath 6K 17
St Catherines. Arg 5J 59
St Clears. Carm 2G 15
St Cleer. Corn 3D 4
St Clement. Corn 5F 3
St Clether. Corn 7D 6
St Colmac. Arg 3J 53
St Columb Major. Corn 3A 4
St Columb Minor. Corn 3F 3
St Columb Road. Corn 4A 4
St Combs. Abers 3L 73
St Cross. Hants 3E 10
St Cross South Elmham. Suff 3J 29
St Cyrus. Abers 7H 67
St Davids. Pemb 1B 14
St David's. Per 3E 60
St Day. Corn 5E 3
St Dennis. Corn 4A 4
St Dogmaels. Pemb 7D 22
St Dominick. Corn 3E 4
St Donat's. V Glam 7B 16
St Edith's Marsh. Wilts 7M 17
St Endellion. Corn 8A 6
St Enoder. Corn 4F 3
St Erme. Corn 5F 3
St Erney. Corn 4E 4
St Erth. Corn 6C 3
St Erth Praze. Corn 6C 3
St Ervan. Corn 2F 3
St Eval. Corn 3F 3
St Ewe. Corn 5A 4
St Fagans. Card 6D 16
St Fergus. Abers 4L 73
St Fillans. Per 3B 60
St Florence. Pemb 3E 14
St Gennys. Corn 6C 6
St George. Cnwy 2J 31
St Georges. N Som 7F 16
St Georges. V Glam 6C 16
St George's Hill. Surr 7L 19
St Germans. Corn 4E 4
St Giles in the Wood. Devn 4G 7
St Giles on the Heath. Devn 6E 6
St Giles's Hill. Hants 3E 10
St Gluvias. Corn 6E 3
St Harmon. Powy 4M 23
St Helena. Warw 1A 26
St Helen Auckland. Dur 1A 44
St Helens. Cumb 8H 49
St Helen's. E Sus 6G 13
St Helens. IOW 7G 11
St Helens. Mers 6C 38
St Hilary. Corn 6C 3
St Hilary. V Glam 6C 16
Saint Hill. Devn 5M 7
Saint Hill. W Sus 4B 12
St Illtyd. Blae 3E 16
St Ippolyts. Herts 1M 19
St Ishmael. Carm 3H 15
St Ishmael's. Pemb 3C 14
St Issey. Corn 8A 6
St Ive. Corn 3E 4
St Ives. Cambs 4M 27
St Ives. Corn 5C 3
St Ives. Dors 5B 10
St James' End. Nptn 5F 26
St James South Elmham. Suff 3K 29
St Jidgey. Corn 3A 4
St John. Corn 4F 4
St John's. IOM 5C 46
St Johns. Worc 6J 25
St John's Chapel. Devn 3G 7
St John's Chapel. Dur 8D 50
St John's Fen End. Norf 8M 35
St John's Hall. Dur 8F 50
St John's Town of Dalry. Dum 3D 48
St Judes. IOM 4D 46
St Just. Corn 6F 3 (nr. Falmouth)
St Just. Corn 6A 3 (nr. Penzance)
St Just in Roseland. Corn 6F 3
St Katherines. Abers 6H 73
St Keverne. Corn 7E 3
St Kew. Corn 8B 6
St Kew Highway. Corn 8B 6
St Keyne. Corn 3D 4
St Lawrence. Corn 3B 4
St Lawrence. Essx 3H 21
St Lawrence. IOW 8F 10
St Leonards. Buck 3K 19
St Leonards. Dors 5B 10
St Leonards. E Sus 7F 12
St Levan. Corn 7A 3
St Lythans. V Glam 6D 16
St Mabyn. Corn 8B 6
St Madoes. Per 3G 61
St Margarets. Here 8D 24
St Margaret's. Herts 2L 19 (nr. Hemel Hempstead)
St Margarets. Herts 2B 20 (nr. Hoddesdon)
St Margaret's. Wilts 7B 18
St Margaret's at Cliffe. Kent 3M 13
St Margaret's Hope. Orkn 8C 78
St Margaret South Elmham. Suff 3K 29
St Mark's. IOM 6C 46
St Martin. Corn 7E 3 (nr. Helston)
St Martin. Corn 4D 4 (nr. Looe)
St Martins. Per 2G 61
St Martin's. Shrp 6A 32
St Mary Bourne. Hants 8E 18
St Marychurch. Torb 3L 5
St Mary Church. V Glam 6C 16
St Mary Cray. G Lon 7C 20
St Mary Hill. V Glam 6B 16
St Mary Hoo. Medw 6G 21
St Mary in the Marsh. Kent 5J 13
St Mary's. Orkn 7C 78
St Mary's Bay. Kent 5J 13
St Maughan's Green. Mon 2G 17
St Mawes. Corn 6F 3
St Mawgan. Corn 3F 3
St Mellion. Corn 3E 4
St Mellons. Card 5E 16
St Merryn. Corn 2F 3
St Mewan. Corn 4A 4
St Michael Caerhays. Corn 5A 4
St Michael Penkevil. Corn 5F 3
St Michaels. Kent 4G 13
St Michaels. Torb 4K 5
St Michaels. Worc 5F 24
St Michael's on Wyre. Lanc 1C 38
St Michael South Elmham. Suff 3K 29
St Minver. Corn 8A 6
St Monans. Fife 5L 61
St Neot. Corn 3C 4
St Neots. Cambs 5K 27
St Newlyn East. Corn 4F 3
St Nicholas. Pemb 8B 22
St Nicholas. V Glam 6C 16
St Nicholas at Wade. Kent 7L 21
St Nicholas South Elmham. Suff 3K 29
St Ninians. Stir 6D 60
St Olaves. Norf 2L 29
St Osyth. Essx 2K 21
St Osyth Heath. Essx 2K 21
St Owen's Cross. Here 1H 17
St Paul's Cray. G Lon 7C 20
St Paul's Walden. Herts 1M 19
St Peter's. Kent 7M 21
St Peter The Great. Worc 6J 25
St Petrox. Pemb 4D 14
St Pinnock. Corn 3D 4
St Quivox. S Ayr 7B 54
St Ruan. Corn 8E 3
St Stephen. Corn 4A 4
St Stephens. Corn 7E 6 (nr. Launceston)
St Stephens. Corn 4F 4 (nr. Saltash)
St Teath. Corn 7B 6
St Thomas. Devn 6L 7
St Thomas. Swan 4L 15
St Tudy. Corn 8B 6
St Twynnells. Pemb 4D 14
St Veep. Corn 4C 4
St Vigeans. Ang 1M 61
St Wenn. Corn 3A 4
St Weonards. Here 1G 17
St Winnolls. Corn 4E 4
St Winnow. Corn 4C 4
Salcombe. Devn 6J 5
Salcombe Regis. Devn 7A 8
Salcott. Essx 2H 21
Sale. G Man 6F 38
Saleby. Linc 8L 41
Sale Green. Worc 6K 25
Salehurst. E Sus 5F 12
Salem. Carm 1L 15
Salem. Cdgn 3J 23
Salen. Arg 1C 58
Salen. High 7L 63
Salesbury. Lanc 2E 38
Saleway. Worc 6K 25
Salford. C Beds 8H 27
Salford. G Man 6G 39 & **Manchester 97**
Salford. Oxon 1C 18
Salford Priors. Warw 6L 25
Salfords. Surr 3A 12
Salhouse. Norf 6K 37
Saligo. Arg 3A 52
Saline. Fife 6F 60
Salisbury. Wilts 2B 10 & 101
Salkeld Dykes. Cumb 8A 50
Sallachan. High 7B 64
Sallachy. High 1H 71 (nr. Lairg)
Sallachy. High 8B 70 (nr. Stromeferry)
Salle. Norf 5H 37
Salmonby. Linc 8K 41
Salmond's Muir. Ang 2L 61
Salperton. Glos 1A 18
Salph End. Bed 6J 27
Salsburgh. N Lan 3G 55
Salt. Staf 7G 33
Salta. Cumb 7H 49
Saltaire. W Yor 2K 39
Saltash. Corn 4F 4
Saltburn. High 5K 71
Saltburn-by-the-Sea. Red C 1F 44
Saltby. Leics 7E 34
Saltcoats. Cumb 4B 42
Saltcoats. N Ayr 5A 54
Saltdean. Brig 7B 12
Salt End. E Yor 3H 41
Salter. Lanc 7H 43
Salterforth. Lanc 1G 39
Salters Lode. Norf 1B 28
Salterswall. Ches W 3D 32
Salterton. Wilts 2B 10
Saltfleet. Linc 6L 41
Saltfleetby All Saints. Linc 6L 41
Saltfleetby St Clements. Linc 6L 41
Saltfleetby St Peter. Linc 7L 41
Saltford. Bath 7J 17
Salthouse. Norf 3G 37
Saltmarshe. E Yor 3D 40
Saltmead. Card 6D 16
Saltness. Orkn 9A 78
Saltness. Shet 7C 79
Saltney. Flin 3A 32
Salton. N Yor 6G 45
Saltrens. Devn 3F 6
Saltwick. Nmbd 4G 51
Saltwood. Kent 4K 13
Salum. Arg 8B 62
Salwarpe. Worc 5J 25
Salwayash. Dors 6D 8
Samalaman. High 6L 63
Sambourne. Warw 5L 25
Sambourne. Wilts 1H 9
Sambrook. Telf 7E 32
Samhia. W Isl 5B 68
Samlesbury. Lanc 2D 38
Samlesbury Bottoms. Lanc 3E 38
Sampford Arundel. Som 4A 8
Sampford Brett. Som 1M 7
Sampford Courtenay. Devn 5H 7
Sampford Peverell. Devn 4M 7
Sampford Spiney. Devn 8G 7
Samsonslane. Orkn 5E 78
Samuelston. E Lot 2D 56
Sanaigmore. Arg 2A 52
Sancreed. Corn 7B 3
Sancton. E Yor 2F 40
Sand. High 2B 70
Sand. Shet 7D 79
Sand. Som 1D 8
Sandaig. Arg 8A 62
Sandaig. High 3M 63
Sandale. Cumb 7K 49
Sandal Magna. W Yor 4M 39
Sandavore. High 5J 63
Sanday Airport. Orkn 3E 78
Sandbach. Ches E 3E 32
Sandbank. Arg 1K 53
Sandbanks. Pool 7A 10
Sandend. Abers 3F 72
Sanderstead. G Lon 7B 20
Sandfields. Neat 4M 15
Sandford. Cumb 2J 43
Sandford. Devn 5K 7
Sandford. Dors 7J 9
Sandford. Hants 5B 10
Sandford. IOW 7F 10
Sandford. N Som 8G 17
Sandford. Shrp 7A 32 (nr. Oswestry)
Sandford. Shrp 6C 32 (nr. Whitchurch)
Sandford. S Lan 5F 54
Sandfordhill. Abers 5M 73
Sandford-on-Thames. Oxon 3F 18
Sandford Orcas. Dors 3F 8
Sandford St Martin. Oxon 1E 18
Sandgate. Kent 4K 13
Sandgreen. Dum 6C 48
Sandhaven. Abers 3K 73
Sandhead. Dum 6K 47
Sandhill. Cambs 3B 28
Sandhills. Dors 4F 8
Sandhills. Oxon 3F 18
Sandhills. Surr 2K 11
Sandhoe. Nmbd 5E 50
Sand Hole. E Yor 2E 40
Sandholme. E Yor 2E 40
Sandholme. Linc 6K 35
Sandhurst. Brac 7J 19
Sandhurst. Glos 1L 17
Sandhurst. Kent 5F 12
Sandhurst Cross. Kent 5F 12
Sandhutton. N Yor 5C 44 (nr. Thirsk)
Sand Hutton. N Yor 8F 44 (nr. York)
Sandiacre. Derbs 6A 34
Sandilands. Linc 7M 41
Sandiway. Ches W 8E 38
Sandleheath. Hants 4B 10
Sandling. Kent 8F 20
Sandlow Green. Ches E 3E 32
Sandness. Shet 6B 79
Sandon. Essx 3F 20
Sandon. Herts 8M 27
Sandon. Staf 7G 33
Sandonbank. Staf 7G 33
Sandown. IOW 7F 10
Sandplace. Corn 4D 4
Sandridge. Herts 2M 19
Sandringham. Norf 5C 36
Sandsend. N Yor 2H 45
Sandside. Cumb 6E 42
Sandsound. Shet 7D 79
Sands, The. Surr 1J 11
Sandtoft. N Lin 5D 40
Sandvoe. Shet 2D 79
Sandway. Kent 8G 21
Sandwich. Kent 8M 21
Sandwick. Cumb 2F 42
Sandwick. Orkn 6A 78 (on Mainland)
Sandwick. Orkn 9C 78 (on South Ronaldsay)
Sandwick. Shet 9E 79 (on Mainland)
Sandwick. Shet 5F 79 (on Whalsay)
Sandwith. Cumb 2A 42
Sandy. Carm 3J 15
Sandy. C Beds 7K 27
Sandy Bank. Linc 4J 35
Sandycroft. Flin 3A 32
Sandy Cross. Here 6G 25
Sandygate. Devn 8K 7
Sandygate. IOM 4D 46
Sandy Haven. Pemb 3C 14
Sandyhills. Dum 6F 48
Sandylands. Lanc 7F 42
Sandylane. Swan 5K 15
Sandy Lane. Wilts 7M 17
Sandystones. Bord 7E 56
Sandyway. Here 1G 17
Sangobeg. High 3M 75
Sangomore. High 3M 75
Sankyn's Green. Worc 5H 25
Sanna. High 7J 63
Sanndabhaig. W Isl 5E 74 (on Isle of Lewis)
Sanndabhaig. W Isl 7C 68 (on South Uist)
Sannox. N Ayr 5J 53
Sanquhar. Dum 8F 54
Santon. Cumb 3B 42
Santon Bridge. Cumb 3C 42
Santon Downham. Suff 3E 28
Sapcote. Leics 2C 26
Sapey Common. Here 5H 25
Sapiston. Suff 4F 28
Sapley. Cambs 4L 27
Sapperton. Derbs 6J 33
Sapperton. Glos 3M 17
Sapperton. Linc 6G 35
Saracen's Head. Linc 7K 35
Sarclet. High 5J 77
Sardis. Carm 3K 15
Sardis. Pemb 3D 14 (nr. Milford Haven)
Sardis. Pemb 3F 14 (nr. Tenby)
Sarisbury. Hants 5F 10
Sarn. B'end 5B 16
Sarn. Powy 2C 24
Sarnau. Carm 1J 15
Sarnau. Cdgn 6F 22
Sarnau. Gwyn 6J 31
Sarnau. Powy 8A 24 (nr. Brecon)
Sarnau. Powy 8M 31 (nr. Welshpool)
Sarn Bach. Gwyn 7C 30
Sarnesfield. Here 6D 24
Sarn Meyllteyrn. Gwyn 6B 30
Saron. Carm 2L 15 (nr. Ammanford)
Saron. Carm 8F 22 (nr. Newcastle Emlyn)
Saron. Gwyn 3E 30 (nr. Bethel)
Saron. Gwyn 4D 30 (nr. Bontnewydd)
Sarratt. Herts 4L 19
Sarre. Kent 7L 21
Sarsden. Oxon 1C 18
Satley. Dur 7G 51
Satron. N Yor 4L 43
Satterleigh. Devn 3H 7
Satterthwaite. Cumb 4E 42
Satwell. Oxon 5H 19
Sauchen. Abers 2G 67
Saucher. Per 2G 61
Saughall. Ches W 3A 32
Saughtree. Bord 2A 50
Saul. Glos 3K 17
Saundby. Notts 7D 40
Saundersfoot. Pemb 3F 14
Saunderton. Buck 3H 19
Saunderton Lee. Buck 4J 19
Saunton. Devn 2F 6
Sausthorpe. Linc 3K 35
Saval. High 1H 71
Saverley Green. Staf 6G 33
Sawbridge. Warw 5D 26
Sawbridgeworth. Herts 2C 20
Sawdon. N Yor 5J 45
Sawley. Derbs 6A 34
Sawley. Lanc 1F 38
Sawley. N Yor 7B 44
Sawston. Cambs 7A 28
Sawtry. Cambs 3K 27
Saxby. Leics 7E 34
Saxby. Linc 7G 41
Saxby All Saints. N Lin 4F 40
Saxelby. Leics 7C 34
Saxelbye. Leics 7C 34
Saxham Street. Suff 5G 29
Saxilby. Linc 8E 40
Saxlingham. Norf 4G 37
Saxlingham Green. Norf 2J 29
Saxlingham Nethergate. Norf 2J 29
Saxlingham Thorpe. Norf 2J 29
Saxmundham. Suff 5K 29
Saxondale. Notts 5C 34
Saxon Street. Cambs 6C 28
Saxtead. Suff 5J 29
Saxtead Green. Suff 5J 29
Saxthorpe. Norf 4H 37
Saxton. N Yor 2A 40
Sayers Common. W Sus 6A 12
Scackleton. N Yor 6F 44
Scadabhagh. W Isl 2F 68
Scaftworth. Notts 6C 40
Scagglethorpe. N Yor 6H 45
Scaitcliffe. Lanc 3F 38
Scaladal. W Isl 7B 74
Scalasaig. Arg 6A 58
Scalby. E Yor 3E 40
Scalby. N Yor 4K 45
Scalby Mills. N Yor 4K 45
Scaldwell. Nptn 4F 26
Scaleby. Cumb 5M 49
Scaleby Hill. Cumb 5M 49
Scale Houses. Cumb 7A 50
Scales. Cumb 6D 42 (nr. Barrow-in-Furness)
Scales. Cumb 1E 42 (nr. Keswick)
Scalford. Leics 7D 34
Scaling. Red C 2G 45
Scaling Dam. Red C 2G 45
Scalloway. Shet 8D 79
Scalpaigh. W Isl 2G 69
Scalpay House. High 1L 63
Scamblesby. Linc 8J 41
Scamodale. High 6A 64
Scampston. N Yor 6H 45
Scampton. Linc 8F 40
Scaniport. High 8J 71
Scapa. Orkn 7C 78
Scapegoat Hill. W Yor 4J 39
Scar. Orkn 3E 78
Scarasta. W Isl 2E 68
Scarborough. N Yor 5K 45
Scarcliffe. Derbs 3A 34
Scarcroft. W Yor 1M 39
Scardroy. High 6E 70
Scarfskerry. High 2H 77
Scargill. Dur 2M 43
Scarinish. Arg 8B 62
Scarisbrick. Lanc 4B 38
Scarning. Norf 6F 36
Scarrington. Notts 5D 34
Scarth Hill. Lanc 5C 38
Scartho. NE Lin 5J 41
Scarvister. Shet 7D 79
Scatness. Shet 10D 79
Scatwell. High 6F 70
Scaur. Dum 6F 48
Scawby. N Lin 5F 40
Scawby Brook. N Lin 5F 40
Scawsby. S Yor 5B 40
Scawton. N Yor 5E 44
Scayne's Hill. W Sus 5B 12
Scethrog. Powy 1D 16
Scholar Green. Ches E 4F 32
Scholes. G Man 5D 38
Scholes. W Yor 3K 39 (nr. Bradford)
Scholes. W Yor 5K 39 (nr. Holmfirth)
Scholes. W Yor 2M 39 (nr. Leeds)
Scholey Hill. W Yor 3M 39
School Aycliffe. Dur 1B 44
School Green. Ches W 3D 32
School Green. Essx 8D 28
Scissett. W Yor 4L 39
Scleddau. Pemb 8B 22
Scofton. Notts 7C 40
Scole. Norf 4H 29
Scolpaig. W Isl 4B 68
Scolton. Pemb 1D 14
Scone. Per 3G 61
Sconser. High 8K 69
Scoonie. Fife 5J 61
Scopwick. Linc 4G 35
Scoraig. High 2C 70
Scorborough. E Yor 1G 41

Scorrier—Staindrop

Scorrier. Corn 5E 3
Scorriton. Devn 3J 5
Scorton. Lanc 1D 38
Scorton. N Yor 3B 44
Sco Ruston. Norf 5J 37
Scotbheinn. W Isl 6C 68
Scotby. Cumb 6M 49
Scotch Corner. N Yor 3B 44
Scotforth. Lanc 7F 42
Scot Hay. Staf 5F 32
Scothern. Linc 8G 41
Scotland End. Oxon 8B 26
Scotlandwell. Per 5G 61
Scot Lane End. G Man 5E 38
Scotsburn. High 4K 71
Scotsburn. Mor 3C 72
Scotsdike. Cumb 4L 49
Scot's Gap. Nmbd 3F 50
Scotstoun. Glas 3D 54
Scotstown. High 7A 64
Scotswood. Tyne 5H 51
Scottas. High 3M 63
Scotter. Linc 5E 40
Scotterthorpe. Linc 5E 40
Scottlethorpe. Linc 7G 35
Scotton. Linc 6E 40
Scotton. N Yor 4A 44 (nr. Catterick Garrison)
Scotton. N Yor 8C 44 (nr. Harrogate)
Scottow. Norf 5J 37
Scoulton. Norf 1F 28
Scounslow Green. Staf 7H 33
Scourie. High 5J 75
Scourie More. High 5J 75
Scousburgh. Shet 10D 79
Scout Green. Cumb 3G 43
Scouthead. G Man 5H 39
Scrabster. High 2F 76
Scrafield. Linc 3K 35
Scrainwood. Nmbd 1E 50
Scrane End. Linc 5K 35
Scraptoft. Leic 1E 26
Scratby. Norf 6M 37
Scrayingham. N Yor 7G 45
Scredington. Linc 5G 35
Scremby. Linc 3L 35
Scremerston. Nmbd 5K 57
Screveton. Notts 5D 34
Scrivelsby. Linc 3J 35
Scriven. N Yor 8C 44
Scronkey. Lanc 1C 38
Scrooby. Notts 6C 40
Scropton. Derbs 6J 33
Scrub Hill. Linc 4J 35
Scruton. N Yor 4B 44
Scuggate. Cumb 4M 49
Sculamus. High 1L 63
Sculcoates. Hull 2G 41
Sculthorpe. Norf 4E 36
Scunthorpe. N Lin 4E 40
Scurlage. Swan 5J 15
Sea. Som 4C 8
Seaborough. Dors 5D 8
Seabridge. Staf 5F 32
Seabrook. Kent 4K 13
Seaburn. Tyne 5K 51
Seacombe. Mers 6B 38
Seacroft. Linc 3M 35
Seacroft. W Yor 2M 39
Seadyke. Linc 6K 35
Seafield. High 3M 71
Seafield. Midl 3L 55
Seafield. S Ayr 7B 54
Seafield. W Lot 3J 55
Seaford. E Sus 8C 12
Seaforth. Mers 6B 38
Seagrave. Leics 8C 34
Seaham. Dur 7K 51
Seahouses. Nmbd 6M 57
Seal. Kent 8D 20
Sealand. Flin 3A 32
Seale. Surr 1J 11
Seamer. N Yor 5K 45 (nr. Scarborough)
Seamer. N Yor 2D 44 (nr. Stokesley)
Seamill. N Ayr 5K 53
Sea Mills. Bris 6H 17
Sea Palling. Norf 5L 37
Searby. Linc 5G 41
Seasalter. Kent 7J 21
Seascale. Cumb 3B 42
Seaside. Per 3H 61
Seater. High 2J 77
Seathorne. Linc 3M 35
Seathwaite. Cumb 2D 42 (nr. Buttermere)
Seathwaite. Cumb 4D 42 (nr. Ulpha)
Seatle. Cumb 5E 42
Seatoller. Cumb 2D 42
Seaton. Corn 4E 4
Seaton. Cumb 8H 49
Seaton. Devn 6B 8
Seaton. Dur 6J 51
Seaton. E Yor 1H 41
Seaton. Nmbd 4J 51
Seaton. Rut 2H 27
Seaton Burn. Tyne 4H 51
Seaton Carew. Hart 1E 44
Seaton Delaval. Nmbd 4J 51
Seaton Junction. Devn 6B 8
Seaton Ross. E Yor 1D 40
Seaton Sluice. Nmbd 4J 51
Seatown. Abers 3F 72
Seatown. Dors 6D 8
Seatown. Mor 3F 72 (nr. Cullen)
Seatown. Mor 2C 72 (nr. Lossiemouth)
Seave Green. N Yor 3E 44
Seaview. IOW 6G 11
Seaville. Cumb 6J 49
Seavington St Mary. Som 4D 8
Seavington St Michael. Som 4D 8
Seawick. Essx 2K 21
Sebastopol. Torf 4E 16
Sebergham. Cumb 7L 49
Seckington. Warw 1A 26
Second Coast. High 2B 70
Sedbergh. Cumb 4H 43
Sedbury. Glos 4H 17
Sedbusk. N Yor 4K 43
Sedgeberrow. Worc 8L 25
Sedgebrook. Linc 6E 34
Sedgefield. Dur 1C 44
Sedgeford. Norf 4D 36
Sedgehill. Wilts 3H 9
Sedgley. W Mid 2K 25
Sedgwick. Cumb 5G 43
Sedlescombe. E Sus 6F 12
Seend. Wilts 7M 17
Seend Cleeve. Wilts 7M 17
Seer Green. Buck 4K 19
Seething. Norf 2K 29
Sefster. Shet 6D 79
Sefton. Mers 5B 38
Sefton Park. Mers 7B 38
Segensworth. Hants 5F 10
Seggat. Abers 5H 73
Seghill. Nmbd 4H 51
Seifton. Shrp 3E 24
Seighford. Staf 7F 32
Seilebost. W Isl 2E 68
Seisdon. Staf 2J 25
Seisiadar. W Isl 5F 74
Selattyn. Shrp 6M 31
Selborne. Hants 2H 11
Selby. N Yor 2C 40
Selham. W Sus 3K 11
Selkirk. Bord 7D 56
Sellack. Here 1H 17
Sellafirth. Shet 2F 79
Sellick's Green. Som 4B 8
Sellindge. Kent 4K 13
Selling. Kent 8J 21
Sells Green. Wilts 7M 17
Selly Oak. W Mid 3L 25
Selmeston. E Sus 7D 12
Selsdon. G Lon 7B 20
Selsey. W Sus 6J 11
Selsfield Common. W Sus 4B 12
Selside. Cumb 4G 43
Selside. N Yor 6J 43
Selsley. Glos 3L 17
Selsted. Kent 3L 13
Selston. Notts 4A 34
Selworthy. Som 1L 7
Semblister. Shet 6D 79
Semer. Suff 7G 29
Semington. Wilts 7L 17
Semley. Wilts 3H 9
Sempringham. Linc 6H 35
Send. Surr 8L 19
Send Marsh. Surr 8L 19
Senghenydd. Cphy 4D 16
Sennen. Corn 7A 3
Sennen Cove. Corn 7A 3
Sennicotts. W Sus 5J 11
Sennybridge. Powy 1B 16
Serlby. Notts 7C 40
Sessay. N Yor 6D 44
Setchey. Norf 6C 36
Setley. Hants 5D 10
Setter. Shet 3E 79
Settiscarth. Orkn 6B 78
Settle. N Yor 7K 43
Settrington. N Yor 6H 45
Seven Ash. Som 2A 8
Sevenhampton. Glos 1A 18
Sevenhampton. Swin 4C 18
Sevenoaks. Kent 8D 20
Sevenoaks Weald. Kent 8D 20
Seven Sisters. Neat 3A 16
Seven Springs. Glos 2M 17
Severn Beach. S Glo 5H 17
Severn Stoke. Worc 7J 25
Sevington. Kent 3J 13
Sewards End. Essx 8B 28
Sewardstone. Essx 4B 20
Sewell. C Beds 1K 19
Sewerby. E Yor 7M 45
Seworgan. Corn 6E 3
Sewstern. Leics 7E 34
Sgallairidh. W Isl 4A 62
Sgarasta Mhor. W Isl 2E 68
Sgiogarstaigh. W Isl 2F 74
Sgreadan. Arg 6A 58
Shabbington. Buck 3G 19
Shackerley. Shrp 1J 25
Shackerstone. Leics 1B 26
Shackleford. Surr 1K 11
Shadforth. Dur 7J 51
Shadingfield. Suff 3L 29
Shadoxhurst. Kent 4H 13
Shadsworth. Bkbn 3E 38
Shadwell. Norf 3F 28
Shadwell. W Yor 2M 39
Shaftesbury. Dors 3H 9
Shafton. S Yor 4M 39
Shafton Two Gates. S Yor 4M 39
Shaggs. Dors 7H 9
Shakesfield. Glos 8G 25
Shalbourne. Wilts 7D 18
Shalcombe. IOW 7D 10
Shalden. Hants 1G 11
Shaldon. Devn 8L 7
Shalfleet. IOW 7E 10
Shalford. Essx 1F 20
Shalford. Surr 1L 11
Shalford Green. Essx 1F 20
Shallowford. Devn 1J 7
Shallowford. Staf 7F 32
Shalmsford Street. Kent 8J 21
Shalstone. Buck 8E 26
Shamley Green. Surr 1L 11
Shandon. Arg 1A 54
Shandwick. High 4L 71
Shangton. Leics 2F 26
Shankhouse. Nmbd 4H 51
Shanklin. IOW 7F 10
Shannochie. N Ayr 7H 53
Shap. Cumb 2G 43
Shapwick. Dors 5J 9
Shapwick. Som 2D 8
Sharcott. Wilts 8B 18
Shardlow. Derbs 6A 34
Shareshill. Staf 1K 25
Sharlston. W Yor 4M 39
Sharlston Common. W Yor 4M 39
Sharnal Street. Medw 6F 20
Sharnbrook. Bed 6H 27
Sharneyford. Lanc 3G 39
Sharnford. Leics 2C 26
Sharnhill Green. Dors 5G 9
Sharoe Green. Lanc 2D 38
Sharow. N Yor 6C 44
Sharpenhoe. C Beds 8J 27
Sharperton. Nmbd 1E 50
Sharpness. Glos 3J 17
Sharp Street. Norf 5K 37
Sharpthorne. W Sus 4B 12
Sharrington. Norf 4G 37
Shatterford. Worc 3H 25
Shatton. Derbs 7L 39
Shaugh Prior. Devn 3G 5
Shavington. Ches E 4E 32
Shaw. G Man 5H 39
Shaw. W Ber 7E 18
Shaw. Wilts 7L 17
Shawbirch. Telf 8D 32
Shawbury. Shrp 7C 32
Shawdon Hall. Nmbd 8K 57
Shawell. Leics 3D 26
Shawford. Hants 3E 10
Shawforth. Lanc 3G 39
Shaw Green. Lanc 4D 38
Shawhead. Dum 4F 48
Shaw Mills. N Yor 7B 44
Shawwood. E Ayr 7D 54
Shearington. Dum 5H 49
Shearsby. Leics 2E 26
Shearston. Som 2B 8
Shebbear. Devn 5F 6
Shebdon. Staf 7E 32
Shebster. High 3F 76
Sheddocksley. Aber 3J 67
Shedfield. Hants 4F 10
Shedog. N Ayr 6H 53
Sheen. Staf 3J 33
Sheepbridge. Derbs 8M 39
Sheep Hill. Tyne 6G 51
Sheepscar. W Yor 2M 39
Sheepscombe. Glos 2L 17
Sheepstor. Devn 3G 5
Sheepwash. Devn 5F 6
Sheepwash. Nmbd 3H 51
Sheepway. N Som 6G 17
Sheepy Magna. Leics 1B 26
Sheepy Parva. Leics 1B 26
Sheering. Essx 2D 20
Sheerness. Kent 6H 21
Sheerwater. Surr 7L 19
Sheet. Hants 3H 11
Sheffield. S Yor 7M 39 & 102
Sheffield Bottom. W Ber 7G 19
Sheffield Green. E Sus 5C 12
Shefford. C Beds 8K 27
Shefford Woodlands. W Ber 6D 18
Sheigra. High 3J 75
Sheinton. Shrp 1G 25
Shelderton. Shrp 4E 24
Sheldon. Derbs 3J 33
Sheldon. Devn 5A 8
Sheldon. W Mid 3M 25
Sheldwich. Kent 8J 21
Sheldwich Lees. Kent 8J 21
Shelf. W Yor 3K 39
Shelfanger. Norf 3H 29
Shelfield. Warw 5M 25
Shelfield. W Mid 1L 25
Shelford. Notts 5C 34
Shelford. Warw 3C 26
Shell. Worc 6K 25
Shelley. Suff 8G 29
Shelley. W Yor 4L 39
Shell Green. Hal 7D 38
Shellingford. Oxon 4D 18
Shellow Bowells. Essx 3E 20
Shelsley Beauchamp. Worc 5H 25
Shelsley Walsh. Worc 5H 25
Shelthorpe. Leics 8B 34
Shelton. Bed 5J 27
Shelton. Norf 2J 29
Shelton. Notts 5D 34
Shelton. Shrp 8B 32
Shelton Green. Norf 2J 29
Shelton Lock. Derb 6L 33
Shelve. Shrp 2D 24
Shelwick. Here 7F 24
Shelwick Green. Here 7F 24
Shenfield. Essx 4E 20
Shenington. Oxon 7B 26
Shenley. Herts 3M 19
Shenley Brook End. Mil 8G 27
Shenleybury. Herts 3M 19
Shenley Church End. Mil 8G 27
Shenmore. Here 8D 24
Shennanton. Dum 5A 48
Shenstone. Staf 1M 25
Shenstone. Worc 4J 25
Shenstone Woodend. Staf 1M 25
Shenton. Leics 1B 26
Shenval. Mor 1C 66
Shepeau Stow. Linc 8K 35
Shephall. Herts 1A 20
Shepherd's Bush. G Lon 5A 20
Shepherd's Gate. Norf 8M 35
Shepherd's Green. Oxon 5H 19
Shepherd's Port. Norf 4C 36
Shepherdswell. Kent 3L 13
Shepley. W Yor 5K 39
Sheppardstown. High 5G 77
Shepperdine. S Glo 4J 17
Shepperton. Surr 7L 19
Shepreth. Cambs 7M 27
Shepshed. Leics 8A 34
Shepton Beauchamp. Som 4D 8
Shepton Mallet. Som 1F 8
Shepton Montague. Som 2F 8
Shepway. Kent 8F 20
Sheraton. Dur 8K 51
Sherborne. Bath 8H 17
Sherborne. Dors 4F 8
Sherborne. Glos 2B 18
Sherborne Causeway. Dors 3H 9
Sherborne St John. Hants 8G 19
Sherbourne. Warw 5A 26
Sherburn. Dur 7J 51
Sherburn. N Yor 6J 45
Sherburn Hill. Dur 7J 51
Sherburn in Elmet. N Yor 2A 40
Shere. Surr 1L 11
Shereford. Norf 5E 36
Sherfield English. Hants 3C 10
Sherfield on Loddon. Hants 8G 19
Sherford. Devn 5J 5
Sherford. Dors 6J 9
Sheriffhales. Shrp 8E 32
Sheriff Hutton. N Yor 7F 44
Sheriffston. Mor 3C 72
Sheringham. Norf 3H 37
Sherington. Mil 7G 27
Shermanbury. W Sus 6A 12
Shernal Green. Worc 5K 25
Shernborne. Norf 4D 36
Sherrington. Wilts 2J 9
Sherston. Wilts 5L 17
Sherwood. Nott 5B 34
Sherwood Green. Devn 3G 7
Shettleston. Glas 3E 54
Shevington. G Man 5D 38
Shevington Moor. G Man 4D 38
Shevington Vale. G Man 5D 38
Sheviock. Corn 4E 4
Shide. IOW 7F 10
Shiel Bridge. High 2B 64
Shieldaig. High 4A 70 (nr. Charlestown)
Shieldaig. High 6A 70 (nr. Torridon)
Shieldhill. Dum 3H 49
Shieldhill. Falk 2G 55
Shieldhill. S Lan 5J 55
Shieldmuir. N Lan 4F 54
Shielfoot. High 7L 63
Shielhill. Abers 4L 73
Shielhill. Ang 8E 66
Shifnal. Shrp 1H 25
Shilbottle. Nmbd 1G 51
Shilbottle Grange. Nmbd 1H 51
Shildon. Dur 1B 44
Shillford. E Ren 4C 54
Shillingford. Devn 3L 7
Shillingford. Oxon 4F 18
Shillingford St George. Devn 7L 7
Shillingstone. Dors 4H 9
Shillington. C Beds 8K 27
Shillmoor. Nmbd 1D 50
Shilton. Oxon 3C 18
Shilton. Warw 3C 26
Shilvinghampton. Dors 7F 8
Shilvington. Nmbd 3G 51
Shimpling. Norf 3H 29
Shimpling. Suff 6E 28
Shimpling Street. Suff 6E 28
Shincliffe. Dur 7H 51
Shiney Row. Tyne 6J 51
Shinfield. Wok 7H 19
Shingay. Cambs 7M 27
Shingham. Norf 1D 28
Shingle Street. Suff 7K 29
Shinner's Bridge. Devn 3J 5
Shinness. High 8A 76
Shipbourne. Kent 8D 20
Shipdham. Norf 1F 28
Shipham. Som 8G 17
Shiphay. Torb 3K 5
Shiplake. Oxon 6H 19
Shipley. Derbs 5A 34
Shipley. Nmbd 8L 57
Shipley. Shrp 2J 25
Shipley. W Sus 3M 11
Shipley. W Yor 2K 39
Shipley Bridge. Surr 3B 12
Shipmeadow. Suff 2K 29
Shippon. Oxon 4E 18
Shipston-on-Stour. Warw 7A 26
Shipton. Buck 1H 19
Shipton. Glos 2A 18
Shipton. N Yor 8E 44
Shipton. Shrp 2F 24
Shipton Bellinger. Hants 1C 10
Shipton Gorge. Dors 6D 8
Shipton Green. W Sus 6J 11
Shipton Moyne. Glos 5L 17
Shipton-on-Cherwell. Oxon 2E 18
Shiptonthorpe. E Yor 1E 40
Shipton-under-Wychwood. Oxon 2C 18
Shirburn. Oxon 4G 19
Shirdley Hill. Lanc 4B 38
Shire. Cumb 8B 50
Shirebrook. Derbs 3B 34
Shiregreen. S Yor 6M 39
Shirehampton. Bris 6H 17
Shiremoor. Tyne 4J 51
Shirenewton. Mon 4G 17
Shireoaks. Notts 7B 40
Shires Mill. Fife 1H 55
Shirkoak. Kent 4H 13
Shirland. Derbs 4L 33
Shirley. Derbs 5K 33
Shirley. Sotn 4E 10
Shirley. W Mid 4M 25
Shirleywich. Staf 7G 33
Shirl Heath. Here 6E 24
Shirrell Heath. Hants 4F 10
Shirwell. Devn 2G 7
Shiskine. N Ayr 7H 53
Shobdon. Here 5D 24
Shobnall. Staf 7K 33
Shobrooke. Devn 5K 7
Shoby. Leics 7C 34
Shocklach. Ches W 5B 32
Shoeburyness. S'end 5H 21
Sholden. Kent 8M 21
Sholing. Sotn 4E 10
Sholver. G Man 5H 39
Shoot Hill. Shrp 8B 32
Shop. Corn 4D 6 (nr. Bude)
Shop. Corn 2F 3 (nr. Padstow)
Shop. Devn 4E 6
Shopford. Cumb 4A 50
Shoreditch. G Lon 5B 20
Shoreditch. Som 3B 8
Shoregill. Cumb 3J 43
Shoreham. Kent 7D 20
Shoreham-by-Sea. W Sus 7A 12
Shoresdean. Nmbd 5J 57
Shoreswood. Nmbd 5J 57
Shore, The. Fife 4H 61
Shorncote. Glos 4A 18
Shorne. Kent 6E 20
Shorne Ridgeway. Kent 6E 20
Shortacombe. Devn 7G 7
Shortbridge. E Sus 5C 12
Shortgate. E Sus 6C 12
Short Green. Norf 3G 29
Shorthampton. Oxon 1D 18
Short Heath. Leics 8L 33
Short Heath. W Mid 2L 25 (nr. Erdington)
Short Heath. W Mid 1K 25 (nr. Wednesfield)
Shortlanesend. Corn 5F 3
Shorton. Torb 3K 5
Shortstown. Bed 7J 27
Shortwood. S Glo 6J 17
Shorwell. IOW 7E 10
Shoscombe. Bath 8K 17
Shotesham. Norf 2J 29
Shotgate. Essx 4F 20
Shotley. Suff 8J 29
Shotley Bridge. Dur 6F 50
Shotleyfield. Nmbd 6F 50
Shotley Gate. Suff 8J 29
Shottenden. Kent 8J 21
Shottermill. Surr 2J 11
Shottery. Warw 6M 25
Shotteswell. Warw 7C 26
Shottisham. Suff 7K 29
Shottle. Derbs 5L 33
Shotton. Dur 8K 51 (nr. Peterlee)
Shotton. Dur 1C 44 (nr. Sedgefield)
Shotton. Flin 3M 31
Shotton. Nmbd 4H 51 (nr. Morpeth)
Shotton. Nmbd 6H 57 (nr. Town Yetholm)
Shotton Colliery. Dur 7J 51
Shotts. N Lan 3G 55
Shotwick. Ches W 8B 38
Shouldham. Norf 1C 28
Shouldham Thorpe. Norf 1C 28
Shoulton. Worc 6J 25
Shrawardine. Shrp 8A 32
Shrawley. Worc 5J 25
Shreding Green. Buck 5L 19
Shrewley. Warw 5A 26
Shrewsbury. Shrp 8B 32 & 102
Shrewton. Wilts 1A 10
Shripney. W Sus 5K 11
Shrivenham. Oxon 5C 18
Shropham. Norf 2F 28
Shroton. Dors 4H 9
Shrub End. Essx 1H 21
Shucknall. Here 7F 24
Shudy Camps. Cambs 7C 28
Shulishadermor. High 7J 69
Shulista. High 4J 69
Shurdington. Glos 2M 17
Shurlock Row. Wind 6J 19
Shurrery. High 4F 76
Shurton. Som 1B 8
Shustoke. Warw 2A 26
Shute. Devn 6B 8 (nr. Axminster)
Shute. Devn 5K 7 (nr. Crediton)
Shutford. Oxon 7B 26
Shut Heath. Staf 7F 32
Shuthonger. Glos 8J 25
Shutlanehead. Staf 5F 32
Shutlanger. Nptn 7F 26
Shutt Green. Staf 1J 25
Shuttington. Warw 1A 26
Shuttlewood. Derbs 8A 40
Shuttleworth. G Man 4G 39
Siabost. W Isl 4C 74
Siabost bho Dheas. W Isl 4C 74
Siabost bho Thuath. W Isl 4C 74
Siadar. W Isl 3D 74
Siadar Uarach. W Isl 3D 74
Sibbaldbie. Dum 3J 49
Sibbertoft. Nptn 3E 26
Sibdon Carwood. Shrp 3E 24
Sibertswold. Kent 3L 13
Sibford Ferris. Oxon 8B 26
Sibford Gower. Oxon 8B 26
Sible Hedingham. Essx 8D 28
Sibsey. Linc 4K 35
Sibsey Fen Side. Linc 4K 35
Sibson. Cambs 2J 27
Sibson. Leics 1B 26
Sibster. High 4J 77
Sibthorpe. Notts 5D 34
Sibton. Suff 5K 29
Sicklesmere. Suff 5E 28
Sicklinghall. N Yor 1M 39
Sid. Devn 7A 8
Sidbury. Devn 6A 8
Sidbury. Shrp 3G 25
Sidcot. N Som 8G 17
Sidcup. G Lon 6C 20
Siddick. Cumb 8H 49
Siddington. Ches E 8G 39
Siddington. Glos 4A 18
Side of the Moor. G Man 4F 38
Sidestrand. Norf 4J 37
Sidford. Devn 6A 8
Sidlesham. W Sus 6J 11
Sidley. E Sus 7F 12
Sidlow. Surr 3A 12
Sidmouth. Devn 7A 8
Sigford. Devn 8J 7
Sigglesthorne. E Yor 1H 41
Sighthill. Edin 2K 55
Sigingstone. V Glam 6B 16
Signet. Oxon 2C 18
Silchester. Hants 7G 19
Sildinis. W Isl 7C 74
Sileby. Leics 8C 34
Silecroft. Cumb 5C 42
Silfield. Norf 2H 29
Silian. Cdgn 6H 23
Silkstone. S Yor 5L 39
Silkstone Common. S Yor 5L 39
Silksworth. Tyne 6J 51
Silk Willoughby. Linc 5G 35
Silloth. Cumb 6J 49
Sills. Nmbd 1D 50
Sillyearn. Mor 4F 72
Silpho. N Yor 4J 45
Silsden. W Yor 1J 39
Silsoe. C Beds 8J 27
Silverbank. Abers 4H 67
Silverburn. Midl 3L 55
Silverdale. Lanc 6F 42
Silverdale. Staf 5F 32
Silverdale Green. Lanc 6F 42
Silver End. Essx 2G 21
Silver End. W Mid 3K 25
Silvergate. Norf 5H 37
Silver Green. Norf 2J 29
Silverhillocks. Abers 3H 73
Silverley's Green. Suff 4J 29
Silverstone. Nptn 7E 26
Silverton. Devn 5L 7
Silverton. W Dun 2C 54
Silvington. Shrp 4G 25
Simm's Cross. Hal 7D 38
Simm's Lane End. Mers 6D 38
Simonburn. Nmbd 4D 50
Simonsbath. Som 2J 7
Simonstone. Lanc 2F 38
Simprim. Bord 5H 57
Simpson. Pemb 2C 14
Simpson Cross. Pemb 2C 14
Sinclairston. E Ayr 8C 54
Sinclairtown. Fife 6H 61
Sinderby. N Yor 5C 44
Sinderhope. Nmbd 6D 50
Sindlesham. Wok 7H 19
Sinfin. Derb 6L 33
Singleborough. Buck 8F 26
Singleton. Kent 3H 13
Singleton. Lanc 2B 38
Singleton. W Sus 4J 11
Singlewell. Kent 6E 20
Sinkhurst Green. Kent 3G 13
Sinnahard. Abers 2E 66
Sinnington. N Yor 5G 45
Sinton Green. Worc 5J 25
Sipson. G Lon 6L 19
Sirhowy. Blae 2D 16
Sisland. Norf 2K 29
Sissinghurst. Kent 4F 12
Siston. S Glo 6J 17
Sithney. Corn 7D 3
Sittingbourne. Kent 7H 21
Six Ashes. Staf 3H 25
Six Bells. Blae 3E 16
Six Hills. Leics 7C 34
Sixhills. Linc 7H 41
Six Mile Bottom. Cambs 6B 28
Sixpenny Handley. Dors 4J 9
Sizewell. Suff 5L 29
Skail. High 5C 76
Skaill. Orkn 6A 78
Skaills. Orkn 7D 78
Skares. E Ayr 8D 54
Skateraw. E Lot 2G 57
Skaw. Shet 5F 79
Skeabost. High 7J 69
Skeabrae. Orkn 5A 78
Skeeby. N Yor 3A 44
Skeffington. Leics 1F 26
Skeffling. E Yor 4K 41
Skegby. Notts 3A 34 (nr. Mansfield)
Skegby. Notts 8D 40 (nr. Tuxford)
Skegness. Linc 3M 35
Skelberry. Shet 10D 79 (nr. Boddam)
Skelberry. Shet 3D 79 (nr. Housetter)
Skelbo. High 2K 71
Skelbo Street. High 2K 71
Skelbrooke. S Yor 4B 40
Skeldyke. Linc 6K 35
Skelfhill. Bord 1M 49
Skellingthorpe. Linc 8F 40
Skellister. Shet 6E 79
Skellorn Green. Ches E 7H 39
Skellow. S Yor 4B 40
Skelmanthorpe. W Yor 4L 39
Skelmersdale. Lanc 5C 38
Skelmorlie. N Ayr 3K 53
Skelpick. High 4C 76
Skelton. Cumb 8M 49
Skelton. E Yor 3D 40
Skelton. N Yor 3M 43 (nr. Richmond)
Skelton. N Yor 7C 44 (nr. Ripon)
Skelton. Red C 2F 44
Skelton. York 8E 44
Skelton Green. Red C 2F 44
Skelwick. Orkn 3C 78
Skelwith Bridge. Cumb 3E 42
Skendleby. Linc 3L 35
Skendleby Psalter. Linc 8L 41
Skenfrith. Mon 1G 17
Skerne. E Yor 8K 45
Skeroblingarry. Arg 7F 52
Skerray. High 3B 76
Skerricha. High 4K 75
Skerries Airport. Shet 4G 79
Skerton. Lanc 7F 42
Sketchley. Leics 2C 26
Sketty. Swan 4L 15
Skewen. Neat 4M 15
Skewsby. N Yor 6F 44
Skeyton. Norf 5J 37
Skeyton Corner. Norf 5J 37
Skiall. High 3F 76
Skidbrooke. Linc 6L 41
Skidbrooke North End. Linc 6L 41
Skidby. E Yor 2G 41
Skilgate. Som 3L 7
Skillington. Linc 7E 34
Skinburness. Cumb 6J 49
Skinflats. Falk 1H 55
Skinidin. High 7G 69
Skinnet. High 3A 76
Skinningrove. Red C 1G 45
Skipness. Arg 4G 53
Skippool. Lanc 1B 38
Skiprigg. Cumb 7L 49
Skipsea. E Yor 8L 45
Skipsea Brough. E Yor 8L 45
Skipton. N Yor 8L 43
Skipton-on-Swale. N Yor 6C 44
Skipwith. N Yor 2C 40
Skirbeck. Linc 5K 35
Skirbeck Quarter. Linc 5K 35
Skirlaugh. E Yor 2H 41
Skirling. Bord 6J 55
Skirmett. Buck 4H 19
Skirpenbeck. E Yor 8G 45
Skirwith. Cumb 8B 50
Skirwith. N Yor 6J 43
Skirza. High 3J 77
Skitby. Cumb 5M 49
Skitham. Lanc 1C 38
Skittle Green. Buck 3H 19
Skroo. Shet 1G 78
Skulamus. High 1L 63
Skullomie. High 3B 76
Skyborry Green. Shrp 4C 24
Skye Green. Essx 1G 21
Skye of Curr. High 1M 65
Slack. W Yor 3H 39
Slackhall. Derbs 7J 39
Slack Head. Cumb 6F 42
Slackhead. Mor 3E 72
Slackholme End. Linc 8M 41
Slacks of Cairnbanno. Abers 5J 73
Slack, The. Dur 1A 44
Slad. Glos 3L 17
Slade. Swan 5J 15
Slade End. Oxon 4F 18
Slade Field. Cambs 3M 27
Slade Green. G Lon 6D 20
Slade Heath. Staf 1K 25
Slade Hooton. S Yor 7B 40
Sladesbridge. Corn 8B 6
Slade, The. W Ber 7F 18
Slaggyford. Nmbd 6B 50
Slaidburn. Lanc 8J 43
Slaid Hill. W Yor 1M 39
Slaithwaite. W Yor 4J 39
Slaley. Derbs 4K 33
Slaley. Nmbd 6E 50
Slamannan. Falk 2G 55
Slapton. Buck 1K 19
Slapton. Devn 5K 5
Slapton. Nptn 7E 26
Slattocks. G Man 5G 39
Slaugham. W Sus 5A 12
Slaughterbridge. Corn 7C 6
Slaughterford. Wilts 6L 17
Slawston. Leics 2F 26
Sleaford. Hants 2J 11
Sleaford. Linc 5G 35
Sleagill. Cumb 2G 43
Sleap. Shrp 7B 32
Sledmere. E Yor 7J 45
Sleightholme. Dur 2L 43
Sleights. N Yor 3H 45
Slepe. Dors 6J 9
Slickly. High 3H 77
Sliddery. N Ayr 7H 53
Sligachan. High 1J 63
Slimbridge. Glos 3K 17
Slindon. Staf 6F 32
Slindon. W Sus 5K 11
Slinfold. W Sus 2M 11
Slingsby. N Yor 6F 44
Slip End. C Beds 2L 19
Slipton. Nptn 4H 27
Slitting Mill. Staf 8H 33
Slochd. High 1L 65
Slockavullin. Arg 6F 58
Sloley. Norf 5J 37
Sloncombe. Devn 7J 7
Sloothby. Linc 8L 41
Slough. Slo 5K 19
Slough Green. Som 3B 8
Slough Green. W Sus 5A 12
Sluggan. High 1L 65
Slyne. Lanc 7F 42
Smailholm. Bord 6F 56
Smallbridge. G Man 4H 39
Smallbrook. Devn 6K 7
Smallburgh. Norf 5K 37
Smallburn. E Ayr 7E 54
Smalldale. Derbs 8J 39
Small Dole. W Sus 6A 12
Smalley. Derbs 5A 34
Smallfield. Surr 3B 12
Small Heath. W Mid 3L 25
Smallholm. Dum 4J 49
Small Hythe. Kent 4G 13
Smallrice. Staf 6G 33
Smallridge. Devn 5C 8
Smallwood Hey. Lanc 1B 38
Smallworth. Norf 3G 29
Smannell. Hants 1D 10
Smardale. Cumb 3J 43
Smarden. Kent 3G 13
Smarden Bell. Kent 3G 13
Smart's Hill. Kent 3D 12
Smeatharpe. Devn 4B 8
Smeeth. Kent 4J 13
Smeeth, The. Norf 8M 35
Smeeton Westerby. Leics 2E 26
Smeircleit. W Isl 2B 62
Smerral. High 6G 77
Smestow. Staf 2J 25
Smethwick. W Mid 3L 25
Smirisary. High 6L 63
Smisby. Derbs 8L 33
Smitham Hill. Bath 8H 17
Smith End Green. Worc 6H 25
Smithfield. Cumb 5M 49
Smith Green. Lanc 8F 42
Smithies, The. Shrp 2G 25
Smithincott. Devn 4M 7
Smith's Green. Essx 1D 20
Smithstown. High 4M 69
Smithton. High 7K 71
Smithwood Green. Suff 6F 28
Smithy Bridge. G Man 4H 39
Smithy Green. Ches E 8F 38
Smithy Lane Ends. Lanc 4C 38
Smockington. Warw 3C 26
Smoogro. Orkn 7B 78
Smyth's Green. Essx 2H 21
Snaigow House. Per 1F 60
Snailbeach. Shrp 1D 24
Snailwell. Cambs 5C 28
Snainton. N Yor 5J 45
Snaith. E Yor 3C 40
Snape. N Yor 5B 44
Snape. Suff 6K 29
Snape Green. Lanc 4B 38
Snapper. Devn 2G 7
Snarestone. Leics 1B 26
Snarford. Linc 7G 41
Snargate. Kent 5H 13
Snave. Kent 5J 13
Sneachill. Worc 6K 25
Snead. Powy 2D 24
Snead Common. Worc 5H 25
Sneaton. N Yor 3H 45
Sneatonthorpe. N Yor 3J 45
Snelland. Linc 7G 41
Snelston. Derbs 5J 33
Snetterton. Norf 2F 28
Snettisham. Norf 4C 36
Snibston. Leics 8A 34
Sniseabhal. W Isl 8B 68
Snitter. Nmbd 1F 50
Snitterby. Linc 6F 40
Snitterfield. Warw 6A 26
Snitton. Shrp 4F 24
Snodhill. Here 7D 24
Snodland. Kent 7E 20
Snods Edge. Nmbd 6F 50
Snowdonia. Gwyn 6G 31
Snowshill. Glos 8L 25
Snow Street. Norf 3G 29
Snydale. W Yor 4A 40
Soake. Hants 4G 11
Soar. Carm 1L 15
Soar. Gwyn 6F 30
Soar. IOA 2C 30
Soar. Powy 8M 23
Soberton. Hants 4G 11
Soberton Heath. Hants 4G 11
Sockbridge. Cumb 1F 42
Sockburn. Darl 3C 44
Sodom. Den 2K 31
Sodom. Shet 5F 79
Soham. Cambs 4B 28
Soham Cotes. Cambs 4B 28
Solas. W Isl 4C 68
Soldon Cross. Devn 4E 6
Soldridge. Hants 2G 11
Solent Breezes. Hants 5F 10
Sole Street. Kent 7E 20 (nr. Meopham)
Sole Street. Kent 3J 13 (nr. Waltham)
Solihull. W Mid 4M 25
Sollers Dilwyn. Here 6E 24
Sollers Hope. Here 8G 25
Sollom. Lanc 4C 38
Solva. Pemb 1B 14
Somerby. Leics 8D 34
Somerby. Linc 5G 41
Somercotes. Derbs 4A 34
Somerford. Dors 6B 10
Somerford. Staf 1J 25
Somerford Keynes. Glos 4A 18
Somerley. W Sus 6J 11
Somerleyton. Suff 2L 29
Somersal Herbert. Derbs 6J 33
Somersby. Linc 8K 41
Somersham. Cambs 4M 27
Somersham. Suff 7G 29
Somerton. Oxon 1E 18
Somerton. Som 3D 8
Somerton. Suff 6E 28
Sompting. W Sus 5M 11
Sonning. Wok 6H 19
Sonning Common. Oxon 5H 19
Sonning Eye. Oxon 6H 19
Sookholme. Notts 3B 34
Sopley. Hants 6B 10
Sopworth. Wilts 5L 17
Sorbie. Dum 7B 48
Sordale. High 3G 77
Sorisdale. Arg 7G 63
Sorn. E Ayr 7D 54
Sornhill. E Ayr 6D 54
Sortat. High 3H 77
Sotby. Linc 8J 41
Sots Hole. Linc 3H 35
Sotterley. Suff 3L 29
Soudley. Shrp 2E 24 (nr. Church Stretton)
Soudley. Shrp 7E 32 (nr. Market Drayton)
Soughton. Flin 3M 31
Soulbury. Buck 1J 19
Soulby. Cumb 2J 43 (nr. Appleby)
Soulby. Cumb 1F 42 (nr. Penrith)
Souldern. Oxon 8D 26
Souldrop. Bed 5H 27
Sound. Ches E 5D 32
Sound. Shet 7E 79 (nr. Lerwick)
Sound. Shet 6D 79 (nr. Tresta)
Soundwell. Bris 6J 17
Sourhope. Bord 7H 57
Sourin. Orkn 4C 78
Sour Nook. Cumb 7L 49
Sourton. Devn 6G 7
Soutergate. Cumb 5D 42
South Acre. Norf 6E 36
Southall. G Lon 6M 19
South Allington. Devn 6J 5
South Alloa. Falk 6D 60
Southam. Glos 1M 17
Southam. Warw 5C 26
South Ambersham. W Sus 3K 11
Southampton. Sotn 4E 10 & 102
Southampton International Airport. Hants 4E 10
Southannan. N Ayr 4A 54
South Anston. S Yor 7B 40
South Ascot. Wind 7K 19
South Baddesley. Hants 6D 10
South Balfern. Dum 6B 48
South Ballachulish. High 8C 64
South Bank. Red C 1E 44
South Barrow. Som 3F 8
South Benfleet. Essx 5F 20
South Bents. Tyne 5K 51
South Bersted. W Sus 5K 11
Southborough. Kent 3D 12
Southbourne. Bour 6B 10
Southbourne. W Sus 5H 11
South Bowood. Dors 6D 8
South Brent. Devn 3J 5
South Brewham. Som 2G 9
South Broomage. Falk 1G 55
South Broomhill. Nmbd 1H 51
Southburgh. Norf 1F 28
South Burlingham. Norf 1K 29
Southburn. E Yor 8J 45
South Cadbury. Som 3F 8
South Carlton. Linc 8F 40
South Cave. E Yor 2F 40
South Cerney. Glos 4A 18
South Chard. Som 5C 8
South Charlton. Nmbd 7L 57
South Cheriton. Som 3F 8
South Church. Dur 1B 44
Southchurch. S'end 5H 21
South Cleatlam. Dur 2A 44
South Cliffe. E Yor 2E 40
South Clifton. Notts 8E 40
South Clunes. High 7H 71
South Cockerington. Linc 7K 41
South Common. Devn 5C 8
South Common. E Sus 6B 12
South Cornelly. B'end 5A 16
Southcott. Corn 4F 6 (nr. Great Torrington)
Southcott. Devn 6G 7 (nr. Okehampton)
Southcott. Wilts 8B 18
Southcourt. Buck 2J 19
South Cove. Suff 3L 29
South Creagan. Arg 1G 59
South Creake. Norf 4E 36
South Crosland. W Yor 6K 39
South Croxton. Leics 8C 34
South Dalton. E Yor 1F 40
South Darenth. Kent 7D 20
Southdean. Bord 1B 50
Southdown. Bath 7K 17
South Downs. W Sus 7A 12
South Duffield. N Yor 2C 40
Southease. E Sus 7C 12
South Elkington. Linc 7J 41
South Elmsall. W Yor 4A 40
Southend. Arg 8E 52
South End. Cumb 7D 42
Southend. Glos 4K 17
South End. N Lin 3H 41
South End. W Ber 6F 18
Southend (London) Airport. Essx 5G 21
Southend-on-Sea. S'end 5G 21
Southerfield. Cumb 7J 49
Southerhouse. Shet 8D 79
Southerly. Devn 7G 7
Southernden. Kent 3G 13
Southerndown. V Glam 6A 16
Southerness. Dum 6G 49
South Erradale. High 4M 69
Southerton. Devn 6M 7
Southery. Norf 2C 28
Southey Green. Essx 8D 28
South Fambridge. Essx 4G 21
South Fawley. W Ber 5D 18
South Feorline. N Ayr 7H 53
South Ferriby. N Lin 3F 40
South Field. E Yor 3G 41
Southfleet. Kent 6E 20
South Garvan. High 6B 64
Southgate. Cdgn 3H 23
Southgate. G Lon 4B 20
Southgate. Norf 5H 37 (nr. Aylsham)
Southgate. Norf 4E 36 (nr. Fakenham)
Southgate. Swan 5K 15
South Gluss. Shet 4D 79
South Godstone. Surr 3B 12
South Gorley. Hants 4B 10
South Green. Essx 4E 20 (nr. Billericay)
South Green. Essx 2J 21 (nr. Colchester)
South Green. Kent 7G 21
South Hanningfield. Essx 4F 20
South Harting. W Sus 4H 11
South Hayling. Hants 6H 11
South Hazelrigg. Nmbd 6K 57
South Heath. Buck 3K 19
South Heath. Essx 2K 21
South Heighton. E Sus 7C 12
South Hetton. Dur 7J 51
South Hiendley. W Yor 4M 39
South Hill. Corn 8E 6
South Hill. Som 3D 8
South Hinksey. Oxon 3F 18
South Hole. Devn 3D 6
South Holme. N Yor 6G 45
South Holmwood. Surr 1M 11
South Hornchurch. G Lon 5D 20
South Huish. Devn 5H 5
South Hykeham. Linc 3F 34
South Hylton. Tyne 6J 51
Southill. C Beds 7K 27
Southington. Hants 1F 10
South Kelsey. Linc 6G 41
South Kessock. High 7J 71
South Killingholme. N Lin 4J 41
South Kilvington. N Yor 5D 44
South Kilworth. Leics 3E 26
South Kirkby. W Yor 4A 40
South Kirkton. Abers 3H 67
South Knighton. Devn 8K 7
South Kyme. Linc 5H 35
South Lancing. W Sus 5M 11
South Ledaig. Arg 2G 59
Southleigh. Devn 6B 8
South Leigh. Oxon 3D 18
South Leverton. Notts 7D 40
South Littleton. Worc 7L 25
South Lopham. Norf 3G 29
South Luffenham. Rut 1H 27
South Malling. E Sus 6C 12
South Marston. Swin 5B 18
South Middleton. Nmbd 7K 57
South Milford. N Yor 2A 40
South Milton. Devn 5J 5
South Mimms. Herts 3A 20
Southminster. Essx 4H 21
South Molton. Devn 3J 7
South Moor. Dur 6G 51
Southmoor. Oxon 4D 18
South Moreton. Oxon 5F 18
South Mundham. W Sus 5J 11
South Muskham. Notts 4D 34
South Newbald. E Yor 2F 40
South Newington. Oxon 8C 26
South Newsham. Nmbd 4J 51
South Newton. N Ayr 4H 53
South Newton. Wilts 2A 10
South Normanton. Derbs 4B 34
South Norwood. G Lon 7B 20
South Nutfield. Surr 3B 12
South Ockendon. Thur 5D 20
Southoe. Cambs 5K 27
Southolt. Suff 5H 29
South Ormsby. Linc 8K 41
Southorpe. Pet 1J 27
South Otterington. N Yor 5C 44
South Owersby. Linc 6G 41
Southowram. W Yor 3K 39
South Oxhey. Herts 4M 19
South Perrott. Dors 5D 8
South Petherton. Som 4D 8
South Petherwin. Corn 7E 6
South Pickenham. Norf 1E 28
South Pool. Devn 5J 5
South Poorton. Dors 6E 8
South Port. Arg 3H 59
Southport. Mers 4B 38
Southpunds. Shet 10E 79
South Queensferry. Edin 2K 55
South Radworthy. Devn 2J 7
South Rauceby. Linc 5G 35
South Raynham. Norf 5E 36
Southrepps. Norf 4J 37
South Reston. Linc 7L 41
Southrey. Linc 3H 35
Southrop. Glos 3B 18
Southrope. Hants 1G 11
South Runcton. Norf 1C 28
South Scarle. Notts 3E 34
Southsea. Port 6G 11
South Shields. Tyne 5J 51
South Shore. Bkpl 2B 38
Southside. Orkn 5D 78
South Somercotes. Linc 6L 41
South Stainley. N Yor 7C 44
South Stainmore. Cumb 2K 43
South Stifford. Thur 6D 20
South Stoke. Bath 7K 17
South Stoke. Oxon 5F 18
South Stoke. W Sus 4L 11
South Street. E Sus 6B 12
South Street. Kent 8J 21 (nr. Faversham)
South Street. Kent 7H 21 (nr. Whitstable)
South Tawton. Devn 6H 7
South Thoresby. Linc 8L 41
South Tidworth. Wilts 1C 10
South Town. Devn 7L 7
South Town. Hants 2G 11
Southtown. Norf 1M 29
Southtown. Orkn 8C 78
South View. Shet 7D 79
Southwaite. Cumb 7M 49
South Walsham. Norf 6K 37
South Warnborough. Hants 1H 11
Southwater. W Sus 3M 11
Southwater Street. W Sus 3M 11
Southway. Som 1E 8
South Weald. Essx 4D 20
South Weirs. Hants 5C 10
Southwell. Dors 8F 8
Southwell. Notts 4C 34
South Weston. Oxon 4H 19
South Wheatley. Corn 6D 6
South Wheatley. Notts 7D 40
Southwick. Hants 5G 11
Southwick. Nptn 2J 27
Southwick. Tyne 6J 51
Southwick. W Sus 7A 12
Southwick. Wilts 8L 17
South Widcombe. Bath 8H 17
South Wigston. Leics 2D 26
South Willingham. Linc 7H 41
South Wingfield. Derbs 4L 33
South Witham. Linc 8F 34
Southwold. Suff 4M 29
South Wonston. Hants 2E 10
Southwood. Norf 1K 29
Southwood. Som 2E 8
South Woodham Ferrers. Essx 4G 21
South Wootton. Norf 5C 36
South Wraxall. Wilts 7L 17
South Zeal. Devn 6H 7
Soval Lodge. W Isl 6D 74
Sowerby. N Yor 5D 44
Sowerby. W Yor 3J 39
Sowerby Bridge. W Yor 3J 39
Sowerby Row. Cumb 7L 49
Sower Carr. Lanc 1B 38
Sowley Green. Suff 6D 28
Sowood. W Yor 4J 39
Sowton. Devn 6L 7
Soyal. High 2H 71
Soyland Town. W Yor 3J 39
Spacey Houses. N Yor 8C 44
Spa Common. Norf 4J 37
Spalding. Linc 7J 35
Spaldington. E Yor 2D 40
Spaldwick. Cambs 4K 27
Spalford. Notts 3E 34
Spanby. Linc 6G 35
Sparham. Norf 6G 37
Sparhamhill. Norf 6G 37
Spark Bridge. Cumb 5E 42
Sparket. Cumb 1F 42
Sparkford. Som 3F 8
Sparkwell. Devn 4G 5
Sparrow Green. Norf 6F 36
Sparrowpit. Derbs 7J 39
Sparrow's Green. E Sus 4E 12
Sparsholt. Hants 2E 10
Sparsholt. Oxon 5D 18
Spartylea. Nmbd 7D 50
Spath. Staf 6H 33
Spaunton. N Yor 5G 45
Spaxton. Som 2B 8
Spean Bridge. High 5E 64
Spear Hill. W Sus 4M 11
Speen. Buck 4J 19
Speen. W Ber 7E 18
Speeton. N Yor 6L 45
Speke. Mers 7C 38
Speldhurst. Kent 3D 12
Spellbrook. Herts 2C 20
Spelsbury. Oxon 1D 18
Spencers Wood. Wok 7H 19
Spennithorne. N Yor 5A 44
Spennymoor. Dur 8H 51
Spernall. Warw 5L 25
Spetchley. Worc 6J 25
Spetisbury. Dors 5J 9
Spexhall. Suff 3L 29
Speybank. High 3L 65
Spey Bay. Mor 3D 72
Speybridge. High 1A 66
Speyview. Mor 5C 72
Spilsby. Linc 3K 35
Spindlestone. Nmbd 6L 57
Spinkhill. Derbs 8A 40
Spinney Hills. Leic 1E 26
Spinningdale. High 3J 71
Spital. Mers 7B 38
Spitalhill. Derbs 5J 33
Spital in the Street. Linc 6F 40
Spithurst. E Sus 6C 12
Spittal. Dum 6A 48
Spittal. E Lot 2D 56
Spittal. High 4G 77
Spittal. Nmbd 4K 57
Spittal. Pemb 1D 14
Spittalfield. Per 1G 61
Spittal of Glenmuick. Abers 5D 66
Spittal of Glenshee. Per 6B 66
Spittal-on-Rule. Bord 8E 56
Spixworth. Norf 6J 37
Splatt. Corn 7D 6
Spofforth. N Yor 8C 44
Spondon. Derb 6A 34
Spon End. W Mid 4B 26
Spooner Row. Norf 2G 29
Sporle. Norf 6E 36
Spott. E Lot 2F 56
Spratton. Nptn 4F 26
Spreakley. Surr 1J 11
Spreyton. Devn 6J 7
Spridlington. Linc 7G 41
Springburn. Glas 3E 54
Springfield. Dum 5L 49
Springfield. Fife 6J 61
Springfield. High 5J 71
Springfield. W Mid 3L 25
Springhill. Staf 1K 25
Springholm. Dum 4F 48
Springside. N Ayr 6B 54
Springthorpe. Linc 7E 40
Spring Vale. IOW 6G 11
Spring Valley. IOM 6D 46
Springwell. Tyne 6H 51
Sproatley. E Yor 2H 41
Sproston Green. Ches W 3E 32
Sprotbrough. S Yor 5B 40
Sproughton. Suff 7H 29
Sprouston. Bord 6G 57
Sprowston. Norf 6J 37
Sproxton. Leics 7E 34
Sproxton. N Yor 5E 44
Sprunston. Cumb 7L 49
Spurstow. Ches E 4C 32
Squires Gate. Bkpl 2B 38
Sraid Ruadh. Arg 8A 62
Srannda. W Isl 3E 68
Sron an t-Sithein. High 7A 64
Sronphadruig Lodge. Per 6K 65
Sruth Mor. W Isl 5D 68
Stableford. Shrp 2H 25
Stackhouse. N Yor 7K 43
Stackpole. Pemb 4D 14
Stackpole Elidor. Pemb 4D 14
Stacksford. Norf 2G 29
Stacksteads. Lanc 3G 39
Staddiscombe. Plym 4G 5
Staddlethorpe. E Yor 3E 40
Staddon. Devn 5E 6
Staden. Derbs 8J 39
Stadhampton. Oxon 4G 19
Stadhlaigearraidh. W Isl 8B 68
Stafainn. High 5J 69
Staffield. Cumb 7A 50
Staffin. High 5J 69
Stafford. Staf 7G 33
Stafford Park. Telf 1H 25
Stagden Cross. Essx 2E 20
Stagsden. Bed 7H 27
Stag's Head. Devn 3H 7
Stainburn. Cumb 1B 42
Stainburn. N Yor 1L 39
Stainby. Linc 7F 34
Staincliffe. W Yor 3L 39
Staincross. S Yor 4M 39
Staindrop. Dur 1A 44

Staines-upon-Thames—Thetford

Staines-upon-Thames. Surr 6L 19
Stainfield. Linc 7G 35
(nr. Bourne)
Stainfield. Linc 8H 41
(nr. Lincoln)
Stainforth. N Yor 7K 43
Stainforth. S Yor 4C 40
Staining. Lanc 2B 38
Stainland. W Yor 4J 39
Stainsacre. N Yor 3J 45
Stainton. Cumb 6L 49
(nr. Carlisle)
Stainton. Cumb 5G 43
(nr. Kendal)
Stainton. Cumb 1F 42
(nr. Penrith)
Stainton. Dur 2M 43
Stainton. Midd 2D 44
Stainton. N Yor 4A 44
Stainton. S Yor 6B 40
Stainton by Langworth. Linc 8G 41
Staintondale. N Yor 4J 45
Stainton le Vale. Linc 6H 41
Stainton with Adgarley. Cumb 6D 42
Stair. Cumb 1D 42
Stair. E Ayr 7C 54
Stairhaven. Dum 6M 47
Staithes. N Yor 2G 45
Stakeford. Nmbd 3H 51
Stake Pool. Lanc 1C 38
Stakes. Hants 5G 11
Stalbridge. Dors 4G 9
Stalbridge Weston. Dors 4G 9
Stalham. Norf 5K 37
Stalham Green. Norf 5K 37
Stalisfield Green. Kent 8H 21
Stallen. Dors 4F 8
Stallingborough. NE Lin 4J 41
Stalling Busk. N Yor 5L 43
Stallington. Staf 6G 33
Stalmine. Lanc 1B 38
Stalybridge. G Man 6H 39
Stambourne. Essx 8D 28
Stamford. Linc 1J 27
Stamford. Nmbd 8M 57
Stamford Bridge. Ches W 3B 32
Stamford Bridge. E Yor 8G 45
Stamfordham. Nmbd 4F 50
Stamperland. E Ren 4D 54
Stanah. Lanc 1B 38
Stanborough. Herts 2A 20
Stanbridge. C Beds 1K 19
Stanbridge. Dors 5A 10
Stanbury. W Yor 2J 39
Stand. N Lan 3F 54
Standburn. Falk 2H 55
Standeford. Staf 1K 25
Standen. Kent 3G 13
Standen Street. Kent 4G 13
Standerwick. Som 8L 17
Standford. Hants 2J 11
Standford Bridge. Telf 7E 32
Standingstone. Cumb 7K 49
Standish. Glos 3L 17
Standish. G Man 4D 38
Standish Lower Ground. G Man 5D 38
Standlake. Oxon 3D 18
Standon. Hants 3E 10
Standon. Herts 1B 20
Standon. Staf 6F 32
Standon Green End. Herts 2B 20
Stane. N Lan 4G 55
Stanecastle. N Ayr 6B 54
Stanfield. Norf 5F 36
Stanford. C Beds 7K 27
Stanford. Kent 4K 13
Stanford Bishop. Here 6G 25
Stanford Bridge. Worc 5H 25
Stanford Dingley. W Ber 6F 18
Stanford in the Vale. Oxon 4D 18
Stanford-le-Hope. Thur 5E 20
Stanford on Avon. Nptn 4D 26
Stanford on Soar. Notts 7B 34
Stanford on Teme. Worc 5H 25
Stanford Rivers. Essx 3D 20
Stanfree. Derbs 8A 40
Stanghow. Red C 2F 44
Stanground. Pet 2L 27
Stanhoe. Norf 4E 36
Stanhope. Dur 8E 50
Stanhope. Bord 6K 55
Stanion. Nptn 3H 27
Stanley. Derbs 5A 34
Stanley. Dur 6G 51
Stanley. Per 2G 61
Stanley. Shrp 3H 25
Stanley. Staf 4G 33
Stanley. W Yor 3M 39
Stanley Common. Derbs 5A 34
Stanley Crook. Dur 8G 51
Stanley Hill. Here 7G 25
Stanlow. Ches W 8C 38
Stanmer. Brig 7B 12
Stanmore. G Lon 4M 19
Stanmore. Hants 3E 10
Stanmore. W Ber 6E 18
Stannersburn. Nmbd 3C 50
Stanningfield. Suff 6E 28
Stannington. Nmbd 4H 51
Stannington. S Yor 7M 39
Stansbatch. Here 5D 24
Stansfield. Suff 6D 28
Stanshope. Staf 4J 33
Stanstead. Suff 7E 28
Stanstead Abbotts. Herts 2B 20
Stansted. Kent 7E 20
Stansted (London) Airport. Essx 1D 20 & 105
Stansted Mountfitchet. Essx 1D 20
Stanthorne. Ches W 3D 32
Stanton. Derbs 8K 33
Stanton. Glos 8L 25
Stanton. Nmbd 2G 51
Stanton. Staf 5J 33
Stanton. Suff 4F 28
Stanton by Bridge. Derbs 7L 33
Stanton by Dale. Derbs 6A 34
Stanton Chare. Suff 4F 28
Stanton Drew. Bath 7H 17
Stanton Fitzwarren. Swin 4B 18
Stanton Harcourt. Oxon 3E 18
Stanton Hill. Notts 3A 34
Stanton in Peak. Derbs 3K 33
Stanton Lacy. Shrp 4E 24
Stanton Long. Shrp 2F 24
Stanton-on-the-Wolds. Notts 6C 34
Stanton Prior. Bath 7J 17
Stanton St Bernard. Wilts 7A 18
Stanton St John. Oxon 3F 18
Stanton St Quintin. Wilts 6M 17
Stanton Street. Suff 5F 28
Stanton under Bardon. Leics 8A 34
Stanton upon Hine Heath. Shrp 7C 32
Stanton Wick. Bath 7J 17
Stanwardine in the Fields. Shrp 7B 32
Stanwardine in the Wood. Shrp 7B 32
Stanway. Essx 1H 21
Stanway. Glos 8L 25
Stanwell. Surr 6L 19
Stanwell Green. Suff 4H 29
Stanwell Moor. Surr 6L 19
Stanwick. Nptn 4H 27
Stanydale. Shet 6C 79
Staoinebrig. W Isl 8B 68
Stape. N Yor 4G 45
Stapehill. Dors 5A 10
Stapeley. Ches E 5D 32
Stapenhill. Staf 7K 33
Staple. Kent 8L 21
Staple Cross. Devn 3M 7
Staplecross. E Sus 5F 12
Staplefield. W Sus 5A 12
Staple Fitzpaine. Som 4B 8
Stapleford. Cambs 6A 28
Stapleford. Herts 2B 20
Stapleford. Leics 8E 34
Stapleford. Linc 4E 34
Stapleford. Notts 6A 34
Stapleford. Wilts 2A 10
Stapleford Abbotts. Essx 4D 20
Stapleford Tawney. Essx 4D 20
Staplegrove. Som 3B 8
Staplehay. Som 3B 8
Staple Hill. S Glo 6J 17
Staplehurst. Kent 3F 12
Staplers. IOW 7F 10
Stapleton. Bris 6J 17
Stapleton. Cumb 4A 50
Stapleton. Here 5D 24
Stapleton. Leics 2C 26
Stapleton. N Yor 2B 44
Stapleton. Shrp 1E 24
Stapleton. Som 3D 8
Stapley. Som 4A 8
Staploe. Bed 5K 27
Staplow. Here 7G 25
Star. Fife 5J 61
Star. Pemb 8E 22
Starbeck. N Yor 8C 44
Starbotton. N Yor 6L 43
Starcross. Devn 7L 7
Stareton. Warw 4B 26
Starkholmes. Derbs 4L 33
Starling. G Man 4F 38
Starling's Green. Essx 8A 28
Starston. Norf 3J 29
Start. Devn 5K 5
Startforth. Dur 2M 43
Start Hill. Essx 1D 20
Startley. Wilts 5M 17
Stathe. Som 3C 8
Stathern. Leics 6D 34
Station Town. Dur 8K 51
Staughton Green. Cambs 5K 27
Staughton Highway. Cambs 5K 27
Staunton. Glos 1K 17
(nr. Cheltenham)
Staunton. Glos 2H 17
(nr. Monmouth)
Staunton in the Vale. Notts 5E 34
Staunton on Arrow. Here 5D 24
Staunton on Wye. Here 7D 24
Staveley. Cumb 4F 42
Staveley. Derbs 8A 40
Staveley. N Yor 7C 44
Staveley-in-Cartmel. Cumb 5E 42
Staverton. Devn 3J 5
Staverton. Glos 1L 17
Staverton. Nptn 5D 26
Staverton. Wilts 7L 17
Stawell. Som 2C 8
Stawley. Som 3M 7
Staxigoe. High 4J 77
Staxton. N Yor 6K 45
Staylittle. Powy 2L 23
Staynall. Lanc 1B 38
Staythorpe. Notts 4D 34
Stean. N Yor 6M 43
Stearsby. N Yor 6F 44
Steart. Som 1B 8
Stebbing. Essx 1E 20
Stebbing Green. Essx 1E 20
Stedham. W Sus 3J 11
Steel. Nmbd 6E 50
Steel Cross. E Sus 4D 12
Steelend. Fife 6F 60
Steele Road. Bord 2A 50
Steel Heath. Shrp 6C 32
Steen's Bridge. Here 6F 24
Steep. Hants 3H 11
Steep Lane. W Yor 3J 39
Steeple. Dors 7J 9
Steeple. Essx 3H 21
Steeple Ashton. Wilts 8M 17
Steeple Aston. Oxon 1E 18
Steeple Barton. Oxon 1E 18
Steeple Bumpstead. Essx 7C 28
Steeple Claydon. Buck 1G 19
Steeple Gidding. Cambs 3K 27
Steeple Langford. Wilts 2A 10
Steeple Morden. Cambs 7L 27
Steeton. W Yor 1J 39
Stein. High 6G 69
Steinmanhill. Abers 5H 73
Stelling Minnis. Kent 3K 13
Stembridge. Som 3D 8
Stemster. High 3G 77
(nr. Halkirk)
Stemster. High 3F 76
(nr. Westfield)
Stenalees. Corn 4B 4
Stenhill. Devn 4M 7
Stenhouse. Edin 2L 55
Stenhousemuir. Falk 1G 55
Stenigot. Linc 7J 41
Stenscholl. High 5J 69
Stenso. Orkn 5B 78
Stenson. Derbs 7L 33
Stenson Fields. Derbs 6L 33
Stenton. E Lot 2F 56
Stenwith. Linc 6E 34
Steòrnabhagh. W Isl 5E 74
Stepaside. Pemb 3F 14
Stepford. Dum 3F 48
Stepney. G Lon 5B 20
Steppingley. C Beds 8J 27
Stepps. N Lan 3E 54
Sterndale Moor. Derbs 3J 33
Sternfield. Suff 5K 29
Stert. Wilts 8A 18
Stetchworth. Cambs 6C 28
Stevenage. Herts 1A 20
Stevenston. N Ayr 5A 54
Stevenstone. Devn 4G 7
Steventon. Hants 1F 10
Steventon. Oxon 4E 18
Steventon End. Cambs 7C 28
Stevington. Bed 6H 27
Stewartby. Bed 7J 27
Stewarton. Arg 8E 52
Stewarton. E Ayr 5C 54
Stewkley. Buck 1J 19
Stewkley Dean. Buck 1J 19
Stewley. Som 4C 8
Stewton. Linc 7K 41
Steyning. W Sus 4M 11
Steynton. Pemb 3D 14
Stibb. Corn 4D 6
Stibbard. Norf 5F 36
Stibb Cross. Devn 4F 6
Stibb Green. Wilts 7C 18
Stibbington. Cambs 2J 27
Stichill. Bord 6G 57
Sticker. Corn 4A 4
Stickford. Linc 3K 35
Sticklepath. Devn 6H 7
Sticklinch. Som 2E 8
Stickling Green. Essx 8A 28
Stickney. Linc 4K 35
Stiffkey. Norf 3F 36
Stifford's Bridge. Here 7H 25
Stileway. Som 1D 8
Stillingfleet. N Yor 1B 40
Stillington. N Yor 7E 44
Stillington. Stoc T 1C 44
Stilton. Cambs 3K 27
Stinchcombe. Glos 4K 17
Stinsford. Dors 6G 9
Stiperstones. Shrp 1D 24
Stirchley. Telf 1H 25
Stirchley. W Mid 3L 25
Stirling. Abers 5M 73
Stirling. Stir 6C 60 & 102
Stirton. N Yor 8L 43
Stisted. Essx 1F 20
Stitchcombe. Wilts 7C 18
Stithians. Corn 6E 3
Stittenham. High 4J 71
Stivichall. W Mid 4B 26
Stixwould. Linc 3H 35
Stoak. Ches W 8C 38
Stobo. Bord 6K 55
Stobo Castle. Bord 6K 55
Stoborough. Dors 7J 9
Stoborough Green. Dors 7J 9
Stobs Castle. Bord 1A 50
Stobswood. Nmbd 2H 51
Stock. Essx 4E 20
Stockbridge. Hants 2D 10
Stockbridge. W Yor 1J 39
Stockbury. Kent 7G 21
Stockcross. W Ber 7E 18
Stockdalewath. Cumb 7L 49
Stocker's Head. Kent 8H 21
Stockerston. Leics 2G 27
Stock Green. Worc 6K 25
Stocking. Here 8G 25
Stockingford. Warw 2B 26
Stocking Green. Essx 8B 28
Stocking Pelham. Herts 1C 20
Stockland. Devn 5B 8
Stockland Bristol. Som 1B 8
Stockleigh English. Devn 5K 7
Stockleigh Pomeroy. Devn 5K 7
Stockley. Wilts 7A 18
Stocklinch. Som 4C 8
Stockport. G Man 7H 39
Stocksbridge. S Yor 6L 39
Stocksfield. Nmbd 5F 50
Stocks, The. Kent 5H 13
Stockstreet. Essx 1G 21
Stockton. Here 5F 24
Stockton. Norf 2K 29
Stockton. Shrp 2H 25
(nr. Bridgnorth)
Stockton. Shrp 1C 24
(nr. Chirbury)
Stockton. Telf 8E 32
Stockton. Warw 5C 26
Stockton. Wilts 2J 9
Stockton Brook. Staf 4G 33
Stockton Cross. Here 5F 24
Stockton Heath. Warr 7E 38
Stockton-on-Tees. Stoc T 2D 44
Stockton on Teme. Worc 5H 25
Stockton-on-the-Forest. York 8F 44
Stockwell Heath. Staf 7H 33
Stockwood. Bris 7J 17
Stock Wood. Worc 6L 25
Stodmarsh. Kent 7L 21
Stody. Norf 4G 37
Stoer. High 7H 75
Stoford. Som 4E 8
Stoford. Wilts 2A 10
Stogumber. Som 2M 7
Stogursey. Som 1B 8
Stoke. Devn 3D 6
Stoke. Hants 8E 18
(nr. Andover)
Stoke. Hants 5H 11
(nr. South Hayling)
Stoke. Medw 6G 21
Stoke. W Mid 4B 26
Stoke Abbott. Dors 5D 8
Stoke Albany. Nptn 3G 27
Stoke Ash. Suff 4H 29
Stoke Bardolph. Notts 5C 34
Stoke Bliss. Worc 5G 25
Stoke Bruerne. Nptn 7F 26
Stoke by Clare. Suff 7D 28
Stoke-by-Nayland. Suff 8F 28
Stoke Canon. Devn 6L 7
Stoke Charity. Hants 2E 10
Stoke Climsland. Corn 8E 6
Stoke Cross. Here 6G 25
Stoke D'Abernon. Surr 8M 19
Stoke Doyle. Nptn 3J 27
Stoke Dry. Rut 2G 27
Stoke Edith. Here 7G 25
Stoke Farthing. Wilts 3A 10
Stoke Ferry. Norf 2D 28
Stoke Fleming. Devn 5K 5
Stokeford. Dors 7H 9
Stoke Gabriel. Devn 4K 5
Stoke Gifford. S Glo 6J 17
Stoke Golding. Leics 2B 26
Stoke Goldington. Mil 7G 27
Stokeham. Notts 8D 40
Stoke Hammond. Buck 1J 19
Stoke Heath. Shrp 7D 32
Stoke Holy Cross. Norf 1J 29
Stokeinteignhead. Devn 8L 7
Stoke Lacy. Here 7G 25
Stoke Lyne. Oxon 1F 18
Stoke Mandeville. Buck 2J 19
Stokenchurch. Buck 4H 19
Stoke Newington. G Lon 5B 20
Stokenham. Devn 5K 5
Stoke on Tern. Shrp 7D 32
Stoke-on-Trent. Stoke 5F 32 & 102
Stoke Orchard. Glos 1M 17
Stoke Pero. Som 1K 7
Stoke Poges. Buck 5K 19
Stoke Prior. Here 6F 24
Stoke Prior. Worc 5K 25
Stoke Rivers. Devn 2H 7
Stoke Rochford. Linc 7F 34
Stoke Row. Oxon 5G 19
Stoke St Gregory. Som 3C 8
Stoke St Mary. Som 3B 8
Stoke St Michael. Som 1F 8
Stoke St Milborough. Shrp 3F 24
Stokesay. Shrp 3E 24
Stokesby. Norf 6L 37
Stokesley. N Yor 3E 44
Stoke sub Hamdon. Som 4D 8
Stoke Talmage. Oxon 4G 19
Stoke Town. Stoke 5F 32 & 102
Stoke Trister. Som 3G 9
Stoke Wake. Dors 5G 9
Stolford. Som 1B 8
Stondon Massey. Essx 3D 20
Stone. Buck 2H 19
Stone. Glos 4J 17
Stone. Kent 6D 20
Stone. Som 2E 8
Stone. Staf 6G 33
Stone. Worc 4J 25
Stonea. Cambs 2A 28
Stoneacton. Shrp 2F 24
Stone Allerton. Som 8G 17
Ston Easton. Som 8J 17
Stonebridge. N Som 8F 16
Stonebridge. Som 1G 9
Stonebridge. Surr 1M 11
Stone Bridge Corner. Pet 1L 27
Stonebroom. Derbs 4A 34
Stonebyres. S Lan 5G 55
Stone Chair. W Yor 3K 39
Stone Cross. E Sus 7E 12
Stone Cross. Kent 4D 12
Stone-edge-Batch. N Som 6G 17
Stoneferry. Hull 2G 41
Stonefield. Arg 2G 59
Stonefield. S Lan 4E 54
Stonegate. E Sus 5E 12
Stonegate. N Yor 3G 45
Stonegrave. N Yor 6F 44
Stonehall. Worc 7J 25
Stonehaugh. Nmbd 4C 50
Stonehaven. Abers 5J 67
Stone Heath. Staf 6G 33
Stone Hill. Kent 4J 13
Stone House. Cumb 5J 43
Stonehouse. Glos 3L 17
Stonehouse. Nmbd 6B 50
Stonehouse. S Lan 5F 54
Stone in Oxney. Kent 5H 13
Stoneleigh. Warw 4B 26
Stoneley Green. Ches E 4D 32
Stonely. Cambs 5K 27
Stonepits. Worc 6L 25
Stoner Hill. Hants 3H 11
Stonesby. Leics 7E 34
Stonesfield. Oxon 2D 18
Stones Green. Essx 1K 21
Stone Street. Kent 8D 20
Stone Street. Suff 8F 28
(nr. Boxford)
Stone Street. Suff 3K 29
(nr. Halesworth)
Stonethwaite. Cumb 2D 42
Stoneyburn. W Lot 3H 55
Stoney Cross. Hants 4C 10
Stoneyford. Devn 5M 7
Stoneygate. Leic 1E 26
Stoneyhills. Essx 4H 21
Stoneykirk. Dum 6K 47
Stoney Middleton. Derbs 8L 39
Stoney Stanton. Leics 2C 26
Stoney Stoke. Som 2G 9
Stoney Stratton. Som 2F 8
Stoney Stretton. Shrp 1D 24
Stoneywood. Aber 2J 67
Stonham Aspal. Suff 6H 29
Stonnall. Staf 1L 25
Stonor. Oxon 5H 19
Stonton Wyville. Leics 2F 26
Stonybreck. Shet 1G 78
Stony Cross. Devn 3G 7
Stony Cross. Here 7H 25
(nr. Great Malvern)
Stony Cross. Here 5F 24
(nr. Leominster)
Stony Houghton. Derbs 3A 34
Stony Stratford. Mil 7F 26
Stoodleigh. Devn 2H 7
(nr. Barnstaple)
Stoodleigh. Devn 4L 7
(nr. Tiverton)
Stopham. W Sus 4L 11
Stopsley. Lutn 1M 19
Stoptide. Corn 8A 6
Storeton. Mers 7B 38
Stormontfield. Per 3G 61
Stornoway. W Isl 5E 74
Stornoway Airport. W Isl 5E 74
Storridge. Here 7H 25
Storrington. W Sus 4L 11
Storrs. Cumb 4E 42
Storth. Cumb 5F 42
Storwood. E Yor 1D 40
Stotfield. Mor 2C 72
Stotfold. C Beds 8L 27
Stottesdon. Shrp 3G 25
Stoughton. Leics 1E 26
Stoughton. Surr 8K 19
Stoughton. W Sus 4J 11
Stoul. High 4M 63
Stoulton. Worc 7K 25
Stourbridge. W Mid 3J 25
Stourpaine. Dors 5H 9
Stourport-on-Severn. Worc 4J 25
Stour Provost. Dors 3G 9
Stour Row. Dors 3H 9
Stourton. Staf 3J 25
Stourton. Warw 8A 26
Stourton. W Yor 2M 39
Stourton. Wilts 2G 9
Stourton Caundle. Dors 4G 9
Stove. Orkn 4E 78
Stove. Shet 9E 79
Stoven. Suff 3L 29
Stow. Linc 6G 35
(nr. Billingborough)
Stow. Linc 7E 40
(nr. Gainsborough)
Stow. Bord 5D 56
Stow Bardolph. Norf 1C 28
Stow Bedon. Norf 2F 28
Stowbridge. Norf 1C 28
Stow cum Quy. Cambs 5B 28
Stowe. Glos 3H 17
Stowe. Shrp 4D 24
Stowe. Staf 8J 33
Stowe-by-Chartley. Staf 7H 33
Stowell. Som 3F 8
Stowey. Bath 8H 17
Stowford. Devn 1H 7
(nr. Combe Martin)
Stowford. Devn 7M 7
(nr. Exmouth)
Stowford. Devn 7F 6
(nr. Tavistock)
Stowlangtoft. Suff 5F 28
Stow Longa. Cambs 4K 27
Stow Maries. Essx 4G 21
Stowmarket. Suff 6G 29
Stow-on-the-Wold. Glos 1B 18
Stowting. Kent 3K 13
Stowupland. Suff 6G 29
Straad. Arg 3J 53
Strachan. Abers 4G 67
Stradbroke. Suff 4J 29
Stradishall. Suff 6D 28
Stradsett. Norf 1C 28
Stragglethorpe. Linc 4F 34
Stragglethorpe. Notts 6C 34
Straid. S Ayr 2L 47
Straight Soley. Wilts 6D 18
Straiton. Edin 3L 55
Straiton. S Ayr 1A 48
Straloch. Per 7A 66
Stramshall. Staf 6H 33
Strang. IOM 6D 46
Strangford. Here 1H 17
Stranraer. Dum 5K 47
Strata Florida. Cdgn 5K 23
Stratfield Mortimer. W Ber 7G 19
Stratfield Saye. Hants 7G 19
Stratfield Turgis. Hants 8G 19
Stratford. Glos 8J 25
Stratford. G Lon 5B 20
Stratford St Andrew. Suff 5K 29
Stratford St Mary. Suff 8G 29
Stratford sub Castle. Wilts 2B 10
Stratford Tony. Wilts 3A 10
Stratford-upon-Avon. Warw 6A 26 & 102
Strath. High 4M 69
(nr. Gairloch)
Strath. High 4H 77
(nr. Wick)
Strathan. High 4B 64
(nr. Fort William)
Strathan. High 7H 75
(nr. Lochinver)
Strathan. High 3A 76
(nr. Tongue)
Strathan Skerray. High 3B 76
Strathaven. S Lan 5F 54
Strathblane. Stir 2D 54
Strathcanaird. High 1D 70
Strathcarron. High 7B 70
Strathcoil. Arg 2D 58
Strathdon. Abers 2D 66
Strathkinness. Fife 4K 61
Strathmashie House. High 4H 65
Strathmiglo. Fife 4H 61
Strathmore Lodge. High 5G 77
Strathpeffer. High 6G 71
Strathrannoch. High 4F 70
Strathtay. Per 8M 65
Strathvaich Lodge. High 4F 70
Strathwhillan. N Ayr 6J 53
Strathy. High 4J 71
(nr. Invergordon)
Strathy. High 3D 76
(nr. Melvich)
Strathyre. Stir 4A 60
Stratton. Corn 5D 6
Stratton. Dors 6F 8
Stratton. Glos 3A 18
Stratton Audley. Oxon 1G 19
Stratton-on-the-Fosse. Som 8J 17
Stratton St Margaret. Swin 5B 18
Stratton St Michael. Norf 2J 29
Stratton Strawless. Norf 5J 37
Stravithie. Fife 4L 61
Stream. Som 2M 7
Streat. E Sus 6B 12
Streatham. G Lon 6A 20
Streatley. C Beds 1L 19
Streatley. W Ber 5F 18
Street. Corn 6D 6
Street. Lanc 8G 43
Street. N Yor 3G 45
Street. Som 5C 8
(nr. Chard)
Street. Som 2D 8
(nr. Glastonbury)
Street Ash. Som 4B 8
Street Dinas. Shrp 6A 32
Street End. Kent 8K 21
Street End. W Sus 6J 11
Street Gate. Tyne 6H 51
Streethay. Staf 8J 33
Streethouse. W Yor 4M 39
Streetlam. N Yor 4C 44
Street Lane. Derbs 5L 33
Streetly. W Mid 2L 25
Streetly End. Cambs 7C 28
Street on the Fosse. Som 2F 8
Strefford. Shrp 3E 24
Strelley. Notts 5B 34
Strensall. York 7F 44
Strensall Camp. York 8F 44
Stretcholt. Som 1B 8
Strete. Devn 5K 5
Stretford. G Man 6G 39
Stretford. Here 6F 24
Strethall. Essx 8A 28
Stretham. Cambs 4B 28
Stretton. Ches W 4B 32
Stretton. Derbs 3L 33
Stretton. Rut 8F 34
Stretton. Staf 8F 32
(nr. Brewood)
Stretton. Staf 7K 33
(nr. Burton upon Trent)
Stretton. Warr 7E 38
Stretton en le Field. Leics 8L 33
Stretton Grandison. Here 7G 25
Stretton Heath. Shrp 8A 32
Stretton-on-Dunsmore. Warw 4C 26
Stretton-on-Fosse. Warw 8A 26
Stretton Sugwas. Here 7E 24
Stretton under Fosse. Warw 3C 26
Stretton Westwood. Shrp 2F 24
Strichen. Abers 4K 73
Strines. G Man 7H 39
Stringston. Som 1A 8
Strixton. Nptn 5H 27
Stroanfreggan. Dum 2D 48
Stroat. Glos 4H 17
Stromeferry. High 8A 70
Stromemore. High 8A 70
Stromness. Orkn 7A 78
Stronachie. Per 5F 60
Stronachlachar. Stir 4M 59
Stronchreggan. High 6C 64
Strone. Arg 1K 53
Strone. High 1H 65
(nr. Drumnadrochit)
Strone. High 3K 65
(nr. Kingussie)
Stronenaba. High 5E 64
Stronganess. Shet 1F 79
Stronmilchan. Arg 3J 59
Stronsay Airport. Orkn 5E 78
Strontian. High 7A 64
Strood. Kent 4G 13
Strood. Medw 7F 20
Strood Green. Surr 3A 12
Strood Green. W Sus 3L 11
(nr. Billingshurst)
Strood Green. W Sus 2M 11
(nr. Horsham)
Strothers Dale. Nmbd 6E 50
Stroud. Glos 3L 17
Stroud. Hants 3H 11
Stroud Green. Essx 4G 21
Stroxton. Linc 6F 34
Struan. High 8H 69
Struan. Per 7L 65
Struanmore. High 8H 69
Strubby. Linc 7L 41
Strugg's Hill. Linc 6J 35
Strumpshaw. Norf 1K 29
Strutherhill. S Lan 4F 54
Struy. High 8F 70
Stryd. IOA 1B 30
Stryt-issa. Wrex 5M 31
Stuartfield. Abers 5K 73
Stubbington. Hants 5F 10
Stubbins. Lanc 4F 38
Stubble Green. Cumb 4B 42
Stubb's Cross. Kent 4H 13
Stubbs Green. Norf 2K 29
Stubhampton. Dors 4J 9
Stubton. Linc 5E 34
Stubwood. Staf 6H 33
Stuckton. Hants 4B 10
Studham. C Beds 2L 19
Studland. Dors 7A 10
Studley. Warw 5L 25
Studley. Wilts 6M 17
Studley Roger. N Yor 7B 44
Stuntney. Cambs 4B 28
Stunts Green. E Sus 6E 12
Sturbridge. Staf 6F 32
Sturgate. Linc 7E 40
Sturmer. Essx 7C 28
Sturminster Marshall. Dors 5J 9
Sturminster Newton. Dors 4G 9
Sturry. Kent 7K 21
Sturton. N Lin 5F 40
Sturton by Stow. Linc 7E 40
Sturton le Steeple. Notts 7D 40
Stuston. Suff 4H 29
Stutton. N Yor 1A 40
Stutton. Suff 8H 29
Styal. Ches E 7G 39
Stydd. Lanc 2E 38
Styrrup. Notts 6C 40
Suainebost. W Isl 2F 74
Suardail. W Isl 5E 74
Succoth. Abers 6E 72
Succoth. Arg 5K 59
Suckley. Worc 6H 25
Suckley Knowl. Worc 6H 25
Sudborough. Nptn 3H 27
Sudbourne. Suff 6L 29
Sudbrook. Linc 5F 34
Sudbrook. Mon 5H 17
Sudbrooke. Linc 8G 41
Sudbury. Derbs 6J 33
Sudbury. Suff 7E 28
Sudgrove. Glos 3M 17
Suffield. Norf 4J 37
Suffield. N Yor 4J 45
Sugnall. Staf 6E 32
Sugwas Pool. Here 7E 24
Suisnish. High 8K 69
Sulaisiadar. W Isl 5F 74
Sùlaisiadar Mòr. High 7J 69
Sulby. IOM 4D 46
Sulgrave. Nptn 7D 26
Sulham. W Ber 6G 19
Sulhamstead. W Ber 7G 19
Sullington. W Sus 4L 11
Sullom. Shet 4D 79
Sully. V Glam 7D 16
Sumburgh. Shet 10E 79
Sumburgh Airport. Shet 10D 79
Summer Bridge. N Yor 7B 44
Summercourt. Corn 4F 3
Summergangs. Hull 2H 41
Summerhill. Aber 3K 67
Summerhill. Pemb 3F 14
Summer Hill. W Mid 2K 25
Summerhouse. Darl 2B 44
Summersdale. W Sus 5J 11
Summerseat. G Man 4F 38
Summit. G Man 4H 39
Sunbury. Surr 7M 19
Sunderland. Cumb 8J 49
Sunderland. Lanc 8F 42
Sunderland. Tyne 6J 51 & 102
Sunderland Bridge. Dur 8H 51
Sundon Park. Lutn 1L 19
Sundridge. Kent 8C 20
Sunk Island. E Yor 4J 41
Sunningdale. Wind 7K 19
Sunninghill. Wind 7K 19
Sunningwell. Oxon 3E 18
Sunniside. Dur 8G 51
Sunniside. Tyne 6H 51
Sunny Hill. Derb 6L 33
Sunnyhurst. Bkbn 3E 38
Sunnylaw. Stir 6C 60
Sunnymead. Oxon 3F 18
Sunnyside. S Yor 6A 40
Sunnyside. W Sus 4B 12
Sunton. Wilts 8C 18
Surbiton. G Lon 7M 19
Surby. IOM 6C 46
Surfleet. Linc 7J 35
Surfleet Seas End. Linc 7J 35
Surlingham. Norf 1K 29
Surrex. Essx 1G 21
Sustead. Norf 4H 37
Susworth. Linc 5E 40
Sutcombe. Devn 4E 6
Suton. Norf 2G 29
Sutors of Cromarty. High 5L 71
Sutterby. Linc 8K 41
Sutterton. Linc 6J 35
Sutterton Dowdyke. Linc 6J 35
Sutton. Buck 6L 19
Sutton. Cambs 4A 28
Sutton. C Beds 7L 27
Sutton. E Sus 8C 12
Sutton. G Lon 7A 20
Sutton. Kent 3M 13
Sutton. Norf 5K 37
Sutton. Notts 6D 34
Sutton. Oxon 3E 18
Sutton. Pemb 2D 14
Sutton. Pet 2J 27
Sutton. Shrp 3H 25
(nr. Bridgnorth)
Sutton. Shrp 6D 32
(nr. Market Drayton)
Sutton. Shrp 7A 32
(nr. Oswestry)
Sutton. Shrp 8C 32
(nr. Shrewsbury)
Sutton. Som 2F 8
Sutton. S Yor 4B 40
Sutton. Staf 7E 32
Sutton. Suff 7K 29
Sutton. W Sus 4K 11
Sutton. Worc 5G 25
Sutton Abinger. Surr 1M 11
Sutton at Hone. Kent 7D 20
Sutton Bassett. Nptn 2F 26
Sutton Benger. Wilts 6M 17
Sutton Bingham. Som 4E 8
Sutton Bonington. Notts 7B 34
Sutton Bridge. Linc 7L 35
Sutton Cheney. Leics 1C 26
Sutton Coldfield. W Mid 2M 25
Sutton Corner. Linc 7L 35
Sutton Courtenay. Oxon 4F 18
Sutton Crosses. Linc 7L 35
Sutton cum Lound. Notts 7C 40
Sutton Gault. Cambs 4A 28
Sutton Grange. N Yor 6B 44
Sutton Green. Surr 8L 19
Sutton Howgrave. N Yor 6C 44
Sutton in Ashfield. Notts 4A 34
Sutton-in-Craven. N Yor 1J 39
Sutton Ings. Hull 2H 41
Sutton in the Elms. Leics 2D 26
Sutton Lane Ends. Ches E 8H 39
Sutton Leach. Mers 6D 38
Sutton Maddock. Shrp 1H 25
Sutton Mallet. Som 2C 8
Sutton Mandeville. Wilts 3J 9
Sutton Montis. Som 3F 8
Sutton-on-Hull. Hull 2H 41
Sutton on Sea. Linc 7M 41
Sutton-on-the-Forest. N Yor 7E 44
Sutton on the Hill. Derbs 6K 33
Sutton on Trent. Notts 3D 34
Sutton Poyntz. Dors 7G 9
Sutton St Edmund. Linc 8K 35
Sutton St Edmund's Common. Linc 1M 27
Sutton St James. Linc 8K 35
Sutton St Michael. Here 7F 24
Sutton St Nicholas. Here 7F 24
Sutton Scarsdale. Derbs 3A 34
Sutton Scotney. Hants 2E 10
Sutton-under-Brailes. Warw 8B 26
Sutton-under-Whitestonecliffe. N Yor 5D 44
Sutton upon Derwent. E Yor 1D 40
Sutton Valence. Kent 3G 13
Sutton Veny. Wilts 1J 9
Sutton Waldron. Dors 4H 9
Sutton Weaver. Ches W 8D 38
Swaby. Linc 8K 41
Swadlincote. Derbs 8K 33
Swaffham. Norf 1E 28
Swaffham Bulbeck. Cambs 5B 28
Swaffham Prior. Cambs 5B 28
Swafield. Norf 4J 37
Swainby. N Yor 3D 44
Swainshill. Here 7E 24
Swainsthorpe. Norf 1J 29
Swainswick. Bath 7K 17
Swalcliffe. Oxon 8B 26
Swalecliffe. Kent 7K 21
Swallow. Linc 5H 41
Swallow Beck. Linc 3F 34
Swallowcliffe. Wilts 3J 9
Swallowfield. Wok 7H 19
Swallownest. S Yor 7A 40
Swampton. Hants 8E 18
Swanage. Dors 8A 10
Swanbister. Orkn 7B 78
Swanbourne. Buck 1J 19
Swanbridge. V Glam 7D 16
Swan Green. Ches W 8F 38
Swanland. E Yor 3F 40
Swanley. Kent 7D 20
Swanmore. Hants 4F 10
Swannington. Leics 8A 34
Swannington. Norf 6H 37
Swanpool. Linc 8F 40
Swanscombe. Kent 6D 20
Swansea. Swan 4L 15 & 103
Swansmoor. Staf 7H 33
Swan Street. Essx 1G 21
Swanton Abbott. Norf 5J 37
Swanton Morley. Norf 6G 37
Swanton Novers. Norf 4G 37
Swanton Street. Kent 8G 21
Swanwick. Derbs 4A 34
Swanwick. Hants 5F 10
Swanwick Green. Ches E 5C 32
Swarby. Linc 5G 35
Swardeston. Norf 1J 29
Swarister. Shet 3F 79
Swarkestone. Derbs 7L 33
Swarland. Nmbd 1G 51
Swarraton. Hants 2F 10
Swartha. W Yor 1J 39
Swarthmoor. Cumb 6D 42
Swaton. Linc 6H 35
Swavesey. Cambs 5M 27
Sway. Hants 6C 10
Swayfield. Linc 7F 34
Swaythling. Sotn 4E 10
Sweet Green. Worc 5G 25
Sweetham. Devn 6K 7
Sweetholme. Cumb 2G 43
Sweets. Corn 6C 6
Sweetshouse. Corn 3B 4
Swefling. Suff 5K 29
Swell. Som 3C 8
Swepstone. Leics 8L 33
Swerford. Oxon 8B 26
Swettenham. Ches E 3F 32
Swetton. N Yor 6A 44
Swffryd. Cphy 4E 16
Swiftsden. E Sus 5F 12
Swilland. Suff 6H 29
Swillington. W Yor 2M 39
Swimbridge. Devn 3H 7
Swimbridge Newland. Devn 2H 7
Swinbrook. Oxon 2C 18
Swincliffe. N Yor 8B 44
Swincliffe. W Yor 3L 39
Swinderby. Linc 3E 34
Swindon. Glos 1M 17
Swindon. Nmbd 2E 50
Swindon. Staf 2J 25
Swindon. Swin 5B 18 & 103
Swine. E Yor 2H 41
Swinefleet. E Yor 3D 40
Swineford. S Glo 7J 17
Swineshead. Bed 5J 27
Swineshead. Linc 5J 35
Swineshead Bridge. Linc 5J 35
Swiney. High 6H 77
Swinford. Leics 4D 26
Swinford. Oxon 3E 18
Swingate. Notts 5B 34
Swingbrow. Cambs 3M 27
Swingfield Minnis. Kent 3L 13
Swingfield Street. Kent 3L 13
Swingleton Green. Suff 7F 28
Swinhill. S Lan 5F 54
Swinhoe. Nmbd 7M 57
Swinhope. Linc 6J 41
Swinister. Shet 3D 79
Swinithwaite. N Yor 5M 43
Swinmore Common. Here 7G 25
Swinscoe. Staf 5J 33
Swinside Hall. Bord 8G 57
Swinstead. Linc 7G 35
Swinton. G Man 5F 38
Swinton. N Yor 6G 45
(nr. Malton)
Swinton. N Yor 6B 44
(nr. Masham)
Swinton. Bord 5H 57
Swinton. S Yor 6A 40
Swithland. Leics 8B 34
Swordale. High 5H 71
Swordly. High 3C 76
Sworton Heath. Ches E 7E 38
Swyddffynnon. Cdgn 5J 23
Swynnerton. Staf 6F 32
Swyre. Dors 7E 8
Sycharth. Powy 7M 31
Sychdyn. Flin 3M 31
Sychnant. Powy 4M 23
Sychtyn. Powy 1M 23
Syde. Glos 2M 17
Sydenham. G Lon 6B 20
Sydenham. Oxon 3H 19
Sydenham. Som 2C 8
Sydenham Damerel. Devn 8F 6
Syderstone. Norf 4E 36
Sydling St Nicholas. Dors 6F 8
Sydmonton. Hants 8E 18
Sydney. Ches E 4E 32
Syerston. Notts 5D 34
Syke. G Man 4G 39
Sykehouse. S Yor 4C 40
Sykes. Lanc 8H 43
Syleham. Suff 4J 29
Sylen. Carm 3K 15
Sylfaen. Powy 1B 24
Symbister. Shet 5F 79
Symington. S Ayr 6B 54
Symington. S Lan 6H 55
Symondsbury. Dors 6D 8
Symonds Yat. Here 2H 17
Synod Inn. Cdgn 6G 23
Syre. High 5B 76
Syreford. Glos 1A 18
Syresham. Nptn 7E 26
Syston. Leics 8C 34
Syston. Linc 5F 34
Sytchampton. Worc 5J 25
Sywell. Nptn 5G 27

T

Tabost. W Isl 7D 74
(nr. Cearsiadar)
Tabost. W Isl 2F 74
(nr. Suainebost)
Tachbrook Mallory. Warw 5B 26
Tackley. Oxon 1E 18
Tacleit. W Isl 5B 74
Tacolneston. Norf 2H 29
Tadcaster. N Yor 1A 40
Taddington. Derbs 8K 39
Taddington. Glos 8L 25
Taddiport. Devn 4F 6
Tadley. Hants 7G 19
Tadlow. Cambs 7L 27
Tadmarton. Oxon 8B 26
Tadwick. Bath 6K 17
Tadworth. Surr 8A 20
Tafarnaubach. Blae 2D 16
Tafarn-y-bwlch. Pemb 8C 22
Tafarn-y-Gelyn. Den 3L 31
Taff's Well. Rhon 5D 16
Tafolwern. Powy 1L 23
Taibach. Neat 5M 15
Tai-bach. Powy 7L 31
Taigh a Ghearraidh. W Isl 4B 68
Taigh Bhuirgh. W Isl 2E 68
Tain. High 3K 71
(nr. Invergordon)
Tain. High 3H 77
(nr. Thurso)
Tai-Nant. Wrex 5M 31
Tai'n Lon. Gwyn 4D 30
Tairbeart. W Isl 2F 68
Tairgwaith. Neat 2M 15
Takeley. Essx 1D 20
Takeley Street. Essx 1D 20
Talachddu. Powy 8A 24
Talacre. Flin 1L 31
Talardd. Gwyn 7H 31
Talaton. Devn 6M 7
Talbenny. Pemb 2C 14
Talbot Green. Rhon 5C 16
Taleford. Devn 6M 7
Talerddig. Powy 1M 23
Talgarreg. Cdgn 6G 23
Talgarth. Powy 8B 24
Talisker. High 8H 69
Talke. Staf 4F 32
Talkin. Cumb 6A 50
Talladale. High 4B 70
Talla Linnfoots. Bord 7K 55
Tallaminnock. S Ayr 2B 48
Tallarn Green. Wrex 5B 32
Tallentire. Cumb 8J 49
Talley. Carm 8J 23
Tallington. Linc 1J 27
Talmine. High 3A 76
Talog. Carm 1H 15
Talsarn. Carm 1M 15
Talsarn. Cdgn 6H 23
Talsarnau. Gwyn 6F 30
Talskiddy. Corn 3A 4
Talwrn. IOA 2D 30
Talwrn. Wrex 5M 31
Tal-y-bont. Cdgn 3J 23
Tal-y-Bont. Cnwy 3G 31
Tal-y-bont. Gwyn 2F 30
(nr. Bangor)
Tal-y-bont. Gwyn 7E 30
(nr. Barmouth)
Talybont-on-Usk. Powy 1D 16
Tal-y-cafn. Cnwy 2G 31
Tal-y-coed. Mon 2G 17
Tal-y-llyn. Gwyn 1K 23
Talyllyn. Powy 1D 16
Talysarn. Gwyn 4D 30
Tal-y-waenydd. Gwyn 5F 30
Talywain. Torf 3E 16
Tal-y-Wern. Powy 1L 23
Tamerton Foliot. Plym 3F 4
Tamworth. Staf 1A 26
Tamworth Green. Linc 5K 35
Tandlehill. Ren 3C 54
Tandridge. Surr 8B 20
Tanerdy. Carm 1J 15
Tanfield. Dur 6G 51
Tanfield Lea. Dur 6G 51
Tangasdal. W Isl 3A 62
Tang Hall. York 8F 44
Tangiers. Pemb 2D 14
Tangley. Hants 8D 18
Tangmere. W Sus 5K 11
Tangwick. Shet 4C 79
Tankerness. Orkn 7D 78
Tankersley. S Yor 6M 39
Tankerton. Kent 7K 21
Tan-lan. Cnwy 3G 31
Tan-lan. Gwyn 5F 30
Tannach. High 5J 77
Tannadice. Ang 8E 66
Tanner's Green. Worc 4L 25
Tannington. Suff 5J 29
Tannochside. N Lan 3F 54
Tan Office Green. Suff 6D 28
Tansley. Derbs 4L 33
Tansley Knoll. Derbs 3L 33
Tansor. Nptn 2J 27
Tantobie. Dur 6G 51
Tanton. N Yor 2E 44
Tanvats. Linc 3H 35
Tanworth-in-Arden. Warw 4M 25
Tan-y-bwlch. Gwyn 5F 30
Tan-y-fron. Cnwy 3J 31
Tanyfron. Wrex 4M 31
Tanygrisiau. Gwyn 5F 30
Tan-y-groes. Cdgn 7E 22
Tan-y-pistyll. Powy 7K 31
Tan-yr-allt. Den 1K 31
Taobh a Chaolais. W Isl 2B 62
Taobh a Deas Loch Aineort. W Isl 1B 62
Taobh a Ghlinne. W Isl 7D 74
Taobh a Tuath Loch Aineort. W Isl 1B 62
Taplow. Buck 5K 19
Tapton. Derbs 8M 39
Tarbert. Arg 1E 52
(on Jura)
Tarbert. Arg 3G 53
(on Kintyre)
Tarbert. W Isl 2F 68
Tarbet. Arg 5L 59
Tarbet. High 4M 63
(nr. Mallaig)
Tarbet. High 5J 75
(nr. Scourie)
Tarbock Green. Mers 7C 38
Tarbolton. S Ayr 7C 54
Tarbrax. S Lan 4J 55
Tardebigge. Worc 5L 25
Tarfside. Ang 6E 66
Tarland. Abers 3E 66
Tarleton. Lanc 3C 38
Tarlogie. High 3K 71
Tarlscough. Lanc 4C 38
Tarlton. Glos 4M 17
Tarnbrook. Lanc 8G 43
Tarnock. Som 8F 16
Tarns. Cumb 7J 49
Tarporley. Ches W 3C 32
Tarpots. Essx 5F 20
Tarr. Som 2A 8
Tarrant Crawford. Dors 5J 9
Tarrant Gunville. Dors 4J 9
Tarrant Hinton. Dors 4J 9
Tarrant Keyneston. Dors 5J 9
Tarrant Launceston. Dors 5J 9
Tarrant Monkton. Dors 5J 9
Tarrant Rawston. Dors 5J 9
Tarrant Rushton. Dors 5J 9
Tarrel. High 3L 71
Tarring Neville. E Sus 7C 12
Tarrington. Here 7G 25
Tarsappie. Per 3G 61
Tarscabhaig. High 3K 63
Tarskavaig. High 3K 63
Tarves. Abers 6J 73
Tarvie. High 6G 71
Tarvin. Ches W 3B 32
Tasburgh. Norf 2J 29
Tasley. Shrp 2G 25
Taston. Oxon 1D 18
Tatenhill. Staf 7K 33
Tathall End. Mil 7G 27
Tatham. Lanc 7H 43
Tathwell. Linc 7K 41
Tatling End. Buck 5L 19
Tatsfield. Surr 8C 20
Tattenhall. Ches W 4B 32
Tatterford. Norf 5E 36
Tattersett. Norf 4E 36
Tattershall. Linc 4J 35
Tattershall Bridge. Linc 4H 35
Tattershall Thorpe. Linc 4J 35
Tattingstone. Suff 8H 29
Tattingstone White Horse. Suff 8H 29
Tattle Bank. Warw 5M 25
Tatworth. Som 5C 8
Taunton. Som 3B 8 & 103
Taverham. Norf 6H 37
Taverners Green. Essx 2D 20
Tavernspite. Pemb 2F 14
Tavistock. Devn 8F 6
Tavool House. Arg 3B 58
Taw Green. Devn 6H 7
Tawstock. Devn 3G 7
Taxal. Derbs 7J 39
Tayinloan. Arg 5E 52
Taynish. Arg 1F 52
Taynton. Glos 1K 17
Taynton. Oxon 2C 18
Taynuilt. Arg 2H 59
Tayport. Fife 3K 61
Tay Road Bridge. Fife 3K 61
Tayvallich. Arg 1F 52
Tealby. Linc 6H 41
Tealing. Ang 2K 61
Teams. Tyne 5H 51
Teangue. High 3L 63
Teanna Mhachair. W Isl 5B 68
Tebay. Cumb 3H 43
Tebworth. C Beds 1K 19
Tedburn St Mary. Devn 6K 7
Teddington. Glos 8K 25
Teddington. G Lon 6M 19
Tedsmore. Shrp 7A 32
Tedstone Delamere. Here 6G 25
Tedstone Wafer. Here 6G 25
Teesport. Red C 1E 44
Teesside. Stoc T 1E 44
Teeton. Nptn 4E 26
Teffont Evias. Wilts 2J 9
Teffont Magna. Wilts 2J 9
Tegryn. Pemb 8E 22
Teigh. Rut 8E 34
Teigncombe. Devn 7H 7
Teigngrace. Devn 8K 7
Teignmouth. Devn 8L 7
Telford. Telf 8D 32
Telham. E Sus 6F 12
Tellisford. Som 8L 17
Telscombe. E Sus 7C 12
Telscombe Cliffs. E Sus 7B 12
Tempar. Per 8J 65
Templand. Dum 3H 49
Temple. Corn 8C 6
Temple. Glas 3D 54
Temple. Midl 4M 55
Temple Balsall. W Mid 4A 26
Temple Bar. Carm 2K 15
Temple Bar. Cdgn 6H 23
Temple Cloud. Bath 8J 17
Templecombe. Som 3G 9
Temple Ewell. Kent 3L 13
Temple Grafton. Warw 6M 25
Temple Guiting. Glos 1A 18
Templehall. Fife 6H 61
Temple Hirst. N Yor 3C 40
Temple Normanton. Derbs 3A 34
Temple Sowerby. Cumb 1H 43
Templeton. Devn 4K 7
Templeton. Pemb 2F 14
Templeton. W Ber 7D 18
Templetown. Dur 7G 51
Tempsford. C Beds 6K 27
Tenandry. Per 7M 65
Tenbury Wells. Worc 5F 24
Tenby. Pemb 3F 14
Tendring. Essx 1K 21
Tendring Green. Essx 1K 21
Tenga. Arg 1C 58
Ten Mile Bank. Norf 2C 28
Tenterden. Kent 4G 13
Terfyn. Cnwy 2J 31
Terhill. Som 2A 8
Terling. Essx 2F 20
Ternhill. Shrp 6D 32
Terregles. Dum 4G 49
Terrick. Buck 3J 19
Terrington. N Yor 6F 44
Terrington St Clement. Norf 7M 35
Terrington St John. Norf 8M 35
Terry's Green. Warw 4M 25
Teston. Kent 8F 20
Testwood. Hants 4D 10
Tetbury. Glos 4L 17
Tetbury Upton. Glos 4L 17
Tetchill. Shrp 6A 32
Tetcott. Devn 6E 6
Tetford. Linc 8K 41
Tetney. Linc 5K 41
Tetney Lock. Linc 5K 41
Tetsworth. Oxon 3G 19
Tettenhall. W Mid 2J 25
Teversal. Notts 3A 34
Teversham. Cambs 6A 28
Teviothead. Bord 1M 49
Tewel. Abers 5J 67
Tewin. Herts 2A 20
Tewkesbury. Glos 8J 25
Teynham. Kent 7H 21
Teynham Street. Kent 7H 21
Thackthwaite. Cumb 1F 42
Thakeham. W Sus 4M 11
Thame. Oxon 3H 19
Thames Ditton. Surr 7M 19
Thames Haven. Thur 5F 20
Thamesmead. G Lon 5C 20
Thamesport. Kent 6G 21
Thanington Without. Kent 8K 21
Thankerton. S Lan 6H 55
Tharston. Norf 2H 29
Thatcham. W Ber 7F 18
Thatto Heath. Mers 6D 38
Thaxted. Essx 8C 28
Theakston. N Yor 5C 44
Thealby. N Lin 4E 40
Theale. Som 1D 8
Theale. W Ber 6G 19
Thearne. E Yor 2G 41
Theberton. Suff 5L 29
Theddingworth. Leics 3E 26
Theddlethorpe All Saints. Linc 7L 41
Theddlethorpe St Helen. Linc 7L 41
Thelbridge Barton. Devn 4J 7
Thelnetham. Suff 4G 29
Thelveton. Norf 3H 29
Thelwall. Warr 7E 38
Themelthorpe. Norf 5G 37
Thenford. Nptn 7D 26
Therfield. Herts 8M 27
Thetford. Linc 8H 35
Thetford. Norf 3E 28

Thethwaite—Upper Neepaback

Thethwaite. Cumb 7L 49
Theydon Bois. Essx 4C 20
Thick Hollins. W Yor 4K 39
Thickwood. Wilts 6L 17
Thimbleby. Linc 8J 41
Thimbleby. N Yor 4D 44
Thingwall. Mers 7A 38
Thirlby. N Yor 5D 44
Thirlestane. Bord 5E 56
Thirn. N Yor 5B 44
Thirsk. N Yor 5D 44
Thirtleby. E Yor 2H 41
Thistleton. Lanc 2C 38
Thistleton. Rut 8F 34
Thistley Green. Suff 4C 28
Thixendale. N Yor 7H 45
Thockrington. Nmbd 4E 50
Tholomas Drove. Cambs 1A 28
Tholthorpe. N Yor 7D 44
Thomas Chapel. Pemb 3F 14
Thomas Close. Cumb 7M 49
Thomastown. Abers 5H 73
Thomastown. Rhon 5C 16
Thompson. Norf 2F 28
Thomshill. Mor 4C 72
Thong. Kent 6E 20
Thongsbridge. W Yor 5K 39
Thoralby. N Yor 5M 43
Thoresby. Notts 8C 40
Thoresway. Linc 6H 41
Thorganby. Linc 6J 41
Thorganby. N Yor 1C 40
Thorgill. N Yor 4G 45
Thorington. Suff 4L 29
Thorington Street. Suff 8G 29
Thorlby. N Yor 8L 43
Thorley. Herts 2C 20
Thorley Street. Herts 2C 20
Thorley Street. IOW 7D 10
Thormanby. N Yor 6D 44
Thorn. Powy 5C 24
Thornaby-on-Tees. Stoc T 2D 44
Thornage. Norf 4G 37
Thornborough. Buck 8F 26
Thornborough. N Yor 6B 44
Thornbury. Devn 5F 6
Thornbury. Here 6G 25
Thornbury. S Glo 5J 17
Thornby. Cumb 6K 49
Thornby. Nptn 4E 26
Thorncliffe. Staf 4H 33
Thorncombe. Dors 5C 8
Thorncombe Street. Surr 1K 11
Thorncote Green. C Beds 7K 27
Thorndon. Suff 5H 29
Thorndon Cross. Devn 6G 7
Thorne. S Yor 4C 40
Thornehillhead. Devn 4F 6
Thorner. W Yor 1M 39
Thorne St Margaret. Som 3M 7
Thorney. Notts 8E 40
Thorney. Pet 1L 27
Thorney. Som 3D 8
Thorney Hill. Hants 6B 10
Thorney Toll. Cambs 1M 27
Thornfalcon. Som 3B 8
Thornford. Dors 4F 8
Thorngrafton. Nmbd 5C 50
Thorngrove. Som 2C 8
Thorngumbald. E Yor 3J 41
Thornham. Norf 3D 36
Thornham Magna. Suff 4H 29
Thornham Parva. Suff 4H 29
Thornhaugh. Pet 1J 27
Thornhill. Cphy 5D 16
Thornhill. Cumb 3B 42
Thornhill. Derbs 7L 39
Thornhill. Dum 2F 48
Thornhill. Sotn 4E 10
Thornhill. Stir 6B 60
Thornhill. W Yor 4L 39
Thornhill Lees. W Yor 4L 39
Thornhills. W Yor 3K 39
Thornholme. E Yor 7L 45
Thornicombe. Dors 5H 9
Thornington. Nmbd 6H 57
Thornley. Dur 8J 51
(nr. Durham)
Thornley. Dur 8G 51
(nr. Tow Law)
Thornley Gate. Nmbd 6D 50
Thornliebank. E Ren 4D 54
Thornroan. Abers 6J 73
Thorns. Suff 6D 28
Thornsett. Derbs 7J 39
Thornthwaite. Cumb 1D 42
Thornthwaite. N Yor 8A 44
Thornton. Ang 1J 61
Thornton. Buck 8F 26
Thornton. E Yor 1D 40
Thornton. Fife 6H 61
Thornton. Lanc 1B 38
Thornton. Leics 1C 26
Thornton. Linc 3J 35
Thornton. Mers 5B 38
Thornton. Midd 2D 44
Thornton. Nmbd 5J 57
Thornton. Pemb 3D 14
Thornton. W Yor 2J 39
Thornton Curtis. N Lin 4G 41
Thorntonhall. S Lan 4D 54
Thornton Heath. G Lon 7B 20
Thornton Hough. Mers 7B 38
Thornton in Craven. N Yor 1H 39
Thornton in Lonsdale. N Yor 6H 43
Thornton-le-Beans. N Yor 4C 44
Thornton-le-Clay. N Yor 7F 44
Thornton-le-Dale. N Yor 5H 45
Thornton le Moor. Linc 6G 41
Thornton-le-Moor. N Yor 5C 44
Thornton-le-Moors. Ches W 8C 38
Thornton-le-Street. N Yor 5D 44
Thorntonloch. E Lot 2G 57
Thornton Rust. N Yor 5L 43
Thornton Steward. N Yor 5A 44
Thornton Watlass. N Yor 5B 44
Thornwood Common. Essx 3C 20
Thornythwaite. Cumb 1E 42
Thoroton. Notts 5D 34
Thorp Arch. W Yor 1A 40
Thorpe. Derbs 4J 33
Thorpe. E Yor 1F 40
Thorpe. Linc 7L 41
Thorpe. Norf 2L 29
Thorpe. N Yor 7M 43
Thorpe. Notts 5D 34
Thorpe. Surr 7L 19
Thorpe Abbotts. Norf 4H 29
Thorpe Acre. Leics 7B 34
Thorpe Arnold. Leics 7D 34
Thorpe Audlin. W Yor 4A 40
Thorpe Bassett. N Yor 6H 45
Thorpe Bay. S'end 5H 21
Thorpe by Water. Rut 2G 27
Thorpe Common. S Yor 6M 39
Thorpe Common. Suff 8J 29
Thorpe Constantine. Staf 1A 26
Thorpe End. Norf 6J 37
Thorpe Fendike. Linc 3L 35
Thorpe Green. Essx 1K 21
Thorpe Green. Suff 6F 28
Thorpe Hall. N Yor 6E 44
Thorpe Hamlet. Norf 1J 29
Thorpe Hesley. S Yor 6M 39
Thorpe in Balne. S Yor 4B 40
Thorpe in the Fallows. Linc 7F 40
Thorpe Langton. Leics 2F 26
Thorpe Larches. Dur 1C 44
Thorpe Latimer. Linc 5H 35
Thorpe-le-Soken. Essx 1K 21
Thorpe le Street. E Yor 1E 40
Thorpe Malsor. Nptn 4G 27
Thorpe Mandeville. Nptn 7D 26
Thorpe Market. Norf 4J 37
Thorpe Marriott. Norf 6H 37
Thorpe Morieux. Suff 6F 28
Thorpeness. Suff 5L 29
Thorpe on the Hill. Linc 3F 34
Thorpe on the Hill. W Yor 3M 39
Thorpe St Andrew. Norf 1J 29
Thorpe St Peter. Linc 3L 35
Thorpe Salvin. S Yor 7B 40
Thorpe Satchville. Leics 8D 34
Thorpe Thewles. Stoc T 1D 44
Thorpe Tilney. Linc 4H 35
Thorpe Underwood. N Yor 8D 44
Thorpe Waterville. Nptn 3J 27
Thorpe Willoughby. N Yor 2B 40
Thorpland. Norf 1C 28
Thorrington. Essx 1J 21
Thorverton. Devn 5L 7
Thrandeston. Suff 4H 29
Thrapston. Nptn 4H 27
Thrashbush. N Lan 3F 54
Threapland. Cumb 8J 49
Threapland. N Yor 7L 43
Threapwood. Ches W 5B 32
Threapwood. Staf 5H 33
Three Ashes. Here 1H 17
Three Bridges. Linc 7L 41
Three Bridges. W Sus 4A 12
Three Burrows. Corn 5E 3
Three Chimneys. Kent 4G 13
Three Cocks. Powy 8B 24
Three Crosses. Swan 4K 15
Three Cups Corner. E Sus 5E 12
Threehammer Common. Norf 5K 37
Three Holes. Norf 1B 28
Threekingham. Linc 6G 35
Three Leg Cross. E Sus 4E 12
Three Legged Cross. Dors 5A 10
Three Mile Cross. Wok 7H 19
Threemilestone. Corn 5E 3
Three Oaks. E Sus 6G 13
Threlkeld. Cumb 1E 42
Threshfield. N Yor 7L 43
Thrigby. Norf 6L 37
Thringarth. Dur 1L 43
Thringstone. Leics 8A 34
Thrintoft. N Yor 4C 44
Thriplow. Cambs 7A 28
Throckenholt. Linc 1M 27
Throcking. Herts 8M 27
Throckley. Tyne 5G 51
Throckmorton. Worc 7K 25
Throop. Bour 6B 10
Throphill. Nmbd 3G 51
Thropton. Nmbd 1F 50
Throsk. Stir 6D 60
Througham. Glos 3M 17
Throughgate. Dum 3F 48
Throwleigh. Devn 6H 7
Throwley. Kent 8H 21
Throwley Forstal. Kent 8H 21
Throxenby. N Yor 5K 45
Thrumpton. Notts 6B 34
Thrumster. High 5J 77
Thrunton. Nmbd 8K 57
Thrupp. Glos 3L 17
Thrupp. Oxon 2E 18
Thrushelton. Devn 7F 6
Thrushgill. Lanc 7H 43
Thrussington. Leics 8C 34
Thruxton. Hants 1C 10
Thruxton. Here 8E 24
Thrybergh. S Yor 6A 40
Thulston. Derbs 6A 34
Thundergay. N Ayr 5G 53
Thundersley. Essx 5F 20
Thundridge. Herts 2B 20
Thurcaston. Leics 8B 34
Thurcroft. S Yor 7A 40
Thurdon. Corn 4D 6
Thurgarton. Norf 4H 37
Thurgarton. Notts 5C 34
Thurgoland. S Yor 5L 39
Thurlaston. Leics 2D 26
Thurlaston. Warw 4C 26
Thurlbear. Som 3B 8
Thurlby. Linc 8L 41
(nr. Alford)
Thurlby. Linc 8H 35
(nr. Baston)
Thurlby. Linc 3F 34
(nr. Lincoln)
Thurleigh. Bed 6J 27
Thurlestone. Devn 5H 5
Thurloxton. Som 2B 8
Thurlstone. S Yor 5L 39
Thurlton. Norf 2L 29
Thurmaston. Leics 1E 26
Thurnby. Leics 1E 26
Thurne. Norf 6L 37
Thurnham. Kent 8G 21
Thurning. Norf 5G 37
Thurning. Nptn 3J 27
Thurnscoe. S Yor 5A 40
Thursby. Cumb 6L 49
Thursford. Norf 4F 36
Thursford Green. Norf 4F 36
Thursley. Surr 2K 11
Thurso. High 3G 77
Thurso East. High 3G 77
Thurstaston. Mers 7A 38
Thurston. Suff 5F 28
Thurston End. Suff 6D 28
Thurstonfield. Cumb 6L 49
Thurstonland. W Yor 4K 39
Thurton. Norf 1K 29
Thurvaston. Derbs 6J 33
(nr. Ashbourne)
Thurvaston. Derbs 6K 33
(nr. Derby)
Thuxton. Norf 1G 29
Thwaite. Dur 2M 43
Thwaite. N Yor 4K 43
Thwaite. Suff 5H 29
Thwaite Head. Cumb 4E 42
Thwaites. W Yor 1J 39
Thwaite St Mary. Norf 2K 29
Thwing. E Yor 6K 45
Tibbermore. Per 3F 60
Tibberton. Glos 1K 17
Tibberton. Telf 7D 32
Tibberton. Worc 6K 25
Tibenham. Norf 3H 29
Tibshelf. Derbs 3A 34
Tibthorpe. E Yor 8J 45
Ticehurst. E Sus 4E 12
Tichborne. Hants 2F 10
Tickencote. Rut 1H 27
Tickenham. N Som 6G 17
Tickhill. S Yor 6B 40
Ticklerton. Shrp 2E 24
Ticknall. Derbs 7L 33
Tickton. E Yor 1G 41
Tidbury Green. W Mid 4M 25
Tidcombe. Wilts 8C 18
Tiddington. Oxon 3G 19
Tiddington. Warw 6A 26
Tiddleywink. Wilts 6L 17
Tidebrook. E Sus 5E 12
Tideford. Corn 4E 4
Tideford Cross. Corn 3E 4
Tidenham. Glos 4H 17
Tideswell. Derbs 8K 39
Tidmarsh. W Ber 6G 19
Tidmington. Warw 8A 26
Tidpit. Hants 4A 10
Tidworth. Wilts 1C 10
Tidworth Camp. Wilts 1C 10
Tiers Cross. Pemb 2D 14
Tiffield. Nptn 6E 26
Tifty. Abers 5H 73
Tigerton. Ang 7F 66
Tighnabruaich. Arg 2H 53
Tigley. Devn 3J 5
Tilbrook. Cambs 5J 27
Tilbury. Thur 6E 20
Tilbury Green. Essx 7D 28
Tilbury Juxta Clare. Essx 7D 28
Tile Hill. W Mid 4A 26
Tilehurst. Read 6G 19
Tilford. Surr 1J 11
Tilgate Forest Row. W Sus 4A 12
Tillathrowie. Abers 6E 72
Tillers Green. Glos 8G 25
Tillery. Abers 1K 67
Tilley. Shrp 7C 32
Tillicoultry. Clac 6E 60
Tillingham. Essx 3H 21
Tillington. Here 7E 24
Tillington. W Sus 3K 11
Tillington Common. Here 7E 24
Tillybirloch. Abers 3G 67
Tillyfourie. Abers 2G 67
Tilmanstone. Kent 8M 21
Tilney All Saints. Norf 8M 35
Tilney Fen End. Norf 8M 35
Tilney High End. Norf 8M 35
Tilney St Lawrence. Norf 8M 35
Tilshead. Wilts 1A 10
Tilstock. Shrp 6C 32
Tilston. Ches W 4B 32
Tilstone Fearnall. Ches W 3C 32
Tilsworth. C Beds 1K 19
Tilton on the Hill. Leics 1F 26
Tiltups End. Glos 4L 17
Timberland. Linc 4H 35
Timbersbrook. Ches E 3F 32
Timberscombe. Som 1L 7
Timble. N Yor 8A 44
Timperley. G Man 7F 38
Timsbury. Bath 8J 17
Timsbury. Hants 3D 10
Timsgearraidh. W Isl 5A 74
Timworth Green. Suff 5E 28
Tincleton. Dors 6G 9
Tindale. Cumb 6B 50
Tindale Crescent. Dur 1B 44
Tingewick. Buck 8E 26
Tingrith. C Beds 8J 27
Tingwall. Orkn 5C 78
Tinhay. Devn 7E 6
Tinshill. W Yor 2L 39
Tinsley. S Yor 6A 40
Tinsley Green. W Sus 4A 12
Tintagel. Corn 7B 6
Tintern. Mon 3H 17
Tintinhull. Som 4E 8
Tintwistle. Derbs 6J 39
Tinwald. Dum 3H 49
Tinwell. Rut 1J 27
Tippacott. Devn 1J 7
Tipperty. Abers 1K 67
Tipps End. Cambs 2B 28
Tiptoe. Hants 6C 10
Tipton. W Mid 2K 25
Tipton St John. Devn 6M 7
Tiptree. Essx 2G 21
Tiptree Heath. Essx 2G 21
Tirabad. Powy 7L 23
Tircoed. Swan 3L 15
Tiree Airport. Arg 8B 62
Tirinie. Per 7L 65
Tirley. Glos 1L 17
Tirnewydd. Flin 2L 31
Tiroran. Arg 3B 58
Tirphil. Cphy 3D 16
Tirril. Cumb 1G 43
Tirryside. High 8A 76
Tir-y-dail. Carm 2L 15
Tisbury. Wilts 3J 9
Tisman's Common. W Sus 2L 11
Tissington. Derbs 4J 33
Titchberry. Devn 3D 6
Titchfield. Hants 5F 10
Titchmarsh. Nptn 4J 27
Titchwell. Norf 3D 36
Tithby. Notts 6C 34
Titley. Here 6D 24
Titlington. Nmbd 8L 57
Titsey. Surr 8C 20
Titson. Corn 5D 6
Tittensor. Staf 6F 32
Tittleshall. Norf 5E 36
Titton. Worc 5J 25
Tiverton. Ches W 3C 32
Tiverton. Devn 4L 7
Tivetshall St Margaret. Norf 3H 29
Tivetshall St Mary. Norf 3H 29
Tivington. Som 1L 7
Tixall. Staf 7G 33
Tixover. Rut 1H 27
Toab. Orkn 7D 78
Toab. Shet 10D 79
Toadmoor. Derbs 4L 33
Tobermory. Arg 8K 63
Toberonochy. Arg 5E 58
Tobha-Beag. W Isl 4D 68
(on North Uist)
Tobha Beag. W Isl 8B 68
(on South Uist)
Tobha Mor. W Isl 8B 68
Tobhtarol. W Isl 5B 74
Tobson. W Isl 5B 74
Tocabhaig. High 2L 63
Tocher. Abers 6G 73
Tockenham. Wilts 6A 18
Tockenham Wick. Wilts 5A 18
Tockholes. Bkbn 3E 38
Tockington. S Glo 5J 17
Tockwith. N Yor 8D 44
Todber. Dors 3H 9
Todding. Here 4E 24
Toddington. C Beds 1L 19
Toddington. Glos 8L 25
Todenham. Glos 8A 26
Todhills. Cumb 5L 49
Todmorden. W Yor 3H 39
Todwick. S Yor 7A 40
Toft. Cambs 6M 27
Toft. Linc 8G 35
Toft Hill. Dur 1A 44
Toft Monks. Norf 2L 29
Toft next Newton. Linc 7G 41
Toftrees. Norf 5E 36
Tofts. High 3J 77
Toftwood. Norf 6F 36
Togston. Nmbd 1H 51
Tokavaig. High 2L 63
Tokers Green. Oxon 6H 19
Tolastadh a Chaolais. W Isl 5B 74
Tolladine. Worc 6J 25
Tolland. Som 2A 8
Tollard Farnham. Dors 4J 9
Tollard Royal. Wilts 4J 9
Toll Bar. S Yor 5B 40
Toller Fratrum. Dors 6E 8
Toller Porcorum. Dors 6E 8
Tollerton. N Yor 7E 44
Tollerton. Notts 6C 34
Toller Whelme. Dors 5E 8
Tollesbury. Essx 2H 21
Tolleshunt D'Arcy. Essx 2H 21
Tolleshunt Knights. Essx 2H 21
Tolleshunt Major. Essx 2H 21
Tollie. High 6H 71
Tollie Farm. High 4A 70
Tolm. W Isl 5E 74
Tolpuddle. Dors 6G 9
Tolstadh bho Thuath. W Isl 4F 74
Tolworth. G Lon 7M 19
Tomachlaggan. Mor 1B 66
Tomaknock. Per 3D 60
Tomatin. High 1L 65
Tombuidhe. Arg 5H 59
Tomdoun. High 3D 64
Tomich. High 1F 64
(nr. Cannich)
Tomich. High 4K 71
(nr. Invergordon)
Tomich. High 1J 71
(nr. Lairg)
Tomintoul. Mor 2B 66
Tomnavoulin. Mor 1C 66
Tomsléibhe. Arg 2D 58
Ton. Mon 4F 16
Tonbridge. Kent 3D 12
Tondu. B'end 5A 16
Tonedale. Som 3A 8
Tonfanau. Gwyn 1H 23
Tong. Shrp 1H 25
Tonge. Leics 7A 34
Tong Forge. Shrp 1H 25
Tongham. Surr 1J 11
Tongland. Dum 6D 48
Tong Norton. Shrp 1H 25
Tongue. High 4A 76
Tongue End. Linc 8H 35
Tongwynlais. Card 5D 16
Tonmawr. Neat 4A 16
Tonna. Neat 4M 15
Tonnau. Neat 4M 15
Ton-Pentre. Rhon 4B 16
Ton-Teg. Rhon 5C 16
Tonwell. Herts 2B 20
Tonypandy. Rhon 4B 16
Tonyrefail. Rhon 5C 16
Toot Baldon. Oxon 3F 18
Toot Hill. Essx 3D 20
Toot Hill. Hants 4D 10
Topcliffe. N Yor 6D 44
Topcliffe. W Yor 3L 39
Topcroft. Norf 2J 29
Topcroft Street. Norf 2J 29
Toppesfield. Essx 8D 28
Toppings. G Man 4F 38
Toprow. Norf 2H 29
Topsham. Devn 7L 7
Torbay. Torb 3L 5
Torbeg. N Ayr 7G 53
Torbothie. N Lan 3G 55
Torbryan. Devn 3K 5
Torcross. Devn 5K 5
Tore. High 6J 71
Torgyle. High 2F 64
Torinturk. Arg 3G 53
Torksey. Linc 8E 40
Torlum. W Isl 6B 68
Torlundy. High 6D 64
Tormarton. S Glo 6K 17
Tormitchell. S Ayr 2M 47
Tormore. High 3L 63
Tormore. N Ayr 6G 53
Tornagrain. High 7K 71
Tornaveen. Abers 3G 67
Torness. High 1H 65
Toronto. Dur 8G 51
Torpenhow. Cumb 8K 49
Torphichen. W Lot 2H 55
Torphins. Abers 3G 67
Torpoint. Corn 4F 4
Torquay. Torb 3L 5
Torr. Devn 4G 5
Torra. Arg 4B 52
Torran. High 7K 69
Torrance. E Dun 2E 54
Torrans. Arg 3B 58
Torranyard. E Ayr 5B 54
Torre. Som 2M 7
Torre. Torb 3K 5
Torridon. High 6B 70
Torrin. High 1K 63
Torrisdale. Arg 6F 52
Torrisdale. High 3B 76
Torrish. High 8E 76
Torrisholme. Lanc 7F 42
Torroble. High 1H 71
Torroy. High 2H 71
Torry. Aber 3K 67
Torryburn. Fife 1J 55
Torthorwald. Dum 4H 49
Tortington. W Sus 5L 11
Tortworth. S Glo 4K 17
Torvaig. High 7J 69
Torver. Cumb 4D 42
Torwood. Falk 1G 55
Torworth. Notts 7C 40
Toscaig. High 8M 69
Toseland. Cambs 5L 27
Tosside. Lanc 8J 43
Tostock. Suff 5F 28
Totaig. High 6G 69
Totardor. High 8H 69
Tote. High 7J 69
Totegan. High 3D 76
Tothill. Linc 7L 41
Totland. IOW 7D 10
Totley. S Yor 8M 39
Totnell. Dors 5F 8
Totnes. Devn 3K 5
Toton. Derbs 6A 34
Totronald. Arg 8F 62
Totscore. High 5H 69
Tottenham. G Lon 4B 20
Tottenhill. Norf 6C 36
Tottenhill Row. Norf 6C 36
Totteridge. G Lon 4A 20
Totternhoe. C Beds 1K 19
Tottington. G Man 4F 38
Totton. Hants 4D 10
Touchen-end. Wind 6J 19
Toulvaddie. High 3L 71
Towans, The. Corn 6C 3
Toward. Arg 3K 53
Towcester. Nptn 7E 26
Towednack. Corn 6B 3
Tower End. Norf 6C 36
Tower Hill. Mers 5C 38
Tower Hill. W Sus 3M 11
Towersey. Oxon 3H 19
Towie. Abers 2E 66
Towiemore. Mor 5D 72
Tow Law. Dur 8G 51
Town End. Cambs 2A 28
Town End. Cumb 3F 42
(nr. Ambleside)
Town End. Cumb 1H 43
(nr. Kirkby Thore)
Town End. Cumb 5F 42
(nr. Lindale)
Town End. Cumb 5E 42
(nr. Newby Bridge)
Town End. Mers 7C 38
Townend. W Dun 2C 54
Townfield. Dur 7E 50
Towngate. Cumb 7A 50
Towngate. Linc 8H 35
Town Green. Lanc 5B 38
Town Head. Cumb 3E 42
(nr. Grasmere)
Town Head. Cumb 2H 43
(nr. Great Asby)
Townhead. Cumb 8A 50
(nr. Lazonby)
Townhead. Cumb 8H 49
(nr. Maryport)
Townhead. Cumb 8B 50
(nr. Ousby)
Townhead. Dum 7D 48
Townhead of Greenlaw. Dum 5E 48
Townhill. Fife 1K 55
Townhill. Swan 4L 15
Town Kelloe. Dur 8J 51
Town Littleworth. E Sus 6C 12
Town Row. E Sus 4D 12
Towns End. Hants 8F 18
Townsend. Herts 3M 19
Townshend. Corn 6C 3
Town Street. Suff 3D 28
Town, The. IOS 2B 3
Town Yetholm. Bord 7H 57
Towthorpe. E Yor 7H 45
Towthorpe. York 8F 44
Towton. N Yor 2A 40
Towyn. Cnwy 2J 31
Toxteth. Mers 7B 38
Toynton All Saints. Linc 3K 35
Toynton Fen Side. Linc 3K 35
Toynton St Peter. Linc 3L 35
Toy's Hill. Kent 8C 20
Trabboch. E Ayr 7C 54
Traboe. Corn 7E 3
Tradespark. High 6L 71
Tradespark. Orkn 7C 78
Trafford Park. G Man 6F 38
Trallong. Powy 1B 16
Tranent. E Lot 2D 56
Tranmere. Mers 7B 38
Trantlebeg. High 4D 76
Trantlemore. High 4D 76
Tranwell. Nmbd 3G 51
Trapp. Carm 2L 15
Traquair. Bord 6M 55
Trash Green. W Ber 7G 19
Trawden. Lanc 2H 39
Trawscoed. Powy 8A 24
Trawsfynydd. Gwyn 6G 31
Trawsgoed. Cdgn 4J 23
Treaddow. Here 1H 17
Trealaw. Rhon 4C 16
Treales. Lanc 2C 38
Trearddur. IOA 2B 30
Treaslane. High 6H 69
Treator. Corn 8A 6
Trebanog. Rhon 4C 16
Trebanos. Neat 3M 15
Trebarber. Corn 3F 3
Trebartha. Corn 8D 6
Trebarwith. Corn 7B 6
Trebetherick. Corn 8A 6
Treborough. Som 2M 7
Trebudannon. Corn 3F 3
Trebullett. Corn 8E 6
Treburley. Corn 8E 6
Treburrick. Corn 2F 3
Trebyan. Corn 3B 4
Trecastle. Powy 1A 16
Trecenydd. Cphy 5D 16
Trecott. Devn 5H 7
Trecwn. Pemb 8B 22
Trecynon. Rhon 3B 16
Tredaule. Corn 7D 6
Tredavoe. Corn 7B 3
Tredegar. Blae 3D 16
Trederwen. Powy 8M 31
Tredington. Glos 1M 17
Tredington. Warw 7A 26
Tredinnick. Corn 3C 4
(nr. Bodmin)
Tredinnick. Corn 4D 4
(nr. Looe)
Tredinnick. Corn 8A 6
(nr. Padstow)
Tredogan. V Glam 7C 16
Tredomen. Powy 8B 24
Tredunnock. Mon 4F 16
Tredustan. Powy 8B 24
Treen. Corn 7A 3
(nr. Land's End)
Treen. Corn 6B 3
(nr. St Ives)
Treeton. S Yor 7A 40
Trefaldwyn. Powy 2C 24
Trefasser. Pemb 8A 22
Trefdraeth. IOA 2D 30
Trefdraeth. Pemb 8C 22
Trefecca. Powy 8B 24
Trefechan. Mer T 3C 16
Trefeglwys. Powy 2M 23
Trefenter. Cdgn 5J 23
Treffgarne. Pemb 1D 14
Treffynnon. Flin 2L 31
Treffynnon. Pemb 1C 14
Trefil. Blae 2D 16
Trefilan. Cdgn 6H 23
Trefin. Pemb 8A 22
Treflach. Shrp 7M 31
Trefnant. Den 2K 31
Trefonen. Shrp 7M 31
Trefor. Gwyn 5C 30
Trefor. IOA 1C 30
Treforest. Rhon 5C 16
Trefrew. Corn 7C 6
Trefriw. Cnwy 3G 31
Tref-y-Clawdd. Powy 4C 24
Trefynwy. Mon 2H 17
Tregada. Corn 7E 6
Tregadillett. Corn 7E 6
Tregare. Mon 2G 17
Tregarne. Corn 7E 3
Tregaron. Cdgn 6J 23
Tregarth. Gwyn 3F 30
Tregear. Corn 4F 3
Tregeare. Corn 7D 6
Tregeiriog. Wrex 6L 31
Tregele. IOA 1C 30
Tregeseal. Corn 6A 3
Tregiskey. Corn 5B 4
Tregole. Corn 6C 6
Tregolwyn. V Glam 6B 16
Tregonetha. Corn 3A 4
Tregonhawke. Corn 4F 4
Tregony. Corn 5A 4
Tregoodwell. Corn 7C 6
Tregorrick. Corn 4B 4
Tregoss. Corn 3A 4
Tregowris. Corn 7E 3
Tregoyd. Powy 8B 24
Tregrehan Mills. Corn 4B 4
Tre-groes. Cdgn 7G 23
Tregullon. Corn 3B 4
Tregurrian. Corn 3F 3
Tregynon. Powy 2A 24
Trehafod. Rhon 4C 16
Trehan. Corn 4F 4
Treharris. Mer T 4D 16
Treherbert. Rhon 4B 16
Trehunist. Corn 3E 4
Trekenner. Corn 8E 6
Trekenning. Corn 3A 4
Treknow. Corn 7B 6
Trelales. B'end 5A 16
Trelan. Corn 8E 3
Trelash. Corn 6C 6
Trelassick. Corn 4F 3
Trelawnyd. Flin 2K 31
Trelech. Carm 8E 22
Treleddyd-fawr. Pemb 1B 14
Trelewis. Mer T 4D 16
Treligga. Corn 7B 6
Trelights. Corn 8A 6
Trelill. Corn 8B 6
Trelissick. Corn 6F 3
Trellech. Mon 3H 17
Trelleck Grange. Mon 3G 17
Trelogan. Flin 1L 31
Trelystan. Powy 1C 24
Tremadog. Gwyn 5E 30
Tremail. Corn 7C 6
Tremain. Cdgn 7E 22
Tremaine. Corn 7D 6
Tremar. Corn 3D 4
Trematon. Corn 4E 4
Tremeirchion. Den 2K 31
Tremore. Corn 3B 4
Tremorfa. Card 6E 16
Trenance. Corn 3F 3
(nr. Newquay)
Trenance. Corn 8A 6
(nr. Padstow)
Trenarren. Corn 5B 4
Trench. Telf 8D 32
Trencreek. Corn 3F 3
Trendeal. Corn 4F 3
Trenear. Corn 6D 3
Treneglos. Corn 7D 6
Trenewan. Corn 4C 4
Trengune. Corn 6C 6
Trent. Dors 4E 8
Trentham. Stoke 5F 32
Trentishoe. Devn 1H 7
Trentlock. Derbs 6A 34
Treoes. V Glam 6B 16
Treorchy. Rhon 4B 16
Treorci. Rhon 4B 16
Tre'r-ddol. Cdgn 2J 23
Tre'r llai. Powy 1C 24
Trerulefoot. Corn 4E 4
Tresaith. Cdgn 6E 22
Trescott. Staf 2J 25
Trescowe. Corn 6C 3
Tresham. Glos 4K 17
Tresigin. V Glam 6B 16
Tresillian. Corn 5F 3
Tresimwn. V Glam 6C 16
Tresinney. Corn 7C 6
Treskillard. Corn 6D 3
Treskinnick Cross. Corn 6D 6
Tresmeer. Corn 7D 6
Tresparrett. Corn 6C 6
Tresparrett Posts. Corn 6C 6
Tressady. High 1J 71
Tressait. Per 7L 65
Tresta. Shet 2G 79
(on Fetlar)
Tresta. Shet 6D 79
(on Mainland)
Treswell. Notts 8D 40
Treswithian. Corn 6D 3
Tre Taliesin. Cdgn 2J 23
Trethomas. Cphy 5D 16
Trethosa. Corn 4A 4
Trethurgy. Corn 4B 4
Tretio. Pemb 1B 14
Tretire. Here 1H 17
Tretower. Powy 1D 16
Treuddyn. Flin 4M 31
Trevadlock. Corn 8D 6
Trevalga. Corn 6B 6
Trevalyn. Wrex 4A 32
Trevance. Corn 8A 6
Trevanger. Corn 8A 6
Trevanson. Corn 8A 6
Trevarrack. Corn 6B 3
Trevarren. Corn 3A 4
Trevarrian. Corn 3F 3
Trevarrick. Corn 5A 4
Tre-vaughan. Carm 1J 15
(nr. Carmarthen)
Trevaughan. Carm 2F 14
(nr. Whitland)
Treveighan. Corn 8B 6
Trevellas. Corn 4E 3
Trevelmond. Corn 3D 4
Treverva. Corn 6E 3
Trevescan. Corn 7A 3
Trevethin. Torf 3E 16
Trevia. Corn 7B 6
Trevigro. Corn 3E 4
Trevilley. Corn 7A 3
Treviscoe. Corn 4A 4
Trevivian. Corn 7C 6
Trevone. Corn 2F 3
Trevor. Wrex 5M 31
Trevor Uchaf. Den 5M 31
Trew. Corn 7D 3
Trewalder. Corn 7B 6
Trewarlett. Corn 7E 6
Trewarmett. Corn 7B 6
Trewassa. Corn 7C 6
Treween. Corn 7D 6
Trewellard. Corn 6A 3
Trewen. Corn 7D 6
Trewennack. Corn 7D 3
Trewern. Powy 8M 31
Trewetha. Corn 8B 6
Trewidland. Corn 3D 4
Trewint. Corn 6C 6
Trewithian. Corn 6F 3
Trewoofe. Corn 7B 3
Trewoon. Corn 4A 4
Treworthal. Corn 6F 3
Trewyddel. Pemb 7D 22
Treyarnon. Corn 2F 3
Treyford. W Sus 4J 11
Triangle. Staf 1L 25
Triangle. W Yor 3J 39
Trickett's Cross. Dors 5A 10
Trimdon. Dur 8J 51
Trimdon Colliery. Dur 8J 51
Trimdon Grange. Dur 8J 51
Trimingham. Norf 4J 37
Trimley Lower Street. Suff 8J 29
Trimley St Martin. Suff 8J 29
Trimley St Mary. Suff 8J 29
Trimpley. Worc 4H 25
Trimsaran. Carm 3J 15
Trimstone. Devn 1G 7
Trinafour. Per 7K 65
Trinant. Cphy 4E 16
Tring. Herts 2K 19
Trinity. Ang 7G 67
Trinity. Edin 2L 55
Trisant. Cdgn 4K 23
Triscombe. Som 2A 8
Trislaig. High 6C 64
Trispen. Corn 4F 3
Tritlington. Nmbd 2H 51
Trochry. Per 1E 60
Troedrhiwdalar. Powy 6M 23
Troedrhiwfuwch. Cphy 3D 16
Troedrhiwgwair. Blae 3D 16
Troedyraur. Cdgn 7F 22
Troedyrhiw. Mer T 3C 16
Trondavoe. Shet 4D 79
Troon. Corn 6D 3
Troon. S Ayr 6B 54
Troqueer. Dum 4G 49
Troston. Suff 4E 28
Trottiscliffe. Kent 7E 20
Trotton. W Sus 3J 11
Troutbeck. Cumb 3F 42
(nr. Ambleside)
Troutbeck. Cumb 1E 42
(nr. Penrith)
Troutbeck Bridge. Cumb 3F 42
Troway. Derbs 8M 39
Trowbridge. Wilts 8L 17
Trowell. Notts 6A 34
Trowle Common. Wilts 8L 17
Trowley Bottom. Herts 2L 19
Trowse Newton. Norf 1J 29
Trudoxhill. Som 1G 9
Trull. Som 3B 8
Trumaisgearraidh. W Isl 4C 68
Trumpan. High 5G 69
Trumpet. Here 8G 25
Trumpington. Cambs 6A 28
Trumps Green. Surr 7K 19
Trunch. Norf 4J 37
Trunnah. Lanc 1B 38
Truro. Corn 5F 3
Trusham. Devn 7K 7
Trusley. Derbs 6K 33
Trusthorpe. Linc 7M 41
Tryfil. IOA 1D 30
Trysull. Staf 2J 25
Tubney. Oxon 4E 18
Tuckenhay. Devn 4K 5
Tuckhill. Staf 3H 25
Tuckingmill. Corn 5D 3
Tuckton. Bour 6B 10
Tuddenham. Suff 4D 28
Tuddenham St Martin. Suff 7H 29
Tudeley. Kent 3E 12
Tudhoe. Dur 8H 51
Tudhoe Grange. Dur 8H 51
Tudorville. Here 1H 17
Tudweiliog. Gwyn 6B 30
Tuesley. Surr 1K 11
Tufton. Hants 1E 10
Tufton. Pemb 1E 14
Tugby. Leics 1F 26
Tugford. Shrp 3F 24
Tughall. Nmbd 7M 57
Tulchan. Per 3E 60
Tullibardine. Per 4E 60
Tullibody. Clac 6D 60
Tullich. Arg 4H 59
Tullich. High 7B 70
(nr. Lochcarron)
Tullich. High 4L 71
(nr. Tain)
Tullich. Mor 5D 72
Tullich Muir. High 4K 71
Tulliemet. Per 8M 65
Tulloch. Abers 6J 73
Tulloch. High 2J 71
(nr. Bonar Bridge)
Tulloch. High 5F 64
(nr. Fort William)
Tulloch. High 2M 65
(nr. Grantown-on-Spey)
Tulloch. Per 3F 60
Tullochgorm. Arg 6G 59
Tullybeagles Lodge. Per 2F 60
Tullymurdoch. Per 8B 66
Tullynessle. Abers 2F 66
Tumble. Carm 2K 15
Tumbler's Green. Essx 1G 21
Tumby. Linc 3J 35
Tumby Woodside. Linc 4J 35
Tummel Bridge. Per 8K 65
Tunbridge Wells, Royal. Kent 4D 12
Tunga. W Isl 5E 74
Tungate. Norf 5J 37
Tunley. Bath 8J 17
Tunstall. E Yor 2K 41
Tunstall. Kent 7G 21
Tunstall. Lanc 6H 43
Tunstall. Norf 1L 29
Tunstall. N Yor 4B 44
Tunstall. Staf 7E 32
Tunstall. Stoke 4F 32
Tunstall. Suff 6K 29
Tunstall. Tyne 6J 51
Tunstead. Derbs 8K 39
Tunstead. Norf 5J 37
Tunstead Milton. Derbs 7J 39
Tunworth. Hants 1G 11
Tupsley. Here 7F 24
Tupton. Derbs 3L 33
Turfholm. S Lan 6G 55
Turfmoor. Devn 5B 8
Turgis Green. Hants 8G 19
Turkdean. Glos 2B 18
Turkey Island. Hants 4F 10
Tur Langton. Leics 2F 26
Turleigh. Wilts 7L 17
Turlin Moor. Pool 6J 9
Turnastone. Here 8D 24
Turnberry. S Ayr 1M 47
Turnchapel. Plym 4F 4
Turnditch. Derbs 5K 33
Turners Hill. W Sus 4B 12
Turners Puddle. Dors 6H 9
Turnford. Herts 3B 20
Turnhouse. Edin 2K 55
Turnworth. Dors 5H 9
Turriff. Abers 5H 73
Tursdale. Dur 8J 51
Turton Bottoms. Bkbn 4F 38
Turtory. Mor 5F 72
Turves Green. W Mid 4L 25
Turvey. Bed 6H 27
Turville. Buck 4H 19
Turville Heath. Buck 4H 19
Turweston. Buck 8E 26
Tushielaw. Bord 8M 55
Tutbury. Staf 7K 33
Tutnall. Worc 4K 25
Tutshill. Glos 4H 17
Tuttington. Norf 5J 37
Tutts Clump. W Ber 6F 18
Tutwell. Corn 8E 6
Tuxford. Notts 8D 40
Twatt. Orkn 5A 78
Twatt. Shet 6D 79
Twechar. E Dun 2F 54
Tweedale. Telf 1H 25
Tweedmouth. Nmbd 4J 57
Tweedsmuir. Bord 7J 55
Twelveheads. Corn 5E 3
Twemlow Green. Ches E 3E 32
Twenty. Linc 7H 35
Twerton. Bath 7K 17
Twickenham. G Lon 6M 19
Twigworth. Glos 1L 17
Twineham. W Sus 5A 12
Twinhoe. Bath 8K 17
Twinstead. Essx 8E 28
Twinstead Green. Essx 8E 28
Twiss Green. Warr 6E 38
Twiston. Lanc 1G 39
Twitchen. Devn 2J 7
Twitchen. Shrp 4D 24
Two Bridges. Devn 8H 7
Two Bridges. Glos 3J 17
Two Dales. Derbs 3K 33
Two Gates. Staf 1A 26
Two Mile Oak. Devn 3K 5
Twycross. Leics 1B 26
Twyford. Buck 1G 19
Twyford. Derbs 7L 33
Twyford. Dors 4H 9
Twyford. Hants 3E 10
Twyford. Leics 8D 34
Twyford. Norf 5G 37
Twyford. Wok 6H 19
Twyford Common. Here 8F 24
Twyncarno. Cphy 3D 16
Twynholm. Dum 6D 48
Twyning. Glos 8J 25
Twyning Green. Glos 8K 25
Twynllanan. Carm 1M 15
Twyn-y-Sheriff. Mon 3G 17
Twywell. Nptn 4H 27
Tyberton. Here 8D 24
Tyburn. W Mid 2M 25
Tyby. Norf 5G 37
Tycroes. Carm 2L 15
Tycrwyn. Powy 8L 31
Tyddewi. Pemb 1B 14
Tydd Gote. Linc 8L 35
Tydd St Giles. Cambs 8L 35
Tydd St Mary. Linc 8L 35
Tye. Hants 5H 11
Tye Green. Essx 1D 20
(nr. Bishop's Stortford)
Tye Green. Essx 1F 20
(nr. Braintree)
Tye Green. Essx 8B 28
(nr. Saffron Walden)
Tyersal. W Yor 2K 39
Ty Issa. Powy 7L 31
Tyldesley. G Man 5E 38
Tyler Hill. Kent 7K 21
Tylers Green. Buck 4J 19
Tyler's Green. Essx 3D 20
Tylorstown. Rhon 4C 16
Tylwch. Powy 3M 23
Ty-nant. Cnwy 5J 31
Tyndrum. Stir 2L 59
Tyneham. Dors 7H 9
Tynehead. Midl 4M 55
Tynemouth. Tyne 5J 51
Tyneside. Tyne 5H 51
Tyne Tunnel. Tyne 5J 51
Tynewydd. Rhon 4B 16
Tyninghame. E Lot 2F 56
Tynron. Dum 2F 48
Ty'n-y-bryn. Rhon 5C 16
Tyn-y-celyn. Wrex 6L 31
Tyn-y-cwm. Swan 3L 15
Tyn-y-ffridd. Powy 6L 31
Tynygongl. IOA 1E 30
Tynygraig. Cdgn 5J 23
Tyn-y-groes. Cnwy 2G 31
Ty'n-yr-eithin. Cdgn 5J 23
Tyn-y-rhyd. Powy 8K 31
Tyn-y-wern. Powy 7K 31
Tyrie. Abers 3K 73
Tyringham. Mil 7G 27
Tythecott. Devn 4F 6
Tythegston. B'end 6A 16
Tytherington. Ches E 8H 39
Tytherington. Som 1G 9
Tytherington. S Glo 5J 17
Tytherington. Wilts 1J 9
Tytherleigh. Devn 5C 8
Tywardreath. Corn 4B 4
Tywardreath Highway. Corn 4B 4
Tywyn. Cnwy 2G 31
Tywyn. Gwyn 1H 23

U

Uachdar. W Isl 6C 68
Uags. High 8M 69
Ubbeston Green. Suff 4K 29
Ubley. Bath 8H 17
Uckerby. N Yor 3B 44
Uckfield. E Sus 5C 12
Uckinghall. Worc 8J 25
Uckington. Glos 1M 17
Uckington. Shrp 1F 24
Uddingston. S Lan 3E 54
Uddington. S Lan 6G 55
Udimore. E Sus 6G 13
Udny Green. Abers 1J 67
Udny Station. Abers 1K 67
Udston. S Lan 4F 54
Udstonhead. S Lan 5F 54
Uffcott. Wilts 6B 18
Uffculme. Devn 4M 7
Uffington. Linc 1J 27
Uffington. Oxon 5D 18
Uffington. Shrp 8C 32
Ufford. Pet 1J 27
Ufford. Suff 6J 29
Ufton. Warw 5B 26
Ufton Nervet. W Ber 7G 19
Ugadale. Arg 7F 52
Ugborough. Devn 4H 5
Ugford. Wilts 2A 10
Uggeshall. Suff 3L 29
Ugglebarnby. N Yor 3H 45
Ugley. Essx 1D 20
Ugley Green. Essx 1D 20
Ugthorpe. N Yor 2G 45
Uidh. W Isl 4A 62
Uig. Arg 8F 62
Uig. High 5H 69
(nr. Balgown)
Uig. High 6F 68
(nr. Dunvegan)
Uigshader. High 7J 69
Uisken. Arg 4A 58
Ulbster. High 5J 77
Ulcat Row. Cumb 1F 42
Ulceby. Linc 8L 41
Ulceby. N Lin 4H 41
Ulceby Skitter. N Lin 4H 41
Ulcombe. Kent 3G 13
Uldale. Cumb 8K 49
Uley. Glos 4K 17
Ulgham. Nmbd 2H 51
Ullapool. High 2D 70
Ullenhall. Warw 5M 25
Ulleskelf. N Yor 2B 40
Ullesthorpe. Leics 3D 26
Ulley. S Yor 7A 40
Ullingswick. Here 7F 24
Ullinish. High 8H 69
Ullock. Cumb 1B 42
Ulpha. Cumb 4C 42
Ulrome. E Yor 8L 45
Ulsta. Shet 3E 79
Ulting. Essx 3G 21
Ulva House. Arg 2B 58
Ulverston. Cumb 6D 42
Ulwell. Dors 7A 10
Umberleigh. Devn 3H 7
Unapool. High 6K 75
Underbarrow. Cumb 4F 42
Undercliffe. W Yor 2K 39
Underdale. Shrp 8C 32
Underhoull. Shet 1F 79
Underriver. Kent 8D 20
Under Tofts. S Yor 7M 39
Underton. Shrp 2G 25
Underwood. Newp 5F 16
Underwood. Notts 4A 34
Underwood. Plym 4G 5
Undley. Suff 3C 28
Undy. Mon 5G 17
Union Mills. IOM 6D 46
Union Street. E Sus 4F 12
Unstone. Derbs 8M 39
Unstone Green. Derbs 8M 39
Unthank. Cumb 7L 49
(nr. Carlisle)
Unthank. Cumb 7B 50
(nr. Gamblesby)
Unthank. Cumb 8M 49
(nr. Penrith)
Unthank End. Cumb 8M 49
Upavon. Wilts 8B 18
Up Cerne. Dors 5F 8
Upchurch. Kent 7G 21
Upcott. Devn 5G 7
Upcott. Here 6D 24
Upend. Cambs 6D 28
Up Exe. Devn 5L 7
Upgate. Norf 6H 37
Upgate Street. Norf 2G 29
Uphall. Dors 5E 8
Uphall. W Lot 2J 55
Uphall Station. W Lot 2J 55
Upham. Devn 5K 7
Upham. Hants 3F 10
Uphampton. Here 5D 24
Uphampton. Worc 5J 25
Up Hatherley. Glos 1M 17
Uphill. N Som 8F 16
Up Holland. Lanc 5D 38
Uplawmoor. E Ren 4C 54
Upleadon. Glos 1K 17
Upleatham. Red C 2F 44
Uplees. Kent 7H 21
Uploders. Dors 6E 8
Uplowman. Devn 4M 7
Uplyme. Devn 6C 8
Up Marden. W Sus 4H 11
Upminster. G Lon 5D 20
Up Nately. Hants 8G 19
Upottery. Devn 5B 8
Uppat. High 1L 71
Upper Affcot. Shrp 3E 24
Upper Arley. Worc 3H 25
Upper Armley. W Yor 2L 39
Upper Arncott. Oxon 2G 19
Upper Astrop. Nptn 8D 26
Upper Badcall. High 5J 75
Upper Bangor. Gwyn 2E 30
Upper Basildon. W Ber 6F 18
Upper Batley. W Yor 3L 39
Upper Beeding. W Sus 4M 11
Upper Benefield. Nptn 3H 27
Upper Bentley. Worc 5K 25
Upper Bighouse. High 4D 76
Upper Boddam. Abers 6G 73
Upper Boddington. Nptn 6C 26
Upper Bogside. Mor 4C 72
Upper Booth. Derbs 7K 39
Upper Borth. Cdgn 3J 23
Upper Boyndlie. Abers 3K 73
Upper Brailes. Warw 8B 26
Upper Breinton. Here 7E 24
Upper Broadheath. Worc 6J 25
Upper Broughton. Notts 7C 34
Upper Brynamman. Carm 2M 15
Upper Bucklebury. W Ber 7F 18
Upper Bullington. Hants 1E 10
Upper Burgate. Hants 4B 10
Upper Caldecote. C Beds 7K 27
Upper Canterton. Hants 4C 10
Upper Catesby. Nptn 6D 26
Upper Chapel. Powy 7A 24
Upper Cheddon. Som 3B 8
Upper Chicksgrove. Wilts 3J 9
Upper Church Village. Rhon 5C 16
Upper Chute. Wilts 8C 18
Upper Clatford. Hants 1D 10
Upper Coberley. Glos 2M 17
Upper Coedcae. Torf 3E 16
Upper Cokeham. W Sus 5M 11
Upper Common. Hants 1G 11
Upper Cound. Shrp 1F 24
Upper Cudworth. S Yor 5M 39
Upper Cumberworth. W Yor 5L 39
Upper Cuttlehill. Abers 5E 72
Upper Cwmbran. Torf 4E 16
Upper Dallachy. Mor 3D 72
Upper Dean. Bed 5J 27
Upper Denby. W Yor 5L 39
Upper Derraid. High 6A 72
Upper Diabaig. High 5A 70
Upper Dicker. E Sus 7D 12
Upper Dinchope. Shrp 3E 24
Upper Dochcarty. High 5H 71
Upper Dounreay. High 3E 76
Upper Dovercourt. Essx 8J 29
Upper Dunsforth. N Yor 7D 44
Upper Dunsley. Herts 2K 19
Upper Eastern Green. W Mid 3A 26
Upper Elkstone. Staf 4H 33
Upper Ellastone. Staf 5J 33
Upper End. Derbs 8J 39
Upper Enham. Hants 1D 10
Upper Farmcote. Shrp 2H 25
Upper Farringdon. Hants 2H 11
Upper Framilode. Glos 2K 17
Upper Froyle. Hants 1H 11
Upper Gills. High 2J 77
Upper Glenfintaig. High 5E 64
Upper Godney. Som 1D 8
Upper Gravenhurst. C Beds 8K 27
Upper Green. Essx 8A 28
Upper Green. W Ber 7D 18
Upper Green. W Yor 3L 39
Upper Grove Common. Here 1H 17
Upper Hackney. Derbs 3K 33
Upper Hale. Surr 1J 11
Upper Halliford. Surr 7L 19
Upper Halling. Medw 7E 20
Upper Hambleton. Rut 1H 27
Upper Hardres Court. Kent 8K 21
Upper Hardwick. Here 6E 24
Upper Hartfield. E Sus 4C 12
Upper Haugh. S Yor 6A 40
Upper Hayton. Shrp 3F 24
Upper Heath. Shrp 3F 24
Upper Hellesdon. Norf 6J 37
Upper Helmsley. N Yor 8F 44
Upper Hengoed. Shrp 6M 31
Upper Hergest. Here 6C 24
Upper Heyford. Nptn 6E 26
Upper Heyford. Oxon 1E 18
Upper Hill. Here 6E 24
Upper Hindhope. Bord 1C 50
Upper Hopton. W Yor 4K 39
Upper Howsell. Worc 7H 25
Upper Hulme. Staf 3H 33
Upper Inglesham. Swin 4C 18
Upper Kilcott. Glos 5K 17
Upper Killay. Swan 4K 15
Upper Kirkton. Abers 6H 73
Upper Kirkton. N Ayr 4K 53
Upper Knockando. Mor 5B 72
Upper Knockchoilum. High 2G 65
Upper Lambourn. W Ber 5D 18
Upper Langford. N Som 8G 17
Upper Langwith. Derbs 3B 34
Upper Largo. Fife 5K 61
Upper Latheron. High 6G 77
Upper Layham. Suff 7G 29
Upper Leigh. Staf 6H 33
Upper Lenie. High 1H 65
Upper Lochton. Abers 4H 67
Upper Longdon. Staf 8H 33
Upper Longwood. Shrp 1G 25
Upper Lybster. High 6H 77
Upper Lydbrook. Glos 2J 17
Upper Lye. Here 5D 24
Upper Maes-coed. Here 8D 24
Upper Midway. Derbs 7K 33
Uppermill. G Man 5H 39
Upper Millichope. Shrp 3F 24
Upper Milovaig. High 7F 68
Upper Minety. Wilts 4A 18
Upper Mitton. Worc 4J 25
Upper Nash. Pemb 3E 14
Upper Neepaback. Shet 3F 79

Upper Netchwood—Whasset

Upper Netchwood. Shrp 2G 25
Upper Nobut. Staf 6H 33
Upper North Dean. Buck 4J 19
Upper Norwood. W Sus 4K 11
Upper Nyland. Dors 3G 9
Upper Oddington. Glos 1C 18
Upper Ollach. High 8K 69
Upper Outwoods. Staf 7K 33
Upper Padley. Derbs 8L 39
Upper Pennington. Hants 6D 10
Upper Poppleton. York 8E 44
Upper Quinton. Warw 7M 25
Upper Rissington. Glos 2C 18
Upper Rochford. Worc 5G 25
Upper Rusko. Dum 5C 48
Upper Sandaig. High 2M 63
Upper Sanday. Orkn 7D 78
Upper Sapey. Here 5G 25
Upper Seagry. Wilts 5M 17
Upper Shelton. C Beds 7H 27
Upper Sheringham. Norf 3H 37
Upper Skelmorlie. N Ayr 3K 53
Upper Slaughter. Glos 1B 18
Upper Sonachan. Arg 3H 59
Upper Soudley. Glos 2J 17
Upper Staploe. Bed 6K 27
Upper Stoke. Norf 1J 29
Upper Stondon. C Beds 8K 27
Upper Stowe. Nptn 6E 26
Upper Street. Hants 4B 10
Upper Street. Norf 6K 37 (nr. Horning)
Upper Street. Norf 6K 37 (nr. Hoveton)
Upper Street. Suff 8H 29
Upper Strensham. Worc 8K 25
Upper Studley. Wilts 8L 17
Upper Sundon. C Beds 1L 19
Upper Swell. Glos 1B 18
Upper Tankersley. S Yor 6M 39
Upper Tean. Staf 6H 33
Upperthong. W Yor 5K 39
Upperthorpe. N Lin 5D 40
Upper Thurnham. Lanc 8F 42
Upper Tillyrie. Per 5G 61
Upperton. W Sus 3K 11
Upper Tooting. G Lon 6A 20
Uppertown. Derbs 3L 33 (nr. Ashover)
Upper Town. Derbs 4K 33 (nr. Bonsall)
Upper Town. Derbs 4K 33 (nr. Hognaston)
Upper Town. Here 7F 24
Uppertown. High 2J 77
Upper Town. N Som 7H 17
Uppertown. Nmbd 4D 50
Uppertown. Orkn 8C 78
Upper Tysoe. Warw 7B 26
Upper Upham. Wilts 6C 18
Upper Upnor. Medw 6F 20
Upper Urquhart. Fife 5G 61
Upper Wardington. Oxon 7C 26
Upper Weald. Mil 8G 27
Upper Weedon. Nptn 6E 26
Upper Wellingham. E Sus 6C 12
Upper Whiston. S Yor 7A 40
Upper Wield. Hants 2G 11
Upper Winchendon. Buck 2H 19
Upperwood. Derbs 4K 33
Upper Woodford. Wilts 2B 10
Upper Wootton. Hants 8F 18
Upper Wraxall. Wilts 6L 17
Upper Wyche. Here 7H 25
Uppincott. Devn 5K 7
Uppingham. Rut 2G 27
Uppington. Shrp 1F 24
Upsall. N Yor 5D 44
Upsettlington. Bord 5H 57
Upshire. Essx 3C 20
Up Somborne. Hants 2D 10
Upstreet. Kent 7L 21
Up Sydling. Dors 5F 8
Upthorpe. Suff 4F 28
Upton. Buck 2H 19
Upton. Cambs 4K 27
Upton. Ches W 3B 32
Upton. Corn 5D 6 (nr. Bude)
Upton. Corn 8D 6 (nr. Liskeard)
Upton. Cumb 8L 49
Upton. Devn 5M 7 (nr. Honiton)
Upton. Devn 5J 5 (nr. Kingsbridge)
Upton. Dors 6J 9 (nr. Poole)
Upton. Dors 7G 9 (nr. Weymouth)
Upton. E Yor 8L 45
Upton. Hants 8D 18 (nr. Andover)
Upton. Hants 4D 10 (nr. Southampton)
Upton. IOW 6F 10
Upton. Leics 2B 26
Upton. Linc 7E 40
Upton. Mers 7A 38
Upton. Norf 6K 37
Upton. Nptn 5F 26
Upton. Notts 8D 40 (nr. Retford)
Upton. Notts 4D 34 (nr. Southwell)
Upton. Oxon 5F 18
Upton. Pemb 3E 14
Upton. Pet 1K 27
Upton. Slo 6K 19
Upton. Som 3D 8 (nr. Somerton)
Upton. Som 3L 7 (nr. Wiveliscombe)
Upton. Warw 6M 25
Upton. W Yor 4A 40
Upton. Wilts 2H 9
Upton Bishop. Here 1J 17
Upton Cheyney. S Glo 7J 17
Upton Cressett. Shrp 2G 25
Upton Crews. Here 1J 17
Upton Cross. Corn 8D 6
Upton End. C Beds 8K 27
Upton Grey. Hants 1G 11
Upton Heath. Ches W 3B 32
Upton Hellions. Devn 5K 7
Upton Lovell. Wilts 1J 9
Upton Magna. Shrp 8C 32
Upton Noble. Som 2G 9
Upton Pyne. Devn 6L 7
Upton St Leonards. Glos 2L 17
Upton Scudamore. Wilts 1H 9
Upton Snodsbury. Worc 6K 25
Upton upon Severn. Worc 7J 25
Upton Warren. Worc 5K 25
Upwaltham. W Sus 4K 11
Upware. Cambs 4B 28
Upwell. Cambs 1A 28
Upwey. Dors 7F 8
Upwick Green. Herts 1C 20
Upwood. Cambs 3L 27
Urafirth. Shet 4D 79
Uragaig. Arg 6A 58
Urchany. High 7L 71
Urchfont. Wilts 8A 18
Urdimarsh. Here 7F 24
Ure. Shet 4C 79
Ure Bank. N Yor 6C 44
Urgha. W Isl 2F 68
Urlay Nook. Stoc T 2D 44
Urmston. G Man 6F 38
Urquhart. Mor 3C 72
Urra. N Yor 3E 44
Urray. High 6H 71
Usan. Ang 8H 67
Ushaw Moor. Dur 7H 51
Usk. Mon 3F 16
Usselby. Linc 6G 41
Usworth. Tyne 6J 51
Utkinton. Ches W 3C 32
Uton. Devn 6K 7
Utterby. Linc 6K 41
Uttoxeter. Staf 6H 33
Uwchmynydd. Gwyn 7A 30
Uxbridge. G Lon 5L 19
Uyeasound. Shet 1F 79
Uzmaston. Pemb 2D 14

V

Valley. IOA 2B 30
Valley End. Surr 7K 19
Valley Truckle. Corn 7C 6
Valsgarth. Shet 1G 79
Valtos. High 5K 69
Van. Powy 3M 23
Vange. Essx 5F 20
Varteg. Torf 3E 16
Vatsetter. Shet 3F 79
Vatten. High 7G 69
Vaul. Arg 8B 62
Vauld, The. Here 7F 24
Vaynol. Gwyn 2E 30
Vaynor. Mer T 2C 16
Veensgarth. Shet 7E 79
Velindre. Powy 8B 24
Vellow. Som 2M 7
Velly. Devn 3D 6
Veness. Orkn 5D 78
Venhay. Devn 4J 7
Venn. Devn 5J 5
Venngreen. Devn 4E 6
Vennington. Shrp 1D 24
Venn Ottery. Devn 6M 7
Venn's Green. Here 7F 24
Venny Tedburn. Devn 6K 7
Venterdon. Corn 8E 6
Ventnor. IOW 8F 10
Vernham Dean. Hants 8D 18
Vernham Street. Hants 8D 18
Vernolds Common. Shrp 3E 24
Verwood. Dors 5A 10
Veryan. Corn 6A 4
Veryan Green. Corn 5A 4
Vicarage. Devn 7B 8
Vickerstown. Cumb 7C 42
Victoria. Corn 3A 4
Vidlin. Shet 5E 79
Viewpark. N Lan 3F 54
Vigo. W Mid 1L 25
Vigo Village. Kent 7E 20
Vinehall Street. E Sus 5F 12
Vine's Cross. E Sus 6D 12
Viney Hill. Glos 3J 17
Virginia Water. Surr 7K 19
Virginstow. Devn 6E 6
Vobster. Som 1G 9
Voe. Shet 5E 79 (nr. Hillside)
Voe. Shet 3D 79 (nr. Swinister)
Vole. Som 1C 8
Vowchurch. Here 8D 24
Voxter. Shet 4D 79
Voy. Orkn 6A 78
Vulcan Village. Warr 6D 38

W

Waberthwaite. Cumb 4C 42
Wackerfield. Dur 1A 44
Wacton. Norf 2H 29
Wadbister. Shet 7E 79
Wadborough. Worc 7K 25
Wadbrook. Devn 5C 8
Waddesdon. Buck 2H 19
Waddeton. Devn 4K 5
Waddicar. Mers 6B 38
Waddingham. Linc 6F 40
Waddington. Lanc 1F 38
Waddington. Linc 3F 34
Waddon. Devn 8K 7
Wadebridge. Corn 8A 6
Wadeford. Som 4C 8
Wadenhoe. Nptn 3J 27
Wadesmill. Herts 2B 20
Wadhurst. E Sus 4E 12
Wadshelf. Derbs 8M 39
Wadsley. S Yor 6M 39
Wadsley Bridge. S Yor 6M 39
Wadswick. Wilts 7L 17
Wadwick. Hants 8E 18
Wadworth. S Yor 6B 40
Waen. Den 3L 31 (nr. Llandyrnog)
Waen. Den 3J 31 (nr. Nantglyn)
Waen. Powy 2M 23
Waen Fach. Powy 8M 31
Waen Goleugoed. Den 2K 31
Wag. High 7F 76
Wainfleet All Saints. Linc 4L 35
Wainfleet Bank. Linc 4L 35
Wainfleet St Mary. Linc 4L 35
Wainhouse Corner. Corn 6C 6
Wainscott. Medw 6F 20
Wainstalls. W Yor 3J 39
Waitby. Cumb 3J 43
Waithe. Linc 5J 41
Wakefield. W Yor 3M 39
Wakerley. Nptn 2H 27
Wakes Colne. Essx 1G 21
Walberswick. Suff 4L 29
Walberton. W Sus 5K 11
Walbottle. Tyne 5G 51
Walby. Cumb 5M 49
Walcombe. Som 1E 8
Walcot. Linc 6G 35
Walcot. N Lin 3E 40
Walcot. Swin 5B 18
Walcot. Telf 8C 32
Walcot. Warw 6M 25
Walcote. Leics 3D 26
Walcot Green. Norf 3H 29
Walcott. Linc 4H 35
Walcott. Norf 4K 37
Walden. N Yor 5M 43
Walden Head. N Yor 5L 43
Walden Stubbs. N Yor 4B 40
Walderslade. Medw 7F 20
Walderton. W Sus 4H 11
Walditch. Dors 6D 8
Waldley. Derbs 6J 33
Waldridge. Dur 6H 51
Waldringfield. Suff 7J 29
Waldron. E Sus 6D 12
Wales. S Yor 7A 40
Walesby. Linc 6H 41
Walesby. Notts 8C 40
Walford. Here 4D 24 (nr. Leintwardine)
Walford. Here 1H 17 (nr. Ross-on-Wye)
Walford. Shrp 7B 32
Walford. Staf 6F 32
Walford Heath. Shrp 8B 32
Walgherton. Ches E 5D 32
Walgrave. Nptn 4G 27
Walhampton. Hants 6D 10
Walkden. G Man 5F 38
Walker. Tyne 5H 51
Walkerburn. Bord 6M 55
Walker Fold. Lanc 1E 38
Walkeringham. Notts 6D 40
Walkerith. Linc 6D 40
Walkern. Herts 1A 20
Walker's Green. Here 7F 24
Walkerton. Fife 5H 61
Walkerville. N Yor 4B 44
Walkford. Dors 6C 10
Walkhampton. Devn 3G 5
Walkington. E Yor 2F 40
Walkley. S Yor 7M 39
Walk Mill. Lanc 2G 39
Wall. Corn 6D 3
Wall. Nmbd 5E 50
Wall. Staf 1M 25
Wallaceton. Dum 3F 48
Wallacetown. Shet 6D 79
Wallacetown. S Ayr 7B 54 (nr. Ayr)
Wallacetown. S Ayr 1M 47 (nr. Dailly)
Wallands Park. E Sus 6C 12
Wallasey. Mers 6B 38
Wallaston Green. Pemb 3D 14
Wallbrook. W Mid 2K 25
Wallcrouch. E Sus 4E 12
Wall End. Cumb 5D 42
Wallend. Medw 6G 21
Wall Heath. W Mid 3J 25
Wallingford. Oxon 5G 19
Wallington. G Lon 7A 20
Wallington. Hants 5F 10
Wallington. Herts 8L 27
Wallis. Pemb 1E 14
Wallisdown. Pool 6A 10
Walliswood. Surr 2M 11
Wall Nook. Dur 7H 51
Walls. Shet 7C 79
Wallsend. Tyne 5J 51
Wallsworth. Glos 1L 17
Wall under Heywood. Shrp 2F 24
Wallyford. E Lot 2M 55
Walmer. Kent 8M 21
Walmer Bridge. Lanc 3C 38
Walmersley. G Man 4G 39
Walmley. W Mid 2M 25
Walnut Grove. Per 3G 61
Walpole. Suff 4K 29
Walpole Cross Keys. Norf 8M 35
Walpole Gate. Norf 8M 35
Walpole Highway. Norf 8M 35
Walpole Marsh. Norf 8L 35
Walpole St Andrew. Norf 8M 35
Walpole St Peter. Norf 8M 35
Walsall. W Mid 2L 25
Walsall Wood. W Mid 1L 25
Walsden. W Yor 3H 39
Walsgrave on Sowe. W Mid 3B 26
Walsham le Willows. Suff 4G 29
Walshaw. G Man 4F 38
Walshford. N Yor 8D 44
Walsoken. Cambs 8L 35
Walston. S Lan 5J 55
Walsworth. Herts 8K 27
Walter's Ash. Buck 4J 19
Walterston. V Glam 6C 16
Walterstone. Here 1F 16
Waltham. Kent 3K 13
Waltham. NE Lin 5J 41
Waltham Abbey. Essx 3B 20
Waltham Chase. Hants 4F 10
Waltham Cross. Herts 3B 20
Waltham on the Wolds. Leics 7E 34
Waltham St Lawrence. Wind 6J 19
Waltham's Cross. Essx 8C 28
Walthamstow. G Lon 5B 20
Walton. Cumb 5A 50
Walton. Derbs 3L 33
Walton. Leics 3D 26
Walton. Mers 6B 38
Walton. Mil 8G 27
Walton. Pet 1K 27
Walton. Powy 6C 24
Walton. Som 2D 8
Walton. Staf 7F 32 (nr. Eccleshall)
Walton. Staf 6F 32 (nr. Stone)
Walton. Suff 8J 29
Walton. Telf 8C 32
Walton. Warw 6A 26
Walton. W Yor 4M 39 (nr. Wakefield)
Walton. W Yor 1A 40 (nr. Wetherby)
Walton Cardiff. Glos 8K 25
Walton East. Pemb 1E 14
Walton Elm. Dors 4G 9
Walton Highway. Norf 8L 35
Walton-in-Gordano. N Som 6G 17
Walton-le-Dale. Lanc 3D 38
Walton-on-Thames. Surr 7M 19
Walton-on-the-Hill. Staf 7G 33
Walton on the Hill. Surr 8A 20
Walton-on-the-Naze. Essx 1L 21
Walton on the Wolds. Leics 8B 34
Walton-on-Trent. Derbs 8K 33
Walton West. Pemb 2C 14
Walwick. Nmbd 4E 50
Walworth. Darl 2B 44
Walworth Gate. Darl 1B 44
Walwyn's Castle. Pemb 2C 14
Wambrook. Som 5B 8
Wampool. Cumb 6K 49
Wanborough. Surr 1K 11
Wanborough. Swin 5C 18
Wandel. S Lan 7H 55
Wandsworth. G Lon 6A 20
Wangford. Suff 3D 28 (nr. Lakenheath)
Wangford. Suff 4L 29 (nr. Southwold)
Wanlip. Leics 8C 34
Wanlockhead. Dum 8G 55
Wannock. E Sus 7D 12
Wansford. E Yor 8K 45
Wansford. Pet 2J 27
Wanshurst Green. Kent 3F 12
Wanstead. G Lon 5C 20
Wanstrow. Som 1G 9
Wanswell. Glos 3J 17
Wantage. Oxon 5E 18
Wapley. S Glo 6K 17
Wappenbury. Warw 5B 26
Wappenham. Nptn 7E 26
Warbleton. E Sus 6E 12
Warblington. Hants 5H 11
Warborough. Oxon 4F 18
Warboys. Cambs 3M 27
Warbreck. Bkpl 2B 38
Warbstow. Corn 6D 6
Warburton. G Man 7E 38
Warcop. Cumb 2J 43
Warden. Kent 6J 21
Warden. Nmbd 5E 50
Ward End. W Mid 3M 25
Ward Green. Suff 5G 29
Ward Green Cross. Lanc 2E 38
Wardhedges. C Beds 8J 27
Wardhouse. Abers 6F 72
Wardington. Oxon 7C 26
Wardle. Ches E 4D 32
Wardle. G Man 4H 39
Wardley. Rut 1G 27
Wardley. W Sus 3J 11
Wardlow. Derbs 8K 39
Wardsend. Ches E 7H 39
Wardy Hill. Cambs 3A 28
Ware. Herts 2B 20
Ware. Kent 7L 21
Wareham. Dors 7J 9
Warehorne. Kent 4H 13
Warenford. Nmbd 7L 57
Waren Mill. Nmbd 6L 57
Warenton. Nmbd 6L 57
Wareside. Herts 2B 20
Waresley. Cambs 6L 27
Waresley. Worc 5J 25
Warfield. Brac 6J 19
Warfleet. Devn 4K 5
Wargate. Linc 6J 35
Wargrave. Wok 6H 19
Warham. Norf 3F 36
Wark. Nmbd 6H 57 (nr. Coldstream)
Wark. Nmbd 4D 50 (nr. Hexham)
Warkleigh. Devn 3H 7
Warkton. Nptn 4G 27
Warkworth. Nptn 7C 26
Warkworth. Nmbd 1H 51
Warlaby. N Yor 4C 44
Warland. W Yor 3H 39
Warleggan. Corn 3C 4
Warlingham. Surr 8B 20
Warmanbie. Dum 5J 49
Warmfield. W Yor 3M 39
Warmingham. Ches E 3E 32
Warminghurst. W Sus 4M 11
Warmington. Nptn 2J 27
Warmington. Warw 7C 26
Warminster. Wilts 1H 9
Warmley. S Glo 6J 17
Warmsworth. S Yor 5B 40
Warmwell. Dors 7G 9
Warndon. Worc 6J 25
Warners End. Herts 3L 19
Warnford. Hants 3G 11
Warnham. W Sus 2M 11
Warningcamp. W Sus 5L 11
Warninglid. W Sus 5A 12
Warren. Ches E 8G 39
Warren. Pemb 4D 14
Warrenby. Red C 1E 44
Warren Corner. Hants 1J 11 (nr. Aldershot)
Warren Corner. Hants 3H 11 (nr. Petersfield)
Warren Row. Wind 5J 19
Warren Street. Kent 8H 21
Warrington. Mil 6G 27
Warrington. Warr 7E 38
Warsash. Hants 5E 10
Warse. High 2J 77
Warslow. Staf 4H 33
Warsop. Notts 3B 34
Warsop Vale. Notts 3B 34
Warter. E Yor 8H 45
Warthermarske. N Yor 6B 44
Warthill. N Yor 8F 44
Wartling. E Sus 7E 12
Wartnaby. Leics 7D 34
Warton. Lanc 6F 42 (nr. Carnforth)
Warton. Lanc 3C 38 (nr. Freckleton)
Warton. Nmbd 1F 50
Warton. Warw 1A 26
Warwick. Warw 5A 26
Warwick Bridge. Cumb 6M 49
Warwick-on-Eden. Cumb 6M 49
Warwick Wold. Surr 8B 20
Wasbister. Orkn 4B 78
Wasdale Head. Cumb 3C 42
Wash. Derbs 7J 39
Washaway. Corn 3B 4
Washbourne. Devn 4K 5
Washbrook. Suff 7H 29
Wash Common. W Ber 7E 18
Washerwall. Staf 5G 33
Washfield. Devn 4L 7
Washfold. N Yor 3M 43
Washford. Som 1M 7
Washford Pyne. Devn 4K 7
Washingborough. Linc 8G 41
Washington. Tyne 6J 51
Washington. W Sus 4M 11
Washington Village. Tyne 6J 51
Waskerley. Dur 7F 50
Wasperton. Warw 6A 26
Wasp Green. Surr 3B 12
Wasps Nest. Linc 3G 35
Wass. N Yor 6E 44
Watchet. Som 1M 7
Watchfield. Oxon 4C 18
Watchgate. Cumb 4G 43
Watchhill. Cumb 7J 49
Watcombe. Torb 3L 5
Watendlath. Cumb 2D 42
Water. Devn 7J 7
Water. Lanc 3G 39
Waterbeach. Cambs 5A 28
Waterbeach. W Sus 5J 11
Waterbeck. Dum 4K 49
Waterditch. Hants 6B 10
Water End. C Beds 8J 27
Water End. E Yor 2D 40
Water End. Essx 7B 28
Water End. Herts 3A 20 (nr. Hatfield)
Water End. Herts 2L 19 (nr. Hemel Hempstead)
Waterfall. Staf 4H 33
Waterfoot. E Ren 4D 54
Waterfoot. Lanc 3G 39
Waterford. Herts 2B 20
Water Fryston. W Yor 3A 40
Waterhead. Cumb 3E 42
Waterhead. E Ayr 8D 54
Waterhead. S Ayr 2A 48
Waterheads. Bord 4L 55
Waterhouses. Dur 7G 51
Waterhouses. Staf 4H 33
Wateringbury. Kent 8E 20
Waterlane. Glos 3M 17
Waterlip. Som 1F 8
Waterloo. Cphy 5D 16
Waterloo. Corn 8C 6
Waterloo. Here 7D 24
Waterloo. High 1L 63
Waterloo. Mers 6B 38
Waterloo. Norf 6J 37
Waterloo. N Lan 4G 55
Waterloo. Pemb 3D 14
Waterloo. Per 2F 60
Waterloo. Pool 6A 10
Waterloo. Shrp 6B 32
Waterlooville. Hants 5G 11
Watermead. Buck 2J 19
Watermillock. Cumb 1F 42
Water Newton. Cambs 2K 27
Water Orton. Warw 2M 25
Waterperry. Oxon 3G 19
Waterrow. Som 3M 7
Watersfield. W Sus 4L 11
Waterside. Buck 3K 19
Waterside. Cambs 4C 28
Waterside. Cumb 7K 49
Waterside. E Ayr 1B 48 (nr. Ayr)
Waterside. E Ayr 5C 54 (nr. Kilmarnock)
Waterside. E Dun 2E 54
Waterstein. High 7F 68
Waterstock. Oxon 3G 19
Waterston. Pemb 3D 14
Water Stratford. Buck 8E 26
Waters Upton. Telf 8D 32
Water Yeat. Cumb 5D 42
Watford. Herts 4L 19
Watford. Nptn 5E 26
Wath. Cumb 3H 43
Wath. N Yor 7A 44 (nr. Pateley Bridge)
Wath. N Yor 6C 44 (nr. Ripon)
Wath Brow. Cumb 2B 42
Wath upon Dearne. S Yor 6A 40
Watlington. Norf 6C 36
Watlington. Oxon 4G 19
Watten. High 4H 77
Wattisfield. Suff 4G 29
Wattisham. Suff 6G 29
Wattlesborough Heath. Shrp 8A 32
Watton. Dors 6D 8
Watton. E Yor 8K 45
Watton. Norf 1F 28
Watton at Stone. Herts 2A 20
Wattston. N Lan 2F 54
Wattstown. Rhon 4C 16
Wattsville. Cphy 4E 16
Wauldby. E Yor 3F 40
Waulkmill. Abers 4G 67
Waun. Powy 8M 31
Waunarlwydd. Swan 4L 15
Waun Fawr. Cdgn 3J 23
Waunfawr. Gwyn 4E 30
Waungilwen. Carm 8F 22
Waunlwyd. Blae 3D 16
Waun-y-Clyn. Carm 3J 15
Wavendon. Mil 8H 27
Waverbridge. Cumb 7K 49
Waverley. Surr 1J 11
Waverton. Ches W 3B 32
Waverton. Cumb 7K 49
Wavertree. Mers 7B 38
Wawne. E Yor 2G 41
Waxham. Norf 5L 37
Waxholme. E Yor 3K 41
Wayford. Som 5D 8
Way Head. Cambs 3A 28
Waytown. Dors 6D 8
Way Village. Devn 4K 7
Wdig. Pemb 8B 22
Wealdstone. G Lon 5M 19
Weardley. W Yor 1L 39
Weare. Som 8G 17
Weare Giffard. Devn 3F 6
Wearhead. Dur 8D 50
Wearne. Som 3D 8
Weasdale. Cumb 3H 43
Weasenham All Saints. Norf 5E 36
Weasenham St Peter. Norf 5E 36
Weaverham. Ches W 8E 38
Weaverthorpe. N Yor 6J 45
Webheath. Worc 5L 25
Webton. Here 8E 24
Wedderlairs. Abers 6J 73
Weddington. Warw 2B 26
Wedhampton. Wilts 8A 18
Wedmore. Som 1D 8
Wednesbury. W Mid 2K 25
Wednesfield. W Mid 1K 25
Weecar. Notts 3E 34
Weedon. Buck 2J 19
Weedon Bec. Nptn 6E 26
Weedon Lois. Nptn 7E 26
Weeford. Staf 1M 25
Week. Devn 3G 7 (nr. Barnstaple)
Week. Devn 5H 7 (nr. Okehampton)
Week. Devn 4J 7 (nr. South Molton)
Week. Devn 3J 5 (nr. Totnes)
Week. Som 2L 7
Weeke. Devn 5J 7
Weeke. Hants 2E 10
Week Green. Corn 6D 6
Weekley. Nptn 3G 27
Week St Mary. Corn 6D 6
Weel. E Yor 2G 41
Weeley. Essx 1K 21
Weeley Heath. Essx 1K 21
Weem. Per 1D 60
Weeping Cross. Staf 7G 33
Weethly. Warw 6L 25
Weeting. Norf 3D 28
Weeton. E Yor 3K 41
Weeton. Lanc 2B 38
Weeton. N Yor 1L 39
Weetwood Hall. Nmbd 7K 57
Weir. Lanc 3G 39
Welborne. Norf 6G 37
Welbourn. Linc 4F 34
Welburn. N Yor 5F 44 (nr. Kirkbymoorside)
Welburn. N Yor 7G 45 (nr. Malton)
Welbury. N Yor 3C 44
Welby. Linc 6F 34
Welches Dam. Cambs 3A 28
Welcombe. Devn 4D 6
Weld Bank. Lanc 4D 38
Weldon. Nptn 3H 27
Weldon. Nmbd 2G 51
Welford. Nptn 3E 26
Welford. W Ber 6E 18
Welford-on-Avon. Warw 6M 25
Welham. Leics 2F 26
Welham. Notts 7D 40
Welham Green. Herts 3A 20
Well. Hants 1H 11
Well. Linc 8L 41
Well. N Yor 5B 44
Welland. Worc 7H 25
Wellbank. Ang 2K 61
Well Bottom. Dors 4J 9
Welldale. Dum 5J 49
Wellesbourne. Warw 6A 26
Well Hill. Kent 7C 20
Wellhouse. W Ber 6F 18
Welling. G Lon 6C 20
Wellingborough. Nptn 5G 27
Wellingham. Norf 5E 36
Wellingore. Linc 4F 34
Wellington. Cumb 3B 42
Wellington. Here 7E 24
Wellington. Som 3A 8
Wellington. Telf 8D 32
Wellington Heath. Here 7H 25
Wellow. Bath 8K 17
Wellow. IOW 7D 10
Wellow. Notts 3C 34
Wellpond Green. Herts 1C 20
Wells. Som 1E 8
Wellsborough. Leics 1B 26
Wells Green. Ches E 4D 32
Wells-next-the-Sea. Norf 3F 36
Wellswood. Torb 3L 5
Wellwood. Fife 1J 55
Welney. Norf 2B 28
Welsford. Devn 3D 6
Welshampton. Shrp 6B 32
Welsh End. Shrp 6C 32
Welsh Frankton. Shrp 6A 32
Welsh Hook. Pemb 1D 14
Welsh Newton. Here 2G 17
Welsh Newton Common. Here 2H 17
Welshpool. Powy 1C 24
Welsh St Donats. V Glam 6C 16
Welton. Bath 8J 17
Welton. Cumb 7L 49
Welton. E Yor 3F 40
Welton. Linc 7G 41
Welton. Nptn 5D 26
Welton Hill. Linc 7G 41
Welton le Marsh. Linc 3L 35
Welton le Wold. Linc 7J 41
Welwick. E Yor 3K 41
Welwyn. Herts 2A 20
Welwyn Garden City. Herts 2A 20
Wem. Shrp 7C 32
Wembdon. Som 2B 8
Wembley. G Lon 5M 19
Wembury. Devn 5G 5
Wembworthy. Devn 5H 7
Wemyss Bay. Inv 2K 53
Wenallt. Cdgn 4J 23
Wenallt. Gwyn 5J 31
Wendens Ambo. Essx 8B 28
Wendlebury. Oxon 2F 18
Wendling. Norf 6F 36
Wendover. Buck 3J 19
Wendron. Corn 6D 3
Wendy. Cambs 7M 27
Wenfordbridge. Corn 8B 6
Wenhaston. Suff 4L 29
Wennington. Cambs 4L 27
Wennington. G Lon 5D 20
Wennington. Lanc 6H 43
Wensley. Derbs 3K 33
Wensley. N Yor 5M 43
Wentbridge. W Yor 4A 40
Wentnor. Shrp 2D 24
Wentworth. Cambs 4A 28
Wentworth. S Yor 6M 39
Wenvoe. V Glam 6D 16
Weobley. Here 6E 24
Weobley Marsh. Here 6E 24
Wepham. W Sus 5L 11
Wereham. Norf 1C 28
Wergs. W Mid 1J 25
Wern. Gwyn 5E 30
Wern. Powy 2D 16 (nr. Brecon)
Wern. Powy 8M 31 (nr. Guilsfield)
Wern. Powy 8J 31 (nr. Llangadfan)
Wern. Powy 7M 31 (nr. Llanymynech)
Wernffrwd. Swan 4K 15
Wernyrheolydd. Mon 2F 16
Werrington. Corn 7E 6
Werrington. Pet 1K 27
Werrington. Staf 5G 33
Wervin. Ches W 8C 38
Wesham. Lanc 2C 38
Wessington. Derbs 4L 33
West Aberthaw. V Glam 7C 16
West Acre. Norf 6D 36
West Allerdean. Nmbd 5J 57
West Alvington. Devn 5J 5
West Amesbury. Wilts 1B 10
West Anstey. Devn 3K 7
West Appleton. N Yor 4B 44
West Ardsley. W Yor 3L 39
West Arthurlie. E Ren 4C 54
West Ashby. Linc 8J 41
West Ashling. W Sus 5J 11
West Ashton. Wilts 8L 17
West Auckland. Dur 1A 44
West Ayton. N Yor 5J 45
West Bagborough. Som 2A 8
West Bank. Hal 7D 38
West Barkwith. Linc 7H 41
West Barnby. N Yor 2H 45
West Barns. E Lot 2F 56
West Barsham. Norf 4F 36
West Bay. Dors 6D 8
West Beckham. Norf 4H 37
West Bennan. N Ayr 7H 53
Westbere. Kent 7K 21
West Bergholt. Essx 1H 21
West Bexington. Dors 7E 8
West Bilney. Norf 6D 36
West Blackdene. Dur 8D 50
West Blatchington. Brig 7A 12
Westborough. Linc 5E 34
Westbourne. Bour 6A 10
Westbourne. W Sus 5H 11
West Bowling. W Yor 2K 39
West Brabourne. Kent 3J 13
West Bradford. Lanc 1F 38
West Bradley. Som 2E 8
West Bretton. W Yor 4L 39
West Bridgford. Notts 6B 34
West Briggs. Norf 6C 36
West Bromwich. W Mid 2K 25
Westbrook. Here 7C 24
Westbrook. Kent 6M 21
Westbrook. Wilts 7M 17
West Buckland. Devn 2H 7 (nr. Barnstaple)
West Buckland. Devn 5H 5 (nr. Thurlestone)
West Buckland. Som 3A 8
West Burnside. Abers 6H 67
West Burrafirth. Shet 6C 79
West Burton. N Yor 5M 43
West Burton. W Sus 4L 11
Westbury. Buck 8E 26
Westbury. Shrp 1D 24
Westbury. Wilts 8L 17
Westbury Leigh. Wilts 1H 9
Westbury-on-Severn. Glos 2K 17
Westbury on Trym. Bris 6H 17
Westbury-sub-Mendip. Som 1E 8
West Butsfield. Dur 7G 51
West Butterwick. N Lin 5E 40
Westby. Linc 7F 34
West Byfleet. Surr 7L 19
West Caister. Norf 6M 37
West Calder. W Lot 3J 55
West Camel. Som 3E 8
West Carr. N Lin 5D 40
West Chaldon. Dors 7G 9
West Challow. Oxon 5D 18
West Charleton. Devn 5J 5
West Chelborough. Dors 5E 8
West Chevington. Nmbd 2H 51
West Chiltington. W Sus 4L 11
West Chiltington Common. W Sus 4L 11
West Chinnock. Som 4D 8
West Chisenbury. Wilts 8B 18
West Clandon. Surr 8L 19
West Cliffe. Kent 3M 13
Westcliff-on-Sea. S'end 5G 21
West Clyne. High 1L 71
West Coker. Som 4E 8
Westcombe. Som 2F 8 (nr. Evercreech)
Westcombe. Som 3D 8 (nr. Somerton)
West Compton. Dors 6E 8
West Compton. Som 1E 8
West Cornforth. Dur 8J 51
Westcot. Oxon 5D 18
Westcott. Buck 2H 19
Westcott. Devn 5M 7
Westcott. Surr 1M 11
Westcott Barton. Oxon 1E 18
West Cowick. E Yor 3C 40
West Cranmore. Som 1F 8
West Croftmore. High 2M 65
West Cross. Swan 5L 15
West Cullerlie. Abers 3H 67
West Culvennan. Dum 5M 47
West Curry. Corn 6D 6
West Curthwaite. Cumb 7L 49
Westdean. E Sus 8D 12
West Dean. W Sus 4J 11
West Dean. Wilts 3C 10
West Deeping. Linc 1K 27
West Derby. Mers 6B 38
West Dereham. Norf 1C 28
West Down. Devn 1G 7
Westdowns. Corn 7B 6
West Drayton. G Lon 6L 19
West Drayton. Notts 8D 40
West Dunnet. High 2H 77
West Ella. E Yor 3G 41
West End. Bed 6H 27
West End. Cambs 2A 28
West End. Dors 5J 9
West End. E Yor 7K 45 (nr. Kilham)
West End. E Yor 2H 41 (nr. Preston)
West End. E Yor 2F 40 (nr. South Cove)
West End. E Yor 8L 45 (nr. Ulrome)
West End. G Lon 5A 20
West End. Hants 4E 10
West End. Herts 3A 20
West End. Kent 7K 21
West End. Lanc 7F 42
West End. Linc 5K 35
West End. Norf 6L 37
West End. N Som 7G 17
West End. N Yor 8A 44
West End. S Glo 5K 17
West End. S Lan 5H 55
West End. Surr 7K 19
West End. Wilts 3J 9
West End. Wind 6J 19
West End. Worc 8L 25
West End Green. Hants 7G 19
Westenhanger. Kent 4K 13
Wester Aberchalder. High 2H 65
Wester Balgedie. Per 5G 61
Wester Brae. High 5J 71
Wester Culbeuchly. Abers 3G 73
Westerdale. High 4G 77
Westerdale. N Yor 3F 44
Wester Dechmont. W Lot 2J 55
Wester Fearn. High 3J 71
Westerfield. Suff 7H 29
Wester Galcantray. High 7L 71
Westergate. W Sus 5K 11
Wester Gruinards. High 2H 71
Westerham. Kent 8C 20
Westerleigh. S Glo 6J 17
Westerloch. High 4J 77
Wester Mandally. High 3E 64
Wester Quarff. Shet 8E 79
Wester Rarichie. High 4L 71
Wester Shian. Per 2D 60
Wester Skeld. Shet 7C 79
Westerton. Ang 8G 67
Westerton. Dur 8H 51
Westerton. W Sus 5J 11
Westerwick. Shet 7C 79
West Farleigh. Kent 8F 20
West Farndon. Nptn 6D 26
West Felton. Shrp 7A 32
Westfield. Cumb 1A 42
Westfield. E Sus 6G 13
Westfield. High 3F 76
Westfield. Norf 1F 28
Westfield. N Lan 2F 54
Westfield. W Lot 2H 55
Westfields. Dors 5G 9
Westfields of Rattray. Per 1G 61
West Fleetham. Nmbd 7L 57
Westford. Som 4A 8
West Garforth. W Yor 2M 39
Westgate. Dur 8E 50
Westgate. Norf 3F 36
Westgate. N Lin 5D 40
Westgate on Sea. Kent 6M 21
West Ginge. Oxon 5E 18
West Grafton. Wilts 7C 18
West Green. Hants 8H 19
West Grimstead. Wilts 3C 10
West Grinstead. W Sus 3M 11
West Haddlesey. N Yor 3B 40
West Haddon. Nptn 4E 26
West Hagbourne. Oxon 5F 18
West Hagley. Worc 3J 25
West Hall. Cumb 5A 50
Westhall. Suff 3L 29
West Hallam. Derbs 5A 34
Westhall Terrace. Ang 2K 61
West Halton. N Lin 3F 40
Westham. Dors 8F 8
Westham. E Sus 7E 12
West Ham. G Lon 5B 20
Westham. Som 1D 8
Westhampnett. W Sus 5J 11
West Handley. Derbs 8M 39
West Hanney. Oxon 4E 18
West Hanningfield. Essx 4F 20
West Hardwick. W Yor 4A 40
West Harnham. Wilts 3B 10
West Harptree. Bath 8H 17
West Harting. W Sus 3H 11
West Harton. Tyne 5J 51
West Hatch. Som 3B 8
Westhay. Som 1D 8
Westhead. Lanc 5C 38
West Head. Norf 1B 28
West Heath. Hants 8F 18 (nr. Basingstoke)
West Heath. Hants 8J 19 (nr. Farnborough)
West Helmsdale. High 8F 76
West Hendred. Oxon 5E 18
West Heogaland. Shet 4C 79
West Heslerton. N Yor 6J 45
West Hewish. N Som 7F 16
Westhide. Here 7F 24
Westhill. Abers 3J 67
West Hill. Devn 6M 7
West Hill. E Yor 7L 45
Westhill. High 7K 71
West Hill. N Som 6G 17
West Hill. W Sus 4B 12
West Hoathly. W Sus 4B 12
West Holme. Dors 7H 9
Westhope. Here 6E 24
Westhope. Shrp 3E 24
West Horndon. Essx 5E 20
Westhorp. Nptn 6D 26
Westhorpe. Linc 6J 35
Westhorpe. Suff 5G 29
West Horrington. Som 1E 8
West Horsley. Surr 8L 19
West Horton. Nmbd 6K 57
West Hougham. Kent 3L 13
Westhoughton. G Man 5E 38
West Houlland. Shet 6C 79
Westhouse. N Yor 6H 43
Westhouses. Derbs 4A 34
West Howe. Bour 6A 10
Westhumble. Surr 8M 19
West Huntspill. Som 1C 8
West Hyde. Herts 4L 19
West Hynish. Arg 9A 62
West Hythe. Kent 4K 13
West Ilsley. W Ber 5E 18
Westing. Shet 1F 79
West Itchenor. W Sus 5J 11
West Keal. Linc 3K 35
West Kennett. Wilts 7B 18
West Kilbride. N Ayr 5A 54
West Kingsdown. Kent 7D 20
West Kington. Wilts 6L 17
West Kirby. Mers 7A 38
West Knapton. N Yor 6H 45
West Knighton. Dors 7G 9
West Knoyle. Wilts 2H 9
West Kyloe. Nmbd 5K 57
Westlake. Devn 4H 5
West Lambrook. Som 4D 8
West Langdon. Kent 3M 13
West Langwell. High 1J 71
West Lavington. W Sus 3J 11
West Lavington. Wilts 8A 18
West Layton. N Yor 3A 44
West Leake. Notts 7B 34
West Learmouth. Nmbd 6H 57
Westleigh. Devn 3F 6 (nr. Bideford)
Westleigh. Devn 4M 7 (nr. Tiverton)
West Leigh. Devn 5H 7 (nr. Winkleigh)
Westleigh. G Man 5E 38
West Leith. Buck 2K 19
Westleton. Suff 5L 29
West Lexham. Norf 6E 36
Westley. Shrp 1D 24
Westley. Suff 5E 28
Westley Waterless. Cambs 6C 28
West Lilling. N Yor 7F 44
West Lingo. Fife 5K 61
Westlington. Buck 2H 19
Westlinton. Cumb 5L 49
West Linton. Bord 4K 55
West Littleton. S Glo 6K 17
West Looe. Corn 4D 4
West Lulworth. Dors 7H 9
West Lutton. N Yor 7J 45
West Lydford. Som 2E 8
West Lyng. Som 3C 8
West Lynn. Norf 6C 36
West Mains. Per 4E 60
West Malling. Kent 8E 20
West Malvern. Worc 7H 25
Westmancote. Worc 8K 25
West Marden. W Sus 4H 11
West Markham. Notts 8D 40
Westmarsh. Kent 7L 21
West Marsh. NE Lin 5J 41
West Marton. N Yor 8K 43
West Meon. Hants 3G 11
West Mersea. Essx 2J 21
Westmeston. E Sus 6B 12
Westmill. Herts 1B 20 (nr. Buntingford)
Westmill. Herts 8K 27 (nr. Hitchin)
West Milton. Dors 6E 8
Westminster. G Lon 6A 20
West Molesey. Surr 7M 19
West Monkton. Som 3B 8
Westmoor End. Cumb 8H 49
West Moors. Dors 5A 10
West Morden. Dors 6J 9
West Muir. Ang 7F 66 (nr. Brechin)
Westmuir. Ang 8D 66 (nr. Forfar)
West Murkle. High 3G 77
West Ness. N Yor 6F 44
Westness. Orkn 5B 78
Westnewton. Cumb 7J 49
West Newton. E Yor 2H 41
West Newton. Norf 5C 36
Westnewton. Nmbd 6J 57
West Newton. Som 3B 8
West Norwood. G Lon 6B 20
Westoe. Tyne 5J 51
West Ogwell. Devn 3K 5
Weston. Bath 7K 17
Weston. Ches E 4E 32 (nr. Crewe)
Weston. Ches E 8H 39 (nr. Macclesfield)
Weston. Devn 5A 8 (nr. Honiton)
Weston. Devn 7A 8 (nr. Sidmouth)
Weston. Dors 8F 8 (nr. Weymouth)
Weston. Dors 5E 8 (nr. Yeovil)
Weston. Hal 7D 38
Weston. Hants 3H 11
Weston. Here 6D 24
Weston. Herts 8L 27
Weston. Linc 7J 35
Weston. Nptn 7D 26
Weston. Notts 3D 34
Weston. Shrp 2F 24 (nr. Bridgnorth)
Weston. Shrp 4D 24 (nr. Knighton)
Weston. Shrp 7C 32 (nr. Wem)
Weston. S Lan 5J 55
Weston. Staf 7G 33
Weston. Suff 3L 29
Weston. W Ber 6D 18
Weston Bampfylde. Som 3F 8
Weston Beggard. Here 7F 24
Westonbirt. Glos 5L 17
Weston by Welland. Nptn 2F 26
Weston Colville. Cambs 6C 28
Westoncommon. Shrp 7B 32
Weston Coyney. Stoke 5G 33
Weston Ditch. Suff 4C 28
Weston Favell. Nptn 5F 26
Weston Green. Cambs 6C 28
Weston Green. Norf 6H 37
Weston Heath. Shrp 8E 32
Weston Hills. Linc 8J 35
Weston in Arden. Warw 3B 26
Westoning. C Beds 8J 27
Weston-in-Gordano. N Som 6G 17
Weston Jones. Staf 7E 32
Weston Longville. Norf 6H 37
Weston Lullingfields. Shrp 7B 32
Weston-on-Avon. Warw 6M 25
Weston-on-the-Green. Oxon 2F 18
Weston-on-Trent. Derbs 7A 34
Weston Patrick. Hants 1G 11
Weston Rhyn. Shrp 6M 31
Weston-sub-Edge. Glos 7M 25
Weston-super-Mare. N Som 7F 16
Weston Town. Som 1G 9
Weston Turville. Buck 2J 19
Weston under Lizard. Staf 8F 32
Weston under Penyard. Here 1J 17
Weston under Wetherley. Warw 5B 26
Weston Underwood. Derbs 5K 33
Weston Underwood. Mil 6G 27
Westonzoyland. Som 2C 8
West Orchard. Dors 4H 9
West Overton. Wilts 7B 18
Westow. N Yor 7G 45
Westown. Per 3H 61
West Panson. Devn 6E 6
West Park. Hart 8K 51
West Parley. Dors 6A 10
West Peckham. Kent 8E 20
West Pelton. Dur 6H 51
West Pennard. Som 2E 8
West Pentire. Corn 3E 3
West Perry. Cambs 5K 27
West Pitcorthie. Fife 5L 61
West Plean. Stir 1G 55
West Poringland. Norf 1J 29
West Porlock. Som 1K 7
Westport. Som 4C 8
West Putford. Devn 4E 6
West Quantoxhead. Som 1A 8
Westra. V Glam 6D 16
West Rainton. Dur 7J 51
West Rasen. Linc 7G 41
West Ravendale. NE Lin 6J 41
Westray Airport. Orkn 2C 78
West Raynham. Norf 5E 36
Westrigg. W Lot 3H 55
West Rounton. N Yor 3D 44
West Row. Suff 4C 28
West Rudham. Norf 5E 36
West Runton. Norf 3H 37
Westruther. Bord 4F 56
Westry. Cambs 2M 27
West Saltoun. E Lot 3D 56
West Sandford. Devn 5K 7
West Sandwick. Shet 3E 79
West Scrafton. N Yor 5M 43
Westside. Orkn 5B 78
West Sleekburn. Nmbd 3H 51
West Somerton. Norf 6L 37
West Stafford. Dors 7G 9
West Stockwith. Notts 6D 40
West Stoke. W Sus 5J 11
West Stonesdale. N Yor 3K 43
West Stoughton. Som 1D 8
West Stour. Dors 3G 9
West Stourmouth. Kent 7L 21
West Stow. Suff 4E 28
West Stowell. Wilts 7B 18
West Strathan. High 3A 76
West Stratton. Hants 1F 10
West Street. Kent 8H 21
West Tanfield. N Yor 6B 44
West Taphouse. Corn 3C 4
West Tarbert. Arg 3G 53
West Thirston. Nmbd 1G 51
West Thorney. W Sus 5H 11
West Thurrock. Thur 6D 20
West Tilbury. Thur 6E 20
West Tisted. Hants 3G 11
West Tofts. Norf 2E 28
West Torrington. Linc 7H 41
West Town. Bath 7H 17
West Town. Hants 6H 11
West Town. N Som 7G 17
West Tytherley. Hants 3C 10
West Tytherton. Wilts 6M 17
West View. Hart 8L 51
Westville. Notts 5B 34
West Walton. Norf 8L 35
Westward. Cumb 7K 49
Westward Ho!. Devn 3F 6
Westwell. Kent 3H 13
Westwell. Oxon 3C 18
Westwell Leacon. Kent 3H 13
West Wellow. Hants 4C 10
West Wemyss. Fife 6J 61
Westwick. Cambs 5A 28
Westwick. Dur 2M 43
Westwick. Norf 5J 37
West Wick. N Som 7F 16
West Wickham. Cambs 7C 28
West Wickham. G Lon 7B 20
West Williamston. Pemb 3E 14
West Willoughby. Linc 5F 34
West Winch. Norf 6C 36
West Winterslow. Wilts 2C 10
West Wittering. W Sus 6H 11
West Witton. N Yor 5M 43
Westwood. Devn 6M 7
Westwood. Kent 7M 21
Westwood. Pet 2K 27
Westwood. S Lan 4E 54
Westwood. Wilts 8L 17
West Woodburn. Nmbd 3D 50
West Woodhay. W Ber 7D 18
West Woodlands. Som 1G 9
West Woodside. Cumb 7L 49
Westwoodside. N Lin 5D 40
West Worldham. Hants 2H 11
West Worlington. Devn 4J 7
West Worthing. W Sus 5M 11
West Wratting. Cambs 6C 28
West Wycombe. Buck 4J 19
West Wylam. Nmbd 5G 51
West Yatton. Wilts 6L 17
West Yell. Shet 3E 79
West Youlstone. Corn 4D 6
Wetheral. Cumb 6M 49
Wetherby. W Yor 1A 40
Wetherden. Suff 5G 29
Wetheringsett. Suff 5H 29
Wethersfield. Essx 8D 28
Wethersta. Shet 5D 79
Wetherup Street. Suff 5H 29
Wetley Rocks. Staf 5G 33
Wettenhall. Ches E 3D 32
Wetton. Staf 4J 33
Wetwang. E Yor 8J 45
Wetwood. Staf 6E 32
Wexcombe. Wilts 8C 18
Wexham Street. Buck 5K 19
Weybourne. Norf 3H 37
Weybourne. Surr 1J 11
Weybread. Suff 3J 29
Weybridge. Surr 7L 19
Weycroft. Devn 6C 8
Weydale. High 3G 77
Weyhill. Hants 1D 10
Weymouth. Dors 8F 8 & 104
Weythel. Powy 6C 24
Whaddon. Buck 8G 27
Whaddon. Cambs 7M 27
Whaddon. Glos 2L 17
Whaddon. Wilts 3B 10
Whale. Cumb 1G 43
Whaley. Derbs 8B 40
Whaley Bridge. Derbs 7J 39
Whaley Thorns. Derbs 8B 40
Whalley. Lanc 2F 38
Whalton. Nmbd 3G 51
Wham. N Yor 7J 43
Whaplode. Linc 7K 35
Whaplode Drove. Linc 8K 35
Whaplode St Catherine. Linc 7K 35
Wharfe. N Yor 7J 43
Wharles. Lanc 2C 38
Wharley End. C Beds 7H 27
Wharncliffe Side. S Yor 6L 39
Wharram-le-Street. N Yor 7H 45
Wharton. Ches W 3D 32
Wharton. Here 6F 24
Whashton. N Yor 3A 44
Whasset. Cumb 5G 43

Whatcote—Zouch

Whatcote. Warw 7A 26
Whateley. Warw 2A 26
Whatfield. Suff 7G 29
Whatley. Som 5C 8 (nr. Chard)
Whatley. Som 1G 9 (nr. Frome)
Whatlington. E Sus 6F 12
Whatmore. Shrp 4G 25
Whatstandwell. Derbs 4L 33
Whatton. Notts 6D 34
Whauphill. Dum 7B 48
Whaw. N Yor 3L 43
Wheatacre. Norf 2L 29
Wheatcroft. Derbs 4L 33
Wheathampstead. Herts 2M 19
Wheathill. Shrp 3G 25
Wheatley. Devn 6K 7
Wheatley. Hants 1H 11
Wheatley. Oxon 3F 18
Wheatley. S Yor 5B 40
Wheatley. W Yor 3J 39
Wheatley Hill. Dur 8J 51
Wheatley Lane. Lanc 2G 39
Wheatley Park. S Yor 5B 40
Wheaton Aston. Staf 8F 32
Wheatstone Park. Staf 1J 25
Wheddon Cross. Som 2L 7
Wheelerstreet. Surr 1K 11
Wheelock. Ches E 4E 32
Wheelock Heath. Ches E 4E 32
Wheelton. Lanc 3E 38
Wheldrake. York 1C 40
Whelford. Glos 4B 18
Whelpley Hill. Buck 3K 19
Whelpo. Cumb 8L 49
Whelston. Flin 8A 38
Whenby. N Yor 7F 44
Whepstead. Suff 6E 28
Wherstead. Suff 7H 29
Wherwell. Hants 1D 10
Wheston. Derbs 8K 39
Whetsted. Kent 3E 12
Whetstone. G Lon 4A 20
Whetstone. Leics 2D 26
Whicham. Cumb 5C 42
Whichford. Warw 8B 26
Whickham. Tyne 5H 51
Whiddon. Devn 5F 6
Whiddon Down. Devn 6H 7
Whigstreet. Ang 1K 61
Whilton. Nptn 5E 26
Whimble. Devn 5E 6
Whimple. Devn 6M 7
Whimpwell Green. Norf 5K 37
Whinburgh. Norf 1G 29
Whin Lane End. Lanc 1B 38
Whinnyfold. Abers 6L 73
Whinny Hill. Stoc T 2C 44
Whippingham. IOW 6F 10
Whipsnade. C Beds 2L 19
Whipton. Devn 6L 7
Whirlow. S Yor 7M 39
Whisby. Linc 3F 34
Whissendine. Rut 8E 34
Whissonsett. Norf 5F 36
Whisterfield. Ches E 8G 39
Whistley Green. Wok 6H 19
Whiston. Mers 6C 38
Whiston. Nptn 5G 27
Whiston. S Yor 6A 40
Whiston. Staf 5H 33 (nr. Cheadle)
Whiston. Staf 8F 32 (nr. Penkridge)
Whiston Cross. Shrp 1H 25
Whiston Eaves. Staf 5H 33
Whitacre Heath. Warw 2A 26
Whitbeck. Cumb 5C 42
Whitbourne. Here 6H 25
Whitburn. Tyne 5K 51
Whitburn. W Lot 3H 55
Whitburn Colliery. Tyne 5K 51
Whitby. Ches W 8B 38
Whitby. N Yor 2H 45
Whitbyheath. Ches W 8B 38
Whitchester. Bord 4G 57
Whitchurch. Bath 7J 17
Whitchurch. Buck 1J 19
Whitchurch. Card 6D 16
Whitchurch. Devn 8F 6
Whitchurch. Hants 1E 10
Whitchurch. Here 2H 17
Whitchurch. Pemb 1C 14
Whitchurch. Shrp 5C 32
Whitchurch Canonicorum. Dors 6C 8
Whitchurch Hill. Oxon 6G 19
Whitchurch-on-Thames. Oxon 6G 19
Whitcombe. Dors 7G 9
Whitcot. Shrp 2D 24
Whitcott Keysett. Shrp 3C 24
Whiteash Green. Essx 8D 28
Whitebog. High 5K 71
Whitebridge. High 2G 65
Whitebrook. Mon 3H 17
Whitecairns. Abers 2K 67
White Chapel. Lanc 1D 38
Whitechurch. Pemb 8D 22
White Colne. Essx 1G 21
White Coppice. Lanc 4E 38
White Corries. High 8E 64
Whitecraig. E Lot 2M 55
Whitecroft. Glos 3J 17
White Cross. Corn 7D 3 (nr. Mullion)
Whitecross. Corn 8A 6 (nr. Wadebridge)
Whitecross. Falk 2H 55
White End. Worc 8H 25
Whiteface. High 3K 71
Whitefarland. N Ayr 5G 53
Whitefaulds. S Ayr 1M 47
Whitefield. Dors 6J 9
Whitefield. G Man 5G 39
Whitefield. Som 3M 7
Whiteford. Abers 1H 67
Whitegate. Ches W 3D 32
Whitehall. Devn 4A 8
Whitehall. Hants 8H 19
Whitehall. Orkn 5E 78
Whitehall. W Sus 3M 11
Whitehaven. Cumb 2A 42
Whitehaven. Shrp 7M 31
Whitehill. Hants 2H 11
Whitehill. N Ayr 4A 54
Whitehills. Abers 3G 73
Whitehills. Ang 8E 66
White Horse Common. Norf 5K 37
Whitehough. Derbs 7J 39
Whitehouse. Abers 2G 67
Whitehouse. Arg 3G 53
Whiteinch. Glas 3D 54
Whitekirk. E Lot 1E 56
White Kirkley. Dur 8F 50
White Lackington. Dors 6G 9
Whitelackington. Som 4C 8
White Ladies Aston. Worc 6K 25
White Lee. W Yor 3L 39
Whiteley. Hants 4F 10
Whiteley Bank. IOW 7F 10
Whiteley Village. Surr 7L 19
Whitemans Green. W Sus 5B 12
White Mill. Carm 1J 15
Whitemire. Mor 6M 71
Whitemoor. Corn 4A 4
Whitenap. Hants 3D 10
Whiteness. Shet 7E 79
White Notley. Essx 2F 20
Whiteoak Green. Oxon 2D 18
Whiteparish. Wilts 3C 10
White Pit. Linc 8K 41
Whiterashes. Abers 1J 67
White Rocks. Here 1G 17
White Roding. Essx 2D 20
Whiterow. High 5J 77
Whiterow. Mor 4A 72
Whiteshill. Glos 3L 17
Whiteside. Nmbd 5C 50
Whiteside. W Lot 3H 55
Whitesmith. E Sus 6D 12
Whitestaunton. Som 4B 8
Whitestone. Abers 4G 67
Whitestone. Devn 6K 7
White Stone. Here 7F 24
Whitestones. Abers 4J 73
Whitestreet Green. Suff 8F 28
Whitewall Corner. N Yor 6G 45
White Waltham. Wind 6J 19
Whiteway. Glos 2M 17
Whitewell. Lanc 1E 38
Whitewell Bottom. Lanc 3G 39
Whiteworks. Devn 8H 7
Whitewreath. Mor 4C 72
Whitfield. D'dee 2K 61
Whitfield. Kent 3M 13
Whitfield. Nptn 8E 26
Whitfield. Nmbd 6C 50
Whitfield. S Glo 4J 17
Whitford. Devn 6B 8
Whitford. Flin 2L 31
Whitgift. E Yor 3E 40
Whitgreave. Staf 7F 32
Whithorn. Dum 7B 48
Whiting Bay. N Ayr 7J 53
Whitington. Norf 2D 28
Whitkirk. W Yor 2M 39
Whitland. Carm 2G 15
Whitleigh. Plym 4F 4
Whitletts. S Ayr 7B 54
Whitley. N Yor 3B 40
Whitley. Wilts 7L 17
Whitley Bay. Tyne 4J 51
Whitley Chapel. Nmbd 6E 50
Whitley Heath. Staf 7F 32
Whitley Lower. W Yor 4L 39
Whitley Thorpe. N Yor 3B 40
Whitlock's End. W Mid 4M 25
Whitminster. Glos 3K 17
Whitmore. Dors 5A 10
Whitmore. Staf 5F 32
Whitnage. Devn 4M 7
Whitnash. Warw 5B 26
Whitney. Here 7C 24
Whitrigg. Cumb 6K 49 (nr. Kirkbride)
Whitrigg. Cumb 8K 49 (nr. Torpenhow)
Whitsbury. Hants 4B 10
Whitsome. Bord 4H 57
Whitson. Newp 5F 16
Whitstable. Kent 7K 21
Whitstone. Corn 6D 6
Whittingham. Nmbd 8K 57
Whittingslow. Shrp 3E 24
Whittington. Derbs 8A 40
Whittington. Glos 1A 18
Whittington. Lanc 6H 43
Whittington. Shrp 6A 32
Whittington. Staf 3J 25 (nr. Kinver)
Whittington. Staf 1M 25 (nr. Lichfield)
Whittington. Warw 2A 26
Whittington. Worc 6J 25
Whittington Barracks. Staf 1M 25
Whittlebury. Nptn 7E 26
Whittleford. Warw 2B 26
Whittle-le-Woods. Lanc 3D 38
Whittlesey. Cambs 2L 27
Whittlesford. Cambs 7A 28
Whittlestone Head. Bkbn 4F 38
Whitton. N Lin 3F 40
Whitton. Nmbd 1F 50
Whitton. Powy 5C 24
Whitton. Bord 7G 57
Whitton. Shrp 4F 24
Whitton. Stoc T 1C 44
Whittonditch. Wilts 6C 18
Whittonstall. Nmbd 6F 50
Whitway. Hants 8E 18
Whitwell. Derbs 8B 40
Whitwell. Herts 1M 19
Whitwell. IOW 8F 10
Whitwell. N Yor 4B 44
Whitwell. Rut 1H 27
Whitwell-on-the-Hill. N Yor 7G 45
Whitwick. Leics 8A 34
Whitwood. W Yor 3A 40
Whitworth. Lanc 4G 39
Whixall. Shrp 6C 32
Whixley. N Yor 8D 44
Whoberley. W Mid 4A 26
Whorlton. Dur 2A 44
Whorlton. N Yor 3D 44
Whygate. Nmbd 4C 50
Whyle. Here 5F 24
Whyteleafe. Surr 8B 20
Wibdon. Glos 4H 17
Wibtoft. Warw 3C 26
Wichenford. Worc 5H 25
Wichling. Kent 8H 21
Wick. Bour 6B 10
Wick. Devn 5A 8
Wick. High 4J 77
Wick. Shet 8E 79 (on Mainland)
Wick. Shet 1F 79 (on Unst)
Wick. Som 1B 8 (nr. Bridgwater)
Wick. Som 8F 16 (nr. Burnham-on-Sea)
Wick. Som 3D 8 (nr. Somerton)
Wick. S Glo 6K 17
Wick. V Glam 6B 16
Wick. W Sus 5L 11
Wick. Wilts 3B 10
Wick. Worc 7K 25
Wick Airport. High 4J 77
Wicken. Cambs 4B 28
Wicken. Nptn 8F 26
Wicken Bonhunt. Essx 8A 28
Wickenby. Linc 7G 41
Wicken Green Village. Norf 4E 36
Wickersley. S Yor 6A 40
Wicker Street Green. Suff 7F 28
Wickford. Essx 4F 20
Wickham. Hants 4F 10
Wickham. W Ber 6D 18
Wickham Bishops. Essx 2G 21
Wickhambreaux. Kent 8L 21
Wickhambrook. Suff 6D 28
Wickhamford. Worc 7L 25
Wickham Green. Suff 5G 29
Wickham Heath. W Ber 7E 18
Wickham Market. Suff 6K 29
Wickhampton. Norf 1L 29
Wickham St Paul. Essx 8E 28
Wickham Skeith. Suff 5G 29
Wickham Street. Suff 5G 29
Wick Hill. Wok 7H 19
Wicklewood. Norf 1G 29
Wickmere. Norf 4H 37
Wick St Lawrence. N Som 7F 16
Wickwar. S Glo 5K 17
Widdington. Essx 8B 28
Widdrington. Nmbd 2H 51
Widdrington Station. Nmbd 2H 51
Widecombe in the Moor. Devn 8J 7
Widegates. Corn 4D 4
Widemouth Bay. Corn 5D 6
Wide Open. Tyne 4H 51
Widewall. Orkn 8C 78
Widford. Essx 3E 20
Widford. Herts 2C 20
Widham. Wilts 5A 18
Widmer End. Buck 4J 19
Widmerpool. Notts 7C 34
Widnes. Hal 7D 38
Widworthy. Devn 6B 8
Wigan. G Man 5D 38
Wigbeth. Dors 5A 10
Wigborough. Som 4D 8
Wiggaton. Devn 6A 8
Wiggenhall St Germans. Norf 8M 35
Wiggenhall St Mary Magdalen. Norf 8M 35
Wiggenhall St Mary the Virgin. Norf 8M 35
Wiggenhall St Peter. Norf 6C 36
Wiggens Green. Essx 7C 28
Wigginton. Herts 2K 19
Wigginton. Oxon 8B 26
Wigginton. Staf 1A 26
Wigginton. York 8E 44
Wigglesworth. N Yor 8K 43
Wiggonby. Cumb 6K 49
Wiggonholt. W Sus 4L 11
Wighill. N Yor 1A 40
Wighton. Norf 3F 36
Wightwick. Staf 2J 25
Wigley. Hants 4D 10
Wigmore. Here 5E 24
Wigmore. Medw 7G 21
Wigsley. Notts 8E 40
Wigsthorpe. Nptn 3J 27
Wigston. Leics 2E 26
Wigtoft. Linc 6J 35
Wigton. Cumb 7K 49
Wigtown. Dum 6B 48
Wigtwizzle. S Yor 6L 39
Wike. W Yor 1M 39
Wilbarston. Nptn 3G 27
Wilberfoss. E Yor 8G 45
Wilburton. Cambs 4A 28
Wilby. Norf 3G 29
Wilby. Nptn 5G 27
Wilby. Suff 4J 29
Wilcot. Wilts 7B 18
Wilcott. Shrp 8A 32
Wilcove. Corn 4F 4
Wildboarclough. Ches E 3G 33
Wilden. Bed 6J 27
Wilden. Worc 4J 25
Wildern. Hants 4E 10
Wilderspool. Warr 7E 38
Wilde Street. Suff 4D 28
Wildhern. Hants 8D 18
Wildmanbridge. S Lan 4G 55
Wildmoor. Worc 4K 25
Wildsworth. Linc 6E 40
Wildwood. Staf 7G 33
Wilford. Nott 6B 34
Wilkesley. Ches E 5D 32
Wilkhaven. High 3M 71
Wilkieston. W Lot 3K 55
Wilksby. Linc 3J 35
Willand. Devn 4M 7
Willaston. Ches E 4D 32
Willaston. Ches W 8B 38
Willaston. IOM 6D 46
Willen. Mil 7G 27
Willenhall. W Mid 4B 26 (nr. Coventry)
Willenhall. W Mid 2K 25 (nr. Wolverhampton)
Willerby. E Yor 2G 41
Willerby. N Yor 6K 45
Willersey. Glos 8M 25
Willersley. Here 7D 24
Willesborough. Kent 3J 13
Willesborough Lees. Kent 3J 13
Willesden. G Lon 5A 20
Willesley. Wilts 5L 17
Willett. Som 2A 8
Willey. Shrp 2G 25
Willey. Warw 3C 26
Willey Green. Surr 8K 19
Williamscot. Oxon 7C 26
Williamsetter. Shet 9D 79
Willian. Herts 8L 27
Willingale. Essx 3D 20
Willingdon. E Sus 7D 12
Willingham. Cambs 4A 28
Willingham by Stow. Linc 7E 40
Willingham Green. Cambs 6C 28
Willington. Bed 7K 27
Willington. Derbs 7K 33
Willington. Dur 8G 51
Willington. Tyne 5J 51
Willington. Warw 8A 26
Willington Corner. Ches W 3C 32
Willisham Tye. Suff 6G 29
Willitoft. E Yor 2D 40
Williton. Som 1M 7
Willoughbridge. Staf 5E 32
Willoughby. Linc 8L 41
Willoughby. Warw 5D 26
Willoughby-on-the-Wolds. Notts 7C 34
Willoughby Waterleys. Leics 2D 26
Willoughton. Linc 6F 40
Willow Green. Worc 6H 25
Willows Green. Essx 2F 20
Willsbridge. S Glo 6J 17
Willslock. Staf 6H 33
Wilmcote. Warw 6M 25
Wilmington. Bath 7J 17
Wilmington. Devn 6B 8
Wilmington. E Sus 7D 12
Wilmington. Kent 6D 20
Wilmslow. Ches E 7G 39
Wilnecote. Staf 1A 26
Wilney Green. Norf 3G 29
Wilpshire. Lanc 2E 38
Wilsden. W Yor 2J 39
Wilsford. Linc 5G 35
Wilsford. Wilts 2B 10 (nr. Amesbury)
Wilsford. Wilts 8B 18 (nr. Devizes)
Wilsill. N Yor 7A 44
Wilsley Green. Kent 4F 12
Wilson. Here 1H 17
Wilson. Leics 7A 34
Wilsontown. S Lan 4H 55
Wilstead. Bed 7J 27
Wilsthorpe. E Yor 7L 45
Wilsthorpe. Linc 8G 35
Wilstone. Herts 2K 19
Wilton. Cumb 2B 42
Wilton. N Yor 5H 45
Wilton. Red C 2E 44
Wilton. Bord 8E 56
Wilton. Wilts 7C 18 (nr. Marlborough)
Wilton. Wilts 2A 10 (nr. Salisbury)
Wimbish. Essx 8B 28
Wimbish Green. Essx 8C 28
Wimblebury. Staf 8H 33
Wimbledon. G Lon 6A 20
Wimblington. Cambs 2A 28
Wimboldsley. Ches W 3D 32
Wimborne Minster. Dors 5A 10
Wimborne St Giles. Dors 4A 10
Wimbotsham. Norf 1C 28
Wimpole. Cambs 7M 27
Wimpstone. Warw 7A 26
Wincanton. Som 3G 9
Winceby. Linc 3K 35
Wincham. Ches W 8E 38
Winchburgh. W Lot 2J 55
Winchcombe. Glos 1A 18
Winchelsea. E Sus 6H 13
Winchelsea Beach. E Sus 6H 13
Winchester. Hants 3E 10 & 103
Winchet Hill. Kent 3F 12
Winchfield. Hants 8H 19
Winchmore Hill. Buck 4K 19
Winchmore Hill. G Lon 4B 20
Wincle. Ches E 3G 33
Windermere. Cumb 4F 42
Winderton. Warw 7B 26
Windhill. High 7H 71
Windle Hill. Ches W 8B 38
Windlesham. Surr 7K 19
Windley. Derbs 5L 33
Windmill. Derbs 8K 39
Windmill Hill. E Sus 6E 12
Windmill Hill. Som 4C 8
Windrush. Glos 2B 18
Windsor. Wind 6K 19 & 103
Windsor Green. Suff 6E 28
Windyedge. Abers 4K 67
Windygates. Fife 5J 61
Windyharbour. Ches E 8G 39
Windyknowe. W Lot 3H 55
Wineham. W Sus 5A 12
Winestead. E Yor 3K 41
Winfarthing. Norf 3H 29
Winford. IOW 7F 10
Winford. N Som 7H 17
Winforton. Here 7C 24
Winfrith Newburgh. Dors 7H 9
Wing. Buck 1J 19
Wing. Rut 1G 27
Wingate. Dur 8J 51
Wingates. G Man 5E 38
Wingates. Nmbd 2G 51
Wingerworth. Derbs 3L 33
Wingfield. C Beds 1L 19
Wingfield. Suff 4J 29
Wingfield. Wilts 8L 17
Wingfield Park. Derbs 4L 33
Wingham. Kent 8L 21
Wingmore. Kent 3K 13
Wingrave. Buck 2J 19
Winkburn. Notts 4D 34
Winkfield. Brac 6K 19
Winkfield Row. Brac 6J 19
Winkhill. Staf 4H 33
Winklebury. Hants 8G 19
Winkleigh. Devn 5H 7
Winksley. N Yor 6B 44
Winkton. Dors 6B 10
Winlaton. Tyne 5G 51
Winlaton Mill. Tyne 5G 51
Winless. High 4J 77
Winmarleigh. Lanc 1C 38
Winnal Common. Here 8E 24
Winnard's Perch. Corn 3A 4
Winnersh. Wok 6H 19
Winnington. Ches W 8E 38
Winnington. Staf 6E 32
Winnothdale. Staf 5H 33
Winscales. Cumb 1B 42
Winscombe. N Som 8G 17
Winsford. Ches W 3D 32
Winsford. Som 2L 7
Winsham. Devn 2G 7
Winsham. Som 5C 8
Winshill. Staf 7K 33
Winsh-wen. Swan 4L 15
Winskill. Cumb 8A 50
Winslade. Hants 1G 11
Winsley. Wilts 7K 17
Winslow. Buck 1H 19
Winson. Glos 3A 18
Winson Green. W Mid 3L 25
Winsor. Hants 4D 10
Winster. Cumb 4F 42
Winster. Derbs 3K 33
Winston. Dur 2A 44
Winston. Suff 5H 29
Winstone. Glos 3M 17
Winswell. Devn 4F 6
Winterborne Clenston. Dors 5H 9
Winterborne Herringston. Dors 7F 8
Winterborne Houghton. Dors 5H 9
Winterborne Kingston. Dors 6H 9
Winterborne Monkton. Dors 7F 8
Winterborne St Martin. Dors 7F 8
Winterborne Stickland. Dors 5H 9
Winterborne Whitechurch. Dors 5H 9
Winterborne Zelston. Dors 6J 9
Winterbourne. S Glo 5J 17
Winterbourne. W Ber 6E 18
Winterbourne Abbas. Dors 6F 8
Winterbourne Bassett. Wilts 6B 18
Winterbourne Dauntsey. Wilts 2B 10
Winterbourne Earls. Wilts 2B 10
Winterbourne Gunner. Wilts 2B 10
Winterbourne Monkton. Wilts 6A 18
Winterbourne Steepleton. Dors 7F 8
Winterbourne Stoke. Wilts 1A 10
Winterbrook. Oxon 5G 19
Winterburn. N Yor 8L 43
Winter Gardens. Essx 5F 20
Winterhay Green. Som 4C 8
Winteringham. N Lin 3F 40
Winterley. Ches E 4E 32
Wintersett. W Yor 4M 39
Winterton. N Lin 4F 40
Winterton-on-Sea. Norf 6L 37
Winthorpe. Linc 3M 35
Winthorpe. Notts 4E 34
Winton. Bour 6A 10
Winton. Cumb 2J 43
Winton. E Sus 7D 12
Wintringham. N Yor 6H 45
Winwick. Cambs 3K 27
Winwick. Nptn 4E 26
Winwick. Warr 6E 38
Wirksworth. Derbs 4K 33
Wirswall. Ches E 5C 32
Wisbech. Cambs 8L 35
Wisbech St Mary. Cambs 1A 28
Wisborough Green. W Sus 3L 11
Wiseton. Notts 7D 40
Wishaw. N Lan 4G 55
Wishaw. Warw 2M 25
Wisley. Surr 8L 19
Wispington. Linc 8J 41
Wissenden. Kent 3H 13
Wissett. Suff 4K 29
Wistanstow. Shrp 3E 24
Wistanswick. Shrp 7D 32
Wistaston. Ches E 4D 32
Wiston. Pemb 2E 14
Wiston. S Lan 6H 55
Wiston. W Sus 4M 11
Wistow. Cambs 3L 27
Wistow. N Yor 2B 40
Wiswell. Lanc 2F 38
Witcham. Cambs 3A 28
Witchampton. Dors 5J 9
Witchford. Cambs 4B 28
Witham. Essx 2G 21
Witham Friary. Som 1G 9
Witham on the Hill. Linc 8G 35
Witham St Hughs. Linc 3E 34
Withcall. Linc 7J 41
Witherenden Hill. E Sus 5E 12
Withergate. Norf 5J 37
Witheridge. Devn 4K 7
Witheridge Hill. Oxon 5G 19
Witherley. Leics 2B 26
Withermarsh Green. Suff 8G 29
Withern. Linc 7L 41
Withernsea. E Yor 3K 41
Withernwick. E Yor 1H 41
Withersdale Street. Suff 3J 29
Withersfield. Suff 7C 28
Witherslack. Cumb 5F 42
Withiel. Corn 3A 4
Withiel Florey. Som 2L 7
Withington. Glos 2A 18
Withington. G Man 6G 39
Withington. Here 7F 24
Withington. Shrp 8C 32
Withington. Staf 6H 33
Withington Green. Ches E 8G 39
Withington Marsh. Here 7F 24
Withleigh. Devn 4L 7
Withnell. Lanc 3E 38
Withnell Fold. Lanc 3E 38
Withybrook. Warw 3C 26
Withycombe. Som 1M 7
Withycombe Raleigh. Devn 7M 7
Withyham. E Sus 4C 12
Withypool. Som 2K 7
Witley. Surr 1K 11
Witnesham. Suff 6H 29
Witney. Oxon 2D 18
Wittering. Pet 1J 27
Wittersham. Kent 5H 13
Witton. Norf 1K 29
Witton. Worc 5K 25
Witton Bridge. Norf 4K 37
Witton Gilbert. Dur 7H 51
Witton-le-Wear. Dur 8G 51
Witton Park. Dur 8G 51
Wiveliscombe. Som 3M 7
Wivelrod. Hants 2G 11
Wivelsfield. E Sus 5B 12
Wivelsfield Green. E Sus 6B 12
Wivenhoe. Essx 1J 21
Wiveton. Norf 3G 37
Wix. Essx 1K 21
Wixford. Warw 6L 25
Wixhill. Shrp 7C 32
Wixoe. Suff 7D 28
Woburn. C Beds 8H 27
Woburn Sands. Mil 8H 27
Woking. Surr 8L 19
Wokingham. Wok 7J 19
Wolborough. Devn 8K 7
Woldingham. Surr 8B 20
Wold Newton. E Yor 6K 45
Wold Newton. NE Lin 6J 41
Wolferlow. Here 5G 25
Wolferton. Norf 5C 36
Wolfhill. Per 2G 61
Wolf's Castle. Pemb 1D 14
Wolfsdale. Pemb 1D 14
Wolgarston. Staf 8G 33
Wollaston. Nptn 5H 27
Wollaston. Shrp 8A 32
Wollaston. W Mid 3J 25
Wollaton. Nott 5B 34
Wollerton. Shrp 6D 32
Wollescote. W Mid 3K 25
Wolseley Bridge. Staf 7H 33
Wolsingham. Dur 8F 50
Wolstanton. Staf 5F 32
Wolston. Warw 4C 26
Wolsty. Cumb 6J 49
Wolterton. Norf 4H 37
Wolvercote. Oxon 3E 18
Wolverhampton. W Mid 2K 25 & 103
Wolverley. Shrp 6B 32
Wolverley. Worc 4J 25
Wolverton. Hants 8F 18
Wolverton. Mil 7G 27
Wolverton. Warw 5A 26
Wolverton. Wilts 2G 9
Wolverton Common. Hants 8F 18
Wolvesnewton. Mon 4G 17
Wolvey. Warw 3C 26
Wolvey Heath. Warw 3C 26
Wolviston. Stoc T 1D 44
Womaston. Powy 5C 24
Wombleton. N Yor 5F 44
Wombourne. Staf 2J 25
Wombwell. S Yor 5M 39
Womenswold. Kent 8L 21
Womersley. N Yor 4B 40
Wonersh. Surr 1L 11
Wonson. Devn 7H 7
Wonston. Dors 5G 9
Wonston. Hants 2E 10
Wooburn. Buck 5K 19
Wooburn Green. Buck 5K 19
Wood. Pemb 1C 14
Woodacott. Devn 5E 6
Woodale. N Yor 6M 43
Woodall. S Yor 7A 40
Woodbank. Ches W 8B 38
Woodbastwick. Norf 6K 37
Woodbeck. Notts 8D 40
Woodborough. Notts 5C 34
Woodborough. Wilts 8B 18
Woodbridge. Devn 6A 8
Woodbridge. Dors 4G 9
Woodbridge. Suff 7J 29
Wood Burcote. Nptn 7E 26
Woodbury. Devn 7M 7
Woodbury Salterton. Devn 7M 7
Woodchester. Glos 3L 17
Woodchurch. Kent 4H 13
Woodchurch. Mers 7A 38
Woodcock Heath. Staf 7H 33
Woodcombe. Som 1L 7
Woodcote. Oxon 5G 19
Woodcote Green. Worc 4K 25
Woodcott. Hants 8E 18
Woodcroft. Glos 4H 17
Woodcutts. Dors 4J 9
Wood Dalling. Norf 5G 37
Woodditton. Cambs 6C 28
Woodeaton. Oxon 2F 18
Wood Eaton. Staf 8F 32
Wood End. Bed 5J 27
Woodend. Cumb 4C 42
Wood End. Herts 1B 20
Woodend. Nptn 7E 26
Woodend. Staf 7J 33
Wood End. Warw 3A 26 (nr. Bedworth)
Wood End. Warw 2A 26 (nr. Dordon)
Wood End. Warw 4M 25 (nr. Tanworth-in-Arden)
Woodend. W Sus 5J 11
Wood Enderby. Linc 3J 35
Woodend Green. Essx 1D 20
Woodfalls. Wilts 3B 10
Woodfield. Oxon 1F 18
Woodfields. Lanc 2E 38
Woodford. Corn 4D 6
Woodford. Devn 4J 5
Woodford. Glos 4J 17
Woodford. G Lon 4B 20
Woodford. G Man 7G 39
Woodford. Nptn 4H 27
Woodford. Plym 4G 5
Woodford Green. G Lon 4C 20
Woodford Halse. Nptn 6D 26
Woodgate. Norf 6G 37
Woodgate. W Mid 3K 25
Woodgate. W Sus 5K 11
Woodgate. Worc 5K 25
Wood Green. G Lon 4A 20
Woodgreen. Hants 4B 10
Woodgreen. Oxon 2D 18
Wood Hall. E Yor 2H 41
Woodhall. Inv 2B 54
Woodhall. Linc 3J 35
Woodhall. N Yor 4L 43
Woodhall Spa. Linc 3H 35
Woodham. Surr 7L 19
Woodham Ferrers. Essx 4F 20
Woodham Mortimer. Essx 3G 21
Woodham Walter. Essx 3G 21
Woodhaven. Fife 3K 61
Wood Hayes. W Mid 1K 25
Woodhead. Abers 3K 73 (nr. Fraserburgh)
Woodhead. Abers 6H 73 (nr. Fyvie)
Woodhill. N Som 6G 17
Woodhill. Shrp 3H 25
Woodhill. Som 3C 8
Woodhorn. Nmbd 3J 51
Woodhouse. Leics 8B 34
Woodhouse. S Yor 7A 40
Woodhouse. W Yor 2L 39 (nr. Leeds)
Woodhouse. W Yor 3M 39 (nr. Normanton)
Woodhouse Eaves. Leics 8B 34
Woodhouses. Ches W 8D 38
Woodhouses. G Man 5H 39 (nr. Failsworth)
Woodhouses. G Man 6F 38 (nr. Sale)
Woodhouses. Staf 8J 33
Woodhuish. Devn 4L 5
Woodhurst. Cambs 4M 27
Woodingdean. Brig 7B 12
Woodland. Devn 3J 5
Woodland. Dur 1M 43
Woodland Head. Devn 6J 7
Woodlands. Abers 4H 67
Woodlands. Dors 5A 10
Woodlands. Hants 4D 10
Woodlands. Kent 7D 20
Woodlands. N Yor 8C 44
Woodlands. S Yor 5B 40
Woodlands Park. Wind 6J 19
Woodlands St Mary. W Ber 6D 18
Woodlane. Shrp 7D 32
Woodlane. Staf 7J 33
Woodleigh. Devn 5J 5
Woodlesford. W Yor 3M 39
Woodley. G Man 6H 39
Woodley. Wok 6H 19
Woodmancote. Glos 1M 17 (nr. Cheltenham)
Woodmancote. Glos 3A 18 (nr. Cirencester)
Woodmancote. W Sus 5H 11 (nr. Chichester)
Woodmancote. W Sus 6A 12 (nr. Henfield)
Woodmancote. Worc 7K 25
Woodmancott. Hants 1F 10
Woodmansey. E Yor 2G 41
Woodmansgreen. W Sus 3J 11
Woodmansterne. Surr 8A 20
Woodmanton. Devn 7M 7
Woodmill. Staf 7J 33
Woodminton. Wilts 3A 10
Woodnesborough. Kent 8M 21
Woodnewton. Nptn 2J 27
Woodnook. Linc 6F 34
Wood Norton. Norf 5G 37
Woodplumpton. Lanc 2D 38
Woodrising. Norf 1F 28
Woodrow. Cumb 7K 49
Woodrow. Dors 4G 9 (nr. Fifehead Neville)
Woodrow. Dors 5G 9 (nr. Hazelbury Bryan)
Wood Row. W Yor 3M 39
Woods Eaves. Here 7C 24
Woodseaves. Shrp 6D 32
Woodseaves. Staf 7E 32
Woodsend. Wilts 6C 18
Woodsetts. S Yor 7B 40
Woodsford. Dors 6G 9
Wood's Green. E Sus 4E 12
Woodshaw. Wilts 5A 18
Woodside. Aber 3K 67
Woodside. Brac 6K 19
Woodside. Derbs 5L 33
Woodside. Dum 4H 49
Woodside. Dur 1A 44
Woodside. Fife 5K 61
Woodside. Herts 3A 20
Woodside. Per 2H 61
Wood Stanway. Glos 8L 25
Woodstock. Oxon 2E 18
Woodstock Slop. Pemb 1E 14
Woodston. Pet 2K 27
Wood Street. Norf 5K 37
Wood Street Village. Surr 8K 19
Woodthorpe. Derbs 8A 40
Woodthorpe. Leics 8B 34
Woodthorpe. Linc 7L 41
Woodthorpe. Notts 5B 34
Woodthorpe. York 1B 40
Woodton. Norf 2J 29
Woodtown. Devn 3F 6 (nr. Bideford)
Woodtown. Devn 3F 6 (nr. Littleham)
Woodvale. Mers 4B 38
Woodville. Derbs 8L 33
Woodwalton. Cambs 3L 27
Woodwick. Orkn 5B 78
Woodyates. Dors 4A 10
Woody Bay. Devn 1H 7
Woofferton. Shrp 5F 24
Wookey. Som 1E 8
Wookey Hole. Som 1E 8
Wool. Dors 7H 9
Woolacombe. Devn 1F 6
Woolage Green. Kent 3L 13
Woolage Village. Kent 8L 21
Woolaston. Glos 4H 17
Woolavington. Som 1C 8
Woolbeding. W Sus 3J 11
Woolcotts. Som 2L 7
Wooldale. W Yor 5K 39
Wooler. Nmbd 7J 57
Woolfardisworthy. Devn 3E 6 (nr. Bideford)
Woolfardisworthy. Devn 5K 7 (nr. Crediton)
Woolfords. S Lan 4J 55
Woolgarston. Dors 7J 9
Woolhampton. W Ber 7F 18
Woolhope. Here 8G 25
Woolland. Dors 5G 9
Woollard. Bath 7J 17
Woolley. Bath 7K 17
Woolley. Cambs 4K 27
Woolley. Corn 4D 6
Woolley. Derbs 3L 33
Woolley. W Yor 4M 39
Woolley Green. Wilts 7L 17
Woolmere Green. Worc 5K 25
Woolmer Green. Herts 2A 20
Woolminstone. Som 5D 8
Woolpit. Suff 5F 28
Woolridge. Glos 1L 17
Woolscott. Warw 5C 26
Woolsery. Devn 3E 6
Woolsington. Tyne 5G 51
Woolstaston. Shrp 2E 24
Woolsthorpe By Belvoir. Linc 6E 34
Woolsthorpe-by-Colsterworth. Linc 7F 34
Woolston. Devn 5J 5
Woolston. Shrp 3E 24 (nr. Church Stretton)
Woolston. Shrp 7A 32 (nr. Oswestry)
Woolston. Som 3F 8
Woolston. Sotn 4E 10
Woolston. Warr 6E 38
Woolstone. Glos 8K 25
Woolstone. Oxon 5C 18
Woolston Green. Devn 3J 5
Woolton. Mers 7C 38
Woolton Hill. Hants 7E 18
Woolverstone. Suff 8H 29
Woolverton. Som 8K 17
Woolwell. Devn 3G 5
Woolwich. G Lon 6C 20
Woonton. Here 6D 24 (nr. Kington)
Woonton. Here 5F 24 (nr. Leominster)
Wooperton. Nmbd 7K 57
Woore. Shrp 5E 32
Wooth. Dors 6D 8
Wooton. Shrp 3H 25
Wootton. Bed 7J 27
Wootton. Hants 6C 10
Wootton. IOW 6F 10
Wootton. Kent 3L 13
Wootton. Nptn 6F 26
Wootton. N Lin 4G 41
Wootton. Oxon 3E 18 (nr. Abingdon)
Wootton. Oxon 2E 18 (nr. Woodstock)
Wootton. Shrp 4E 24 (nr. Ludlow)
Wootton. Shrp 7A 32 (nr. Oswestry)
Wootton. Staf 7F 32 (nr. Eccleshall)
Wootton. Staf 5J 33 (nr. Ellastone)
Wootton Bridge. IOW 6F 10
Wootton Common. IOW 6F 10
Wootton Courtenay. Som 1L 7
Wootton Fitzpaine. Dors 6C 8
Wootton Rivers. Wilts 7B 18
Wootton St Lawrence. Hants 8F 18
Wootton Wawen. Warw 5M 25
Worcester. Worc 6J 25 & 103
Worcester Park. G Lon 7A 20
Wordsley. W Mid 3J 25
Worfield. Shrp 2H 25
Work. Orkn 6C 78
Workhouse Green. Suff 8F 28
Workington. Cumb 1A 42
Worksop. Notts 8B 40
Worlaby. N Lin 4G 41
Worlds End. Hants 4G 11
Worldsend. Shrp 2E 24
World's End. W Ber 6E 18
Worlds End. W Mid 3M 25
World's End. W Sus 6B 12
Worle. N Som 7F 16
Worleston. Ches E 4D 32
Worlingham. Suff 2L 29
Worlington. Suff 4C 28
Worlingworth. Suff 5J 29
Wormbridge. Here 8E 24
Wormegay. Norf 6C 36
Wormelow Tump. Here 8E 24
Wormhill. Derbs 8K 39
Wormingford. Essx 8F 28
Worminghall. Buck 3G 19
Wormington. Glos 8L 25
Worminster. Som 1E 8
Wormit. Fife 3J 61
Wormleighton. Warw 6C 26
Wormley. Herts 3B 20
Wormley. Surr 2K 11
Wormshill. Kent 8G 21
Wormsley. Here 7E 24
Worplesdon. Surr 8K 19
Worrall. S Yor 6M 39
Worsbrough. S Yor 5M 39
Worsley. G Man 5F 38
Worstead. Norf 5K 37
Worsthorne. Lanc 2G 39
Worston. Lanc 1F 38
Worth. Kent 8M 21
Worth. W Sus 4B 12
Wortham. Suff 4G 29
Worthen. Shrp 1D 24
Worthenbury. Wrex 5B 32
Worthing. Norf 6F 36
Worthing. W Sus 5M 11
Worthington. Leics 7A 34
Worth Matravers. Dors 8J 9
Worting. Hants 8G 19
Wortley. Glos 4K 17
Wortley. S Yor 6M 39
Wortley. W Yor 2L 39
Worton. N Yor 4L 43
Worton. Wilts 8M 17
Wortwell. Norf 3J 29
Wotherton. Shrp 1C 24
Wothorpe. Nptn 1J 27
Wotter. Devn 3G 5
Wotton. Glos 2L 17
Wotton. Surr 1M 11
Wotton-under-Edge. Glos 4K 17
Wotton Underwood. Buck 2G 19
Wouldham. Kent 7F 20
Wrabness. Essx 8H 29
Wrafton. Devn 2F 6
Wragby. Linc 8H 41
Wragby. W Yor 4A 40
Wramplingham. Norf 1H 29
Wrangbrook. W Yor 4A 40
Wrangle. Linc 4L 35
Wrangle Lowgate. Linc 4L 35
Wrangway. Som 4A 8
Wrantage. Som 3C 8
Wrawby. N Lin 5G 41
Wraxall. N Som 6G 17
Wraxall. Som 2F 8
Wray. Lanc 7H 43
Wraysbury. Wind 6L 19
Wrayton. Lanc 6H 43
Wrea Green. Lanc 2B 38
Wreay. Cumb 7M 49 (nr. Carlisle)
Wreay. Cumb 1F 42 (nr. Penrith)
Wrecclesham. Surr 1J 11
Wrecsam. Wrex 4A 32
Wrekenton. Tyne 6H 51
Wrelton. N Yor 5G 45
Wrenbury. Ches E 5C 32
Wreningham. Norf 2H 29
Wrentham. Suff 3L 29
Wrenthorpe. W Yor 3M 39
Wrentnall. Shrp 1E 24
Wressle. E Yor 2D 40
Wressle. N Lin 5F 40
Wrestlingworth. C Beds 7L 27
Wretton. Norf 2C 28
Wrexham. Wrex 4A 32
Wreyland. Devn 7J 7
Wrickton. Shrp 3G 25
Wrightington Bar. Lanc 4D 38
Wright's Green. Essx 2D 20
Wrinehill. Staf 5E 32
Wrington. N Som 7G 17
Writtle. Essx 3E 20
Wrockwardine. Telf 8D 32
Wroot. N Lin 5D 40
Wrotham. Kent 8E 20
Wrotham Heath. Kent 8E 20
Wroughton. Swin 5B 18
Wroxall. IOW 7F 10
Wroxall. Warw 4A 26
Wroxeter. Shrp 1F 24
Wroxham. Norf 6K 37
Wroxton. Oxon 7C 26
Wyaston. Derbs 5J 33
Wyatt's Green. Essx 4D 20
Wybers Wood. NE Lin 5J 41
Wyberton. Linc 5K 35
Wyboston. Bed 6K 27
Wybunbury. Ches E 5D 32
Wychbold. Worc 5K 25
Wych Cross. E Sus 4C 12
Wychnor. Staf 8J 33
Wychnor Bridges. Staf 8J 33
Wyck. Hants 2H 11
Wyck Hill. Glos 1B 18
Wyck Rissington. Glos 1B 18
Wycliffe. Dur 2A 44
Wycombe Marsh. Buck 4J 19
Wyddial. Herts 8M 27
Wye. Kent 3J 13
Wyesham. Mon 2H 17
Wyfold Grange. Oxon 5G 19
Wyfordby. Leics 8D 34
Wyke. Devn 6K 7
Wyke. Dors 3G 9
Wyke. Shrp 1G 25
Wyke. Surr 8K 19
Wyke. W Yor 3K 39
Wyke Champflower. Som 2F 8
Wykeham. Linc 7J 35
Wykeham. N Yor 6H 45 (nr. Malton)
Wykeham. N Yor 5J 45 (nr. Scarborough)
Wyken. Shrp 2H 25
Wyken. W Mid 3B 26
Wyke Regis. Dors 8F 8
Wyke, The. Shrp 1H 25
Wykey. Shrp 7A 32
Wykin. Leics 2C 26
Wylam. Nmbd 5G 51
Wylde Green. W Mid 2M 25
Wylye. Wilts 2A 10
Wymering. Port 5G 11
Wymeswold. Leics 7C 34
Wymington. Bed 5H 27
Wymondham. Leics 8E 34
Wymondham. Norf 1H 29
Wyndham. B'end 4B 16
Wynford Eagle. Dors 6E 8
Wyng. Orkn 8B 78
Wynyard Village. Stoc T 1D 44
Wyre Piddle. Worc 7K 25
Wysall. Notts 7C 34
Wyson. Here 5F 24
Wythall. Worc 4L 25
Wytham. Oxon 3E 18
Wythenshawe. G Man 7G 39
Wythop Mill. Cumb 1C 42
Wyton. Cambs 4L 27
Wyton. E Yor 2H 41
Wyverstone. Suff 5G 29
Wyverstone Street. Suff 5G 29
Wyville. Linc 7E 34
Wyvis Lodge. High 4G 71

Y

Yaddlethorpe. N Lin 5E 40
Yafford. IOW 7E 10
Yafforth. N Yor 4C 44
Yalding. Kent 8E 20
Yanley. N Som 7H 17
Yanwath. Cumb 1G 43
Yanworth. Glos 2A 18
Yapham. E Yor 8G 45
Yapton. W Sus 5K 11
Yarburgh. Linc 6K 41
Yarcombe. Devn 5B 8
Yarde. Som 2M 7
Yardley. W Mid 3M 25
Yardley Gobion. Nptn 7F 26
Yardley Hastings. Nptn 6G 27
Yardley Wood. W Mid 3M 25
Yardro. Powy 6C 24
Yarhampton. Worc 5H 25
Yarkhill. Here 7G 25
Yarlet. Staf 7G 33
Yarley. Som 1E 8
Yarlington. Som 3F 8
Yarm. Stoc T 2D 44
Yarmouth. IOW 7D 10
Yarnbrook. Wilts 8L 17
Yarnfield. Staf 6F 32
Yarnscombe. Devn 3G 7
Yarnton. Oxon 2E 18
Yarpole. Here 5E 24
Yarrow. Nmbd 3C 50
Yarrow. Bord 7M 55
Yarrow. Som 1C 8
Yarrow Feus. Bord 7M 55
Yarrow Ford. Bord 6D 56
Yarsop. Here 7E 24
Yarwell. Nptn 2J 27
Yate. S Glo 5K 17
Yateley. Hants 7J 19
Yatesbury. Wilts 6A 18
Yattendon. W Ber 6F 18
Yatton. Here 5E 24 (nr. Leominster)
Yatton. Here 8G 25 (nr. Ross-on-Wye)
Yatton. N Som 7G 17
Yatton Keynell. Wilts 6L 17
Yaverland. IOW 7G 11
Yawl. Devn 6C 8
Yaxham. Norf 6G 37
Yaxley. Cambs 2K 27
Yaxley. Suff 4H 29
Yazor. Here 7E 24
Y Bala. Gwyn 6J 31
Y Bont-Faen. V Glam 6B 16
Y Clun. Neat 3A 16
Y Dref. Gwyn 6D 30
Y Drenewydd. Powy 2B 24
Yeading. G Lon 5M 19
Yeadon. W Yor 1L 39
Yealand Conyers. Lanc 6G 43
Yealand Redmayne. Lanc 6G 43
Yealand Storrs. Lanc 6F 42
Yealmpton. Devn 4G 5
Yearby. Red C 1F 44
Yearngill. Cumb 7J 49
Yearsett. Here 6H 25
Yearsley. N Yor 6E 44
Yeaton. Shrp 8B 32
Yeaveley. Derbs 5J 33
Yeavering. Nmbd 6J 57
Yedingham. N Yor 6H 45
Yeldersley Hollies. Derbs 5K 33
Yelford. Oxon 3D 18
Yelland. Devn 2F 6
Yelling. Cambs 5L 27
Yelsted. Kent 7G 21
Yelvertoft. Nptn 4D 26
Yelverton. Devn 3G 5
Yelverton. Norf 1J 29
Yenston. Som 3G 9
Yeoford. Devn 6J 7
Yeolmbridge. Corn 7E 6
Yeo Mill. Devn 3K 7
Yeovil. Som 4E 8
Yeovil Marsh. Som 4E 8
Yeovilton. Som 3E 8
Yerbeston. Pemb 3E 14
Yesnaby. Orkn 6A 78
Yetlington. Nmbd 1F 50
Yetminster. Dors 4E 8
Yett. N Lan 4F 54
Yett. S Ayr 7C 54
Yettington. Devn 7M 7
Yetts o' Muckhart. Clac 5F 60
Y Fali. IOA 2B 30
Y Felinheli. Gwyn 3E 30
Y Fenni. Mon 2F 16
Y Ferwig. Cdgn 7D 22
Y Fflint. Flin 8A 38
Y Ffor. Gwyn 6C 30
Y Fron. Gwyn 4E 30
Y Gelli Gandryll. Powy 7C 24
Yielden. Bed 5J 27
Yieldshields. S Lan 4G 55
Yiewsley. G Lon 5L 19
Yinstay. Orkn 6D 78
Ynysboeth. Rhon 4C 16
Ynysddu. Cphy 4D 16
Ynysforgan. Swan 4L 15
Ynyshir. Rhon 4C 16
Ynyslas. Cdgn 2J 23
Ynysmaerdy. Rhon 5C 16
Ynysmeudwy. Neat 3M 15
Ynystawe. Swan 3L 15
Ynyswen. Powy 2A 16
Ynys-wen. Rhon 4B 16
Ynys y Barri. V Glam 7D 16
Ynysybwl. Rhon 4C 16
Ynysymaerdy. Neat 4M 15
Yockenthwaite. N Yor 6L 43
Yockleton. Shrp 8B 32
Yokefleet. E Yor 3E 40
Yoker. Glas 3D 54
Yonder Bognie. Abers 5F 72
Yonderton. Abers 6K 73
York. York 8F 44 & 103
Yorkletts. Kent 7J 21
Yorkley. Glos 3J 17
Yorkshire Dales. N Yor 6K 43
Yorton. Shrp 7C 32
Yorton Heath. Shrp 7C 32
Youlgreave. Derbs 3K 33
Youlthorpe. E Yor 8G 45
Youlton. N Yor 7D 44
Young's End. Essx 2F 20
Young Wood. Linc 8H 41
Yoxall. Staf 8J 33
Yoxford. Suff 5K 29
Yr Hob. Flin 4A 32
Y Rhws. V Glam 7C 16
Yr Wyddgrug. Flin 3M 31
Ysbyty Cynfyn. Cdgn 4K 23
Ysbyty Ifan. Cnwy 5H 31
Ysbyty Ystwyth. Cdgn 4K 23
Ysceifiog. Flin 2L 31
Yspitty. Carm 4K 15
Ystalyfera. Neat 3M 15
Ystrad. Rhon 4B 16
Ystrad Aeron. Cdgn 6H 23
Ystradfellte. Powy 2B 16
Ystradffin. Carm 7K 23
Ystradgynlais. Powy 2M 15
Ystradmeurig. Cdgn 5K 23
Ystrad Mynach. Cphy 4D 16
Ystradowen. Carm 2M 15
Ystradowen. V Glam 6C 16
Ystumtuen. Cdgn 4K 23
Ythanbank. Abers 6K 73
Ythanwells. Abers 6G 73
Y Trallwng. Powy 1C 24
Y Tymbl. Carm 2K 15
Y Waun. Wrex 6M 31

Z

Zeal Monachorum. Devn 5J 7
Zeals. Wilts 2G 9
Zelah. Corn 4F 3
Zennor. Corn 6B 3
Zouch. Notts 7B 34

INDEX TO SELECTED PLACES OF INTEREST

(1) A strict alphabetical order is used e.g. Benmore Botanic Gdn. follows Ben Macdui but precedes Ben Nevis.

(2) Entries shown without a main map index reference have the name of the appropriate Town Plan and its page number;
e.g. Ashmolean Mus. of Art & Archaeology (OX1 2PH) .... Oxford 100
The Town Plan title is not given when this is included in the name of the Place of Interest.

(3) Entries in italics are not named on the map but are shown with a symbol only.
Entries in italics and enclosed in (brackets) are not shown on the map.
Where this occurs the nearest town or village may also be given, unless that name is already included in the name of the Place of Interest.

SAT NAV POSTCODES

Postcodes (in brackets) are included as a navigation aid to assist Sat Nav users and are supplied on this basis.
It should be noted that postcodes have been selected by their proximity to the Place of Interest and that they may not form part of the actual postal address. Drivers should follow the Tourist Brown Signs when available.

ABBREVIATIONS USED IN THIS INDEX

Garden : Gdn.	Museum : Mus.
Gardens : Gdns.	National : Nat
	Park : Pk.

Copyright of Geographers' A-Z Map Company Ltd.

© Crown copyright and database rights 2014 Ordnance Survey 100017302